HEAD OF

THE MEMOIR OF SYDNEY NEWMAN

DRAMA

SYDNEY NEWMAN

with contributions by Graeme Burk
and a foreword by Ted Kotcheff

Published by ECW Press
665 Gerrard Street East
Toronto, ON M4M 1Y2
416-694-3348 / info@ecwpress.com

Cover design: Tania Craan
Interior images: courtesy Deirdre Newman,
    except where otherwise indicated
Type: Rachel Ironstone

Printing: Friesens   5   4   3   2   1

To the best of his abilities, the author has related
experiences, places, people, and organizations from his
memories of them. In order to protect the privacy of
others, he has, in some instances, changed the names of
certain people and details of events and places

Library and Archives Canada
Cataloguing in Publication

Newman, Sydney, author
Head of drama : the memoir of Sydney Newman / Sydney
Newman.

Issued in print and electronic formats.
ISBN 978-1-77041-304-7 (softcover)
ISBN 978-1-77305-052-2 (PDF)
ISBN 978-1-77305-053-9 (EPUB)

1. Newman, Sydney. 2. Television producers and directors—Canada—Biography. 3. Autobiographies. I. Title.

PN1992.4.N49A3 2017   791.45092   C2017-902396-9
C2017-903161-9

The publication of *Head of Drama* has been generously supported by the Canada Council for the Arts, which last year
invested $153 million to bring the arts to Canadians throughout the country, and by the Government of Canada through
the Canada Book Fund. *Nous remercions le Conseil des arts du Canada de son soutien. L'an dernier, le Conseil a investi 153
millions de dollars pour mettre de l'art dans la vie des Canadiennes et des Canadiens de tout le pays. Ce livre est financé en
partie par le gouvernement du Canada.* We also acknowledge the support of the Ontario Arts Council (OAC), an agency of
the Government of Ontario, which last year funded 1,737 individual artists and 1,095 organizations in 223 communities
across Ontario for a total of $52.1 million, and the contribution of the Government of Ontario through the Ontario Book
Publishing Tax Credit and the Ontario Media Development Corporation.

Printed and bound in Canada

to Betty

CONTENTS

From the Saturday Serial, to the Wednesday Play, to the
October Crisis, and Beyond *by Graeme Burk*

TED KOTCHEFF

FOREWORD

Sydney Newman's *Head of Drama* is an engrossing book, delineating the extraordinary odyssey of a Toronto polyglot slum-boy who ascended to the vertiginous heights of being the sovereign ruler of British broadcasting television drama. In command of over 400 top creative people, he performed the daunting task of producing 370 hours of high-quality dramatic entertainment every year, always under the harsh scrutiny of tough TV critics — would he be able to manage this Herculean task or would he topple from the high wire?

I have to declare that I cannot be dispassionate about Sydney Newman, for he was my mentor. If it was not for him, I have no idea what I would be doing now, or even who I might be.

In 1954, I had been working as a stagehand for two years at the Canadian Broadcasting Corporation Television Network (CBC Television). I heard that Sydney Newman, head of documentaries and outside broadcasts, was planning to produce twelve one-hour documentaries about new currents of thought and discoveries at the

University of Toronto, from which I had recently graduated. I asked to see him and he graciously met me.

I offered to be his assistant, doing the research and legwork, and then writing a draft of the show. I was twenty-three, and not just wet but *soaking* behind the ears. I think Sydney was amused by my cheekiness in asking for this job in an arena in which I had no track record, no knowledge whatsoever. Sydney asked me what was my ultimate goal: I said I wanted to be a poet. His eyes twinkled — he hired me. This was the beginning of a long, close and fruitful friendship.

Sydney remembers this first encounter of ours in these memoirs. I think he was also amused, as he says, by my disheveled, unkempt stagehand wardrobe, my bare elbows poking through the worn-out sleeves of my turtleneck pullover. I myself had forgotten this detail, but not Sydney. The acute memory he displays concerning my clothing informs this whole book — everything is remembered with incredible accuracy and vivid verisimilitude. I can attest to it.

Our working together was a great learning experience for me. Sydney was a great documentary filmmaker at the National Film Board of Canada. He was extremely generous in passing on his omniscient knowledge of documentaries to me. I wrote twelve shows, and he rewrote all twelve shows.

Then, out of nowhere, the CBC made Sydney the head of the drama department. He rushed up to me: "Ted, I need your help! I'm a documentarian, I know sweet Fanny Adams about drama! You're an English major; come along and be my script editor." Of course, I jumped at the chance.

Sydney was in charge of two anthology drama series, *General Motors Theatre* and *The Chase and Sanborn Hour*. He had a very clear vision of the kind of dramas he wanted. He gave me my marching orders: "I want plays about Canada, that deal with what's going on around us *right now*. I want intensely real plays about people like us: their hopes, their needs, their ambitions, their failures." He ended by surprisingly quoting Hamlet's advice to his actors: "The purpose of playing . . . is to hold as 'twere the mirror up to nature . . . and the very age and body of the time." So much for his supposed ignorance of drama.

Under his brilliant leadership, both shows were successful. One of his dramas, Arthur Hailey's *Flight into Danger*, became famous worldwide, making him known to everyone in the TV business in the United States and Great Britain.

One day, after my being a year at the job, Sydney came into my office. "Ted! You're doing a great job running the script department. And you're a pretty good writer — not a *great* writer," he added, smiling, "but a pretty good one. But, do you know what you'd be really good at?" I shook my head. "You have all the necessary qualities to be a fine director." I was taken aback, totally perplexed. "I'll tell you what. I'll let you direct one play — if I like it, I'll give you a year's contract. If I don't like it, you're out on the street; you can't come back to this job. If you don't want to risk it, of course you can continue here." Well, obviously I said I'd risk it.

So, that's how I became a director: he made me one. What he saw in me, I do not know, and I still kick myself for never having asked him.

Sydney liked his directors to have a strong point of view. Once, Sydney fired a director, and I asked him why. Sydney replied, "He was always agreeing with me." Sydney liked the sparks to fly. He felt that was the only way that interesting, innovative work could be achieved. On one occasion, Sydney and I had a strong disagreement. He said to me, "Don't talk to me like that, Kotcheff. I pulled you out of the gutter!" I replied, "From the gutter to you is up?" Sydney laughed uproariously — he loved disagreement.

After two years of directing for Sydney, I went to England, in hopes of branching out into theatre and film. I got a job with ABC TV directing on their anthology series, *Armchair Theatre*. One day, Howard Thomas, the head of ABC TV, called me in, informing me he wanted to find a new producer for *Armchair Theatre* and someone had suggested Sydney Newman. Knowing we had worked together, he canvassed my opinion. Of course, I gave Sydney top marks: "No one better in the whole world," I said. And at the end of it, he was hired. Sydney had made me. Now I could partially return the favour.

When he started producing on *Armchair Theatre*, Sydney saw that British television drama was staid, with static camera work, and was mostly using tired, out-of-date stage plays for scripts — scripts that were full of gross errors about working-class British life. As in Canada, Sydney immediately implemented his personal TV drama philosophy. Gathering his whole English staff together, he enunciated it: "TV is a new medium: it needs new plays that reflect what is presently going on in society and its culture. Britain is in a state of ferment and flux" — these were the Carnaby Street years — "and our plays should reveal this new quintessential England to the whole country."

Sydney's idealism about the role of drama in the lives of the audience stoked all of his creative co-workers. He laid down the law: "No stage plays, even if they were written by Terence Rattigan or Dodie Smith. Only original plays by new writers." So he instantly commissioned a bunch of plays from young, untested British writers that Sydney divined could fulfill his vision.

At first, disaster: there were inexperienced dramatists experimenting in an unfamiliar style — it was a shambles. We were universally panned by the critics, Sydney's directors were in revolt, Howard Thomas was pulling his hair out. But Sydney was not to be deterred. He stubbornly persevered in his radical new policy. And then, after a few months and almost magically out of nowhere, came Harold Pinter, Alun Owen, John Mortimer, Clive Exton, and many other fresh TV playwrights who turned out to be great.

Armchair Theatre became hugely successful, with fascinating new plays that were brilliantly produced, receiving great reviews and whopping ratings. It was Sydney's apotheosis. He illuminated a changing Britain. He was a cultural hero.

Sydney's career soared and soared. He subsequently went to the BBC and continued to produce fabulously memorable dramas there: *The Forsyte Saga*, *Doctor Who*, *The Wednesday Play*, *Z Cars*, Shakespeare, operas, and more.

One of the reasons Sydney enjoyed such extraordinary success was because he always surrounded himself with extremely talented people. But this was not happenstance, not something accidental. Sydney had an uncanny intuitive ability to spot talent. It was almost supernatural. He saw endowments in people that were totally invisible to everyone else, including the persons concerned — like me.

Case in point: Verity Lambert. At the BBC, Sydney was looking for someone to produce a new sci-fi series he was developing. He interviewed several men, but none of them excited him. Suddenly, he selected Verity Lambert to produce the show. Everyone, myself included, was surprised at Sydney's choice. I knew Verity very well; she had been my assistant for two years. She was a lovely woman and a wonderful assistant. But what did Sydney see in this polite, intelligent, middle-class Englishwoman? What did he see in her — a woman who so far had always been someone's assistant, so totally untested as a producer— that would lead him to think she had it in her to handle this mammoth undertaking — *Doctor Who*! No one could figure it out. Like mild-mannered Clark Kent becoming Superman, Ms. Polite-Middle-Class was transformed into a wildly imaginative, creative dynamo, full of new ideas and stories, and she made *Doctor Who* into a colossal mega success in Great Britain and all over the world. And Verity also gave it "legs." It's still running! How did Sydney know? Furthermore, Verity was the first woman to produce a drama in the BBC; Sydney scored a point for feminism.

I am so glad that this book of Sydney's memoirs is being published, so that the record of his extraordinary achievements is available to everyone. Sydney Newman was a visionary, incredibly innovative, supremely creative, and totally original. He was a man of integrity, with great courage in pursuing and realizing his vision of the world.

He was the most influential person in television in the '60s, someone who made an incalculable contribution to British culture. He was truly a great man.

HEAD OF

DRAMA

CHAPTER ONE

HIS UNKNOWN QUEEN STREET

He was born ass-backwards, as it were, in the fourth year of World War I.[1]

It is just after midnight on, wouldn't you guess, April Fool's Day. History records that he emerged from the warm body of his mother, Bessie, feet first. The legs had to be pushed in again to reverse the as-yet-unborn baby, head down. The doctor barely suppresses a curse as he faces yet more trouble — the baby's right arm is somehow entangled under its chin. With a shrug and a murmured "what the hell," the doctor fumbles in and deliberately breaks the arm, and a moment later the boy emerges and begins bawling lustily. The life-giving ordeal over and the child seemingly well, Bessie, the Austrian-born mother sighs, *Gott sei dank*.

There's no record that Bessie sang aloud to the child in utero,

---

1   Newman wrote this autobiography in 1987-88 after moving back to Britain in 1983 following the death of his wife.

which might not augur well for the kid. Sir Yehudi Menuhin said that "a baby which does not receive these melodic vibrations from its mother's voice suffers from emotional starvation, just as lack of food leads to physical starvation" (*Daily Telegraph*, December 30, 1986). Sir Yehudi, wunderkind, as indeed he is, knew because his mother and father had sung to him before he was born and he believed this was a factor in his musical development. Well, that's not to be sneezed at, so sure enough, as an adult, as far as Bessie's son's musical knowledge went, he was never able to honestly claim more than "but, I know what I like." It is good to know that despite the lack of musical nurturing, the infant had plenty of eye-contact bonding with his mother as he greedily sucked at her milk-laden breast.

Considering the stumbling, often torturous path this babe was to trod in the years ahead — sometimes painful, often bewildering, a few blinding moments of revelation — makes the circumstances of his birth a field day, a rich cornucopia of psychological insights for pre- and post-natal experts. Those he offended (likely more than he was to know) and those he loved and the many he tolerated might take note of the circumstances of his birth.

The question of naming him was not difficult because the infant's father Mordecai (anglicized to Morris) had a passionate admiration for Shimshon Hagibor, which to a Hebrew scholar is, of course, Samson the Great. This was no doubt due to the shit that was kicked out of him as a Yid in the land of his birth, good old Czarist Russia. But, thought the father, we can't saddle *unser kind* in Anglo Canada with a ludicrous handle like Samson. So he picked a name that the child was to hate most of his life — Sidney. When he entered into school, Sidney became Sydney,[2] because what foreign-born parents would dare correct the spelling of the school principal?

---

2   Not only was the spelling of Sydney Newman's first name changed, but Newman's last name was anglicized as well — it was originally Nudelman. It was Newman's surname as late as 1932, when he was fifteen, when "Sydney Nudelman" was listed amongst the prize winners for a National soap sculpture competition — though by that point he was certainly Sydney Newman at school.

So, to his father, Sydney was always Shimshon ben Mordecai; to his mother, Shimon; and until he was in his early twenties, to his older sister and brother, he was always Shim. Through life he was called variously Syd (accepted only from siblings and intimate friends); Sydney; Chink (when a child); Newman; Genghis Khan, due to the somewhat Tatar cast to his features, and more likely by the people he couldn't tolerate — pretentious creative types. In his teens and early twenties, his excessive energy directed at the opposite sex earned him the name of — wait for it — Jo-Jo, The Bouncing Boy. By him, his mother and father were always simply called Ma and Pa. His sister Ruth's name was no problem. But his brother's name, Wilfred, was. It was anglicized from Wolfgang, a relative of his mother and she always called him Volf. And so to Sydney the child, his brother was always Wolf.

Down the seven steps from the kitchen and through his father's shoe store facing Beverly Street at 331 Queen Street West, the child emerged daily, eager for what was new.

While his mother and father hated the district they were forced to live in, to Sydney it was exciting — a world of discovery. How could he know that that part of Queen Street in the 1920s was a George Grosz nightmare of broken, confused people? Here were the post-war immigrant families mainly from Finland, a sprinkling of Ukrainians and Jews and some English, Irish and Scots too poor to move. In the midst by the dozen were the disoriented wrecks — the vets of World War I, crippled or shell-shocked or victims of mustard gas. That was up to his thirteenth year. After

Little Shim.

that, in the '30s, were the dispossessed, the "Buddy, can you spare a dime" unemployed who had fled the Depression from across Canada believing that they would find work in Toronto, or "Hogtown" as it was known to other Canadians.

To escape the harsh, sordid conditions, booze or its equivalent was often the solution for the men and women on the street. Prohibition was in force but from local drugstores, with scarce pennies, they would buy their dreams in Lydia E. Pinkham Syrup for Ladies and paregoric — both, it was said, contained opium to help ease menstrual pain — and Bay Rum hair tonic, largely a wood alcohol, as was Sterno in a can, a waxy mixture containing alcohol which, when set alight, heated food.

Oh, it was a great education the kid got, all right. Before he was ten, he learned how to get the alcohol out of a can of Sterno by endlessly watching the alcoholics in back lanes empty a can into a stocking used as a filter then squeezing the juice out of the wax back into the can. Presto! When drunk, it wasn't exactly nectar — it was dynamite. Sydney learned that the stuff could blind one. What he couldn't know was that, perhaps, that was the reason for drinking it.

It was an everyday occurrence — sometimes three, four times a day — seeing a policeman frog-marching a stumbling drunk past 331 to the police telephone call-box fixed to a sturdy wood telephone pole just down the street. The copper would prop the sad, sodden, usually passive wreck against the pole with one hand while phoning for the Black Maria with the other. Sometimes the drunk would be fighting mad and resist. With hoots and jeers from onlookers — little Sydney, goggle-eyed in their midst — they would appraise the struggle with expert eyes to see who would win. Rarely did anyone help the cop. Pure tragicomedy was the drink-crazed woman Sydney watched one night wrestling an embarrassed but determined copper as he struggled to drag her to his call-box a street and a half away.

The word *wrestle* is no exaggeration: trying to get away, she literally turned cartwheels. The copper, with half the buttons on his uniforms torn off and helmet gone, never completely lost his hold on her. That was the first time Sydney discovered that a woman was anatomically different from a man — she was wearing no underpants, and he was surprised to note that there was nothing between her legs!

To his mother, the streets were a constant danger to *der kinder*. When his sister, Ruth, got a job as a stenographer, she was relieved that the place of work was just around the corner.

Wilfred, Sydney's brother, was a real worry. He was a member of the John Street gang. Nothing special, it was just a typical slum neighbourhood bunch of kids who hung out together and who used to shoot craps in the back lanes. Canada, in those days, was more Presbyterian than Glasgow — gambling was a sin, illegal. The beat policeman used to break up their games, the boys running away before he could grab them.

One night in the kitchen, the air was thick with fear. Ruth, tense. Mother, grim — worried. Where was Father?

Apparently, the craps game that night was broken up, but this time the boys fought with the policeman and were arrested. What provoked it, Sydney never found out. His father felt so much shame that when he brought Wilfred back from the police station he marched him upstairs and whipped the hell out of him. His screams still echo in Sydney's ears. A month later, underage and without any warning, Wilfred ran away.

For six months, nothing was heard from him. Then, an enormous parcel arrived containing gifts for all, including roller skates for Sydney. Wilfred was in Flint, Michigan, working for the Graham-Page car company that didn't know he was underage and according to him, he was making "big money." He was a paint stripper, adding those thin, cream-coloured lines that used to decorate car bodies' windows.

Except for the Canadian-born kids who spoke English, the district was a babel of thick accents and foreign languages. True or not, the Finns were thought to be terrible drinkers and when sloshed become violent. One Sunday morning the deadly silence on Queen Street was intruded upon by a growing bedlam (it might be noted that because of the English-Canadian Lord's Day Observance Act, Quebeckers would quip, *Last Sunday we spent a fortnight in Toronto*). The Newman family rushed from their kitchen, down the seven steps and out the locked store to see what was what. A mob was running down Beverly

Street, coming directly toward the Newman store. They were in the slipstream of a fight between two Finns. When Sydney's parents saw the opened straight razor in the hand of the pursuer and the blood-covered face of the pursued, with one ear half cut off, they quickly herded the children back into 331 Queen Street.

How could there not be prostitutes on that part of Queen Street parading up and down after the cop had passed? They were on the bottom level of their profession, most of them well over forty, cheap scents coping bravely with the odour of their hefty bodies. One was called Scabby Ass and the going rate was twenty-five cents. It wasn't until Sydney was ten that he found out how they earned their daily bread. One day a new whore turned up on the street, but this one was young! In the early evenings she'd come literally bouncing down the street, tits and ass proclaiming joyously the goodies she was prepared to offer the hobos, the unemployed or whoever. Her fee? One buck! And she did well. Gladys was her name and soon renamed Glad Ass. In the mornings, the kids would see her as any young woman doing her shopping. Once, out of a paper bag she withdrew a lovely red apple and gave it to little Sydney. Shades of Eve! Gurgling with laughter she offered him a student's rate and before he could ask her what for, his mother, seeing this and knowing her bible, pulled him away, threatening that he was "never to have anything to do with girls like that!" Sydney never did, which one supposes goes to show the benefits of a proper upbringing.

Seven years later coming home to see the folks, and not incidentally to scrounge a free supper, he saw Gladys. Alas, gone the bouncing beauty. Her work told; Gladys had become a somewhat thinner and wasted Scabby Ass.

The lane behind the stores was where the real unknown lay. Out of sight of parents, he would play doctor-patient with the girl up the street; gaze at prostrate drunks sleeping it off; collect empty Bay Rum and paregoric bottles from among the litter of opened Sterno tins and garbage — the local druggist paid one cent for each unchipped bottle. Eleven a week got one into the local cinema. And, in that same lane, joining a ring of kids from three to seven years old, Sydney wondered why a man was taking so long just to take a pee — turns out, he was masturbating.

One of the great days of the year for Sydney was July 12 — the Orange Day Parade,[3] all three hours of it. In a blaze of colour, it marched to the music of brass, fife and bagpipe along Queen Street right past 331. Families on Sydney's block had a special reason to wait for this day, though most didn't have a clue why the parade was held. Just down the street from 331 was Toronto's last fire station, whose engine was still being pulled by dray horses. One of its firemen was the drum major of one of the bands, and they were all waiting to see him do his stuff.

In Toronto on July 12, it's usually a scorcher — a day so hot it was said, "you could fry an egg on the pavement!" (Once Sydney and his pals tried it.) When their fireman appeared, Sydney's parents stopped handing their wax paper cups of homemade lemonade to paraders and onlookers. Cheers went up when the fireman stopped the band directly in front of his fire station, backing up the 10,000 marchers behind him along Queen Street and up University Avenue to Dundas Street. The show he put on was worthy of the best of the London Palladium. The crowd went wild as he twirled and tossed his baton as if the orange sash his father wore was at stake.

Years later, when Sydney met Catholic Alun Owen and when he saw on television Ian Paisley ranting and saw the tragic events in Ulster, he would remember those innocent Orange Day parades in Protestant Toronto. At the time though, it was just another exciting day — better than any movie.

The first movie he had ever seen was certainly a questionable one. His father was not too good at picking them. It was Lon Chaney in *London after Midnight* and Sydney was four. This so frightened the wits out of him that for months he was afraid to go up the unlit stairs

---

3   One aspect of staunchly Protestant life in the province of Ontario was the presence of Irish Protestant Orange Order, which was pervasive at the time. Toronto's Orangemen's Day parade, celebrated on July 12, was, until the 1970s, the largest Orangemen's parade outside of Ireland. It still continues today — the longest running parade in North America — though in fewer numbers.

to bed unless the lights were turned on. Another film he would never forget was Charlie Chaplin's *The Kid* with Jackie Coogan. How he cried when the authorities took the orphan away from the Tramp (shades of *Cathy Come Home*) and how he admired the Tramp's genius for the way he solved the problem of getting the Kid a pair of trousers that would fit. In the film, the Tramp took a pair of his own, measured them against the little boy, then carefully laid them on the tram tracks. When the trolley-car rolled over them — lo and behold, the trousers fit the Kid to a T. It was a connection with this film which, not many years later, became a turning point in Sydney's life.

The Pickford Theatre at the corner of Queen and Spadina was sheer heaven to him. To see Tom Mix and his next best hero, Ken Maynard[4]! How he and his pals would breathlessly wait for the next episode of the Saturday matinee serial to find out whether *The Green Archer*[5] would free himself from the villain's trap! Every means by which he could escape were argued out in meticulous and elaborate detail.

The Pickford was a grubby little hall that held, at most, about 250 bodies. As will be guessed, the cinema was named after America's Sweetheart, Mary Pickford, who made Canadian chests swell with pride because she was really theirs, born Gladys Smith on University Avenue in Toronto. Inside the cinema, the air was rank with the smell of urine and sweat, the floor sticky with layers of chewing gum — none of which curbed the boys' and girls' excitement at the thought of going. On Saturdays it was jam-packed with as many kids outside waiting to get in as there were inside. Trouble was, many inside wouldn't leave when the program was over and hung on to see the films over again. Sydney was no different and often had to clutch his parts to prevent peeing.

It was on such an occasion it must be observed that there was a greedy streak in him. He'd been queuing outside for a long time and finally was allowed to plunk down his eleven cents (one cent

---

4 Maynard was a stuntman and actor who appeared in Westerns mostly in the silent era.

5 *The Green Archer* was a 1926 serial starring Allene Ray and Walter Miller.

provincial tax) and enter the cinema. When he had just managed to find a seat and was about to sit down, he paused when a slide was flashed up on the screen:

ANY BOY OR GURL
WHO LEAVES NOW
WILL BE GIVEN ONE CENT!

"Holy cats," he thought, "I can get a cent for nothin'!" He quickly moved, wiggled his way past the knees of kids and dashed up the aisle to collect his free penny. Only outside, as he looked at the penny in his hand, did he realize what a stupid jerk he had been.

CHAPTER TWO

HIS DREADED THREE R'S

It was September 2, 1922, 8:45 a.m. The boy was five. Washed and scrubbed, he was taken by his mother through the rushing cars, trucks, clanging streetcars and along the far side of Queen Street through the crowds of people blankly rushing to work, and then up Peter Street, past Widmer and then along Ogden. He was about to get the first taste of the externally imposed, fixed daily routine that for most of his life he was to abhor. On this day he entered a new world: school.

Ogden Street Public School was a huge, Victorian building since replaced with an even uglier, though smaller, one.[6] It housed forty writhing boys and girls in each of its many classrooms. The school was unique, and annually praised as such by the *Toronto Evening Telegram*: anxious to woo new readers among the thousands of Europeans who

---

6   Odgen Street Public School (now Ogden Junior Public School) is one of
Toronto's oldest schools, though the original building was torn down and
replaced in 1957.

fled to Canada after the war, each Christmas it would publish a photo to prove that more kids from more foreign-born parents were in this school than any other in Toronto. Sydney was grateful that he was not selected for that group shot. The poor little bleeders had to dress in the natural costume of their parents!

So there they were in the *Tely*, ironically, as chauvinistic a newspaper as one can imagine, the hyphenated Canadian kids with shining faces, as commanded, shouting "cheese" — some looking suspiciously as if they had yelled "crap." The boys were ludicrously wearing oversized, elaborately embroidered blouses, pantaloons tucked into Cossack boots, white Greek skirts, boarded Bulgarian vests, lederhosen and, because there were few Brits in that district, only one wearing a Scottish kilt with his sporran practically touching the ground. The girls, likewise, were dressed in the finest provided by their proud matkas, mutters, mas and mothers.

Kindergarten (only mornings) Sydney quite looked forward to — the games, the pictures and the painting. But, as the years rolled by, somehow, he began to dislike school; it was the academic subjects he had no patience for.

At age seven, he was struck down with the mumps and quarantined in the house for fourteen days. The days of idleness caused him to do something that was to radically propel him into a previously unimagined direction.

After finishing reading *The Green Fairy Tales*, and with nothing else to read or do, his eyes lit on one of his most prized possessions. It was a fifteen-inch high, cheaply painted plaster statuette of Jackie Coogan as *The Kid* in Chaplin's film, which his father had bought him as a memento. Idly, he thought he might draw it. He found a stub of a pencil, licked the lead and proceeded to draw it on a torn-open and flattened brown paper bag. Finished, he then wondered what else he might do.

Whether his family was only being kind to him because he was ill, or because the drawing wasn't bad, he'll never know. From the praise lavished on him — especially from Ruth, who was positively ecstatic about it — one might think that Leonardo da Vinci (it's almost certain that no one in the family knew who the hell da Vinci was) had been reborn on Queen Street. He knew he was loved because he was the baby in the family (seven years younger than his brother and nine younger than his sister). But people cannot get enough love, it is said, and Sydney was clearly no exception. Gradually he became aware that the more he drew, the more he'd get an equal measure of love in return. No piece of paper in the house escaped his hand.

At school he couldn't wait for the Friday afternoons when his teachers, tired after the week's work, found it easier to hand out paper, pencils and paint and give the pupils free rein. He and his Finnish buddy, Kultimo, were top of the art class, each getting fifty out of fifty marks.

Sydney would never forget one teacher, a Mr. Greer, a long lean gaunt man who with a small beard might have looked like Abe Lincoln. This teacher actually looked forward to Friday not because he was pooped after the week's work, but because he was a closet artist. He had taken a summer course at the Ontario College of Art and when he saw Sydney was drawing people with noses and heads with ears, and was not drawing as the other boys and girls were — featuring airplanes firing guns or houses with curlicue smoke above chimneys — he gave special attention to the boy.

Mr. Greer, guessing that there might be some talent in Sydney, told him that on his recommendation, the Art Gallery of Toronto (much bigger today and re-named the Art Gallery of Ontario) had accepted him for their children's Saturday morning art classes. Two hundred or so, each year, were selected from the city's public schools, not so much because they were talented, but to increase their interest in art. Sydney, of course, would have to get his parents' permission. He was so excited that he raced home, nearly killing himself crossing Queen Street. Little did he know . . .

He rushed into the store yelling out his good luck as he passed his father, up the seven steps two at a time into the kitchen, and breathlessly told the news to a pleased, but strangely guarded mother. His Pa entered the kitchen and said, "Do I understand that the classes are on Saturday morning?"

"Yeah?"

"Well, I hoped you would know better. No Jewish boy draws

on the Shabbat." Ma looked at Pa, said nothing. Sydney anguished, pleaded. Cried. Made a big scene to no avail. "No boy of mine will take art classes on Saturday." His father turned and left the kitchen to return to the store. Sydney was poleaxed. The vibes of that scene shook him for the rest of his life.

It was sheer persistence over eighteen months before Sydney finally got his father to cave and allow him to take the Saturday morning art classes.

During those unhappy months a lot more was happening than his worsening relationship with his father. Sydney only lived to draw and paint, and he displayed what looked to the casual observer a blasé attitude to his formal education. In fact, he was charging toward a precipice, tentatively aware that he was committing suicide by not learning the three R's.

His penmanship was abominable; geography, just fair; and as for arithmetic, geometry and grammar, the very thought of them — their precise abstraction, ephemeral exactness — filled him with dread. He enjoyed English composition and English literature because he was already an avid reader, consuming at least three books a week as well as his brother's daily newspaper fix, the *New York Daily Mirror*. This tabloid gave him an advantage over all his pals, and more important, filled his thrill-seeking mind with the stuff of the real today! He was now Queen Street's expert on gangsters — Dutch Schultz, Baby Face Nelson, John Dillinger and Detroit's Blue Gang, whose tentacles stretched to Canada's Hamilton. He even knew the exact thickness of the glass in Al Capone's bullet-proof Cadillac.

Rich food for him too were Wilfred's pulp magazines such as *True Detective Fiction Weekly*. The kid was attracted to the stories of the unsung talents of Dashiell Hammett and Raymond Chandler and other writers by the vivid pen-and-ink action drawings illustrating the stories. His favourite private eye was a guy called "Candid Jones."[7]

---

7   The adventures of Terence "Candid" Jones were written by Richard B.
     Sale in *Detective Fiction Weekly* starting in 1936. He was a former insurance
     troubleshooter and professional photographer. Candid Jones not only used guns
     and cameras, he adapted a camera to fire bullets!

There he was, this young private eye, leaping forward with his blazing .38 Colt in his right hand and in his left, a candid camera held up to his eye snapping the crucial evidence of the crook committing the crime. To this day, he gets a frisson remembering the feel of turning over those crisp, pulp pages to gobble up the next hairy adventure.

The thought of a ten- or eleven-year-old reading this sort of literature no doubt sends shivers up the backs of the likes of Mary Whitehouse.[8] "Heavens, the child will learn to live by the gun." Instead, this child learned to live by the camera and not the gun. Whatever, no one paid much attention to what he read anyway. Except, perhaps, his brother, but he finally gave up trying to hide the magazines; a difficult job, since he was settled with sharing the same room and sleeping in the same bed with his squirming kid brother.

As for school, this kind of reading sure gave zest to Sydney's composition writing. He did enjoy English literature, but studying for exams was a real bugbear. He didn't mind boning up on *Ivanhoe*, or that kind of book, but it was memorizing poems that stuck in his craw. He never did learn to enjoy verse and no doubt it was the memory work that killed poetry for him forever.

At the age of eleven he began to use his noggin and thought of a way out. Here he was, before an exam, spending all his time trying to memorize poems instead of cramming on the stories he truly enjoyed. Looking at old returned exam papers he found that memory work, even if he had been perfect at it, could never earn him more than ten marks. Besides, out of the six poems they had studied, who could predict which one of them the teacher would ask for on the exam paper? All that work for a lousy ten marks out of a hundred. Why not, he figured, forget those ten marks and only study what he enjoyed? And that's what he did! His English literature marks jumped into the eighties among the best in his class. In art he was already consistently getting fifty out of fifty. (It was an omen of the future that art was

---

8   Mary Whitehouse was for decades the head of the National Listeners and Viewers Association in Britain, a conservative organization that wanted standards of decency and morality enforced on television. She would be the bane of Newman's existence when he worked for the BBC.

always worth half of any other endeavour.)

The Settlement ran Copper Beech, a summer camp, and when Sydney was ten, his parents gratefully allowed him to escape Queen Street's scalding pavements for the ten days offered to the underprivileged. At camp, Sydney was unlike the other kids who were out there batting baseballs, learning the Australian crawl or going on hikes through clouds of blackflies and mosquitoes. He would more likely be found under a shady tree weaving a basket or doing burnt-leather work using the sun's heat focused through a magnifying glass.

A young Sydney Newman.

It was during his second summer that he recalls most vividly when, not for the last time, he broke a rule. It was on a three-day canoe trip.

After paddling on silent lakes connected by whitewater streams through miles and miles of awe-inspiring wilderness, the campers found a place to bed down for the night. When they bivouacked, they had been trained to pitch their tents on flat ground so that if it rained, they wouldn't find themselves lying in a pool of water. Sydney, looking for physical comfort — a lifelong desire — couldn't resist the promise of a hollow filled with soft, fallen pine needles, and so pitched his pup tent exactly over it. It rained. He awoke at 4 a.m. soaked to the bone and cold. He might have asked himself why he could not take advice and must always find things out for himself. But, as usual, he didn't.

All the boys and the counsellors asleep, and despite the strictly enforced injunction against any boy going out alone in the canoe, Sydney thought, "Heck, why not? It's my only chance!" No, there was no tragedy to report. Not even a near drowning. Just simply, it was one of the most awe-inspiring, almost religious experiences he would ever have.

He put on some dry clothes, crept down to the shore, quietly turned the canoe right side up, slid it into the water and pushed off. With the J-stroke he had learned, he expertly dipped his paddle into the black, still water, silently gliding the canoe through the grey mist lying on the lake until the shore disappeared from sight. In truth, he felt the world had slipped away. Gone. It was so still! So eerie, beautiful. The *silence*! He felt that God Himself must surely be present. Then slowly his thoughts turned outwards, his reverie broken as he became aware of hearing for the first time in his life, the cry of a loon — that haunting cry that no Canadian can ever forget.

He could see it, a solitary black silhouette floating on the silky water 200 yards away, just under a bank of lifting mist. He thought he should get closer. Maybe even catch it. But when he oh-so-silently paddled halfway to it, it disappeared with a barely heard plop, diving into the water. Furiously he paddled to the centre of the ever-widening ripples, expecting the loon to emerge right alongside his canoe, and hopefully, with a fish in its mouth. It didn't. Where was it? He feared that perhaps a snapping turtle had grabbed it by one of its legs and pulled it under to drown! Anxiously, he scanned the lake. Would it never come up?

Then suddenly he heard that cry again. His head swivelled around scanning the narrow strip between the water and this mist and he saw it — as far away from him as before, alone. And again, that cry. And again it dived to emerge and cry, again. After two more tries to at least get close to it, frustrated by his efforts, he finally gave up. He accepted that no one was going to catch that solitary loon. It made him think.

The light on the distant hills told him that the sun was coming up and he'd better not be caught out in the canoe. Thoughtfully, he paddled back to the campsite. That cry was to remain with him forever — that sound that said like no other, you are alone. Many years later when he heard John Jacob Niles sing a Woody Guthrie song, the words triggered his memory of that dawn morning.

As he beached his canoe, one of the counsellors came charging down and tore a real strip off him. His absence, his disobedience — if he went through life that way! — the whole schmear was thrown at him. Sydney tried to explain but gave up. He didn't have the words. All he wanted now was to get to the bonfire where he could smell burning wood mixed with the salivating aroma of frying bacon and eggs.

Two days later, while the other boys were boasting about their adventures, Sydney was in a chair, tilted against the massive trunk of the camp's giant copper-beech tree, dozing in the bronze, leaf-filtered sun. He was beat from the canoe trip and half asleep, his other half hearing the cry of that elusive, solitary loon.

CHAPTER THREE

HIS SINFUL SATURDAYS

It was a year after the incident with the loon that Sydney finally got his father to give in and allow him to join the Saturday morning art classes.

To get to the art gallery he had to pass through Grange Park, which he knew like the back of his hand. During the summers he would be in the park watching the tennis players, running to catch their missed balls as they played on the clay courts on both sides of the gravel walk. Often he would earn fifty cents an hour (big money in those days) as a model for the students of the College of Art. He finally gave up trying to explain that he was not a cute "little Chinese boy."

In winter, the clay courts were flooded and became ice-skating rinks, with Sydney whizzing over the ice in his brother's cast-off skates, colliding with the hundred others also speeding and colliding. Under the glaring overhead lights it was joyously noisy and a wonderful blaze of colour. No L.S. Lowry painting, that. It was pure Bruegel. In the bushes on the rim of the park there was a lot of hanky-panky between the boys and girls. He and his pals sniggered about what went on, but later in his teens Sydney was to experience his own hanky-panky in those same bushes.

But there were years when Grange Park was unforgettably grim. During the Depression years when it wasn't cold, it was only here that the unemployed were able to bed down, take stock, smoke, curse the system, count the pennies they'd panhandled and think of their families. Imprinted on Sydney's mind was the sight of men queuing at the steady but thin stream of water from the park's only drinking fountain, patiently waiting for their turn to wash themselves or their socks and bits of clothing. Winter for them was a half-assed blessing when at least they'd get work in gangs as shovellers to rid Toronto of the mountains of snow that annually blanketed it.

It was a red-letter day the first time he stepped into the Art Gallery of Toronto for the much pined-for art classes. He knew the outside of the building well enough; it was so close to where he lived. If his parents had to live in a poor district, it was for Sydney the most fortuitous poor district in the whole of Toronto.

He would run 100 yards east from 331 to John Street (where the police call-box was) and then 200 yards up John to the dead end — Grange Park. Beyond its great grilled cast-iron gates, at the north end of a broad gravelled path bordered by flowers and huge elm trees, was the Grange — an eighteenth-century manor house looking as if it had been transplanted, brick by brick, from England. Behind it, somewhat dwarfing it, but tastefully so, was Sydney's destination, the relatively newly-built art gallery.

As if that wasn't enough for a budding artist, immediately to the right of the Grange House was the main entrance to the Ontario College of Art. And facing Grange Park was the University Settlement, part of the social studies activities of the University of Toronto. Where better could student social workers practise their best than on the scruffy children living in that depressed area? It was during those frustrating months he spent begging his father to rescind the Sabbath ruling that the Settlement House kept him alive. Its young staff never condescended to the children of the "underprivileged" class — that lovely circumlocution for the shit poor.

How greedily the boy consumed what the place offered! Its earnest librarians shoved books at him — books that blew his mind, opening a vast world far beyond Queen Street. Not for him though, was its modest, sweat-smelling gymnasium where skinny, freely perspiring youths were hoping to equal the strength of their idol, Charles Atlas. No, there he was in its art class run by a gentle, strange (Sydney had never met one before) Japanese student, Tatsuo Misoumi. The broken English the teacher spoke in no way inhibited his conveying the art of lino-cuts and the means of printing many colours on one original lino block. In later years when Sydney was making anti-Axis war propaganda films under John Grierson, he often pondered the frightful notorious "Nip" atrocities with his warm recollection of Tatsuo.

The early years of the Saturday mornings at the art gallery are a blurred but happy, mind-expanding memory for Sydney. The Long Gallery's polished, mahogany floor was a sea of boys and girls with their pots of paint and sheets of paper. It was so quiet one might think that the gallery was peopled by mutes — so intense are the children painting their notions of reality or their fantasies. In the marble-floored sculpture gallery, others are drawing the astonishingly ugly yet beautiful pregnant woman sculpted in stone by Meštrović or Michelangelo's giant bronze head of Moses.

On the walls of the different rooms he saw for the first time original, framed paintings — silky smooth old Masters of Kings and Queens and gentry and Christ crucified and Christ risen. He thought these oily and didn't like them. One painting that excited him was of a red-haired, somewhat wild-looking aristocratic woman by Augustus John. It wasn't until many years later that he understood why he liked it even though she was no beauty. What he sensed was the way the paint was so vividly and passionately applied that it seemed to match exactly the character of the woman portrayed.

Giddy-making as well were the bold swirls of paint in many of the works of the Canadian Group of Seven, which would imprint on him indelibly the extraordinary wild beauty of Canada's north. It would come to him that, in those paintings, no living creatures, man or beast, were ever seen. It was uninhabited land of rugged solitary pines fighting a harsh wind, or vast skies over silent icebergs or lakes reflecting the dazzling autumn wilderness of dark evergreens blotting red and translucent, golden yellow trees. But no people. If Sydney ever wondered what country was in his blood, it was those Group of Seven paintings that left him in no doubt.

It was a painter of the Group who organized and ran the classes. What a lovely man was Arthur Lismer[9] and how he made exciting the very act of catching life with pencil and paint. And with what chemistry he managed to infuse his staff with the same excitement to help that large bunch of what might have been unruly children. Then there was Norah McCullough, Lismer's chief assistant, whose serene smile, it seemed to Sydney, was reserved only for him. And kind Gordon Webber, with his Byronic, beautiful head and stunted body needing canes to walk, was always there to gently encourage and inspire.

It's easy to imagine that the city fathers and the directors of the gallery would be fearful that the paintings and sculptures might be defaced by the kids or the floors stained with spilled paint. It simply never happened, as far as Sydney could recall. But once, Arthur Lismer shocked all the children with an act that was typical of his exuberant nature.

He had just returned from a visit to Africa and all the children were sitting on the Long Gallery floor eagerly listening to his adventures. Spellbound, they ate up his every word as he described the wild animals he had seen and how the tribes used spears to catch animals for food and shields for protection when they fought. From behind a screen specially placed there, he brought out a beautifully decorated elongated shield and then, from behind that, he withdrew an enormous seven-foot spear.

To prove how sharp it was, he proceeded to sharpen a pencil with it. Then, frighteningly, he lifted it high as if to throw it to the far end of the gallery, shook his head and to the gasps of all, drove it

---

9   Arthur Lismer (1885-1969) was a painter and one of the original members of the Group of Seven, a collective of Canadian landscape painters who worked together from 1920 to 1933 and revolutionized landscape painting. Lismer founded the children's art class Newman attended in 1934.

right into the mahogany floor at his feet where it stood, quivering. He did this so theatrically that no child who was lucky enough to be at the art gallery in Lismer's days would ever forget it. Just as they would never forget the revelation and beauty of life when it was interpreted on canvas or paper, stone and clay by and for themselves and for others.

Sydney had more reasons later to be forever indebted to Arthur Lismer.

But now, his dream of entering the Ontario College of Art was a forlorn hope. To enter it, a student required university entrance qualifications. To get these he would need high school entrance grades. And even if he got all these, aside from the fact that his father thought being an artist was a one-way ticket to poverty, in no way did his parents have the money to pay the college fees.

He was sick in the knowledge that he'd never get his high school entrance. He was consistently failing in arithmetic and grammar and a few more subjects he disliked. All seemed lost until one Saturday morning he told Gordon Webber that his marks were so bad he'd never get into high school, and so, for him, there would be no art school. Webber suggested a solution by explaining that there were other art courses; to take the Central Technical School[10] art course, no high school qualifications were required.

Some of its teachers were friends of his and were good artists. Besides, they were mostly younger than those at the college and were academically less rigid. Elizabeth Wyn Wood, its head of sculpture, was already regarded as one of Canada's best sculptors. Up and coming was Carl Schaefer, a fine watercolour painter, who pointed at the wall where there hung a portrait of him by Charles Comfort. Another was Robert Ross, who could get more feeling out of a conté pencil than most artists with the most expensive palette of Windsor and Newton oil paint. And he told of others.

---

10 Central Technical School was developed as a school where adolescents could learn a trade. Even so, it had a burgeoning commercial art program. Many leading artists of the '30s, '40s and '50s in Canada got their start at Central Tech, and more still do today.

Sydney was somewhat disappointed when he heard that this was not primarily a fine art course with a capital A. He would also be required to study commercial art such as industrial design, lettering, batik and other applied arts. Its purpose was to prepare students for industry — to be a useful citizen. It never occurred to him, as it wouldn't to any eleven-year-old, that life wasn't a free ride. It demanded that one must earn a living, something that his father kept trying to drum into his head. Then, that old, ground-glass feeling in the pit of his stomach. He groaned upon learning that he could not escape the tedious academic subjects that he would be forced to take. Clearly, Toronto's Board of Education, in their Presbyterian earnestness, were intent on preparing children for all of life's eventualities, even if, as he thought, it killed them in the process.

Well, Sydney figured, he'd take the bad with the good and was overjoyed at what lay ahead after public school. *Freedom!* He couldn't wait! For the next year he totally disregarded all the subjects he found hateful. His teachers were disgusted by his poor marks. They'd be more so if they knew his mind: phooey to high school entrance qualifications.

It was around this time that Sydney first saw his name in print. Mr. Greer encouraged him to make a sculpture and enter it in an international soap-carving competition sponsored by Ivory soap. In the largest bar of Ivory laundry soap he could buy he carved the figure of a chef striding proudly holding aloft a roast turkey on a tray. It won third place in the Junior class. His prize was a sturdy, khaki-coloured Scout flashlight, which he cherished. He was heartbroken when twenty years later it was smashed by his three-year-old daughter, Deirdre, who with childish glee dropped it out of the window of a ninth-floor apartment in New York to see if it would bounce.

It would be sheer grandiosity on the part of the reader to think that at this age it ever occurred to Sydney that he was a potential Rembrandt. At best he might aspire to be a James Montgomery Flagg, or a Leyendecker, who painted those slickly Brilliantined, squeaky-clean American men and women in the Arrow shirt collar ads. Or an Arthur Rackham, whose illustrations of fairy tales thrilled with his gnarled and evil-looking oak trees that seemed alive and about to grab a child fleeing for its life. But Sydney had no doubt he would become a cartoonist.

Endlessly he copied the popular cartoonists of the day — John Held, Jr., with his men wearing trousers with the fashionable thirty-inch bottoms of the day and G. Russell Patterson, with his smart-set men and women. The daily newspaper's strip cartoons *Tillie the Toiler*, *Dick Tracy* or *Mutt and Jeff* he shunned because he thought them inferior. The *Tarzan* drawings excited him tremendously but all those muscles and charging lions, he found, were somewhat beyond him. It was teaching he needed; the Art Gallery classes were no good for an aspiring cartoonist. Then he noticed attractive ads at the back of magazines:

> YOU TOO CAN BECOME A CARTOONIST!
> In only twelve easy lessons mailed to you
> our TOP-NAME cartoon instructors will take you,
> step-by-step, to BIG MONEY!
> EARN AS YOU LEARN MORE THAN $75 A WEEK
> Send the enclosed special offer coupon NOW
> and receive the first lesson FREE!

Soon, 331 was inundated with thick envelopes addressed to Mr. Sydney Newman from all parts of the United States. He diligently followed each of the free, first lessons as they arrived. He became quite adept at drawing in crow-quill pen, brush and India ink. He depicted men and women running, jumping, slouching and climbing, their heads the standard cartoon proportion of one-quarter the height of the figure. He learned the symbols of emotion — *Grrr!* for hatred and rage, a heart above a head for love and a flashing light bulb for an idea. His family reacted to his efforts each in their own way — Ruth ecstatic; Mother monosyllabically pleased; Wilfred quipping, "How come one eye's got a squint?"; and Father . . . he just smiled and went back into the store. The idea of their buying him the other eleven lessons was, of course, out of the question.

During this period Sydney began a friendship that was to last many years. This was with a boy whose name was also Sidney, but spelled with an "i," who lived on Beverly Street opposite Grange Park. He was a starved-looking youth of fifteen, darkly handsome in a "spiv" fashion with his pencil moustache, big-toothed, ready-flashing grin and, surprisingly for one so young, dark smudges under his eyes. He never seemed to get enough sleep. He was in his second year of high school and to earn money he was a jazz musician playing non-union gigs for a pittance. What drew them together was that Sidney, too, wanted to become an artist.

A drum set was his instrument, and he would allow Sydney free rein on his set of percussion gear. This consisted of a glittering array of waxed chrome, brass, wood and inlaid artificial mother-of-pearl décor, which was not an accident — his full name was Sidney Pearl. "PEARL, get it?" Sydney eventually did. Later, while still in his teens, Sidney lived the high life. He criss-crossed the Atlantic on the palatial *Isle de France* during summer seasons as drummer in the Bert Simmons jazz band playing for third-class passengers.

He was a randy guy, was Sidney. Often, sitting resplendently in the midst of his percussion gear, he would regale his younger friend with stories of his many and varied sexual experiences, which came easy to him as a musician playing weddings, bar mitzvahs, coming-out dances and such. In meticulous detail he would musically punctuate each stage of his conquests. A wham on his bass drum meant a connection had been made to get laid; a sneaky, vibrato slide of his brushes on the snare drum was a hand sliding up a skirt; a tinkle on a triangle was tweaking a nipple. The orgasm? For that he would go berserk. With maniacal glee he would hit everything in sight, a veritable, premature, Gene Krupa in full flight. After ending with a diminuendo gliss on his marimba he'd sag, depleted, and gaze at his admiring friend with a glazed look on his face. These moments excited Sydney in ways he didn't fully understand.

Totally incomprehensible were other tales where Sidney, to continue getting jobs, would have to evade the amorous passes of a notorious old queen of a society bandleader who never tired of offering more money and jobs for a young man's bottom. Confused, Sydney would bring the talk back to art; that is to say, to cartooning.

They began dreaming up cartoon gags, some of them so funny, so excruciatingly hilarious, they'd end up in helpless, screaming, eye-watering laughter. Why, Sydney often wondered later in life, do grown-ups so rarely find a moment so funny as to release such intense laughter? Some of their jokes they felt were as good as, if not infinitely better than, the ones in the popular American humour magazines of the day: *Judge*, *Life* (somewhat similar to England's *Punch*), *College Humor* and *College Life* (both reprinting the best cartoons from university newspapers) and the somewhat raunchy *Ballyhoo*. *The New Yorker* was new and had not yet crossed their path. Hey, they thought, a bulb flashing above their heads. Why not take a crack at sending a cartoon they would do themselves? "Why not?" they shouted. "Yeah!"

Because Sidney was a jazz musician, they would parody and give funny meanings to the popular songs of the day. Its title would be its caption and would contrast with the cartoon. They drew a cartoon showing an angry man chasing another who has a gallon jug of hooch with three X's marked on it clutched to his chest captioned SOMEBODY STOLE MY GAL. Another for the song "I Covered the Waterfront" showed a very fat lady in a bathing suit standing on the seashore. They were certain that any magazine, well at least the editor of *College Humor*, forced to use crappy drawings by amateur university students, would absolutely grab theirs like a shot! They would guarantee a page of five cartoons a month. No pain! The supply of songs was endless.

Within a week they completed seven cartoons and mounted the best five on a sheet of illustration board. With returned postage enclosed, they wrapped it most carefully and sent it off to The Editor, c/o *College Humor* in New York. They waited and waited. Then one day it came back somewhat battered, containing a pink rejection slip thanking the artist (singular!) for thinking (thinking!) of *College Humor*. The damn pink slip didn't even explain why it was not accepted. They reasoned that their cartoons were rejected because they were not university students. Undaunted, they decided to try again, but this time they'd send the page of drawings to a classy magazine, which might even pay more: *Judge* magazine. One can guess. It too was returned — this time the rejection slip was blue. After a rainbow of rejection slips they decided to give up their joint efforts.

While Sidney Pearl pondered whether to leave high school and go to Tech when his young friend did, Sydney thought he'd try a cartoon of his own. Perhaps their song idea was too corny. After all, he was reading the *New York Daily Mirror* and big-time stuff like that. He felt he knew what American readers wanted. A good question. Was this the first sign that Newman was becoming aware of audiences and the market?

He dreamed up an idea he thought fabulous and his friend thought so too. He drew a quadriplegic, empty sleeves and trousers neatly safety-pinned, sitting in a wheelchair looking up, startled, at a white-coated doctor with the inevitable stethoscope hanging from his neck, speaking. The caption under the cartoon read, "I am sorry. I am afraid we shall have to amputate."

Sydney could not understand why the cartoon was rejected. Was it too cruel? Tasteless? It was 1930 and black comedy was yet to be tried. The boy was clearly ahead of his time.

By June 1931, Sydney was into his third month of his thirteenth year. As expected, he learned that he had failed in three subjects, and would not be going to high school. To his amazement he got a pass in arithmetic, one mark above failure. But he couldn't care less. Because he was going to continue his schooling, his family was not particularly disturbed.

Ruth was concerned with more immediate matters. She was preparing to get married to Edmond Saffron, a hotshot shoe salesman from Buffalo. She would move there, a mere 125 miles away just inside the American border beyond Niagara Falls. Buffalo was where inhibited Torontonians would shuffle off to, to escape their own blue Sundays and have a hot time in the old town or buy the latest fashions at bargain prices. Today, of course, the traffic is reversed: Buffalonians come to Toronto.

Eddie was regarded as a "good catch." Hearing him talk, one knew he had prospects. Sydney's parents were busy preparing for a wedding reception they could ill afford and which wouldn't shame them. His father, by now, had given up trying to dissuade Sydney from becoming an artist. Wilfred was beginning to forge his own career. On his elegant, black bicycle — a Planet, which only the Toronto police could afford — he was whizzing around Toronto as a collection boy for Canadian Pacific telegrams.

September 2, 1931, 8:15 a.m. Sydney bounced out of 331 heading for the art course at Central Technical school. On his way up University Avenue, Sydney watched the Labour Day parade, with its endless union floats covered with flowers and happy, pretty girls and macho men in work clothes, massed bands and dignitaries riding in open Cadillacs.

His walk slowed as he saw the state of Queen Street where it broadened between Peter Street and Spadina Avenue. It looked as if a hurricane had passed through it. Here, 500 yards west of University Avenue, a different labour event had been planned. A happy one? In the Depression? Who the hell had a job in that district? What an opportunity this day was for the illegal Communist Party.

Tim Buck, the leader of the party, was behind bars in Kingston Penitentiary, along with seven other communists. To protest and demand the release of the imprisoned eight, a core of communists attracted hundreds of unemployed, many from central and eastern Europe — both "red" Ukrainians who wanted their release and "white" Ukrainians who hated the "reds" and wanted the communists to be kept in jail, if not hanged. From the look of the street, Sydney knew that the police had also been present.

Had he seen Eisenstein's *Ten Days That Shook the World*, he would have noted the similarity between scenes in it and Queen Street. He remembered what he saw months earlier when walking home from Ogden School. As he passed the Elder Carriage Works, suddenly out from its wide gates a squad of mounted policemen came charging down Soho toward Queen Street followed by three open trucks filled with cops. Sydney ran like mad to see what was going on. They were breaking up a protest meeting of left-wing unemployed. He would never forget seeing mounted police above the crowd with batons bending up and down, clobbering right and left. A horse would rear up and come down, cries and screams rising above the noise of the melee. Sydney was terrified and sickened. "Just like Russia," he could still hear his father say, "only here, the Kossakim are the good guys."

This morning, Sydney, now old enough to understand, sighed as he picked his way through the mess of broken glass, torn DEFEND THE SOVIET UNION! MORE JOBS! and FREE THE EIGHT! banners and leaflets littering the ground, as well as stains that he guessed were dried blood. Bad, he thought, but today, it's art for me. Forever! And kept going.

Central Technical School was about a mile from 331 but for Sydney it was the beginning of a trip to be measured in light years. He carried within him the feelings of plain simple caring, love even. But also buried within him were the sensations of frustration, estrangement, poverty and helplessness that lead to irrational escape or violence — a grab bag of latent seeds that could germinate and flower into a human vegetable, a gardenia . . . or poison ivy.

CHAPTER FOUR

MY FATHER OF THE DOORSTEP

Whenever one reads an autobiography, one inevitably wonders how much of what is recounted by the author of his childhood can be taken as gospel. I do.

The pre-perception years up to the ages of ten to twelve cannot help but be a hopeless blur for those less fortunate than, say, Anthony Burgess, who seems able to salivate over his incredible total recall. I'm convinced that for most, childhood memories of events and relationships are what's left over after rejecting what one dares not, for the sake of sanity or vanity, remember. If I'm wrong, psychoanalysts' couches would be as empty as their owners' pockets. In recalling my childhood, it would be a waste of time to question if I have consciously tried to clean up my B.G. (background, to anyone who has not read a film script). I don't have to these days, and besides, a juicy, lurid background being an illegitimate, or the victim of incest or being beaten by a drunken father seems obligatory, being in showbiz. No, as a politician would proclaim, my life is an open book. If you believe him, why not believe me?

If there was drama in my young life it was the kind that John Grierson used to describe as the drama of the doorstep — the stuff that is under one's nose, commonplace, a yawn and therefore unseen. Unseen, that is, until its significance is noted and held aloft in some creative means. At around twelve years of age, I began to think.

Those old children of Israel were pretty smart when they dreamed up the notion of the Bar Mitzvah for boys when they became thirteen. Not so smart was making it such a traumatic experience (I'm sure they didn't have kids like me in mind). For that ceremony I had to learn things I never understood, and write and deliver a speech from memory to the entire congregation. (That damned chore, memory, was to dog me all my life.) What I thought really smart though, and still do, was that this event declared the boy a man. Bar Mitzvah was proof positive that I had now fully reached the age of perception, which I read to mean that I no longer had to obey my father. He didn't like it, but Judaic law was on my side. Henceforth, I was to go my own way. Inescapable, though, were the sometimes dubious rewards of eating the apple of awareness. I gradually put together the bits and pieces that seeped from my memories.

Was I a happy child? I think so, but perhaps masochistically so, because the joys seem to be outweighed by frustrations and wounds that clearly bit deep. My mother was always an enfolding presence; Wolf, uncommunicative but warmly indulgent; and Ruth always on top, cuddling when happy with me, her girl's nails scratching when she was not. My father —

Wolf, Ruth and Sydney Newman.

how could I make sense out of what, in later years, I recognized was a subconscious hatred of him. I find it truly awe-inspiring; the natural, blind incomprehension children have of their parents. That's me, in spades!

I knew who I was. My father told me. I was Shimshon ben Mordecai, but he, he was Mordecai ben . . . what?

He was an orphan, born in Russia and raised, it was said, by an aunt. From her, he received a modicum of Jewish religious teaching, and was booted off boardwalks and into muddy roads by too many plain, fun-loving Russian folk. Jews crucified Christ, didn't they? Jew or not, he was good enough to be press-ganged into the army to fight for Holy Russia. When conscripted he was an apprentice cobbler, and he became a fully-fledged shoemaker in the Service Corps of the Imperial Army of Czarist Russia. He was reliable and skilled enough, and so he earned a lance-corporal hook and the responsibility for the work of a squad of shoe repairers. It's a cliché that an army marches on its stomach, but my father knew differently: it marches on its boots. And the Russians wore out a lot of them in 1904 as they went to fight the Japanese in the far east of Asia. The Japanese won that war and the Czarist Army fled, trudging 10,000 miles westward to home.

My father reached home safely, but Russia was not for him. He kept right on going. He'd had enough of those *verdammt Cossacks*! He didn't stop until he reached Hamburg, but only long enough to take the first boat leaving Europe; its destination happened to be Montreal. That wasn't far enough for him and so, going as far as his little money would sensibly take him, he finally came to Toronto. Somehow he managed to set up a tiny shoe-repair shop on York Street and live in one room above a Chinese restaurant where meals were thrown in as part of his rent. That meant he was eating food forbidden to Jews. I found this out years later, just after I had learned to use chopsticks.

We were in the kitchen and my mother was shelling some peas. In an attempt to show off my new and somewhat crude skill to my parents, I fumbled it. My father saw this, "Gimme those chopsticks. I'll show you!" and to my utter amazement, with easy dexterity, he proceeded to pick up some peas, even putting one in my mouth. He was good! I asked him how he knew how to use them and he explained. It did not occur to me then that Pa had broken the Jewish dietary laws! Anyway, there he was, in 1906, a fine, somewhat Tatar-ish looking man of twenty-six starting a new life in a new country, and he did not know a single word of either of its two languages.

Flashback to 1898. Sailing past the Statue of Liberty, a ship from Europe carried a girl of fourteen, gazing rapturously at New York's buildings, which seemingly reached for heaven. Except for her jet-black hair and blue eyes she can be best described as looking, I imagine, somewhat like those young, pretty, Titian-haired girls Renoir painted. She had come all the way from Austria, near Vienna, in a manner typical of immigrant families. The oldest émigré of the family would arrive and save money for the fare to bring over a brother or a sister. The two would then save and bring over more family and so on. She was Bessie Fibus, my mother, the second youngest of nine brothers and sisters, who crossed half of Europe and the Atlantic to give birth to me some nineteen years later.

She lived with her brothers and sisters in a cold-water-only, cockroach-ridden railway flat, in New York's Rivington and Orchard Streets, where most European immigrants were living within sight of the American dream. Bessie went to school and was soon speaking English well, albeit with a "Toidy-toid Street" New York accent. For reasons not known, perhaps an unwillingness to become dissolved into the much-heralded American melting pot, or, more likely, to get away from what they felt a stifling ghetto, Bessie, four sisters and a brother left in 1905 and took a third-class train up to Canada. Two sisters settled in Hamilton, while Bessie and two sisters and a brother moved to Toronto.

It was there that the seven-year North American Bessie met the three-months immigrant, Mordecai. One can imagine their courtship — he, not knowing more than twenty words of English and she, no Russian or Polish. Here's where the lingua franca of the Jews came in handy. With her native tongue of German and his Yiddish, verbal communication, as they say, was happily established to help fill in the gap of their love and they married. Mordecai became Morris and some years later they made a down payment on a store with living quarters above it. With their two young children, Ruth and Wilfred, they moved to Queen Street. The mortgage payments and taxes, later in the depressed '30s, were to cause them great anxiety, so poor were they. Now, Morris was determined to mend only the shoes his family wore. His cobbler's bench with all its iron lasts, hammers, knives, stropping board, flies and rasps, boxes of tacks and assorted pieces of leather were set up at the back of what became a retail outlet — Morris was going to sell footwear in his own place! He named it The Right Shoe Store. My Uncle Schlein, of whom I was fond, was a wagster and couldn't resist ribbing, "Morris, what's the matter? Don't you sell any shoes for left feet?"

The year I was born, 1917, it was joked by Ma and endless relatives that I was conceived only to save my father from being conscripted because rumours were rife that men with two children were about to be called up. That may be true, because in his mind, even though an Ally, not a finger was he going to lift to help Russia. "Russia? Those *momsers*? Never!" Later, in the promising years of the Popular Front and when I was in my teens, it never occurred to me why my father became apoplectic at the mere mention of Soviet Russia when I firmly believed then that the sun shone out of Joe Stalin's ass.

My father's intransigence about my art on the Sabbath, which nearly drove me mad, would make any reasonable person ask what lifeline had he to a normal existence. He did not have a single blood relative anywhere that he knew of. He was constantly submerged by the endless visits of my mother's brothers and sisters in Toronto, or those who drove up from New York or down from Hamilton, most with their endless number of offspring. They were great breeders, those Fibus siblings. I had so many cousins that I think that it wasn't until I was ten that I was able to count so high. And couldn't they talk and argue! Unless they spoke Yiddish, my father's broken English only allowed him to occasionally chip in. As well, he was illiterate, unable to write in any language and only able to read Yiddish and Hebrew. In the latter, he only understood the gist of the prayers and not the literal meaning of the words. (The little English he did speak he learned from my mother and consequently, to the amusement of many, had a Toid Avenue flavour even though he had never set foot in New York.)

The whole essence of his existence, it came to me so much later, was the daily, unconsciously tedious grind of maintaining his family. The only outside event he looked forward to was the weekly Saturday ritual of going to shul. Here, there was not only communion with his "dare-not-be-named" God, but there were mates, men like himself who had fled the soul-destroying anti-Semitism of Eastern Europe; he could speak Yiddish here, share experiences, argue, praise and, above all, be a mensch as a man should be.

Every Saturday morning, fifty-two times a year, he would put on his finest — crisp shirt, grey tie, black jacket and striped trousers — and take me (also dressed to kill, and clean as a whistle) by the hand to go to shul. I'm sure we looked like a banker and his son out for a brisk walk as we'd stride eastward along slummy Queen Street, past John, McCaul, Simcoe Streets and then up University Avenue past the Osgoode Hall Law School and the Armouries to what I feel was my father's second home: the Goel Tzedec Synagogue[11] that he and nine others had founded in 1907. There they'd sit in the founders' pew alongside others looking just as correct and prosperous. But not all were prosperous — least of all, my father.

When the service was over and they had bid each other a *gutten Shabbos*, I gradually became aware that not all obeyed the stricture against riding in a car on the Sabbath. Some I would see enter a black, chauffeur-driven limousine discreetly parked around the corner to be driven home. In contrast, my father and I would retrace our way home through the Saturday noon crowds. On arrival, he would immediately go upstairs, take off his shul finery and don his shoe-selling work clothes, relieving my mother who had been minding the store. She would then make sure that I got out of my Sabbath best and into my play clothes.

---

11 Goel Tzedec merged with another synagogue in the 1950s and still exists today as the Beth Tzedec congregation.

My father thought he had the solution to my ignorance about the sacredness of the Sabbath. He decided that *der kind* needed further religious instruction; further, because I already went unprotestingly to parochial classes each day for an hour after school. Now, for two hours on Saturday afternoon, when all the other kids were out playing or going to the Pickford, I had to go to a special rabbi — a frightening, near hunchbacked, ancient gnome of a man who was noted for his rabbinical wisdom. He would point to the Hebrew words in books beyond the first five of the Old Testament and with a bony finger, the joints horribly swollen by arthritis, force me to read them aloud. Should I make a mistake, which was not infrequent, *wham!*, that gnarled hand would come down on me like a blunt axe. I was sure that old man detested me as much as I hated him.

I must admit, though, that occasionally when the rabbi (who spoke an educated English) revealed his interpretation of an event involving those ancient Jews and the shenanigans they got up to, it sure made me sit up and made my eyes pop in wonderment. Imagine, it was mighty King David who was so strong that when he struck his enemy with his sword diagonally on the left shoulder, not only did he lop off the head but the right fighting arm as well! Now that kind of religious instruction I enjoyed, and it showed. Seeing this, the rabbi would be encouraged and, forgetting that I was only ten years old, told me things that would have shaken my mother rigid. Wasn't it Esther, a nice Jewish girl who became the concubine of a goy king? That was okay, I learned, because her position made it possible for her to later save her people. Too bad it never occurred to me to ask what price virginity is, though, if it transpired that later her people did not need saving. Alas, those memorable moments were all too rare.

A year later I was no further ahead. I could not conceive why anyone could regard drawing on the Sabbath a sin. True, the Bible did forbid Jews to make graven images, but I was not going to draw God. I wouldn't dare. Besides, nobody, least of all Jews, knew what He looked like. His appearance was totally irrelevant to their (my) inherited faith. To no avail, the religious teaching that was drummed into me did not ease my frustration. Worse, it was like prescribing large doses of sugar to a diabetic.

Deep in my gut, the nerve endings of the realities of my father's survival were beginning to twitch like mad at the time of my Bar Mitzvah. Jews were not allowed to eat *treif*, or non-kosher food and yet my father had eaten Chinese food; hardly Kosher. Jews were not allowed to drive cars on the Sabbath, but some did, including father's respected friends. Business was forbidden on Shabbos, and yet my own father sold shoes on the Sabbath! (As poor as it was, Saturday, in fact, was the only decent selling day of the week.) This was my instinctive reasoning — the start of a conscious rift, a growing crack in the armour that bonded me to my father and to his beliefs.

Not surprisingly, my first resolve upon reaching the age of perception was that I would never again enter a house of worship to pray. It's not that I had any doubts about the existence of God, I just figured that He knew this and would allow me to relate (that word!) to him in my own way. For me, the Ten Commandments said it all for all religions; the rest I thought to be hocus-pocus and hypocrisy — the ritual, the often false sense of bonhomie, the conformity, the reserving of goodness for the day of worship only.

Other perceptions that grew in my mind then, and on which I acted, surprise me when I think of them today. No one enjoyed being a Cub in the 59th Pack more than I did with its Akela ritual, its green uniform, the passing of tests to win badges and all the rest. Becoming twelve I was allowed to join and was accepted into the 59th Boy Scout Troop. It should have been a great day, but I found it just plain silly — a change of mind that literally happened overnight. I never went back again.

One route to the Central Technical School was to walk up Spadina Avenue, which throbbed with Jewish life, and was the centre of the needle trades. But on hot days I would go up Beverly Street in the shade of its enormous elm and chestnut trees past the Art Gallery at Dundas and then further north to College Street, where I would come to what I used to call The Big Library: the Central Circulating Branch of Toronto's Public Library. At twelve I was, at long last, entitled to join it. And I did — a red-letter day!

I now giggle at the thought of my first request of a librarian: "Miss? Miss, is there a book I can borrow which — which kinda — which kinda tells you how to tell what kind of person a person is by the features on his face?" With sweet solemnity the darling looked down at me and asked me to follow her. She led me to the stacks titled Psychology and hauled out a few tomes, some of them out of my reach, and handed them to me. To my dismay they were all dense with words. "Miss — Miss?" I asked. "Don't you have any with pictures in them? You know, with noses and eyes and things like that?" Would you believe it? She found a book that had exactly what I wanted! It was written by a German around 1880 and was well illustrated. After considerable research, his results, he claimed, were scientifically accurate and would be of value to those contemplating choosing a partner or identifying a criminal.

Studying the many clear drawings in both full face and profile, and reading the accompanying text, I learned that a high forehead denoted high intelligence; slit eyes, someone not to be trusted; full lips, a passionate nature and blah blah blah. I believed every bit of it — for a couple of years anyway. It seemed like Hoyle to me because it verified what the correspondence cartoon courses had taught.

Believe it or not, by the time I was sixteen, I ploughed through many a book on those stacks, not excluding Sigmund Freud's lectures on psychoanalyses. I didn't understand a damned bit of it, but found it fascinating stuff. Maybe through a kind of osmosis some of it stuck. One piece of his I did understand was an analysis of laughter in which he stated that one laughs as a relief from fright. He cited a baby that is pleased when confronted with a pretty Jack-in-the-Box when it is closed. When the button is pressed and Jack springs out, the baby is terrified and sucks in air about to cry; once it sees that the toy is harmless, then miraculously the baby's inhaled air emerges as laughter. What a revelation, proven to me a thousand times when in an audience laughing at the antics of Chaplin, Harold Lloyd and other great comedians.

CHAPTER FIVE

NUDES, MADE EASY

There was certainly no nonsense in the minds of the descendants of the Scots, English and United Empire Loyalists of Toronto when they built the Central Technical School. To them, idleness was a sin and existence without paid work was strictly a non-starter. Training of skills for the young was clearly no laughing matter. Its jut-jawed purpose was reflected in the rough blocks of granite that enclosed more than a thousand students in the massive, grey structure. Inside were classrooms by the score, but most impressive were the mind-boggling number and variety of training laboratories, kitchens, studios and workshops for every conceivable trade from bricklaying to cooking, commercial art, chemistry, cabinet and die-cast making. In one vast room I saw an entire house being built and in another, the construction of the fuselage of an airplane. In retrospect, those honest Ontarians had their eyes on the future. Who would imagine it — aircraft construction in 1931!

But it was the art department that grabbed me. It was built as a kind of penthouse that sat four-square, four floors above the main entrance, so that no art room was without natural daylight. And rising above it, all by itself, was the life class. On its roof was the flagstaff, flying the Canadian flag — the Red Ensign.

Here, my fellow art students and I were truly in seventh heaven in more ways than one. We would look out over the city and be constantly surprised that, except for church spires, the newly built Royal York Hotel (claimed to be the largest in the British Empire), the Bank of Commerce building (likewise, the highest) and the Park Plaza Hotel, Central Tech seemed to be placed bang in the middle of a green forest that fingered out onto Toronto's islands, into the blue sheen of Lake Ontario. We also felt somewhat superior to the thousand or so students below us hammering, sawing and welding their way to a skill. And while taking a shortcut from one side of the vast building to the other through our corridor, which was lined with our sculptures, the uncultured bums couldn't resist pencilling in eyeglasses, moustaches, armpit and pubic hair on our precious works of art. Why, oh why, many of us felt, didn't the rest of the world appreciate *art* like us?

It never occurred to me or my family that most art supplies were not free. For the price of a sheet of Whatman's watercolour paper you could take a girl out for a meal and each have a hot beef sandwich with peas and chips well larded with HP sauce, plus a slice of coconut-cream pie with your coffee. I pleaded and got enough money from my father to buy the barest minimum of required art supplies; it wasn't because he was ungenerous or resented my wanting to become an artist (he'd long given that up), it was because he simply didn't have enough money, like others in those dark, depressed years. I carefully doled out the few bucks he could afford, and those added by my brother, to buy a portfolio with an oil-cloth cover to protect it from the rain. I filled it with a dozen sheets of large, cheap cartridge paper, two precious sheets of watercolour paper, a frightfully expensive (about $1.75, I recall) set of drafting instruments and, of course, a drawing board set and T-square. Loaded with all this in my portfolio, my thirteen-year-old arm barely long enough to grasp it, would be carried each day for a mile to the school and back again to 331. Funny!

Being as abhorrent as I am about any kind of physical exertion, I have no recollection whatsoever of resenting that. Hell, for the first time in my life homework was a pleasure.

In the course, whether you were good at art or not made no difference with regard to which of the two "streams" you were put into. The clunks, as we called my stream, was made of those who did not have their high-school entrance, were therefore very young, aged thirteen to fifteen, and usually too poor to pay the College of Art fees. In the first year we were allowed only half our periods on art (in the last year, 4/5ths) and the rest of the time on my bête noir, the academic subjects.

The lucky stiffs in the other stream were as different as could be. To begin with, they acted differently, especially the girls — women really but with a lot of girl in them. They were curious about us hoi polloi kids — a sort of Lady Chatterley–Mellors attraction — which they expressed both intellectually and sexually. Mellors, that's me, was happy to reciprocate on both. Most came from affluent families. Some even drove their own cars and spent money as if there was no tomorrow. Over the four years at school I never got over being disturbed when many of them would throw away an expensive piece of art paper because they felt they had started a drawing badly. It was not envy; to be casual about materials for creative work was sick. It was disrespect in some off-putting way I still find hard to explain. In most art subjects I did well, perhaps because I couldn't afford to start a work badly — some of it, of course, even done on scavenged paper I couldn't resist recirculating.

In one respect though, I profoundly envied them — they weren't required to take any academic subjects. Imagine me in the middle of life class drawing an interesting model in an unusual pose: I knew she was unlikely to be given that pose to take again and I would be feeling really pleased at my progress when the gong, like the death knell, rose from down below! While my mates in the other stream kept on cheerfully working, I unpinned my drawing from my drawing board, carefully put it into my portfolio, rose, apologized — "Sorry. Excuse me. S'cuse me" — as I slithered past precariously poised easels and joined the other clunks who had to leave. We trudged down the stairs into the bowels of the building to take a class in mathematics or French or other subjects I thought totally irrelevant. (Later, I was to pay a heavy penalty for my disregard of what was to become an official language of Canada: French.)

The pattern was set in my first year. Despite failing in six subjects, I passed because of my high marks in most art subjects. The same happened in years two and three. In my fourth and final year, even though I was among the top three in the class, my failures in academia could not be excused; the art department's authorities, with touching regret, had to deny me my graduation certificate. Being artists themselves, I don't think they thought they were depriving me of a pot of gold. I couldn't have cared less.

After about a year of feeling my oats as a better than average student and gorging on great works of art — Goya, El Greco, Picasso and Cézanne (da Vinci, Michelangelo and other Renaissance painters, generally, bored me) — the idea of becoming a mere cartoonist in my young mind was out — not creative enough. My aim was to become a fine artist.

Two years after leaving, I found out that being a struggling artist was romantic crap. I had left home, so no more free meals, no free bed and worse, I couldn't even afford to buy a girl a beer. Inevitably I began accepting the occasional teaching job and commercial art assignment. Gradually these took over and I found that, having a one-track mind, I couldn't solve the problem of pleasing myself by pleasing others. Later in life and dealing with creative people, there was nothing original in my problem. I painted less and less. There was also, I must confess, the sick-making feeling that I would never be as good as the artist I most admired: Picasso. I think now that that reality outweighed the poverty thing. Being second best was not to be even thought of.

While my teachers at Central Technical School encouraged me to become a painter, the course also provided a comprehensive back-up. It made sure that no matter what, I would be given at least rudimentary skills in all manner and means of making a living as a creative person.

We learned all about printing processes, styles and usage of typefaces; lettering by hand (I was terrible at this, the finish of my work was crude, but they said my spacing was great); wallpaper, textile design and hand-painted batik; sculpture and casting processes; drafting; ad layout; poster design and illustration. Whether talented creatively or not, we were all given no excuse for being unemployed. Most wonderful of all though, was my getting a sense of space, the arrangement and relationship of different shapes, textures, and colours and the capacity to express an idea — observed, felt or imagined. I also learned a lot about myself.

Going to my first life drawing class, in which the female model would be nude, worried me like mad. Suppose I got an erection? I'd look pretty silly, like a toff, standing nonchalantly behind my easel with my right hand drawing and my left hand in my trouser pocket. A right Charlie needing a monocle! No sweat: she turned out to be an old lush with a body like a half-empty bag of flour. There was something so positive about her shape that she was a delight to draw. The young models with attractive bodies were difficult to get right, avoiding making them look like *Esquire* pin-up, pretty girls. I very quickly became positively blasé about seeing a naked woman — in the classroom, that is.

Most teachers were as Gordon Webber described them — young or youngish in spirit and they infused us (they did me, anyway) with a sense of excitement about capturing life in paint and pencil.

On my first look at Elizabeth Wyn Wood, head of sculpture, I fell instantly in love. I thought her beautiful, with a face that could have been sculpted by the ancient Egyptians with the same quality of eternal serenity that nothing could faze. Her chief technical assistant, Simpson — whom we all called Simmie — would go to endless trouble, teaching us to cast our almost uncastable work with impossible undercutting, and making sure our clay figures wouldn't collapse when their metal and wire innards were not clearly thought out in advance.

There was always a sense of mystery to me surrounding the private life of Robert Ross, a part-time teacher who taught only drawing. A stocky man in his early thirties, with his thin black moustache looking like George Raft's strong-arm in a Warner Brother's movie, he'd often turn up at life class unshaven and somewhat bleary-eyed as if the night before had been a helluva one. After setting the model's pose (I was sure he slept with one of them and no doubt with some of the girls in the class), he would climb up onto the broad window ledge, make himself comfortable and begin reading the morning *Mail and Empire* before falling into a doze. As I worked, I'd often look up at him, newspaper fallen to the floor, silhouetted against the green panorama of Toronto, hoping he'd awake soon and look at my drawing. He worried us because rumours were continually rife that the head of the art department, Peter Howarth, was about to fire him. He wasn't. Not in my day. Howarth must never have confused the choice between personal behaviour and talent. Ross's drawings were the most beautiful of any artist I ever knew personally. No shading was needed by him. His sensitive line expressed the three-dimensional form in lovely perfection.

After about an hour he'd climb down from the windowsill and begin making his rounds from pupil to pupil. In criticizing your work, he'd never touch your drawing, but alongside it would show you how it could be done. He held the conté pencil in a most unusual way. Not as one would when writing, but as a surgeon would a scalpel, with the length of the pencil under his palm, guiding it with his arm and not his fingers. Depending on the shape of the form, his line would vary in a continuous motion from a touch of barely seen lightness to a darker and thicker presence; sometimes he would turn the long point sideways and almost achieve a brush-stroke. Miracle of miracles, he was able to create an equally beautiful drawing by starting at the bottom and pushing his pencil upwards, too. Simply breathtaking — a way of drawing I adopted but never equalled.

Another teacher whom I got to know and liked many years later was one I disliked intensely at the time. Not only did he correct my drawing by drawing right on top of it, but he did so with a blunt stub of a pencil. How I fiercely resented him and his occasional nasty, dumb sarcasm. Dumb because he was insensitive. He knew nothing of my background. I'm still amused at my cheeky response to his, "Newman, perfectly dreadful drawing. Unless you do better, you'll end up being a shoe salesman!" I replied, "Sir, you may mock me all you want but leave my father out of it. He sells shoes." He stonily looked at me, said nothing and moved to the next student.

On another occasion in the class on advertising art, he assigned us to design an ad that would express in the most original way the product sold. I rose to the challenge and to this day, think it one of the best ideas I've ever had. I conceived of an ad to sell fresh fish. Since fish bought at an open market was always wrapped in newspaper, why not paint the fish on an actual page of newspaper? That's what I did.

On a want-page, uncluttered by bold ads, I painted two fish lying on the paper in limpid watercolour so that the print could still be seen through them. It looked like a Japanese silk painting. Everyone admired it, but what I got from that teacher was, "We all know that fish smell, but that's no excuse for doing a painting that stinks!" The sting of that comment burned into my brain. Years later I can't count the times I was about to say the same, but didn't, to a drama director doing a lousy job who blamed his results on the poorish play rather than on his direction.

We students were cruel, too. One of the dearest teachers we had was Carl Schaefer, a fine watercolour painter who later became one of the Canada's most distinguished war artists. I suppose he must have been in his late twenties and had the most endearing, conscientious, gentle and almost child-like nature. What bunch of students could resist ragging him? When with great seriousness he'd turn to the blackboard to illustrate a point, we'd throw chalk at him, carefully hoarded and saved for just his classes. His dark jacket would look as if he'd just come through a snowstorm and, the funny thing is, he either didn't care, or, I suspect, was unaware that it had happened. I'm embarrassed remembering the idiotic things we did to him.

In life class the easels we used were of the three-legged kind and, if not set up right — that is, when the single rear leg is too close to the front two and accidentally jostled, which happened frequently — it would come crashing down with an irritating clatter. Sometimes a falling easel hit another one and both would collapse, which gave us a great idea. In one of Schaefer's classes we set up four easels, and pushed the first one; like a row of dominoes they all toppled over, one by one making a splendid clatter. Oddly enough, or perhaps not surprisingly, Schaefer, hunched over a drawing board and helping a student, was totally unaware of what happened. That obliviousness egged us on. Twenty minutes later we set up twenty easels that arced right to where it was hoped he would pass. At the right moment the first easel was pushed and clatter, clatter, clatter — like a speeding train the onrushing falling easels came charging toward him. Only because of the ear-splitting din did he become aware and see it coming. Did he jump out of the way? Not Carl Schaefer! He reached up to stop the last one from falling and succeeded in looking like someone holding up a ski slope. "Hmm, how did that happen? Tsk, tsk," we fake wondered as we helped him out from under the mountain of easels. He showed not a bit of rancour. What cruel shits we were.

To the teachers, the imaginative ones anyway, we must have been a fascinating challenge. After a teacher had helped me, a fourteen-year-old kid from Queen Street with elbows about to poke through sleeves, and others like me, he'd move to the pupil alongside. As likely or not she would be a Rosedale debutante filling a Jaeger sweater and matching Creed skirt, who drove to class in her own cream convertible with a rumble seat. Next to her was a would-be Gauguin type, who would decide at forty that art, "Nude models!" or "Ah, la vie Bohème!" was to be his. And next to him the teacher would have to linguistically wrestle with another kid like me, but this one just off the boat from Hungary, who barely spoke English. What a microcosm it was of a growing Toronto.

I made some lifelong friends during those four years and became reacquainted with some of them a long time later — Marion Porter was one who turned out to be the sister of George Johnston, who married my wife's sister, Jeanne. Another was Alison Grant, who was to become a friend of my wife's brother Robert McRae, George Johnston and Jack Harris (a good friend and novelist whom I met through my wife) when they were all in London during the war. It was rumoured Alison was in some kind of spook, intelligence activity. Later she married the distinguished Canadian diplomat George Ignatieff. Ironically, someone in my class turned out to have lived on Queen Street and almost directly across from 331 in my early years. We had never met because we were both too young to be allowed to cross the busy street. He was Laurence Hyde, who became a noted graphic illustrator and designer of some nifty stamps for Canada Post.

My dearest personal friend was Jack Olsen — a cheerful little guy whose five-foot height made him an ideal rear gunner for two tours in a Lancaster during the war. On one flight, his plane was so badly shot up, he was the crew's only survivor. Before he signed up for the RCAF, we shared an apartment for two years. One might imagine that being as short as he was would inhibit Ollie (as we called Olsen) in the stakes of getting laid, but that wasn't the case. The sounds of revelry, the giggles, suppressed screams and heaving bedsprings that emanated from Olsen's room too often made me green with envy as I sat alone in mine.

Jack did everything with great panache. I was always terrified as a passenger when he drove a car. He wasn't accident-prone, but I always felt that anyone with him was. Once, driving into Ottawa from the Gatineau Hills in his open, British racing green MG with Nancy Watson (who later married Thom Benson, the CBC radio and television producer — not short of panache, himself!), Ollie took a turn just a titch too fast and went off the road; the car flipped over and landed upside down. Wouldn't you guess? The car landed straddling a ditch and Nancy, who was at least ten inches taller than Ollie, has, to this day, only a small scar on her forehead to show for it.

Ollie wanted to sail, so he and I shared ownership of a small, somewhat disreputable-looking, second-hand sailboat. It was moored at the breakwater opposite the Toronto Canoe and Sailing Club Ollie had joined. Neither of us knew much about sailing, although you couldn't have known that from Olsen. In April, after work, he and I were in it, puttering about, as sailing aficionados never seem to stop doing, when Jack said, "Why don't we take her out just for a little spin?"

"That's crazy, Olsen. It's after eight. It's getting dark." I was always afraid.

"Ah, c'mon. Just a little one. Just off the shore and back again."

"Listen Olsen, NO! Besides, it's gusting like hell."

Little did we appreciate how badly it was gusting. We were soon to find out.

Olsen was irresistible in making everything seem like an adventure, which is one reason why I love the guy. And so we raised the sail, cast off and, oh! did that offshore wind drive toward the shore! Olsen had the tiller, but in trying to bring the boat about we capsized before you could say "Boo!" Olsen, being on the windward side, was able to clamber onto the gunwale getting only one shoe wet while I, in a brand new tweed suit, was totally submerged with the sail and rigging above me, snarling my efforts to surface. It might be noted that Lake Ontario water in April is just above freezing. So with my teeth chattering like castanets, frozen to the bone and my soaking tweed suit smelling more and more of sheep's urine, I sat on that capsized boat for half an hour with Olsen, drifting about a mile, night coming on fast before the harbour police boat picked us up. Odd thing is that fifty years later, I have no recollection of being angry at Olsen. That's the kind of guy he is. The best I could manage was to hate myself for agreeing to go with him.

After being de-mobbed, I helped get Olsen into the Film Board of Canada where he made many fine films; then he got married and left to become photo editor for the *Toronto Star*. After a few years and wanting change, he accepted a one-year assignment from UNESCO to teach audio-visual aids in Egypt's hinterland with his wife, Joy, and two children hardly more than babes. Unsurprisingly, knowing Ollie, just after getting settled there Suez happened and they had to flee to Alexandria with the few belongings they were able to pack into their station wagon. They were evacuated on a British destroyer, their station wagon shipped separately to Italy. When they got to the dock in Naples to get the car, it had been picked clean of everything in it. I can see Ollie concerned about his loss for about half a day — only ten minutes if he hadn't a wife and children. He has no time for regrets and is now retired in Italy, busily rebuilding a ruined seventeenth-century villa with his own hands after serving FAO as its head of audio-visual for many years.

Jack Olsen and Sydney Newman in Italy.

Another friend I cherished was an odd one for me. He was Heckle Faessler, older than me and gentle, with a gimp leg because of a childhood shooting accident in Switzerland. He was in the other stream at school. His father, it was said, owned half the ships that plied the Great Lakes. He, Ollie and I hung out together and sometimes with Laurence Hyde. Both Olsen and I ribbed Heckle and Laurence mercilessly, the latter for his almost humourless seriousness and Heckle for his astonishing naïveté. Being poor, Ollie and I were also naïve in our mistaken notion that if you were rich, you were automatically sophisticated. Heckle had a pretty sister Dilly, whom Olsen and I ogled, but as his sister she was out of bounds for us. Besides, she was too young. Years later she married Mavor Moore and is now the mother of Tedde Moore, the actress.

Despite excelling at art in school, Heckle was never able to make a go of it as a sculptor or a commercial artist. One felt it had something to do with his highly successful father. Heckle and his second wife left

Canada to teach art at a private school in Scotland. Prior to this he had many passionate and exciting stormy years with the most astonishingly different woman a WASP could ever find and whom he eventually married. Together they were something to behold — he tall, blondish, handsome and shy and Shirley Faessler, a tiny Jewess who is larger than life in every respect. Her black hair framed a face that radiated a vivacious, witty intelligence. Heckle was always enchanted and amused by her remarkable and highly theatrical (for many years she ran a theatrical boarding-house) way of recounting stories, some of them malicious, of the ludicrous incidents and behaviour of an odd lot of acquaintances ranging from gamblers, gangsters and communists to actors. I've often wondered if it was Heckle's influence that started her writing because she became an outstanding writer.

Someone I lost touch with after leaving school was William (Bill) Penovacz, who arrived at Central Tech a year or two after coming to Canada from Hungary. He could draw like a dream, but what I remember most was his taking me often to the Ukrainian Worker's Temple at 300 Bathurst Street. This was the red "Ukes," the pro–Soviet Ukranian's main club and perhaps its communist headquarters. Bill was an enthusiastic gymnast and I often was a dilatory companion of his and its well-equipped gym. The smell of sweat was overpowering in the gym — in fact it was throughout the somewhat untidy building — which I eventually learned to accept. "It is worker's sweat," I was told. The inside of the place radiated a wonderful air of comradely oneness, especially when sitting in the audience watching my first Russian films. Oh how we adored the films of Eisenstein, Pudovkin and Dovzhenko. We cheered when the Winter Gates were stormed and smiled admiringly at Chapaev's peasant cunning as he explained his plan of attack, using potatoes as lines of soldiers. It must have been in that cinema that I first became dimly aware that the movies could be more than escapist entertainment.

Many years later, as the Canadian Government Film Commissioner, I paid an official visit to the Soviet Union. Going to see the Ukraine's much-praised documentary film centre, my fellow Canucks and I were met at Kiev airport by one of the local party bigwigs. Incidentally, except for his language, he was a carbon copy of a Tammany Hall politician. Driving into Kiev, through the chauffeur who acted as translator, he gave us a ten-dollar tour guide's explanation of the sights. At one point when he was about to identify a huge bronze statue of a man, I exclaimed, "That's Taras Shevchenko, your national hero poet." He was dumbfounded. So were my companions André Lamy and Gerry Graham. And so was I! It had popped into my mind where it had lain asleep for forty years after I had seen a four-hour epic film on the poet in the cinema of the Ukranski Robotnik Temple.

CHAPTER SIX

GREETINGS, COMRADE

Some of the most valuable, indeed mind-opening, times of that period of my life were spent with Nathan Petroff, who was my friend at school and then my business partner for two years. Like Penovacz, Petroff was a recent newcomer to Canada, but he came from Poland. In my mind he was not just a damn good artist in the general sense of craft, but without a shadow of a doubt he was the most inventive and creative student in our class. He was smart too. Wanting to become Canadian as rapidly as possible, and despite an initial language handicap, he shamed me completely in most academic subjects. So, in fact, did Jack Olsen. (Though shamed may be the wrong word, because I didn't have any with respect to that subject.) One drawing that Petroff did when he was seventeen was good enough to be exhibited at the Art Gallery of Toronto. It was of a beautifully executed head that combined the front view of a face with its profile. Today, that may not sound unusual, but the kind of imagination Petroff had, thinking of the ordinary and expressing it in an extraordinary way, blew my mind then and still does today.

Of equal importance was the fact that my friendship with Petroff brought me close to the relationship between art and social content; he was deeply political — that is, as much as a teenager can be called political. Penovacz also had a political bent and because we were among the top three in the class, we were drawn together. Toward the end of the first year, Petroff and I became friends. By the end of the second year I learned that he was painting banners for May Day parades and protest rallies. The stuff he was doing was more than just sign painting. He was doing large, graphically executed portraits of Lenin, Marx, Stalin and Canadian Communist Party leaders I had never before heard of — Tim Buck, Sam Carr, Jose Salsberg. One could almost say that Petroff was the official artist of the party. Soon I was helping him and even getting paid a little; it was money I very much needed. By 1935, he and I were a going concern. We shared a studio on Brunswick Avenue and did a tremendous amount of work in partnership, creating work for The Movement under the name of Ward and Mann. If he was the main artist, the name Ward came first. If I was, Mann came first. We thought we were clever, but I bet we never fooled the Royal Canadian Mounted Police who were charged with rooting out the Reds. From 1934 to 1938, in parades and rallies, in the Young Communist League's magazine *The Advance* and in *The Daily Worker* newspaper, those two names were seen hundreds of times.

Our clients — it sounds odd to my ears today to be calling the CPC and their friend groups *clients* — couldn't afford expensive metal cuts for printing, so we created illustrations for magazines, leaflets and posters. Petroff and I became extremely good at doing marvels with lino and rubber-cuts to suit the printing presses and we were whizzes at silkscreen design, execution and printing (why today this process is ennobled with the name "serigraph" truly escapes me). It must be understood that while we were sometimes paid for what we did, that wasn't our reason for doing it — and besides, the money was damn little. We did it out of idealism and belief in The Cause, something that only teenagers, the IRA, militant Arabs, Muslims, Israelis, Rev. Ian Paisley and perhaps Mary Whitehouse fully understood. While I believed in The Cause passionately (to the disgust of my father), for some inexplicable reason I never joined the Party and never knew if Petroff did.

One piece of history worth recording is about another Toronto artist, a cartoonist really, whose work was seen in all sorts of publications, including the communist *Daily Worker*, for which he did a daily strip cartoon. He was good, drew in a variety of styles and was genuinely funny. Through our left-wing work, Petroff and I got to know him and when he left Toronto for a big job in New York, even though we were kids, he generously gave us all his contacts to continue the work for his clients. His name was Richard Taylor, and his goggle-eyed woman cartoons were making millions of *New Yorker* readers laugh for thirty or more years over the signature of R. TAYLOR.

In retrospect it's hard to believe the number of doors that were starting to open for me. Many of my friends were joining something called the Theatre of Action, which put on plays of social contact. Their first play was *Waiting for Lefty* by New York writer Clifford Odets. I found it damned exciting and so did many of the critics. Up to this time my only experience with theatre had been when, as an art student, I was allowed backstage to sketch the actors as they performed, thanks to a non–left-wing artist friend, Eric Aldwinckle. Aldwinckle acted in the amateur Toronto Shakespearean Society on the Hart House stage; very legit it was indeed. I had fun learning to roll my R's as I watched its English director, G. Wilson Knight, act Othello from the lighting gallery, his eyes gleaming madly up at me through black makeup before strangling Desdemona. Even at seventeen I knew you didn't have to be a Jew to recognize a ham when you saw it. I loved their production of *Henry VIII* with its "Had I but served my God with half the zeal/ I served my king, he would not in mine age/ Have left me naked to mine enemies," and especially Shaw's play, *The Devil's Disciple*, with Eric playing the lead.

In the Theatre of Action they sure did not roll their R's. This was the gutsy language of the street. Petroff and I were soon doing their posters and then were asked by its New York director, David Pressman, if we'd like to take a crack at designing the set for Irwin

A teenaged Sydney makes his start behind the scenes.

Shaw's *Bury the Dead*. Like a shot, we were off. For two years, before Petroff and I split, we designed, built and painted set after set. One year, the company's production of *Steel* by Wexler won the Dominion Drama Festival award with special commendation for its sets by Petroff and Newman. We had designed it so that all scenes, whether in kitchens, on the street or in the boardroom were set against an ever-present backdrop of belching chimneys, ladies pouring hot metal, and overhead gantries dangling giant hooks all looming over the action. We were paid about twenty-five dollars for doing each play — more than enough for the fun of creating.

It was also exciting and interesting being designers, a part of and yet not in the group. We were close to Pressman, who was a Stanislavsky exponent and a talented, nice guy to boot. We were not part of the jealousies vying for acting roles, endemic in most theatrical groups. Best of all, when the curtain went up, the actors did the work and all we had to do was watch. It was there that I first met Johnny

Wayne and Frank Shuster and Sidney Banks. For the fun of it I took a few classes in improvisation that embarrassed me, so I never went back. In one class we each had to imagine ourselves to be a vegetable. Pressman asked me, "Sydney, what are you?" When I replied, "A stalk of celery," his murmured "Hmm" said it all.

His correcting our sense-memory work was pure magic. He demonstrated threading a needle — with nothing in his hands you knew exactly what he was doing: spooling out the thread, biting it off, wetting the point with his lips, failing at first and then succeeding in getting the thread through the tiny eye of the needle, and tying the knot at the thread's end. Breathtaking. And then, to our laughter, "Want to see me do it behind my back?" With the roar of assent, he would appear to examine the thread in one hand, wet the point, examine the needle then twist both arms behind his back, concentrate on his task, then suddenly with a look of success one arm would come flashing out victoriously holding aloft the successfully threaded but invisible needle. He and I met up many times after the war when I visited or worked in New York.

During this period, Petroff and I did other work as well. To stay alive, we had to. We did window displays — why not, we were stage designers, weren't we? We tried to get the highly lucrative and prestigious Toronto Skating Carnival design job, too. We worked for weeks trying to match our designs to our understanding of the choreography of the skaters. Since we were going to contract the whole job, costing its construction was a headache. We failed. We succeeded, however, in getting the job of design and decor for the 1937 Book Fair, held annually by the Association of Canadian Bookmen, whose president was Hugh Ayres, Canadian head of Macmillan. There I met Jack MacLaren's father and that most incredible Englishman who looked more like an Indian than any Indian ever could, Grey Owl.

Foreign films were beginning to be seen in Toronto and their distributor, Leo Clavir, head of the tiny Cosmopolitan Film Company, needed advertising posters in English as well as in the languages of the ethnic minorities who most wanted to see them. Petroff and I became his answer. Most films were from Russia — *We Are from Kronstadt*,

Sydney's poster for We Are from Kronstadt.

Gypsy — and for those and a dozen more we made all the posters, some of them the large twenty-four sheet billboards, which we hand-painted. Most challenging were the lithographed posters. Because Cosmopolitan Films seemed always to be short of money (they were the most charming and persuasive cheapskates — no different really from most small film distributors) our artwork could not be photographically engraved to the printing plates. No, we had to draw the artwork and lettering ourselves with grease crayons right onto the lithographic zinc plates. All were in two or three colours, and with each colour plate having to be drawn separately, one can imagine the difficulty of anticipating the final colour of the three, over-printed plates. Good old Central Tech teachers. Couldn't have done it without them.

There were a great many parties in those left-wing, theatrical circles that I went to — usually held to collect money for this cause or that. Taking a bottle was obligatory. It didn't matter what was in the bottle as long as it was something to drink. After upchucking a couple of times I learned to not mix grape with spirits. Once, a party ran out of drink and a collection was taken up — I chipped in twenty-five cents — and Roy Chappelle, one of the flyest guys in the Theatre of Action, went off to a bootlegger to get some booze.

I saw him return with a wrapped bottle and awaited my turn to get my two bits' worth. When I didn't get the call I asked Roy, "How about me?" Conspiratorially, he whispered, "Sorry, in a moment come to the bedroom. Don't want to upset the others who didn't chip in." I joined him in the bedroom and he gave me a jigger of a clear liquid I assumed to be gin (vodka not being fashionable then) and hurriedly left the room. Like the man I was (eighteen), I threw it right down my throat, gasped, clamped my hand over my mouth and rushed out into the garden and puked my guts out. I lay on the grass sicker than I have ever been, before or since. Roy, that bum, had doled out all the gin, forgetting that I was one of the contributors. Not knowing what to do, he had given me some of the hostess's eau de cologne.

Inevitably, a hat was passed around at these parties to collect money for strike funds, money for the starving in Greece, for the unemployed, the Party, defence of the arrested and very definitely money for the Spanish Loyalists whose democratically elected socialist government was overthrown by Generalissimo Franco and his Falangists.

Late in 1938, I was taken to a party by a girlfriend who was a member of the Young Communist League. The guest of honour was Dr. Norman Bethune, famed Canadian hero of the Spanish Civil War who had pioneered the system of mobile blood banks, which had saved the lives of many Loyalist soldiers. He had just arrived from the front lines in Spain and was in Canada on a fundraising mission. When we arrived with our thirteen-ounce bottle of rye, the party was in full swing. Rising above the din, inevitably we heard bits of conversation breaking the air, thick with smoke, as we sweat in eager anticipation, waiting for the man's arrival:

"Engel said . . ."

". . . NOT Tim Buck!"

"Franco, the Soviets are!"

"Ah, but the negation of the negation . . ."

I feel inadequate at describing the intensity, the humbleness and awe we all felt about meeting a genuine hero of the working-class struggle.

The room suddenly became quiet. We craned our necks toward the door and there he was, this ex-Montreal society surgeon who had left a lucrative practice to fight for justice and freedom. He looked different from what I had imagined. Shorter, stockier, hair shaved off or bald. Surprisingly, he wore a black shirt. The party noise rose again as many of us were led, or sidled up, to be introduced to him. When it was my turn, his surgeon's hand crushed mine briefly. When he took the hand of the girl who brought me, though, he didn't let go and with his other hand covering hers, he asked what she did for a living. Hell to blazes, the bugger was making a pass at her!

I left the party alone. There was no way of tearing her away from him. I was angry. At her. At him. I also felt guilty. Hell, he was probably sexually frustrated as hell. Why not? No time to get laid, giving blood transfusions in the middle of the horrors of war. I just didn't like his shirt. Too reminiscent of Mussolini's fascist Black Shirts.

CHAPTER SEVEN

LOVE AND OTHER DISCOVERIES

During this period between 1935 and '38, there were other awakenings. While at art school I had completely lost touch with my Jewish friends and now I rediscovered them and they were a revelation, unlike any I had ever met before. Petroff was one, but gave the feeling of being more middle European than Jewish. He was also an atheist. For the first time in my life — and how it came about I cannot recall — I became friends with a group of Jewish University of Toronto students. They had nothing to do with political activity or with the world of art or theatre, but they quickened me with their lively, wonderful curiosity about life, literature and social ways. Among them there was not a stitch of the humourless dogmatism I came later to judge in Petroff and other friends I liked of the extreme left. I guess I simply do not believe in certainties. The more ironclad the beliefs, the faster I seem to run away.

We used to meet most Saturday nights at the home of Joe Orenstein, a tall, shambling and spectacled second-year medical student who, after graduating, became a practising psychiatrist in New York. But, at this time, he aspired to become a novelist. He figured that doctors, like A.J. Cronin and others, made good writers. He never wrote his book and tragically died while still under forty.

I remember another friend, Ben Keyfitz, being gleefully excited as he recounted to us the way he had charted the moves westward and north of ethnic minorities away from the districts they first lived in. Ben later became general secretary of the Canadian Jewish Congress.

Danny Drutz's jutted jaw belied the wryest sense of humour about the foibles of mankind. Danny's sister Pauline was an untouchable, lean, black-haired beauty who later married Jack Nichols, the painter.

It was knowing these fellows that I got to reading André Malraux's *Man's Fate*, which I found as exciting and as fast a piece of storytelling as Hammett. I loved the books of Romain Rolland and will never forget something he said in the introduction to one of the volumes of a series of connected novels he wrote. He apologized that his heroine had taken over and was not doing what he had planned she would do. When writing her, he simply had to let her have her own way! Romain Rolland thought of that character as if she were real, and he had created her! What an eye-opener that was about the creative problem of writing believable characters. Saint-Exupéry was pure poetry to me. Camus's *The Plague* I liked but didn't understand.

While I found Thomas Mann's *Buddenbrook* (for which he won the Nobel Prize) somewhat heavy going, his *Magic Mountain* was pure magic to me — especially the chapter called "Snow," which, as a Canadian, sharpened my appreciation of its beauty, which had been to me, except when skiing, a drafted pain in the neck. We endlessly chewed over why its central character was never referred to by his author as Hans or Castorp but always by his full name, Hans Castorp.

There were a few other delightful chaps who joined our Saturday nights. Bill Snitman was a pharmacist and so we used to get our French safes (condoms), from him without embarrassment and at cut-rate prices. Often our sessions would continue at the steam baths on Bathurst Street a little north of the Ukrainian Labour Temple. Clean and in our wrapped sheets feeling like Roman senators, we'd gorge ourselves on ice-cold Cokes and hot pastrami sandwiches sold in the baths. We'd eventually break up at 3 or 4 a.m. I'd wend my way home, alone, through deathly silent streets, occasionally stopped, questioned and allowed to go my way by the police, my mind awhirl with the thoughts of the evening.

What astonishes me in retrospect is that there was never a dull or empty moment in my teens. Even with all the activities I was engrossed in, the Art Gallery of Toronto was still part of my life. When I entered Central Tech, Arthur Lismer asked if I would like to stay on and help with the Saturday morning art classes. For four years I fetched art materials for the kids and cleaned up after them. As well, I learned that you don't have to teach kids how to paint. You merely get them enthusiastic about an idea or a story, give them the paint and brushes and they just do it — sometimes to exhaustion. It was here at the Gallery that I fell in love for the first time in my life.

Like me, Patricia FitzGerald was one of the helpers. She had come to Toronto to take advanced piano lessons and she was seventeen and about my size, meaning she had a big frame and was my height. First came the animal attraction — I asked to paint her and did so, badly. Then, our backgrounds being so different, the social curiosity needed satisfying — and so it went. Pat had a pug nose and when she smiled at me her brown eyes and the curve of her mouth would make me feel sick with love. In the movies or in the Gallery when no one could see us we couldn't help holding and touching one another. Walking together, our bodies from hips to knees would be pressed together closer than Siamese twins. We even discovered ways of confirming our animal warmth in restaurants concealed by the drooping tablecloth, startling or making ourselves smirk with innovative caresses.

She was a romantic, larger than life and wonderfully passionate about what interested her. We talked and ruminated about every conceivable matter — her music, the way she saw the world, my leftist leanings, my art. The exception was her father, L. Lemoine FitzGerald, whom I never met, as he was safely far away in Winnipeg. Pat suspected that I did not like his paintings, which, indeed, I didn't because I thought them cold. Her responses to my thoughts and ideas caused them to soar to heights that only young love could inspire. When she played the piano, she could attack it with such intensity or play with such delicacy; when it was Chopin, I was absolutely and totally besotted with her.

Making love beyond the serious petting was an unspoken but mutual desire. Not for me the stand-up quickies of the Central Tech cloakrooms, or the unzip skirmishes in the bushes of Grange Park in which one partner inevitably was left excited but unsatisfied. I decided it must be in a real bed, a first for me, and for Pat the first time, period. To this end, a friend lent me his cottage along the lakefront at Port Credit.

The Day was a typical, southern Ontario hot and sticky day. The damn bed, still with the winter damp in it, was lumpy, creaked and sagged in the middle so badly that even if we had wanted to part our perspiring bodies we couldn't. To this day when I hear creaking bedsprings, I think of her wild, seemingly never-ending thrashings on that afternoon. It was a nightmare. Was it that she wanted more and more or hadn't I satisfied her at all? On our streetcar ride back to Toronto, we didn't speak much. Her face was flushed and I sensed she sneaked the odd look at me. It was the same in the restaurant as we silently ate our dinner. Then halfway through our coconut cream pie I began to be aware of a toe pushing its way up the inside of my thigh toward my genitals. I looked up at Pat and there was that mischievous, glorious smile on her face and I knew that everything was all right.

We were together until I went to Hollywood in 1938, and I remember proposing in a letter to her that she and I go off to the Soviet Union where she could continue her piano studies while I trained as a cinematographer. I can't remember why she refused, and when I returned to Toronto she had left, address unknown. Four years later, travelling to do some reconnaissance ("recce") for a documentary on radar for the National Film Board in Vancouver, I heard that she was there. We met, and my heart pounded in the same way it had before. Same with her, but she was now married and unhappy. Years later I heard that she had remarried and lived in Montreal. And even later, I learned that she had taken her own life in 1952. I never found out why.

After leaving Central Tech, I developed an intense interest in photography alongside my increasing graphic artwork and set design — I was painting less and less, for reasons I do not yet fully understand. So, at the Gallery I became the unofficial photographer of the children's art classes and some of its social events and activities.

One day, Lismer, admiring my latest batch of enlargements, wondered, "Sydney, why don't you make a movie of our classes?"

"Can't," I replied, "I don't know how."

"Nonsense. You take photographs, don't you?"

Getting a brainwave and hoping to stop the unknown and possibly dangerous direction he was pushing me in, I said, "I don't have a movie camera."

Quick as a flash, Lismer jumped in: "We'll get you a camera and film."

"Lights?"

"Good. That's settled. We'll get you lights."

I was stuck. I'd have to make a movie. I certainly couldn't let Lismer, or the Gallery, down.

Sure enough, Lismer came up with a beautiful little 16mm Bell and Howell Camera with a swivelling turret that had three lenses of different focal lengths mounted on it. With great curiosity I shot a roll of precious film. While the exposure and focus were okay and I knew you could swing the camera from one person to another as long as you did so smoothly, I felt there had to be more to it than that. So, to the Central Library I went, and came home with all the books on film I could find. From Rudolf Arnheim, Paul Rotha, Pudovkin and more, I learned about Grierson and British documentaries and Russian and German films. Hollywood films didn't seem worth considering; their best film directors, I figured, including von Stroheim, Fritz Lang, Slavko Vorkapich, and Billy Wilder, came from Europe, anyway. I thought of Charlie Chaplin only as a comedian, and not the director of his own films, which he was.

I became excited as I slowly began to sense the power of the movie camera and above all, montage — that incredible process of putting pieces of different film together in a calculated order to create tempo, pace, emotional and intellectual clarity — the very heart of motion pictures.

While I was able to see the connection between a still photograph and a painting, it never occurred to me that there was one fundamental similarity to a movie, which artists and film directors would deny until they took a minute to think about it.

I approached filmmaking as an artist and after many years eventually divined the connection. Why did I bother to care about such niceties? Perhaps it was that I had to rationalize my giving up painting. No matter. The difference is basically how the artist and filmmaker copes with time — the time it takes to see a painting compared with the time it takes to see a movie.

A painting is composed; that is, its creator has so arranged the shapes and colours in it so that one's eye is led, on a merry chase, from bit to bit of the composition. To absorb each bit before moving on to the next has, of course, taken time, albeit a fraction of a fraction of a second. All these split seconds add up and you know whether you like the painting or not almost instantly. A ninety-minute movie has its own unique kinds of "bits" — the close-ups; long, pan and tracking shots; the actors; and music and sounds. Each takes their own length of time and in the right order makes the film you hate or love. I didn't have a clue about any of this as I began to make my first film — the start of an adventure that would obsess and own me for the rest of my life.

There was no script. Didn't think of it. As his partner, I naturally shared the joys of shooting with Petroff. We just shot everything — the kids receiving art supplies, happily painting, intensely painting, talking, looking at the head of Moses, Lismer and the other teachers talking and helping, the kids arriving and departing past the gates to the sometimes worried looks of the guards and Pat playing the piano, which unfortunately was out of focus. (It's not a cop-out when I say the focus error was not mine. All shots taken on this lens were soft — which we discovered after the shooting was completed — and the cause of the problem was the camera's mounting.)

Having no Movieola — or in fact knowing such a thing existed — we edited the film on a hand-cranked viewer peering at the flickering

16mm images on its three-by-four-inch screen. The film's story was simple. The kids arrived full of enthusiasm, they listened to Lismer (it was a silent film), they painted, they departed happy — hardly an original structure and as old as the first Robert Flaherty film.[12] In editing, it became clear that by cutting together a lot of short shots you could create a sense of excitement, whether the shots themselves were exciting or not. So, just before the end of the ten-minute film, when the kids left the Gallery, we gave the film a climax by recapping the best moments of the film, very short shots, some lasting as little as a second, including bits and pieces of film cuts and trims and even out-of-focus ones. To add to the frenzy of the climax, it seemed appropriate to use a close-up of Pat's hands playing the piano, cut in so that it was upside down, deliberately. To me, at the time, the process of editing the shots and finding the shape of the film was an experience without parallel.

Most remarkable was the discovery that by placing two unconnected shots together, a new meaning was given to each and the two together provided a third insight. I had a close-up of a young girl looking up at Lismer, who is out of shot. She is pleased and then not quite understanding him. On another day I had taken a shot of Mestrovich's very pregnant woman as she gazed inscrutably into the unknown. What magic it was to place the shot of the girl just before the one of the pregnant woman. Now the audience saw the girl looking not at Lismer, but is instead wondering, "Did my mother look like that before I was born?" Or, "Will I look like that?" Or even, "Poor dear. She must be sick. Her tummy is so blown up!"

It absolutely proved an experiment by Pudovkin[13] I found when I reread his short but immensely valuable book on film technique. He took a close-up of the impassive face of a woman and when he cut it

---

12   Robert Flaherty (1884-1951) was one of the first documentary filmmakers. He produced the first feature-length documentary film, *Nanook of the North* (1922).

13   Vsevolod Pudovkin (1893-1953) was one of the early proponents of the montage form of editing technique. He noted that it was in juxtaposing two images together that film was unlike most art forms and felt this juxtaposition could be used to create emotion in the viewer.

into the scene of a wedding, she looked happy. But when he cut her into a funeral, her face expressed infinite sadness.

The genius of film is truly the controlled effect of creating new meanings — shock by the juxtaposition of disparate images.

Lismer was effusive in his praise when he saw the little ten-minute documentary. Everyone else who saw it was pleased. The praise was unstinted. Fifty years later, I'd give my eye teeth to see my first film.[14] Innocent as I was, the film was cut in the original reversal stock, no prints were struck, and it was the master cutting copy that was screened time and time again. It probably no longer exists, which is, perhaps, just as well. It was probably terrible. But at the time I thought it was good and people said so. I was irrevocably hooked on filmmaking.

---

14 Decades later, Newman wrote to the Ontario College of Art, searching for the film. But it was long destroyed.

CHAPTER EIGHT

HELLO, HOLLYWOOD!

Early in 1938, Petroff and I decided to split. Or rather, he did. He hankered after New York where he thought his chances of recognition as a painter were better. Initially I was disappointed but soon got over that. Why shouldn't I become a cinematographer? I'd need to learn, though, and where best to learn? Hollywood, Hol-lee-wood, here I come.

Being somewhat timid about travelling so far alone, I asked my friends if they, or anyone they knew, would be interested in joining me. I was lucky. It turned out that Joe Orenstein, my medical student friend, not only had relatives who were Los Angelenos, but his kid brother, Leo, would like to go with me as well. I didn't know him well, even though he too had taken art at Tech only two years behind me. He appeared amiable enough, and besides, we would be able to live with his relatives, which was a real bonus.

In preparation for the trip, I got a letter of introduction to the head of the Cinematographers Union. Cosmopolitan Films gave me one for the Russian in charge of Soviet film distribution in the USA and a fine one from Charles Chaplin[15] (not *that* Charles Chaplin), who was the Canadian distributor of Selznick International films. His letter was for a man called Russell Birdwell, whom I later learned was Hollywood's top PR and advertising genius. The selling of *Gone with the Wind* was one film that he handled. I never did get to see him.

After many farewells, a sad one with Pat whom I was intent upon convincing to join me there later, with about $30 I had saved in my pocket (my brother, Wilf, staked me the $37.95 fare) and my things in a battered tin suitcase my mother gave me, Leo and I set out for the three and a half days' non-stop journey by Greyhound Bus. We were warmly welcomed by Leo's relatives who lived in a small house on Vineyard Avenue near Washington and La Brea. It was a poorish street but pretty and quiet — a far cry from the cement of Toronto's Queen Street and even leafy Brunswick Avenue. Its stunted, desiccated palm trees gave welcome shade from the fierce sun shining through its as-yet-unpolluted air. Strange and pleasant too was hearing in the night the dew dripping off the roof of the house. We quickly settled in.

It didn't take long to find out that Hollywood was no land of opportunity for the likes of an unskilled kid of twenty-one — not in 1938, anyway. A year or two earlier the Depression had finally come to Hollywood. Ironically, during the blackest days of the '30s, the film business boomed. Warner's action-filled gangster pictures, the flowering of sound and well-crafted fiction had helped people escape the miseries of the times and swelled box-office receipts to an all-time high. Especially grateful for the movies were the impoverished and the unemployed. A cinema was the only place where they could be cool in summer and get some warmth in winter. So bad was business when I arrived, though, the States was in the middle of a mammoth publicity campaign financed by industry moguls designed to re-capture their lost audience. Their highly publicized slogan "Movies are your best entertainment" was quickly shot down by cynical critics

---

15 The "other" Charles Chaplin was a friend of Newman's who worked in film distribution for the next 40 years. By the 1970s, he was Canadian head of distribution for Warner Brothers.

who felt the slogan's acronym, which spelled MAYBE, was more realistic. Just as quickly and at great cost the slogan was changed to "Motion pictures are your best entertainment."

First thing I did was to follow up with my few contacts. Most important to me was the Cinematographers Union, which I would have to join and which would, if I was lucky, get me a job. The union's secretary was very kind to me at first. Somehow he had misunderstood my letter of recommendation and declared me smart to transfer my membership from their east coast, New York Branch, which he clearly didn't think much of. Like the innocent I was, I corrected him. "You mean," he stuttered as if I had lied, "you're not a member?" Outraged, I muttered, "No, if you look again at the IATSE . . ." and before I could continue, I was dumbfounded to hear, "To join will cost you 500 smackeroos." Then, softening a bit, "Nothing against Canadians, you understand. We like them. Same for anyone." Today, that would be like asking for $5,000, or more, and I couldn't even put up fifty bucks! It was not a good start to my Hollywood future.

Perhaps that Russell Birdwell guy might help me get into the union, I thought. He's important, they say. Ten phone calls later, it was clear that he would never see me. What a dope I am to have explained to his secretary the reason for my calls.

I was getting desperate. I needed to earn some money. Leo and I thought we might make some money by selling watercolour sketches of people's houses. We'd do the sketch first, then go up to the door and ask the owner to buy it. And that's what we did and gave up after a week and ten sketches later, Leo having sold only one sketch for one miserable dollar, and me, none.

It was worth a try getting in touch, I thought, with the Russian film people. Maybe they'll give me some poster work to do. (I had brought with me some of my posters and a batch of skills.) When I phoned their office, I had great difficulty in making it clear why I wanted an appointment, the understanding of English on the other end of the line being somewhat sketchy. When I arrived at the address given me, it was not in a business district but was a handsome, slightly dour-looking mansion on a fine hilly street. Above the door was a plaque:

Consulate
The Union
Of
Soviet Socialist
Republics

To my surprise, even before I had finished knocking on the brass-studded oak door, an oblong slot in the door slid open and a pair of eyes under black brows peered at me and a heavily accented, basso-profondo voice asked what I wanted. What skin I could see around his eyes was dark and pockmarked. Jeez-us, I'm in a Hollywood movie being examined before being allowed into a speakeasy. Spooky! After explaining that I had an appointment, the slit snappily slid shut after his comment, "You wait!" After what seemed like a long time, the massive door swung open.

Inside, coming toward me with outstretched arms and a warm smile on his face was a youngish man slightly running to fat and about thirty-five, wearing a loose Hawaiian shirt, white cotton trousers and sandals. "Come in, mn. Davi! Davi! Hi! Mn, good you to come in, mn," he said as he led me across the shiny parquet floor and into a large living room. Igor's grammatical English was better than his accent, which made me feel that I was back at the Ukrainian Workers Temple in Toronto. "On phone, mn, you said letter. I see, please?" and bade me to sit. I sank into the corner of the largest and softest sofa I'd ever seen — if only Pat were here — and looked around the elegant room as he read my letter, nodding his head as he did so. "Ah, you are an artist! Good. In the Soviet Union, mn, artists, mn, are very much respectful, mn." I'm sure he meant, respected. "Would you like a drink? Tea? Ah, something cold." In a moment, unbidden, as far as I could see, Mr. Pockmark silently entered with two tall glasses of lemonade, each wrapped with a napkin to contain the condensation, and a bowl of cheese crackers all on a silver tray. He glanced at me and departed. Boy, this was the life!

As we sipped our drinks through long straws I found myself utterly charmed. He's so interested in me, craving attention. When he looked at Petroff's and my posters of the Russian films he would exclaim, "Good. Horosho. Ochin horosho." He especially liked the one of *Baltic Deputy*, saying, "Cherkasov [the actor who played the part of the old professor portrayed on the poster]. A fine actor. One of our most respectful. Now, he is shooting Nevsky in new film of Eisenstein's." After about half an hour chatting about what I thought of Soviet films, was Petroff a Russian, how long would I remain in Hollywood, that kind of thing, he said he would see whether any new films needed posters and would get in touch with me, and he was "very glad to meet such an interesting Canadian. An artist."

When I emerged from the house I was blinded by the scorching sun and by what I thought a most promising prospect of finally getting some work. Not just any old work, but work that would be seen all over the United States. And, I was sure, I'd be paid more than Leo Clavir ever would! What a charming man.

A week later I was asked to come back, and did. My high hopes were somewhat dashed when he told me that there was no immediate need for artwork. Seeing the look of a disappointed twenty-one-year-old, he quickly assured me that there was a good chance for some in a month or two. We talked and I confessed that I had really come to Hollywood to become a movie cameraman, and that making some money by doing posters would keep me alive until I could get people to help me get into the union. He sympathized, regretted that he couldn't help with the union but could he help me in any other way? He'd be happy to lend me some money, he said. What a nice man! Hell, there wasn't a chance in a million that I'd ever be able to pay it back. With deep gratitude I refused his generous offer. (Vivid in my mind was my mother's injunction about being in debt.) In the blazing sun, I kicked myself for refusing his loan because Leo and I needed some money, fast. After two or three more meetings, both flattering and frustrating, I received an invitation to go there for tea.

When I arrived, outside the Consulate were many fancy European limos and low-slung cars I envied. One day I'd be rich enough to have one. He invited me for tea, but it turned out to be a cocktail party. The martinis and Manhattans flowed easily, consumed or sipped by as elegant a crowd of informally dressed Hollywood types as I could never have imagined. I was introduced to some who displayed no interested in me whatsoever. I hadn't a clue as to who they were, didn't recognize any stars, but all the talk was about diminishing box-office grosses, John Garfield being difficult, Gable seeing Carole Lombard on the sly, the poor Spanish Loyalists and what would be Hitler's last territorial demand — the world?

When the party was breaking up, Igor came over and suggested I stay behind and have a quiet drink with him. Why not? Maybe he'd ask me for stay for dinner. I could sure use a good, square meal. Later, we went upstairs into what was obviously his office. After reassuring me that his offer to lend me money was still open, he said he had thought of an alternative way to help by getting me a job — something to enable me to earn some money until he needed posters. The job would involve travel, which sounded interesting to me. They had a spot open for someone to carry diplomatic material from different points in Canada to the United States. In fact, he thought so well of me that later on, he thought he might be able to swing a scholarship for me at one of Russia's world-renowned film schools where I could learn camera work from men like Eduard Tisse, Eisenstein's cameraman. Fabulous! I couldn't believe it!

Because in one of our meetings I had mentioned that I had a girlfriend, quick like a bunny I asked whether she could come with me and go to a music conservatory, which I hoped would be in the same city as the film school. He thought that was very possible. We even discussed how Pat and I would travel to the Soviet Union — by sea on a tramp steamer sailing from New York to Leningrad. Me and Pat. What a wonderful way to start a new life! It was left that all he had to do was get the okay of the ambassador, which was only a formality. I wasn't invited for dinner, but didn't care. I couldn't wait to tell Leo and to write Pat with the incredible news. Me, going to where Pa came from! I couldn't tell my folks — it'd kill him if he knew. I would worry about that later.

I wrote Pat spelling out all the details, including travelling by ship, feeling certain she'd be as excited as I was. Leo was dubious. Leave

North America? I knew he didn't think as highly as I did of Russia. Or, was he jealous?

After two weeks had gone by and I hadn't heard from Igor, I phoned the consulate several times but was told that he was away. A few weeks later, they told me they didn't have anyone in the consulate by the name of Igor and hung up. The rude bastards. What happened to my friend Igor? That put an end to that dream; the episode is as vivid in my mind as if it had happened yesterday.

By now Leo and I had been in Los Angeles for four months and his uncle and aunt were making it pretty obvious that we were perhaps overstaying our welcome. Leo and I were getting to be somewhat like Simon's *Sunshine Boys*, finding that we didn't always quite like one another. We both missed the opposite sex. Once we dated two very proper Jewish girls. After frustrating hours of futile necking, we were barely able to walk home, so aching were our gorged loins, balls as blue as monkeys.

As well as breakfast and the off meal we were able to cajole from Leo's relatives, we were living on oranges (ten cents a dozen!), grapes, dates and biscuits. My brother was beginning to complain about the odd ten bucks my letters were asking for. Getting into a studio was harder than breaking into the Bank of England. I saw the Warner Brothers Outdoor Lot, though, and was amazed. Those were the days when shooting a film away from Hollywood out on location, in real settings, was regarded as the fantasy of a madman. It wouldn't then occur to me either and looking around I could see why. Here was every kind of setting a director could wish for. Except for a lick of paint, each part seemed ready for the camera from an entire frontier town to chunks of ancient Rome, streets of old New York to an English thatched cottage. At least that's the way they would have appeared if the camera was put in the planned spot. So economically were they built that the wrong camera position would reveal the scaffolding that supported their three-dimensional, perfectly fabricated façades.

If I couldn't get a job in film production I felt lucky that I could fall back on my being an artist, as I had tried to do with the Russians. I designed stage sets, so why not take a crack at sets for feature films?

Through a connection Leo made, he and I were promised jobs as draftsmen on a new Mae West picture as soon as the art director got the go-ahead. He never got it.

I met a friendly art director of the Goldwyn Studios. He might have been the owner's son-in-law, I don't know, but through him I saw the studios and learned how Sam Goldwyn worked. This came about when he showed me a book of beautifully drawn depictions of each shot for an upcoming production of theirs of *Marco Polo*, which was to star Gary Cooper. I asked, "Did you say upcoming? The drawings look as if they were made after the film was shot."

Many years later I was to profit from my recollections of that visit. It gave me an insight into the controls that must be put into the hands of one person when creating art in a group, as film and theatre is created; it is totally different from the process of creating as a painter or a writer, in which the artist does his own thing by himself. A Goldwyn production bore Sam Goldwyn's mark and his mark alone, whether you admired or hated the film.

Compared to giants like MGM, Twentieth Century-Fox and even Columbia, Goldwyn's output, like Selznick's, was tiny by comparison. Because he not only owned the studios and financed his pictures with his own money, he was able to exercise to the full his own taste and judgement of what would win audiences without the interference of partners, banks or investors. I have always thought of him as Hollywood's best example of balancing tasteful and reasonably socially worthwhile material with popular appeal.

Goldwyn made most of his films to capitalize on the five or six stars he owned under exclusive contract such as Gary Cooper, Danny Kaye, Merle Oberon and his mistake, Anna Sten. After his personal taste in material, they were his main capital and therefore his starting point. He'd commission a script that he thought would precisely suit the unique qualities of his star. Only after the blood of many a writer was shed, no doubt, and he was satisfied that the script was right, did he proceed to the next stage.

Contrary to what I then expected, and contrary to what I now believe, he was not yet ready to hire the director. No, the film was his. Any other way was, as he might have put it, to "Include me out." The next person he hired was the art director who, under his direction, would make fully detailed shaded drawings interpreting the story from the style of furniture to the precise mood to be achieved in each and every camera set-up. After he approved these, eight-by-ten glossies of the drawings in proper sequence were bound into a book — a static though complete visualization of the film. Even at this stage, Goldwyn would not choose his director. The book would be given to the director of cinematography to get his approval — not of its creative elements such as mood, but for the down-to-earth practicalities of shooting. Changes might be made and only then was it time to hire the director he thought most suitable for the specific mood and genre of story. He would give the director the package containing the name of the star, the lead players, the script and the book and say, in effect, "That's what I want. Can you do it? Well, get on with it." When I'd first arrived in L.A. I had looked up a young artist's friend from Toronto whom I met through Eric Aldwinckle. He was Eric Gurney, who had recently left Toronto to work for Walt Disney as an animator. He and his wife were damn nice to me and I was given many a good meal at their home. To my astonishment, Disney was an enormous establishment with thousands of employees. My mind boggled when I realized that a Donald Duck or Mickey Mouse cartoon lasting eight minutes needs 11,520 painted drawings! Each year they were producing twelve of these cartoons, about eight *Silly Symphonies*, and had just completed *Fantasia* with Leopold Stokowski after the phenomenally successful *Snow White and the Seven Dwarfs*. While I was there, *Bambi* was also in full production with *Pinocchio* being planned.

The atmosphere in the plant was warm and electric, giving a sense that the work being done was fun and important — that is, in the departments where the creative work took place. They even had their own tiny zoo to draw and study the movements of the animals that *Bambi* was to feature. The animators, the cartoon-film equivalent of the director of a photographed film, were the kingpins of the place. Around them were the idea, story and layout artists, the background artists, composers and actors who voiced the drawn characters and the in-betweeners who did the step-by-step drawings required to bridge the key action drawings of the animator. Eric, being new, was learning and so was an in-betweener. The lucky stiff was working in the midst of some of the world's best illustrators, whom Disney had lured to his shop.

In other areas were all the backup technicians running an incredible array of specialized equipment to make still pictures move. In one room was a vast machine they had designed and built — the multi-plane camera, which provided different speeds to many layers of backgrounds to give the effect of, say, Snow White walking to running swiftly. Little did I know that years later at Canada's Film Board I would help Norman McLaren paint backgrounds for his own designed and crudely built multi-plane apparatus. Thanks to my visits with Disney, I was one of the few who understood what the "eccentric" McLaren was trying to do.

I did not like everything I saw. In contrast to the freedom and seeming fun of the creative people I met, my heart sank when I was led into the vast rooms where hundreds of artists were hunched over lit-from-underneath glass drawing boards doing the menial trace and paint work. I shuddered at the thought of having to paint Donald Duck's feet yellow thousands of times. Someone had to do it, but not me. I needed work but I'd rather starve than do that.

Eric knew that I was hard up and suggested that I come and work at Disney, which was hiring new people like mad. "For you, it'll be easy to pass the test you'll have to take." Well, what's to lose? Through him, I met a friendly man, Mr. George Drake,[16] in charge of personnel and training. They were hiring so many people that they actually gave would-be employees a beautifully illustrated booklet to teach them how to draw Mickey Mouse, Minnie, Pluto etc., which one had to do well to be hired. I passed the test with flying colours and was offered a three-year contract as an animator starting at $18 a week (Canada's

---

16 Newman was invited on September 15, 1938, to attend the interview with Drake "at his convenience." Newman kept the envelope, on the back of which are his own doodles of Donald Duck and Mickey Mouse.

minimum wage for men at that time was $12.50 per week) and rising to $350 per week! I was dumbfounded. Okay, to hell with being a movie cameraman. I like drawing and this is Hollywood. "Gee, that's great! Can I start tomorrow?"

There was a slight snag though. Since Eric had introduced me as a Canadian, I couldn't start until I had a work permit gotten by leaving the United States and then re-entering. Easy, I was told, if done via Tijuana, near the U.S.-Mexican border. Since this was going to be a permanent move, I preferred to go back to Toronto, say goodbye to my folks, work on Pat to join me — why hadn't she answered my letter of five weeks ago about Russia, by the way? — and no doubt, enjoy boasting to my friends the bonanza that had come my way. Drake assured me their offer would hold until I returned.

By now, we had been in Los Angeles about five months and Leo was ready to go home anyway. And so, with a soaring heart, my fare money provided by my brother, Leo and I boarded the Greyhound Bus. Since it would be winter in the north, we decided to go by the southern route, which would take us east along the Mexican border to El Paso, then north to Chicago, east again to Buffalo and over the border to Toronto. We carried with us in large brown paper bags the food we'd need on the trip spending half of our last $4 on nutritious fruitcake, various biscuits and oranges. Also I had stashed away an avocado, which I had never seen in Canada, as a gift for Pat.

Over beautiful mountains and equally beautiful scrub desert our half-empty bus sped us eastward. I noticed a cute blonde who seemed to be sneaking odd looks at us. Or, was it me? I got to talking to her, ending up, as night began, sitting next to her. She was returning home, a failed Hollywood starlet who lived two hundred miles further on. For some totally inexplicable reason I said I was a French Canadian and I told her all about Disney. When the desert cold seeped into the dark and silent bus we shared a blanket and with the help of some pillows we did what young people do so naturally. We said goodbye when she left the bus at 6 a.m. I returned to my seat next to Leo.

At the next re-fuelling stop, Las Cruces, just when we were about to start, the bus doors reopened and two big men in tan uniforms wearing

Stetsons entered. One of them looked just like Broderick Crawford in *Highway Patrol*. Slung beneath their sagging bellies were half-holstered guns on bullet-studded belts. They looked at the passengers and then came up the narrow aisle looking right at me. "What's your name?" My heart in my mouth, I told them and explained that I was returning to Canada. Broderick, looking at Leo, said, "You with him?" Leo nodded. "Okay, you two, get your things and come with us." We took our few belongings, including the bags of uneaten food, and left the bus to be put into the back of a very dusty, tan police car. To our exclamations of "What? Why?" all we got was, "You'll be more comfortable with us. We're taking you to El Paso for questioning." The engine was gunned and we took off. Silence. Except, that is, for the rattle of gravel hitting the underside of the car.

I was afraid. Frightened stiff. What had we done? I know I should have had a visa to stay in the States as long as we had, but it was only illegal if we'd been in the U.S. over six months without permission and we were returning in five and a half! Having a somewhat uncontrollable imagination, I couldn't help but see myself as Paul Muni in *I Am a Fugitive From a Chain Gang*, incarcerated, beaten and no one knowing where I was to help get me out. It sounds fanciful but we were as far south in the States as one could get — this was he-man country, not an area noted for its kindness to law-breakers, non-conformists and vagrants. Leo and I had less than two dollars between us.

My morbid thoughts were interrupted and became even darker when Leo suddenly asked, "Have you read any good books lately? Have you had any lynchings around here, lately?" I kicked Leo and frowned a *shut up* at him. That idiot! I suppose he was as frightened shitless as I was — his bravado a way of hiding his fear. Then, from the front seat: "Naw . . . Jeb, remember that nigger? That was nine, oh ten months ago."

"Oh yeah. The one up on the charge of fooling with McReady's kid."

To change the subject, I jumped in with, "The bullets in your belt. There seem to be two kinds. What's the difference?" The officer in the passenger seat fiddled with his belt and then turned around toward us, holding two bullets in his stubby fingers. "This here's for people and this copper-tipped baby'll rip through a car like cheese."

All we got out of those guys on that sixty-mile dusty ride was that headquarters wanted to question us. They volunteered that maybe it was that we were illegal entrants. I also learned that people on the border could pick up an easy $25 when they informed; in this neck of the woods, it was usually about Mexicans. My God, it must be that broad on the bus! She thought me a Mexican. This was not a ridiculous imagining of mine.[17] Writing this today, after a lot of sun, I may look like a balding dentist back from holidays; when young, however, with my black hair and Asian appearance I always looked like an outsider. As a child I was often called "Chink." As a teenager I was thrown out of a dancehall in Orillia, Ontario, because they thought I was an Indian from the local Rama Reserve. Recently in Los Angeles I had been evicted from a place because they thought I was Filipino. No one can dispute my claim of understanding what it's like to be "different." That dopey girl might easily have imagined me, burned black by the California sun, a Mexican.

As we entered the outskirts of El Paso, a nasty viper of a thought began wiggling its way out of my stupid twenty-one-year-old brain. It's my dealings with the Russians! The FBI had the consulate bugged and to them, I'm a Soviet courier. How can I prove I'm not? I was fucked. We asked the cops if we would be able to catch a bus later on in the day and they assured us that if we missed it we shouldn't worry. "At the expense of Uncle Sam," chuckling, "we'll put you up in a hotel."

Before we could go to the toilet in the headquarters of the New Mexico state police, Leo and I were photographed and fingerprinted. Then, over four or five hours with pauses between questioning us, sometimes separately, they found out who we were, where we came from, what we did while in the States — that kind of thing. Except for my abortive dealings with Igor, we scrupulously told all. I was

---

17 He wasn't joking. Newman's obituary in the *Independent*, by Leonard Miall, actually begins, "Sydney Newman was a Canadian who looked like a Mexican."

terrified that Leo might, in his own flippant manner, make a quip that would lead to the subject of Russia; he didn't.

By early evening I was no closer to finding out why we were in custody than I was when we were taken off the bus at 8 a.m. that morning. The script could have been written by Kafka. Before and since, I have never been as frightened. Leo didn't seem to be — perhaps, being younger than me, he didn't realize the potential seriousness of my position, or, was he cool in covering his fear?

Told that we could not leave, we were handcuffed and were taken to where we would spend the night. The "hotel" of Broderick's chuckle became clear. It was the county jail. Inside we were divested of anything in our possessions that could be used as a weapon; in my case, a nail file and a tiny penknife I used to sharpen my pencils. (I always carried a sketchpad with me.) The prison was a high-rise and going up in the elevator we were separated by wire mesh from our guard and the operator. We were taken along a corridor that had cell doors along one side and finally told to stop. The guard pressed a button and a bell rang. Through the opening in the door I could see men sitting on the floor playing cards or just lounging about. At the sound of the bell, in unison like Pavlov's dogs, they all moved and disappeared into different cells along one side of the room. The guard, assuring himself that the room was empty, pulled a lever, and with a deafening noise all the cell doors in the room slid shut. Then with a key, he opened the door of what was a prison within a prison and morosely waved an arm at us to enter. He saw our bewilderment. "You'll find beds in there. Make yourselves at home."

We entered and the door behind us slammed shut and immediately, the six or so cell doors ground open. The bell rang and, as if choreographed, all the inmates simultaneously emerged. Heads swivelled at us, curious to see who we were.

I have never felt more like a stupid git than I did standing there not knowing what to do, holding my carryall and overcoat and inwardly cursing the blasted paper bag of food clutched to my chest, which was now limp and close to collapsing. We looked each other over. They were all disreputable, a dangerous looking lot as the mind of a frightened, over-imaginative twenty-one-year-old could conceive. To many of them, I was sure, we looked ripe for the plucking. Satisfied, all but one went back to what they had been doing. A seedy, unshaven runt sidled up to us and told us to grab a bunk. "You," he said to me, "can share my cell."

Bravely, I said, "M-my friend and I would p-p-prefer, uh, can't we s-stay together?"

"Yeah," he said, grinning over nicotined teeth, "but someone's in each cell." To Leo, he pointed out a cell with an empty bunk in it and I followed him to his. It was about six by nine feet. "Top bunk for you, okay?"

"Sure," I replied, "would you like some fruit?" Christ, I was frightened.

Just as he picked out an orange, suddenly a man came running to our doorway and said, "Get your things. They want you." What was it now? When I left the cell, Leo was also out of his and then the bell rang. As the others began to mechanically go into their cells, I turned, bewildered, and started to return as well. A voice shouted out, "Not you two. Stay there!" In a moment all the cell doors split the air and shut, the main door opened and the same guard who had brought us told us to come out. As he locked the door and pulled the lever to open the inner doors, he said, "Made a mistake. Shouldn't have put you in with them bums." The bell rang behind us as he told us, "Putting you into our grand suite. Two adjoining rooms — reserved for the poor fucker who goes to the chair." He cheerfully assured us we would be comfortable.

It was a large room roughly divided in half by a wall of bars that had a door left open in it. In the larger area there was a table, two chairs, a cot and a small barred window through which we could see below us the twinkling lights of El Paso at night. In the other room where the condemned prisoner spent his last days was a cot, a concrete toilet bowl with no seat on it, a concrete wash basin cemented to the wall and high above it a heavy nickeled faucet sticking out with no visible means of turning it on.

We made ourselves as comfortable as we could, me losing the

toss and getting the condemned prisoner's cell next to the toilet. When I went to wash I finally found a button set into the wall to turn the water on. When I pressed it the water came down with such force that when it hit the side of the bowl it rose to the other and completely inundated the front of my trousers and one complete leg. Shit! They were the only pants I had with me. I took them off and as best I could, wrung the wet out of them. The buggers hadn't fed us and when we were on our second orange and fig bars, suddenly the lights went out. When we crawled into our cots I discovered that there were no sheets, the mattress was stained and the blanket was as sticky as a wet Ryvita. Yech! I couldn't bear the thought of that against my skin, and so, reluctantly, I put on my damp trousers and covered myself with my overcoat.

Lying there in the stygian blackness we ruminated about what was happening and why, our voices quietly reverberating from wall to wall passing through the bars between us. Even if I get safely out of this mess, would the fact of it affect my going to Disney? As our talk slowed down we became aware of the sounds of the prison. It was a gentle hum of hundreds of voices broken occasionally by a loud laugh. Once we heard someone crying and then even a quavering voice singing what sounded like a mighty, sad song in Spanish. Later in life, I figured that if I put that into a drama, I'd be accused of sentimentalizing prison.

We were awakened at 6 a.m. by the noise of a tray containing our breakfast pushed through a large slot at the bottom of the iron door. On it were two bowls of uneatable cold porridge, two half loaves of dodgy white bread and two king-sized tin cups of steaming black coffee. I raised my cup to drink and to my disgust my lips felt some food, or whatever, stuck to the rim of the cup. I didn't touch a bit of that breakfast and ate an orange and a fig bar. We washed after standing well back from the sink when the water gushed down, cleaned our teeth and, except for the fact that my right trouser leg looked like an accordion, I was ready to face whatever the day would bring.

Two hours later, with a rattle of keys, our door was swung open and we were told to get our things. Down below after they had returned our "weapons," we were handcuffed, only this time while I was attached to Leo, my right wrist was also firmly handcuffed to a twitchy little Mexican fellow. He looked ill. His face was drawn and around his colourless lips the skin had that whiteness that usually precedes the moment someone is about to vomit. We were led up some stairs and out of the jail.

The early morning New Mexico sunlight was blinding and soon, to my utter astonishment, I discovered that our prison was right in the centre of El Paso. A main street with noises of traffic and crowds of people. It was a surrealist dream. Here were ordinary people perhaps wondering if we were murderers, bank robbers or layabouts — or maybe they were just irritated because they might be late for work as they were stopped by the police to make way for three handcuffed characters being herded across the pavement and motioned to climb up into the back of an open, wire-meshed truck. In Toronto it was the kind of truck used by dog-catchers! This was a nightmare.

We quickly left the city and began speeding over a bumpy, unpaved road, the truck shaking our guts to pieces and drowning us in clouds of scorching dust. The driver must have hated the world, the way he was driving. The Mexican was looking worse than ever. When I asked him if there was anything wrong, which was a damn silly thing to ask, he either didn't understand English or didn't care to answer.

The three of us, manacled together, were, perforce, sitting side-by-side on the jouncing wooden bench and I was becoming very worried — my Mexican co-prisoner seemed to be at death's door. I had to extend my right hand to accommodate his hunching over to rest his head on his knees. Leo and I saw to our horror that the poor fucker's cream-coloured jacket was stuck to his back by a large stain of dried blood. As awful as this was, I was more concerned that as he and I were as close together as Siamese twins, if he were to throw up . . .

We were taken to what was the border immigration point where people entered the United States from Mexico. When we were put into a large screened room, the moment the cuffs were taken off, the Mexican rushed into the toilet and we could hear him retch. It was awful. After a bit, we heard the sounds of great splashing of water, then silence. When he emerged, he'd clearly gotten his colour back and was a considerably more presentable-looking guy. He came up to us and with only the faintest Mexican accent, straightforwardly asked if one of us would lend him a comb. The idea of giving him a comb was anathema to me. His nits or whatever, on my comb! Leo seemed to not have one, and I couldn't seem able to refuse so I reached into my pocket and gave him mine. To my utter astonishment, when he turned and walked back to the washroom I could see him looking at my comb and with his fingers was attempting to clean it. I was furious. The nerve of the guy to think my hair dirty and his hair cleaner than mine. And then it hit me — what a rotten vain snob I am. How dare I think I am clean and he is not? Why shouldn't he have the same right to judge me? The shame I felt at that moment was, in retrospect, worth all the frustrations, frights and joys of the whole Hollywood trip.

When he returned he was cleaning my comb with a paper towel. We asked him about his back. He lived in Juarez, the Mexican town just across the Rio Grande River. Two weeks earlier he had gone on a wine binge with some friends. The drinking went on for days and at some time during the two weeks he had somehow crossed the border. Last night he had gotten into a fight with a gringo, was stabbed in the back, arrested, and without any medical attention was unceremoniously thrown into jail. "No, my friends, it wasn't the stab wound that made me sick. It was two weeks of wine. Not for me again will I get such a hangover." He was called out first by the authorities and we never saw him again.

In our interrogation by the immigration authorities, and by sheer luck, I was able to prove that we had been in the States less than six months because I found the stub of my ticket dating our entry. After a severe dressing down we were to be shipped out on the next bus. Our tickets would be retained by each successive bus driver to make sure we left the blessed country. On top of all that we were given a letter, which had to be given to immigration at the U.S.–Canadian border signifying our legal exit. "Until out of the States, for the rest of the trip, no stops anywhere, y'hear?"

Who the hell would want to!

The nightmare was not yet over. Being older than Leo, I took possession of the letter and carefully put it into my wallet. Two days later, as we were approaching Chicago, somebody picked my pocket and gone was the letter, and my last dollar. We managed to lie ourselves out of the States, but it was ridiculous — a farce comedy that wasn't funny at all.

CHAPTER NINE

HOME, AT LAST

It was snowing like mad when we arrived in Toronto. Worse, it was one of those bitter December days when the temperature is just above freezing and there's about three inches of slush you must slither and plough through. Lugging my suitcases in and out of streetcars and having no galoshes on my shoes I was soaked to the ankles by the time I reached the safety of 331. When I embraced my mother and father I was shivering. God, it was good to see them. While they seemed happy at my telling them about Disney, which I described in confusing technical detail far beyond their understanding, they were certain I was exaggerating or misunderstood the salary being offered. They did not like the idea of my going to live so far away. Unstoppable, I was burbling on and on about all the rest when my mother reached over and pressed her hand against my forehead, "Into bed, Mr. Hollywood. You're running a fever." And indeed I was. Whether it was the relief at the end of the traumatic five and half months, the excitement of my Disney future or the radical change from sunny California to Toronto's ice and snow, I became bedridden for two weeks with the flu.

Just before Christmas Leo and I went to the Consulate of the United States on University Avenue and to a bored official declared ourselves officially out of the U.S. Alone, I went to the passport section to get a visa to enable me to move to the States. To my dismay, I learned that I couldn't until I presented them with a Disney job-offer letter. Without such a letter there were two other ways I could enter. Someone in the States would have to indicate by their financial worth a guarantee that I would not become a "charge" of the U.S. government. The other was an accord between Canada and the States that 10,000 persons each year were allowed to immigrate to the other country without any qualifications, assuming no criminal record. "There's a waiting list. Shall I put your name on it?" I was asked. "Sure," I replied. "By the way, how long is the list?" The chap looked me straight in the eye and said, "Oh, about 50,000 people ahead of you."

Fat lot of good that would do me. Not overly worried, I immediately wrote to Mr. Drake. Two weeks later he replied telling me that they couldn't give me an offer-of-job letter because they dare not appear to be favouring hiring a foreigner; the offer was still open if I could be in the States legally. To my next impassioned letter, Drake explained that only if they could show that my talents were unobtainable in the U.S. would they give me such a letter and regrettably, the test I had taken was not sufficient for such a purpose. He then outlined a different test that he strongly urged me to take because he had faith in me.

The test was to find out how original and imaginative I was and if I successfully completed it I would be taken on in the story and layout department. I had to devise four original, one-reel cartoons, one each featuring Mickey Mouse and Donald Duck, another of any other Disney character and one featuring a character of my own creation. I was to do the key drawings of the stories and provide some of them in colour.

It amazes me, the arrogance of youth. Unfazed, I went right to work. Over a period of two months I did exactly as requested. I dreamed up four stories involving 400 drawings in pencil of the key moments elucidating the funny (I hoped) incidents exactly in the manner I had seen them done in the studio in Hollywood, and about fifteen large paintings in full colour showing mood and to prove my general skills as an artist. I wasn't smug about my efforts but felt okay. One concept I thought especially original: Since this was in March 1939, the Nazi menace was looming large, day by day. In my story a Nazi submarine enters New York Harbour to spy. When its periscope emerges from the water I put a roving, darting eye in it and my drawings show the periscope twisting and turning, looking around just as a human eye would.

The enormous parcel, carefully packaged, went off in April by special delivery post and costing my brother, Wolf, a whopping $7.50. Now, the waiting began. I became an insomniac. Finally, after about six weeks a letter arrived regretting exceedingly that while they thought me a good and imaginative artist, they couldn't in all honesty claim that no one in the States had what I had; after all, I was young and should I be able to enter the States legally and fairly quickly, their original offer of the animator's job was still open.

I didn't contemplate suicide but I was sure desolated. What did that chap on the U.S. Consulate say about a visa and no "charge" on the State? I dashed off a letter to my sister Ruth who lived in Buffalo; would she and her husband, Eddie, stand surety for me? She phoned long distance to say that they would if they could but were having enough trouble paying their income taxes and so were unable to give the necessary guarantees. It was truly the end of the world for me. So unusual was a long distance call in our family that my folks and brother had come near the phone and had listened. Dear Wolf volunteered he might ask some fellow bellhops at the Royal York Hotel if they had an angle to get me into the States. I knew that if there was an angle they'd know it. After all, at the drop of a hat they were able to supply hotel guests with the names of call girls, bootlegged liquor, contraceptives and sundry at all hours of the day or night. They represented my last avenue of hope.

Sure enough, there was an angle but it was risky. Wolf found out that an American Consul in one of the Canadian cities would place your name at the top of the list (of 50,000) if you padded his palm with $700! It usually worked but you couldn't be certain; sometimes the guy took the dough and then did nothing. Having insomnia and trying so hard for five months to get to Disney, I didn't give a damn whether it was legal or not. Like a shot I asked my brother to lend me the money. He was shocked. "Seven hundred dollars! You must be joking. I haven't got seventy-five bucks in the bank!"

What to do? I decided I'd make the money. I'd take any goddamned crappy commercial art jobs I could get. In the past, Petroff and I had been very snooty about the kind of paying art jobs we would accept. Now, I was hungry. No job was too low in my esteem as long as it paid. From finicky airbrush drawings of shoes for glossy catalogues that paid fifty bucks a crack to the equally tedious lettering backwards the names of stores to the inside of their plate-glass shop windows — all were meat for me. I find it hard to believe today, but by mid-August I was able to give Wolf the entire $700 to get to the crook that would lead me to Disney.

What happened next was like one of those captions in a silent movie: Then came the war! Within days of Canada declaring war on Germany, newspapers carried stories of families sneaking their sons into the States hoping to avoid the draft, which they thought was imminent. (In fact, Canada did not have conscription during the entire war.) Holy cats! If I get to the States now, people'll think I'm chicken. A coward! No job at Disney is worth that. I ran to my brother and told him I had changed my mind and please get the money back. To my intense relief, the bellhop who had the connection was on holiday and so Wolf still had the money.

The start of WWII kept me from Disney[18] but the fates were in

---

18   The situation was slightly more complicated than Newman lets on: Drake wrote Newman just after the start of the war on September 7, 1939, telling him that he would have to submit more test material to the studio. It turned out, though, that Disney didn't want Newman. Newman received a letter on December 21, 1939, from Vernon Caldwell, who had inherited George Drake's correspondence with Newman. "When Mr. Drake opened negotiations with you, he did so in good faith as he had no way of knowing what the future would bring . . . It now becomes my duty to inform you that our present production schedule does not allow for the hiring of new people at this time or in the near future." Caldwell explained that the expansion the Disney studio was doing to recruit artists was now over and "comparatively few men will be brought into the training group in future."

my corner. A year later, at Disney, those hundreds of paint and trace artists I pitied went on a strike that lasted four months, which they eventually lost. Knowing my strong pro-union stance at that time, I likely would have been on the side of the strikers and probably fired for it. A year later, another strike. Walt Disney lost financial control of the studio he had built. Even if none of this had affected me, I can't, even now, avoid the morbid thought that as a U.S. citizen I would have been conscripted and probably would have died in action at Iwo Jima.

Before the end of September, my brother joined the Governor General's Horse Guards regiment. He loved horses, but one month later they switched to motorcycles and when they got to England two months later, they switched again, this time to tanks. He fought through Italy and then in Europe from Caen to Holland and on. Five years later, while he was still in uniform and very much in one piece, he came to visit me in Ottawa and to meet my wife, Betty. I noticed that he was still a private. "Wolf," I asked, "you've been in the army five years, how come you haven't even got one hook on your sleeve?" He solemnly looked at me and said, "I fought and did my job. As good as anyone, I guess. I was in the colonel's tank. I just didn't want any responsibility." Several years later in his early forties he married out of the faith. Like me, he had a questioning relationship to religious rituals, but surprisingly his wife, Marie, adopted Judaism. She loved him, she said. That's Wolf, Wilfred my brother, the most honest, humble and decent man I shall ever know.

Even with the whole Hollywood experience indelibly imprinted on my mind — the Russians, the Disney fiasco, the night in the condemned prisoner's cell — all capped by the absence of Pat, somehow I was able to gradually stop licking my wounds. Olsen, I think, with his perky, obstinate optimism had a lot to do with it. Optimism is perhaps the wrong word. An absolute refusal to worry about tomorrow is more like it, and it was starting to rub off on me. He and I decided to share an apartment. Olsen had a steady job as art editor of catalogues for the Levy Auto Parts Company. I, at first, fell into the old pre-Disney routine of work, meaning picking and choosing art jobs so my income shrank to almost nil. And I took up with my old mates again, but with the war, relationships with friends on the far left thinned out.

Those on the left were in total disarray. The shock of the German-Soviet pact amazed and stunned everyone, not excluding me. The diehard's explanation that Stalin did it to save his own country just didn't wash with many. My Saturday night Jewish friends, who at best had been sympathetic to the Soviet Union, now turned violently against it. The very thought of holding hands with those anti-Semitic Nazi bastards was sickening. I found myself in a cleft-stick position with them when one Saturday evening I brought with me a friend, Maurice Constant.

In 1936, I had met Maurice, who was some years older than me — he was an intellectual, which was far, far different from me. On park benches or over coffee in night cafés I'd listen, fascinated by his dissection of politics and the books I had read and not understood. When the Spanish Civil War broke out, Maurice left university and joined Canada's Mackenzie-Papineau battalion to fight Franco. When the defeated remnants of the battalion returned to Canada, Maurice was the colonel in charge. Although he never spoke of it, for him to have become an officer it was likely that he had to join and be a member of the Spanish Communist Party. So brilliant did I find his analysis of the military situation that I was sure my Jewish friends would be equally entranced. Like hell they were. Many of them thought him to be a cold fish, unsympathetic to our side in the war. I felt he wasn't unsympathetic, but the enthusiastic way he described German tactics, in their use of tanks and aircraft that he fought against in Spain, made him appear so.

In his own quiet, unemotional way (making him appear even more heartless), Maurice considered wishful thinking about our military strength foolish. We shuddered when he declared the British and French armed forces weak and old-fashioned. The Germans had planned the war so that their war industries would reach their maximum productivity by 1941 when they would unleash their full might against us. The Russians joined with Nazi Germany only to give themselves time to prepare for their war, which Maurice felt inevitable, against Germany. Their plan for maximum war production was designed to reach its peak by 1943! It was all heady and serious argument that infuriated us with his manner and disturbed us with his seeming logic and facts. He was not only a "premature anti-fascist," but to my friends he looked like a kind of premature Dr. Strangelove. There was guilt on our part too — he had already done his bit against the Germans in Spain. And worse, he had his own plan for his participation in the war against Germany, which he knew was going to be fought in the air. He had already enrolled at the University of Toronto in something none of us had ever thought or heard of — aeronautical navigation.

During this time, I looked up my old contacts for the work that I liked doing — namely making films and creating film posters and stage sets. I was troubled. Whenever Petroff and I worked together, I always quite happily took the role of the subsidiary partner. How good would I be without Petroff? Hell, he was such a genius, with so many good ideas and such passionate drive. I'd soon find out.

My efforts to get a film commission were futile. Alas, there were too few Arthur Lismers.

During my absence from Canada, the Theatre of Action had disappeared and some of its members formed a new group under the direction of Sidney Banks. I designed the stage sets for it. One of the most successful was the set for *Of Mice and Men*, which was performed on one of the lousiest stages in Toronto. One of the play's key scenes, where Lennie eventually strangles the randy wife of the ranch owner, called for an enormous barn. How could I do that effectively on the stage of Margaret Eaton Hall, which is about thirty feet wide but at most twelve to fifteen feet deep? Got it! In the foreground I would build part of a horse stall, use some bales of hay, and behind this, if I could manage to do it right, design and paint a trompe l'oeil backdrop with perfect perspective of the largest barn I could imagine. It would have to include part of the barn's roof and its wooden structural beams. At stage floor level in the centre of the painted backdrop I'd have the barn door half open, showing blue sky and sunny wheat fields beyond it. The doors would have to look to be twenty feet high, but in perspective, would have the painted height of only two feet. And that's what I did.

When the scene begins, Lennie is sitting on one of the bales of hay with some rabbits, sad that he has just accidentally strangled one of

Sydney's poster for Alexander Nevsky.

them. To my utter amazement and no small pleasure, when the curtain rose revealing the setting, the audience burst into applause lasting for a full minute! This happened performance after performance to which I came as a bee to a succulent flower. My pleasure eventually gave way to shame. That poor fucker who played Lennie had to sit there fooling with the rabbit's ad libbing action until the applause stopped. The things you learn about yourself.

The realization gradually came to me that I didn't need Petroff. Any inhibition I felt that he was superior to me in ideas and craftsmanship was foolish. If our former clients had ever thought me Petroff's junior partner, they now knew otherwise.

Leo Clavir of Cosmopolitan Films was happy to give me work to do. He was amazed to hear of my experience with Igor in Hollywood and couldn't understand it at all. I was pleased with my posters for the Russian film *Professor Mamlock* and thought the ones for *Alexander Nevsky* not merely my best but as good a design as one made by the world's best graphic artists. To my shame I misspelled a word in a sub-paragraph; I still wonder if the Russians noticed it, because the large poster is in the Sergei Eisenstein archives in Moscow.

My connection with Clavir gave me an extraordinary insight into the business side of film distribution. His film checker on *Nevsky* was ill — would I like to make a few bucks as a checker for a few weeks? Needing the money, I quickly agreed after finding out what the hell a checker did. He explained: "You see, foreign films are usually shown in third-rate, flea-trap cinemas. We get a percentage of the movie house take and y'can't always trust the bums to report honestly the number of admissions. Here's what you do. You gotta be there as long as the box office is open. When you first arrive, be sure to take down the first number on each of the ticket rolls in the box office. There'll be different prices, for kids etc. What? You didn't know there were numbers on each ticket? Well, there are! At the end of the day you take the last numbers and the difference between the two sets, voilà, gives you — gives us — the number of admissions."

As if this wasn't enough, and to Clavir it clearly wasn't: "Now, see this gadget? Keep it in your hand and stand next to the ticket taker and every time he takes a ticket, you press it, see? It's a counter, a double check on the ticket totals. Be sure that the ticket taker shreds each ticket. And, oh yes, before I forget, take a gander every now and then at the tickets to see that the numbers run consecutively. You see, sometimes those crooks sell tickets from the inside of the roll. Y'see?"

I nearly turned the job down when I learned that there were matinees and so I would have to be in the cinema when it opened at noon until a little after nine in the evening. I did this work for several foreign films. While the job was mostly boring it was interesting to see the kinds of people who went in and hearing their comments as they left. Years later when I met Betty, who became my wife, she said she remembered seeing me standing at the back of the Standard Theatre on Spadina Avenue when she went to see *Professor Mamlock*. One day, I got a good laugh when a guy about my age came through the ticket door carrying a Rolleiflex camera with an enormous flash gun mounted on it. "Sorry," the ticket taker said, "you can't take that in with you. You'll have to leave it in the box office." Curious, I asked the guy what he was going to shoot in the cinema. "Oh, the movie. It's so beautiful."

"Oh, you'll need a faster lens. That 4.5 lens on the Rollei is too slow," I said, showing this guy I knew a lot about cameras.

"Of course it's too slow," he replied pityingly, as if talking to a moron. "I'm not stupid. That's why I brought the flash gun!"

Once, I became involved in a bit of drama. I asked the ticket taker to show me a ticket to verify its number; it did not run on from the previous number. When I queried him, he airily answered that the guy had probably bought his ticket earlier. I accepted that, but felt that I was being had. Soon, two more tickets, also out of order, turned up. When I said I would keep them, he said he had to go to the john and would I take tickets for a short while? Being a gent, I obliged, and noticed that en route to the toilet, he popped his head into the ticket booth for what looked like a quick help to the cashier. There were no more out of order tickets, but in my report, I mentioned the discrepancy.

When I arrived the next day, there was a new cashier. It was the owner's wife and the ticket taker had metamorphosed into the cinema owner. He thanked me for reporting what had happened the day before. Grateful, he gave me a bottle of whiskey. For months he'd been suspicious that the box office receipts didn't seem to match the size of the audience. When Clavir phoned him about my report he had a rough session with the cashier, who finally broke down and confessed that she was in cahoots with the ticket taker. He would palm the tickets and sneak them back to the cashier who would then resell them. He figured that for months he was probably robbed at least twenty to thirty bucks a week. "I wanted to call the cops, but didn't. It would have killed my wife. Can you imagine? That son-of-a-bitch is my brother-in-law!" This was the first time I learned that no industry could teach the movie business anything about financial chicanery and nepotism.

In those tiny movie houses, the ticket taker stands at the rear of the hall so that as a checker I could not avoid seeing the movies over and over again. People think I'm lying when I say I've seen *Alexander Nevsky* 180 times, but it's true. It's no idle boast when I say that much of Eisenstein's book *Film Sense*, in which he described how he made *Nevsky*, merely confirmed what I had already figured out.

The $20 a week I earned as a checker was worth a thousand times more because of what I began to learn about what makes a scene tick with the audience. It is simple: I learned to listen — to hear the audience actually breathe. I waited for more than the obvious laughter, snores or coughs, but also the intake of breath and the deathly silence of intense concentration — these are what alerted me to look for the why and how of filmmaking. As a bonus, I began to revere the audience, to hear them gasp in a large group or, many years later when I was in television, hear them in my mind's ear when they were alone at home in front of a TV set. A new discovery for me was music, which could so powerfully or delicately give new meaning to a scene by invoking the past, or counterpoint a character's expression. I sensed the power of the moving images, their length and distance from the object for clarity, and often the redundancy of dialogue when the visuals already said it.

A revelation to me was discovering how to get a sure response from an audience: compassion. A character responding understandingly to the plight of another who doesn't expect it will almost always bring tears to an audience. Chaplin understood this so well, as demonstrated, for example, in his last scene in *City Lights* when the blind girl recognizes Charlie, the tramp, as her rich benefactor.

Jack Olsen got me a commission to paint a portrait. It had to be done from photographs, which to me as a somewhat purist artist was anathema. There was good reason for it — the man I was to paint was dead. He was the son of the owner of the company Olsen worked for who was killed while training as a pilot in the Royal Canadian Air Force. Out of sympathy for their boss, Olsen's fellow employees had taken up a collection to get the portrait painted. Olsen warned me against any impressionist, van Gogh look. It had to be a conventional "academic" type portrait — the kind that hangs in boardrooms.

As loathsome as I found the job, I needed the money and so I went to work, basing it on a two-and-a-half by two-and-a-half colour photograph of the poor kid in his flight-sergeant's uniform. I had trouble getting that "academic" look, especially with the face. I got my old friend Sidney Pearl who was an academic whiz to come in and give the portrait the final professional touch — right down to the obligatory window highlight on the chap's nose.

The day arrived when Olsen and the delegation of workers came to my studio to approve the painting. My place was spic and span, the painting on my easel in the heavy, somewhat gaudy, gold-leafed frame I had bought — compensating, no doubt, for the ghoulish shame I felt for having accepted this unpleasant job. There were six of them. They stood back and with humility appraised it, me anxiously waiting for their approval. Despite the, "Mmn. That's just like him . . . " and the "It's more real than life . . ." comments, I sensed that there was something wrong. They were guarded. Then they huddled together, mumble mumble, and then turned and faced me. One man stepped forward, cleared his throat and said, "We think you should make a small change. He should be in an officer's uniform with wings."

I was flummoxed, "B-but, the photograph . . . Oh, did he become a pilot officer? I thought he was killed before he —" I was interrupted: "He was. But he would have become one." Silence. They waited. Bewildered, I looked at Olsen for help. His eyes implored me to agree with their request. I did.

When they left I wanted to be sick. What a ghoul I was. What a shit! I painted the appropriate stripe on the uniform cuffs and carefully painted wings on the left breast — suitably highlighted. Of the one hundred dollar fee, twenty-five went for the frame and I gave Sidney twenty-five for his help. The needed fifty that came to me was the most unwelcome fifty bucks I ever earned.

Life went on and I did more and more commercial art jobs. Olsen decided to enlist. The army wouldn't have him because he was too short, but the air force was glad to get him. He was the ideal height for a rear gunner. I was now earning enough to pay our flat's rent by myself, but niggling me was whether or not I should enlist. I was terrified at the thought of having to heel to discipline, but my best friend had gone and my brother had been in England in the army for over a year. Each month I was reminded forcibly of him when I'd hollow out a loaf of bread to protect a bottle of Canadian rye to send to him in England along with a carton of cigarettes.

One evening, at a movie, there was a short Canadian film — an absolute rarity, something Canadians never, ever saw. Out of a hundred films shown in Canada, about ninety of them were American and the remainder came from England and France. This little twenty-minute film was all about Canada, my own country! Simply unbelievable. I stayed to see it again. It was called *Canada Carries On*[19] and by God, it seemed that it was made in Ottawa.

I hauled out my sketchpad and pencil on seeing it the third time, scribbled, "Produced by the National Film Board of Canada" and the one name on the credits, Graham McInnes, which rang a faint bell in my mind. Wasn't he the art critic I knew slightly?

---

19 *Canada Carries On* was a series of theatrical short films made by the National Film Board of Canada. The films were each ten minutes or so and were originally part of the war effort, offering Canadians their own perspective on the conflict overseas and the home front. The series was distributed by Columbia Pictures where it was shown on a monthly basis to over 800 theatres across Canada. The series persisted well after the Second World War and continued until 1960.

CHAPTER TEN

ON BOARD THE FILM BOARD

Graham McInnes, when he was the art critic for *Saturday Night*[20] (which was then printed newspaper size) came to Petroff's and my studio to see our work. He had been commissioned by England's *Studio Magazine* to write a special edition on Canadian art. Believe me, as a seventeen-year-old it was quite a thrill to be mentioned in it among top graphic artists even though it was only in a footnote.

I wrote to him care of the Board in Ottawa asking whether he remembered me, did he write the film, was it actually made in Canada, were any more going to be made and, if so, might there possibly be a job there for me? He answered warmly almost immediately with

---

20 *Saturday Night* was Canada's longest-running general interest magazine, lasting from 1887 to 2005.

a yes to every question. He told me that a John Grierson[21] (whose name I recalled reading about in Paul Rotha's book *The Film Till Now*) had been brought from England and was in charge of film for the Canadian government. He suggested that I write to him and ask for a job. "Better," he went on, "why not come up and see him? He'd like that."

Write? No, this was too good a chance to miss.[22] I would go there, in person. And dammit, no bus or train. I'm going to go in style — by airplane! A dream. I'd fly there in the early morning and wow, back in Toronto on the same day! This was 1940, and to go by plane was daring. And I was flush enough from all the work I had been doing to blow the exorbitant fare, $28 return. I put together a batch of still pictures I had taken, examples of my posters, photographs of my stage sets — but sadly, without my little film, which the gallery couldn't find.

In the TCA Lockheed 14, it was high drama. Half the passengers were officers of different Canadian armed forces. The other half were dollar-a-year men perusing papers from briefcases. My mind was awhirl with a mixture of thoughts: what kept the plane aloft; what a marvel were the wonderful patterns of the ground 5,000 feet below; how would I manage to get a job from Mr. Grierson? Before landing

---

21 John Grierson (1898-1972) was a pioneer in documentary film. In Britain in the 1930s, he established a film unit within the Empire Marketing Board and then another within the General Post Office that made documentaries about British life, including the heralded films *Night Mail* (1936) and *Coal Face* (1935). In 1938, Grierson was invited by the Canadian government to look at film production in Canada. He recommended that Canada establish a national body for filmmaking, the result of which was the National Film Commission, founded in 1939, which later became the National Film Board of Canada. Grierson would serve as the first government film commissioner.

22 Newman did in fact write Grierson as well, on January 14, 1941. He told him the story of his work to date and his attempt to get a job at Disney before talking about seeing a *Canada Carries On* short. "It was on becoming acquainted with the series of films you are doing that I became aware that, at last, films were being produced in Canada. I am particularly anxious to participate in their production. Hence this letter — to find out what the possibilities are of doing film work with you."

we were given hard candies to suck; to clear the eardrums, I was told. At Ottawa's Uplands airport you knew there was a war on. Yellow Royal Canadian Air Force Ansons and Piper Cubs with their training crews were buzzing and coughing all over the place landing and taking off. I was fascinated but I had to leave to face what I came for.

In Ottawa I took the Rockcliffe streetcar east and when I got off at John Street I began to walk to a very handsome building that I thought appropriate for a National Film Board. It was not. It was the French Embassy. Across from it was the crummiest decrepit-looking building with a corroded sign beside its door that read, "THE MOTION PICTURE BUREAU." Under the sign was a huge box that I later learned was filled with sand to prevent one from breaking one's neck on the icy pavement in Ottawa's fierce winter. Inside its gloomy, shit-brindled corridors I passed a few young men purposefully carrying a piece of paper or a can of 35mm film and one old man carrying three cans of film whom John Bird, the journalist, would have described as looking like an old scrotum, the wrinkled retainer.

I was shattered to learn from a Miss Scellen, Mr. Grierson's secretary, that the government film commissioner was not in. In fact, he was out of town. So was Graham McInnes. She thought Mr. McLean, the deputy film commissioner, might see me. This, after I explained that I was a filmmaker hoping to work for the board. Gosh, she was kind. I hoped Mr. McLean was too.

Ross McLean airily invited me into his office. When he was looking at my still photographs and posters I saw a conservatively dressed man — he was even wearing a vest. No Hollywood type, he! Neat and trim in his mid-thirties, with a scrubbed pink face under thinning hair he was almost handsome with an aquiline nose I rather envied. As he'd flip over my stuff murmuring polite approval, he would nervously hunch his shoulders every now and then as if making certain that his jacket sat properly, or shoot a cuff or wave a cigarette in a holder. A meticulous sort of guy.

When finished he looked across the desk at me and thought Grierson (he didn't use the Mr.) might like to meet me and see my work. In fact, Grierson would be back tomorrow and, "Would that be all right with you?" Would it! Darn right it would. Except, where would I sleep? I explained that I had a problem, I was flying out on an 8 p.m. flight . . . his eyebrows lifted at the flight mention. Clearly he thought me no slouch. They dropped when I continued, "But unfortunately I'm short of cash for a hotel room." He lent me a fiver! I stayed awhile, talking. He was amused at my Hollywood experiences, and he amazed me in turn by telling me that the entire Film Board of Canada consisted of no more than four people — Grierson, himself and their secretaries! Their job was to coordinate all government film activities. The films themselves were actually being made by the few people they were able to place in the Motion Picture Bureau. My heart sank at that. With Miss Scellen a time was set for me to come tomorrow and meet the man who was to influence me more than any other: John Grierson.

The next day in his office with large windows overlooking the Ottawa River and the green Gatineau hills beyond in Quebec, Grierson didn't get up when I entered. He was leaning back in his chair with his feet crossed on the desk. If his feet looked tiny his eyes looked enormous as they sized me up. He looked almost fierce; his mouth, under a short clipped moustache, seemed to suggest that there was a faint smell of shit in the air. Before I could sit down, he rapped out with a bare Scottish accent, "I know about you, Newman. Syd? What have you got to show me?" He studied me as I leaned across the desk and opened my portfolio. "Sit down, sit down," he said, as if I was silly waiting to be invited.

My artwork was on top and he unfolded the *Baltic Deputy* poster. Without looking at me he said, "Cherkasov, fine actor. Started as an acrobat in a circus. Where Chaplin started. Who's Petroff?" He looked up at me. I told him that he was once a partner of mine. Maybe he thought the posters were not mine. I was relieved when he came to *Professor Mamlock* and *Alexander Nevsky*, which were clearly signed Sydney Newman and prayed he would not notice the misspelled word. If he did he made no comment, but murmured, "Good. Mmn, not bad. Not bad!" as he looked at the rest and at my colour Disney work. To keep my nervousness in check I volunteered a truncated version of my Disney experience. With some small pride he mentioned that he had commissioned Disney to make a training film for the Canadian Army on how to use a Bren Gun. By the time he finished looking at my still photographs, I was worried. On the third shot when I heard "ver-ry hearty" again I wondered, hearty? My Canadian ears! What Grierson is saying is arty! And from the way he is saying it, artiness is something he clearly does not approve of. I must have heard "Very arty . . . Very arty," five more times as he quickly perused the remaining ten shots. He sighed as he closed the portfolio.

Grierson leaned back in his chair, put his feet back on the desk looking at me somewhat less fiercely now with his blue-grey eyes and said, "So you want to make films." I quickly said, "Yes," and described the documentary I had made. He asked me a few questions about how I went about it and then suddenly asked, "Could you do some war posters?" My heart sank. "B-but is there . . . I mean, I want to . . . can't I—" He cut me off: "Sorry, not now. No film openings. Could you do some war posters?" A flat statement, not a question. I gulped and said I could. "Right thing. Nice meeting you, laddie. McLean will write to you."

I flew back to Toronto feeling rotten. Dammit, what the hell was wrong with those stills? They're bloody good, I know it! Anyway, it was a connection. After three tries I finally penned a very polite letter of thanks to Ross McLean, not forgetting to enclose a five-dollar bill, and asked him to mention again to Mr. Grierson my desire to be of service as a filmmaker, or in any other way, should an opening occur.

Our letters must have crossed in the mail because I received one from him the day after I sent mine. They needed full-colour posters to promote the sale of War Savings Stamps and War Bonds to be used as slides in movie houses; would I send sketches of ideas? By May I had produced two — McLean told me that Grierson was very happy with them. One was of an army tank whose treads were made of war savings stamps rolling over and crushing a Nazi soldier. The other had Canada in the foreground and, stretching from it over the Atlantic to Britain, was a bridge of War Bonds on which marched proud Canadian armies; over the bridge the sky was black with our planes and under it our vast navy all advanced to save Britain.

Still no word of a film job despite my constant reminders to Ross McLean. For years I had taken a summer job teaching art at a children's camp. There was nothing left to do but go again that summer.

Ever since my four ten-day holidays at the University Settlement Camp I had managed to get summer jobs as a counsellor teaching art at camps, most of them at one that was run by the B'nai B'rith organization for underprivileged (that word again!) Jewish boys, some from broken homes and so on. When they arrived, the kids would break your heart — grey-skinned, skinny, and some lice-ridden with nits in their hair. After ten days of sun, swimming, lots of food, some do-good activity like my art classes, they went back to the same environment they came from with perhaps a bit more zest for life. Twenty years later in England I met one of England's outstanding drama directors — Alvin Rakoff.[23] "You don't remember me, do you?" he asked. I didn't, and he grinned. "I was one of your kids at Camp B'nai B'rith."

When I was younger, I made some good lifelong friends among the counsellors at that camp, most of whom were in high school or university. One was Louis Applebaum, then seventeen, who wanted to become a composer. In the evenings after the campers were snug in their cots I would go with Lou to the large meeting hall where there was a piano. I'd sit and watch him painfully try to master *Clair de Lune* on the piano. Leo Orenstein, with whom I later went to Hollywood, was another.

Most fun to be with was Louis Weingarten, later to become Johnny Wayne of Wayne and Shuster.[24] It never surprised me that he became a top comedian — it was all there at camp. He was the one who dubbed our Jewish camp "Camp Bonnie Brae." He and I used to entertain the kids from the stage, he giving the comic patter while I drew chalk cartoons. One unforgettable moment was Johnny's comeback

---

23 Rakoff's wife, Jacqueline Hill, would play Barbara Wright, one of the first companions on *Doctor Who*.

24 At the time, he was still Lou Weingarten. Newman kept in his papers a note from him dated October 16, 1941, just after Newman had started at the NFB. "Dear Eisenstein," it began. It adds the postscript "My radio name is Johnny Wayne."

to our head counsellor who was a strict disciplinarian and somewhat pompous on the psychology of handling children. He went too far once in instructing us, prompting Johnny to say, "Harold, you're being a prick." Harold, furious at this insubordination said, "You take that back!" Johnny's instant rejoinder that broke us up was, "Okay, I withdraw my prick!"

We weren't paid much for the summer's work but it was well worth it. I felt good that somehow I was paying back the good times I was given as an underprivileged kid. As well, working with the kids was fun, and the sun and the food I stored up were enabling me to face another hard winter.

The need for money drew me to a handsomely paying camp for rich kids near Algonquin Park — Camp Winnebago. It was run by Mrs. Danson, the mother of Barney Danson, who later became Canada's Minister of Defence. The year I had been there, I had carved for her a totem pole out of an old log using hardly more than a hatchet. With no Film Board job in sight I agreed to go back to her camp for another summer of sun, food and fun with nubile girls. (Keeping the boys and girls apart is another story needing a Mordecai Richler to write.)

Mrs. Danson had so liked my eight-foot, winged totem pole that she imposed a condition that I next carve a really huge one. I agreed, as long as she provided me with proper chisels, a mallet, rasps and a decent, not worm-eaten, log. I spent a small fortune on the best wood carving tools and supervised the expensive hauling by tractor of an equally expensive thirty-foot tree trunk to the camp. It was June 29, 1941, and just after it had been laboriously set up on special trestles and I was about to begin carving, I was called to the camp's office. It was my mother calling long distance from Toronto. Oh God, something's happened to Wolf overseas! I thought. It wasn't anything like that at all. A telegram had come for me saying, NFB JOB OPEN STOP START JULY FIRST MCLEAN.

That old darling, Mrs. Danson, concealed her disappointment. She understood. She allowed me to leave. For all I know, that log is still on its trestles today, well-seasoned and waiting for the hands of a sculptor. I hitchhiked to Ottawa the next day.

How did a job suddenly open at the Film Board? I found out later that Grierson's original good relations as Government Film Commissioner with Captain Badgley, head of the Motion Picture Bureau, had gone sour. The Bureau's staff was old fashioned and incapable of meeting Grierson's sense of urgency to get the right films made quickly and of a standard and style that would grab the minds of a wartime public. He made his case to the prime minister, William Lyon Mackenzie King, whose ear he had. Grierson was ready to return to England, but King, a shy, wily introvert, in some inexplicable way identified with the larger-than-life Grierson and his ideas for using film to unite Canada and as a force for the war effort. He wouldn't let the feisty Scot go.

He increased Grierson's powers in many ways, but most specifically as it was to affect me, put the Bureau under his direct control, taking effect on July 1. Knowing Grierson as well as I got to know him, I'd bet my life that after he saw the Bureau's unwillingness to cooperate, the powers that came to him were exactly what he had planned to get. Canada reaped the benefits and so did I. In spades! Now, Grierson could hire the people he wanted and had a field day in doing so.

In my mind's eye I can see clearly the scene in Ottawa as everyone prepared for the day when Grierson's kiss would turn the froggy Motion Picture Bureau into the princely National Film Board of Canada: Grierson and Ross McLean huddle over a desk littered with letters, bits of paper with names scribbled on them, applications, newspaper clippings — who to hire? They argue — Grierson wants them young, while McLean is concerned that there be a regional and French-

Sydney Newman at the NFB, 1948.

Canadian balance. Grierson strides back and forth looking into his address book for the name of that pimply, amateur filmmaker he met in Kamloops; the pretty girl who worked for the *Winnipeg Tribune*; that librarian in Toronto, what is her name?; the bearded school teacher he had drinks with in Quebec's Chateau Frontenac, the one who wouldn't take communion because the Pope blessed Franco's tanks. Janet Scellen is driven mad looking for addresses, phone numbers. Finally, a list! Ross begins sending out telegrams to the four corners of Canada, similar, I imagine, to the one I received.

The first two (I believe) of the new Film Boarders who turned up on July 1, Doug Sinclair from Canada's west coast and me, were the cause of some mirth for Grierson and the English colleagues that he had lured to Canada to teach us young Turks how to make films. Whenever these English blokes wanted something done, they'd poke their heads out of their cutting rooms and shout out, "Newman? Sinc-leh?" And usually laugh when they did so. Or other Englishmen would laugh when they heard the "Newman Sinc-leh" cry. Why was this so funny to them? The camera that had been brought up to use in England was called the Newman-Sinclair camera.

On my first day at the Board I was signed in by the controller, A.G. McLean, a sweet little roly-poly man who turned out to be Ross McLean's brother. My salary was to be $100 a month — a drop of $300 from what I had been earning as an artist. I didn't give a damn: this was a job I wanted. A.G., as he was called, was the father of Grant McLean, who joined the Board after A.G. left and who became a fine cameraman/director. At great danger to himself he crossed the Japanese war front to get the West's first movie shots of Mao Tse Tung and the beleaguered Chinese Liberation Army holed up in the caves of China's Yunnan province.

I was assigned to a J.D. Davidson, whom I learned was a noted cameraman who had shot some of England's finest documentaries. I'm not sure I liked him at first. He was a lean man with a thin red face and scrappy moustache who rapped out words rather than speak them — when he did, he used few of them, as if each cost him. One of his arms and hand seemed twisted, a result, I was told, of shooting a film in the raging, winter sea of the North Atlantic. He was being transferred in a sling on a cable from one ship in a convoy to be in a destroyer. Something broke and he fell into the icy Atlantic between the two ships. Luckily, he was only partially crushed and kept afloat by his duffle coat until rescued.

When I met him he led me into a large, nearly empty room, but there in a corner was an immense pile of 35mm cans, fifty or sixty of them. "There's footage of the brass of the Forces. Make a three-minute film of each in sync sound. It's for cinema. Use the third cutting room from the end." And he left! In trepidation I picked up one of the cans and lifted out a four-hundred foot roll on a spool, the centre of which fell out and the whole damn thing collapsed into a mountain of film on the floor. Not only had I never edited any 35mm film nor spliced any, but hell, I'd never even held a piece of it in my hand. As the saying goes, I didn't know my ass from a sprocket hole. My first day, too! I wanted to cry when into the room came a thin, light brown-haired guy carrying a piece of paper. With his Adam's apple bobbing up and down as he spoke, he said, "Hi! I'm Tom Daly." Here I was caught with my film pants down. Thank God he was Canadian.

Seeing the mess of film, he said, "I'll un-clamp a rewind from a cutting room and give you a hand." When he returned, he clamped the rewind onto the edge of a desk, put a reel on the spindle and asked me to start handing him the film. I couldn't find the end or the start in the pile and when I finally did and handed it to him, he looked at me very upset and said, "Oh dear. This is negative. I'll go and get some gloves." And he left.

Gloves? Why gloves? When Daly returned, he was putting them on and to my bewilderment, handed me a pair. He picked up the lid of the empty can and said, "Tsk tsk, just as I thought. It's not labelled negative." And cheerfully, "Not your fault." When he took the piece of film from my hand to thread into the spool, he said, "Oh no, not from the inside." He looked searchingly at me as we both looked for the outside end of the roll. As we began painfully winding the film onto the spool he guardedly asked me, his Adam's apple bobbing furiously, "Did you work in sixteen or thirty-five?"

"Sixteen," I replied.

Satisfied that this was a good reason for my ineptness he went on: "What kind of films were they?"

"Films? Film. Only one."

He shot a look at me. "One," he said.

Grierson had pulled the same trick on his staff as I was to observe many times over the years. Whether it was because he never wanted to be seen as having made a mistake in hiring someone, or because he hoped that by stating something firmly and often enough it would become a fact, or because he thought it might instill a competitive spirit in his staff, is anyone's guess. Prior to my arrival at the Board he had sung my praises. He had found an artist, a genius of a filmmaker! That was why Davidson assumed I was able to go right to work and make three short films out of stock footage.

Tom Daly and the other two Canadians Grierson had placed in the Bureau, Jim Beveridge and Donald Fraser, helped me learn all about the physical rolls of editing film and a lot more. We were all about the same age. Joining strips of film together on a hot splicer was tricky. I nearly crushed a finger several times when learning. At first, as a junior, Davidson and the other Brits had me splicing day and night so that by the end of three weeks the hot splicer became "user-friendly." I learned to use synchronisers — two-way, three-way and four-way — to match the sound to picture and the most wonderful magic machine of all, a Movieola, for editing film.

An editor is the most unsung creative hero in the entire process of filmmaking. To peer through that Movieola lens, see the images flickering by, grabbing the side wheel with a gloved hand to stop it running at the point of the cut, reversing the film to make sure, then forward again and stop, lift the lens and mark the crucial film frame with an orange grease pencil, slap the lens back down then going on to find the next cutting point — nothing in filmmaking has ever thrilled me as much. The most valued employee in the Board in the early days was the editor, who was, essentially, the director of the film, especially when the basic footage is made of library stock shots — the foundation of most of the early Film Board films for *Canada Carries On* and *World in Action*.

Jim Beveridge was a real charmer who came from Vancouver. At request he'd drop whatever he was doing to help me — he was a natural teacher, a good listener and a great word-spinner. With appropriate facial expression and body movement he would recount an experience to make it alive and funny. I've wondered all these years why he never made his mark as a great film director using his incredible personal means of expression and observation of life. I feel his métier, perhaps, was drama and not documentary. No matter, he is a great teacher — perhaps of more value. I had already met Don Fraser in Toronto. When I left Central Tech, the Ontario Government had set up a six-month course in Industrial Design to provide jobs during the Depression, which I was allowed to take. Don taught photography. Being a camera nut, he became a friend of mine. He told me that he had tried to get a job with Grierson in England and so was the first Canadian filmmaker Grierson hired. He was a shy, slow-speaking fellow, short, stocky and blond, whose eyes smiled at you through spectacles. I was his assistant when we both directed and shot an army film designed to show its troops that the food they were getting was peachy — as good as Mom's. Of the three "originals" I followed into the Board, I was closest to Don.

Doug Sinclair was younger than me. Months earlier he had shown Grierson a longish film he had made in Kodachrome of a trip through Canada's Rocky Mountains. The film demonstrated that for one so young he had guts and that he could handle a camera well. To me, in retrospect, it showed no imagination in structure — in fact it wasn't any better than a travelogue but without the schmaltzy narration of a FitzPatrick[25] to carry it off. To get along in the Film Board in those days you had to be either very creative and exciting in your work or heavily dedicated to doing society good, whether it was in winning the war or helping farmers to grow fatter pigs. Some ideally combined both. Even without these qualities, charm and wit could help — but

---

25 James A. FitzPatrick was a producer of filmed travelogues shown between feature films. He was best known for filming these in colour and for his distinctive narration for which he became known as the "voice of the globe."

not for long. It's sad to say, Doug fitted none of these categories and so after a few years became a ho-hum filmmaker. He left the NFB a bitter man.

He eventually hit back in the silliest way imaginable, writing a letter to no less than the prime minister accusing the Board of making films that leaned in the direction of fascism and cited films and the attitudes of certain individuals as evidence. Of course the charge was seen to be — and was — ludicrous, which further inflamed the spurned lover. Undaunted, over the years he broadsided letters to anyone, or any organization that hated the brash NFB (and there were quite a few of these as the Film Board became more and more successful). His letters even went to the FBI in the United States in which the charge of fascism was replaced by the more fashionable one of communism. Later, these letters were to hurt Grierson terribly.

Most vivid in my mind are the experienced filmmakers Grierson brought to Canada from England. They came to make films, but they found they had to become teachers, so green were we Canadians in the art and techniques of film. Prior to Grierson, Canada could only, at best, muster raw footage of Canadian events that would be shipped to New York and edited there for hoped-for insertion into Canadian editions of the five U.S. newsreels. The two laboratories that could process 35mm black-and-white film survived by printing and developing American films for distribution in Canada, as well as the occasional Canadian-made tourist and travel film sponsored by the provinces and the CP and CN railways.

By the time I arrived in 1941, the NFB was commissioning a few armed forces' training and indoctrination films from outfits such as Associated Screen News in Montreal, Audio Pictures in Toronto and Crawley Films in Ottawa. As well as making some of these itself, the big, public feather in the Film Board's cap was the twenty-minute films of the *Canada Carries On* series, which were seen in over 800 movie houses across Canada each month.

To Grierson there was no point in making films if they were not seen. He succeeded in getting Columbia Pictures of Canada (then wholly Canadian and owned by Louis Rosenfeld) to distribute the series. Even better, Grierson had learned in Britain that because the government gave away their informational propaganda films to the cinemas, being free was no guarantee that they would be screened. The son of a gun actually got Columbia Pictures and the cinemas to pay good hard cash for each and every issue of *CCO*. He also knew that if the pictures were pious in intention but boring and irrelevant to the urgencies of the times, no amount of con or salesmanship would get them seen. Grierson had the right man in the right frame of mind to produce the series: Stuart Legg.

Legg and Grierson made the series so relevant that Legg's *Canada Carries On: War Clouds in the Pacific*, about the coming danger of the Japanese, was shown in Canada one week before the attack on Pearl Harbor. The Americans wanted it for immediate U.S. release, but they couldn't have a film title with the word "Canada" in it. In finding a solution, a thought occurred to Grierson and probably Legg: "Why not a new monthly series with *War Clouds* as the opener for the United States? A U.S. distribution deal!" And so a new series called *World in Action*[26] was born. Canada had at last found a voice that would be heard, and was heard, for the first time in the United States.

Legg now had his work doubled.

Legg frightened the hell out of me for the four years we were together at the Board. Why was he always so arrogantly above it all? Only those close to him or who worked for him may have felt at home with him — Tom Daly, his production assistant; Margaret Ann Adamson (now Lady Elton), his researcher who found most of the spectacular footage for the *CCO* and *World in Action* films; and a few other assistants who came and went. By 1943, Legg's *World in Action* series was wowing them all over the United States (J.G. made sure the Americans paid for them), and to lighten Legg's burden of work, a few Canadians were given a crack at making the occasional *Canada Carries On*. I was one of them.

---

26 *World in Action* was a companion series to *Canada Carries On*, though its focus was more global. That series didn't continue after the war.

I was asked to go to see Mr. Legg. (It wasn't until he left the Board that I had the courage to call him Stuart as Tom and Margaret Ann did.) He was a tall man, slightly stooped as if he carried the troubles of the world on his shoulders. When I hated him most, I thought his perpetually frowning pink face looked like a peeled grape. He told me that there was about 4,000 feet of film of Vancouver's successful efforts at setting up an air-raid warning system to protect Canada against a Japanese airstrike. He wanted a two-reel *CCO* out of that material and told me to use any library material I felt necessary. I had made many films, some fairly good, but nothing as challenging or as exciting had ever been offered to me before. I didn't expect to fail and approached the task with relish. That didn't last long. I knew I had a dog on my hands when I screened the Vancouver footage.

There was no action in any of it, no guns being fired, mostly men marching or being reviewed by their commanding officer. One series of grey shots showed two old home guard types wearing oversized raincoats walking at a snail's pace on a roof and peering through binoculars at the Pacific beyond, looking more ridiculous than Laurel and Hardy. Well, I gave it my best shot, as they say. I sparked it up with shots of how the Londoners were coping with their blitz, firing ack-ack guns or how our boys are fighting overseas while our chaps are protecting the home front. When I had finished drafting the narration, I told Mr. Legg I was ready to screen the cutting copy for him. When the time came, my only fear when I gave the film to the projectionist was that some of the splices might come apart; an irritating but common experience.

When Legg strolled into the screening room, he looked as if he'd rather be anywhere else but there to see my film. And when he walked up to the screen, lifted a leg and farted, I knew I was in trouble. Geez, you might fart in Cambridge or in an English public school, but you don't fart in public in Canada.

The best thing I can say of the screening was that the film did not break. As I attempted to read the narration aloud from the back of the darkened screening room I couldn't help but be distracted, in fact destroyed by Legg's frequent exclamations of "Shit." "Oh fuck."

"This is SHIT!" At the end of the screening before the lights came on, Legg jumped to his feet and looked at me as if he could kill me. The others in the screening room fled. Then striding to the door not looking at me, Legg, in a deadly voice said, "Bring the cutting copy to my cutting room along with all the outs and trims you've got. When you've done that, call me." And was gone.

I have never before, nor since, felt so shamed and beside myself with such a deep and violent anger. After I had rolled my film bins with the outs and trims into his cutting room and with the cutting copy in my hand, I went to his office and told him I had done as he asked. As he got up from his desk, where he had obviously been making some notes, he walked toward me and stopped and looked at me, not at my eyes but at a point just above them, and told me that I would be with him until he had finished re-cutting the film. When he entered his cutting room, he violently swept the top of a filing cabinet clean of dirty coffee cups, empty Coke bottles and scripts, sending them flying and crashing onto the floor. He took the two cans of film from me and, speaking to my forehead, said, "Get a broom and clean it up."

When I returned, he was sitting at his cutting table tearing my film apart, shot by shot, and hanging each shot on a nail above an empty film bin. After I swept up the mess, he handed me the shots to hang on the nails reminding me to make sure I knew where each one was when he wanted it. Boy! What a guy this was. Suddenly I was back where I was two years ago — a lousy production assistant!

For thirty-six hours, with the exception of visits to the toilet or the screening room downstairs, we never left the cutting room. Doggedly, he worked non-stop, cutting and re-cutting with me getting more and more tired, never speaking except when saying, "Get me the second, night take." "Find me that Hitler shot from *Triumph*." "No, not this, the other long shot." And so it went on and on as he painfully edited twenty minutes of screen time.

I noticed something unique about the way he varied the pace of the film. After he had selected the shots he wanted for a sequence, he would use his arms to measure the length of a shot. The longest shot would stretch the distance between his two outstretched arms, making sure, of course, that it contained the action he wanted. The next shot would be, say, from one outstretched arm to his nose, the next to his shoulder, the shortest shot would be to the middle of his forearm — a foot in length. Another trick I learned was the way he heightened the visual impact of an explosion. He inserted at the moment of flash two clear frames of leader, followed by two black ones, the variations of this depending on the size of the bang he wanted.

After finishing the editing, he went into his office to have a short nap in his tilted chair while I went ahead making a detailed shot list of the film, translating the feet and frame length of each shot to minutes and seconds. This was to help him write his commentary, and for composer Lucio Agostini to write and conduct this music. Then I finally left the sawmill on John Street, went across Sussex to my room above the Nichols Grocery Store and Snack Emporium and fell into my bed, dead beat.

Ten days later Lorne Greene came to Ottawa to read Legg's narration for the re-recording session marrying Greene's voice, the music and the sound effects for the *Canada Carries On* edition, which Legg had titled *Banshees Over Canada*. I didn't dare ask Legg, "What the hell is a banshee?" I wonder now how many other non-Irish Canadians knew. Maybe Legg's film was better than mine, but it was one of his poorest. Small wonder, to use a phrase he used so often in his commentaries, considering the speed with which he had to put the stupid thing together. At the end of that experience, it's an understatement to say that I had no affection for that man. You have to admire his steadfastness. Pure genius the way his commentary words gave new meaning to dull images, with no corny waiting for the pictures to catch up. But how could he treat any human being the way he treated me!

Three years later when he was living in New York, and when I had become the producer of *Canada Carries On*, I bumped into him there. He couldn't have been more gracious and charming, making plenty of eye contact and not talking to the dead end of my forehead. Not only did he give me a splendid lunch but insisted on pointing out the sights to me from the top of the Empire State Building. He was that same friendly self when my wife and I saw him with his wife and family when I lived in England.

How to understand this Jekyll and Hyde character? First thought that comes to mind is obvious: he was close to the breaking point because he was vastly overworked and his films were no off-the-cuff, easy, win-the-war propaganda. They were deeply thought out and inspired revelations about war strategies, but also about the democratic imperatives of the war and post-war aspirations. His fanatical dedication to work was shared by the other Brits at the Board, and we Canadians and the few Americans with us could do no less than work as hard and as long as they did. Also, there's now trickling into my mind another factor that motivated them, which did not occur to me during the war. It was guilt, or something like it. Here, they were living in what was to them a Garden of Eden under Canada's blue skies — food plentiful, whisky available — while in England their friends and relatives were eating meagre rations under the constant threat of death raining down from the skies. I learned more than craft from Stuart Legg — I learned the toughness and the will to never give up. And never, around a junior whose work isn't up to scratch, give way to emotional extremes.

If Legg appeared an arrogant patrician, Stanley Hawes was a totally different kind of Englishman. He was stocky, dark-haired, warm and avuncular — a working-class in feel kind of guy. In his Birmingham ("Brummigan") accent he was always ready to stop his work to help you. When I would bleat to him about my search for a creative or craft solution, or even talk to him about a personal problem such as I had with Legg, his deadpan, almost Buster Keaton–like, slate-grey look of earnest concern would gradually warm and a solution would be given. He was the first chain-smoker I met. It always amused us to see his flagrant disregard for the explosive dangers of smoking in a nitrate film–filled cutting room. A cigarette was always dangling from his lips even when working over a synchronizer. When an ash fell onto it (only positive film!) he'd casually blow it away and go on working.

At war's end, which came suddenly, Hawes led a large team to make a fifty-minute film to recap the entire war for immediate release to the cinemas. Miraculously, over a period of four days and nights the film was completed. During the final re-recording session in the middle of the night, after recording one reel, so exhausted was the team of Canadians that when the lights came on — with the exception of the sound recordist, Lorne Greene and Hawes — we were all fast asleep. When Stan saw us, his face cracked into a smile. He woke us to get the next reel ready, made himself comfortable on a bed of three chairs and fell dead asleep himself.

Raymond Spottiswoode was the fourth Englishman, an Oxford graduate to Legg's Cambridge with the resulting coolness between them occasionally on display. He was thin, somewhat ungainly and peered at you through glasses that I swear were a quarter of an inch thick. Uncomfortable with people, only Raymond's loud, haw-haw English laugh would signal that he felt liked. He appeared to be comfortable only around Red (Goldie) Myers, his secretary, and Gordon Weisenborn, his production assistant, perhaps because they were both teenagers and he was under thirty at the time. It was said that Legg, Arthur Elton, Edgar Anstey, Basil Wright and the others in the early Grierson days in England originally thought Spottiswoode, who was younger than they were, a cheeky upstart because he had the nerve to write a book called *A Grammar of the Film* (the first edition) before he had ever made a film himself. They thought that Grierson hired him so that they could rag him rotten.

Raymond might have wanted to make films, but Grierson saw that he was a sucker for all things technical. If Raymond were a character in a *Boy's Own* magazine story, his mates would have nicknamed him "Stinks" — the brainy kid who'd rather fool with chemicals than play rugger. Grierson did what he thought right, and it was. I firmly believe that Raymond, as the NFB's first technical coordinator, set the standards for the Board's subsequent worldwide reputation, which it held for many years. I should know: my wife Betty McRae succeeded him in that job.

There was a fifth English person who was incredibly important to the morale, tone and skill of the place — Grierson's wife, Margaret. There was a serenity and a warmth that she radiated; and her bemused

Jack Olsen, Sydney Newman and Nick Balla, early 1950s.

smile, as if that of a tolerant mother, when told of Grierson's often outrageous behaviour made most of us adore her. She was never fazed when Grierson would come to their flat at 30 Cooper Street with a slew of staff. She was never caught short and would always be able to find a ham in the fridge to feed us. The same on Saturdays, which was a kind of "open house" where young jerks like me would find ourselves talking to Cabinet Minister Brooke Claxton and other, usually out of sight, bigwigs. In terms of craft, it was Margaret Grierson who came to the Board for a few days to teach the new negative cutters-to-be and who stayed six months. She was a true gentlewoman who reminded me of Norah McCullough at the Art Gallery of Toronto.

After I arrived on July 1, new recruits began arriving in droves in answer to McLean's telegrams. With only a pause now and then, the forty at the start of the NFB grew to over seven hundred by the end of the war. In the first two weeks I made two lifelong friends — Beth Bertram and Norman McLaren.

Beth was a Toronto bluestocking, the kind of woman I first met in the second stream in my Central Tech art days. It was her straightforwardness and competence that made me enjoy her company, especially when my uneducated, Queen Street vulgarity made her laugh. What often made me laugh was her reaction every time we compared salary increases and she learned that mine was greater than hers. She had been a senior librarian in Toronto, and like the earnest Toronto WASP she was, she felt she could do more for the war effort than be a librarian and so came to Ottawa. Somehow Grierson found her and, you guessed it, hired her to become a librarian — to organize a film library. But not for long. She wanted a more active, hands-on, filmmaking job and so she was the first one whom Margaret Grierson taught to cut negative.

Beth cut the negative of the first film I made at the Board. I think it was her first too. It became a joke between us because we were editing a film to be shown in Quebec and I didn't know a word of French, which she did, and also because she had made a mistake in cutting the negative and a frame bar was seen when the test print was screened. Beth became head negative cutter and hired several women, training them to cut negative. With a cute snobbishness she made sure that most of these women had university degrees — Kay Simmonds, Daphne Lilly (who married Edgar Anstey), Marion Meadows and more, including Betty McRae who became my wife. Later, Beth went on to more and more senior jobs. After the war she went to the Public Service of Canada before another ex–Film Boarder, Pierre Juneau, brought her to the Canadian Radio and Television Commission as its chief of personnel.

What is there to say about Norman McLaren, the most famous of all Film Board employees, that isn't already known? The delightful "cartoons" drawn directly on clear film — *Hen Hop, Buy Victory Bonds* — or scratched on black leader to the music of the then-unknown Oscar Peterson; his pastel "paintings" to Quebec's *Chants Populaires* drawn and animated frame by frame directly under the camera; his 3D animated film for the Festival of Britain; innovative pixilation films of live action looking like animation, including *A Chairy Tale* and the Oscar-winning

Neighbours; dozens of delightful films illuminating music and arithmetic; his live-action, stroboscopic dancers in *Pas de Deux*.

He turned up, a fragile-looking, horn-rimmed young chap who spoke in a quiet and hesitating voice with a faint Scottish accent. The fact that I was an artist drew us immediately together. I remember once going to his room when he was living at the YMCA and he showed me many of his drawings and paintings, which filled me with awe, so beautiful were they. I remember too his speaking of a Canadian friend of his, Guy Glover, who was dear to him. With a barely perceptible catch in his throat, which I didn't understand until months later when Guy did join the Board, he told me that Grierson would not hire Glover because he disapproved of their relationship. It says a lot about Grierson that he was able to overcome his Scottish Puritanism in going along with McLaren's wishes. Glover not only paid his dues in full to the NFB by helping, indeed protecting McLaren, but also in dozens of ways by the films he made, promoted and inspired. He did everything with humour, and sometimes with cutting, wicked wit, right up to his retirement in 1978.

McLaren was the basis for the Film Board's animation department. Young artists began arriving — Jim MacKay, George Dunning (who made the Beatles' feature *Yellow Submarine*), Bob Verrall — all learning from McLaren how to put their skills as artists into drawings that moved. The place, being short of sophisticated equipment, became a source of inspiration for devising new ways of animating without expensive equipment and the hordes of cell animation, menial paint and trace artists of Disney and other cartoon shops. As their work was seen in cinemas and in the NFB's growing non-theatrical circuits, more artists came and the department grew. McLaren had no stomach for office work and so Guy Glover became its boss. For over forty years and under ten film commissioners — remarkable for a government to be so intelligent and liberal a patron — McLaren was allowed to go his own way, never told what to do, but steadily made one memorable film after another. So internationally known was he that when Prime Minister Indira Gandhi of India came to Canada she insisted upon a visit to the Film Board to meet Norman McLaren.

Sydney Newman in Ottawa to film
Prime Minister William Lyon Mackenzie King (behind him).

During my first weeks Norman helped me with a small amount of animation for some maps I had been asked to do for a film on the Great Lakes. I sandwiched it in between my splicing chores. But when I was immediately asked to do more maps, I went to McLean (Grierson being away as he so often was) and reminded him that I had come to the Board as a filmmaker and not an artist. No sweat! I was never again asked to do any artwork, despite the impression I received that Grierson had hired me for just that purpose. That was one of the intelligent things about the way the NFB was run in those days. Grierson and McLean's instinct was that better work would be gotten out of people if they were allowed to work in areas of their choice; that is, until it was seen that they couldn't hack it.

What audacity, desperation or downright foolishness it was when they assigned me to direct my first film. I'd barely been there two months and prominent in the film was to be the prime minister himself! The seven-minute film was to be of an event celebrating something called Consecration Day, held in front of the Parliament Buildings. The film would either make me or kill me.

The way I prepared, Cecil B. DeMille readying the shoot of *The Ten Commandments* was nothing by comparison. I deployed two 35mm cameras. One was to cover the sync-sound speech of the PM; Ernie Wilson was on it. He was an old duffer, often cantankerous but very reliable, who had been with the Bureau for donkey's years. I got a new kid on an Eyemo[27] camera to get colour, intercut shots of the crowds, bands and a fly-past of three Hurricanes — to be used to cover the times when Ernie had to reload his camera.

Ross had warned me that while the PM had great respect for the power of the camera, for the same reason and with justification, he hated it. No Roosevelt or Reagan was King! Before he made his speech I would respond to his fleeting, nervous smiles to me with a confident grin and thumbs-up sign — more to conceal my fright than to encourage him. Well, when William Lyon Mackenzie King got up to face that audience of five thousand and heard his own voice booming back to him, like the true politician he was, he forgot the camera and took off!

Even though the Eyemo shots were largely useless, the old duffer's were excellent. Three days later, with the help of Spottiswoode to get the shots to match the sync-sound, I was able to get the cutting copy to Beth Bertram, who cut the negative overnight and a day later the prints went off to the distributor. The film was certainly not art. It was clean, clear and square and I had not loused up the assignment. No one said that for the first effort it was remarkable. To Grierson and McLean the thought of anyone failing appeared to be inconceivable. Ho hum.

Before I could take a breath I was assigned to assist in the making of an army training film on how to clean, handle, load and fire a rifle. The director was also the writer and cameraman — there would only

---

27 The Eyemo was the camera of choice at the NFB (and by newsreel cameramen and documentary filmmakers). Made by Bell and Howell, it was rugged, durable and lightweight, which made it ideal because it could be used handheld, without a tripod. It would hold about 100 feet of film stock, which came out to about one minute's worth of film.

be the two of us on it. Wow, what a chance! I'm to be the assistant writer, the assistant cameraman and the assistant director. The director is a hotshot from New York, according to Grierson: Julian Roffman.[28] I hadn't heard of him. Hmn, according to *Grierson*. I wondered if it was the same kind of bullshit Grierson spieled to us then as he did the others before I came? Turns out, it was no bullshit!

Roffman was a likeable, totally bald, sallow-faced, short guy who had earlier left Montreal to become a filmmaker and now returned a wisecracking, brassy New Yorker. He left behind him a few distinguished documentary film credits to make his contribution to the war effort. He took his work very seriously, although you'd never know it once we'd left Camp Petawawa after the day's shoot.

Each day we would turn up at the camp at 8 a.m. after leaving our hotel at 7:30, and work until 6 p.m. or later (no union hours for us or the army!), and return to our hotel. I'd be dead beat in contrast to Roffman, a real pro. After a soak in a hot bath I'd go to his room to go over the plans for the next day. He didn't drink, Coca-Cola being his tipple, so I'd have to bring with me my tumbler of rotgut Canadian rye: Seagram's One Star, the cheapest.

I'd find him, virtually every evening, sprawled on his bed, having a great old long-distance schmooze with his wife in New York. As I thinned my rye with one of his Cokes I'd listen to him tell her about the great backlit shots he'd taken in deep-focus of the lined up gun sights (when I saw the developed film, it was no exaggeration — what Julian got out of a hundred-foot turret Eyemo camera was truly amazing); describe the pompous, finicky, liaison officer assigned to us as Himmler in disguise; grin at me as he parodied my smoking with a rolled-up bit of cardboard; complain about his being saddled with an assistant from Toronto who didn't know his ass from a sprocket hole. You just couldn't take offence. He was a cute bugger and good. I'd leave, go back to my room for more rye and when I returned, he was still at it.

---

28   Today, Roffman is best known as the director of the 1961 produced-in-Canada horror film *The Mask*.

When we (he) finished the film, seeing it, a recruit would have been a moron if he couldn't clean, handle, load and fire a rifle. It was as good an instruction film as I have ever seen.

Roffman's second film was also for the army. With Norway now being occupied by the Germans, it was necessary for us and the Allied armies to know how to fight in the snow. Who better to make a film to be called *Winter Warfare* than we Canadians? Roffman's script, with a tiny assist from me, was simple: we'd follow a patrol on skis in training for twenty-four hours. I still feel the cold in my bones and am amused to recall the non-drinking Roffman's sallow face with his cold nose as red as an old boozer's. On some days it was so cold, −20 degrees, that the film would become brittle and break in the camera. Often, the camera itself would freeze and either not run up to speed or not run at all. The adverse shooting conditions were far beyond Roffman's experience.

We had to go back to Ottawa to get advice from J.D. Davidson for a solution. He said it was the grease in the camera that became stiff as gum. He opened the camera and poured carbon tetrachloride into it and flushed out all the oil and grease. He then advised that we put a Coleman, kerosene-burning, cooking heater under the camera, and over the camera place a tent-like shroud with two slits in it for the cameraman's hands, with a hold for the viewfinder and for the lens outside the tent — to avoid condensation inside it. Believe it or not but this Rube Goldberg–Emett contraption worked — most of the time. Trouble was, there being only two of us and me being the assistant, I was the one who would operate the explosive thing and get it ready before Roffman put his hands into its warm interior.

The first freezing day we used the heated tent started well. It was windy, helping to delineate the shapes of the blindingly white mounds and hills of snow lit by a brilliant sun. The sky was an intense blue and cloudless.

The snow was so dry it squeaked when you walked on it. Except for the cold, it was perfect for our film. The action for the camera was to see a patrol on skis appear over the brow of a hill and swiftly slalom down it toward and then past us. After Roffman found the right, snow-covered hill, he wanted his camera placed halfway up it. We had to carry our gear from our station wagon about 400 yards up the hill. As the assistant, I was loaded with the camera; the cumbersome, heavy tripod; cases of film and camera batteries — only about a hundred pounds, if not more! Our Himmler liaison officer carried about fifteen pounds on top of his round self: a walkie-talkie set, field glasses and a clipboard. Roffman carried the can of kerosene, the heater and tent — a light load — to which, I, as the assistant director-cameraman, did not object.

While the hill looked smooth enough, it had been ploughed so that one step would be up into eighteen inches of snow and the next down to two feet of snow at the bottom of the furrow. Being overdressed to beat the weather and no Atlas, clouds of steam panted out of my mouth like a 6400 CNR train engine climbing the Rockies; carrying my load up that serrated hill just about killed me.

While I was setting up the gear, our liaison chappie and Roffman established contact by walkie-talkie with the patrol who by now was waiting out of sight below the far side of the crest of the hill waiting for the Go! command. Finally, I got the tripod levelled on the far-from-level hill, the camera on it under its shroud with the heater going full blast. Roffman took his reading of the light, corrected the aperture of his lens, put his hands inside the tent and peering to the viewfinder, started the camera rolling and said, "Go!" Our lighting operator shouted into his walkie-talkie, "GO." We waited. Again the L.O.: "GO! Come on patrol; go!" And suddenly, sweeping over the crest of the hill they came, their backpacks and rifles and snow goggles gleaming. The long blue, undulating shadows they cast were breathtaking. Halfway through the shot, the camera began to go slower and slower and then stopped. The L.O. said, "What happened?" Roffman stood up, his nose even redder against his white face, and looked at me. "I guess I shoulda' waited longer for the camera to warm up." And taking a deep breath he said, "This one's no good now. C'mon, let's go find another hill."

Two tries later we finally got the shot. It was a good one too because it was late in the day and the sky was filled with fast-moving clouds, the shadows rolling over the snow-covered hills with the sun backlighting the kicked-up powdery snow of the army skiers.

Later, going back to our hotel, the sweat having dried inside my clothes, I was shuddering with cold, which I didn't stop doing until I had lain in my hot tub for forty-five minutes sipping rum. When I went to Roffman's room to get a Coke for my rum, he was on the phone telling his wife that he was going to be useless to her from now on. "My thing got frozen and broke off." He waved his rolled cardboard cigarette in the air and in sudden inspiration, "Hey, baby. How about knitting me a woollen jockstrap? Double that order. Newman could use one. In angora!"

Roffman did so well on these army training films he was put onto more complex films. I remained in the armed forces training films unit and this time was assigned to Don Fraser on army messing. My father as a shoemaker believed that an army marches on its boots, but now I was to learn that it doesn't; it marches on its stomach. Don wasn't as much fun to work for as Julian but I learned a lot from him. Because I now knew more, and the kind of good guy he was, he gave me a lot more leeway so that I did some direction and editing.

Suddenly, after being in the NFB for ten months, I was promoted to what was at first a frighteningly challenging job. I was made responsible for producing a three-minute film each week and with no one to assist me!

Grierson, in his most persuasive manner, had gotten an agreement from the five American newsreels to include a direct propaganda message film in each of their weekly Canadian editions. They were not strictly news but had to be timely. In effect they were government-sponsored commercials. As it turned out, I truly grew up as a filmmaker while making them, even though it was an eighteen-hours-a-day, seven-day job. Even today I can't figure out how I was able to succeed. Not only did I have to write them, but also direct them or find the appropriate stock-shots, edit, record and deliver the negatives to the two top laboratories, one each in Toronto and Montreal. I rarely missed a deadline. The subjects of the filmlets dealt with everything from how to make margarine look like butter to convincing people to buy war bonds.

Most educative was my having to deal with the newsreel people who demanded that my stuff not bore the audiences — and so I got my first whiff of what it was like trying to grab audiences. What a thrill it was to go to any cinema in Canada and see my work up there on the big screen. It's pretty humble making, however, when your stuff comes up and the audience response is to get up and go home! I learned to say a lot in a short time and grab them fast. As an audience member, when I'd have to get up to let someone wiggle past me to take a seat just when my clip appeared, by the time I had risen to allow them to pass me and about to sit down again, my clip had finished! It's extraordinary how much one can pack into a few seconds of screen time: the power of the image and sound.

Frightening at first was my having to deal directly with the brass of the armed forces, government departments and often their cabinet ministers. About the latter, Grierson very carefully warned me against allowing a cabinet minister to make a direct speech to the screen. He said it was boring and no doubt the opposition parties in the House would accuse the government of using the NFB for party political purposes and not the war effort. Should I be unable to prevent it, before agreeing, I was to let him or McLean know so that they could intercede. As I got to know him better, it was clear that he wanted the NFB to live long after the war — if it ever became a political football, Parliament would kill it.

Three men I dealt with during this period I will never forget. George Davidson, when I first met him, was deputy minister of welfare in Paul Martin's department of health and welfare. Because I did many news clips for his department, I got to rather like the way he showed his trust in my judgement. I felt he envied my work because it was creative and his was administration.

One day he asked me if I would introduce him to Mr. Grierson. I set this up and after the introduction I didn't leave Grierson's office right away. Grierson had his feet on his desk listening as George expressed his interest in creative work; that he wasn't giving society his best — "I guess I'm stuck in my small admin corner." Grierson never liked any form of self-abnegation, and, as was his wont, immediately acted to bolster George's will. He rapped out, "What'd y'do before becoming deputy minister?" George: "I was general secretary of the Community Chest of Canada." Grierson: "And before that?" George: "I was professor of history. Classics mostly." Grierson swung his feet off the desk and leaned forward and snapped out, "D'you remember the motto of ancient Athens?" and before poor George could answer, Grierson cited it in Greek, which I gathered meant something like, "We are tiny but the world is ours!" I felt it was time to leave. And did. [29]

Tiny in stature, Grierson could change the world to believe that film was more than escapist fare but clearly he couldn't change George. Later George became secretary of Canada's Treasury Board, then president when I sat on the Board of the Canadian Broadcasting Corporation. He left it to become Deputy Director-General of Administration of the United Nations under Kurt Waldheim. George, no doubt, felt his life a waste.

I liked Paul Martin, who always came down to the Board to see the news clips I made for his department. When he spoke to me he'd look at me through his thick glasses to really see me, and he never forgot my name. Maybe it was only because he was the politician par excellence. They tell the story that before visiting his farm constituents it was the job of his political aid to get a pail of cow shit and paint Martin's pant legs with it so that he'd look *jes' like plain farm folk.*

Now Herb Richardson was totally different — he was not really in public service, nor was he a politician. He and his wife became personal friends of my wife and me. He was a hi-fi nut and had installed in the living room of his house one wall of lead in which was embedded no fewer than thirty speakers, ranging in size from one-inch tweeters to fifteen-inch giants. He required special pillars in his cellar just to support it. I never thought to ask him what his neighbours thought when the speakers were all going full blast, belting out "Ride

---

29 Davidson would have revenge, of a sort. More than two decades later Newman was passed over as President of the Canadian Broadcasting Corporation in favour of Davidson.

of the Valkyries." What drew us together was that before becoming Secretary of the Bank of Canada, in charge of promoting each year's Canada Savings Bond war loan campaigns, he had been art director of Canada's largest graphic art studio: Rapid, Grip and Batten. He inspired me to produce some nifty clips selling war bonds. I did a set of three for him, each one powerfully ending with a commando dagger piercing a war bond, striking Berlin in the centre of a military map.

During this period, Grierson taught me something I can never forget. I had made a clip to encourage women to take jobs in industry. Before the final re-recording I was lucky to get him, usually away on a trip, to come and see it in the screening room.

To my horror, within ten seconds of it starting and hearing the commentary, Grierson leaped to his feet shouting at me, "How dare you? What are you, a fascist? Only fascists tell people what to do!" By now he was in front of the screen, the projector images flickering on his face, his arms punctuating each word all exaggerated by his black shadow behind him. He bawled the hell out of me. "What you say is the people, with their own will — that women, knowing that their husbands, their loved ones, are fighting overseas risking their lives for their loved ones — that Canadian women know their duty, and are doing their bit by the thousands by going to work, by working in factories." He was beside himself and even continued after the lights came on. I felt so ashamed. If there had been anywhere to hide in that screening room, I would have done so. He ended with, "You must give people reasons for an action and they will likely do the right thing. Don't ever use the 'you' in your commentary. No finger pointing. Say, intelligent Canadians are doing . . ."

Absolutely chastened, when we were going up the stairs, Grierson, seeing my crushed state, put his arm on my shoulder and said, "I wouldn't talk" — talk! — "to you the way I did if I thought you weren't worth it." And then he sped away from me toward his office.

That incident summed up for me Grierson at his very best, which took me many years to fully appreciate. His cleverness at understanding what motivates people was combined with a profound compassion. I thank God that his morality was on the side of the angels. His words to me were basically that I should be telling people, flatteringly, what action to take, while making them believe that it was their own idea. And who could not love the man, the way he handled me?

About halfway through this nine-month period, since I seemed to be getting along well with the newsreel people, I was given the additional responsibility of assigning crews to cover news events. So, in a sense, I became an embryonic newsman, but thank heaven they finally got a top pro, Robinson (Bob) McLean to take it over. But, before that happened, I was able to convince Ross McLean that I needed an assistant. He even allowed me to find my own man from outside the Film Board. It was Nick Balla.

I found Nicholas Balla on the recommendation of my old Central Tech friend, Laurence Hyde, who was now at the Board working as a graphic artist. It was the first time in my life that I was to interview people who wanted a job; not surprisingly, I felt important doing so. Holed up in the Royal York Hotel, I interviewed the candidates, who turned up at half-hourly intervals. I certainly asked some stupid questions but generally looked for someone who had a background in the visual arts. One of the problems was that the person selected would have to move to Ottawa at his own expense. None really suited the job, but Nick Balla, who was at the time the photo editor of the *Toronto Daily Star*, seemed okay. Moving away from Toronto was ideal for him because he had just gotten married. Ross McLean accepted Nick. He and his wife, Lillian, who, in contrast to Nick's somewhat introverted nature, turned out to be a delightfully exuberant dame, turned up in Ottawa. It was lucky! It was one of the best appointments I ever recommended, because Nick Balla became the finest film editor and film finisher I've ever worked with, and later followed me in my job when I left the NFB. He and his wife became lifelong friends of my wife and me.

CHAPTER ELEVEN

LOVE + ART = NFB

The hard daily grind of work and its stimulating nature made it inevitable that release be found in get-togethers — bottle parties, gab sessions in pubs and dinner parties. We talked, argued, made sexual passes (sometimes successfully), skied and swam in the Gatineau Hills, played as hard as we worked. If we hadn't, I'm sure we would have gone bonkers. Besides, most of us were single and in our twenties — the bohemians, which was the word of the day that described us orchids in Ottawa's sea of dandelions. Much of our goings-on shocked the staid and earnest civil (often called servile) servants of the Capital, the politicians, armed forces types and diplomatic corps. Of these, some would find their way to us looking to break their own routine grind of war work. It's amusing to recall that later, in the 1950s, when there was talk of moving the NFB to Montreal, the honest burghers of Ottawa fought the move, fearing the loss to the city of such colourful(!) types.

For reasons I don't understand, I never feel quite happy at parties — don't now and didn't then. In somebody's apartment there'd be dancing in one room, attempted seduction in the bathroom or on a heap of coats in the bedroom, and in the study someone listening to Burl Ives, John Jacob Niles or Fats Waller records. I would be casing the joint, wondering who I would accompany home and whether there'd be a chance of nookie (a splendid word little heard today). I'd wander into the kitchen, where the inevitable crowd would be jamming the booze counter while, sitting on the floor, Grierson would be ringed by a few others having a violent argument, agreeing or disagreeing about citizen participation, participatory citizenship, Churchill handling Stalin (whom he'd recently called a guttersnipe), conscription in Quebec, the People's War, art, no time during war for self-expression. I rarely participated in these but was very much all ears. My God, were my colleagues articulate!

One party in the depths of winter nearly ended in tragedy. One of our younger production assistants had too much to drink, went outside to get some air — or be sick — and was found hours later covered by a thin layer of snow lying in a snowbank. He was fast asleep. Somewhat sheepishly he turned up at work the next day.

Another party became a nightmare. It was decided that a *Canada Carries On* edition celebrate the first Canadian-built Lancaster bomber. Brought back to Canada, much publicized, was an RCAF air crew who had flown two tours over Germany, and who would be flying our Lancaster to England. The crew, a typical bunch of young Canadians, home after three years away, understandably exploited their freedom to the hilt. They voraciously set out to consume what they had been deprived of for so long: food, booze and Canadian girls. Grant McLean, the director of the film, thought a party for them was obligatory. A great idea!

At the party, mayhem suddenly broke out. One of the crew members, pissed to the hilt, ranted that he and his mates were fighting the war to save the Jews. A non-Jewish Film Boarder tried to set the record straight and a moment later fists were flying, the enraged crew member going berserk and hitting out right and left. It was Eugene "Jack" Kash of our music department who got a stranglehold on the wild crewman and hissed, "You shut up! Quiet down or I'll break your goddamned neck!"

Jack was so enraged that I believe he would have. Among other things I learned at that party was that violinists weren't weaklings.

Jack Kash had come to the Film Board after being first violin with the Toronto Symphony Orchestra under Sir Ernest MacMillan. Square-built, he was as strong as the proverbial ox. He also changed my ideas about the fiddle, which I had always thought a somewhat namby-pamby instrument.

One Boxing Day, Norman McLaren and Guy Glover, both spectacular cooks, gave a dinner. Jack and Nina Finn, Jack's intimate friend, were there. After dinner, we were so satiated by the scrumptious food and wine that we were exhausted — to the point where to even utter a monosyllable was too much. Guests were sprawled on the sofa, reclining in deep chairs or lying on the floor as I was. Guy, hoping to liven us up, made a catty crack about an MP who had attacked one of our films in the House of Commons. We couldn't bring ourselves to rise to it. Dead silence.

At some point Jack Kash quietly left the living room, went to his flat, which was next door, and in the silence we could hear him tune his fiddle and begin playing it. He returned, and while continuing playing, didn't stop walking until he stood right over me. I don't know what the music was, but looking up at him — seeing his square fingers moving on the strings, the strained muscles in his neck and face — the music he produced on that fragile violin blew me away. The intense, penetrating sounds, sometimes delicate as a whisper and sometimes loud, with the authority of a thirty-two-foot diapason, woke us up. No matter how I express it, it was one of the great musical discoveries of my life. The fiddle and its master would never again be namby-pamby for niminy-piminies.

My first Film Board party was on New Year's Eve in 1941, and my going to it was quite accidental. I had met a rather nice girl, and she agreed to spend the evening with me. The plan was that we would drop in on the Griersons at 30 Cooper Street, bid them a happy new year and then have dinner. When I picked her up, to my horror she was dressed looking like Tenniel's Alice come to life — lacy frills on all hems, white stockings (white stockings!) and black pumps — and spoke a kind of baby talk. No matter; she rarely spoke. At Grierson's it was suggested that we join them at Jane Marsh's — Margaret Grierson was sure that we would be welcome. We didn't go by taxi. That night, on New Year's Eve, Grierson wanted to travel with the hoi polloi on a public conveyance, so we hopped on a Sussex streetcar.

At the party were John and Margaret Grierson's closest Film Board friends and others strange to me. Jane Marsh, who later married Jim Beveridge, was a staff writer and director. She was from one of Ottawa's old established families and lived in a duplex apartment above Hazen Sise, an architect, whose father it was said, was a major stockholder of Northern Electric. He was new, and what his job was I didn't know. Don Fraser and Jim Beveridge were present. The atmosphere was pleasant — a sense of Film Board family, people at ease with one another. I thought Jane Marsh most attractive, but her sardonic smile, her way of looking at me, made me feel somewhat uncomfortable. And then, there was my Alice clone.

There was another girl present whom I thought so beautiful she took my breath away. I say girl because she looked seventeen, with flowing blonde hair and a long, diaphanous white dress that delineated her fairy-tale slender body. Gosh, she was fantastic. Who was she? Just when I was about to ask Beveridge, there was a great hullabaloo on the arrival of a couple being greeted with hugs, kisses and congratulations as they shed their overcoats and galoshes. They were Alan Adamson and "Baby" Bjornson, who had just returned that day from Winnipeg after being married. Alan was new to the group, but Margaret Ann, whom most called Baby, was already on the staff as Stuart Legg's main researcher. Years later, she and Alan divorced, and more years later she married Sir Arthur Elton. Both were to become good friends, and would remain such after we were working colleagues.

Just when I was again about to ask Beveridge about the blonde, my sweet Alice clone told me that she had to be home by midnight. Damn! I was goin' to miss ringing in the new year and a chance to kiss that girl. I decided to take her home and then come right back to the party. It was snowing and streetcars were few and far between, so we didn't reach her house until 12:30. Believe it or not, her father, a distinguished journalist, opened the front door wearing only his long johns and bawled the hell out of me for bringing his daughter home so late. Luckily, I was able to find an empty cab, and returned to the party that by now was slowing down. Luckily, the beautiful woman was still there.

I sidled up to Beveridge and asked, "Who is that gorgeous girl?" "Oh," he replied, "she's Elizabeth Smart, Jane's sister. The one who wrote *By Grand Central Station I Sat Down and Wept.*" Seeing the look of sex on my face, he said, with that cheerful chipmunk-like smile of his, "Forget it. She's the mother of endless kids. The father is the English poet George Barker." Then, mischievously, he added, "They're not married. She's only here because of the bombings in England. C'mon, I'll introduce you." I was shocked. To speak so blithely about having illegitimate children! I gulped and thanked Jim, "Thanks. Not now. Must get a drink."

There was a sad undercurrent in the party. I noticed that Don Fraser, not the most cheerfully extroverted of guys at best, seemed especially quiet. Jim told me later that the party put an end to Don's love affair with Margaret Ann. For me though, with or without my sweet Alice clone, it was a great start to 1942 (though a black year for Canada — the Dieppe raid fiasco!), and a warm introduction to the centre of the Film Board's social life. 1942 was also the year when two atoms collided to produce a flash that lasted forty years and is still dimly visible today. More prosaically, I met the woman I married.

A few of us were lolling about, sitting on or around the sand box outside the main door of our ex-sawmill building having a smoke. 'Twas a fine sunny May day when a smart coupé pulled up on the French Embassy side of John Street. A young woman emerged wearing a white blouse and a navy blue skirt and began walking toward our front door. She wore one of those tiny Empress Eugenie hats and carried a navy blue bag, the hat signifying that she was applying for a job. As she passed us to enter, she appeared to take no notice of us whatsoever. Mmn, what a womanly body. That erect yet graceful walk, those understated swaying hips. A classy lady with a classy chassis. "Very nice," said Stan Jackson (ex-school teacher from Winnipeg) as he fumbled inside his jacket searching for a Life Saver.

Gordon Weisenborn, the kid from Chicago, wisecracked, "I bet she's another one of Beth Bertram's debutramps from Toronto."

Weisenborn was only half right. When Betty (Margaret Elizabeth) McRae turned up a few weeks later, it was as a trainee negative-cutter under Beth Bertram. But no debutante, she. Betty was typical of most clergyman's daughters: financially poor, yet raised and educated as of the very rich — the money provided by her father's church. Dr. Duncan McRae was born in Glengarry County, Ontario, and met and married Susan Rodgers while he was at the University of Manitoba. In 1914, after his ordination as a Presbyterian minister (later becoming a part of the United Church of Canada), he, his young wife and three-month-old son went as missionaries to carry the faith to Buddhist China.

Many years later, I said to him, "You know, Duncan, you're the only true Christian I've ever met." The dear man, embarrassed, said, "Oh? Uh, why do you say that?" I replied, "It's because you spent most of your life among heathens and not contaminated by other Christians in the West." He lifted his head and laughed so hard I thought his false teeth would pop out. He was a good man in the best sense of the word. He respected the Buddhists and people of other faiths. While he didn't smoke or drink, he was never censorious about people who did. Betty was born in a Hong Kong hospital where wives of missionaries went to have their babies. Because they all had their primary education at an English boarding school for the children of Westerners, Betty's origins confused people — her English a's came out as *cahn't* instead of *can't*.

Betty and her family crossed

Betty McRae as a teenager.

the Pacific Ocean many times for Duncan's furlough. When each child reached the age of twelve, they were shipped back to Canada for further education. Robert became a Ph.D. Professor of Philosophy and an authority on Leibnitz; Mary, an interior designer; Jeanne a nurse; and the woman I married, an M.A. in philosophy and English, who became a negative cutter. It was as a negative cutter that I got to know her — but not in the biblical sense. That came later.

Later, indeed. When I first saw Betty, I was in the middle of a reasonably torrid affair with a gentle and lovely girl who was a fine film director. When Betty began cutting the negative of my films, the stirrings of something deeper than an affair began over a hot-splicer. She really was special. Before I knew anything much about her background, I took her to the Canton Inn for dinner. When the chopsticks were placed on the table, she asked the waiter for a fork. "Nonsense," I said, "we will use chopsticks, and I will teach you how." I did, and fool me! I did not twig at the speed of her adeptness. Being in China all those years, chopsticks had probably touched her lips long before a spoon ever did. Months later when our relationship was becoming more than casual, I asked her, "At the Chinese restaurant, why did you ask for a fork?" She replied, "Well, I didn't know whether you knew how to use them and so I . . ." I knew right there and then that this was one extraordinary lady.

It was a rough time — the three-month affair was being superseded by my growing love for Betty. I don't suppose anyone is an expert at knowing how to drop someone whom you have genuinely liked. But no one could have been more stupid than I was — once I inadvertently invited each of them to have lunch with me at the same restaurant, one hour apart. Luck was on my side, though. Girl #1 had to leave early and dashed off. As I was paying the bill at the counter near the door, Girl #2 entered and apologized for being late. What is she talking about? Oh . . . my god. What a dope I was! The penny dropping, I pretended to be at the cash counter buying cigarettes. On my second lunch, Girl #2 wondered if I was well because I didn't seem to have my usual hearty appetite. It became apparent to all that our affair was over when I rented a small apartment on the top floor of a house that was directly over the room Betty shared with her older sister Mary.

Among her many virtues, Betty had a mind like a whip (most gently applied), was a superb map-reader (for the many trips we took) and a near-professional seamstress (making her own clothes and shirts for me). She also had an undemanding love and tolerance of me (constantly shown or implied) and was well-versed in the art of cooking. Living in the same house, and in line with the times, the proprieties were observed and we gave many a fine dinner party prepared in my primitive kitchen after being refurbished and exploited by McRae. (During this time, as a fellow worker, she was McRae.)

Betty McRae in a news article, c.1950.

One evening we had invited a new Film Boarder, who had become my boss, and his wife for dinner. He was an ex-journalist, part of Grierson's wave of hiring newspapermen who were unlike "you creative laddies who lack the sense of today." Also present was a very young production assistant who worked in my unit. (The same kid who was found half-frozen in the snowbank.) He was an artist and sculptor, gentle but gay, which made our new boss feel uncertain. Our young assistant had just discovered James Joyce and, after coffee, couldn't resist singing Joyce's praises. I had not read *Ulysses* and was interested. But not Boss: "Crap! Literature? That's disgusting, perverted filth!" he passionately vomited, totally destroying the kid.

While I was mewling a defence of the rights of a creative person blah, blah, blah, I failed to distract Boss away from the kid who, as a junior employee, wouldn't dare defend himself, even if he had the words to do so. McRae had been in the kitchen, clearing up, and, hearing the raised voices, came back to join us. "More coffee, anyone?" Most ladylike, she quietly entered the fray by citing the legal clearing of *Lady Chatterley's Lover* and *Well of Loneliness*, and even threw in Galileo as a case and related these to Joyce. Boss, of course, agreed that history was right, but still! Best of all, McRae gently set it up so that Boss confessed that he had not read *Ulysses*. McRae opined that he might read the book and "no doubt enjoy it." I learned later that she hadn't read it either.

After that evening, and after word got around about what happened, Boss did not remain boss for much longer. Not over me, anyway. If nothing else, the Film Board was intolerant of illiberal people. Betty? Well, that was Betty!

During this period Betty had become head of the negative cutting room and one of her new charges was a young, attractive girl from Montreal — an aspiring writer, Mavis Gallant. I can't recall the exact circumstances, but late one evening after work, walking by my house as I accompanied her home, Mavis offered to fry up some eggs. Great idea! We quietly went up the stairs, past the room Betty shared with her sister, to get to my flat. A good fryer, Mavis was, and she left. The next day, rumours flew that I had made a pass at her. I hadn't so much as thought of touching her. That bum, Mavis. Anything for a laugh!

It's astonishing to recall the number and kinds of people at the Board and what became of them. Mavis, of course, is the elegant prose writer; Norman McLaren, Louis Applebaum, Eugene Kash, Morris Blackburn, Eldon Rathburne, Bob Fleming, Jean Palardy, Jack Olsen, Gudrun Parker, the Jacques brothers, Ken Johnstone, Ralph Foster, Daphne Anstey, Lady Elton, Marion Leigh, Stuart Legg, Red (Goldie) Burns, Nick Balla, Jim MacKay, George Dunning, Ernst Bornemann, Grant McLean, George Brandt, Jim Beveridge and Jane Marsh, Raymond Spottiswoode, Hazen Sise, Beth Bertram, Marjorie MacKay, Dan Wallace, Colin Low and others I've already mentioned. What a wonderful mix of brains and talent. Ironic that it was an alien ideology — fascism — that allowed John Grierson to bring them together. And lucky me, I was there.

Grierson's hiring policy was mercurial to say the least, and he did hire some dogs, but generally, he was right. Above all, he looked for people who seemed to be sincere in their regard for society, possessed a proven (or at least showed promise of) required skill and lastly, held a reverence for the arts. It took Grierson only about six months after the first wave of hiring to realize that we weren't entirely up to the standard the Film Board required. He hired us because we were artists, writers, etc. — creative types, closest to his heart. But it became evident to him that our films would be effective only if they had a strong sense of immediacy, of what was happening *now*! Immediately, there was a large influx of hard-core newshounds he wooed from Canada's top newspapers.

From the States there arrived brash newsreel men like Hamilton Wright, known for news stories such as the one in which he sent his veteran cameraman, Joe Gibson, up in a plane to photograph a girl bathing in a tub suspended from a balloon, flying over the Florida Everglades. We'd mutter, "That's hardcore actuality? That's immediacy?" But nonetheless, Grierson harnessed them to the war effort and we learned from them. Hamilton was not satisfied with showcasing Canada's breadbasket for Allied armies merely by showing one harvester doing its stuff. He'd marshal ten of them to simultaneously bring in the wheat to prove that Canada was no slouch when it came to feeding the free world.

Grierson, after a while, became dissatisfied. "Artists? Journalists? The lovely bums have no sense of tomorrow. We've got to know where we are going!" So the next wave of hiring came from the universities and jerks like me began to rub shoulders with philosophy buffs, economists and such. We, of the first wave, knew and never complained that the journalists were paid twice our salary. I didn't feel hard done by when the intellectual group earned even more, because without ever asking for a raise, somehow Grierson gave me one every six months.

One summer Sunday afternoon, I was in my cutting room editing a film. The building was deafeningly silent. I was whistling and peering into my Movieola when I heard my door open and, "Newman, whustle 'n 'yurr stomach!" It was Grierson. And with a twinkle in his eye he said, "As a heathen, I guess the Lord'll forgive you for wurrking on the Sabbath." Grierson had originally studied to become a Minister of the Kirk and so I figured that whistling on Sunday, at least in Scotland, was not allowed. He's reputed to have once said that the pulpit did not give him a big enough audience.

"What film are you working on?" he asked. I ran a bit of the film for him.

I had just gotten a new and handsome raise and so thanked him for it, ending with, "And I suppose that'll be the last raise I shall get." He looked up at me with his huge eyes and asked, "Why'd you say that?" I answered, "Well, with all these Ph.D.'s that have come on staff, I'll never be able to match them."

"Newman," he replied with that sneering smile of his, "you're a jerk!" (He pronounced it *jairrk*.) "With what you've got, you'll be able to buy a man with a Ph.D., anytime." He went on to say that he thought me the Harry Watt (who later directed *The Overlanders*) of Canada. Who couldn't love such a man?

Somehow, Grierson had the notion that I was a whiz with the girls. Where he got that idea from, I don't know, although at the Board I was often referred to as Jo-Jo, the bouncing boy. At one point when Betty and I weren't exactly seeing things eye-to-eye and I needed someone to take to a party, I invited a waitress I knew. She was a smasher, known then as "a dish." She had the body of a young Lana Turner. At the party, when she and I were dancing, Grierson cut in, saying, "May we trip the light fantastic?" Trip the light fantastic, indeed! It was poor Grierson's notion of the with-it language of the day! Anyway, he thought I showed good judgement in women. He thought greatly of my affair girl, whom he personally hired, and he instantly took to Betty who, as a McRae, he claimed must be a cousin, or at least a second cousin of his. (It might be noted that Betty's grandfather was brought to Canada as a child around 1815.)

In my own mind, I became a filmmaker with a *Canada Carries On* documentary called *Trans-Canada Express*.

In the film vaults were about 40,000 feet on Canada's railways. Apparently, several years back, Stan Hawes, with Don Fraser on camera, had set out to make the definitive film on what Canadians regard as the main symbol of the making of Canada — the linking of the Atlantic to the Pacific by steel rails in 1888. In the middle of getting some spectacular footage, they had to break off shooting. Many had been assigned to make a film out of the footage and had failed. I was assigned to take a crack at it, but in partnership with Bob Anderson, who was new to the Board.

Bob had been a top announcer with the CBC in Winnipeg. He was almost too handsome and always spoke with a mellifluous voice, as if his index finger was eternally pressed behind one ear to confirm it to himself. We screened the previous attempts, and he agreed with me that we should strike a brand new print of the original uncut material — the existing outs and trims being in an unholy mess. We talked of various ways of putting the material together, and I went to work on the Movieola. We disagreed at one point, and I amiably put forward my reasons why I was doing whatever it was, which I have since cheerfully forgotten. What I have not cheerfully forgotten, however, was his ordering me to obey him. Ordering! No one orders me to do anything. Besides, we were in this together, or so I believed.

"Bob," suppressing my outrage as I went on, "no one orders anyone here. I am the editor because I know how to edit. You haven't learned yet. We are equal partners."

"Sorry, chum," he said, "I'm the producer of the film. We are not partners. You are only the editor." Well, bugger that. I charged out of the cutting room and saw Ross McLean. Anderson was called and McLean confirmed my understanding. Anderson took the news calmly and a few weeks later found ways to leave the "partnership." It is impossible for me to forget the hurt I felt then. I can take orders, but rarely, and then only from someone I truly respect. Over the years we got along, but only just. Later, Bob went on and cut a reputable swath in the field of mental health films. And later still, he was the main planner of how Parliament was to be daily telecast.

I went back to the problem of the film with relish. Some of the shots were breathtakingly beautiful — long trains like toys dwarfed by the Rocky Mountains as they sped alongside roaring rivers, belching steam that climbed the mountain slopes; trains speeding across the horizon of the flattest, richest wheat fields in the vast prairies; trains winding along the north shore of Lake Superior; freight cars being loaded and unloaded as trains entered and left cities; marshalling yards shown in such detail the shots would make a do-it-yourself film. Most lovingly covered were the washing and oiling of the CNR's proudest engine, the 6400, by little men as it sat on its turntable, gently puffing, waiting to do its day's work.

What was missing were close-ups of driving wheels, ramming pistons, block signals clicking in place, lights flicking from green to red (danger!) and, missing most of all, people! Not merely shots of the engine driver or the crew sitting up in the caboose, but the passengers and people awaiting them. One of the world's finest documentaries ever made on the railways was *Night Mail*. Grierson himself was its producer, and he and Stuart Legg had read its T.S. Eliot commentary to the music of Benjamin Britten. While I never for a moment dreamed of making a film as good as that, I knew that comparisons were inevitable.[30] I had to do my damnedest!

I scoured the library for weeks looking for any shots that had anything to do with railways — especially ones that related to the war. The material I found was robbed from newsreels and feature films, including a train crashing over a broken bridge (from a Hitchcock feature) and — to humanize the railways — a chunk of film from Buster Keaton's railway comedy *The General*. I couldn't find any close-ups of driving wheels and so I shamelessly stole two shots from Grierson's own *Night Mail*. (The fact that the wheels were totally different from those on a North American train troubled me slightly.

---

30 Newman offers a pastiche of *Night Mail* by using its technique of having voiceover speak in the same rhythm as the train.

What Grierson would think of this, I was prepared to worry about later.) The most idiotic material I found was a crowd of people going by train to see the Dionne Quintuplets.

With this mountain of accumulated film added to the 40,000 feet of Hawes-Fraser material, I devised a script. Simply, the film was about a train carrying some domestic goods, but emphasized the journey of military tanks and soldiers speeding from Vancouver to Halifax Harbour to meet the deadline of a waiting Atlantic convoy of ships sailing to England. To break up the headlong journey across the continent I intercut several sequences: Canada's rail history using animation-stand shooting of the famous still pictures of the driving of the last spike; washing and oiling the snorting 6400 engine; the Buster Keaton and Hitchcock clips; Canadian soldiers having a sing-song on an English train (from an English war film). And just to be certain I had conveyed our human need for the railroads, I threw in a Dionne Quintuplets sequence.

On the final twenty-minute film, I used only about eight minutes of the original material, leaving unused about 39,000 feet. I shot or had shot only about two minutes of original material, including one quick shot of Betty asking when a shipment by rail was leaving[31] and a glorious end-sequence shot by old Joe Gibson, showing the train victoriously belching white steam and black smoke as it raced into the sparkling, snowy Halifax Harbour with the ships of Bedford Basin in the background.

I broke tradition in the use of the narrator. Interspersed with the normally used, marvellous dramatic reading of Lorne Greene, I used an actor who, with a gruff, old-timer, working-class voice, read the parts of the narration about the history of the railways and the "care and feeding" of the trains. If *Night Mail* had T.S. Eliot, I had Guy Glover, who, as well as tidying up my narration, wrote for me some doggerel verse à la Robert W. Service, read by the old-timer:

---

31 Betty appears at one minute, forty-two seconds into the film where she says, "Hey Joe! The boss says ship those thirty armour caps right away! Not tonight!"

We'll get it to yah somehow
Sir John A. Macdonald said
'Twas 1880
No railroad yet
to British Columbia led.

He also wrote a group chant read to the rhythm of a specially composed music score: Day. Night. Cloud. Sun. Railways. Job. Never. Done.

Lou Applebaum wrote and conducted a fine score of warm and dramatic go-go-go railway music to equal Honegger, and the picture was adjudged a winner. I had at last come into my own as a filmmaker. If I were to see it today, though, I'd probably die of shame!

Come 1944, my brother Wilfred and his regiment were fighting their way up Italy. D-Day had come and our beach was more than secure. Stuart Legg, who had relinquished any direct influence of the *Canada Carries On* series, was concentrating entirely on *World in Action*, which was now suffering from fewer cinema bookings, just like *CCO*. Fewer, not because of the quality of the films in both series, but mainly, I believed, because film industry people are fearful of the government at the best of times. Victory now seemed certain, and so more and more cinemas were refusing to screen them. In the States, our films were foreign. In Canada, it was American film interests that owned or controlled most cinemas and film distributors. Running a Canadian film meant displacing a "Made in U.S.A." film. Why, therefore, whether they were good or bad, show audiences Film Board films?

Grierson appointed Guy Glover and me as joint producers of *Canada Carries On* with full authority over the films. He gave us a budget that would cover only about eight, which meant we would have to re-cut existing NFB films for cinema exhibition to make up the twelve annual issues. We were intent upon increasing the number of theatre bookings.

Guy and I worked very happily together, but then after about six months, because he spoke French, he left to become head of the French unit. He was a delight to work with and taught me much about the use of language. He was witty, wrote well (where I was very nearly hopeless), had good ideas and an objective critical mind. I think it was the steady grind of deadlines that got him down. He also didn't care much for dealing with our Columbia Pictures of Canada distributor, Harvey Harnick, whom he and others dubbed "Horrible" Harvey.

To we youngish, socially committed, creative types, Harvey, indeed, seemed somewhat horrible. As a manager responsible to his boss, he had to be commercial. "If a picture don't make a buck, what good is it? If it don't make a buck, it means no one wants to get off his ass to see it. You know why?" I could guess, but to make sure, he'd shout out the motherlode of show business refrains: "It's a lousy picture, that's why! It's gotta be lousy if it can't make a dollar!"

Harvey Harnick took great pride in being the distributor to the government's National Film Board films. He enjoyed hopping on a plane to the capital, perhaps hoping to meet a cabinet minister that I'm sure he'd boast about to his Toronto mates at the Variety Club. I figured that if Grierson got along well with him, why shouldn't I? And I did. In fact, I got to like him. I think, secretly, he believed he was helping people by showing our films. He knew the inside and underbelly of film distribution and exhibition. He would watch a film once and would instantly know the best first-run theatres it should play in in each city in Canada, its subsequent runs and, to within a thousand dollars, the profit to be reaped from it. He could do this because the basis of his business was his nose for audiences and the factors that would affect how they watched the films — their location in urban or rural areas, the time of the year, the actors and the story's genre.

He'd come to Ottawa to see previews of *CCO*s, and when I got to know him better, I'd show him one even before it was recorded and would occasionally act on his advice. How often have I heard his: "Sydney, I could have cried. D'you know what half the audience did when your last beautiful film came on the screen? Got up and left!" Or: "Jeez, another waving wheat field. D'you guys up here always get a hard-on when you see a waving wheat field?" Or: "Sydney, when are you goin' to learn that people don't give a damn for oily wheels meshing with oily wheels, machinery going clang-clang. It's people meshing with people that people'll pay bucks to see!" And when I would complain about low cinema bookings, I'd get the whammy: "Listen pal, I can't ram a dog down a theatre manager's throat. If you give me dogs to sell, you keep 'em. I'm not blaming you, Sydney, but some of those *CCO*s don't make enough to pay for the celluloid they're printed on!"

Boy, those were hard words! And I wanted to make artistic films. I realized he wasn't wrong. Audiences meant money to him, but to us, audiences were to be communicated with. We needed them. They needed us. In Legg's heyday, when we were in danger of losing the war, *Canada Carries On* played in over 800 Canadian cinemas each month. When Guy and I took over and it looked certain that we were winning the war, *CCO* was down to fewer than 200 cinemas a month.

It took me as long as six months before I began to think of our shrinking audiences. And it depressed me. I had no idea what others felt about it, so I went and talked to some I knew and trusted in our now large distribution department, with its many innovative non-theatrical circuits. Normally, few of us hoity-toity, creative chaps had anything to do with our distribution colleagues, except to complain when they reported low audience figures and timidly blamed the film. *We made 'em, they showed 'em*, was the general production attitude. These distribution reps, with their 16mm projector in the same room as their audience, could escape its reactions. What I learned was eye-opening, and with Harnick's bitching and my own conscience, I did some very hard thinking.

I was producing films as if I were Stuart Legg, but I did not come close to demonstrating his level of knowledge or his acute analytical mind. I couldn't wring emotion out of library footage. The closest any of us came to succeeding à la Legg was Tom Daly with his powerful film on the Nuremberg trials. But then, Tom had been Legg's assistant for five years. No, I would have to do films with more specially shot sequences and not hope to cobble together films with what could be found in the library. And so, for *Inside Fighting Norway*, which was largely made of stock shots, I was able to give it a human dimension with a specially shot sequence that I directed of Norwegian underground fighters (played by Canadian army demolition experts) dynamiting a bridge as a German troop train speeds over it. I did the same for *Fighting Sea-Fleas*, which was about naval MTBs sinking a German submarine. The film was made largely from specially shot material by Nick Read (a charming American on our staff) whom the Board had posted in England.

Trainbusters was a challenge and exciting to make. It was a two-reeler about the planes that skim across the channel and fly over France and Holland to shoot up trains. The only film footage I had, shot by Julian Roffman in England, was of RCAF pilots horsing around and getting into Hurricane fighters, taking off and landing in England. But, I also had a few terrific shots of the climax of the action — remarkable real gun-camera shots of tracer bullets actually firing at and exploding European trains at practically treetop level.

I wanted to give the audience the sensation of actually being on the train that was being shot at. This meant that I would need three kinds of material: shots from the air, seeing the target train and diving at it; close-ups of the pilot and the plane diving toward the camera; and, the toughest to organize, being on the train itself while it was being attacked.

The air force and army, being PR-conscious, were most cooperative, as was the Canadian National Railway, who lent me a freight train for an entire day. The air shots of the train were easy, the countryside near Ottawa looking near enough like France. From the air, the Canadian train could pass for European. Most complicated was the train itself, which required hidden cameras and demolition experts. Thought was needed as to how to get the close-ups of a fighter plane flying directly at the camera, as if it was flying at the train.

At Rockcliffe Military Airport I managed to get some terrific shots of two Hurricanes flying directly at the camera, which frightened the hell out of me. It did not occur to me or the eager pilots that what I was asking for was sheer madness. I'll never forget the thrill of seeing those Hurricanes come hurtling directly toward us and the totally deafening and terrifying experience of them passing forty feet over us. It so looked as if they were going to hit us that I threw myself on the ground. Joe Gibson, on camera, cool as a cucumber said, "No good. Not low enough. Get 'em to fly lower next time."

I looked at him, "You're kidding!" And somewhat hysterically, and not thinking of the planes and their pilots, I screamed, "You're crazy, Joe. If they fly any lower they'll hit us!"

"No they won't. You want good shots? Get 'em to do it again." On the next pass, I'm afraid I sat on the ground and indeed they must have flown only twenty feet above us. Joe said, "Okay! Not bad. But I want another crack at it. Tell 'em to come in even lower." I gave up.

Then, to my surprise, Joe dismantled the tripod, hauled out an Eyemo from his case and laid down on his back, flat on the ground. With his head lifted, he glued his eye to the viewfinder of his handheld camera and aimed it at the oncoming planes. I was lying flat alongside him, too cowardly to run away when, like the furies, the two planes screamed over us and at the crucial moment, Joe suddenly arched his back, tilting the camera to follow them as they sped away from us. What a remarkable and most lovable old coot was Joe Gibson. Those shots of his were great, but the last Eyemo shot was a revelation to me. When he followed the planes as they flew past and over him, his camera was in fact shooting upside-down, which resulted in the planes themselves suddenly flipping over and flying up into the sky upside-down in the film — a victory roll!

I organized the freight train as a mix of flat and bow cars. On the roof of the caboose car at the end of the train I positioned a well-secured camera; its cameraman was to shoot toward the engine to show German soldiers lying on the roofs of the boxcars with machine guns and rifles to protect the train. Between the boxcars were spaced low flat cars, unseen by the main camera, on which army demolition men were to drop small explosive charges and set off smoke canisters at the appropriate time. With them, also unseen, were two other cameramen. Most tricky of all was timing the train with the arrival of two Hurricane fighters who were to simulate the attack, which I planned to take place near Carp, Ontario.

To my utter amazement the whole thing came off like clockwork. Later, to my horror I saw that clearly visible on one of the boxcars were the letters CNR, on a French train! The solution became simple: Nick Balla who edited almost every *CCO* in my unit suggested optically reversing the shot so that CNR, backwards, became RNC. All the shooting cut together beautifully. To this day I wonder what the local farmers thought when they saw a speeding CNR freight train, on fire, being furiously attacked by two fighter planes defended by helmeted Germans, returning their fire with rifles and machine guns in their peaceful Ontario countryside!

It was getting to me good by now, the feeling of guilt that had been growing because I had not been directly fighting the war. My brother had come through unscathed in Italy, and now his regiment was fighting their way through the Lowlands in Holland. My best friend Jack Olsen was escaping with his life in bombers many times while I was having fun making films. The worst I suffered was drinking cheap rye whiskey and having to sleep in upper berths when going on location.

Every four months during the war, Grierson and McLean had been getting us deferments from being called up. In fear of Quebec, Wiley Willy King devised conscription so that those called up were obligated to defend Canada only if the country itself was physically attacked. To fight overseas, a man had to volunteer. The joke used to go around that conscripts were lined up against a wall and the Sergeant Major would rap out, "Okay you men, any who don't choose to fight overseas, take one step backwards."

Acting on my guilt, I applied to the navy for a commission in their overseas film unit. When it looked fairly certain that I would get it, I told Betty. She was happy for me, knowing that was what I wanted and then said, "What about us?" I was taken aback. "Oh, I hope things'll be the same between us when I come back." And I uttered some words about loving her. Betty carefully said, "I'm not sure that it is good for us to wait. Perhaps we should get married now." The thought of marriage had never occurred to me, but like a shot I said, "Yeah, why not?" Since the navy appointment was imminent we decided to get married right away.

Betty shot letters off to her folks and it was arranged that we would be married in two weeks in the tiny town of White Lake, where

Duncan McRae was minister of its only church. (The United Church of Canada had posted him there when he and Betty's mother had to flee China just ahead of the advancing Japanese.) I had only briefly met Betty's mother, Susan, and to my surprise received a letter from Betty's father, which I opened with some trepidation. In it I was warmly welcomed into the family. That his daughter loved me was proof enough to him and his wife of my goodness. He looked forward to marrying us himself. What a wonderful augur that letter was of my new extended family.

My father had died earlier that year and I shudder to think of his reaction had he known that I was marrying a shiksa! My mother? I couldn't be sure. I decided it would be much smarter to wait and tell her after the wedding.

The day before we were to be married, Betty, her sister Mary and I took the train to where Betty's folks lived. It was a tiny village in the upper reaches of the Ottawa valley, and even though it was close to Canada's enormous Chalk River atomic energy plant, White Lake was still without electricity. The tiny lumbering village was so ingrown, everyone in it was either a McNam or a Fraser.

If I felt nervous when I arrived, I was quickly put at ease by her folks and another sister, Jeanne, whom I had not yet met. We found out that Betty's only brother, Robert, was not there — he was in a German POW camp, the only naval officer captured in the ill-fated Dieppe raid. Also, Murray, Mary's husband, was with the Royal Canadian Air Force in England. Present, though, was Susan's mother, Grandma Rodgers, who had been brought as a child from Ulster in the last century. As she crossed Canada's prairies in a covered wagon, it was pierced by the arrows of attacking Indians. Now in her eighties and looking fit, it was said that she once weighed 280 pounds, but had decided to lose most of it. For three months she drank water and ate only bananas. There was no doubt I was marrying into a hardy family and one full of Canadian history.

That evening, after a fine dinner in the Manse, I was given my own bedroom. When lying in bed, reading by Coleman oil lamp, there was a knock on the door. Surely it was not Betty. Not in her folks' house! I called out, "Yes? Who is it?" It was Betty's father. "Sydney, may I come in?" Oh my God! What does he want? Convert me to Christianity? Will I be able to support his daughter in the manner . . . That sort of thing? "Of course. Do come in." When he entered with a light-springing step (he was aged about sixty), I noticed that he was carrying a black, soft covered book with red edged paper and one finger of his hand in it. Clearly it was a Bible. As he sat down on the edge of the bed he said that he and Susan liked me, and then very pleasantly threw a loop at me by asking, "Have you ever read the Sermon on the Mount?"

I explained, "Well, brought up as a Jew we only read from the five books of the Old Testament. No, I'm not familiar with the Sermon on the Mount."

"Would you read it and tell me what you think of it?" It was clear he was genuinely curious and of course I agreed. He opened the bible where his finger was and handed it to me. I felt him watching me as I read it. Having spent years studying socially committed art, painting communist posters and making war propaganda films, I could not avoid blurting out, "Hey, this is great! What a brilliant piece of persuasive propaganda." Betty's father's eyes popped open. It was the last thing he expected to hear. In full admiration I couldn't stop. "Jesus not only decries the money changers, but rouses everyone to action to throw them out. This is marvellous. Jesus was a communist!"

Dear Duncan lifted his head and gleefully laughed and laughed. "That's a revelation, Sydney; that never occurred to me." And with a "Sleep well, tomorrow's a big day," he cheerfully left me, quietly closing the door behind him.

The next day, May 20, 1944, we emerged from the Manse to be married in brilliant sunshine in the garden. I was in my finest suit, white shirt and tie, and Betty wore a beautiful powder blue jacket and skirt she made herself, with powder blue gloves and a tiny veiled hat. She pinned a carnation to my lapel. Behind Betty and me were her sisters, mother and grandma. From the latter during the service, I could hear the occasional suppressed hiss indicating her Ulster disapproval of her youngest granddaughter marrying a Jew.

Sydney and Betty on their wedding day.

Duncan, the dear man, when he came to the line, "Do you, Betty, take this man . . ." he did the classical parental thing — to the giggles of Betty's sisters: "Do you Mary, er, Jeanne, ah, Betty take this man, Sydney, to be your lawfully wedded . . ." Chez McRae being a teetotalling house, we were toasted with ginger ale, and after a splendid lunch, Betty and I left for Ottawa.

Our marriage was the cause for a great NFB celebration.[32] It's not that there weren't many love affairs or people living together, it's just that we were the first two who met, fell in love and who actually went

---

32 Newman kept the internal memo that proclaimed on May 12: "OYEZ OYEZ
    – The nuptials of Miss Elizabeth McRae of Honan province, and Mr. Syd
    Newman, of Toronna, will be celebrated May 20 (Saturday) in the spacious
    gardens adjoining 42 Stanley Avenue. On this occasion of institutional rejoicing
    and solidarity, we earnestly solicit your cooperation in laying aside or otherwise
    providing one of the following: a bottle of rye whiskey, a bottle of rum (to mix
    with the rye, into a devastating Punch)."

whole hog and got married. Later there were many others. The party was held in the rolling gardens of a palatial Rockcliffe home.

When Betty and I arrived at about three in the afternoon, the hundred or so there were already in full swing. Most had brought bottles of whatever they could lay their hands on to drink, and into a large washtub went whiskey, rye, rum, gin, cider, beer, red, white and rosé wine replenished by latecomers and a great time was had by all. Grierson was on one of his many trips, but his wife, Margaret, was there, along with every other Uncle Tom Cobbly Film Boarder. Despite the absence of any food, the lethal mixture of drink produced no scenes; in fact, it brought together many a former enemy. I still giggle when I see vividly in my mind Arla Saare, a Finnish negative cutter who, still smarting from her country's war with Russia, was joyously dancing with a man called Altsev who used to hang around the Film Board a lot. Whether they were too drunk to care I don't know, but he was the Soviet Union's Cultural Attaché! I was told that a very sedate administrative lady was found asleep under a bush by the owners of the house the following morning.

The party broke up at nine in the evening and about thirty of us went to the Canton Inn where owner Stanley Wong and his father, the chef, outdid themselves in providing a feast for an emperor. Stanley gave Betty and me a gift of Chinese rice-pattern bowls with chopsticks to match. At 2 a.m., laden with food and drink, Betty and I finally hit the sack, merely kissed one another goodnight and instantly fell dead asleep. This reads as if I have perfect recall, but only an idiot could forget such an eventful time.

The following day, on the train, Betty and I found ourselves in the same coach as a bunch of Volkoff ballet dancers returning to Toronto. And there among them was the ubiquitous Soviet Cultural Attaché, Tovarish Altsev, who came over to join us. Among other things, he boasted that he had luckily found a print in mint condition of D.W. Griffith's *Intolerance* lying in a dusty cellar of an old cinema in London, Ontario. He bought it from the cinema owner who did not know its value for $25 and, at this very moment, had it in an American plane (part of U.S. aid to war-torn Russia) flying from Whitehorse,

Canada, over the Arctic to become part of the Russian film archives. It made me mad that a dopey Canadian had let something so valuable slip out of our hands.

Three days later I finally got up enough courage to tell my mother the news of my marriage. From our room at the Royal York Hotel I phoned her in Buffalo, where she was living with my sister. After the usual greetings, I said, "Ma, congratulations are in order. I'm now a married man." Immediately she gave me a hearty, "Mazel Tov! Who's the lucky girl?" I said, "Ma, she's not Jewish but you'll like—" and before I could continue, I heard, *"What?!"* Fool that I was, and wanting to get it over with quickly, I said something like, "It's worse. Her father is a minister but she's—" and my mother began to cry. Ruth got on the phone and, just as she had always been with me, was warmly effusive in her congratulations, wanting to know when she would meet the bride. We agreed that it would be this weekend, but only for a day.

On Sunday, Betty and I crossed Lake Ontario on the *S.S. Cayuga* and then travelled by bus to Buffalo. Betty was nervous and I, terrified, at the thought of meeting my mother. It was she who answered the door, and so help me God, she was positively wonderful. How she screwed up the courage for the meeting was beyond me. She kissed us both and before we even sat down, as if wanting to get it over with as soon as possible, gave us a cheque for fifty dollars, apologizing that she had been unable to buy a proper wedding present for us.

My brother-in-law, Eddie, brought out a bottle of whiskey, and we each had a glass of schnapps as a toast. Eddie, my sister and I had a few more. Betty, knowing she was being closely observed, refused a second one. (She could, in those days, drink me under the table.) They all put on a good front, and the day was helped by Ruth's two children, Rhodelle and Donny, who scampered all over the place making welcomed distracting noises. I admired Betty's bravery and was proud of my dear, dear mother. Over the years, she and Betty got along fine — a happy mother-in-law and grandmother.

CHAPTER TWELVE
TV — FRIEND OR FOE?

Betty and I moved into a tiny house on John Street just one minute's walk from the Joint. It had been Irene and Graham Spry's house, and when the delightful Irene Spry showed it to us, to my amazement, I discovered that her toilet reading was an enormous tome on economics.

At this time, Betty was head negative cutter, and shortly after our wedding, she was promoted to replace Raymond Spottiswoode as the NFB's technical coordinator. One helluva big job it was, with a staff of over 175 responsible for everything technical in the making of films — camera, sound, laboratory, opticals and research. (The latter was also setting technical standards for Canada's burgeoning private film companies.) For good measure, she was also charged with other odds and sods of responsibility for the cleaning staff, our office safety and the film library.

I wasn't idle either. The bookings for *Canada Carries On* were rising, but too slowly to suit me. At this time, too, Grierson was pressing us to move into films that would deal with the problems that would arise at the end of the war and the issues of what our peacetime aspirations would and should be. Men trained to kill — how would they adjust to civilian life? Women in factories — would they now return to the kitchen? How would we bring democratic thinking back to countries that were under fascist regimes for years? How would the many homeless of a ravaged Europe be clothed and fed?

Inspired as we all were by this, I faced a special problem — that of making my *CCO*s so attractive that more theatres would show them, and avoiding the threat of losing the documentaries entirely.[33] How do you make a film exciting without showing the firing of guns? I decided to try to get away from films made of library material and go for broke on as many originally shot films as I could. They might be more expensive, but would be about Canada — the uniquely Canadian things my audiences would identify with and were proud of. To do this and be certain of succeeding, I reluctantly forced myself to take a draconian action that affected a friend and working colleague, Lorne Greene. Yes, Mr. Bonanza himself.

Lorne was a trained actor and singer, had been the Canadian Broadcasting Corporation's senior announcer and was the permanent narrator of the Film Board's major showcased theatrical *CCO* and *World in Action* films. His magnificent voice and authoritative and intelligent reading of commentaries enhanced our good films and saved many a lousy one. In the dark, early days of the war, many dubbed him "The Trans-Atlantic Boom" and sometimes, the "Voice of Doom." Gradually I became more and more convinced that his voice reminded my audiences too much of the days when we thought we might lose the war. I had to break the association between the dark

---

33 Newman may not have been as up for the task as he makes out. He actually sent a memo on April 11, 1945, to his bosses at the NFB, Alan Field and Tom Daly, resigning from *Canada Carries On*. He claimed he was burned out. "If I am to have any value to the Film Board in the future, it is important for me to have a rest, away from film production." He was suggesting he go back to the art department. "Film-making is a personal and emotional experience. I can't go on making them without some kind of re-evaluation of my purpose at the Film Board." Newman was apparently talked out of resigning.

war years and the *CCO* of today in the minds of the audience.

When I told Lorne that he shouldn't count on being the only narrator in future *CCO*s, he was understandably upset and he didn't like me much — happily, though, for only a few years. I used him only when I wanted a strong, authoritative voice, such as on my *Suffer Little Children*, which was a compilation film based largely on marvellous footage of children shot by Nick Read in the aftermath of the war in Greece. I'm proud of that film. The United Nations thought so highly of it they bought and distributed 300 prints of it. I set about and produced a series of films about Canadian cities, immigrants to Canada, returning vets and a sweet little film about a children's camp sensitively directed by Stanley Jackson and written by Len Peterson. There was also one about the family directed by my friend Jack Olsen who, earlier, had been hired quick as a shot by Grierson when I introduced them to one another. I'm amused to think that Grierson hired him not because Jack was still in his air force uniform, but because Grierson, a little guy, was taller than Jack.

Len Peterson was only one of the many talented people I borrowed from Andrew Allan's radio series, *Stage*. Other writers of Allan's I used were Lister Sinclair and Joseph Schule. Allan's actors read some fine character commentaries — Bernie and Barbara Braden, Budd Knapp, Frank Peddie, John Drainie, and not forgetting wonderful Ruth Springford among many others.

One film I cannot forget because it marked the end of the war in Europe was *Headline Hunters*. It was about Canada's war correspondents. Ralph Foster, who came to the Board in the wave of Grierson's journalist hiring, and who later became deputy film commissioner under Ross McLean, was in Europe; with Julian Roffman, he sent back some splendid footage of our newsmen covering the war for press and radio. Men like Ross Munroe and René Lévesque were seen in military briefings, under fire and typing their copy or speaking into microphones. The main material I needed was to show how their stories got to readers and radio listeners. The Canadian Press, the CBC, *Toronto Daily Star* and the *Globe and Mail* cooperated fully. My tiny crew consisted of trainee director Daphne Lilly, the general gofer, Peter Sager and Lorne Batchelor on camera.

With the war's end in sight, I decided that I would time the film's release with the end of the war. The *Toronto Star* at my request generously set up a special edition, the front page of which was headlined "Victory in Europe!" But, just as giant presses were rolling for our camera, believe it or not, a newsflash came: VE Day, at long last! We were glad the damn war was over, but it shot to hell the climax to my film. Nonetheless, we rushed out of the *Star* pressroom, and from the back of a truck, we roamed Toronto, getting shots of the city in a state of delirium celebrating the war's end. We got some great footage but nearly starved that day, because by the time we finished shooting, all the restaurants and shops had closed. The next day the *Star* set up a VJ Day front page, which served my film even better because it pointed to the war in the east, which had still to be won.

In the summer of 1945, Betty suggested, "Isn't it time we had a family? After all, Sydney, I'm getting on." (She was twenty-six.) I didn't want any kids, feeling that their entry into our lives would spoil the perfection of our marriage and the way we lived. I held my position but so did she, gently, and of course, I capitulated. After all, what's a guy to do when he's besotted with love?

Throwing contraception to the wind, caution cheerfully denied, eventually Betty became pregnant. I say *eventually* because this didn't happen easily, which concerned her greatly. She studied the whole question of fertility, menstrual cycle, body temperature and things I still know nothing about, and one night, she said, "Tonight. Tonight's the night!" And, by God, it was.

As she grew larger with child (she worked right up to two weeks before giving birth), it was clear that we needed a larger place. Our landlord, a Mr. Blackburn, who seemed to own half of Ottawa, liked the crazy Film Boarders and offered us an elegant apartment on the top floor of an old, but elegant, Victorian house he had converted into flats. Betty and I knew it well — 30 Cooper Street, where the Griersons still kept their flat on the ground floor.

When we moved into it we discovered that we shared the top floor with the newly married Duntons. Davidson Dunton was Grierson's successor as head of the government's Wartime Information Board and was just becoming president of the CBC. A lusty baby, Deirdre, was soon born to us, Betty having measured her contractions with a stopwatch before telling me when to take her to the Ottawa Civic Hospital. About six months later, I was returning to 30 Cooper and having difficulty hiking the pram, with little Deirdre in it, up the front steps to enter the house. Who should open the front door but MacKenzie King, the prime minister of Canada himself! I guess he was about seventy then. Very courtly and with a sweet smile, he helped me bring the pram inside. What was he doing in our house?

Bursting to find out, that evening Betty and I went downstairs to Grierson's flat, in which the Leggs were temporarily living. I was still in an arm's length but friendly relationship with Stuart, and I told him of the encounter with the PM and asked what he was doing in our house. "Oh," replied Legg, "his retired secretary of thirty-five years, a Mrs. Pattison, lives in the other ground floor flat." And with a lascivious twinkle in his eye, he said, "He visits her quite often." My mind awhirl with scandalous thoughts, I said, "I see. What do they do, I wonder?" And Legg, deadpan, said, "I don't know, but I often hear them play duets on the piano accompanied by the rustle of dry skin."

In August 1945, to our sorrow, John Grierson left the Film Board and Canada. His credit with the prime minister had run out.

Grierson was too cocky and much too forthright for staid Ottawa. Imagine him during the war describing himself as a propagandist when the word was identified with Hitler and Goebbels. To us he explained the word's Roman Catholic origins. On one occasion late in the war, he violently disagreed with the U.S. Secretary of State at a cocktail party in, of all places, the Embassy of the USSR. He was later to rue this when he tried to get a U.S. work permit.

It is to the shame of Canada that he was allowed to leave. Worse, that he was pilloried later for his generosity in transferring a secretary of his to the Board's office in Washington, as if he should have known that she was the mistress of the leader of the spies exposed to the Soviet cipher clerk Igor Gouzenko.[34] Grierson's brilliance and his persuasive powers with the prime minister were bound to make functionaries jealous. Not one to suffer fools gladly, he gained unforgiving enemies, overriding his immense understanding of what makes people tick, which he put to use for society's good. Gradually, over the years, his enemies outnumbered his friends. Canada was simply too small to keep him.

Following Grierson, Legg and Spottiswoode soon joined him in New York, and then Stan Hawes left (with Ralph Foster) to create a film board for the Australian government. The source of our inspiration and our teachers were gone. We Canucks would have to look after ourselves from now on. And we did. Grierson in particular, and his British mates, had so thoroughly inculcated us, not merely in the craft and techniques of filmmaking, but also in the value of film as more than escapist entertainment. The Board's most fruitful work was still to come in the years ahead.

After some government shilly-shallying, debates in the House of Commons and backstage maneuverings of Ross McLean, the postwar future of the NFB was assured. Ross himself was forced to wait two years before being confirmed as our chief executive. McLean may not have had Grierson's inspirational qualities but in every other respect was a superb boss. He, like us, was imbued with Grierson's aims, was accessible, wise, knew and loved Canada. He was not a filmmaker but had confidence in our creative abilities.

As commissioner and the producer of films, McLean had to administer a large and complex distribution department, run an effective skills photography group with its own specialized laboratory, watch expenditures and prepare estimates for the annual vote of money, fend off an increasingly jealous, growing private film industry, liaise with the government departments and public pressure groups and keep a watchful eye on potential political pressure. Ross McLean

---

34 Igor Gouzenko was a cipher clerk at the Soviet embassy in Ottawa. On September 5, 1945, he walked out of the embassy with various documents and defected.

had a lot on his plate despite the help of Marjorie McKay on finance, Beth Bertram on personnel and Paul Theriault as his Quebec guru and political advisor.

Some of us in production felt that the horizontal structure in production needed streamlining. Ross would have to okay what were often minor matters coming to him from twenty or more producers, each responsible for an area of production — agriculture, newsreels, animation, French language films, foreign versions and so on. Don Fraser, Michael Spencer and I wrote a paper recommending the creation of five production units, each to consist of three or four areas of specialized films, headed by an executive producer who would report to him on a regular basis. After weeks of discussion, the proposal was adopted.

I should have been happy at becoming an executive producer, but I wasn't. All I ever wanted to do was create. At first, as an artist. In documentary, that meant being a director. But, hating having a boss over me as I made *CCO* films, I allowed myself to become its producer, which, while allowing me freedom to make my own films unhindered, kept my films fewer in number because I had to supervise the work of other directors. Now, I was to have even fewer opportunities to do my own "thing." As executive producer and the remaining producer of *CCO*, I now had to be responsible as well for the producers in charge of newsreels, travel films and films for children. This promotion was the continuation of a pattern that was to bedevil my entire professional career. Why? I'm positive that it wasn't the increase in money that more senior jobs gave. While I enjoyed the power it gave me, I don't think it was that either. I guess I simply could not stand people breathing down my neck.

Now I had to embark on the precarious journey of learning the give and take required to not crush those responsible to me, even though ultimately I was to be held accountable for what they did. At the very start, and totally unprepared, I was tested.

In making a documentary, the kind of film that the Film Board made in those days, someone in charge had few points of control over what was made. Often, a script was hardly more than scribbles on the back of an envelope written by its director or producer with a gleam in his eye. Without a script, seeing the film rushes (beyond checking the stuff for focus) was not much help. And since few films were shot with sync sound, seeing the cutting copy without its narration was just as useless. So, prior to its final recording, it was the typed commentary approved by Ross McLean that gave a film a go or not. With the thorny problem of control in my mind, I called the first meeting of the producers in my unit.

I picked a Saturday afternoon, knowing the joint would be quiet for this first, most important session with them. If the producers were worried, they didn't show it. We aired most sides of the new scheme, and after about two hours it was all clear and agreed that they would give me their ideas in script, or in some other form, with estimated budgets based on an annual plan. I would secure the unit's global money from the commissioner, then see their edited films before recording and read their commentaries before submitting them to Ross McLean for final approval. We broke up with everyone seeming pretty cheerful. I was surprised when Don Mulholland asked if I wouldn't mind seeing him alone for a few minutes. I agreed.

Don was different from most in production. He was eight years older than me and had come to the Board after being de-mobbed as an air force flight sergeant. Before going into the service, he had been a copywriter for the J. Walter Thompson Advertising Agency in Toronto. He drank dry martinis, new to me. He had a weary, sardonic look about him. We Grierson originals were not certain of him at all! Not our kind. To us blue-eyed idealists, how could we not be wary of a mind that in all seriousness could say, "To sell democracy, you've got to dress it up as you would to sell a can of Heinz beans." Anyway, he was in my unit and in fact was doing a good job with newsreels and had created a successful series called *Eye Witness* that he wrote himself, which covered industrial news.

When the others left he closed the door, sat down and, looking straight at me, declared, "I am not going to show you my commentaries. I'll go along with everything else, but not the commentaries." I was stumped. "But, Don," I said, "that's a rule. I'm responsible to Ross for what you and the other—" Before I could finish he cut in: "I won't have it! Christ! I wanted to make films, I left a good job, was a top copywriter with the promise of a commission in the air force film . . . There, they make me eat shit, cleaning latrines, peeling potatoes for two years — a lousy three hooks — no commission — stuck two fuck'n years takin' orders . . ." His eyes were staring, white flecks of spittle in the corners of his mouth; the man was mad!

"Don! Take it easy! C'mon! Be reasonable. I'm responsible to the commissioner, can't you see that?" I was talking to a stone wall. More quietly, but still deadly, he said he would not do it. "Not my commentary!"

I took a deep breath, and sighed. "Okay, Don, this seems important to you," (the understatement of the year!), "so I won't read your precious commentaries. But, listen hard, should you say anything in it that'll embarrass the Board, I'll kick the shit out of you so hard you'll . . ." I shrugged, "Okay?"

Suspicious, he looked at me. "Okay." No thanks, no smile of victory. We silently left and parted. We worked quite well together, but always with a barrier between us. Pity that, because he had a very sweet wife, Ruth, who knew Betty, and the barrier kept us from ever socializing. But I got to like dry martinis. Years later he and I had a similar encounter, which I shall tell in its proper place in these memoirs, but then, the shoe was on the other foot.

Ross was finally confirmed as government film commissioner in 1947 and seemed happy with the reorganization of production. As his deputy, he had brought back from Australia Ralph Foster, who was a delightful, urbane giant of a man — six-foot-six with enthusiasm to match.

Being in a senior position along with Jim Beveridge, Don Fraser, Mike Spencer, Guy Glover and Tom Daly, now close old friends, we couldn't help but get a much broader perspective on the NFB, its problems and its future value to Canada. My *CCO* series was now beginning to reach six hundred theatre bookings a month, mostly in the Famous Players cinemas, and Don Mullholland's *Eye Witness* series was becoming successful in the Odeon chain.

As government film commissioner, it was McLean's duty to advise the government on all matters affecting film. It was only fair, he felt, for Canada to be exposed to Canadian films, and for both commercial and NFB ones to be shown in the U.S. as a partial counterbalance to Hollywood's gross monopoly in Canada. While pushing the notion of a quota, limiting U.S. films here unless our films were seen in the States, Hollywood retaliated by sending a team of silver-tongued gents who seduced our government to see things their way. Ross couldn't win.

Our films were good. Audiences in the theatres, but especially Canadians in schools, churches, community and union halls wanted them. The problem was getting the films to audiences. There must be, I thought, a better means of delivery. Television!

When man first stepped onto the moon, while thrilling in a basic way, to me it was a so-what achievement. The moon, or even Columbus discovering North America was just finding unthinking area, beautiful perhaps, but mute. It was our genius of being able to see astronauts walking in near airless slow motion and *hearing them talk* at the same time, over vast distances of space — *that* was, to me, the marvel. It was something of a considerably higher order, to be able to see and hear one another. Communication of thought and feeling.

Vivid in my mind is the day in 1938 when I went to Eaton's department store in Toronto to see a demonstration of what was regarded as a newfangled invention from England. I found myself gazing at a five-by-eight-inch, greenish glass screen of blurred images of people moving and talking. Nothing amazing about that until I recognized on the screen some of the people standing near me — then I saw myself. I stuck out my tongue and saw myself doing it on the screen at the same time! Surely it was not done by a clever arrangement of mirrors. How was it done? A miracle!

It was not until 1948 that I saw television again. I had read quite a bit about it and knew that it had started in New York just after the war. I went to Ross McLean and Ralph Foster and suggested that if we couldn't get our films into the American cinemas, why didn't we try to get them on American television? It was worth trying, they thought, and besides, the NFB should know about this new visual medium, since television was bound to come to Canada someday. Since it was my idea, they asked me to go and be prepared to offer the National Broadcasting Company (owned by the Radio Corporation of America, or the RCA, who were big in Canada) first refusal on our films. Joining me on the trip was another Film Boarder, Gordon Burwash, because he knew an ex-BBC chap who was regarded as the hottest TV director in New York.

What I saw there utterly amazed me. Not only was television able to transmit motion pictures into any home, it was doing it with the ease of breathing. Even more remarkable was my feeling that it had creative possibilities when I saw drama and opera being shot using three or even four cameras operating in a planned order, with the results received immediately by the viewer. People were buying television sets by the thousands.

As a filmmaker, one could sneer at the crude black-and-white productions, but it was common sense that said this was only the beginning. Gordon's friend was feted far and wide as the innovative genius of television. It's funny to think today how critics marvelled when he superimposed the head of Toscanini, as he was conducting, over a shot of his entire symphony orchestra; or how they responded when he showed the slippered feet of a ballerina on points supered over the corps de ballet — the sort of thing you would see in films made fifty years earlier! To get that effect in film took days of tricky optical and laboratory work, but in television all you had to do was press two buttons and then a third and presto, there it was immediately seen in the comfort of viewers' homes.

Gordon and I returned to Ottawa with a definite interest from NBC; the negotiations were to be handled by McLean and Foster. I also returned with the memory of an event that still makes me giggle at how wrong I can be.

Gordon's friend had gotten the assignment to direct a variety show for potential sponsorship by the Ford Motor Company. He invited us to come along to the theatre to see how it was done, but asked us to sit with the audience, apologizing that the control room would be too crowded with Ford, CBS and ad agency executives.

After the show, Gordon and I took the director, who was wet with exhaustion, to Sardi's for a drink and a bite to eat. Later a messenger arrived with a note to the director: the Ford Motor Company loved the show and bought it for a year's run. So, our bite to eat became a champagne dinner.

I'm not ashamed to admit that earlier, when the director asked what I thought of the show, I said I thought it good and entertaining, but could use a new MC. The current one was deadly, couldn't talk and was totally lacking in grace and charm. The show was called *The Talk of the Town*, and the MC was Ed Sullivan. Who was I to anticipate the public's taste?

Two months later I was called into Ross McLean's office and asked whether I would like to live in New York for the next year and be on loan from the Board to NBC. I would enjoy staff status, spend time in each of its television departments and send back reports on how it is all done, noting what the implications of television might be on the NFB and its future role in Canada. What a marvellous turn of events it was. New York City! Land of my *Daily Mirror* childhood reading! *The New Yorker*! On the Avenue, *Fifth* Avenue! Broadway Melody! Television! And all expenses paid for me, Betty, Deirdre and our second daughter, Jennifer, who was eight months old. Betty was as keen as I for this new experience.

Preparations were complex. About to move into an unfinished new house in Manor Park, we found an excellent tenant for our Canadian home, a farmer from Western Canada who had just been appointed a commissioner of Canada's Wheat Board. We were lucky, because only a farmer would know what to do with the mud that surrounded the house. Another problem was getting agreement on who would temporarily take over my unit at the NFB. My choice of Nick Balla, who was my deputy and who beautifully finished most of the unit's films, was overridden. Instead, Don Mulholland became acting head — a prophetic choice that would affect the Film Board and my life.

Betty and I agreed that I precede her and the girls to New York City to find a place to live. External affairs got me a special passport marked "Foreign Agent," which indeed I was, since I was an employee of His

Betty and Sydney with their new addition to the family,
Jennifer, and Deirdre in Central Park, New York City.

Majesty's loyal Canadian government. In April 1949, I flew to New York. I had just turned thirty-two and earnestly set out to uncover the mysteries of television for the benefit of Canadian documentary.

While looking for an apartment, where would I stay? The Algonquin Hotel, of course! Home of the famous *New Yorker* roundtable, rubbing shoulders with Dorothy Parker, James Thurber and my old pal from Toronna, Dick Taylor. I lived there for three months — and never caught so much as a sight of them. Mmn, Charles Laughton's was living there, getting his *Galileo* ready for Broadway — but I didn't dare approach him. My most vivid recollection of my stay was the elevator shaft's smell of the kitchens, which assailed my nose and gradually sickened me each morning as I rode down to the hotel's charming, small lobby. The hotel was convenient for me, being only a short walk up Sixth Avenue to the RCA building, where I would spend thousands of air-conditioned hours in endless corridors going to windowless rooms and studios.

At NBC I was warmly welcomed by its new vice-president of programs, Sylvester "Pat" Weaver,[35] who said I should plan my year's stay, check in with him and he would open all necessary doors for me. He even offered attendance to his high-level program-planning meetings, where he told me I was not to divulge what I heard to anyone. I went to some of these, but soon quit. It was too embarrassing when a rancorous argument would break out and eyes darted to me — a "foreign agent" present. I got to know him a little, liked him and was filled with admiration. Tall, urbane and charming (to me), in some respects he resembled Grierson. He was a visionary and recognized the social values of television, albeit in a profit-motivated context. For pure innovation in new programs, no one in television anywhere could, or has, equalled him. The Golden Age of 1950s American television was due to him alone — a visionary — and the pace he set.

He came as a program director for radio and television from a giant advertising agency, Young and Rubicam, where it was his job to defend the sponsor's power to control the shape, and more importantly, the content of programs. Now, surprisingly, he set out to break the sponsor's grip in an effort to make programs innovative and entertainingly informative. New programs he devised, such as *Today*, *Tonight* and dozens more, were designed so that sponsors could only buy portions of each of them, or buy spot commercials — it was divide and rule; ruled, of course, by the makers of the programs, the NBC network.

Being rather thick, it didn't occur to me why NBC was being so nice to me, which indeed they were. At an early meeting with Pat (in my thirteen months at NBC I never heard anyone refer to, or speak to him as anything other than Pat), he expressed great interest in Canada, admiration for the CBC and the latter's relationship to government. He marvelled that the government kept its sticky fingers off the CBC. It was when he asked when TV would start in Canada that

---

35 Pat Weaver was a legend of American television. He eventually would become President of NBC from 1953 to 1955. He came up with the ideas for *Today* and *The Tonight Show*. His main innovation was the practice of networks creating their own programming during which sponsors could advertise, rather than having an ad agency create a program for a sponsor, as was the practice on radio.

the penny dropped. Of course, the parent company was RCA! They wanted Canada to buy their gear, cameras, transmitters and TV sets, and wanted the CBC to take NBC's programs — not those of their powerful competitor, CBS. They thought I could influence the CBC and the Canadian government. Well, I thought, let 'em. What a laugh!

I was given a desk in a large windowless office that I shared with directors and assistants of all kinds. When I needed stationery, pencils or a stopwatch I could get them from the office manager, a young guy called Bobby. It didn't take long to find out that Bobby was Robert Sarnoff, son of the general who was the chairman and major stockholder of RCA. Talk of starting at the bottom! The kid was born with a silver-image orthicon in his mouth, but thankfully acted as if he didn't know it. Four years later he succeeded Pat Weaver as president of NBC and not many years after that became chairman of the board.

Like Grierson in Canada, Weaver was too big for the giant NBC. After he left, television in general started its slippery slope downwards to become "a wasteland," as Chairman Newton Minow of the Federal Communications Commission described it in 1962. When in 1986, *Variety*, the bible of show business, produced an enormous issue celebrating the sixtieth anniversary of the glories of NBC, it pulled the Russian trick of rewriting history. In all its 150 pages there was not a single reference to Pat Weaver. As always, Weaver had his eye on the future. When he left, he set up the world's first pay-TV company. It didn't work out, but this was in 1958!

To get the best overall view of television, Weaver suggested that I start work in Master Control. It was into here that all programs came, whether from dozens of inside studios, remote camera units, or film, which were then channeled out to transmitters.

The co-axial network then hardly covered the country. It extended only south to New Orleans and west to Chicago. Until the national microwave grid was completed, Los Angeles and the few other television stations were airmailed some pretty awful kinescope recordings of the programs made for local transmission. NBC television was on the air from four in the afternoon to close-down near midnight.

For two weeks I became a working part of the team that ran Master Control. Its boss, Ivan Reiner, was a tall, benign and efficient ex–army officer who became, with his wife, lifelong friends of Betty and mine. What helped draw us together was, like so many in such jobs, the fact that Ivan wanted to be a writer and producer. To my amazement he had actually heard of Canada's Film Board. Years later he wrote and produced many feature films. Others in the group also became "creative" names. One of them was a nice young guy, Bill Harbach, who was the son of Otto Harbach, the much-honoured composer of Broadway musicals. Under the guidance of Pat Weaver, Bill brought to the screen the laidback Steve Allen in the highly successful *Tonight Show*.

It was fun being with that team. Seeing everything that went out on the air, the wisecracks about the various shows and their makers and performers gave me a wonderful insight to the inner politics and the television programs of NBC. I also got a sense of what their competitors were putting out, as it was monitored in this same Master Control room. They got a kick, watching a Canadian open the network at 4 p.m. with my, "Okay you guys, time to alert the nation. We'll go in ten seconds. Nine, eight, seven . . ." As the second hand approached the one, I'd should out, "Okay, hit it!" Imagine, pictures flickering into light in thousands of homes from Chicago to New Orleans — at my command! No wonder the top priority for revolutionaries, when they grab a country, is to first occupy their television station.

Ivan helped me work out a plan as to how to spend my year. Since my main concern was documentary, I planned on spending four months with the Outside Broadcast Unit covering everything from a High Pontifical Mass at St. Patrick's Cathedral, through every conceivable sport, to location talk shows. Although not primarily interested in drama and light entertainment, but fascinated by their use of the most complicated television techniques, I allotted two months to each of them. Since news programs at that time seemed more like radio enhanced by the odd film story, and film being a medium I knew, two weeks seemed sufficient for that.

NBC found us a place to live — a two-bedroom, furnished flat in a reasonably fine-looking apartment building with doorman to match on East 84th Street between Park Avenue and Third. By subway it was an easy run to the RCA building, with good shopping just around the corner and, best of all for Betty and the kids, Central Park and the Metropolitan Museum of Art was a two-minute walk away.

Trouble was, Betty and the two girls were going to arrive three days before we could occupy the flat. The Algonquin couldn't take us because they didn't have a crib or means for heating milk for our Jennifer, and so we got a suite in the Essex House, which we hated. No porter, waiter or bellboy would do a damn thing unless he was

Sydney and Deirdre, and Betty and Jennifer in Central Park, New York City, c.1949.

heavily tipped; my Canadian Government money was zilch for that kind of thing. It was said that for a long time during the war, the first two letters of the big electric sign on the roof of the place were broken so that the hotel's name read "Sex House."

Our flat was okay in many respects, but the pretensions of the building were a pain in the ass. The elevator man insisted that Betty use the back elevator when taking our laundry, which included Jennifer's diapers, out to be washed. We were always fearful that our two rambunctious daughters would break things, which indeed, they often did. There was also the perpetual fear that they would fall out of our ninth-floor windows.

The place was also lousy for us — this elegant building was cockroach-ridden. When we moved in, the flat was clean enough, but the well-equipped kitchen and the floorboards seemed dirty and somewhat sticky. In the humid heat of July, Betty and I stripped and scrubbed all the wood surfaces. To our horror, we were immediately inundated with hundreds of cockroaches. The sticky stuff on the woodwork was not grease — it was stuff to keep the creepy things out. All my, and my family's, love for Archy of the musical, *Archy and Mehitabel*, will never mitigate my aversion to cockroaches.

That year I was not the most ideal husband or father. How Betty took it I shall never know. I'd leave her and the children between eight and nine-thirty in the morning and not return until late in the evening, after the show I had been working on had been aired live. So obsessed was I by what I was experiencing that I'd often work seven days a week. Evenings were rarely free. She saw all the shows I worked on and no matter how late my return, there she was, eager to listen to what I had done and mention what she thought of the show. Sometimes the children watched with her.

One big remote show I worked on was the celebration of the UN's *Declaration of Human Rights Day* in Carnegie Hall. On it was Leonard Bernstein, who conducted the Philadelphia Symphony Orchestra; Laurence Olivier, who read the Declaration in his most declamatory fashion; and Eleanor Roosevelt and the President of the Philippines (head of the UN's Security Council that year), who both gave speeches.

As a production assistant on the show my job was very simple. I sat in the very first row of the auditorium and when someone — Olivier, say — would approach the centre of the stage to speak I would leave my seat, step forward and onto a box, reach up and adjust the height of the microphone to suit him. Eleanor Roosevelt, being tall, was followed by the short president of the Philippines. Betty told me that when she and the girls were watching the show and when I reached up to lower the microphone for the president of the Philippines she said, "Look, girls. There's Daddy!" Deirdre, who was aged three said, "Why is he speaking so funny, Mummy?" Even my own kids find me looking like the perpetual outsider, as others do!

My most memorable moments were working with Bill Garden and his directors on shows remote from the studios. I covered their main staple of work, which was sports — the Big Ten eastern football games, boxing at Madison Square Garden, stock car racing, and flat and trotting races. Oddly enough, no baseball. In New York, I found working with sports people a welcome relief from the pretensions and insecurities of creative types. They may not have been cultural heavyweights, but they were a breath of fresh air. No ideological confusions. Just making the sporting event clearly visible was their aim, and they did. They had an uncomplicated, lusty sense of humour, which I discovered I could share. Recollection of the trots at the Roosevelt Raceways still makes me giggle. Right behind our cameras was a radio team covering the races whose announcer had an impediment of speech so that all his R's came out as W's. Each Tuesday evening, the camera crew and I would wait with bated breath to break up with laughter as we'd hear his, "Good evenin' ladies and gen'emen. Welcome to Woosevelt Waceways, as we bwing you the twats."

Even when I spent my months in other program departments such as drama or variety, I'd get myself assigned to one of Bill Garden's shows, so much did I enjoy being with his gang. It was they who introduced me to the standard macho drink: a shot glass of whiskey followed immediately by a swig of beer. These boilermakers were consumed before and after matches in bars I'd never have the courage to enter by myself. The conversation was full of esoteric talk by boxing handlers, managers, last year's white hope, jockeys, racetrack touts and plenty of sports writers betting their reputations on who was going to win this or that. After I assisted on my first *The Gillette Cavalcade of Sports*[36] at Madison Square Garden, I kept coming back Friday after Friday night for the whole year. It wasn't the bloodletting that drew me — it was life. Raw life.

The man who did the boxing commentary was the popular sports writer Jimmy Powers, who was syndicated in over 160 newspapers. He was a real pro and a gent to boot. Before the telecast he, with me on his heels, would go down into the concrete bowels of the Garden

---

36 *The Gillette Cavalcade of Sports* was broadcast live from Madison Square Garden from 1948 to 1960 — the longest-running boxing program on television.

and visit the main contenders in their dressing rooms, wish them luck and get a few lines for his next day's newspaper column. He'd do the same after the show. What a contrast it was seeing the winner and then the loser after the fight. In the corridor outside the winner's dressing room police would be keeping at bay dozens of well wishers. Powers was, of course, immediately recognized and so we'd push through the crowd and enter. Inside the sweat-stench filled room, a bedlam of noise and handlers, managers and reporters surrounded the dazed, glazed, battered winner, who was naked but for a jockstrap, having his back slapped, being congratulated by his joyous owner to the popping flashbulbs of the photographers.

It was a totally different scene visiting the loser, which Powers scrupulously did. Outside the room there were no well wishers, just a solitary, bored cop. Inside, equally smelly, the only sound was that of a manager commiserating or bawling the shit out of his punch-drunk, swollen-faced boxer. Really sad. It always surprised me to see these boxers looking so runty in their dressing rooms when they appeared to be heroic giants in the ring.

My job was simple. I'd sit alongside Jimmy Powers up in the special announcer's booth, high under the roof of the Garden, with a clear view through the cigar smoke–laden air of the excited spectators and the dazzling white, but blood-splattered boxing ring. As well as cueing the commercials announcer, it was my job to hand Powers cue cards that contained snippets of information about each boxer, their style and boxing history. Before the match I'd be briefed by the program's boxing expert on what cards would be required. At a given punch, Jimmy would put his hand over his microphone and whisper to me "Bolo." I'd find him the appropriate card, and into the microphone I'd hear him say in his low-key style, "That Bolo punch, y'know, it was first used by Jake LaMotta in 1946, when he knocked out . . ." Soon I learned a lot about boxing, even the judge's point system. I got so good at the latter that I was able to often to win bets as to which boxer would win on points.

A million words have been written about Mrs. Eleanor Roosevelt, but none begin to approach my personal regard for her. It was with a feeling of intense respect, indeed affection, that I worked with her for fourteen weeks on a talks program.

Television program people wrack their brains trying to devise ways of doing a current affairs program that will be more than what the trade calls a "talking heads" show. Someone had devised a talks program that she agreed to do. It was called *Tea with Mrs. Roosevelt* and took place in a large suite in a major hotel, as if in her home. The format was simple: she would give tea to ten to fifteen guests, usually picked for their "name value" from politics, show business and the arts. During the half-hour, with most of the guests chatting quietly, she would, by prior arrangement, sit down with three of them and chat about a current news issue. Being unaccustomed to being a "performer," she was at first extremely nervous hosting such a show. It was my job to keep her happy and relaxed and to allay her worst fear, which was the timing of each "chat" so that the program came out to its exact time of 29:40 minutes.

To help her, I made up large cards, each one numbered from one to thirty. During the course of the show I would move from camera to camera as they were trained on her, crouching beneath the one with the red light on, revealing the cards that indicated the number of minutes to the end of the program. Only when I dropped the card reading *one* did she know she had sixty seconds to end the show and I was able to stop perspiring. By the third show, she was as professional as a Robert MacNeil, Robin Day and Dick Cavett. When the program was over, she gave me a beautiful book in which she wrote, "Dear Sydney — I simply could not have gone through what at first appeared to be a nightmare without you. Yours, with affection and gratitude, Eleanor Roosevelt." I shall never forget the privilege of having Mrs. Roosevelt needing me, the kid from 331 Queen Street!

So open were TV broadcasters in those days to new ideas that Bill Garden was assigned to do a series of shows that, on the face of it, seemed impossible. It was a series of six docudramas made with electronic cameras that were to go on the air live. In short, the audience would see it as it was being shot, mistakes and all. It started at 11 p.m. and finished at twelve and was called *New York at Midnight!* The stories were based on fact. Even though I was doing my stint in the variety department, I felt that as a documentary bloke, this was a chance I couldn't afford to pass up. I got myself assigned to it. Unless I am mistaken, it was probably the first electronic-camera docudrama to be shot live in the world.

The location of the dramas had to be limited because only one control truck was used and, as usual, it had to be within line-of-sight of the microwave receiver on top of the RCA building. The need for a variety of real settings to make the drama more interesting was a major problem. Each setting could be no farther from the control truck than the length of the three cameras' cables. One drama was ideal because it took place in the YMCA, which allowed settings in its lobby, swimming pool, gymnasium and a bedroom. Another drama took place in the vast garage of a taxi company with its ramps, offices, banks of dispatchers and so on.

But the very first drama was a killer.

The story was based on a Jewish lawyer who had given up his successful New York practice and died fighting in Israel in 1948. The drama itself dealt with the night he made up his mind to go to Israel. In the drama, he returns to the Lower East Side of New York, where he was born, to find out if his Jewish roots are strong enough to risk his career and fight once again, having already been a U.S. officer in WWII. At the play's conclusion he decides to fight. The settings required were an apartment, the street, a synagogue and a shop selling religious items, which was run by an old crony of his dead father.

It was amazing; but with the exception of the shop, the director and the technical director were able to find exactly what was wanted for settings at Rivington and Orchard Streets. Police were laid on to block off the street and extra crew were brought in to move the cameras quickly from setting to setting. In the case of the apartment, a camera had to be moved up and then down one flight of stairs and then into a synagogue — joining another camera already placed there to cover a religious service. The actors, having learned their stuff over a period of two weeks, turned up on the one day allotted to shoot the hour-long drama.

Two other production assistants and I turned up with the director and the technical crew at 8 a.m. to start one hellish, sixteen-hour day. (Union approval? I don't know.) As well as the control truck, there were trucks carrying all the lights for the interior settings and the street, and a huge truck carrying the electricity generator supplying the enormous amount of power required. The street lighting had to be a last-minute operation, since it didn't get dark until nine in the evening, and the trucks and camera cables had to be hidden from the cameras.

By 8 p.m. a stagger-through rehearsal was held, and, by God, just when we thought the show would come off all right, it began to rain! Raincoats had to be gotten in a hurry for the actors who would be seen on the street. Cameramen and crew also had to be kept dry. Worse was the real danger of electrocuting someone handling the lights — water gets into tiniest crevices, including the connectors of the camera cables. Camera after camera went down in the wet.

The problem was solved by the ingenuity of one of the technical crew. He twisted apart the two parts of the leaking cable, withdrew a condom from his wallet, snipped the end off, stretched it over one half of the connector, twisted in the second cable and stretched the remainder of the condom over it. Bob's Your Uncle, the joint was waterproof! After we ran out of "safes," I was the gofer who ran to the drugstore to buy more for the other duff connectors. At precisely 11 p.m., the drama hit the air and we were off!

It being a live show and, consequently, with me unable to see it as I worked, I have no means of judging it. Betty thought it good. Most of the critics gave it a rave review, praising its innovation. Many remarked that the rain gave the drama a reality that no slick studio production could ever equal. For me, it was the start of a conviction that there was no end to the creative possibilities of electronic cameras linked together to produce whatever man wanted to communicate.

My two months in variety were interesting and good for laughs. Not funny though, was seeing the on-camera, loveable, Milton Berle being most unlovable off-camera, going berserk during the one day's camera rehearsal for the *Texaco Hour*. Things were not going right and he screamed aloud, demanding that everyone not working on the show be thrown out of the studio, which included me. I hated him until it dawned on me that making people laugh every Wednesday night, thirty-nine times, year after year, was no laughing matter. Texaco sure got their money's worth out of him.

The best variety show was Max Liebman's *Your Show of Shows* on Saturday nights at 10 p.m. Again, there was only one studio day to put together a magical mix of one semi-classical, musical number such as "Un bel di vedremo," and a remarkable, modern dance pas de deux, both interspersing the inspired and highly creative antics of Sid Caesar, Imogene Coca and Carl Reiner. Liebman was a classy genius and despite the complexity of the shows, and because of the methodical planning they received, I never saw any emotional extremes displayed in rehearsal. I wish that I had paid some attention to the writers of the comedy skits — Woody Allen, Reiner and others.

In drama, I also paid no attention to the writers who were cutting their teeth writing landmark plays in Fred Coe's *NBC Philco Playhouse* — Paddy Chayefsky, Horton Foote and others who set a pace for character drama that dug deep into what makes ordinary American people tick and suited the limits of the smallish studio. The dialogue, except perhaps at the play's climax, was never explicit; the sparse words were only the tip of the iceberg, leaving the mass of meaning and emotion beneath them to be illuminated by the director and actors. And what actors they were — largely unknown then! Paul Newman, Eva Marie Saint, E.G. Marshall, Rod Steiger — the list is endless — all took your breath away. These were plays that you thought about for weeks after seeing them. The full import of what I too casually observed at rehearsals did not hit me for many years.

The subject matter of these Philco plays intrigued me. Unlike most of the plays we had done in the Theatre of Action, which

dealt with large social issues such as labour-management disputes or unemployment, these plays dealt with psychological problems — avarice, mother fixation, incompatibility — problems between one individual and another and never problems arising from social or environmental conditions. While this approach gave wonderful insights to individual behaviour, I gradually came to the irrevocable conclusion that the heavy hand of the sponsor was seen through their front men in the advertising agencies. It was safer, and to their advantage, to pay for plays dealing with notions related to Sigmund Freud than to those of Karl Marx or John Maynard Keynes.

The main drama series I was attached to was a weekly half-hour series called *The Chevrolet Tele-Theatre*. They were plays of a totally different order from Coe's. They were unabashedly escapist, which held the viewers' attention while they were watching, but were immediately forgotten when over. They couldn't be any competition for the commercials, which were, after all, what the sponsors wanted to be remembered! The major promotional gimmick was that the lead actor was a star from stage or screen. It was interesting being handmaiden to the likes of Rex Harrison, Basil Rathbone and Mercedes McCambridge, the latter having scored big in the recent hit film *All the King's Men*. Harrison was not too well known then to American audiences, but gave a memorable performance playing a mousey bank clerk who became a flamboyant rake after inheriting a magical cane.

Basil Rathbone was a delight to work with. I remember walking to a restaurant with him, and even though we were in a hurry, he most courteously signed an autograph book for an adoring fan who recognized him. He played the part of a German student who attempted to get the secret of winning at Monte Carlo by seducing the niece of an old Duchess in the play. The niece was played by Felicia Montealegre, a fine radio actress who later became Mrs. Leonard Bernstein. In the story, based on the famous Russian short story, "The Queen of Spades," for reasons of fate, luck or what have you, the student dies, just when he is about to win at Monte Carlo. The ad agency handling the show felt that to die of fate would not be understood by an American audience. A logical reason for his death had to be given.

A fine professional, Rathbone's approach to acting would make a Stanislavski-trained actor have the heebie-jeebies. At rehearsal, the director, Gary Simpson, raised the problem of the student's death and suggested to Rathbone that early in the play, they plant indications that the student had a problem with his heart — perhaps a heart attack would justify his later inexplicable death.

Basil Rathbone, quick to oblige, asked, "What kind of heart attack?" And before Gary could answer, he said, "I can do this," and twitched his left shoulder. "Or this," and grabbed his left arm with his right and grimaced. On number five, the attack had grown, ending with Basil violently spinning around and falling onto the rehearsal floor. Dusting himself off, as he got up he asked Gary, "Which do you want?" Gary solemnly replied, "Number three." From then on, right up to and including the on-air performance, Basil Rathbone consistently acted number three to perfection.

The fact that Basil Rathbone was well into his sixties at the time didn't seem to bother anyone. Wasn't he perhaps a bit too old to be playing a student? The things you gotta learn. It's the *star* system, dummy!

There were two directors who leap-frogged each other on this drama series, which went out live every Tuesday at 8 p.m. I saw the planning and organization that made the show work flawlessly week after week. The minutes and seconds each director had in the two weeks allotted to him were worked out to a T. I marvel, remembering this acute sense of time that live television demanded.

Once, after Gary had given his final notes to the actors after the dress rehearsal, Gary looked at the clock in the control-room and saw that we were five minutes to airtime. He said, "Mmn. Must go and take a crap," and left. As his production assistant, I became nervous as the minute hand began approaching zero hour. *Christ, one minute to go! Where is he?* I took his director's seat and used the microphone, getting the cameras into their opening positions and watching with dread the second hand inexorably moving to the top of the clock. *My God, am I going to have to start the show! Where is he?* With only four seconds to go, the control-room door opened, and as if he had all the time in the world, Gary ambled to the control desk, leaned into the microphone and said, "Take one" at precisely eight o'clock and sat down. He was a pro.

It's incredible to remember that television audiences in those days were able to choose each week from no fewer than four or five single, one-off, plays. A bonanza for drama-hungry audiences and for writers, directors and actors. I managed to see some of them at work. Many years later in England, Harry Saltzman, founding father with Cubby Broccoli of the James Bond films, told me that not only was he Canadian-born but that we had actually met when he was a director on NBC's *Robert Montgomery Presents*. He'd sat in on a few of Worthington Miner's *Studio One* at CBC, which were much more slickly produced than *Philco*, but without the latter's gritty realism. Reginald Rose's *Twelve Angry Men* and plays by Gore Vidal and others made this one of the top series. *Kraft Television Theatre* at NBC, which catered frankly to an audience accustomed to soap opera–type drama, suddenly astonished everyone with *Patterns*, a hard-hitting, boardroom drama written by Rod Serling.

I managed to reacquaint myself with David Pressman, the brilliant young New Yorker who, eleven years earlier, had been resident director of Toronto's radical Theatre of Action. He was a director of *The Play's the Thing* series at CBS, which presented more challenging, off-beat plays than the others. It couldn't find a sponsor, though, and was dropped by CBS.

David, however, landed on his feet by being taken on as one of the two directors on a new series called *Treasury Men in Action*. At a $1,000 a week, David, for the first time in his life, was earning more than subsistence money. Just after he and his wife, Sasha, left their railway flat and bought a handsome apartment on Central Park West, David's contract was rescinded and he was dropped from the show. The shameful McCarthy witch-hunt was gaining momentum. David's name was mentioned in the scurrilous *Red Channels*[37] booklet, which

---

37 *Red Channels* was an anti-communist pamphlet that claimed to list the names of 151 actors, writers, musicians, broadcast journalists and others who were allegedly communists. It led to many of those cited being blacklisted.

purported to expose communist infiltrators in media. He was only one of hundreds of producers, writers, directors and actors who suddenly found themselves unhireable.

Canada did not escape that wave of hysteria. Even the NFB was caught in the undertow of the Gouzenko exposure of twenty-one Canadians charged with spying for Russia. The hounds were baying at its doors demanding the firing of forty suspected communists on staff.

CHAPTER THIRTEEN

TELEVISION, HERE I COME!

By the autumn of 1948, Betty and I with our two bairns were snugly happy in New York, notwithstanding the odd cockroach here and there.

She and I would go to the theatre, or on the rare days I would not work, we'd pile Deirdre and Jennifer into our tiny English A40 Austin car (the only one in the entire city, at which blasé New Yorkers would ooh! and ah! because it was so cu-ute!) and drive and drive. The great city had so much to offer us hungry Canadians — the Bronx Zoo, museums and galleries, the Queen Mary and other great ships, the car ferry to Staten Island and Coney Island — just for the mixed smells of sea air, hot dogs and mustard. The thought of it still makes my mouth water.

Our social life in New York compared to that in Ottawa was low-key, taking second place to my television work, which, being live, blocked most evenings. I did manage to look up Petroff, but we had grown too far apart and the old relationship could not be renewed.

Sydney and the Austin A40 outside the house in Manor Park, Ottawa, with Jennifer, c.1950.

He'd had an interesting war; as an artist he worked in Patton's headquarters, drawing maps for the General. He was now designing sets for television commercials.

Occasionally Betty and I dined with new NBC friends, mainly the Reiners. More rarely, ex-NFBers who were living there — Jane Marsh, Ted Scythes, Nick and Bunty Read (in the unhappy process of separating) and occasionally the Andersons, Bob cutting quite a swath with Irving Jacoby as they made some fine films on mental health. We enjoyed a few evenings with Boris Kaufman and his wife and even bumped into Helen van Dongen.

During the war years, Grierson gave refuge to many European filmmakers. Some he had extricated from Canadian internment camps — young Germans who had been students or were making films in England at the outbreak of war and sent to Canada by Churchill as potential saboteurs. Among these were George Brandt, Werner Schott and Ernst Bornemann who earlier, under the name of Cameron McCabe, had written the cult mystery thriller, *The Face on the Cutting-Room Floor*.

The two most outstanding professionals Grierson gave a home to were Joris Ivens and his cameraman, Johnny Fernhout. Ivens was the brilliant Dutch documentary director of *Zuiderzee, Heart of Spain* (with Ernest Hemingway) and *400 Million*. Betty and I got to know Ivens well, because she cut the negative of the exciting film he made for us on the Canadian Navy. The other was Boris Kaufman, famed French cameraman of, among his other films, Jean Vigo's *L'Atalante* and *Zero de Conduite*.

Ivens was not in New York, but his editor, Helen van Dongen, was. I bumped into her while she was editing John Flaherty's *Louisiana Story*, and, as is my unfortunate wont, I really put my foot into it. When she told me what she was editing, I exclaimed, "Terrific! I'm so glad you are editing it because I couldn't stand the editing of his last film, *The Plains*, with its tedious, sixty-four frame dissolves." Through thin lips, she spat out, "You didn't like it, eh? I edited it!"

I couldn't make amends, and beat a hasty retreat.

It was an honour when Boris Kaufman was assigned to me as cameraman just after he arrived in Canada. It was when I was as green as green could be, when I was making those three-minute news clips, but stuffed with my own ideas of what I wanted. I was working on a clip to support Canada's Community Chest, encouraging people to contribute money to the unfortunate. The night before the shoot, I was giving Boris my ideas about the style of camerawork I wanted as we walked along Montreal's St. Catherine Street. "At the beginning, Boris, when we see the poor in their slum background, the shooting should be crystal sharp with infinite focus. Then, when we see the people after they are helped, I would like the pictures to be soft, little depth of field, almost as if shot through a silk stocking. You know, like those romantic effects you've gotten in so many of your French films?"

He looked at me in gratitude with his sad Russian eyes, and with his poor English, heavily larded with French and Russian accents said, "Zidney, you are ze first Canadien who treat me like ze art-eest I am. All ze udders, all zey want is quvick shootink. And, ze camera zey give me! An Eyemo! You know wat I do wis ze Eyemo in France? I tell you." Boris, one arm on my shoulder, the other free to punctuate his words, continued: "Vigo. He tell me he want image with girl as she kill herself jumpink off cliff. I take Eyemo to edge cliff, wind it, press button and throw it over. I go down to bottom. Ze camera, she is broken open, ze film no good, exposed. Again I go to top of cliff, I say to assistant, 'Gimme anozzer Eyemo,' wind it up, press button and throw it. Zis time, ze camera, she no break, pas? Vigo, he like shot, like from girl's eye. Zat is wat your Film Board Eyemo iz good for!" A truly lovely man.

When he first came to New York after the war, it's hard to believe but he had difficulty getting into the Cinematographers Union. Elia Kazan got him to shoot his *On the Waterfront*, which won six Academy Awards. It pleased Betty and me to see Boris receiving his Oscar for cinematography.

In response to my reports on my TV activities and letters to friends in Ottawa, disquieting news came. The Film Board was being accused by some press in the House of Commons of being profligate with money, inefficiency and worse — that it was a hotbed of socialists and communists. The *Financial Post* devoted several full pages to attacking the Board.

One day, a letter came from our personnel department asking me to fill out an enclosed form, which all members of the staff were asked to complete and return immediately to Ottawa. It was a security clearance form from the Royal Canadian Mounted Police Subversion Division. The form didn't ask for much: they only wanted to know where I, my wife, my mother, my father and *all* blood relatives lived for the previous ten years, our places of birth and answers to a host of similar questions!

Well, I sweated plenty filling out that damn form. To say that I was worried sick is an understatement. I was sure that my adolescent years of communist involvement would come back to haunt me, that Hollywood's Russian Consulate business would kill me dead.[38] With leaden heart

---

38 One of the astonishing things about Newman's connections with communists and fellow travellers in the 1930s is it never came up when he was vetted in the 1950s, nor when he was even further vetted when he came to work for the CRTC in 1970 and then became Government Film Commissioner at the National Film Board in 1971.

I sent it off to Ottawa and threw myself even more vigorously into experiencing television to escape thinking of the impending axe that would fall. The news from Ottawa became increasingly bad. I felt I should be back there, but a part of me was glad to be far from it.

Then Betty and I heard the most incredible news of all. In the *Ottawa Gazette*, we found out that a shocked Ross McLean, the boss whom we loved, had been fired. The new Government Film Commissioner would take up his post in a month's time. His name was Arthur W. Irwin, editor of *Maclean's* magazine. Why him? He was a journalist, not a filmmaker. Poor Ross! What the hell happened?

I eventually pieced together the whole gory story. Apparently, the government minister to whom Ross McLean reported had asked Ross to fire forty members of the staff who were cited by the RCMP as endangering the security of Canada. Ross, flatly or not, refused. Only after he had personally seen and judged the evidence would he remove anyone he thought a danger to Canada's security.[39] This rank insubordination was further exacerbated by the fact that Ross had earlier, against the wishes of his Minister, publicly attacked a claim made in favour of the Canadian Broadcasting Corporation running television in Canada; he felt that, as a visual medium, the NFB should run television, not the radio-oriented CBC.

---

39 Newman doesn't possess a complete picture of the politics going on at the time. There were other contributing factors to McLean's removal. While the minister responsible for the NFB, Brooke Claxton (who served as minister of national health and welfare) actually supported Ross McLean becoming permanent government film commissioner, Claxton's predecessor in the portfolio, James Joseph McCann, despised John Grierson and felt McLean was tainted by his connection to Grierson. This was a view shared by Prime Minister Louis St. Laurent, who believed Grierson to be a communist sympathizer and felt the NFB was a communist nest. (Most in the prime minister's office felt Grierson had been merely indiscreet and careless.) Making matters worse, Ross McLean was not highly regarded for his leadership or organizational skills. It was determined the solution was to completely reorganize the Film Board. A more detailed assessment of the skulduggery going on at the time can be found in Gary Evans's *In The National Interest: A Chronicle of the National Film Board of Canada from 1949 to 1989*.

We learned that in the month between Ross's firing and the arrival of Arthur Irwin, my fellow Film Boarders were in a state of pandemonium. Ralph Foster, the deputy film commissioner who was equally loved by us, resigned in protest. Allan Field, the first director in the NFB newsreel unit, spearheaded a small group who wanted the staff itself to root out the communists as a means of proving the Board's loyalty to the government. Shades of McCarthy! Friends became enemies. And who, everybody wondered, were the forty on the secret list? Nobody knew. Perhaps I was one of them!

To show its affection, the staff threw a mammoth going-away party for Ross and Ralph that was talked about for years. Betty and I could not attend, but we contributed money for it and for gifts. The size of the gifts, enormous even by today's standards, were evidence of our feelings. Ralph Foster was given a $1,200 hi-fi ring (a high-fidelity speaker), and for Ross McLean, who had already been grabbed by UNESCO as its head of film, the staff's gift of a motor car was waiting for him when he arrived in Paris. We understood that it was a very emotional party, but I was not unhappy being away from Ottawa during those dreadful days.

About two months later, I received a phone call from Mr. Irwin's secretary, Reta Kilpatrick, to tell me that he was coming to New York to look over the NFB's distribution office and that he would like to meet me. Also, would I get tickets to T.S. Eliot's *The Cocktail Party* with its brilliant London cast and join him to see it?

We met very briefly in the Board's New York offices. A little taller than me, he had the well-scrubbed, pink look of a well-to-do Toronto businessman in his mid-forties. He seemed to approach me cautiously.

When I tried to find out his views about the Board, he fielded my questions, saying that it was too early for him to form any opinions. While he thought many of the films he had seen were good, he seemed more concerned about the NFB's film circulation. Idiot that I was, I blurted out that *distribution* was the film term, not *circulation*. I found it easy to like him when he smiled and excused himself, saying that he had a lot to learn.

Trying to warm him up further, I told him of my connection

with print and that years earlier I had done some caricatures for Floyd Chalmers, the editor of the *Financial Post*, a sister publication owned by *Maclean's* whom I figured Irwin knew. Chalmers was now chairman of the *Maclean's* board. Feeling on safer ground, he talked a bit about his intentions as editor of *Maclean's* magazine, explaining that we Canadians, as northern North Americans, were different from our neighbours to the south. I liked that, and said so. When I began to enthuse about television he apologized that he had to go to another appointment. We agreed to meet in the lobby prior to seeing *The Cocktail Party*, and I looked forward to having a relaxed drink with him after the play.

Before curtain time, I nervously waited for him to turn up. He didn't. I left his ticket at the box office, entered the theatre and began to watch the play. About twenty minutes after the curtain had risen, he quietly took his seat next to mine, murmuring an apology for being late. Whether it was that he didn't like the play, or me, during the act break he regretted that he had to meet someone, thanked me for getting the tickets and left.

Disturbed as hell, I returned to my seat and found the play totally incomprehensible. That I was able to place my overcoat on his empty seat was no consolation. It was a totally disappointing evening, and I did not see him again in New York.

About a month later he phoned me from Ottawa; he had decided on a reorganization. In future there would be five divisions, each under a director. On my return from New York, he wanted me to continue doing the good work he understood I had been doing as executive producer of the theatrical films unit. It concerned him, and he wanted an assurance that I would be happy to work under the man he had chosen as director of production — Don Mulholland!

Holy cats! The one guy in my unit I was not close to; the guy who temporarily filled my shoes while I was chasing rainbows in New York City. Damn Ross and Ralph for choosing Don. What could I do? Should I say I'd call him back? No, I couldn't do that. So out it came: "Of course, Mr. Irwin, as you wish. I'll be (gulp) happy to work under Don Mullholland."

It was now March 1949, and my year of New York adventure would end in about three months' time. While I had been sending back reports on the different aspects of television, I set about writing a definitive report summing up my recommendations for its exploitation to ensure the Film Board's place in television, which I understood would start in Canada soon. (It started in 1952.)

In my somewhat illiterate fashion, I stated that television had a powerful capacity to disseminate information and ideas very easily. Its two main advantages were that it was an ideal method for reaching mass audiences and that film, as a one-camera production method, was inefficient compared to television's multi-camera techniques. The latter, while somewhat crude at present, was bound to improve, as would the technique of kinescope recording on the film of electronically recorded images (no video tape existed then) for use with specialized small audiences, such as classrooms. I sent the report off to Ottawa.

While continuing my work on television shows and writing the report, I thought long and hard; why, of the executive producers Irwin had met, had he picked Mulholland as chief of production?

It was only a guess, but I was sure that the one person the staff would have picked, Jim Beveridge, would be in Irwin's eyes too fanciful — an artsy, idealistic dreamer; Don Fraser would be too gentle; Mike Spencer, earnest but uncreative; Tom Daly, nice but square; and Guy Glover... Irwin, for political reasons, would be fearful of Guy's sexual orientation. I reasoned that Irwin, as a sophisticated Torontonian, would feel completely at home with Don's populist approach in his films — his mixture of Board loyalty leavened by a non-precious, ad-agency vernacular and martini-drinking manner.

I couldn't help thinking that, had I been in Ottawa, Irwin might have picked me. I'm efficient and make popular films; I am definitely not precious in my approach to documentary. *To hell with it*, I thought, *I've still got good films to make*! I was a good boss to Don; he would be the same with me. As Pierre Trudeau said years later, "Life will enfold, as it will."

In May, I received permission to make a short trip to Ottawa to prepare for our return and see the house that Betty and I bought in Manor Park, in which we had never yet lived.

I found that our tenants had done wonders with it. The farmer had planted clover, then dug it in, and the mud that had surrounded the house now had the greenest, healthiest grass of any lawn in the housing development.

At the Board, things were different. The place, while busy, had a kind of wait-and-see atmosphere. Irwin was rarely seen in the John Street headquarters, having taken an office in downtown Ottawa. Friends told me that he might not be too bad a commissioner — he had stemmed the government's demand to fire the forty so-called communists by removing three members of the staff. Jim Beveridge was gone, having asked for, and gotten, the post as head of the NFB office in England. There was the odd wisecrack made about Don, but he was gradually being accepted. When we met, it was with a wary friendliness. Nick Balla was, I think, happily ready to step down as acting head of my unit.

To my surprise, Irwin invited me to have dinner with him at his apartment. He was a gracious host and had cooked the dinner himself. I learned that one of the reasons he had been attracted to the government's offer of the commissionership was that his wife had died the previous year, and change was just right for him. I learned too that he had a bad stomach, and he would only have a glass of white wine. It was touching to see him enviously watching me enjoy the peach melba, drowned in brandy, that he had made for me.

After dinner, we sat on the porch in the warm May air. He expressed his appreciation for my willingness to return to my old job, and thought my reports on television most valuable. So much so, that he had sent copies of them to Davidson Dunton, president of the CBC. He told me that the Board would not be involved in the running of television, that it was the government's wish that it be in the hands of the CBC. I jumped up and told Irwin what I had learned about film and the BBC in England: when the Government's Crown Film Unit refused to give news footage to the BBC's burgeoning television service, the latter was forced to buy cameras and set up a film department of its own.

As a result, the BBC rarely ran Crown Unit films and were now even making their own films. The same might happen in Canada, which could mean the end of the NFB. Irwin murmured, "Interesting," but went on to say that a joint committee on television was being planned, made of senior CBC and NFB staff, and he knew that when I returned, I would be a valuable member of it.

When I got back to New York, I told Betty all the news about the house, the exit of Jim and Margaret Beveridge, that TV was a dead duck as far as the NFB was concerned and also, that I thought I might get to like Arthur Iwrin.

There were farewell parties for Betty and me, and we in turn made our goodbyes to Ivan and Peggy Reiner and David and Sasha Pressman. One of the gifts I received I value to this day: the NBC engineering department gave me an early Mark image orthicon tube, mounted on a walnut stand.

Getting our furnished flat ready for the next owners was an expensive chore, making good the evidence of the vigorous behaviour of our growing girls. Jennifer, at twenty-one months, was fully mobile, while Deirdre, now four, was chattering non-stop in a mixture of a New York accent and Betty's English one. Once, when having a bath, I heard her complain, "Mummy, the bahth waddeh is too hot!" We said farewell to our cockroaches and flew home to Ottawa. I didn't know it, but that was the year that was to change my life.

Within days I was back into the familiar routine of work, especially with the backing of Nick Balla. The theatre bookings of the *Canada Carries On* and *Eye Witness* series had continued to grow during my absence. However, we were still well under Stuart Legg's wartime high of *CCO*'s 900 theatre bookings a month. Even if it killed me, I not only intended to beat his record, but aimed to do so without the aid of the flash and boom of screaming spitfires and exploding shells that sparked up so many of the wartime films. My experience in New York observing the ad agency and TV programmer's reverence for numbers — that is, audiences — sharpened my sense of the need to win the viewers over. (The advertising people still had much to learn regarding how to talk down to television audiences!)

I set out to make fast, exciting films, emphasizing people, that would engage the audience's imaginations by showing them little-known aspects of their own country. By 1951, we exceeded the magical number of 900. In fact, that year our theatrical bookings were just short of 16,000 for *Canada Carries On*, *Eye Witness* and Tom Daly's *Royal Journey*, which covered the Canadian visit of Princess Elizabeth and the Duke of Edinburgh.

Television was still the bee in my bonnet, while to most of my colleagues it was as remote as the thought of man being able to walk on the moon. A joint CBC–NFB committee on television, of which I was a member, was set up and a bit of a farce. The CBC was naïve about what lay ahead of them in terms of programs and what they would cost. Funnily they were worried like mad about keeping at bay what they thought was a voracious NFB, which generally, couldn't care less.

The meetings were alternately chaired by Ernie Bushnell, CBC's general manager, and Arthur Irwin, film commissioner. Members included Don Mullholland as director of production and Gerry Graham as the NFB's director of technical services. The only two on the committee who could claim any expertise were myself and Alphonse Ouimet, the brilliant engineering head of the CBC and chief architect of the Television Service.

The CBC was planning to hit the air in the autumn of 1952.

I went to Don Mulholland with an idea that would make the CBC depend on the NFB for all their film-made programs. I told him that, should the CBC ever buy one film camera, our Film Board would become just another supplier, and I repeated what I had said months earlier to Irwin about the British experience of the Crown Film Unit's refusal to have anything to do with the BBC's upstart medium.

We must learn from that, I said, because today, the BBC had a vast and creative film department, which had grown from the first cameras and staff initially only used for the purpose of news coverage.

To circumvent this happening, the NFB should submit a plan

with costs to the CBC, in which we would provide them with news stories from across Canada. Further, I explained, we would be able to make double use of the news stories we were already placing in the American weekly cinema newsreels. Our contacts with the U.S. and UK reels would also enable us to secure some of their international stories for our newsreel for the CBC. Mulholland saw the sense of this and agreed that since covering news was a part of my responsibilities, I should draw up such a plan.

After endless weeks of figuring, consultations with my staff and some discreet phone calls to New York, I arrived at a scheme in which we would provide five, ten-minute daily newsreels a week of Canadian and world coverage to the CBC. The trouble was I thought the cost I had arrived at might be regarded as being too high — $2,200 per ten-minute newscast. After some discussion with Don, I got him to agree that this was so vitally important to us that we deduct from the price the money we were already spending on news — it was all public funds anyway. And so the proposal, agreed to by Irwin, went to the CBC; each reel would cost them only $1,500 — a rock-bottom price they would be unable to refuse.

Or so I thought.

At the next CBC–NFB joint meeting on television I waited for their reaction to what I thought was a brilliant and economical solution for the CBC but also for the future of the Film Board. They turned it down. Ernie Bushnell explained that it was too expensive. "You see," he explained, "we are planning on spending in television an average of $400 per hour on programs."

I was flabbergasted and blurted out, "You'll never be able to hold to that, Ernie. Not for news coverage all across Canada!" My mind full of what I had learned in New York, I added, "That might cover a cheap outside broadcast, but it won't come anywhere near the cost of news, variety or drama." *Oh hell*, I thought, *this is a farce comedy! They haven't a clue!*

It seems to me today that the CBC brass did have a clue. They were not going to share their responsibilities with anyone. Especially not with a sister government body, the NFB.

During this period my relations with Mulholland were going from neutral to bad. Basically my relations with a boss only work if he gives me a brief as to what is wanted and then leaves me alone to execute the job. I accept interference or more specific detailed instruction only if I feel he has demonstrated superior judgement, taste and experience to mine. While amiable enough, and excellent in practical administrative matters, in no way did I feel that Don's creative abilities matched mine. Our relations became a minefield, with me treading more warily than he.

As soon as I returned to work from New York, the question arose about the thorny question of his requirement that he vet my scripts and commentaries. I had recorded my first *CCO* without showing him my director's commentary, which I had approved. After the film was completed, he called me into his office and told me that in future I must get his approval before the final re-recording took place. Not expecting any difficulties, I said, "Don, isn't that a needless duplication?"

"It might be," he replied, "but that is the way it must be."

I, very reasonably, replied, "Why must it be? If I were new to film, or as a new Film Boarder, I could understand."

He was intractable.

I blew my top. "F'r Chris' sake, I've had ten times more experience than you and you know it. Now leave me be!"

"Sorry, Sydney," he replied, "but that's the way Mr. Irwin wants it. I'm responsible."

I jumped in. "That I understand. But, you won't make an exception with me?"

"I can't. I'm responsible," he replied.

Furious, I hissed at him, "Listen, you sonofabitch, cast your mind back to when I became your boss and you went into an emotional tirade about not taking orders from anyone. I too had my instructions from the commissioner, do you remember? You were so beside yourself and what did I do? I let you go your own way. Ross McLean, I made him understand. You bloody well can do the same with Irwin!"

It was no dice. He was immovable, the silly bugger. I'll never be able to understand such a mind. After that, I did show him all the commentaries and, of course, paid no attention whatsoever to his comments.

One of my directors in the *CCO* unit, Roger Blais, came to me with what I thought a damn good idea. It was to make a film about Canada's official carillonneur, who sat up high in the Parliament Tower and rang out his clanging bells. Roger's script was, as most of our scripts were in those days, hardly more than a bunch of notes, but seeing the glint in his eye, I knew that we had a winner in that idea.

The script went to Mulholland. He called me in and said that the ending was no good. This led to words, which led to his forbidding me to proceed until he had approved the script. I tore the script out of his hand with a "Fuck you, Mulholland. Just you try to stop me!" I can't remember whether or not I slammed the door as I left his office.

Should I appeal to the commissioner? I wondered. No, I wouldn't. This was between Donald and me. I gave in to him once, and if he had any good sense on his part he'll give in to me. Eternal optimist, that's me.

I instructed Roger to go ahead with the film knowing that if I was wrong about Don, this was my chance to get Irwin to free me from Mulholland's idiotic use of his powers — that is, if the film was a good one, and if, a very large if, Mulholland didn't use those same powers to prevent me from assigning cameramen and equipment, which he could do.

He didn't.

When shooting started, I noticed that Don's administrative assistant, Desmond Dew, would sidle into the darkened screening room when Roger's rushes were being run. What the hell! I then instructed that no outsiders be allowed to see the rushes. The locked door of the screening room didn't stop Don. Often, I could see Desmond's nose pressed against one of the glass portholes of the projection room peering out at our rushes.

Nick Balla did a beautiful job editing the film. Eldon Rathburne wrote some great music and used the newly formed Ottawa Symphony Orchestra to accompany the carillonneur's playing. I got Lister Sinclair to write and speak a wittily dry and illuminating commentary. At the re-recording session, Roger, Nick and I, as well as Guy Glover who dropped in, felt that we had made a fine film. I couldn't lose.

Irwin rarely came from his downtown office to visit the production building on John Street. He had the irritating habit of very occasionally phoning senior production people at lunchtime, which, because of his rum stomach, we knew he spent contenting himself with a glass of milk in his office. With our stomachs rumbling with hunger, he'd keep us talking.

When *The Man in the Peace Tower* was in its final stage of editing, Irwin phoned me just as I was going to lunch. We chatted about this and that for about twenty minutes and then he asked how the Peace Tower film was progressing. Since the film did not appear as a working project in any of the schedules, I replied, "What film is that, Mr. Irwin?"

"You're making a film about the carillonneur, aren't you?" he asked.

I said, "There's no such film in the schedule. I don't know what you are referring to."

"Sydney," he said somewhat firmly, "if you were making a film about the man in the Peace Tower, how would it be coming along?"

With my stomach twisting in wild knots, I carefully said, "Well, if I were making such a film, it would be a humdinger!"

There must have been a twinkle in his eye as he solemnly said, "Thank you, Sydney. Enjoy your lunch." He hung up.

Although the test print was slightly defective it showed that we were right; it was a good film. While waiting for a new test print I got a call from Irwin's secretary that Mr. Irwin wanted to see the film that very morning and screen it for the members of his Board who were in Ottawa for their quarterly meeting!

"Reta!" I screamed. "Tell Mr. Irwin that the test print is no good. Have them come late this afternoon and I'll have a good one then."

Reta cut in, "You know Mr. Irwin. He wants it this morning — at twelve noon!"

"Reta, please . . ."

"At twelve noon, Sydney. He'll understand."

Hell, hell, hell.

At about 12:15 they arrived, Irwin friendly as he introduced me to the Board members I didn't know. Just before the lights in the screening room went down, Don Mulholland shuffled in, took a seat at the back and, as was our fashion, propped his legs over the seats in front of him. I signalled the projectionist to start and held my breath.

Holy of holies, even as the end titles appeared on the screen the members began to applaud this film. When the lights came on, Charles Band, Deputy Chairman (whom we all called Charlie "Rubber" Band because he was head of Goodyear Tires), jumped to his feet applauding and said, "By God, Newman, that's a damn fine film!" Others rose, praising its "capturing the essence of Canada" and "amalgam of Canada's cultural grandeur" and suchlike. Irwin beamed at me, and Don Mulholland, as he shuffled out of the theatre, nodded to me his approval.

That afternoon I sent a carefully composed memorandum to Irwin explaining my difficulties with Mulholland, which was why I had illegally, as it were, made the Peace Tower film without the latter's approval and I asked that he relieve me of Don's method of supervision. Within a day, Reta phoned saying that Mr. Irwin would like to give me lunch at Ottawa's exclusive Rideau Club, habitat of MPs, senior public servants and tycoons.

In going to that lunch I knew I was in a do-or-die situation. If Irwin would not agree to my request, I was prepared to leave the Film Board rather than work for a man whose ideological and creative notions I did not respect. What no one but Nick Balla and of course Betty knew, was that months before, the CBC, having been impressed by my report from New York on television's Outside Broadcast Unit, had interviewed me and offered me a contract to become its producer of outside broadcasts when television was to begin the following year, which I turned down.

Wearing my best bib and tucker, I entered the portals of that sacrosanct club. Irwin was most charming and plied me with drink as he sipped a sherry. During lunch, we talked about everything except what I wanted to talk about until we sat in the lounge having coffee.

Irwin told me he regarded me as the senior production executive he valued most, because I made documentary accessible to ordinary people. No one else had my touch, or something to that effect. My request, he went on, placed him in a most difficult position and he wanted to know how seriously I took the matter of Don.

I explained that I was deadly serious. I had proven my worth to the Board for over ten years; I loved making films and honoured the NFB's role in Canada. While I respected Don in many ways, I frankly could not work with any kind of zest under his kind of supervision. "Without zest, it is no job for me."

Irwin, surprised, looked at me and said, "You mean, because of this, you would leave?"

I took a deep breath and probably gulped. "Yes, as reluctant as I am to leave, I would. Yes."

Arthur Irwin sighed and said he would have to think about it and would get back to me in a few days. We parted, and I left feeling that I had made my case well and that Irwin was bound to get Don to let me go my own way.

Two weeks later, we had another lunch at the Rideau Club. Irwin repeated that I had posed him with a most difficult decision. He asked again if I was still intent upon leaving on the question of supervision. When I said I was, he told me that with a heavy heart he could not find a way of acceding to my request. It was just after Christmas 1951. It was agreed that I would leave on April 1. My birthday. Three months' notice.

My head whirling, I took a Rockcliffe streetcar to John Street, and not wishing to go inside, hopped into my A40 Austin and went tearing home to Betty in Manor Park to tell her all. Gone were the more than ten years' seniority; gone was the secure civil service pension. To boot, I could not have picked a worse time for this to happen: Betty was in her sixth month of pregnancy and here was I looking for a new job in a city 260 miles from our home in Ottawa. Was it vanity? Pride? Sheer bloody-mindedness that made me stand up and fight to be myself? Whatever went on inside my pinhead, the fates were driving me in a new direction.

That evening I sent a telegram to CBC television in Toronto: IF STILL OPEN HAPPY ACCEPT OUTSIDE BROADCAST JOB OFFER STOP READY DISCUSS TERMS DATES TORONTOWISE. A phone call from Stuart Griffiths, designated program director, confirmed his pleasure at my acceptance and a date was set for our negotiations. These went well. I was wanted in Toronto by mid-February. Goodbye NFB, Grierson's child.

I left the Board with a reverence for the craft and the sheer act of doing. The shaping with eye, hand and mind, the tools of film and the skills of dozens of talented people. But more stuck on me than that. Craft is subservient to intention and content. A poet or a painter, as I learned at art school, may be concerned with pleasing only himself — valid enough for some. For me there had to be more. Thanks to John Grierson's influence, which somehow suited me, I pleased myself by pleasing my audience.

My wife once said to me that I was happier when concerned about the many and rarely so when concerned about the individual. That may be true. I have always been dogged by the nagging question of talking to people through media. It is no easy ride. For a start who are they, those people out there? An amorphous, great unwashed mass? Are they intelligent? To what extent are they educated? What do they know or care for the process of creating?

Good questions! But now, my intentions: Does one create to make a buck? Flatter a boss? A sponsor? Get rid of personal angst of which I undoubtedly have? Or, is it what is ingrained in me during my years at the National Film Board: to give people something valuable, of use in daily life, a revelation of an obvious but unrecognized truth directed to help people cope with a screwed up world? A final, thorny question is that of who I am — what authority do I have to determine what people need? Am I what is now too frequently denigrated — an elitist?

So what? How else shall I use my membership in the human race and the privilege of having skills and abilities? Shall I hide them?

These ruminations about the Grierson baggage I carried with me to television never entered my mind. They resided in the seat of my pants. Only hindsight tells me that from my experience in New York, television was bound to test me severely. Television — its many components creating the masses of mass media, flinging ideas, attitudes, facts, information and shit faster and further than everything else ever devised by man.

Television, here I come!

AMONG JARVIS STREET VIRGINS

After Toronto's gentry moved north to pleasant Rosedale, many of the handsome mansions they left became brothels. Some of those people surreptitiously returned with many others who could pay to get their jollies up. When I turned up in late February at the Canadian Broadcasting Corporation, the broad, leafy street was now denuded of its giant trees under which elegant people and whores had once strolled. Six lanes of cars sped up and down between the now tatty-looking mansions. If the street had seen better days, hope for the future sparkled like crystal among those starting television in English-speaking Canada.

The main spark, I found, was clearly Stuart Griffiths, its program director. Short, stocky and strong as an ox, he was no beauty. But when he passionately waxed rhapsodic about what television could do for Canada, and when I saw that he owned an original Henry Moore sculpture, I knew that he was positively beautiful and the man I would be happy working for.

To top it off, Stuart's wife, Alice, was a sweet woman and, like Betty, was born in China. They became good friends.

How it was that the CBC brass made what appeared at the time such a good appointment in Stuart is wrapped in mystery. It was rumoured that in that Canadian-style, Senator McCarthy era, Stuart was too dangerously left to remain in his previous senior position in the CBC's International Radio Service in Montreal. His previous boss, Ira Dilworth, a highly respected man, had just been moved to Toronto as Ontario Regional boss and it was figured that Dilworth could safely handle the radio-oriented but flamboyant Griffiths bringing television into program fruition.

To make doubly sure of keeping Griffiths in line, they appointed as director of television — his immediate superior — one helluva nice guy, Fergus Mutrie, who had been national supervisor of Radio Farm Programs. No two men could have been more different. Mutrie, a retiring, gentle, playing-it-by-the-book sort of guy, could probably more easily control a hurricane than he could Griffiths. Those of us on staff could not avoid sensing, if not seeing, the tension between the two.

Under Stuart as chief producer was the man of many talents — writer, performer and stage director Mavor Moore — who could so smoothly pour oil on the roughest staff waters when conflicts arose. He was the one person at the top who understood the idiocies and problems of creative types and he was a willing shoulder to cry on. It was more than his creative bent that drew me to him. His attractive wife, Dilly, was the kid sister of my Central Tech mate, Heckle Faessler. Mavor had been in the same year at Victoria College as my wife, Betty.

The rules for who could be hired for the Television Service were both wise and tough. Rule number one was that regardless of any seemingly useful talents or other qualifications, no one was to be older than thirty-five. Unlike the rest of CBC employees who were permanent staff, rule number two made it obligatory that all television personnel not in the executive class be on a contract that was negotiated annually, meaning no permanency and no pension.

The age limit was a good one, I thought, especially as I just got in by a whisker — I was thirty-five and the oldest in the first group of twenty starters. I didn't feel even vaguely older than the majority who were in their twenties — not even when I met the eternally twenty-three-year-old Norman Jewison. Besides, the young don't have to unlearn anything and catch on quick, as was well proven by those Stuart and Mavor chose.

The rule about non-permanency didn't bother those who had never had a nine-to-five job or who had just left university. I got over that news in about five minutes. It was cruel, though, to the many talented staff members who had brought kudos to CBC radio for many years for their many brilliantly produced radio programs. If attracted to television, as many were, they would be forced to give up within a year their staff seniority and security and accept the termination of their pension. No doubt the CBC brass adopted this policy in fear of losing valuable radio talent — at least until television as a popular, widespread service, was a certainty. Some thought, in those pioneering days, that television might not catch on.

One who should have, but didn't go into television at its very start due to this policy was the much loved and internationally respected Andrew Allan. His radio *Stage* series was unequalled in its talent. I, and thousands more, blocked off Sunday evenings to listen and talk for days about his shows. There were others who should have crossed over from the radio to the TV building on Jarvis Street.

Many in the first batch of twenty who did give up their seniority never lived to regret it. Peter MacDonald became CBC's national program director and went on to become a vice-president of the giant MCA as did Gunnar Rugheimer, who came from the CBC's International Radio Service. And how many young drama directors have not been helped by Robert Allen, Franz Kraemer, John Barnes — and too many others to mention? Among those who later exchanged their ears for square eyeballs was Arthur Hiller, who today is one of Hollywood's most sought-after feature film directors. *Love Story* and dozens of other films, including *The Americanization of Emily* starring James Garner and Julie Andrews in her first film, were his.

The CBC Brass allotted six months of training for us potential directors. Brought in from New York to teach us were Gilbert Seldes and Rudy Bretz. Seldes was the famed author of *The 7 Lively Arts* and as demonstrated in his book, he marvellously communicated, with wit and illustration, the creative and social possibilities inherent in this new medium. Even before the war had ended, the Columbia Broadcasting System had hired him and given him a small studio and crew to "find out what television was all about."

Bretz had written a book called *A Handbook of Television*, which quickly became dog-eared in our hands. A pleasant, studious man, he knew his video from electronics to lenses, and also knew tricks such as using mirrors for high-angle shots with a camera at ground level. Stuff I knew as a filmmaker about lenses and the area each focal length would cover quickly became known to others through his ingenious "Bretz Box" — a black box into which you peered through different sized square holes and saw the field a lens would cover.

I thought it very clever of Stuart and Mavor to have the trainee technical crew join the twenty members of the production gang for most lectures and practical exercises. Job functions were juggled so that cameramen were given the chance to direct and future directors could handle cameras, allowing each to experience the other's problems. As well, Stuart and Mavor were able to spot future directors among the cameramen. Wilf Fielding, Bill Bolt, and George Retzlaff were some who later crossed over to the production side. The six months passed all too rapidly; it was fun and all on a first-name basis.

While drama production was not of direct interest to me, actuality and documentary being more my thing, I did have ideas of my own about it. Most fascinating was hearing the talk from drama buffs Mavor Moore, Peter MacDonald and Bob Allen about the handling of actors and the experience of most of them being in steam — that is, old-fashioned sound radio.

My problem when I first arrived in Toronto was to find a temporary place to live and then a house to buy. At the same time, Betty, despite being in her seventh month of pregnancy, faced the nasty business of selling our Ottawa house.

Luckily for me, one of the trainee producers offered me room and board for a most modest sum. He was Gunnar Rugheimer, a Swede who became a lifelong friend. He had left his job as head of the TV news. Oh how we talked — marvellous and stimulating arguments about TV and about news gathering, about which I knew a fair amount. About film he knew virtually nothing but, without it appearing obvious, day after day he picked my brains dry.

His new wife, Gillian (pronounced with a hard G), was a superb cook and Gunnar introduced me to food and drink that was strange to me: aquavit, endless varieties of marinated fish and the Swedish mulled wine, glug. I lived and ate like a king.

And, happily, I found and bought a splendid three-bedroom house in the postwar-developed Governor's Bridge area for $16,500[40] — a lot of money for Betty and me. It became a cliffhanger situation, because I bought it with a completion date on April 3 before Betty had sold our Ottawa house. Worse still, I wondered if Betty would not only be able to sell it before that date, but if she would be able to arrive in time for the baby, due on April 10, to be born in a Toronto hospital.

It was sold in time all right, but for only $11,500, leaving me the problem of securing a third mortgage. Our plans were snagged when, probably due to the nerve-wracking business of selling and getting ready to move Betty gave birth to a baby girl on March 31.

Gunnar and Gillian insisted on a celebratory drink, and on the following morning I sped through slush and sleet, travelling the 260 miles to Ottawa in just under five hours. What a happy April Fool's Day: mother and baby were fine. Betty happily agreed that the newborn child be named Gillian, after Gunnar's wife.

Soon after my return to Toronto, the furniture arrived and I moved into 3 Nesbitt Drive. Over the next seven days, Peter McFarlane, Norman Jewison and their wives, along with the Rugheimers and Ross McLean (the Toronto Ross, not my ex-NFB boss) helped me get the house in order. Betty then turned up by sleeper train from Ottawa with the baby, her mother and our girls, Deirdre and Jennifer, and the Newman family was complete. I was finally ready to dive back into

---

40 Newman would keep that home, at 3 Nesbitt Drive, for the rest of his life, renting it out during his sojourns to Britain, Montreal and Ottawa.

Sydney Newman at the CBC.

work to make my third professional career, television, my own.

By the end of summer I was officially declared supervising producer of Outside Broadcasts — meaning that I was supervising myself since I was destined to direct all the programs. Since CBLT, the "flagship" station of CBC's English television network, was slated to open on September 8, it was decided to go on the air two weeks prior to the official opening, so that Toronto TV aerials would be turned to Canada's own transmitter and away from the seductive foreign stuff coming from Buffalo. The shows became my baby. I was to do as many programs as I could from the Canadian National Exhibition.

I was given assistants. Harvey Hart, a former ballroom dance instructor, I assigned to direct some of the shows; Harry Rasky I made my advance man to research upcoming ones; and Desmond Smith, who had just gotten off the boat from England, became my production secretary — the only male production secretary on staff.

My years at the Film Board as executive producer and especially the year in New York on remotes sure paid off. I organized matters so that my team and the technical crew produced two half-hour shows on each of fourteen days from different CNE locations. We were proud of what we thought of as a real nifty title for the series — *Ex Marks the Spot!* Still making amends for having dropped Lorne Greene from *Canada Carries On* years earlier, who better than he to open the first *Ex* show. So his manly mug was the first native face to grace English Canada's television. As was to be expected, he'd shame Richard Dimbleby.

The very first show of mine started with a clanger. The station identification slide reading CBLT went out nice and sharp, but upside down! Many thought it was my fault, but that wasn't so. In New York I had seen title cards, customarily shot on location, often tremble in the wind if not actually be blown away. I thought it would be better if they came from Jarvis Street, and that's where the mistake occurred. For years I ribbed Murray Chercover, because he was in charge of the facilities studio on that historic day.

I've often wondered, when in a whimsical frame of mind, if that upside-down announcement was an augury of the future — that the CBC might get things ass-backwards in its struggle with its competitors? Was the finger of fate pointing at Murray on that day knowing that he would eventually become president of the CTV Network, Canada's privately owned commercial competitor of the publicly owned CBC?

It's a thought for Pierre Juneau[41] to ponder but I don't expect that on that day it entered the mind of Davidson Dunton, CBC's first television president. Dunton had come down from Ottawa to see his staff produce the first show, and while I was directing it, to my utter amazement, I found him standing next to me in the sticky, hot, mobile control truck. Not knowing who he was, a crew member asked him to leave. Since he and I had shared the top floor at 30 Cooper Street in Ottawa, I screamed out, "No! For heaven's sake, that's our president!" Then, with a "Hi, Davy," I continued directing my first on-air program.

So, for two weeks we churned out program after program, each

---

41   Pierre Juneau was, at the time Newman wrote this autobiography, the president of the CBC. He was a longtime friend of Newman's.

one, except for the odd stinker, a little better than the last. We covered acts in the Grandstand, the guy who guesses your weight, the shills and hawkers on the midway, cattle judging and everything from industry displays to the RCMP Musical Ride. Harvey Hart was keen, humble and showed talent; Harry Rasky, infuriatingly oblivious to his own enthusiasm; and Desmond Smith found our Canadian ways and slang both confusing and ridiculous. To this day, Des cannot refrain from hooting with laughter when he recalls me shouting, "Okay Harvey, cue the elephant!"[42]

One show I will never forget. It was about the compound where lost children were kept until their distraught parents found them. My hope was that I would capture the happy moment when a lost child was reunited with his parents. To do this I had our cameras concealed, a pre-cinéma vérité coup, but alas, by the time our half-hour program was about finished, we had seen many a lost kid brought to the compound but not one single child found by a parent! I phoned Stuart Griffiths and asked him to allow me to extend the program until a reunion would take place. He gave his okay "but, only by fifteen minutes." We continued to shoot the kids playing, interviewing yet another child minder, and with only three minutes of my time left, over my earphones I heard one of the cameramen whisper, "Sydney, look at what's coming down the street!" Sure enough, on the control truck's monitor of Wilf's concealed camera, I could see in the distance coming toward us a policeman shepherding an agitated woman to the lost children's compound.

"Wilf, stay on them! Wow!" And then to another concealed

---

42   Newman is being slightly reticent and possibly self-censorious here. In fact, it was this situation that became the title of Knowlton Nash's 1996 chronicle of the early days of CBC television, *Cue the Elephant!* As Nash explains, "The title comes from the beginning of Canadian television, when neophyte CBC-TV producer Sydney Newman was urging an elephant to prance and wave its trunk in the opening scene of an experimental television show at the Canadian National Exhibition in Toronto. In spite of the anxious producer's pleas of 'Cue the elephant!' the reluctant pachyderm was camera shy; it refused to perform and instead had an elephantine bowel movement. As TV producers would have to do a million times in the years ahead, Newman improvised and got on with the show."

cameraman, "Camera three. There's a mother coming. Get your camera on the kids in the compound. Stay on the kid who'll spot the mother and follow him until they come together. Camera two, rack over to your 100 millimetre lens and get close to the kid camera three finds, and stay with him."

I intercut the mother and the kid recognizing each other and then flying to one another. Oh boy. This is great! Real Eisenstein stuff! Just when I thought they were going to embrace, she held off the kid and smacked him a good one right in the face! The ways of love, I thought, are sure mysterious. It was one of the finest endings of any program I ever produced.

The great day on which Canada's first English language station hit the air arrived on September 8, 1952. So significant was it in my mind that today I cannot remember a damn thing about my role in it. No regrets. I'd left that kind of po-faced chore I had to do a decade earlier. They tell me that I was the director of the official ceremonial part of the evening covering speeches by Prime Minister Louis St. Laurent (pre-recorded on film), CBC Chairman and President Davidson Dunton, Director-General of Programs Ernie Bushnell and CBLT's man in charge, Fergus Mutrie.

Others faced greater challenges that evening. My friend Rugheimer produced the first *Newsmagazine*, which in a recent nostalgic piece about that evening was described as "a selection of original and slightly used material." But, it also gave an update on that day's major news story, "the big bust-out from Don Jail of the notorious Boyd Gang," covered by Rasky, cameraman Stan Clinton and film editor, ex-NFB's Arla Saare under Gunnar's instruction. I understand that when Davy Dunton saw this he quipped, "The Boyd Gang, you see, we're dedicated to featuring Canadian talent." As an aside, Dunton, thanks to a benign government, was the last totally self-confident president of the CBC — good reason for the ebullience of the early television breed of creative types.

That evening audiences also saw Norman Campbell's *Let's See*, which promo'd upcoming programs; a weather report by the electric Percy Saltzman; and a poor man's *Howdy Doody* that was called

Uncle Chichimus. The main feature of the night was a mammoth thing called *Kaleidoscope*, bravely directed by Drew Crossan. It gave bits and pieces of what audiences could expect in the future from Canada's own television. It included Glenn Gould playing the piano; a funny skit from Ross McLean's upcoming and highly original series, *Stopwatch and Listen*; Jan Rubeš singing an aria from *Don Giovanni*; the incredibly funny Jane Mallett doing a comedy bit; Don Harron giving a dramatic reading; Wally Koster singing; and Dave Price interviewing the veteran sports writer Ted Reeve. There was also the first Leslie Bell Singers program with Howard Cable conducting the orchestra and a salute from CBFT Montreal, which had opened two days earlier, directed by Pierre Petel who, like myself, flew the NFB coop to exchange celluloid for electrons.

That week saw Don Hudson's *The Big Review* and I can remember only three things about that eminently successful variety show. Don, in his excitement, drove his floor manager, Norman Jewison, totally insane. It was written by Frank Peppiatt and John Aylesworth, two junior copywriters who later, as part of the Hugh Horler-MacLaren Advertising team, were to bug me good. Ah, but in the chorus line was the lissome, lovely Lorraine Thomson (today Mrs. Knowlton Nash).

We had a lot of drama too. Peter MacDonald directed the ninety-minuter *Call It a Day* with Toby Robins, Peggy Brown and Toby Tarnow. It was sponsored and went out as the *Ford TV Theatre*. Bob Allen began his half-hour, weekly *Stephen Leacock Sunshine Sketches*. Silvio Narizzano started *20,000 Leagues Under the Sea* and many other kinds of shows directed by Don Brown, Peter McFarlane, Franz Kraemer and Harvey Hart. I think I did some dumb thing I can't even remember called *In Town Tonight*.

Considering that the programs were produced live — that is, the audience saw them as they were actually being performed — and 90% of the directors and crews had not even seen a television camera eight months previously, the output was miraculously good, which was a testimonial to the quality of the leadership of Griffiths, Moore and Mutrie. The critics were mostly upbeat, one going so far as to boast that U.S. television had better look to its laurels — the Canadians were now in the game too! Ron Poulton, TV columnist from the *Toronto Evening Telegram*, warned the CBC of the dangers of too much culture.

In charge of all shows coming from locations away from the studios, I discovered soon enough that my main steady grind was not going to be what I knew and cared deeply about — documentary — but sporting events. To me, it was reducing my potential and felt like limiting Baryshnikov to Morris dancing.

Growing up as one of those kids who'd rather strike a lino-cut print than a home run, sports were never my bag either as spectator or perspiring participant. The fast action and danger of Grand Prix racing excited me as much as when Joe Louis knocked out Max Schmeling, but my interest of the latter had probably more to do with the Brown Bomber being a black man from neighbouring Detroit vanquishing Hitler's master-race darling. My stint in New York gave me some sense of boxing and allowed me to see my first football games, admiring its orchestrated team plays, but without a clue as to how it was done.

To my shame, equally ignorant was I about Canada's national sport, ice hockey. Hockey to me was like hearing symphonic music — sounds, not pictures. For year after year, millions of Canadians stayed home on Saturday nights, ears strained to their radios for *Hockey Night in Canada!* and the thrill of Foster Hewitt's "He shoots, he scor-r-es!" His emotionally charged comments electrified me as well, but did so as music only. The pictures it evoked in my mind were non-representational Kandinsky.

And that was about it as I faced the prospect of covering sports for the Canadian Broadcasting Corporation. Hockey was to start in October, and the other national mania in November — the Grey Cup game in which the best Western football team would play the best Eastern club in Toronto. Canadians might forgive television if its drama or variety shows were not up to scratch, but *hockey* . . . if that was badly done, the CBC would be slaughtered and I would be the first to go. How the hell did I get myself into this position?

Well, I had made successful films about cooking when I didn't know how to cook, on weather when I didn't know a mackerel sky from a cumulonimbus. I figured a bit of research plus a camera team that knew hockey well and a couple of dummy runs would be enough for me. How innocent I was! I did not figure on the weight, the big dough, the crushing importance the mere covering of a sport would have on its sponsor, Imperial Oil of Canada; the owners of the club; Maple Leaf Gardens; the advertising agency, MacLaren's, and Foster Hewitt himself, who was as nervous as a cat anticipating a bath.

I asked that I be allowed to shoot a trial hockey match so that I could figure out the best camera positions. It was granted. Trouble was, crowding me in the temporary control room were dozens of experts representing the principals, the senior CBC engineers, and my crew incessantly yakking into my earphones at me to do this and do that. The thoughtless bastards wouldn't give me a chance to think. I got my crew to shut up but the others . . . not a square eyeball among them, incapable of seeing the game in anything more than a series of long shots reducing the fastest game in the world into ants scurrying on white ice.

I prevented myself from blowing my stack out of fear that I might fail, and also fear of the sponsor, the ad agency and Conn Smythe, major owner of the team and Maple Leaf Gardens. No politician, not even the prime minister, had frightened me in the past. Here, in the crowded control room it was money, the smell of big bucks that choked me. No chance they were going to allow me to lose them one penny. *Get a hold of yourself, Newman!*

Two other factors complicated matters: the same cameras that shot the game had to be used for the commercials, which had to be done live, as well as what was called The Hot-Stove League, in which three sports commentators discussed the game between periods. One final complication was that Foster Hewitt had to be seen from time to time, but he refused to leave his tiny announcer's box way up in the rafters of the Gardens.[43]

---

43 Foster Hewitt had been doing play-by-plays for hockey games on radio since the 1920s. Newman elaborated in a 1983 interview with CKVU producer Emmanuelle Gattuso that the complications with Hewitt were more than logistical: "As a matter of fact, he had a big voice and he was quite a tiny person. He also had a weak chin and he was very nervous and I had to sort of massage his ego and help him in every way. He was worried and I think that's absolutely natural."

All was solved by building a studio for the live action and cameras up in the rafters about thirty feet away from Foster Hewitt, necessitating my having to use a 200mm telephoto lens to get shots of him.

With no replay facility as there is today, everything had to be done right the first time. Except for the fact that the shots of Foster did not do him justice, the coverage of the game and the program as a whole came off well.

I used camera one to follow the puck, including two or three players; a second covered the action on half the rink and general reaction shots of hockey fans; the third camera stayed on the goal or goalie, off-air, in the event the attacking team fired the puck at it. This camera was also used to get tight shots of a player going into and returning to the ice from the penalty box. Normally, a director tells the technical supervisor which camera to switch to. It was too slow for this fast game, so, after a lot of palaver between the engineering and program departments it was agreed that this "program" function would be performed by the switcher, subject to the producer overriding him. This was the beginning of George Retzlaff's program career, leading to his becoming supervising producer of sports years later.

One injunction laid down by the sponsor and the hockey league was that I was to avoid showing any fights on the rink or any player injured, which was deemed bad for the game.

I produced *Hockey Night in Canada* successfully for the whole of the first two seasons, but if you were to ask me today what icing the puck means, I wouldn't be able to tell you.

Televising the Grey Cup game from Varsity Stadium was a terrific experience and one of which I'm proud. To prepare myself I was allowed, without any advice from anyone, to shoot three high school rugby games prior to the big event. With my cameraman, who knew football inside and out, I prepared about five routines for the cameras that I would call out based on the advice given to me by an expert who I had the wit to have sitting next to me in the control truck. For example, I would be told on the third down, "He'll pass it to the right," and I'd tell the cameras, "Plan No. 5," and the cameramen would go into their planned moves. Not once during the game did those lovely guys lose the ball, even though I asked for a lot of close-ups.

As usual, the live commercials were a headache. They were done from a room inside the stadium, and so two of the four cameras that covered the game had to be trundled inside through the crowds, the path cleared by police.

Disaster struck just before the start of the third quarter, when the main transmitter blew. I continued to cover the game, expecting the fault to be remedied at any moment. We giggled hysterically, watching some poor maintenance engineer half a mile away through Wilf Fielding's biggest telephoto lens; he was wearily climbing slower and slower up the 525-foot transmission tower on Jarvis Street to fix the damn thing. He succeeded in time for the final quarter.

After the game was over, I remember standing up, pulling my shirt that was drenched with sweat from my back and being congratulated by all, including phone calls from Griffiths, Moore and — holy of holies — a call from the ad agency. When covering this game, my concentration was such that I concerned myself only with separate seconds of the action. I asked aloud when it was over, "Who won the game?" They all thought I was kidding.

It's hard to believe, but for the two years I was in charge of Remotes I organized and directed well over two hundred programs. Most of them were sports — a season of hockey games, a run of thirteen boxing shows, wrestling and so on. Once the creative part was over — working out the best camera positions and the best order in which they were to cover the sport — each program became for me a repetitive bore.

Definitely not a bore was the High Pontifical Mass I did from St. Michael's Cathedral in Toronto. Even though I had worked as a production assistant in New York when Cardinal Spellman celebrated Mass, I took no chances. I very carefully picked a staff consisting of practising Roman Catholics, and got terrific cooperation from the cardinal's office by having priests do a dummy run of the Mass for me and my crew. Permission was also granted for me to place a camera behind curtains to the side and in front of the cardinal, whose back was to the worshippers, so that television audiences saw a full frame close-up of him as he took the sacraments. Later, I was told that this had never before been seen.

When finished, I was outside the control truck, trying to relax after the nerve-wracking experience, when a young priest came up to me and asked that I come with him — Cardinal McGuigan wished to thank me personally. I turned to Betty McCarthy, my production secretary, and Wilfred Hayden, floor manager, and told them to come with me.

"I'm sorry," said the priest who overheard me, "His Eminence only asked for you."

"Oh, in that case," I replied, "please give His Eminence my appreciation for his kindness, but I regret I'll not be able to see him."

The priest looked at me, turned and began walking away, but then paused, turned back and said, "I think it will be all right for your assistants to come as well."

Inside, the cardinal was changing out of his vestments when we arrived. As he was thanking me, he held out his hand. As we shook hands he seemed to be pulling me toward him. I resisted and didn't understand until I introduced Betty and then Wilfred. When he held out his hand to them, they immediately dropped to one knee and kissed the ring on his finger. The things I learned on that day.

At one point, Cardinal McGuigan looked at Betty (twenty-three years old and pretty), and said "McCarthy? McCarthy. Do you come from Edmonton?" Bewildered, Betty nodded. The cardinal smiled, "You're Seamus McCarthy's daughter! I was a young priest in Edmonton; I baptized you." I learned on that day too, that it takes more than piety to be made a cardinal.

There were many delicious moments during those years. Once I did a program from the Second Mile Club, a social group for the elderly. After a scratch rehearsal and having a half hour before hitting the air, I said to Desmond Smith, my newly promoted floor manager, "C'mon, let's go grab a bite to eat." He replied that he couldn't do so right away, and agreed to meet me at the greasy spoon down the street as soon as he could.

Desmond didn't turn up at the restaurant. When I returned to the club, Des was white-faced. "Where were you?" he asked. "I looked everywhere and couldn't find the restaurant."

"Jeez," I answered, "the only greasy spoon on the block and you couldn't find it?"

"What? What'd you call it?" he asked.

"The greasy spoon!"

Des's shoulders sagged. "Oh, dear," said the new Canadian, fresh from England. "No wonder I couldn't find it. I was looking for a restaurant called the Grecian Spoon."

The only shows I did that came close to documentary were those in a series called *The Varsity Story*, later renamed *University Story*, when my shows alternated with those from Montreal's CBFT. Each one covered the activities of different university departments. Not only were they interesting challenges, but they were particularly memorable because of the extraordinary experience they provided, allowing me to work with Marshall McLuhan who, at that time, was relatively unknown. These projects were also how I first met William T. (Ted) Kotcheff, the noted Hollywood film director.[44]

Not having been to university, I was as ignorant of it as I was of hockey. Needing an assistant who knew the place, someone suggested I look over a young, recent university graduate, Ted Kotcheff, who had just joined the CBC as a stagehand. We met. He was a young, gangly, untidy looking kid with elbows poking through his sweaters, but he was an honours graduate and seemed intelligent. Like me, he was the son of European parents. He was keen to help, and I managed to get him released from stagehand duties for one day a week. And he worked hard, opening doors for me into the most interesting corners of the university. While his major studies were in English, his curiosity had led him into all sorts of lectures from anthropology to science.

Kotcheff was friendly with Ted Carpenter, who was a young anthropology lecturer and a member of the University of Toronto's

---

44 After a stellar career directing television for both the CBC and the BBC and then theatre, Kotcheff's film career would include films such as *The Apprenticeship of Duddy Kravitz*; the first Rambo movie, *First Blood*; *Weekend at Bernie's*; and *North Dallas Forty*. He was also, for a time, showrunner on *Law & Order: Special Victims Unit*. In 2017, his autobiography, *Director's Cut*, was published by ECW Press.

four-man Explorations Group, another one of member being Marshall McLuhan.

When I did a program with McLuhan on language, his narration was so dense and convoluted that to anyone with an IQ under 160 it must have been total gibberish. Even I, who researched him many times before I did the program, got only the barest glimmerings of what he was trying to elucidate. But he carried the program because he shocked and amused with unconscious, intense and almost humourless sincerity. Television fascinated him because of its unique means of delivering messages, information and underlying codes to people, and he was intrigued by how it would inevitably affect society. He felt it proved his theories in his recently published *The Mechanical Bride: Folklore of Industrial Man*.[45] He wondered if I would collaborate with him and the Explorations Group to produce a specially prepared television program designed to test people's capacity to remember information absorbed through different means — aurally, visually, through print and so on. The program sounded like a real dog as an audience winner, but with Grierson's talk of propaganda still alive in my mind, I quickly agreed. To work with this fascinating man and the other members of the Explorations Group he was a part of, would be a chance too good to miss.

The test they devised involved four groups of twenty second-year U of T students, separated from one another. One group would be seated in a studio seeing and hearing Ted Carpenter in front of them deliver a twenty-eight minute talk on the language used by an obscure Pacific tribe, the Trobrianders.[46] I would shoot this as a normal program as it was being broadcast, but with the cameras concealed

---

45 *The Mechanical Bride* was Marshall McLuhan's 1951 collection of essays on popular culture. It was one of the first works to suggest that "lower" forms of culture like newspapers, advertisements, even comic strips, were worthy of consideration. It did not sell well; in fact, most copies were sold by McLuhan himself, who bought 1,000 copies when it went out of print.

46 The Trobrianders were the people of the Trobriand Islands (today officially known as the Kiriwina Islands), an archipelago of coral atolls off the eastern coast of New Guinea.

from the students. I was asked to use only a medium shot of the lecturer showing only his head and arms. The other three groups were each in different rooms: one to see and hear the lecture on a television set, a second to hear it only on the radio and the third to get the lecture in print form to keep and read for the twenty-eight minutes of the program. No student in the four groups was allowed to make any notes. When the program was over, the printed lecture was taken from the fourth group and all eighty students were given an exam paper to test what they had remembered and learned from the lecture.

The audience at home watching the show was asked to participate by writing in for the exam paper and returning it completed. Nothing of statistical value emerged from this, but then, nothing of real value was expected. I thought it a good advertising gimmick, which it was.

In the following week in the program's regular slot, the members of the Explorations Group — McLuhan, Carpenter, Tom Easterbrook and D.C. Williams —revealed the results of the test. Even though they warned that their experiment was not to be taken as definitive, to everyone's surprise, scoring the highest marks were those who saw the lecture by television. This, they ventured, was because a person seeing it on the TV set received the most information — the words they heard were more memorable because they were reinforced by the fixed, medium shot of the facial expressions, hands and body movements of the lecturer. Those in the studio who also saw the lecturer, were perhaps distracted by the artificial environment and their eyes were freer to wander.

People in television were, of course, delighted at the results. In my mind's eye I could see Grierson chortling, "Boyoboy! Can you see an audience in a dark cinema with nothing to look at but that huge lit screen of talking pictures over Wagner's music? Goebbels and Hitler knew that and we'd better learn it fast."

In their handsome quarterly communications, the Group wrote an article on the experiment.[47] My heart swelled when they mentioned my name.

---

47 It appeared in the Explorations Group's magazine, *Explorations: Studies in Culture and Communication*, Issue 3 (August 1954).

CBC remote truck, c.1952 (Sydney is at the front left).

One university story I did is unforgettable, because it was such a disaster in the making and it was Ted Kotcheff who bore the major brunt.

The Banting and Best Institute was part of the University of Toronto and was world famous for its manufacture of insulin, discovered by the late Sir Frederick Banting and Dr. Charles H. Best, the Institute's director at the time of my visit. Scoping out the Institute as a possible university story, I discovered that they were intensely researching different forms of insulin and drugs for other illnesses. Yes, Dr. Best was only too happy to allow us to do a show about their work. Even though our cameras and lights might make a mess, I was not to worry — that was okay by him, he said. Little did he know! Nor did I, considering what happened.

I thought it would be most interesting for audiences to see how they tested the different forms of insulin and the effects of certain drugs on the heart. The plan was that Dr. Best would be followed on camera, explaining the experiments while also communicating valuable information about diabetes and the heart.

During the production of the live show I, of course, would be in the control truck, while five floors above me with our cameras and lighting men, floor manager Ted Kotcheff would ready the action and cue Dr. Best and the lab technicians. One of the insulin tests involved inoculating thirty mice, half of them with the proper drug and half of them with another. Twenty minutes later, if the fifteen with the other drug went into convulsions and died, the proper drug was considered a success. Another experiment was hoping to prove the effectiveness of a heart stimulant. This meant seeing a chicken's heart still pulsating after having been removed earlier (off-camera, of course) from the fowl. When the heart's beating began to weaken, a lab technician would bring it back to normal with the injection of the stimulant.

The program was to go on the air at 8 p.m. During the rehearsal, having worked out the order of the experiments in the program, we realized that the mice would have to be inoculated ten minutes before the program began if they were to convulse ten minutes into the program. For the same reason, the heart would have to be removed from the chicken two minutes before eight o'clock. We were now ready to do the show.

At precisely ten minutes to eight, through my microphone I instructed Ted, "Okay, inoculate mice." And from our live microphone above, I could hear Ted yell out, "Inoculate mice!" Then, just as precisely, at two minutes to eight, Ted heard me say, "Kill chicken," and I heard his response. My titles came upon the screen and we were off! Just as Dr. Best was getting into his stride, though, the phone rang in the truck. It was Stuart Griffiths. "You're off the air," he said. "Something wrong with our microwave receiver. We're filling with a film. I'll tell you when to start the program again."

Into my microphone, I said, "Ted, stop everything. Technical difficulties on Jarvis Street. Put them at ease and get ready to go again." A few minutes later, Ted whispered to me through my headset, "Jeez, Sydney, you should see the mice, they're convulsing like mad! Dr. Best doesn't look too happy either." Then the telephone rang.

It was Stuart. "Okay now, Sydney, we're going to hit your opening."

I screamed at him, "No, don't! Stu, don't. We're not ready. We gotta inoculate some mice and get a chicken killed."

"Are you crazy? Wha'd you mean, kill a——"

I cut him off and explained our situation. We agreed that the program would start again at 8:20. Into my mic, I said, "Ted, are the new batch of mice ready?"

"Yeah."

"Okay, inoculate!"

Then, eight minutes later: "Ted, kill chicken."

At 8:20, we were on the air, but when we got to the chicken's heart, the danged thing wasn't pulsating. It had died before it could be hypo'd into life, which stopped Dr. Best cold. I screamed at Ted through my mic, "Signal Best to keep talking. Keep him talking!" We saw Best's frozen face warm, and he began explaining the tricky nature of experiments.

Then the damned phone rang again.

"I'm sorry, Sydney, the stupid thing's gone again. I'm going to go on with our regular schedule. Can you wait — and when we're ready we'll kinescope you?"

"Yeah," I muttered, "if they've got enough chickens upstairs!" I hung up.

I explained the mess to Ted and told him to get ready to go again. Twenty minutes later, Ted came over my headset, whispering, "How much longer? The lab guys are beginning to foam at the mouth. Dr. Best looks ready to burst a blood vessel. I think you should come up and talk to them."

"No, Ted," I replied. "I can't. Stu may call. Besides, it's your job. You wanted to be in production, didn't you? Well, chum, you're in it now!" Poor guy. I didn't envy him. Days later, Ted asked me to never call him "chum" again.

It wasn't until 9:15 that I got the word from Stuart that they were finally ready for me. So, through his headset, Ted again heard, as cheerful as I was able to sound, "You ready to go, Ted? Okay, inoculate mice."

So, after forty-five dead mice, three dead chickens and many frayed tempers, the show was in the bag. When Ted and I screened the kinescope it didn't look too bad. When it was aired, people wondered why Dr. Best looked so wooden.[48]

There was another disaster, too, but of a different kind.

Stuart Griffiths bought the rights to televise the Canadian Opera Company's first-night performance of Puccini's *Madame Butterfly* live from the stage of the Royal Alexandra Theatre in Toronto. I had only seen about two operas in my life, and so I was delighted at the assignment. I managed to secure my crew for three days' rehearsal in the theatre. After many a fight with the otherwise benign management of the Royal Alex (to remove seats for the cameras), the fire inspector (for safety reasons) and Herman Geiger-Torel, the stage director (to increase the lighting necessary for our cameras), I felt supremely confident as curtain time approached. Over our audio speaker, I could hear the sound of instruments being tuned and the hum of excitement as the last people in the audience were finding their seats. In the control truck, we were tense but eager. And then the phone rang.

It was Stuart Griffiths. "Sydney, pack up! Get the cameras out of the theatre! We're not doing—" I started to argue with him, but he stopped me. Griffiths spat out, "I said we are not doing it. Get your gear and crew out of the theatre. Fast. Now move!"

"Why?!" I shouted, but he had hung up. I was livid with anger — all those fights for nothing, the sound and camera crew and I hot as pistols. We were raring to go, and now we had to quit! In the theatre, with 90% of the seats now filled, my cameramen had to cap their lenses. They slunk out, just as the curtain rose.

The next day, Stuart explained that Walter Murdoch, the president of the Canadian division of the American Federation of Musicians union, had, at the last minute, told him that he would pull his musicians out unless each of the eighty members of the orchestra received an additional $10 because they were going to play in the presence of a live

---

48 Newman would recount in interviews that Best didn't seem so bothered when he talked about the show later, saying, "I have plenty of rats."

TV audience. Another version I heard later, was that Griffiths knew of this days earlier, but because the show had been so well advertised, he thought Murdoch wouldn't dare pull his men out — and so had been bargaining right up to the point when he phoned me. I don't know which story is true but I suspect that it is the latter one.

Stuart was a gambler and I was feeling somewhat ungenerous, to put it mildly, about being the stake in his gamble. Just about everybody in show business knew that no employer of musicians ever won a fight with Murdoch. Even the serious professional musicians hated Murdoch, whose main support came from the bulk of union members who were referred to as "the Sunday cornet players." I knew this from my Film Board days. Why the hell didn't Stuart!

The incident was only one of many that thinned out my regard for him. Not only was he a gambler, he too often acted on a whim or a sudden stroke of inspiration, making a last-minute request. After a year and a half of doing remotes, I got fed up, being told on a Thursday morning to cover a Santa Claus parade on Saturday. After a year and a half, it was beyond me how Stuart could disregard the time needed to find out who and what was in the parade and when it would pass a given point *before* any outside broadcast was made. Worse still, I was the one who had to ask the engineering department to lay on police protection, ask for permission to block streets and park trucks, get a line-of-sight from location to receiving dish on Jarvis Street and get special telephone lines installed. Often, the engineers, in their anger, would shoot the messenger, who was me. And I don't like being disliked! Not for a thoughtless reason, anyway.

At about this time, not only was the thrill of being the chief cook and bottle washer of sports production and outside broadcasts wearing off, but I felt I was going to seed.

I was doing a run of thirteen weeks of boxing, and as usual, it was fun doing the first three shows, working out the best camera positions and shooting routines. For the fourth show to the end of the run it was a mechanical operation. The crew would arrive early and set up in their accustomed positions. Along with my wonderful production secretary, Robi Ivey, I would turn up at the arena in the late afternoon, check everything and then go for an Elizabeth Street smash-up Chinese feast with many a Manhattan cocktail. Somewhat thickheaded, I'd drive us back to the arena. Once, I was so dizzy with drink I couldn't concentrate on the video monitors. George Retzlaff carried the show. My slurred speech broke up the crew but for me it was no laughing matter. Professionally, I felt I was letting the team down; I was going to the dogs but good. At least I knew it.

And Betty knew it, too. Busy with our three girls, with Gillian approaching two and Deirdre and Jennifer going to Bennington Heights Public School, the last thing Betty needed was listening to me agonizing about another damned hockey game, another stock car race. Betty pressed me to become involved in the school's parent teacher association. I didn't. She threw superb dinner parties to which Stuart and Alice Griffiths were often invited, hoping to deal with my growing disenchantment with Stu and to help me sell him on doing genuine documentaries. The closest she ever came to referring to my state was, "Are you sure you want another drink?"

Nothing helped. It stuck in my craw that my whole background dictated that I do programs with some kind of social relevance. Yet, here I was, knocking myself out on sports and Santa Claus parades for viewers needing unthinking relief from their daily struggles to earn a living. Legit enough, but, not for me, dammit. I was going to be thirty-seven soon. My life was more than half over. *Am I gonna be stuck with this for the rest of my life?* I thought. I had to get off this slippery slope. *An obvious thought, Newman, but how?* The fates were on my side.

Suddenly, early in 1954, Stuart Griffiths was dropped as program chief and moved sideways to the thinly disguised post as TV advisor to the top Ontario Region boss, Ira Dilworth. Bob Allen, supervising producer of drama, was appointed program director. The moves were to take place on April 1.

All the speculation we indulged in gave no answer to Stuart's removal. My own guess is that his passionate hurry to make television the best it could be was his downfall. He was too flamboyant and rich for his thin-blooded and methodical, budget-ridden masters at headquarters in Ottawa. All his passion for good television and his demonstrated capacity for picking good people and program ideas were no compensation for his maverick nature. Very simply, Griffiths was his own man, not an organization man.

In appointing Bob Allen, I would guess the brass thought they were cleverly solving two problems. He was a good choice because he was methodical, had a good record as a CBC employee and was liked by his fellow producers. No flash, no sound. Allen himself, I'm sure, would be the first to admit that he was not as inspiring a leader as Stuart, but the place was chock-a-block with good people from whom the inspiration and ideas would continue to flow. His removal from drama would also improve relations with MacLaren's Advertising Agency,[49] who had brought many of their clients into television — the most lucrative being General Motors, who sponsored a weekly one-hour drama series. Rumour had it that Bob's taste in plays didn't suit them, and when they asked for a change in a line of dialogue or in a scene, Bob was less than cooperative. *General Motors Theatre* was a prestige show, and brought in needed revenue to the young service of the CBC. The agency's director of radio and television, Hugh Horler, was a most charming and persuasive chap. Bob became a victim of the false claim that the CBC did not allow sponsor interference. So making Allen program director seemed to be a wise move all around.

One month after announcing the changes in the hierarchy, nothing was said about who was to succeed Bob in drama. Peter MacDonald was suitable, but he was now in Vancouver setting up CBC-TV's station there. Mavor Moore had left television months earlier. By mid-March it was clear the brass thought nobody suitable. As time went on, a crazy idea entered my head: why didn't I take a crack at getting the job? It would get me out of remotes, and even though I had read play scripts only as a designer looking for the mood of the play, figuring out what doors and windows had to be practical in the set, I knew more about camera angles than anyone else in the place. It was a long

---

49 In the era when sponsors, through their ad agencies, devised and approved programming, MacLaren's was top dog in Canada. It not only had General Motors as an account (which sponsored the CBC's main drama, *General Motors Theatre*), but also had Imperial Oil, who sponsored *Hockey Night in Canada*.

shot, but I had nothing to lose by trying. The director of television agreed to see me.

Fergus Mutrie was surprised, saying that I was doing such a good job as head of outside broadcasts. "I thought documentary and current affairs were your specialties?" he asked. I nodded. "I know the schedule doesn't allow you many," he continued, "but later, there'll be more opportunities."

Hell, I'd heard that answer to my pleas many times before.

"Oh, I know that, Ferg," I said, lying, "but I've always liked drama." I'd never given it much thought. "I know you read my New York report on remotes, but didn't you read the one I wrote on drama? I know a lot about it . . . from the backside . . . ah, that is, as a designer — where you really see what makes a play tick. After all, Ferg, I know cameras inside and out. I'm not suggesting that I direct a show, but I can run it."

Ferg, fiddling with a pencil, looked at me thoughtfully and murmured, "Hmmn."

Silence. I studied him. The leitmotif to this nice, conservative man was that the organization be kept safe. I burst out with the only card I had left: "Ferg, I'm the oldest in production. I'm mature and can handle people. Hell, Ferg, I've handled prime ministers! And you know I get along well with Hugh Horler and other advertising agency people."

Would that get him? He thanked me for coming to see him and told me he'd think about it.

The next day I was called into his office and told that the job was mine[50] — for a trial period of four months. The starting date was my birthday, April 1 — the day honouring fools.

---

50 Newman kept Fergus Murtrie's March 30, 1954, memo offering him the promotion on a trial basis. It more or less echoes what Newman has said, but added that "the job of Supervising Producer is about equally divided between safeguarding program quality and maintaining the operating budget within its given boundaries." Murtrie adds, "This aspect of your work will be watched closely and with interest," indicating that Newman's ability to produce drama was perhaps not so big a concern as whether he could do it within a reasonable budget.

CHAPTER FIFTEEN

THE PLAY'S THE THING . . . ?

Once I knew I was going to be head of drama, a new series of questions plagued me: Would I catch the conscience and interest of my viewers? Would I be able to succeed when I really didn't know a damn thing about plays and their construction, actors and acting? In drama, how do you direct a director? I didn't even know the questions to ask! How could I use what I learned in New York as a working member of Chevrolet Teletheatre? How could I use what I observed in theatre as a set designer? What had I learned as a maker of documentary films?

Then there was the sponsor, General Motors, and their ad agency minder, Hugh Horler. Oh, he was amiable enough when discussing the nuances of shooting hockey, or how to make Foster Hewitt look good. Would he be as easy in my choice of plays, or on details in scenes? I knew why Bob had been dropped. And I knew that silly words like *damn* and *hell* were not to be used — too many buyers of Buicks and Chevrolets were churchgoers, and GM was not going to chance being associated with blasphemous talk! Should Horler and I disagree, Bob

Allen as program director would support me against the agency, but that would have been like asking the premier of Ontario to demolish Hitler.

With my mind in a whirl and my fear put away, I entered the sacred precincts of the elite drama department as its supervising producer with a shining face.

I had no conscious plan, and for the first six weeks or so, I found myself getting to know the directors. By watching them work and following the set routines, I got the hang of things . . . except for the small matter of questions about where scripts came from, who wrote them, their cost and rehearsal and studio conditions. I had the good sense to keep my mouth firmly shut about the creative aspects of production of which I was truly ignorant. The directors accepted me on the basis of not appearing even vaguely competitive with their creative sovereignty. How I would, if I ever did, exercise my authority on the interpretive, creative side of production never entered my mind.

It was the advertising agencies, with their often craven notions of how to protect their client, or sometimes even the client himself (one never knew) who made it impossible for me to avoid their interfering on the creative side of my director's work. It was a positive, though, that I was of one mind with the agency on the matter of ratings, which resulted from the creative work. An agency satisfies its clients by the nose count of specific kinds of viewers. The larger the number, the happier the sponsor. No one would have to put much pressure on me for that! It would help tune my sensibilities about winning and holding viewers, too. The kind of play one was able to hold them with, however, was something else again, as far as I was concerned. In the years to come, time and time again, I would have my judgement challenged.

One day after my appointment was announced, I was taken to lunch by Hugh Horler in the King Edward Hotel's elegant restaurant. In the past, as producer of *Hockey Night in Canada*, whenever I met Hugh, he was never alone. In his wake would be a swath of agency copywriters and aids of all sorts, including Peppiatt and Aylesworth, later the originators of the highly successful *Hee Haw* show. This time he was accompanied by only his personal aide, a vivacious brunette.

I'd never met anyone like Hugh before. He was slight, usually in grey flannel suit, button-down shirt and black knitted tie, looking as if he had just left university with a Ph.D. As we sipped huge, dry martinis with a twist, his eyes, through heavy horn-rimmed glasses, radiated confidence and admiration for me. He was a good listener and when he spoke, his few words would be enthusiastically endorsed and amplified by his extroverted assistant. Over our roast beef, rare, and baked potato, filled with butter and sour cream lightly sprinkled with chives, I couldn't believe my ears when he spoke highly of the Film Board and reverentially of the publicly owned CBC. Usually, "his sort," as I thought of Hugh then, deprecated both the NFB, for taking business away from commercial film companies, and the CBC, for its incompetence. Boy, is this guy cool, I thought. To this day, I don't know whether he was telling the truth or not. In the language of the actor, in the years I knew him, he never once broke character.

While I did not disguise my ignorance of drama, I made no claims about it either. I was relieved, but also curious as to why he made no attempt to find out what I knew, or even liked, about theatre. Being of a suspicious nature, it occurred to me that perhaps he felt it in the best interest of the agency that I know little about it.

When I asked him why scripts needed to be sent to the agency in advance of their production, he assured me that it was only for purposes of information and would be used to help advertise the drama. Seeing a look of doubt in my eyes, he said, "You don't mind, do you?"

"No, not at all," I replied, "if it helps advertise the show, the better for all of us."

The only firm agreement he easily extracted from me was that I would not change his approved schedule of plays for the rest of the season, which would end in seven weeks. I hadn't read them and I certainly wasn't going to throw my weight around before I knew which end was up.

After refusing a cigar and while sipping brandy in a huge snifter, it was clear to me that the television expenditures of GM were certainly in good hands. As expected, the lunch was most cordial. Cautiously, I felt I could handle him. Horler was a seducer, all right. I would have to watch myself carefully in the days to come if I was to keep those hands off my neck.

Where the plays came from and what kind of guys the directors were, I was most anxious to find out. Of course, I knew the latter, but only casually. Most of them by now had almost two years of experience behind them. David Greene was regarded as easily the best and most reliable. A tall, glibly charming Englishman, he had conned his way into the CBC claiming to be a stage director. When I got to know him better, I learned that he and his beautiful wife, Katharine Blake, had been experienced actors, even performing in front of BBC cameras. They had come to New York, largely for the trip itself, as members of the cast playing in Laurence Olivier's Old Vic Company's twinned Shaw and Shakespeare's *Cleopatra* plays on Broadway. "Kate," as David quipped, "waved a fan over Cleopatra, and I was a spear carrier for Caesar."

After the tour was over, hearing that TV was starting in Canada, David thought he'd try his luck and applied. Impressing Mavor Moore — David could sell an elephant to a dairy farmer — he was quickly taken on and just as quickly got the hang of directing cameras and pacing a play.

For a long time, I was afraid of him. He was so damn sure of himself and acted as if his opinions on play construction and acting were gospel. Watching him handle actors became an epiphany for me. As a filmmaker of documentaries, the importance of the actor had never occurred to me. They were a blank in my mind. I thought films were mainly camera angles and shots, music and pacing. Once, I praised David for a particularly fine close-up of an actress. It was Kate Reid. He said, "Oh yes, she's a fine actress." When I came back with, "Oh, I know that! It's the skin texture and the lighting I'm referring to that makes it." David said, "Like hell it does. If her face was empty, if the eyes didn't tell what was going on in the character's mind, no matter how beautiful the shot, it would be lousy. It's the actor that makes or breaks a play." For many months, to my shame, I thought that was the ex-actor boasting. I was wrong.

It wasn't until I was head of drama for about a year that it finally sank into my dim, visually-oriented head that a play's the thing — that it is what it is — only after the actors make it so. All other elements are there to extract, enhance and reveal the performance.

Other directors I inherited were Henry (Hank) Kaplan, a delightful guy with a pixie sense of humour and Silvio Narizzano who, years later, was to become one of England's finest award-winning drama directors, working mainly for Granada Television. The feature film, *Georgy Girl*, was one of his. Silvio ran hot and cold then — his work sometimes produced moments of subtle and tender emotion; at other times, confusion. But they were never less than interesting.

Within days of sitting in my drama seat, I got stomach cramps, figuratively speaking, when I say that the means of finding the plays to produce was an unholy, catch-as-catch-can mess. *General Motors Theatre* alone needed thirty-nine one-hour plays for the autumn season, and coming up fast was the summer series calling for thirteen half-hours — and not a single script in sight. It was an unbearable nightmare. What few plays Canadian playwrights submitted were rejected as not good enough. As little as I knew about it, even I could see that Canada had no Paddy Chayefsky, Horton Foote or Reginald Rose. If a writer showed promise, nobody was there to offer help and guidance. My directors looked mostly to do TV plays they had already seen on "the box" from the Buffalo transmitter. My Canadian nationalism, polished to a rosy hue at the Film Board, made me cringe at the thought of our doing Canadian repeats, as excellent as they were, of *Philco Television Playhouse* and *Studio One* productions. I had to fight off suggestions that all we had to do was replace American names so that Philadelphia would become Toronto, a Congressman an MP — that sort of thing. The shortage of plays forced me into this, especially later, when the demand for half-hour plays increased.

MacLaren's was in the game too, usually offering up old Broadway or West End stage plays that required cutting and versioning into something less talky and more visual. The best aspect of this was that it provided work and experience for writers whose only serious drama market up to that time was radio — CBC Radio and, outside that, mainly Al Savage's *Ford Theatre*. These half-baked radio versions, when I learned more about TV drama, made me quip, "It's a radio stew, garnished with pictures!"

I inherited three or four freelance readers whose job it was to synopsise and comment upon the mass of submitted scripts, ideas, stage plays, novels and short stories. It was my job to read their reports, and if a proposal was recommended by them, I would then read the original material and decide whether to buy it or commission it. If something looked promising, but not yet ready for production, I had two choices — assign a director sympathetic to it and the writer, or work with the writer myself. The former rarely worked. Either the director was too busy, or he alienated the writer by wanting the story to go his way rather than the writer's. As to the latter, at that time I was better qualified to advise a cartoonist than a playwright.

Most of the readers were too damn kind, which forced me to read useless submissions. They were paid the ignominious sums of between one dollar and two dollars, fifty cents depending on the length of what they evaluated. I raised the minimum fee to two dollars and paid a double rate for a rejection, because I demanded more detailed reasons why the item was not accepted. I was being canny in doing this. Selfishly, I would have much less to read. On the positive side, reasons for rejection would also prevent writers from submitting similar dumb ideas, and the report would be useful to writers learning their craft.

Among the readers, there were two, Nathan Cohen and George Salvarson, whose judgements I felt were often more sound than the others. Nathan, of course, was later to become a polished, national figure as the host of *Fighting Words*[51] and, eventually, as the entertainment editor and columnist of the *Toronto Daily Star*. At the time, 1954, he was probably the most hated man in theatre circles,

---

51 *Fighting Words* was a popular panel quiz show which ran from 1952-62 on CBC, where panelists had to identify people who wrote or said a particular quotation. The rotating panel often included Canadian literary legends such as Morley Callaghan and Irving Layton. The series defied cancellation multiple times because of its popularity with the Canadian public.

such as it was, for his acerbic and uncompromising theatre criticisms he published in his own six-page newsletter, *The Critic*.

I had met him earlier, but as a playwright when I was doing outside broadcasts. Glen Frankfurter and Len Peterson, executives of Toronto's lively Jupiter Theatre, remembering my pre-war stage sets, asked me whether I would like to design for them. Happy for anything to break the monotony of my work, I quickly agreed. The job was for Nathan Cohen's first play, called *Blue Is for Mourning*, on the pathetically tiny stage of the Royal Ontario Museum; for the play's action, I designed and had built a full, two-storey house. As a critic who didn't conceal his scorn for the opinion of his fellow critics, Nathan was truly asking for it. And boy, he got it. The critics slated it roundly, finding the stage setting the best thing in it! I don't recall it being as bad as they said, but it was dour and downbeat.

After that, in my off-hours, I continued to design sets for many plays, including Cole Porter's *Out of This World* and most memorably, Jean Anouilh's *Ring Round the Moon* at the Royal Alex. So Nathan Cohen was identified in my mind with my very enjoyable work as a designer.

As an aside, on the afternoon of the opening night of *Blue*, I was sitting in the mainly empty theatre, instructing the electrician lighting the set. I began to be aware that someone sitting behind me, clearly not knowing that I was the designer, was knocking the set. Casually, I turned my head and saw a sallow-faced, blond young guy. Later, I asked someone who he was, and I learned that he was an artist who designed most of the company's sets. His name was Harold Town.

Nathan was a Maritimer, a big, overweight, badly shaven, growing man who looked to be forty-five to my thirty-seven. He was at least six years younger than me, though. He didn't know much about television, but he certainly knew theatre.

Happily, he was a bear for work. Later, I learned that he was as poor as a church mouse and needed the money. On a Friday, I would load him up with one novel, two short stories, one one-hour and three half-hour scripts. Come Monday morning, he'd be in my office with sloppily typed but hand corrected, detailed, literate and excellent reports, which I would quickly read and discuss with him. This enabled me to make quick decisions. They also helped educate me, as I was certain they would the writer to whom I might give a copy. Should I see the writer in person, which I often did, I'd break the bad news to him with modest authority and even transmogrify Nathan's criticisms into positive suggestions for improvement.

If Cohen was brusque and bulky, George Salvarson was lean and gentle, with a shy manner. Originally from Winnipeg, he was a professional writer — one of the best — whose plays were regularly heard on Andrew Allan's *Stage* series. He was a faultlessly nice and civilized man who was able to give me precise and practical suggestions to improve a play.

Being burdened with dealing not only with Horler and his lot, but my new staff and a genre I knew little about, to my horror, my CBC bosses committed me to produce two new, sponsored, half-hour drama series to run concurrently with *General Motors Theatre*. In my first season, I knew that I must find another and better way to deal with writers.

General Motors Theatre being uppermost in my mind, I asked Nathan Cohen to come on staff on a non-exclusive basis to deal with writers directly, help them write better stories, and find new plays that suited the show. He agreed. When, weeks later, I was told about the two new autumn shows, I took on George to do the same thing with the half-hour plays. Now I could get on with the other problems while meeting George and Nathan regularly to discuss their progress and thankfully read only the material they recommended for purchase. We used to joke about trying to find a new story editor whose first name was Jean. Then, when calling for my story editors, I would be able to yell out, "Get me George Jean Nathan," the name of America's best-known drama critic in those days.

Of course I didn't always agree with them on the suitability of a play. The buck stopped with me balancing CBC policy with the sponsors. It wasn't until I got to know them well, and until I felt they fully understood the specific style and character of a series, that I gave the editors the power to commission a play on their own. And when I thought it necessary later, after I learned something of play construction and could tell the difference between good and bad dialogue, that I became confident enough to deal directly with a writer for the play's final touch-ups, or discuss its details at the commissioning stage.

The two new half-hour series were *On Camera*, sponsored by Procter & Gamble with the Canadian arm of Benton & Bowles protecting them. The starting date: October. The other series would start in January, sponsored by the Ford Motor Company, with its agency being Cockfield-Brown. Trouble was, not only had I no plays, I hadn't enough directors. I was able to move Murray Chercover from the children's serials he had been successfully directing onto the *On Camera* series. And somehow or other Paul Almond and Arthur Hiller came my way, but neither of them had ever before looked through a viewfinder, let alone handled multiple television cameras.

Paul Almond was a tall, gangly, freely perspiring Montreal amateur stage director who picked up an English accent at Oxford's Balliol College; among his other activities there, he played ice hockey and was involved with the OUDS (Oxford Union Debating Society). He was a lovable fellow whose tastes in plays were hilariously esoteric — the kind of guy who, when he started with me, thought Procter & Gamble, famous for its many daytime soap operas, would jump for joy at the privilege of sponsoring a play by Kafka.

Arthur Hiller, equally lovable, solid and dependable, with a winning grin and, as I was to later learn, stubbornly proud, had come from Alberta to Toronto. Here, he won recognition as an up-and-coming radio drama director. He had given up his CBC staff position and pension to risk his career in television.

I was faced with the problem of mothering Paul and Arthur as they experienced the mysteries of making drama visually effective. What I had learned by watching David Greene and others over the previous six months I passed on to them. I could impart my own experience as a filmmaker as well, which was useful even to David Greene. I explained the psychological effects of different shots on an audience: a high-angle shot diminishes a character and a low angle ennobles him; a crabbing shot gives speed even though the actor doesn't move. Over the years at the CBC, I became adept at teaching people in drama — not how to get a performance out of actors, which I never felt even vaguely qualified to do, but in how to use and orchestrate cameras to achieve clarity and power of visual expression.

With a story editor in place and three directors assigned to the *On Camera* series, other personnel were added to my staff — two script/ production assistants and a floor manager. As Ted Kotcheff was anxious to get into drama, and remembering his intelligence and good work for me on *University Story*, it pleased me to have him promoted from stagehand crew chief to floor manager. In army terms, it was like promoting a sergeant major to second lieutenant — a move that was to launch him and bring me much credit later.

During that first summer, I discovered there were virtually no budgetary controls. With the coming of the additional two series, it wasn't hard to convince Fergus Mutrie that I needed a drama unit manager. For this post I was able to steal Don MacPherson, an amiable twenty-one-year-old from the accounts department who had generously given me some after-hours help in my previous job. At my request, he established an accrual system where I was able, at any time, to know the state of our money situation.

I made Don my own and brought him with me to the control room, script sessions, some rehearsals and meetings with my superiors and agencies. He was like a kid in a candy shop. Soon, he was assisting directors in all sorts of ways and even doing some second-unit direction. Even though he was not an especially "creative" type, I was not surprised when, years later, he rose to the position of CBC vice-president of the English Radio and Television Service.

While Nathan Cohen was able to get a firm hand on getting scripts for the autumn *General Motors Theatre* by using revised radio dramas, cut-down stage plays and the odd U.S. teleplay, George Salvarson was having a tough time. Half-hour plays were not easy to come by — and we needed thirty-nine of them for *On Camera* and thirteen for *Ford Theatre*. Since U.S. television had been chock-a-block for many years with half-hour drama series, most reluctantly I told him to go down to New York and find any suitable scripts that wouldn't look too American. He came back with a trunk full. We selected a batch, bought and revised them, and it was with these that we launched *On Camera*, the CBC's first series of half-hour, commercially sponsored television dramas.

Ron Poulton of the *Evening Telegram* praised the series. So did the *Daily Star*'s Gordon Sinclair — at first. Several weeks in, Sinclair blasted me to hell. His national fervour was assaulted. How dare the CBC pawn off plays that were patently American as Canadian?[52] Who is this guy, Newman, anyway! Taxpayers' money should go to Canadian writers! In this fashion, he ranted in his widely read column. I was sick with anger, and even considered suing him for impugning my patriotism.

It was the lovable Hy Bossin who advised me. "Forget it!" he said. "Don't be a dope and get into a fight with him. For your one letter of complaint against him the *Star* might print, he can get at you in his column every day of the week!" It was advice I took and advice I have never forgotten.

To my utter amazement, a few weeks later, Sinclair devoted most of his column to expressing his regret that he had gotten me wrong. He said that he had received many letters praising me. One of them was from Nathan Cohen, who hadn't told me he'd written in. Another letter he quoted went something like this: "I am a Canadian, age twenty-one. After graduating from an American script-writing course, I submitted a script to the CBC. Mr. Newman rejected it, but told me how to fix it. I went away and did what he told me, but he still didn't think it was good

---

52 Sinclair's column, which appeared in the *Toronto Daily Star* on January 13, 1955, said, "How come so many U.S. yarns and scripts are on CBC drama? . . . When do we see the work of Canadian writers on their own Canadian TV screens? Seldom. Too seldom." Sinclair listed a number of Canadian writers — many of them friends and colleagues of Newman, including Len Peterson, Lister Sinclair, Nathan Cohen and George Salvarson — and asked why their work wasn't on TV before sticking the knife into Newman. "Could it be that supervising producer Sydney Newman has too much authority and too little Canadianism? Is this man, nice guy that he is, a Caesar who can accept or reject without argument?"

enough — and he gave me more advice. When I next took it to him, he not only bought it, but he gave me a down payment on a commission to write another one. Yours truly, Sidney Furie."[53]

I bought many a play from Sidney until he left Canada for England, where later, under the name of Sidney J. Furie, he set the pace for spy thrillers, which helped propel Michael Caine into international stardom with his stylish *The Ipcress File*.

When anyone tells me that sponsorship of programs by commercial organizations is good, he is talking through his hat. Sponsorship is especially bad when a program has social content, which most drama has. It's bad because what sensible sponsor, a pharmaceutical company, say, would allow a play they are paying for be seen by millions in which the hero, a chemist in a drug company, comes to work drunk after a fight with his wife, and approves the wrong batch of chemicals, sending them out in neat bottles only to affect the babies of pregnant women?

---

53 Newman's recollection fails him here somewhat. What Sinclair said in his February 23, 1955, *Toronto Daily Star* column was this: "A couple of weeks back this column let fly at Sydney Newman, supervising drama producer for the CBC, on the ground that Newman didn't use enough Canadian material, didn't encourage Canadian writers, and didn't forget that, drama-wise, he was the corporation's Mr. Big . . . Newman never complained about the article but Nathan Cohen did. Cohen wrote that he spent part of a year as Newman's aide on the drama desk and during that time had personally seen Syd push toward production scripts that would have normally been ditched. But because these were Canadian writers they were used."

Sinclair then writes, "Yesterday an intent looking youth by the name of Sidney Furie dropped in to see me. He had a similar tale." Sinclair then recounts how Furie had wanted to be a playwright and had studied at Carnegie Tech and come back to Canada. "Last June he came home to Toronto and dropped into the Jarvis St. Kremlin, colder than a March toad, to tell the waiting script crew he had some stuff for them. Instead of the 'so what?' treatment, young Mr. Furie (then twenty-one) was encouraged. He talked with people like Newman and Murray Chercover and Leo Orenstein. They thought maybe he had something. Nobody gave him the chill." After much encouragement, "About ten days ago they telephoned to say this kid has clicked. His 'Saturday Night' will be aired on Wednesday, February 23." Furie's episode "Saturday Night" was a tale of teenaged romance featuring Bruno Gerussi.

It's not a play about drug manufacturing, it's a fine, sensitive play about marital relations. Nevertheless, this sponsor will either not buy the play — resulting in wasted time by a talented writer and depriving the public of something that would entertain and enrich their lives — or, liking it, he will say as he inevitably will, "Now, don't get me wrong. It's a good play but why can't the hero work in a bakery or in a car plant?"

It can be bad for the sponsor as well. A brewery introducing a new German beer bravely sponsored a drama about an old Jew who, long after the war, recognizes and accosts the concentration camp guard who tortured him — right at the climax, just before the commercial break. Their following commercial soured the mouth. It showed cheerful contemporary Germans in Lederhosen dancing and yodelling to their oom-pahs with the beer's name superimposed over the action. Who could not help but think of the Nazi Holocaust at that moment? It didn't make one want to go out and buy a six-pack of beer.

Even in sports that are largely free of social comment, sponsorship, I found, affects the televised game. In an ice hockey faceoff, the players wait one to three seconds before the puck is dropped. In a sponsored match, the game is held up because the agency man will slip in a thirty-second commercial before the cue is given to the referee to drop the puck. Maybe the players like the thirty-second pause, but likely also, the pause breaks their concentration. Depending on the game, variations of this are affecting and changing all sports.

Sponsors must look after their own interests, and those interests too often are not in the best interests of drama, documentary and current affairs — not even sports, and definitely not audiences.

After my years of producing sponsored drama in Canada, I realized how wise it was of the British to keep the BBC and even commercial television free of sponsorship. In weighing the experiences I had running drama in Canada, the majority of the fights I had with writers and directors and even designers were because of sponsor interference. Even as I write this, I can still feel the grinding of glass in the pit of my stomach. One occasion was so silly, it defies belief. It involved Sidney Furie.

Even though things worked out well for Furie after he went to England, one of the factors that influenced his decision to leave

Canada was a play he wrote for the *General Motors Theatre* called "The Runaways." The story was about a poor boy and a rich girl who want to get married without the consent of the girl's snobbish father. They run away to Buffalo and get married. The mean father is foiled, and the play ends with the young couple facing the future with shining faces. It was a simple story, but charmingly told. I thought the agency would be very pleased, because it would appeal to the young who buy Chevrolets.

When Furie had finished the script, I assigned a director and scheduled it for production. As was customary, I sent a copy of it to MacLaren's Advertising Agency.

A few days later, Hugh Horler phoned and asked that I delay its production for a while. It was a quick call, and I couldn't get him to say why. Since at that time I was fairly rich with one-hour plays, I could afford to be easy and so I agreed. He was always present on Tuesday evenings when *General Motors Theatre* went out live, and after two or three weeks I mentioned to him that I had to put "The Runaways" into production; Sidney Furie's impatience and many phone calls to me were becoming embarrassing. Yes, Horler said, he liked the script, but would I please bear with him and hold off for a little while longer. And no, he couldn't tell me why.

Three months later, I got really fed up stalling my director and pouring oil on a pent-up Furie, whose surname was becoming more apt each day. I insisted that Hugh meet me for lunch to discuss the matter. In my mind, I was resolved that, unless I got his agreement, he was forcing me to complain to my CBC superiors about his agency blocking me. Over my second martini, I mentioned this threat — and to that he shrugged his shoulders. We both knew that my threat was futile since his counter would be to cancel the series, which would force the CBC to cave in.

"For heaven's sake, Hugh," I said, "at least give me a reason for the hold-up."

He looked at me and, in deadly earnest, said, "I can't."

"Look," I said, really angry, "I've made the series work despite some stupid things you guys have asked for. I can't face a writer with this kind of shit you're throwing at me. You are . . ." And I looked him straight in the eye. I think I was trembling. "You, Hugh, are not being fair with me." He sighed and looked around at the busy dining room and turned back to me.

"All right, I'll tell you why, but only if you keep it to yourself." I nodded. "A promise?"

"Yes, a promise. I'm listening!"

Very quietly he told me that the daughter of one of the most senior, but unpopular executives of GM had run off against his wishes and married a boy of whom he didn't approve. Were the "The Runaways" to go out, this executive would think that his colleagues, seeing that the play's story was almost a carbon copy of his own experiences, had deliberately accepted the play to embarrass him publicly.

"Holy Mother!" I shouted, and seeing people turning heads to look at me, I quietly squeaked, "That's the reason?"

Hugh, with a sickly smile, said, "Yeah."

Disgusted, I said, "So all the work Nat did with Furie, who wrote his guts out . . . it was all for nothing. For the garbage can!"

Horler, finding an upbeat ending to our lunch, said, "GM is renewing for next year. Things are bound to cool. We could use it then."

I don't know what lie I told Sidney, but he demanded the play back and offered to return his fee. In shame, I couldn't refuse and wouldn't accept the return of his fee. What he then did with it is a glorious testimonial of youth. With a friend, Bill Davidson, he scraped up enough money and made a feature film of the story[54] — a very unusual and courageous thing to do in Canada, then. I'm told that for a first film, it was remarkably good.

Thus, a new director was born. Maybe, somehow, the sponsorship of drama has a good side?

Another play, set in Italy, called for its hero to have a love scene

---

54 Furie managed to raise $50,000 to make the production, now called *A Dangerous Age*. He filmed it in Toronto in 1957. It was produced by Meridian Films, a Toronto-based production company co-founded by Newman's old NFB colleague Julian Roffman. As a Canadian independent film — unheard of in the 1950s — it was never able to find distribution in North America, though Furie was able to get a deal to have it released in Britain and Europe.

in his tiny racing Fiat — but showing a car of another make was absolutely verboten, even if it wasn't sold in Canada! We were forced into cramming a monster Corvette into our tiny studio.

One incident had grave repercussions. In a play by an outstanding French-Canadian writer, a teenage gang of kids is caught smuggling American cigarettes. When they are grilled, one of the cops displays a sadistic tendency. Smuggling, being a federal offence, is a matter for the Royal Canadian Mounted Police, and they had to be portrayed as squeaky clean to a man. I made sure that the police were in plainclothes, so that the audience would not know whether they were local, provincial or federal. But the commissioner of the RCMP knew, and that was enough for him.

Ill-advised, he sent a letter of complaint to the president of General Motors and foolishly included a line like, "when considering our next purchase of cars for the force, we will think seriously about which make of car we will buy." One can easily imagine the panic buttons pressed in the GM headquarters in Oshawa and in MacLaren's agency. The GM president shot the letter to Davidson Dunton, CBC president, declaring their innocence and asking him to reply to the RCMP Chief. Dunton did — a splendid, cagey reply that apparently pacified both GM and the RCMP without accepting one iota of blame. My bosses said nothing to me, nor did the agency. Had the latter, I would have slaughtered Hugh Horler because, as usual, there were no fewer than three agency people in the control room when the show was shot and went out live.

Any word of dialogue that suggested irreverence was out. God, Jesus, Holy Mary, even a "damn!" and "Heavens to Betsy" were unacceptable to MacLaren's — and they were easy compared to other agencies, especially the U.S. branch offices in Canada. The Benton & Bowles man minding *On Camera* for Procter & Gamble gave me a slickly printed *Writer's Guide of Do's and Don'ts* for their U.S. "soaps" that I was to heed.

My returning the guide it to him didn't stop him. He knew it by heart: Married couples sleep in separate beds; should they be lying together, one of them should have at least one foot touching the floor. A wardrobe lady must always have available a bit of frilly material in the studio for last minute tucking into a woman's cleavage thought to be too deep. A woman's thighs were never to be seen, but MacLaren's, after persuasion, only no-no'd the inside of the thighs. Open-mouth kissing was forbidden, and chaste ones could last for no more than three seconds.

I have no strong recollections of strictures against violence. Perhaps this was because I myself never liked it. I particularly avoided a character threatening a helpless person, especially with a common, easily available weapon such as an axe or a kitchen knife.

Themes to avoid were those involving named political parties, industrial disputes and drug addiction. I was carefully watched whenever a play touched upon identifiable national institutions, professional bodies and churches of all kinds.

In short, as boss of mainly sponsored drama, my employees and freelance writers were able to fly as high as a bird, but only as high as was allowed, being shackled to a ten-tonne block of Don'ts.

But nothing is truer than Huw Wheldon's[55] saying, "All art is based on chains" — the chains being the things that restrict and limit the creative artist. In discounting all the restrictions placed upon my staff and me, it's amazing how good some of our productions were. We were too innocent, as were our viewers, to know how crippling the limits were. In the main, audiences enjoyed and talked about our work, not having a clue as to what they were being deprived of.

For myself, I listened to the agency suggestions and beefs and often fought with them, but never to the point of no return. The same with my directors, bosses and writers. I just ploughed on with memories of Grierson, not quite dead yet in my mind, that art must say something valuable if it's to be worth the effort.

As irritating and often foolish the restrictions, they gave me something of value — a sensitivity to the people who watch drama. I didn't think of the viewers as some sort of amorphous mass — and certainly didn't

---

55 Huw Wheldon was Controller of BBC 1 for the latter half of Newman's tenure at the BBC. He would later become Managing Director of BBC Television.

join cynics who insinuated that in order to look at it from the viewer's point of view, one had to get down on hands and knees — but I realized that they were specific people, and their education and common cultural bonds determined what they would appreciate and perhaps need.

Just as I discovered the importance of the actor, the recognition of the writer had an even greater impact on me. "In the beginning was the word," is no idle saying. After a year or two, I became fed up with hand-me-down versions of stage plays, short stories and novels written in other countries. I felt I would get bigger and more satisfied audiences if I could dramatize the here and now of their Canadian existence. That meant getting plays specially written for my series. And that meant finding and developing more Canadian writers. This I made Salvarson's and Cohen's main goal. Other than drawing attention to writing, though, we regretfully achieved only moderate success.

Andrew Allan had found excellent radio playwrights, but the pictures created in the listener's mind came only from words, both narrated and spoken. Music and sound effects were crucially important. The more excellent these writers wrote for the ear, the more difficult it was for them to grasp and harness the power and clarity possible when writing for the eye. How often had I tried to explain this to a writer — even going so far as to ask them to write a play about a mute individual to get their reliance upon words out of their system! Len Peterson was one of the few who was able to succeed. One of his best was a play for *General Motors Theatre* about an aging hockey player, which starred Austin Willis. Ted Kotcheff, whom I had promoted from floor manager to director of half-hour plays and then to hour-long ones, directed it with marvellous energy.

The most noteworthy writer we uncovered was Arthur Hailey.

One day, Nathan Cohen came rushing into my office, waving a script in the air and joyously proclaiming, "Boy, have I found a writer! This guy is terrific. Full of suspense and absolutely Canadian."

"Oh wonderful," I said, "I'll read it this weekend."

"Naw," said Nathan. For what he said next, I ribbed him for years: "No point. It needs simplifying, or I'll get him to write something else."

"Nat," I said, "let me read it."

He blustered, not liking his opinions questioned. "It can't be done. It's too tough to produce!"

I got up and tore the script out of his hands. "Let me be the judge of that."

"Flight into Danger" was all Nathan said it was called. While it was simply marvellous as a suspenseful story, it was also dangerously difficult to produce as an episode of *General Motors Theatre* because it needed many filmed inserts crucial to the story. Integrating film into a drama going out live — where the play is seen as it is being made — was risky. Any miscue "rolling" the film, which happened damn often, resulted in the audience suddenly seeing either a blank screen or numbers flashing — six, five, four — in the middle of the play. That could happen twenty-one times in "Flight into Danger."

The first play of Hailey's was typical of the best of his plays and novels — man surviving and vanquishing the perils of technology.

The main action of the play is in the chartered airliner of football fans flying from Toronto to Vancouver to see the Grey Cup game. A choice of two meals, fish or meat, are offered the happy passengers. Everyone who chooses the fish course — about half the passengers and both the pilots — becomes ill. With the two pilots out cold, the first act ends on the pilot's empty seats, with the controls of the plane gently moving back and forth by the plane's automatic pilot. At the end, the airliner is finally safely landed by an unsure, ordinary man talked through it by a professional pilot in Vancouver.

I paid Hailey the going rate for a first play, the princely sum of $600, and assigned it to David Greene, my most accomplished director. If anyone could pull it off, it was David. Little did any of us realize that the dramatic situation Hailey had devised, and the way it was done by us, would become the basis for dozens more as it was immortalized in many feature films, both dramatic and satirical.[56]

---

56 All of what Newman describes is, in fact, in direct succession to "Flight Into Danger," which was broadcast in Canada on April 3, 1956. It was then adapted on American television as part of *The Alcoa Hour* on September 16, 1956, and then, in turn, was then adapted into the film, *Zero Hour!* in 1957. In 1979, the comic film *Airplane!* was a direct parody of *Zero Hour!*

When I first met Arthur to discuss very minor changes in the script, I discovered that he was a relatively new Canadian. He'd come to Canada from England during the war to teach aeronautical navigation to pilots in the Commonwealth Air Training Scheme. Finding the fresh Canadian air more to his liking than the class-ridden land of his birth, at war's end he returned to Canada hoping to fulfill his dream of becoming a novelist. The best he was able to achieve was to write articles for a trade magazine on the road haulage industry.

Apparently he got the idea for the play while eating a meal on a Trans-Canada Air Lines business flight to Montreal. He said that, based on his many rejection slips, he despaired of ever being able to write fiction. "But, hell, a drama needs only bald description to guide the director and dialogue, which I felt I could easily write for the actors."

After arriving in Montreal, he looked up some old wartime buddies at Dorval Airport to get an update on technical data, rented a typewriter and bashed out the play in twenty-four hours, non-stop. Back in Toronto, he did some revisions and sent it off not to the CBC but to the Big Apple. NBC rejected it, and then he tried CBS, who also rejected it.

In despair he finally sent it to the CBC, his last chance.

David Greene, himself, excelled. Every film clip fit in seamlessly, and the casting was bang-on — Jimmy Doohan (later of *Star Trek* fame) played the coward/hero pilot, Cec Linder played the man who talked him down, the delightful Corrine Conley was the stewardess and Sandy Webster appeared as the only doctor on board the plane. Not only was it a tight, tense, compelling production, but its theme of a frightened man conquering a huge monster of a machine riveted anyone who saw it. From all across Canada, letters of praise poured in.

A few letters knocked it, some of them going directly to the sponsor, General Motors. Not surprisingly, these came from different elements of fishery organizations and fish-packing plants for maligning a healthy food — fish. How MacLaren's and GM answered these I don't know. It's a good thing those bums make cars and not boats.

In rapid succession we got Hailey to bash out one thrilling drama after another. "Time Lock" was about a boy locked in a bank's vault, which wouldn't open until after the oxygen was exhausted. In another, the president of the United States, played by Mavor Moore, is in his presidential plane (a Boeing 747 seen by the public for the first time) flying to Moscow on a peace mission, and must set his plane on a "Course for Collision" to intercept a Soviet nuclear bomber mistakenly aimed to blow up Washington. One play sponsored by the Bank of Canada (my old Ottawa friend, Herb Richardson was its minder), was set in Chalk River, one of the world's first nuclear plants. A meltdown is averted, as usual, by human ingenuity.

Somehow, Hailey struck it lucky in getting Maeve Southgate to become his agent. After we did "Flight," Southgate managed to sell it to *The Alcoa Hour* at CBS Television in New York for a fee six times more than what Hailey had gotten from us. Resulting from that production, about which more later, she then sold it to Hollywood for a cool $85,000. She thought the play should be turned into a book. It was, but Arthur thought he wasn't up to it so they got another writer to do it.[57] Writing this in 1987, it's still available.

Hailey was ecstatically waiting to see his very own play televised from New York, which, of course, meant that it would be coming from the Buffalo transmitter. It being more than seventy microwave miles from Toronto, he had himself built a very high aerial tower to get the clearest possible picture. To celebrate the occasion of its airing and finally seeing the U.S. version of his play, he and his charming English wife, Sheila, threw a party for some of us. Betty and I went along with David Greene and Kate, his wife, and some other members of the cast and their wives. Nathan couldn't make it. After booze and good food, with brandies in hand, we waited for it to start.

I knew that David, charmingly self-centred, was bound to think it poor. He was in a bearish mood when he arrived anyway, because he heard that I had given his film clips to CBS without at least extracting a credit line for him or for the CBC. But he grumbled more than I

---

57 The novel was adapted by John Castle and Hailey in 1958 under the title *Runway Zero-Eight*.

thought he would while it was on. When it was over he loudly stated that it was not as good as his. It was a slick production all right, as plays in that series usually were, but somehow I felt it didn't have the suspense and tension that ours had.

Hailey was immensely pleased and only a little disturbed by David's opinion. He came over to me and quietly asked what I thought of it. "Oh it's fine," I said. "A very good show." And thinking of why it lacked tension I realized that the man cast to play the coward/hero was too damned heroic looking. One look at him and one knew from the start of the play they he'd have no trouble whatsoever landing the plane.

"Arthur," I asked, "why did you allow them to change some of the dialogue?"

"What changed?" he asked, somewhat disturbed.

I replied, "Remember when the stewardess says to the doctor that their only hope of being saved is if one of the passengers knows how to fly a plane? The doctor originally says, if I remember correctly, 'Wait a minute! The man sitting next to me. He told me that he flew Spitfires during the war. Maybe he . . . Ah, no good. He was probably boasting!' Why, Arthur, did you allow them to cut the line 'he was probably boasting'?"

"They didn't," Hailey said. "They played the show exactly as I wrote it. *David* was the one who put that line in!"

Well, he can be forgiven. After all, it was his first play!

One day just after we had put his fifth play for us into production, Hailey invited me to lunch. Herbert Brodkin, who had moved from *The Alcoa Hour* to *Studio One*, offered him a commission to write a two-part drama to be called *The Pathologist* for a fee of $7,000 if I would permit him to accept it. How sweet of him, I thought — he didn't owe us anything. Of course I said yes.

To write it, he turned up at an American hospital, his cover being a visiting doctor, and with tape recorder concealed in his pocket he recorded about twenty-four hours of dialogue unbeknownst to the staff. Once, while observing an operation, he was actually offered a chance to continue the surgery! With this massive amount of factual material, Hailey fashioned a drama of the conflict between an old-fashioned pathologist and a young one.

Later, when in production, Brodkin, in a kind way and in the best interests of the show, asked Hailey to not attend any more rehearsals. A troubled Hailey returned to Toronto and asked for my advice. Things were different in New York and not what he was accustomed to in Toronto.

Apparently Hailey had complained when the show's star, Lee J. Cobb, had said that the written dialogue was bad and, without Hailey's permission, Brodkin had allowed Cobb to change many of his lines. What should he do? Hailey asked me. I explained that New York probably felt that the success of the show would largely depend on Cobb's name and that the producer couldn't afford to alienate him. This was the reality of showbiz. Then I reassured him by adding, "Cobb is a fine actor. *Death of a Salesman* showed that. Brodkin can't afford a lousy play and will protect it. Cobb's changes, lines he's gotta believe in, may in fact enrich the dialogue, and it will be to your benefit as the author."

Even though this two-part drama of Hailey's was a great success, I've often wondered if I was right in offering that advice. Was I being pragmatically sensible, or was I suckered into the showbiz way of trading integrity for success?

When the feature film of "Flight" came out (under the title *Zero Hour!*), Hollywood did no better than *Studio One*. Maeve Southgate sold *The Pathologist* to Hollywood and it was the beginning of the end of Hailey writing for the CBC. The *Airport* films and others followed as he finally achieved his goal of becoming a novelist — a bestselling one, at that. Now a multimillionaire, Arthur Hailey and Sheila live in a Nassau estate.[58] He was a lovely guy.

Hailey was not the only one writing for us who went on from those humble, primitive TV days in Canada to extend their talents. Ted Allan, Sidney Furie, Stanley Mann, Len Peterson, Bernard Slade and Mordecai Richler are only some of them. It simply could

---

58 Arthur Hailey died on November 24, 2004, in the Bahamas, at the age of eighty-four.

not have happened without Nathan Cohen, George Salvarson and, later, Ron Hambleton.

Producing plays that go out at the same time as they are performed posed unbelievable problems. To avoid the many possible hazards, the shows had to be meticulously planned. Every move by an actor and camera in relation to the settings had to be precisely fixed before going into the studio, with only one studio day allowed for every thirty minutes of screen time.

Forgetting all the technical things that can go wrong — such as microphones that won't work, cameras out of alignment and lights that blow — the two major concerns for the director of a live show are the length of the program, making sure that it runs to its precisely scheduled time, including the commercial breaks, and the actors, making sure that an actor doesn't forget his or her lines.

In the last days of dry rehearsal — rehearsing without cameras — careful note is taken of the play's running time. If the play seems to run long, cuts are made. If short, bits of action are added. In the studio, when the action gets "on camera" with music and sound effects, the show's length may change and further adjustments are made right up to and including the dress rehearsal, which usually finishes less than an hour before airtime. Trouble comes during the actual performance when the actors, not being robots, play scenes somewhat faster or slower. Therefore, before the show starts, we must plan emergency cuts or means of lengthening the show — the latter more easily rectified by extending the end titles. The former is a headache because it affects what actors and cameramen are supposed to do.

When an actor forgets his lines, which thankfully is rare, it's an unholy nightmare. This and the problem of length hit us one time when Silvio Narizzano directed a *General Motors Theatre*.

The play was an adaptation of *Billy Budd*. Eva Langbord, drama casting director, and Silvio had put together a fine cast with me concerning myself only with the casting of the lead players. Among these were Bill Shatner, a promising young Canadian actor who was to play the title role of Billy (his Captain Kirk role of *Star Trek* still light years away) and Patrick Macnee, the avenger himself, who was living in Toronto then. To play the vital role of Captain Vere, we were lucky to be able to import the famous Basil Rathbone, then close to seventy.

"Dear Boy," Basil Rathbone greeted me when he arrived in Toronto, "New York, *Queen of Spades*, wasn't it? I was wondering if it was you when my agent told me of the Toronto call. Odd, you're being in charge of drama. Frightfully mad about documentary, eh? Y'see, I remember."

We were in a car coming back from the Malton Airport.[59] "Memory. The old grey cells ain't what they used to be. Nearly turned you down. Can quote yards of the old Bard, but new sides don't come easy. Be a good chap and lay on someone to help me with the lines." He saw my startled look. "Oh, after rehearsals. Don't worry, dear heart, I'll be fine on the night."

I mentioned this conversation to Silvio, and told him that if Rathbone seemed uncertain of his lines toward the end of the sixth day of dry rehearsal, Silvio should get someone to work with him during the evenings. It was necessary to have Ted Kotcheff, his floor manager, do so.

Come the night of the show, the dress rehearsal went like clockwork, promising a first-rate, compelling drama. The youthful Shatner had that wonderful quality of good-natured innocence against the stern, brutal character of Claggart, played by Barry Morse. Rathbone was his usual professional best as the regal, yet human, troubled captain. The only thing that bothered me, irrelevant compared to what happened during the live broadcast, were the shadows of the ship's rigging cast on the tiny studio's cyclorama, which was supposed to look like a brooding sky. Silvio and the crew were all in top form. Even Horler and his entourage, usually impassive or worried, ventured smiles of anticipation.

The play started well, but on his first entrance coming down our ship's steep gangway, Basil slipped. He recovered, but every line of

---

59 In 1958, Malton Airport would become Toronto International Airport (now known as Lester B. Pearson Toronto International Airport.)

dialogue that he had painfully learned went right out of his head! Actors are wonderfully resourceful at such moments, and the other actors beautifully revised their dialogue each time poor Rathbone spoke his garbled, often senseless, lines.

By the end of Act 1, I was in a sweat — the big scenes between Shatner and Macnee with Rathbone were still to come. Moreover, the play was running long. I began thinking of cuts that might have to be made, even though, through Kotcheff on the studio floor, Silvo instructed the actors to "pick it up." We blundered through Act 2, losing even more time. The easiest solution was to cut the final commercial, but no agency would allow that! So brainwashed had I become by now, I didn't even ask. I suggested to Silvio possible third-act cuts, but not until he got agreement from Kotcheff were they relayed to cast and crew. By the end of the play, the end titles were zipped through so fast they couldn't be read.

Amazing that the drama was not awful. It merely wasn't as good as it should have been. Rathbone's lines, even though wrong, were spoken with such authority that they were accepted as right, especially with the way the splendid actors playing opposite him ad-libbed their lines. Rathbone, the gent that he is, thanked the cast for helping him and apologized for letting me down.

That's live television!

In another drama, Lloyd Bochner, supposedly dead in a coffin, not having been given the proper cue and thinking the camera was not on him, sat up. Not a word of criticism from the critics or the viewers was heard. It was simply accepted as part of the drama, since the play had an element of the occult. My God, how often have I seen a performer, after a quick costume change, come on camera with her dress or his pants undone, surreptitiously trying to zip up his fly.

As the years rolled by, new directors joined me: Arthur Hiller, Charles Jarrott, Ronnie Weyman (an old NFB colleague), Mel Breen, Basil Coleman, Leo Orenstein (with whom I had gone to Hollywood), and others. Leo directed Ted Allan's tender *Lies My Father Told Me*, where the old decrepit horse required by the play shat on the studio floor during the show. Norman Campbell did a few dramas, one of them a dramatization of Mazo de la Roche's *Whiteoaks Chronicles*. Kotcheff was promoted to director. While he was learning, I insisted that all his now extensive knowledge of the studio was of no use unless he could get good characterization out of his actors. I advised him to take classes in acting, which he did with my old Theatre of Action friend Basya Hunter who taught the Stanislavski method.

In light of his future success as a Hollywood director of such hits as *First Blood* with Sylvester Stallone, it's interesting to recall my assigning Ted one of his first one-hour plays for *General Motors Theatre*.

It was a schlocky but effective whodunit. Kotcheff tried to beg off doing it. I agreed with him that it was not a particularly good play and explained that as a learner, it was an okay vehicle to sharpen his professional teeth on and that it would help his name because it would be popular. Being a nice, humble guy then, he pleaded, "Can't I sharpen my teeth just as well on a good play? Sydney, I don't want to get into the habit of directing crap." He directed it badly. Many good shows later, when I was about to reap the full benefit of his clearly evident talent, he left Canada for a TV job in England.

Meanwhile, Hiller left Canada angry. With no director's agents in Canada we ourselves had to annually renegotiate our contracts with poor Fergus Mutrie, who certainly had no stomach for bargaining.[60]

Hiller was showing great promise, especially after very successfully directing a tricky play by Chuck Israel. *The Mark* was about a child molester, played by Jimmy Doohan, who has just emerged from prison. Hiller's negotiations went badly. Fergus wouldn't go higher than $6,700 for the upcoming year and Hiller thought he was worth more: $7,000. The brass considered fees their business, and besides, they explained, fees might affect a supervisor's relations with his staff. I needed Hiller badly, and so I tried to intervene, but Mutrie was adamant. He wouldn't budge. So upset was Hiller that he took a kinescope of *The Mark* down to New York, screened it and was

---

60 Even Newman was not immune. His papers include a memo from Mutrie trying to convince him that a $500 increase in 1954 was a good thing.

instantly hired by NBC for a new daily anthology drama series, which was to originate in Hollywood. It was a sad loss for Canada and, of course, for me. And all for a lousy 300 bucks!

Sometime during this period I got my first taste of opera. If I didn't produce it, I certainly helped Franz Kraemer, who directed *The Consul* by Gian Carlo Menotti. I also did some interesting major ninety-minute Canada Savings Bond shows for the Bank of Canada. They were omnibus-type programs amalgamating documentary, music and drama, bringing Bernie Braden back from England as host.

Over the years I evolved a fairly good method of working with my directors while keeping sponsors at bay and my bosses happy.

My story editors worked to meet my definition as to what kind of stories were wanted, and they provided me with plays for my approval. These I read, rejecting some and often suggesting they get writers to make changes to others. Originally Nat and George were called script editors. I didn't like that because it suggested, if not encouraged, them to make changes in the script itself. After I made it a rule that only the writer would make the changes, I renamed them story editors.

I would assign the script to a director I thought suitable in terms of skill, style and the genre of play they were best with. Greene could handle anything from a schmaltzy romance to a thriller, Narizzano was best on character plays, and so on. At the time of assigning the director, the director and I would discuss a possible cast that would inevitably reveal to me his understanding of the play and how he was going to interpret it. We sometimes did not agree, but then, he'd only had the script for a week and I had read it perhaps several times since its commissioning. Later, of course, by the end of rehearsals and with the writer often present, he'd know a hell of a lot more about the play than I did. With the exception of the lead actors, I left casting up to him and our casting director, Eva Langbord.

Experienced directors on *General Motors Theatre* did one play every four weeks, and half-hour plays fortnightly. I would sometimes go to the cast read-through, but never missed the rehearsal, which, two days before the show, went into the studio.

This dry rehearsal became my main point of control over the "look" and clarity of the story as it would appear on camera. The director was the camera at these rehearsals, because at my request he stood, or silently indicated with his hands, where the camera would be for each shot as the actors gave what was close to being their final performance, moving from one simulated set to another. As I followed the director throughout the run-through, scribbling notes to discuss with him later, I'd be aware of what he intended to get on camera, but watched more intently the actors' faces and especially their eyes, which would convey to me — and the viewer — the inner depth of their characterizations.

After the rehearsal, the director and I would retire to a corner of the room out of earshot of the actors. I'd give him my notes — first, always in the form of a query, having learned disastrously in my early days that I might momentarily antagonize him if I had misunderstood his direction. My notes often suggested that an actor should speak more clearly but more crucially, and that the camera be on the right actor at the right moment — often, seeing a character listening to a line of dialogue is more important in driving the story forward than seeing the actor who is speaking. I always made sure the director wrote down the results of our note session.

Sometimes we would fiercely disagree, mainly over idiotic details like love scenes that were too frankly played, or script changes made during rehearsal without the permission of the author. Very rarely was it necessary for me to pull my weight and insist a change be made, saying, "Sorry, this is an executive decision."

In coming into a rehearsal room, if the director was working with the cast I'd leave immediately, asking the production assistant to call me when the rehearsal would start. I wanted to see it fresh, with no pre-conceived ideas until the director was ready for me. In general, I found it best to avoid any contact with the cast during production. I didn't think it wise to inadvertently find myself between them and the director. Many of them thought this was arrogance on my part. Like hell it was! Their fragile insecurity frightened me. Directors were bad enough, but actors . . .

Once, at an after-show party, an actor began laboriously explaining to me why I had thought he was bad in the dry rehearsal. I was mystified, because he was good and I said so when I gave my notes to the director. Was the director using me as a club to beat the actor with, something I wised up to early on?

"Whaddya mean I thought you were bad?" I asked.

He replied, "When you were leaving — the way you looked when you said goodbye to me, it was clear enough!"

Jeezus!

I'd usually drop into the studio early on the first day, have a quick look at the sets, say hello to the director and leave. The next day I'd turn up around four o'clock for the stagger-through, which took place before the dress rehearsal. In the announcer's booth that was next to, but still away from the din of the control room, I'd make notes, looking only for necessary improvements to camera positions, music, sound effects and perhaps costume and makeup, if important. After I gave my notes to the director, everyone would break for a quick meal to return made-up and in final costume for the important dress rehearsal at about seven o'clock.

In the control room, there would be several agency people present, but Hugh Horler would join me in the announcer's booth (I couldn't keep him out!). During the dress, if necessary, I'd make notes on acting and touch-ups of this and that. When over, I'd listen to the murmured comments of Hugh Horler, and note only the ones I agreed with. After Horler left, the director would join me for the final discussion on changes. I'd bid the director and his staff a cheery good luck and dash home to see the drama on the air with my wife, just like millions of others. Immediately after the show, I'd phone the control room, and if the show was good I'd tell him it was great! If it was merely okay, I'd congratulate him on some of the performances he got out of the actors. If it was lousy, I wouldn't phone at all, telling him what I thought of it at the office the next morning after I had cooled down.

Each year at the CBC saw me go through that drama routine no fewer than twice with thirty-nine dramas — some years, more. It was a fully packed, fulfilling week, every week.

The only knock-down, drag-out battle I had with my bosses was one over scripts. Just when I was beginning to be sitting comfortably in my seat as head of drama — the plays were going well, sponsors happy, Nathan and George were getting better original scripts — word came down from headquarters in Ottawa that a centralized television script department was going to be created. It would find scripts, work with writers, negotiate fees and assign scripts for production. My first thought was that I would lose my story editors. I was in a panic.

Thinking ahead, I arrived at the conclusion that without control of the content of a play — the script — this was no job for me. In fact, it was no job for any head of drama, so cockeyed a notion it was.

My Toronto bosses were sympathetic to my anger, but to no avail — Ottawa's word was final. In desperation, and with Fergus Mutrie's permission, I bypassed Toronto and wrote directly to Ernest Bushnell, general manager of the CBC, opposing a centralized script department. I said it might look good for the annual report, but that, with the exception of negotiating fees and securing copyright, it was totally impractical.

I went on to explain that what wins the loyalty of audiences week after week is the essential, unique character of a series. Only one person, the producer, can be the guardian of its unique character. Should he fail, it is he who "carries the can" in the eyes of his superiors at the CBC. The procurement of scripts is primarily the function of a story editor, who is responsible only to the producer. The story editor must find a script that will suit the concept of the series and the directors — who are also responsible to the producer — who have an individual style that only the producer knows how to exploit and control.

Fergus Mutrie, unless I imagined it, was happy that Ottawa was reconsidering the matter. I kept control of the scripts. I think the real clincher in my memorandum, which was written with the help of my literate wife, Betty (who expunged some of my pungent language), was my description of the farce (a word I did not use) of the much-vaunted "no sponsor interference" in the selection and interpretation of a script. I queried whether the proposed script department would hammer out arguments with the agency in script matters, leaving me to later argue with the agency on production matters? Who in the CBC would be the Solomon to arbitrate the failure of a poor program?

I had gotten my way before, but in order to win this one I began to realize that I would need the strength to confirm my conviction — and I had it. My life could be my own. Queen Street had receded into a blurred past.

In the summer of 1956, I was asked to see Peter MacDonald, the new national program director, who had recently returned after setting up CBC's Vancouver TV station. With him was my close friend Gunnar Rugheimer, who was in charge of sponsored programs. I was asked whether, in addition to my present drama load, I would create and produce a new and innovative program. With my outside broadcast experience and flair(!), they said, it was right up my alley.

The idea did excite me. It was somewhat similar to the Edward R. Murrow show, *Person to Person*, where he, from the studio, interviewed top personalities in their homes or places of work. Al Savage, Hugh Horler's equal in the Cockfield-Brown Agency and an outstanding radio drama producer in his own right, had dreamed up the idea. The Ford Motor Company was to sponsor it for a twenty-six-week run starting in January. I expressed eagerness, but questioned whether I would have the time to produce *General Motors Theatre*, *On Camera* and the new show. MacDonald said they would give me every possible help. They added that the new half-hour show had a hefty budget, and asked if I would think about it. "And, oh yes," said Peter, "there'll be a $2,500 increase in salary if you take it on."

Well, *that's* the kind of talk that was nice to hear. It would help pay off our third mortgage on the house. But how the hell could I produce three major shows a week? The two I was doing already were killing me! I said I would give them an answer after I had discussed the program more fully with Al Savage.

Of course, I knew Savage when I produced the *Ford Theatre* drama series earlier, and I had found him to be one of the easiest agency men to deal with. We discussed his idea fully. He made it very plain that the program was not to be a stuffy current affairs program, which didn't faze me in the least. I was especially happy when he agreed with me that we needn't stick only to top Canadian personalities, and that if an unknown but interesting ordinary person could be found, they would be interviewed as well. He insisted, however, that one of the two interviewees in each half-hour show must be well known. He was interested in my idea of bridging the two interviews with a one- or two-minute *Candid Camera*–type item shot on film.

He expressed fear that my other work might interfere with his show. It crossed my mind then that my other work involved the sponsor's major competitor, General Motors. I answered by saying that, if I took on the show, I would give it my best — that is, I would if I could figure out the staff and facilities it required and if the CBC would provide them for me.

It was a thrilling assignment, and I never shunned working long hours when it made sense to me. This was an opportunity too good to turn down. These stories weren't fabricated: this was real life. I was back to my documentary origins but now I felt well armed, with a polished sheen from the abrasions of my drama experience, which included the critics, the viewers and Hugh Horler.

The CBC gave me everything I felt I needed. Not only did the show need a studio, it also needed two mobile camera units, a film unit, a top research team, three directors and special telephone switching gear. The craziest thing I asked for and got was a fourteen-piece orchestra to bridge and, if necessary, back each segment of the show. Since there was nothing in common between drama and *Graphic*, as it was later called, I got myself a second secretary and decided the new staff should be housed elsewhere.

Unfortunately, while the CBC gave me handsome quarters, they were down on Front Street[61] in what is now called Film House, making me shunt back and forth endlessly between my two staffs. I planned on

---

61 Until the Canadian Broadcasting Centre was constructed in 1992, the various studios and offices comprising the CBC were in various buildings throughout Toronto, which were repurposed from everything from stately homes to movie theatres to schools to, famously, a former car dealership showroom with a leaky roof which became its Davisville studio.

working three days a week on *Graphic*, and four on drama.

Putting together a staff was a chore, but in the end we did very well. My remote directors were Wilf Fielding, who was one of my best cameramen when I did remotes, Norman Caton and Merv Rosenzweig. Peter McFarlane was the director of the studio portions, and as the writer and chief of research I brought Norman Klenman to the CBC, who later set up CKVU-TV with his partner Daryl Duke in Vancouver.

One thing bothered me. In the eyes of the brass, *Graphic* was a current affairs show that dealt with public figures. To make sure I did nothing to bring disgrace (as I interpreted it) to the corporation, they attached to me Norman DePoe to vet scripts before each show went on the air. He turned out to be a soft nellie, no trouble at all, which didn't stop us from referring to him as our tame political commissar.

Biggest problem was to find our Ed Murrow. With Al Savage, I interviewed and screen-tested dozens. None seemed to combine all the essential qualities needed for the position: knowledge of the world, imagination to ask the questions that the viewer himself would ask, and, most important, that ineffable quality that would command respect and admiration. As a long shot, I thought of a man in Ottawa who had been the commissioner of penitentiaries for the federal government, Joe McCulley. I had met him when I produced Ron Weyman's prize-winning film "After Prison What?" for *Canada Carries On*. Ron, now one of my senior drama directors, said to my pleasant surprise that McCulley was living locally. He was the University of Toronto's Warden of Hart House.

Joe McCulley was a giant of a man with a winning grin on his craggy face. He looked and sounded good in the screen test. He was prepared to stick his neck out for something he'd never done before. Al and I had finally found our Ed Murrow.

To compose the music and conduct our orchestra, I got Lou Applebaum, my old friend from the Camp Bonnie Brae days, ex-NFB director of music, Oscar winner for his music in *The Story of G.I. Joe*, and later, co-chairman of the unloved Applebaum-Hébert Report on the Arts and Broadcasting.[62] All that was left to do was capture the imaginations of millions with good programming.

Timing live programs is always difficult, but making *Graphic* run to time was a nightmare. Imagine trying to produce over the telephone with two directors, each with his camera crew, doing a different segment of approximately twelve minutes on a person who is inevitably nervous and is being interviewed by someone he can't see, reacting to a voice coming out of a loudspeaker. That was *Graphic*.

Early in the afternoon on the day of the show, I was in the control room with Norman Klenman and a script assistant with a stopwatch in hand, seeing and watching the remote directors in succession on our monitors, rehearsing their segments. Peter McFarlane, in the same room, was cutting back and forth, picking up the cross-chat between McCulley and the person being interviewed. Over the phone, I gave each director comments on possible improvements and sometimes suggested things to cut. Peter, who controlled McCulley, told him of each change. With each remote segment timed and added to studio and commercial times, the show was too long. By now, I'd made up my mind on what was the most interesting item to my viewers. I had to make brutal decisions. I got on the phone to discuss specific cuts with the directors. Peter relayed those cuts for me.

By dress rehearsal, inevitably, the show was still too long. I consciously wiped out of my mind that every change I would demand from this point on would affect Joe McCulley, Lou Applebaum, the people interviewed and dozens more. Wearily, I picked up the phone to order another minute cut, feeling like a real bastard — which the remote director, now sympathizing with his interviewee, confirmed. Once Wilfred Fielding was so angry about my cuts that for a whole week he communicated with me only through his production secretary. That was *Graphic*.

---

62 Released in 1982, the Applebaum-Hébert Report was the first government-appointed review of Canadian cultural policy in thirty years. Among the most controversial of its 101 recommendations was that the CBC relinquish telvision production in favour of acquiring programming from independent production companies.

After the five-month lead-in time, I produced the first twenty-six *Graphic* shows, as well as the normal weekly quota of drama, which didn't suffer at all. And I didn't get an ulcer. The show must have worked, because Ford renewed it for a second year.

I can boast of having produced Canada's first cross-border telecast as an item in *Graphic*. After months of palavering with external affairs in Ottawa, Ma Bell and sundry others, Joe McCulley interviewed the Canadian Ambassador to the United States, who talked of his work as he led our cameras through the majestic rooms of the embassy in Washington. In direct opposition, the accompanying item was Joe interviewing a Polish immigrant, ladling molten metal in The Steel Company of Canada's Hamilton plant. While the visuals were smashing, the interview was close to being as disaster. The din in the vast rolling mill was so great that the steel worker could not make out Joe's questions, and when he spoke, he couldn't be understood because of his accent.

Of the forty-eight items we did, one was unforgettably delicious. At the time I wished it could have gone on for the full half-hour. In the control room, we roared with laughter at Joe's inability to, figuratively speaking, "get into" a young woman.

There in our studio, through the plate-glass window of our control room, we saw our highly articulate Joe McCulley, trying to cope with a young, pretty Montreal stripper who had just finished her nightclub act. As she mopped the sweat from her gorgeous body, she gleefully and ingeniously chattered away about herself and the way men made passes at her. Joe was as unable to get onto her wavelength as she was oblivious to his efforts.

Another, but entirely different memorable item involved the brilliant and eccentric pianist, Glenn Gould, whose *Goldberg Variations* had recently stunned the music world. Because we wanted to get decent shots and good sound we shot this interview in our studio.

When he arrived he was wearing an overcoat so long, it was three inches above the floor, and he did not remove his thick fingerless woollen gloves. When he sat down at the piano, he first lowered his bench — so low that, when he began to play, his gloved hands were raised to the level of his chest. As he played his eyes would glaze, his head moving slowly up and down. Faintly, we and the audience could hear him humming along with the music.

It was an awe-inspiring, almost religious experience, seeing and listening to this strange young genius. Peter was covering it beautifully. At one point he had one camera shooting along the full length of the grand piano so that we saw only the front of Gould's head as it went up and down. To Peter's dismay, Gould's head went so far down it entirely disappeared from sight. As I heard Peter about to switch to another camera to get a side view of Gould, I screamed out, "No, leave it! Leave it. It's good."

Peter did not switch, and viewers, for at least ten seconds, heard a part of Bach's *Goldberg Variations* coming from a playerless grand piano. It was a frisson of spontaneous revelation that makes live television so uniquely incomparable.

Since *Graphic* was all about the unusual in people, I had convinced Al Savage that the program would be enhanced by inserting a gag between the two major interviews — a short filmed item of ordinary people reacting to something unusual. I had McCulley introduce it to the viewers, asking them to guess why, and to what, the filmed people were reacting. One item taken with a concealed camera showed men and women stepping up onto a public scale, putting in their penny and then reacting as they learned their weight. Some were horrified, some shrugged, some were disgusted at themselves and some laughed. Joe then appeared on camera and explained to our viewers that the scales were rigged to add ten pounds to everyone's weight.

Another item took place at the Riverdale Zoo with a camera presumably in a monkey's cage, shooting through the bars at children and adults reacting in astonishing ways — bewilderment, awe, admiration — to something that the viewer at home did not see. The last shot revealed that the camera shooting the people was being operated by a cameraman dressed as a gorilla.

These items provided more than humour, viewer participation and variation from the interviews. Functionally, they gave our genial host a short break, but also, should the first item run a minute longer than expected, these films were designed to be still effective if only the last half was shown.

Years later, I was pleased when producer Patrick Watson told me he used to stand at the back of the control room just to watch how I worked.

If *Graphic* was a complicated show to produce, because it came from three different locations, it was a piece of cake compared to one I later became involved with. And this one would marry my drama work with outside cameras. Pat Weaver, president of NBC, had an idea that unsurprisingly, was so grand and complex it boggled the mind. He planned a live outside broadcast show that would link together for the first time the continent's three largest countries: Canada, the USA and Mexico. It would start on the east coast and progress westward, showing North Americans at work and at play to end on the sun setting behind San Francisco's Golden Gate Bridge. As the saying goes, "He doesn't think big enough!" Appropriately enough, it was named *Wide Wide World*.

The CBC was asked to take on the responsibility of providing twenty minutes on Canada, and Peter MacDonald handed the baby over to me. I went to New York and met those involved in the show; there were about fifty of them, from everywhere. It had been six years since I'd last worked at NBC and I'll admit I was pleased at the warm greetings I received from Pat Weaver, Bob Sarnoff, now NBC's senior vice-president, and Bill Garden, the show's executive producer.

They were quite clear about what they wanted from Canada. Their research told them that Stratford's Shakespeare Festival was it! They wanted an interview with the Festival's founding director Tyrone Guthrie, along with some actors and part of the production of *Julius Caesar*, which they knew had a performance scheduled on the day of the telecast. Everything had to be live, which was okay by me.

On my return, I immediately went to Stratford to see Guthrie. He was happy for us to interview him and the actors, to have cameras on the lawn outside and in the lobby seeing the audience arriving . . . but under no circumstances would he allow us to shoot any of *Julius Caesar*. I worked on him for weeks and got nowhere. New York was adamant. There was nothing else in Canada they would accept. I tried again, even getting Lorne Greene, who was playing Brutus, to intercede. From an actor in the cast I heard that Guthrie had once seen BBC coverage of a live theatre performance and decided that actors acting on a stage, when seen on camera, looked like bad actors. He hated television.

I phoned the show's producer in New York to tell him the bad news, but heard from a saddened Bill Garden that, through worry, he guessed, the producer had died of a heart attack. Small wonder!

After he told me that he was looking for a new producer, I told him my bad news. I added that there might be a slim chance that Guthrie would allow me to shoot part of *Caesar* in advance, but on film.

"Syd, if I put that up to Pat he'll kill me." Bill went on, "His whole idea is that it's live! *Live* as it happens!"

After I tried to sell him on the Niagara Falls, a steel plant, the RCMP Musical Ride and a few more ill-thought-out clichés, he sighed. "Okay. I'll try it out on him."

I jumped in, "Hit him hard, Bill, that *Caesar* would be inserted alongside live stuff of the audience arriving live, Guthrie and Michael Langham, its director, interviewed live and—"

Bill interrupted me, ready to cut his own throat. "Yeah, I know. I'll get back to you." He hung up.

Weaver reluctantly agreed, and with the expenditure of considerably more money, which didn't seem to bother NBC, a chunk of *Caesar* was pre-filmed. My director was Silvio Narizzano, assisted by Ted Kotcheff on NFB 35mm cameras (CBC used only 16mm). The cameraman was my old NFB buddy, Lorne Batchelor — who was especially memorable, because he shot the official film welcoming Newfoundland into Canada, which I directed for *Canada Carries On*.

The live Canadian end of *WWW*, which was directed by Wilf Fielding, came off extremely well. The filmed portion was excellent, and it was top and tailed by people arriving in their finery at the Festival Theatre and by backstage interviews with Michael Langham, Tyrone Guthrie and Lorne Greene in full Brutus makeup and costume, just before actually going onstage.

This first *Wide Wide World* was a landmark program in the history of U.S. television. Its 101 live cameras gave an immediate panorama of a vigorous continent with its variety of people and their different accents, working and playing in different bands of weather and terrain, all within the continuous span of ninety minutes.

I don't think Weaver ever forgave Canada for the only pre-filmed sequence that marred his grand "here and now" concept. And ironically, as the only Canadian who owed a debt to him, I was unable to change the stubborn mind of Tyrone Guthrie!

In the autumn of 1957, a ripple of excitement went through the corridors of the CBC. The mother of all broadcasting organizations, the BBC, gave my drama department its stamp of approval by buying twenty-six of our *General Motors Theatre* dramas for airing as a series called *Canadian Teletheatre*. Such a sale had never before been made. English critics' opinions began trickling in and were passed around. Our work was being admired.

One day, Peter MacDonald asked me if I would like a trip to England.[63] Would I, boy! To see for the first time the country of "God Save the King" and "God Save the Queen," *Comic Cuts*, Ian Fleming, Meccano, Arthur C. Clarke, Land of Hope and Glory! Apparently the BBC was worried about some of the language used in our plays, which was either not understood or offensive. By discussion, perhaps such words could be avoided or paraphrased in upcoming plays. We'd "tank up a car with gas" against their "putting petrol into the motor." Our "elevator" was their "lift." Most hilarious to me was our, "Kick him in the fanny!": we, of course, meant buttocks. But it turns out, in England, only a woman has a fanny, and it's not a word that could be used on television.

I flew to England in a Constellation — which I still think of as the most beautiful looking plane that ever flew — and was met at the airport by Elwyn Jones, who was a senior assistant to the BBC's

---

63 Newman kept his itinerary from that trip, which was from August 18 to 27, 1957. It lists his flights and attempts to explain English money, "Threepenny bit . . . Yellowy coin size of a nickel."

head of drama, Michael Barry. Jones, a tall, laconic Welshman, was assigned to look after me for my week's visit and did so graciously, albeit with a tinge of charming condescension. Barry was as English a gentleman as I could ever imagine, right down to the handkerchief tucked into his left sleeve.

I cannot recall much of our talks about Canadian versus UK language but I remember vividly the trouble they took to show me — their colonial cousin from overseas — a good time.

Jones took me on endless walks just so I could get the feel of London. I think he was relieved that I showed no interest whatsoever in visiting museums, galleries or ancient churches. Instead I was fascinated by the people, the number of them so great, it struck me that Toronto and Montreal were empty deserts by comparison. And I felt like I knew the still-visible vast, bombed-out areas around St. Paul's from the dozens of wartime documentaries I'd seen when at the NFB.

It never bothers me to risk being naïve, which at the time amused Elwyn Jones to no end. When he walked toward the Parliament buildings and I saw the Big Ben tower, I exclaimed, "Holy smokes! It's just like it looks on a bottle of H.P. Sauce!"

He darted a look at me, not sure whether I was pulling his leg. "You mean," he asked, "you never knew what H.P. stands for?"

It took me a second before the penny dropped. "H.P.," I exclaimed, "Houses of Parliament! No, I never made the connection."

He must have wondered what kind of clot I was, this Canadian head of drama.

Even before my first meeting with Michael Barry began, he wanted to make sure that I saw all the things I wished to see on my first trip to London. "Now, I'm sure you want to go to the theatah," he said. "Elwyn, here, will lay on the tickets."

Going to the theatre had not entered my mind. "Oh yes," I said, not really caring. "What do you suggest?"

Barry: "What about Stratford? Suppose I drive you up on Saturday. There's a new production of *Twelfth Night* with John Gielgud, which I'd like to see, anyway. Right?"

I nodded, trying to look eager. I think Elwyn was reading me somewhat better than Barry was, or perhaps he was being mischievous when he said, "Perhaps Sydney would also like to see *Look Back in Anger.*"

"Yes! Yes, of course," said Barry.

What a charming little theatre I thought the Royal Court was as Michael Barry, Elwyn Jones and I took our seats. I was surprised that programs were not free as they were in Toronto and New York. Then the play began, and it completely knocked me out! I thought it just about the finest contemporary play I had ever seen. It was so fresh, so real. So hard, yet tender in its perception of its desperately human characters.

During the intermission in the bar, I was surprised when drinks, already paid for, were waiting for us on a shelf. Elwyn had ordered them earlier. It occurred to me as I sipped my brandy that it was strange no one had swiped them.

"How do you like it?" asked Barry.

"Mn, good. The brandy's fine. French?"

Elwyn smirked. Barry corrected me: "No, Osborne's play. What did you think of it?"

I must have waxed rhapsodic about it for minutes before it occurred to me that Barry did not think as I did. I asked him what he thought of it.

"Can't stand that fellow, Porter. Why does the fellow do nothing but complain and complain all the time! Why doesn't he *do* something?"

It only then entered my mind how considerate a host Michael Barry was. Clearly, he had already seen it, and probably many times, taking out-of-town guests like me to see the play even though he hated it. Years later, after I got to know him better, I wish I had asked him again what he thought of *Look Back in Anger.*

On Saturday, after an endless Tube ride, I met Barry again. In his Volkswagen Beetle, we drove to the famous Stratford-upon-Avon, a town I thought too Tweedle-dee to the Tweedle-dum of tourist trade. Being pretty ignorant of Shakespeare, I didn't voice an opinion about Peter Brook's *Twelfth Night.* The first scene's staging put me off the whole production. Imagine trying to achieve the effect of a ship heaving in a terrible storm by having the actors pretend to be thrown about in time with swaying masts while the stage floor remains horizontal and stable as a rock. How clever I thought it was of Guthrie and Tanya Moiseiwitsch in Stratford, Ontario, to settle for an open stage with no sets, just spectacular costumes and dramatic white light.

In watching Gielgud's left profile and hearing his mellifluous speech, I truly began to admire what Guthrie had gotten out of Canada's young, un-self-conscious, non-classically trained performers belting out a Shakespeare that even I could enjoy.

In driving back to London, Barry thought we might stop off and have tea. In Banbury, of clock fame, we found ourselves peering through dimpled glass, tea-shop window panes, shop after shop at happy people gorging themselves on scones, cream and jam, with Barry becoming more and more apoplectic as he found each tea-shop door locked. Apparently one doesn't drink tea after 5 p.m.! We settled for some peanuts extracted from a publican who couldn't give us a beer until 5:30. Inside I was laughing myself silly, but poor Barry was beside himself with murderous rage at being deprived of a real English tea, especially for my sake.

That was the England I first saw in 1957.

After a farewell dinner with Barry and Jones the night before I was to fly back to Canada, waiting for me at the hotel was a message to call a John Nelson-Burton. On the phone I learned that he wanted to meet me. He agreed that he wouldn't mind talking to me the following morning while I packed.

He was a most amiable fellow and was a producer/director for a television company called ABC. His boss wanted to meet with me before I flew out, which was about three hours away. I could bring my bags to the office, which was nearby on Oxford Street, and after the meeting they would have a car standing by to whip me out to the airport. I was intrigued, to say the least, and so I agreed.

His boss was a jolly, pink-faced, quick-talking charmer who could sell a car to a blind man. He thought my stuff he'd seen on the BBC was great and quickly got to the point. Poor John Nelson-Burton was going bonkers producing a series called *Armchair Mystery Theatre*. John vigorously nodded his head in agreement. His boss wondered if I would move to England, all travel expenses paid including return to Canada for me and my family, so I could take over Nelson-Burton's series for two years. We talked a bit about that and I said that I was interested and would think about it. We exchanged addresses and I left to catch my plane, my mind dizzy with possibilities. Phew, what a week! What a guy was Nelson-Burton's boss, Dennis Vance. I liked him, and thought, I could work for him.

Between naps I had plenty to think about on that eleven-hour flight back to Betty, home and hearth, the CBC and Toronto!

CHAPTER SIXTEEN

LAND OF HOPE AND GLORY

Huw Wheldon once proclaimed to me (whenever that dear man defined anything it was always a proclamation) that there were only three reasons for work: God, mammon or glory. God was working to do society good. Mammon? Filthy lucre. And working for glory? That was vanity, plain and simple.

I may be vain in some ways, and won't deny that I enjoyed glory when it came, but the notion of working for it has never so much as entered my head — I'm too self-centred at trying to get my own way. So self-centred, in fact, that when I was about fourteen, an aunt whom I loathed told me that by painting banners for the May Day parade I was wasting the talent that God gave me. I angrily told her I made my own talent, after which she turned to my mother, saying that what I needed was to be sent to a military academy to be straightened out.

After the basic necessities of life are looked after, money is to be enjoyed — and it's something I have rarely worked for. I'm probably naïve in believing that making money is easy and is for the lazy — an abstraction that frees one from conscience and morality. Masochistically, I revel in the strictures of conscience and morality. Have I then just defined my motives for work as being, in Wheldon's definition, for God? Too simple, I think. God, mammon and glory are the bonuses that come from meeting one's own standards of quality.

None of this was in the front of either Betty's or my mind as we chewed over the pros and cons of moving to England. We were happy in our modest Governor's Bridge house, the kids were happy and at school. I liked the CBC and was eminently satisfied with my work. In England, there was no challenge for me in producing a mystery series, which I felt I could do with my hands tied behind my back. The English money offered was precisely the same as the CBC was paying me. Our attitude at the time is best revealed when one time, after I told Betty that we needed a new garage, I agreed with her when she said that the money it would cost would be better spent on a trip to Greece to see the Parthenon.

So, it was the Parthenon's Marbles in London that we settled upon. We knew the kids might be dislocated for a while, but it would be exciting for us to live in famous London, see a bit of the country and old friends, Grierson, Daphne Lilly who had married Edgar Anstey, Margaret Ann — now Lady Elton — and Betty's closest Film Board friend, Marion Leigh. Besides, it was for only two years with return passage guaranteed, what could we lose?

I wrote to Vance and entered into long-distance negotiations with ABC television. A few weeks before Christmas I received a telegram saying, FLY ENGLAND SOONEST OUR EXPENSE STOP MEET HOWARD THOMAS MANAGING DIRECTOR STOP REGARDS VANCE.

My workload being what it was, I had to wait until I could grab a few days over Christmas. Vance met me at Heathrow with either his first or his second wife, and after putting me up in a top hotel took me to meet Howard Thomas in his Wardour Street office.

He was a tallish, thickset man with thinning hair who looked at me through thick, horn-rimmed glasses. It was clear that he was carefully observing my reactions as he boasted about his company.

I knew that the commercial TV companies were all split up in kooky ways to cover different parts of the country for only part of a week, and to my surprise I learned that ABC was on the air for only two days — Saturdays and Sundays — for the Manchester and Birmingham areas.[64] He was frank in admitting that they needed to get more out of their Saturdays, because advertisers shunned the day before Sunday, when shops were not open. *The Armchair Mystery Theatre* program I was being considered for, if it got mammoth audiences, perhaps would attract more advertisers. Sunday, their big day, was in good shape, because Vance was doing such a good job with their *Armchair Theatre*, which followed *Sunday Night at the London Palladium*, whatever that was.

I was relieved to hear that the Independent Television Authority would not allow sponsorship of programs by companies. I volunteered that that was wise and amused Thomas with some of my gruesome experiences with sponsors. I warmed to him when I learned of his admiration for some of the same people we both knew, including John Grierson, Basil Wright and Edgar Anstey. This was because he had been managing director of Associated British Pathé, which made newsreels and documentaries owned by Associated British Picture Corporation, the same parent company that owned ABC television.

We talked a bit about how I went about being producer of my dramas seen on the BBC, which he much admired. We both smiled at what we had in common — documentary, happy marriages, and daughters, with his two to my three. He told me that he would see me

---

64 The situation with the private, independent television stations, which began in Britain in 1955, was somewhat complicated. This network of regional stations also shared programming between them (sometimes showing at the same time, sometimes not). Programs like *Sunday Night at the London Palladium* were fully networked and shown at the same time, as was *Armchair Theatre*. Other programs would be shown at different times (the first season of *The Avengers*, for example, was shown in other regions about three months after it was first shown in the Midlands and the North of England on ABC). Several of these franchises, like ABC, were limited to broadcasting on weekends while others, like Granada, were limited to weekdays.

again on Monday after Dennis Vance had shown me the studios over the weekend. I thought the meeting had gone well as I cabbed back to my hotel to grab a quick sleep before meeting Dennis for the train trip.

On the train, Vance explained that the main offices were in London, rehearsals were in London, and the sets were designed in London, but they were built in the studios in Manchester, where the technical and camera crews were based. Messy, I thought.

The train trip was riotous fun, because we were on the same train that carried the cast and its production staff. Imagine my surprise when its director amazingly turned out to be Ted Kotcheff. Ted had left my drama department several months earlier to join what I thought was Granada, who had earlier pirated from the CBC some of our best people: Silvio Narizzano, Hank Kaplan, Wilf Fielding, Tom Spaulding and more. This play was going to be Ted's first for *Armchair Theatre* and it starred the lovely Elizabeth Sellars.

Manchester's production centre was a huge converted ABC cinema palace, built in the days when vaudeville acts were an obligatory part of an evening at the flicks. The auditorium's raked floor had been levelled to join the stage. Trouble was, between the main part of the studio and the stage, there was a large lift that used to rise out of the pit to reveal the orchestra. Unfortunately, when raised, its slightly protruding steel rim jarred a camera dollying over it, and so it had to be avoided. The heavy Vinton camera crane had to avoid it as well because it was too heavy. Very messy, I thought.

The sets, however, comprised of a two-level interior of a mansion, impressed me enormously. They were beautifully designed, finished and dressed. Toward the end of the second studio day, the fog outside had crept into the studio and the sets and action looked as if the cameras were shooting through a silk stocking. My English hosts were embarrassed, but I, to be polite, said the shots looked somewhat attractive — which, in fact, they did.

The production was a disaster. There were so many technical breakdowns that the live show had to be cancelled and a feature film found to replace it. I began to feel that I had made a mistake and should hightail it back to Canada.

Ted, accustomed to our smooth studio floor and our swiftly moving cameramen, microphone boom operators and cable handlers, was asking this English crew for shots and at a pace to which they were totally unaccustomed. Why doesn't Vance intervene, I thought. He's the producer, isn't he? Couldn't he foresee this in dry rehearsal? Maybe producers don't do that kind of thing here . . . what the hell am I getting into?

The crew, in trying to please Ted — and he's the kind of guy you want to please — were doing their damnedest to give him what he wanted. In the process, one piece of equipment after another began to break down with consequential loss of valuable time. First, a microphone boom went. Then a second. One had to be borrowed from Granada Television. Then the Vinton crane broke down, nearly injuring its camera operator. The crane was fixed, but an hour later broke down again, too late to get another one from Granada. Vance finally decided enough was enough, and from the fog-bound ABC studios in Didsbury, Manchester, phoned Howard Thomas in London and cancelled the show.

Somewhat downtrodden, we returned to the hotel. Our spirits were quickly revived by the indomitable Dennis Vance, who miraculously produced some booze, and a small party was held in my room with Ted and his production secretary, Verity Lambert. In a corner, quietly, Ted said, "Boy does this place need you! They are great guys but haven't a clue about television drama."

"Ted," I said, "I'm not sure I want this kind of mess."

"Naw," said Ted. "You and Betty will love England. You can cope with them. They're so easy and willing!"

Back in London on the following morning, as arranged, I went to see Howard Thomas, but this time at the Golden Square headquarters of ABPC (Associated British Pictures Corporation). He made no mention of the catastrophic events of the previous night but asked what I thought of the studio. I said I admired the sets, the crew's enthusiasm, and with the exception of the orchestra lift, thought the conversion of the cinema was excellently done. He asked me to have lunch with him, but first he wanted me to meet some members of the executive board of the corporation.

After some quick visits to three of them, Thomas left me alone in an office, saying he'd be back shortly. Half an hour later he returned looking decidedly cheerful and we left for lunch. Outside, we got into his Jag limo and to his chauffeur he said, "Boad, to the Ivy Restaurant."

After our drinks were brought to us in the tiny foyer, Thomas wiped the cat-that-swallowed-a-mouse-look on his face and very solemnly told me that he wished me to join them at ABC. I said that I was pleased. In my letters with ABC, I had not responded to their last offer of five thousand pounds a year. Having had some experience in negotiations, and knowing that it was expected that I ask for more, I told him that their fee was the same as I was getting in Canada, but here the tax bite was considerably bigger. He explained that their offer was most unusual in that they were not only going to pay to bring my family and furniture to England but also pay for our return to Canada at the end of two years.

I was not to worry about taxes, he said — he had a top hat scheme, which I did not understand, [65] which he said would reduce the tax bite. "Besides," he went on, "you'll get a car, and should you want to buy a house, the company will be happy to give you an interest-free mortgage." Well, that shut me up but good. Having worked only for publicly owned Canadian organizations, the idea of a free car had never occurred to me. And an interest-free mortgage! We shook hands on it. He wanted me to start right away but reluctantly agreed that it was only fair that I give CBC three months' notice.

After a final meal, wine, brandy and a cigar, the good Boad was waiting outside and I was driven to my hotel, still smoking the cigar. With mutual wishes for a happy New Year, Thomas left. I flew back to Canada that evening still with the residue of jet lag from four days earlier, bursting to tell Betty the news.

---

65   While Newman would initially have a contract with Associated British Cinemas or the Associated British Picture Corporation (ABPC), he, and the rest of the production staff would be moved to Iris Productions Limited, a shell company set up by ABC in order to achieve possible taxation benefits. Most of the letters Newman has in his papers are on Iris stationery.

As I expected, she was overjoyed. The CBC regretfully accepted my resignation and told me I would be welcomed back at the end of two years. Hugh Horler actually looked worried as he congratulated me. Betty and I had decided all along that if we were going to be gone for only two years, it would be stupid to sell our house. Luckily for us, Joyce Davidson, who had been in our house at parties, wanted to rent it, so it all worked out. But I still had my job to do.

Two memorable events occurred during those last three months, as if the excitement of going to England wasn't enough. One was to challenge my desire for England and the other saddened me.

Michael Sadlier, a friend of Gunnar Rugheimer's, was working in New York for Showcase Productions, one of the most prestigious and successful television producing companies in the United States. The Hollywood arm of the company did, among others, *The Dinah Shore Show*, while its New York half made for NBC the tasteful and innovative ninety-minute *Producer Showcase* series. In it were shows at the level of Mary Martin in *Peter Pan* and a musical version of *Our Town*, which starred Frank Sinatra. Thanks to Michael Sadlier, the New York arm had seen some of my Canadian dramas and now wanted me.

The New York partner of the company, Saul Jaffe, flew me down to New York, installed me in the Waldorf-Astoria and for one and a half days worked on me to join them. The offer sounded too good to refuse, but I did. This tiny, slim, sophisticated man sat dwarfed in a huge chair, surrounded by Chinese antiques in his vast, high-up, Waldorf Towers apartment (the one with the glass greenhouse). He worried himself sick because I turned him down. It was so far out — this, this *Canadian*! Who turns down three times what he currently makes so he can continue to produce a lowdown mystery series in a has-been country — who would turn down an offer to work in the show business capital of the world to produce only four, high-budget dramas with stars? He simply couldn't believe that all I wanted was for Betty and me and our girls to taste England for two years.

Neither before nor after England have I ever had a tinge of regret over my decision. Years later, I heard that six months after my session with Saul Jaffe, he entered hospital with a nervous breakdown.

The other event was a sad one. In January, on a Sunday morning, I received a phone call from Linda Ballantyne, Andrew Allan's wife, asking me to come over right away — Andrew wanted to have a quiet talk with me. Not the following day in the office, but immediately.

Linda opened the door and, after I shed snow, galoshes and overcoat, she led me to Andrew, who rose from his chair with a glass of whiskey in his hand, thanking me for coming. The immaculate, dark apartment had that crushing silence of a childless, uniquely Torontonian, Sunday afternoon. I accepted a drink, and leaving Linda behind I followed him into what was his study. For one so tall and well-built, the head of CBC radio drama had a surprisingly small head, pink and round with wispy blond hair. He sat down at his desk but swivelled his chair around to face me as I sank into mine. I was curious and nervous, still awed by his formidable achievements, his almost old-world manner so close to arrogance — his insistence that actors at rehearsal, and even his friends, call him Mr. Allan. Even after fifteen years we were barely nodding acquaintances. I waited.

Leaning forward slightly, his blue, almost lidless appearing eyes, looked at me for a moment, then, as if wishing to get it over with quickly, he said something along the lines of, "I've waited too long. I must get into television. Will you take me into your department as a director?"

I was dumbfounded. Was he going into this knowing that I was leaving and that my job was now open? Nah, couldn't be. Allan wasn't reputed to be ambitious, seeking high office. Maybe it was because television was getting all the critical attention and radio none at all — the guy was missing the limelight. Why the hell shouldn't he? He certainly earned it ten times over. Obviously too, he wanted the plain and simple fun of creating in a new medium.

"That's terrific, Andrew," I immediately answered. "Just name the day you want to move in and I'll clear an office for you and get you a production secretary."

As we talked, it became obvious to me that there could be trouble ahead. For many years he'd been accustomed to finding and commissioning his own plays, being totally his own man in every respect. No way could I avoid spelling out what he would have to face, and I said, "You know, Andrew, that with me as your producer, you will have to be responsible to me. Because of sponsors and other reasons, you will have to accept the scripts I assign to you."

"I understand that," he said.

Taking a deep breath, I continued, "I will also approve your lead actors and if necessary suggest changes you may have to make during dry rehearsal and in the studio."

Thoughtfully, he nodded his head. It was clear that he had not foreseen how radical the change would be for him, nor how nerve-wracking an experience it would be for me.

To lighten the moment, I went on to say, "Don't be concerned about your greenness about cameras. I'm a good teacher and will help you right down the line. Within a couple of shows you'll beat the pants off everyone."

Two scotches later, Linda saw us emerge, Andrew looking chipper and me relatively cheerful. Once I had my galoshes and overcoat on, Andrew thanked me for the way I responded to him. His last words as I left were, "Don't worry, Sydney. I'll do exactly as you wish. I'll be a good boy."

For his first play, one for *On Camera*, I picked a simple production that was modestly easy to stage for the cameras. It was a courtroom drama, easy to shoot, and with all three cameras generally on the same side of the set, reverse angles — the main pitfall of the novice camera director — would be easy to avoid. I did my usual with Andrew — we agreed on cast and he accepted every bit of my advice after rehearsal quietly in a corner, away from the cast. We continued to consult when in the studio right up to and including the dress rehearsal. As usual, after the dress and relatively confident, I rushed home to see the show on the air with Betty.

He didn't make a single mistake in the camera-work the show required, but the real bonus came in the acting. His long experience as a director showed in the rich characterizations — better than some of my best directors. I was extremely pleased, and I tried to phone the control room to tell him so after it finished. The line was busy for a long time because of the dozens of congratulatory calls he received from his many friends.

The next day, the press raved about the show — along the lines of, "ANDREW ALLAN PROVES HIS METTLE" and "At long last, television has a real, professional director!"

Somewhat unkind to my other directors, I thought, but the acting! It was damn good and hooray for Andrew. I was smug, too, about the way I had handled him.

For his next play, he was critical of the script. I got George Salvarson to find one that Andrew liked. On casting he was completely uncooperative. When I turned up at his dry rehearsal, he loudly greeted me from across the room with all the actors present. "Well, here's the supervising producer of drama himself to see how we are getting along. I'll be with you in a moment, Chief." The sonofabitch! *I'll be a good boy*, my foot! The poor fucker's success had gone to his head. When he disagreed with some of my notes on the rehearsal, I didn't particularly mind, but I had to ask him to lower his voice because the actors, hearing him, were snickering. At me? Him? It didn't matter. It was bad.

The show was a flop. I hoped he'd eventually settle down, but his work in television never did amount to much. I was glad to be away, so I wouldn't have to see the death of a giant. I would be off to England in two weeks' time. What a pity that Andrew Allan had not come into television when it started, six years earlier when he was at his most self-confident.

There were going away parties for Betty and me. My staff gave me a suitcase; Toronto CBC executives gave me — of all things — a floor lamp; MacLaren's agency, a beautiful calf-leather attaché case; and General Motors, a sterling silver, hallmarked cigarette box suitably engraved. GM's name beneath mine was engraved so boldly that I couldn't resist quipping to Hugh Horler that I should charge GM for advertising space, as it would be seen on my desk in England by visitors. It was all rather touching and heartwarming.

Betty and I preceded the children to England by three weeks, leaving them with Betty's folks, to enable us to find someplace to live. Having seen the way Vance and Thomas lived, I made up my mind that never again would Betty and I travel by anything less than first-class. And never having been on a sea voyage I booked one of the four suites on the *Empress of England* sailing from New York. It was in that suite that I saw my first bidet and to this day am not quite sure how to use it. It's great though, I found, for washing one's feet.

Just as in the movies of the day, New York friends came on board carrying bottles of brandy and champagne for a farewell party; finally, we bid farewell to North America. It was the end of March when we left, and Betty and I celebrated my 41st birthday on the ship as it was heaving and tossing like a cork on the giant seas that towered above us in a force-nine gale. It was so bad that, for a day and a half, the 168-seating first-class dining room served only us and a few others. Thanks to Betty's experience, having crossed the Pacific many times, neither of us became seasick. After each meal, she dragged me out onto the sea-sprayed deck and we clutched tightly together as we walked its perimeter in the wind, twice. While invigorating, the mountainous, bilious green seas frightened the hell out of me. I am still a landlubber to the core.

Immediately upon our arrival in London,[66] Howard Thomas assigned to us the company secretary, who was to help Betty and me find a place to live. He was a courtly, tall, white-haired gentleman, Chris Summers, who couldn't have been kinder. With Betty in his good hands, looking for a house, I was ready to go to work.

Before I could take a breath, Howard Thomas called me into his office and told me that he was promoting Dennis Vance, whose creative mind he wanted to exploit, by putting him in charge of program development. He asked me to become his head of drama. After he agreed to my request that I would also personally produce *Armchair Theatre*, I accepted.

My God, they sure did things in style — a far cry from the sparse, Canadian ways I was accustomed to. Thomas threw a cocktail party

---

66 According to UK immigration records, Newman arrived in Liverpool on April 7, 1958, aboard the Canadian Pacific S.S. *Empress of England*.

to introduce Betty and me to the senior staff. During it, I saw Dennis Vance at his most irrepressible self.

In a theatrical whisper, he said to me, "Don't ever hire any queers. You see, Howard hates them." Behind Dennis, I could see Howard Thomas stiffen. I cautioned him that Howard might hear. Dennis, chortling, continued, "What he doesn't know, though, is that there are one or two in the company." By now, Howard Thomas had turned and began to walk toward us.

"Quick, tell me," I whispered. "Who are they?"

With Howard now joining us, Dennis said to me, "First give me a kiss and then I'll tell you!"

Dennis, I became aware, knew damn well what he was doing. He roared with laughter which, of course, I couldn't help joining. Howard laughed as well. Clearly, there was a warm bond between them.

Eight or nine months later it was clear that there was really no need for a head of program development — not when ABC was on the air for only two days a week. Howard must have realized that, so why had he appointed Dennis to a non-job? Years later, I got a plausible answer, and it explained my invitation to join ABC television.

As I discovered soon after my arrival, those production weekends in Manchester, after the days' hard work in the studio, often became a kind of bacchanalia. Apparently, a few weeks before I met Dennis Vance, along the broad corridor of the Midland Hotel, a naked, giggling female star was seen being chased by an equally naked, senior ABC executive. This occurrence did not get into the press, but it did get to the staid, po-faced, members of Associated British Picture Corporation's executive board.

Howard Thomas was hauled on the carpet and told to clean up his act. It was likely that Dennis Vance was the inspiration for such goings-on. By now I knew Dennis fairly well and could see that it was possible — likely, in fact — that they were right. So, ebullient and non-conforming Dennis had to go. The only choices open to Howard were to fire him, which he didn't have the heart to do, or promote Dennis out of trouble, with my hiring providing a sufficient excuse to do so.

In all my life, I have never known a more passionate man. Dennis lived his life as if it were fiction sometimes — alas, a soap opera. Once, so beside himself because a woman he loved rejected him, he stabbed her, nearly killing her. He got a three-year suspended sentence, providing he received psychiatric help. When he died in 1986, he left behind his seventh wife.

On my arrival at the offices of the drama department on Oxford Street, I discovered that there was no systematic way of getting scripts. It was almost precisely the same situation as I had found at the CBC four years earlier — directors finding their own material, usually cut-down rehashes of old west-end plays, some Ibsen, the odd O'Neill and New York television hand-me-downs. Worse, any original script given to a director might be the last a writer would hear of it. I needed a Nathan Cohen, and so found a young American screenwriter living in London, who had recently married a lovely Englishwoman. He had reputedly written twenty-one Hollywood features. He became my first "British" story editor.

Within months, he complained that his burden was so great he needed an assistant. I agreed and he recommended a friend of his, Peter Luke, formerly a wine salesman but now a frustrated writer of fiction, reduced to doing a fortnightly page of book reviews for *The Queen* magazine. While he knew nothing about play writing, he seemed amiable enough and as I was in a hurry, so I took him on. I was impressed that not only was his father an ex-colonel governor (whose name I had come across in a biography of T.E. Lawrence when he was deputy governor of Jerusalem), but Peter was an old Etonian. I also liked the fact that he, like me, had once aspired to become an artist.

Early on, my story editor and I had a row over a silly matter irrelevant to these memoirs, resulting in his early departure, but I shall always be indebted to him. My meeting Peter Luke was the beginning of a solid friendship, one that professionally was to enhance the latent qualities we each possessed.

I mustn't forget to mention that Dennis had hired a reader of scripts whom he had borrowed from the company's Elstree Film Studios. She was sweet, chalk to my cheese, who somehow could never get a handle on me. She was frightfully middle-class. I often thought of her as a refugee from an Oscar Wilde play. As much as I liked her, and from what I observed in her about aspects of British high society that I was ignorant of, I had to let her go. She just didn't fit into my as-yet-unresolved notions about the kinds of plays I should be producing in England.

In my first week, Dennis walked me around his, now *my*, drama department to meet the staff. The directors were all on contract, most for one production and some for many. Among them, I was able to greet Ted Kotcheff and John Nelson-Burton again. New to me were Philip Saville, whose name will crop up many times in this saga, and Wilfred Eades, a helluva nice guy whose work was never less than professional. This was in the very early days, before he left for what he thought were greener pastures.

One of the most endearing was George More O'Ferrall, who had left feature films as one of Britain's most eminent directors. His reputation was such that he had been able to draw to *Armchair Theatre* the biggest film stars of the day, such as Ann Todd, Flora Robson, Sarah Churchill, Joan Greenwood and André Morell. O'Ferrall's charming but disarming vagueness resulted in my renaming him George More-or-less O'Ferrall.

In one office, I saw a man in his early fifties hunched over a drawing board manipulating a T-square and a set-square, a scale ruler and a sharp pencil like a pro. "Ah, a designer," I said to Dennis. Dennis told me no, he wasn't a designer, but a much-revered director. Bewildered, I said, "Don't we have any designers? Do directors design their own sets?"

The director answered me. "I can't trust the designers to give me what the script needs. That's why I do my own designing."

"Uh huh," I said and leaned over his shoulder and looked at his floor plan. The old designer in me cringed. What I saw was no better than sets for old-fashioned, stage vaudeville skits — shallow with no depth. As we walked away from the room, I asked Dennis, "Is he on a several show contract or what?"

Dennis explained, "Long-term, but that's his last show on it. We're in the middle of negotiating a new one with his agent."

"I see," I replied. "Any director who thinks he's a better designer than a designer must think he's Gordon Craig and that guy sure ain't. I'm not renewing him."

Half a year later, I heard that the poor guy had died. He had electrocuted himself while rewiring his house.

I met two extraordinary women that first week. Dodo Watts, a former film star, was ABC's casting director. She was a delightful, tiny and highly competent lady on whom my directors and I leaned heavily. Her nose for new talent and new ways of using old talent were remarkable.

The other was the lean, deadly earnest, almost humourless Marie Donaldson, the company's public relations chief. Her loyalty to Howard Thomas, to the company and to me was beyond all expectation. She was inventive, tasteful and wrote stylishly, as evidenced in the books she edited —*Anatomy of a Television Play: An Inquiry* and *Both Sides of the Camera*. About her being "almost humourless," this was only her everyday manner and was happily belied by the photo captions she wrote in those books.

To introduce me to the British press, Thomas instructed Marie to set up a press conference. And what a press conference she laid on. It was nothing less than a full-scale luncheon for at least forty reporters and critics at the Café Royale. After brandy and cigars, Howard rose and along with fulsome praise said that I would have absolute freedom to be as lively and controversial as I liked. *We shall see*, I thought. *And what do I do if I don't?*

In the three weeks I had been in England, I had spent as much time as I could watching both ITA and BBC television dramas. I thought most of them ho-hum, with dull staging, and unimaginative shooting. It would be difficult but I could change that. Something was missing though, something I couldn't put my finger on. I wanted to do something more than a UK version of *General Motors Theatre* in the two years I would be there. I needed some special angle, a hook that would make *Armchair Theatre* different and, dammit, something more relevant than my competitors' dramas. But the hook eluded me.

With a laboriously hand-written speech in my hand, I got to my feet, praying that I wouldn't put my foot into it, even though I had put as much flannel into my speech as possible. The press people, well fed, were sitting back, curious to see what this colonial creature was like. I sneaked a look at Howard, who appeared to me to be trying to look nonchalant.

I opened by mentioning the risk Howard Thomas was taking in hiring me . . . my gratitude at being freed from censorious sponsors . . . what England meant to me as a Canadian . . . the grand tradition of the British theatre . . . Then, it not having even occurred to me to explain that my views were based only on three weeks' viewing, I said of television drama in England (I had not yet learned that by speaking of "England" I was excluding Scotland, Wales and Northern Ireland) that I found its various single-play series less than exciting: the camera-work was timid, standing back from the actors as if afraid of them; there were too many stage plays; while a theatre audience couldn't get close to actors, a camera could, and there was a need for more intimate acting; past theatre grandeur was of no help to TV drama; and so on. I sat down, and I thought I hadn't done badly.

Howard asked if there were any questions, saying I would be glad to answer them.

Someone made an asinine comment, and suggested that the trouble with stage plays was that they were poorly adapted for television — did I agree?

"Maybe," I answered, "but who wants stage plays, anyway?"

Three people spoke up simultaneously, along the lines of, "You mean they are not good? That Noel Coward and R.C. Sherriff aren't good enough for television?"

"Well," I answered, "yes and no."

Then about six voices shouted, "No? What do you mean, no?"

"Well, maybe. If they wrote specifically for television — that would be okay. But that still wouldn't totally satisfy me."

Jesus, what was I getting into? They were shocked.

I took a deep breath and went on. "As good as they are, I believe they don't speak to television audiences. They speak to elegant people who go to the theatre. Their plays are for upper-class people about upper-class people. It's those 'anyone for tennis' kind of plays that don't touch the ordinary man."

I realized I had dropped a bomb in their midst. The questions flew thick and fast as I found myself firing back one wild answer after another.

"Snobs and intellectuals here look down on television . . . the working man likes it . . . the English theatre uses him as a comic foil . . . ordinary man is confused . . . needs plays for help, not escape . . . to better himself. . ."

In short, the press conference broke up on a high note of controversy.

As we were leaving, Howard congratulated me and before we parted, he asked, "By the way, what you said back there, are they really your views?"

"Yes," I replied.

He darted a mystifying look at me. "Interesting," he said. And with a quick, "G'bye," he left.

For the next few weeks the press had a field day with that conference, which pleased Marie Donaldson immensely.

According to what I read, some stories found me to be a philistine, but most hailed me as the hope of television drama. I was certainly flattered by the attention I received, but wondered if I hadn't made a damn fool of myself.

In rereading those well-thumbed articles, I realized one good thing that emerged from the fray of that press conference: I had found the hook that would motivate my two years in England.

Some quotes from published interviews express my feelings from that May after the press conference — two years before the '60s and swinging London:

"My plays will be more about contemporary themes . . . too many act as if Britain is tired and decadent . . . To me there are exciting subjects here . . . the average person is very much afraid of the brilliant and highly complex work of scientists and engineers. He doesn't understand it and is worried about how he relates to atomic energy, rockets . . . what a fertile field for TV drama! . . . to help the average

Joe better understand the technology his fellow man has created . . . his changing attitudes to marriage, his church, his boss . . . In Canada our plays stemmed from the real everyday world [a lie and a hope only half realized!] . . . Newspapers are a source for themes . . . they build circulation because of their infallible instinct for knowing what interests readers . . . My story editors will study them."

About writers: "The only way to create writers is the slow hard way . . . We must completely change the relationship between writers and the company . . . Story editors will not sit back waiting for writers and scripts to come in. We will woo writers, pay more, even advance money if convinced of their genuineness . . . because ABC's planned writers' competition was scooped by Granada, the money will now go toward higher fees for writers [another lie — I killed it because I think competition's a fake; it was a PR stunt] . . . I hate directors who butcher scripts as if their own."

About actors, they were "generally very fine here in a theatre sense, which doesn't lend too well to intimate TV . . . I don't favour the actor whose technique shows . . . TV actors must act small, deep, leaving it to the director and camera to reveal the size of their actions . . . Dodo Watts will get us big names, but we'll concentrate on new kids who are not spoiled by projecting over theatre footlights."

On directors: "I decry lazy directors who want only to do their own version of the plays they have already seen and understood . . . I have and will find directors who are intelligent and sensitive to dig deep in an original play . . . using cameras as surgeons wield scalpels."

In early June I called a meeting of the senior members of my staff, which included my two story editors, my drama administrator, Tony John, and contract directors. I told them that with Dennis's move to Wardour Street, it was left to me to act as producer until the thirteen-week summer break. Even though I would not take a screen credit, I would be with them on each of the remaining shows — a good chance for them to get to know me and my method of work, which Ted Kotcheff already knew all about. As well, I added, I'd get to know them, so I'd be better able to find or get tailor-made scripts to suit their individual styles.

I told them that during the summer I was going to commission new artwork for the series title, along with original music, which would precede each production when the autumn season would begin in September. Only then would I take my credit as producer.

In slow stages, I proceeded to reveal my hook. "About the plays themselves, I have thought a lot about them and decided that from now on, adaptations of stage plays are out! Caput! Finished!"

There was shocked silence. I went on, saying that while dramatizations of short stories or novels were not ruled out, our main emphasis would be directed toward only original plays by British writers, written specially for television, which we would buy or commission. To that, they practically cheered. Many said, "That's all we ever wanted."

"What about American television plays?" someone asked. "They're good."

"I know they are," I said, "but they'll be done over my dead body." I went on to explain my theory that people want to see themselves on the screen in situations they could identify with, learn from, laugh at. "When you guys do a U.S. play, it reveals its U.S. character, its social ills. You feel you're being daring because it paraphrases your own country, don't you? How about doing the same kind of play about the United Kingdom?"

"Shit," someone said, "there aren't enough writers around. Not good ones, anyway."

"Well," I said as I turned to my two story editors, "we'll bloody well find them, won't we?"

They nodded. "Yeah, it'll be a snap," said the Yank.

"And," I said, "if we can't find 'em, we'll bloody well make them good."

Today, thinking about that meeting with my staff, I realize that, in crossing the Atlantic, a momentous change had occurred in me. I was no longer tentative in my aims. From wanting to be a cartoonist, then an artist, a filmmaker, a television director, a producer, and finally an executive producer — all of my career moves were a part of a process of trying things, testing them, and finding out what they were about. Now, at the age of forty-one, as certain as I knew that the earth was round, I knew exactly what I needed to do. I knew that I was right and my beliefs achievable. So confident was I, the possibility of failure never entered my mind. Was it because England was a distant land and my job was secure in Canada? Was it because of Howard Thomas's arm's length control of me? The willingness of my new staff to follow my lead? The zest of trying through drama to reveal truths (as I saw them) to a new audience in a state of post-Suez shock? Whatever, I was raring to go and nothing I could see would stop me.

While all this was going on, Betty and I had chosen a house, and, as an interim arrangement, we rented a flat on Fitzjohns Avenue in Hampstead just before the arrival of our kids. It was with some excitement that we stood looking through the wire mesh fence of the Trans-Canada Airline terminal in the temporary wartime buildings at Heathrow, watching the Constellation taxi to a stop to see our three girls take their first steps onto English soil.

And there they were, out of the first-class door, coming down the steps looking so damn cute — Deirdre, eleven, Jennifer, nine, and little Gillian, six — each carrying their overnight carry-alls, looking neat as a pin and wearing berets. They spotted us and came running toward us, a look on their faces that no parent can ever forget. But some man seemed to be with them — some character in a cream suit, white Stetson hat, festooned with a camera and binoculars around his neck. As they came closer to us I recognized him. "My god," I said to Betty, "it's Arthur Hailey!"

After immigration, customs, kisses and hugs, and shaking Arthur's hand, I asked him, "What the hell are you doing here?"

He replied, "Remember that two-part play I did for Studio One, *The Pathologist?* The BBC has bought it as a ninety-minuter." He added, grinning, "Fee included return economy fare so I could see it produced. I saw your girls at the airport in Toronto being seen off by your sister-in-law . . . Nora, is it? And Betty's mother. They send their love to you both. You know your girls had their own compartment with berths?"

"Yes, I know," I replied. "But Arthur, the Stetson hat, why the fancy outfit? Your fellow Englishmen'll take you for an American oil tycoon tourist from Texas!"

"Exactly! That's precisely what I want them to think," he replied. "The buggers didn't want me when I was here. Now that I'm a North American, they will!"

Arthur accepted my offer of a ride into London, and I boasted to him how easily I was now driving on the "wrong" side of the road. The car itself reminds me of an amusing story: Unbeknownst to me there was a pecking order that denoted one's status. The group managing director of ABPC rated a Rolls-Royce; executive directors a Bentley; Howard Thomas, as head of his subsidiary company, was allowed a large Jaguar with chauffeur. It was expected that at my level I would buy a Rover, Ford or GM saloon. It wasn't until months later that I found out the car I had chosen was far out of line. It was a smaller and more elegant Jaguar than Howard's. Howard never commented on it, probably attributing it to my Canadian chutzpah, others in the company attributing it to what they assumed was some special seniority I enjoyed; which indeed I did enjoy!

Betty and I, having had the wits scared out of us about state schools by our British friends, most reluctantly entered our girls into St. Christopher's, a private school. This worked out well. Thanks to ABC Television we bought a house on Crediton Hill, NW6, which was in good order, but I insisted on adding central heating. Betty disagreed, fearful that the girls would have friends who would undoubtedly live in underheated houses, and they would become ill and get colds by the radical change in temperature when they came home. I prevailed. Since adding central heating was going to muck up the house, we decided to go whole hog and remake the kitchen, getting rid of its sink, which was more suited to a four-foot-tall scullery maid than Betty's five-foot-six.

During the summer of 1958, I decided that, since England was new to me, we would take our summer holiday in the UK so that I would get a feel for the people who were to watch *Armchair Theatre*. Betty found us a farm family in Cornwall who took in paying guests.

We had a wonderful time enjoying the clean sandy beaches, getting to know Penzance and Mousehole, buying fisherman's shirts and taking the girls out riding horses for the first time. During the two weeks not a single drop of rain fell.

I remember saying to Betty, "Why the hell do the Brits always bitch about their weather? It's perfect, even better than Canada." (The next year we decided to go to the same farm again and it rained solidly for three weeks.)

I looked forward to getting on with my first season. The directors had accepted the fact that they had to indicate to me at rehearsal how and when they were planning on cutting from camera to camera. They mostly accepted my suggested changes of getting in tight on the actors and deepening the sets — so that actors walked toward and away from the camera instead of making right and left entrances and exits. The designers I inherited grabbed at this and began designing wonders. Tim O'Brien, chief of design, helped directors break through the barriers of the tiny flat screen, both through his work and through the work of his designers, Voytek and Reece Pemberton, and those who joined him later: Assheton Gorton, George Haslam, Bob Fuest, Alpho O'Reilly, and Jim Goddard.

Even actors got used to my staring at their faces as I followed the director at rehearsal, scribbling notes about their acting, which I would later quietly give the director.

Once, early on, when I was watching Ann Todd play a love scene with Hugh Williams, she suddenly stopped, glared at me and turned to George More O'Ferrall, saying, "I can't act with that man staring at me."

George took me aside and suggested that I stand well back from her. "After all, Sydney, she is a star!"

I agreed with him, and then slowly resumed my former close position. She did not protest again, and later, she and I became friends when she began directing documentary-type films.

During that period, one of the directors said that I was interfering with his own unique style of directing. "I don't give a damn what style you use," I remember saying, "all I want is clarity of story.

Style without clarity is junk. Just bloody well make sure the audience can hear the dialogue clearly and see the action and actors clearly, especially at the turning points in the story."

When I returned from holiday to set the schedule for my first season, I was dismayed reading the batch of plays the story editors had gathered for me. I knew there were good things in the pipeline, which had been commissioned, but my first few were undistinguished,[67] to say the least! Among the first six, two of them were based on stage plays, to my chagrin — chagrin because Marie Donaldson had publicized widely my intention of using only original writing. I figured I would get away with it by using big close-ups, good sets, dramatic lighting and above all, a fast pace.

I didn't get away with it. The critics tore me to pieces. This Canadian hotshot was just another bigmouth from across the Atlantic.

Ironically, it was the sixth play, a stage play and American to boot, that saved my bacon. I observed later that most critics didn't give a damn whether a play was specially written for TV or whether its subject matter was about their own country. It was stars they wanted and a play that had a reputation. None of this was in my mind when I made my decision. What motivated me was that I hadn't anything really good that was ready to go.

Being an avid reader of *Variety*, the showbiz bible of "Sticks Nix Hick Pix" fame, I read that an all-star American company was performing in the World's Fair in Brussels, courtesy of the U.S. government, to fly its cultural flag. It was William Saroyan's *The Time of Your Life*. In it were no less than three film stars of international fame: Franchot Tone, Dan Dailey and Ann Sheridan, as well as luminaries from the New York stage including its young, newest star, Susan Strasberg. They were about to finish their run at the end of the

---

67   One of the first of Newman's episodes to air was written by a fellow Canadian, Mordecai Richler, who had moved to London by this point. Richler would write four episodes of *Armchair Theatre* over the next three years, including an adaptation of his 1959 novel *The Apprenticeship of Duddy Kravitz* that was directed by Ted Kotcheff; Kotcheff and Richler would later collaborate on the 1974 film adaptation.

following week, and it occurred to me that if I could get them to come to England on their way home and televise the production, I would have a real winner.

I phoned Jean Dalrymple, director and producer of the New York City Centre Theatre, who was in Brussels at the time. I told her about my idea and asked if it was a possibility — it was! In fact, she was most enthusiastic and thought the cast would like a brief respite in London (I hadn't mentioned that the studio was not in London). Uncle Sam would pay for the performers and literary rights and I would only have to pick up the company's expenses while in England. I had little time and said I would call her back.

According to my own rules, this decision would have to be made by Howard Thomas. The expenses alone would be far beyond my budget. But Thomas was out of England and unreachable and I had to act fast. It was too good a chance to miss. I decided to risk it, phoned her and we metaphorically shook hands. I said I would send a director over to Brussels to see the production and work out with her the cuts required to reduce the length of the full stage play.

The idea of *Time of Your Life* fitting into our length of one hour was insane — only Howard Thomas could square a longer period with the network committee of the commercial companies. And how would Howard react to what I had done?

He returned and without expression accepted the fact of my decision. He was a wily one, I found out over the years. Had the production failed it would have been my fault. If a success he'd be happy, but at this stage he was going to reveal neither joy nor disapproval. I suggested to him that ninety minutes was the minimum length suitable for the production, and within half a day, I got his okay. I assigned Philip Saville to direct it and sent him off to Brussels.

Marie Donaldson began having a field day sending out reams of press releases, which the press gobbled up. A press party was arranged for the day of the cast's arrival in England. Even before the play hit the air, Marie boasted to me that if ABC had had to buy the publicity for the show it got, it would have cost them £40,000 — whatever that would be in terms of today's money, it boggles the mind. It didn't occur to me then that, even if the show was lousy, Howard Thomas would win, if only for the enterprise his company had shown.

The plan I had worked out with Philip and Marie was a noon party on the Thursday of their arrival, followed by a rehearsal with the cast to check the cuts in the play and Philip's restaging of the action to suit the cameras. We'd have a second rehearsal on Friday morning before the cast would catch the afternoon train to Manchester. Saturday and most of Sunday would be spent in the studio blocking the camera shots, with dress rehearsal at 6 p.m., finally hitting the air live at 8:30 Sunday evening for a ninety-minute *Armchair Theatre*.

At the party, among a dozen press people, with champagne flowing and the cast revelling and being interviewed in the glare of popping flashbulbs, a tight-lipped Franchot Tone drew me aside. He looked at me as if his fuse was well lit. On behalf of the cast he said they would not rehearse the show for Philip Saville and me that afternoon, because they had just learned the show was being televised from Manchester. It had to be done in London, which was the only reason they agreed to do the show.

I sweated buckets and finally managed to calm him down, along with the other members of the cast. The afternoon's rehearsal was a shambles because of too much discontent and drink. They went out on the town that night, and the Friday rehearsal could not take place because only half the cast turned up. It was a miracle that they all turned up for the train. In Manchester there was complaining from many of them who couldn't be put up at the Midland Hotel. Pacifying Philip, who was justifiably nervous, was also killing me. Everything now depended on him.

That first night, I was sitting totally fraught and exhausted in the Midland lounge at 1 a.m., trying to have a quiet drink with Tom Singleton, when an old night-duty porter came up to me and said, "A long distance call, Sir. I believe it's from London."

"Oh my god," I said, "it's Betty!"

The porter, catching the drift of my worry, quickly added, "The call is from the Savoy Hotel."

I was relieved and told the porter, "Please tell them that you can't find me."

Tom, who was in charge of ABC's religious programs, looked dismayed and said, "Sydney, you can't do that. Suppose it's someone in distress?"

So I took the call and wouldn't you know? — it was from Ann Sheridan's agent. She had just received a long distance call from Miss Sheridan who, at that moment, was three floors above me, complaining that she couldn't sleep in the room she was given. The producer must find another room. And that producer was me.

When I re-joined Tom, I'm afraid I was totally humourless in telling him about the call. I ended by saying, "For heaven's sake, next time please save your compassion for your religious programs."

The two days in the studio were a nightmare, with me fighting hysteria, terrified that Franchot Tone would strangle me and that the whole thing might blow up at any moment. I'll say this though: it was worth it, if only for the affirmation that there is nothing like working with rock-hard professionals. Despite all the complaints, the fouled-up rehearsals, the drinking and the headaches, in the end the acting and the production were nearly flawless.

As for Saville, I saw in him an unimagined, steely strength, infinite patience and a mighty talent that I have revered ever since. Despite our many ups and downs over the years, I have never forgotten that it was he who made my almost impossible idea an overwhelming success. I cannot recall a single bad notice in the press. Praise was lavished on ABC, the series and on me.

Two Sundays later, we had another great success. Still not an original play, still not British, but funny as a satire pertinent to the times. It was Reuben Ship's dramatization of James Thurber's short story "The Greatest Man in the World." Ted Kotcheff was at his liveliest best in directing it. It was about the discovery by an American president (superbly played by Donald Pleasence) that an American had built a rocket, flown it to the moon and was now returning to earth. He decides to publicize this unknown amateur as epitomizing America's best to the world. After the hero (played by Patrick McGoohan with superb relish) lands, to the president's horror, his ideal American is a vulgar, crude slob. To conceal his mistake from the public, he orders the oaf to be killed by having him pushed out of a skyscraper window. I loved that show, but satire aside, it still wasn't what I set out to produce for my series; right content, but wrong country of origin.

But it was during the show that the past haunted me and forced me to change some of my views. It had been ingrained in me at the National Film Board and at the CBC that the head of state of any country was never to be portrayed as a figure of fun. He represented a nation, and making fun of him, or even a country's flag, was showing disrespect to a people.

At the NFB, I had made a war propaganda film about a Canadian Navy Motor Torpedo Boat sinking a German submarine, which had a Swastika flag flying on its conning tower. As it sank beneath the waves, my commentary, "as the Nazi rag sinks . . ." was excised by Ross McLean, my boss, who explained to me that the flag represented the German people at this time, and even though we were at war with Germany, we do not insult the people of Germany.

In *Greatest Man*, Ted Kotcheff, aided and abetted by a willing Donald Pleasence, was sending up rotten a fictional president of the United States; it worried me. I made Ted reduce the hard edge of Pleasence's satirical portrayal. It still went further than I thought proper, but I discovered that, except for a mewling protest from the U.S. Embassy, no British critic gave a damn for such niceties.

What took me longer to shed was another ingrained policy: the avoidance of swearing by characters in my plays, especially blasphemy. This was a continuing bone of contention between writers and me for many years. In the 160 or so *Armchair Theatres* I produced, there was not a single "damn you" or "Jesus!" or even "bloody" as an expletive that was heard by its millions of viewers each Sunday night.

These haunts of mine represented real differences between British and North American audiences. In the U.S. and Canada, at the time of this writing, ridiculing a head of state is confined to small circulation magazines or the nightclub, and blasphemy is still avoided in the mass media. In the UK, not even the royal family is spared and rarely, if ever, does a critic comment on the plethora of religious and other expletives in drama.[68]

Ruminating on these strictures, I think there is something fundamental and even sensible in them; they represent a basic respect for people. If an author dislikes Maggie Thatcher or Brian Mulroney, isn't it more accurate to blame the party that made them leader? In a democratic society, the leader, for better or worse, represents the whole nation. Knocking them, to this brainwashed Canadian, may be an expression of dislike of the nation by the play's author; likewise, the producer can be seen as catering to the self-hatred of his audience. Ruminations, I repeat.

Not a rumination is my belief that, unless one is setting out to represent a nasty, anti-religious villain, blasphemy is silly and irrelevant. Why alienate the portion of the audience who are churchgoing believers by larding the speech of, say, the hero with expletives offensive to them?

The argument usually used by a lesser writer is that he is being truthful in portraying his character's everyday speech. To me, there are small truths and selected truths, and all creative work is a matter of selection. When the small truth of the dialogue he gives his hero distracts the viewer from the larger truth of his main theme — to put it bluntly — he's being an asshole.

Sex and violence separates the U.S. and the UK by a gap much wider than the Atlantic. The United States accepts blood and gore as a staple of its mass media, while sex is better done than seen. In the UK, on the other hand, breasts, bums and bodily functions are fine, while violence on television is not. I come down very much on the side of the Brits.

Explicit sex on the screen is becoming a bit of a bore for audiences. Maybe it's my age, but I don't think so. No director seems able to

---

68 Newman's statement is a little out of touch, even for 1987, when he was writing this memoir. Ridiculing a head of state was a regular occurrence in the U.S. on TV series such as *Saturday Night Live* and in Canada on CBC radio series such as *Royal Canadian Air Farce* (which by the '90s moved to television) and *Double Exposure*. Blasphemy, however, was still taboo.

express anything more relevant to the lovers' characters than ecstasy or rejection, and so it becomes a ho-hum experience for any viewer over the age of fifteen. The best character-revealing, explicit sex I have ever seen on a public screen was in a cinema in Copenhagen with an average audience.

It was in *I Am Curious Yellow*, when its heroine was placidly complying with her love penetrating her while she was yakking away, non-stop, about the Spanish Civil War. That was in 1968 and has still to be bettered today.

Violence is part of the grammar of drama and cannot be avoided. What we can control is how it is used and why it's important. If it makes the audience ill, it's stupid. If it's put in to hype up a flagging story, it's lousy art. That, in essence, is it. I honestly cannot see how violence can be codified and legislated against. If it is, millions risk being deprived of a valuable drama that contains one moment of violence, which might trigger only one who might copy what he has seen. Banning that is about as sensible as banning that murderous weapon, the motor car.

Television is accessible and influential. If it wasn't, advertisers are wasting their millions on it, as are governments in times of war and in combatting AIDS. I believe in what I learned in my twenties from John Grierson, that sound and picture changes minds. And since then, every damn thing in life has come to change minds.

I laid down some simple notions. Some people become physically ill when they see blood, and only a fool wants an audience to puke. Ergo, show blood with care. Some in the audience are daffy with hate, so don't show them how to make a bomb. Viewers will identify with the innocent character, so being bound and helpless and tortured becomes powerfully disturbing, and that kind of reaction is a turn off. And finally, avoid common, easily available weapons such as a kitchen knife, so as not to provoke a viewer who may be feeling a momentary murderous rage to act upon it in the moment.

The first production that made me feel that I was coming close to my objective of producing plays about the turning points in British life was Ray Rigby's "The Boy with the Meat Axe," my eleventh *Armchair*

Theatre. It was about a young, working-class couple. The wife (Sheila Allen) is pregnant but the husband (Richard Pasco) has fallen in love with a Roman Catholic girl (Virginia Maskell) whose brother (Sean Connery) is threateningly opposed to her marrying a divorced man.

The notion of violence was mainly in the title. The play itself had one punch-up between the brother and husband.

The play could be described as one does an iceberg: the action seen was the tip with the murderous feeling implied, latent in the mass of prejudice underneath. Philip Saville gave it pace and searing emotion and captured beautifully its gritty, working-class reality. It got a whopping audience who recognized that this play was no escapist fantasy. It was real and about them. Most discerning critics were impressed. Some weren't, and I believe that it was the first time that the condescending name, "kitchen sink drama," was used. As if only "drawing room comedy" was acceptable!

Considering his present stature, it's amazing to recall that as a struggling actor then, Sean Connery's fee would have been £60.

Not amusing, at the beginning of my first season, was the near revolt of my directors at the original plays I was forcing upon them. "I know I said I would rather do original plays. But this is crap. These writers of Peter's can't write," they would tell me. More times than I'd like to admit, I had to counter with, "The only way writers are going to improve is when they see their own crap on the air, so go and rub their noses in it. Do it — but do it with class!"

The less-than-good scripts quickened the skills of the directors. I used all I had learned in the past to throw production values and directorial dust into the eyes of viewers and critics alike. The play's theme, a cleverly chosen cast, good acting, spectacular camera work, deep sets and a bit of well-chosen background music went a long way to conceal a play's weaknesses.

In January I did a landmark play — the first that I know of in television that dealt with miscegenation. Again, ironically, it was originally a stage play by Ted (now Lord) Willis. I saw it in the West End, liked it, and when I heard that its run was coming to a close, I bought it from Willis's agent, Harvey Unna. I had to, again, ask

Howard Thomas to get from the ITA network a ninety-minute slot. Again, he had no reason to regret it.

In writing the play, Willis pulled no punches. A young West Indian man falls in love with a white girl. She loves him despite the misgivings of her father. Instead of the father being a bigoted redneck, Willis compounded the situation by making him a union general secretary known for his liberal attitude to blacks. Ted Kotcheff, in directing it, brought the acting down to an effective, intimate level and broadened the settings, beautifully denying the play's theatrical origins.

Both Willis and Unna became personal friends. Before I came to England, Willis was a top writer for film and television, writing on contemporary themes. In his credits were films like *Woman in a Dressing Gown*. He also was the creator of *Dixon of Dock Green*. It was *Dixon* that he was noted for when I first met him — when television was being shy about buying his work. It was felt that he was somewhat passé. The accident of my producing "Hot Summer Night" happily revived his reputation. Over the years I produced more of his work.

Some ten years later, he asked me why I was always so kind to him. I told him that I liked his work, but also, "When I first came to England, you and Harvey were the first people here who were kind enough to welcome me by taking me to lunch. It was at the Pastoria Restaurant. Do you remember?"

"I do," said Ted, "but you are crediting me with more than I deserve. I did want to meet you, but it was my job to see what kind of person you were, you who were going to be dealing with writers. You see, at the time, I was the President of the Screenwriters Union."

I'd had no idea.

My 1958–59 season got lots of space in the press, some well-earned. For example, I wasn't hot as an innovative producer of original plays specially written for television, so the newspapers knocked me good. I cannot recall having any sleepless nights over this; I was old enough to know that it would take time.

Plays like "The Boy with Meat Axe" and "Hot Summer Night" and a few others were controversial because they were unvarnished views of working-class life. Marie Donaldson beat the drum whenever we did a writer's first original play, such as those by Donald Giltinan, Jane Arden, Ray Rigby and the partnership of Malcolm Hulke and Eric Paice. Her loudest drumbeat was designed to encourage writers of any sort to turn their skills to drama. To this end, we decided to publicize an unknown writer's first effort in advance of it being aired — in effect, making the audience co-conspirators in judging my decision to produce it.

Stuart Douglass, a left-ish, hoped-to-be playwright had failed to sell any of the four plays he had written. He decided to submit his fifth to us. I liked it, because not only was it pretty good writing, well constructed, but the subject of the play was literally front-page news at that time in 1959. Called "Shadow of the Ruthless," it was about the wheeling and dealing of a Rachmanite bastard who beats the controlled-rent laws by intimidating the poor out of his slum dwellings. Philip Saville gave it his best directorial shot and with its superb cast, Tony Quayle playing the lead, supported by Harry Corbett, Delphi Lawrence and David McCallum, we had an outstanding winner with both critics and audience.

The play was published in the handsome *Armchair Theatre* book, edited by Marie Donaldson with shots of Voytek's splendid sets, additional comments by the authors and criticisms of the play offered by professional writers, Ted Willis and Iain MacCormick.

Armchair Theatre was front-page news for a reason I wish had never happened. An actor died in the middle of a play while it was going out live.

The play was "Underground," based on a story dramatized by James Forsyth. London has been destroyed by an atom bomb, but there are three survivors in the Underground, played by Donald Huston, Patricia Jessel and Gareth Jones.

For three days, they crawl through the rubble-filled Tube tunnels, hoping to find a way out. Exhausted, they reach a large group of starving people in another Tube station now in danger of coming under the control of a would-be dictator. The Gareth Jones character becomes his sycophantic aid in the climax of the play to clinch the dictator's rule. That's the way the play was written, but just before the three survivors are to join the others, Gareth Jones, while he was briefly off-camera having his make-up touched up, suffered a heart attack.

During the transmission, I was watching the on-air television set two rooms away from the control room where Ted Kotcheff was directing, and I saw that something had gone terribly wrong with the action just before the last act break. I left and ran into the control room shouting at Ted, "What the hell's gone wrong?"

Ted, white-faced, turned to me and said, "Gareth's dead! What'll I do?"

All I can recall is blurting out something foolish like, "You gotta finish the show. Shoot it like a football game — just follow the actors!"

"I gotta tell the actors . . ." said Ted, and he rushed out of the control room. I followed him into the studio.

Whatever Ted had to do, he had only two and a half minutes — the length of the commercial break — to do it in, and we had already lost fifteen seconds. Without Gareth Jones, the climax of the play would be like the Last Supper without Judas. I debated whether or not to cancel the show right there and then, but hearing Ted firing out instructions to the actors, I decided to go ahead. During the last act, Ted left Verity Lambert in the control room to run the production while he remained on the studio floor, minute by minute, invisibly instructing actors and cameramen of the changes required to save Forsyth's play.

The actors were incredible, especially Andrew Cruickshank, who played the dictator. His main speech to the survivors depended upon leading questions thrown at him by the now absent actor such as, "How are you going to lead us?" Cruickshank, paraphrasing Gareth's question, ad-libbed, "Now, you might ask, how am I going to lead you?" and then followed it with his own set speech.

The tragedy of Gareth's death reveals some ironies. Newspaper front pages on the following day, in black headlines, bannered "Death Stalks TV Studio, Actor Dies in Drama," while inside on the entertainment pages, the critics who usually phone in their columns right after transmission, not knowing that an actor had died in the middle of our production, criticized me for yet another incomprehensible *Armchair Theatre* play!

In "Underground," as might be expected, some critics saw nothing particularly bad in the show. That's either a testimonial to Kotcheff's genius or it is a reflection on popular criticism.

In recalling that show, it seems to me that it was ill-fated from the start. While Peter Luke and I were satisfied with Forsyth's dramatization, Ted hated the script. It was necessary for me to force him to do it, which led to his being a brutal sonofabitch to the author during rehearsals. Whether or not he hated the assignment, though, he did save the show. That's showbiz!

While we were batting out week after week, Peter Luke was scouring the country for playwrights. And he found them.

In that first season of mine, it worried me that of the forty-eight plays produced, about half of them were by foreign authors. Not nearly good enough if I was to reach my target, my well-publicized goal of dramatizing the turning points in British contemporary life. Only writers living in the UK, writing out of their gut experience could do that, I felt. Waiting for the right plays to come in out of the blue was for the birds.

Out of my annual budget, I peeled off a small amount to be used as down payments on writers that we would commission to write plays on ideas that we would dream up. Having taken on Patrick Brawn to work with Peter, I specifically defined their roles as story editors, not script editors. This distinction of title may appear silly, but it did place emphasis on story, the *what* of the play rather than the *how* it was written — the latter being the business of the writer. Besides the title, the script editor suggested that the editor might blue pencil the script — which is a real turn-off to most writers.

I also defined their roles as defenders of the writers' script, meaning that no director would make a script change without the permission of the story editor, and then only after the latter had gotten the writer's approval. The system I devised was simple: At the end of each day's rehearsal, the director's script assistant will have noted any script changes by copying the changes into the master script in the editor's office. These would be noted daily by him and immediately squared with the writer.

Story editors had access to rehearsals, and writers were encouraged to attend as well. Of course there were disputes, but they were rarely fatal. Writers learned to write better when hearing an actor wrestling with their lines, and they were able to rectify a flaw in their writing much better than the catch-as-catch-can efforts of a director or actor in the heat of rehearsal or studio days.

All this drew writers to us, and once with us, they never left. Many of them were glad to sign over to us an offer of first refusal on their work.

During the summer of '59, Peter Luke suggested I go to the Lyric Hammersmith to see a play by a writer he thought good for us. It was *The Rough and Ready Lot*, written by a relatively unknown ex-actor writer, Alun Owen. Because I had heard that the play had religious overtones, I took along my father-in-law, Reverend Duncan McRae, who was visiting Betty and me at the time.

The play, about some mercenaries in Bolivia in the last century, was hardly anything near what I wanted for *Armchair Theatre*, but my God, the heightened language, the dynamics of the characters and their punchy dialogue knocked me for a loop. This guy could write!

The next day, I vented my enthusiasm and thanks to Peter, and soon we took Owen to lunch. He was a tall, pale-faced, half-Welsh, half-Irish Liverpudlian in his early twenties who had been a "Bevin Boy" working in the mines during the war.[69]

His endearing, warm, upbeat nature didn't quite conceal his insecurity, wondering if I'd asked him to lunch because I might want to buy his stage play. While I waxed lyrical about it, he was downcast when I said that it wasn't for me. I went into my standard pitch, which by now I had down pat; I was not doing any versions of stage plays and definitely wouldn't do a period play. I wanted something relevant about the changing face of Britain. Did he have any ideas that would suit our needs and that he would like to write? Something close to him?

---

69 Bevin Boys were young men during World War Two who were conscripted not to the armed forces but to work in Britain's coal mines. From 1943 to 1945, one in ten recruits were sent to the mines. The name is derived from British politician Ernest Bevin, to whom this scheme is attributed.

Sydney with Ted Kotcheff and Alun Owen.

"Well," he said, "I might think of something that takes place in Liverpool."

"Liverpool!" I exclaimed. "What's so special about Liverpool?"

A comment that Howard Thomas had once made to me crossed my mind — a company should reflect the region of its franchise. ABC's region was the Midlands and the North. Liverpool was in the North!

Owen replied, "You talk about the changing face of Britain. Liverpool is changing so fast you wouldn't believe it. The port is dying." He thought for a moment, and then another change occurred to him. As if unfurling the Union Jack, he said, "There are no trams to Lime Street!"

All I could think of to say to that was, "Hey, that's a good title."

Alun left us certain that he could write a play that would suit me. Four weeks later, a cheerful Peter Luke gave me a script to read. Alun Owen had brought it in that morning, Peter had read it and felt I would like to read it right away. I did, and the dialogue and characters were rich and ready. It was about today, about three ordinary blokes just off a ship in tatty Liverpool. It was thin in plot, but so what! No audience could disregard those three Scousers and the girl one of them takes to bed. And so, "No Trams to Lime Street" was born!

Because of the total untheatrical feel of the play, its not naturalistic but highly selective realism, I decided that it was a play that Ted Kotcheff would handle well. He liked it, but after meeting Alun, came to me with a legitimate doubt. He wasn't sure he could do it justice, because the play demanded a feel for the people and atmosphere of Liverpool, about which he felt ignorant. I saw the sense of that, and taking a leaf out of my film board days I sent Ted and Alun up to Liverpool so that Ted could get the feel of the place and meet Scouse friends of Alun's.

Ted returned so imbued with Alun's love for Liverpool, that he worried me — they intended the actors speak with the local accents. I had been in England for over a year by now, but the Scouse accent was as clear to me as Chinese. Alun assured me that the Brits would have no trouble with it.

Dodo Watts, our casting director, needed assuring too. When casting took place, Ted was smart enough to have Alun with him. When Dodo showed Ted her proposed cast list, it became clear that she expected that the actors would speak with Irish accents. Alun, God bless him, rebelled.

Alun claimed that that Dodo had said, by way of explanation, "Nobody could make love with that dreadful accent!"

Even though she was referring to its effectiveness on the screen, it didn't deter Alun: "How do you think Liverpool babies are born?"

And what a cast we had! Billie Whitelaw, Jack Hedley, Tom Bell and Alfie Lynch. In Voytek's sets, Ted illuminated Owen's play to stunning effect. Having produced by now over 300 dramas, this was the first time I reached the kind of drama I believed in. This was the sort of drama that a wide audience would love and identify with. Small wonder that I felt smug as could be the following morning; I drove to work with the fat batch of favourable newspaper reviews in my briefcase.

As I entered the guarded portals of the Teddington Studios, I was congratulated right and left. In my office, a smiling Valerie Austin, my secretary, told me that Mr. Thomas would like to see me in his office right away. I rushed across, expecting, if not a raise, at least a pat on the back.

When I entered his office, sitting next to him was his boss, C.J. Latta, the ABPC Group managing director. He was an elderly, American bear of a man fronting for Warner Bros., who, at the time, owned 38% of ABPC. Normally, Latta was an amiable man, but he sure wasn't now. And Howard, if anything, looked as if he had been caught with his hands in the cookie jar.

Before I had finished saying, "Good morning, C.J., Howard . . ." Latta belted at me, "What was that crap on the air last night? I couldn't understand a word of it!"

I was taken aback. "Why, C.J., haven't you seen the press? 'No Trams' got rave reviews. I don't . . ." Then the penny dropped. "Oh, the Liverpool accents! Well, C.J., you're an American and even I, as a Canadian, had trouble, and I know this play well—"

Latta cut me off. "Don't soap me. My chauffeur didn't understand it and he's English!" He stabbed a finger at me and said, "Listen to me. Next time, Newman, tell those actors to speak fucking English!"

Not surprisingly, I've been dining out on that story for years. After that astonishing session, neither he nor Howard — who remained silent the whole time — ever brought up the subject again, as regional accents were appropriately heard in play after play in *Armchair Theatre*. "No Trams" beat the Beatles accent by two years.[70]

"No Trams to Lime Street," the sixth play in the second season, was the key *Armchair Theatre* production, which metamorphosed from just another weekly drama into the series people stayed home to watch and talked about for days. I don't forget that I had a golden spot on the air, earning as it did the carryover of the week's top-rated *Sunday*

---

70 Alun Owen, of course, would be nominated for an Academy Award for screenwriting for the first film featuring the four lads from Liverpool, *A Hard Day's Night*.

Night at the London Palladium, which I and my staff exploited fully.

That second season saw us, many times, rated among the ten most-watched shows. There was no let-up. Adding to Philip Saville and Ted Kotcheff, both on an executive contract, I repatriated Alan Cooke from Hollywood and Charles Jarrott from Canada, who had been one of my directors at the CBC. Peter Luke and Patrick Brawn were finding and developing writers with fresh voices. Tim O'Brien and his designers were doing marvels as ABC consolidated its production facilities in beautifully equipped studios in Teddington. Our camera and lighting men were creating pictures as sophisticated as the best of Elstree and Hollywood. Success bred self-confidence and there was no stopping us.

In retrospect it seems to me that I could do nothing wrong. I honestly believe that I was totally oblivious to our success. I just kept my nose to the grindstone, whacking away, trying to get the plays believed in, looking the way I wanted them to look and kicking audiences to life in the process. To quote myself from an ancient article of mine, I wanted to produce drama "for the quick, not the dead." And by God, it seems that that was what I was doing.

Week after succeeding week, audiences grew so strongly that once we even stole the number one spot from the unbeatable *Palladium*. It was a television play I commissioned called "A Night Out" by another ex-actor — an unknown writer called Harold Pinter — that hit the magical first place in the week's ratings.

Again, it was Peter Luke who drew my attention to a play called *The Dumb Waiter*, which was playing at the Hampstead Little Theatre. I couldn't get the hang of it, but was tremendously attracted to it. I'm not sure that Peter understood it better than I did, but we decided that Pinter was a writer we should meet. Pete laid it on and Pinter came out to Teddington.

He was an immaculately dressed and handsome — almost *too* handsome — chap, and I noticed that his jacket sleeves were worn. Clearly, he needed money. Pinter politely hedged explaining his play to us. Perhaps he thought I was a vulgarian who looked down on the audience's intelligence, but nonetheless he agreed to take a crack at a play for us for a small down payment. This was after I made it clear that the play could be as artfully written as he wished, as long as it would not be obscure to the audience I was aiming at. I remember there was some talk of an idea of his about a plain chap who was mother-ridden.

What we were going to get from him only heaven knew, but that was exactly the purpose of the "spec" budget I had set up — to gamble a bit of money in the hopes of striking a vein of original talent.

About six weeks later, and after a contract had been negotiated with his agent, Jimmy Wax, Pinter turned up with "A Night Out." In it, the audience first sees an insecure, self-conscious, white-collar young chap (Tom Bell) preparing for an evening out, being eaten alive by the smothering love of his gabby mother (Madge Ryan). He's all she has in her barren life. He meets two friends he works with (Harold Pinter and Philip Locke) and they go to a staff party given by their paternalistic boss (Arthur Lowe). At the party, the man's masculinity is challenged, and then later he is wrongfully accused of "taking a liberty" with a girl and gets into a near fight with a loudmouth fellow clerk. Dispirited, he leaves the party and goes home to be again assaulted by his mother's incessant whining, cloying attentions. He's close to his breaking point, and on the verge of killing her. Later, on the same night, wanting solace and affirmation of his masculinity, he allows himself to be picked up by a prostitute (Vivien Merchant). In her tatty room, he is offended by her phony, genteel pretentions and finds a kind of frustrated strength in non-sexually dominating her, only to return home as the play ends to be dominated again by his smothering mother.

On the face of it, the paltry synopsis reads as if the play is dour, downbeat and without plot. But it wasn't — not the way Harold wrote it. And not the way Philip Saville, whom I assigned to direct it, handled his wonderful cast in imaginative sets designed by Assheton Gorton.

Pinter's seemingly naturalistic dialogue made one giggle inwardly while never allowing the viewer to forget the agony of the hen-pecked hero. It was full of that best of all drama dialogue, where no character speaks directly what is in his mind, but the audience gets the drift of the subtext clearly. The dialogue makes the viewers strain forward, their minds alive with possibilities that anything might happen next.

Tom Bell gave a performance that no one who saw it could forget. He was like a boiler ready to burst with too big a head of steam, but revealed only a threatening, steady hiss.

Harold himself played under his stage name of David Baron, and was as good as his writing, playing the competitor of the party loudmouth. Madge Ryan as the grasping mother was at her usual best, but almost stealing the show was Harold's real-life wife, Vivien Merchant, who played the class-ridden prostitute, radiating a musky sexuality without revealing a bit of skin.

Harold Pinter was as clever a businessman as he was a writer, which infuriated me at the time. It was a good thing that "A Night Out" was one of our first plays shot live but recorded on tape, because just before the cast list and information about the work of this new writer was to go out, Harold's agent phoned our contracts office and demanded more money for the play. His reason was that the contract called for the play being seen only in ABC's North and Midland regions, but now we were going to televise it throughout the entire United Kingdom. When told this, I phoned Harold, who led me to believe that it was his tough agent who controlled his affairs.

With some trouble, I had to pull the play out of my schedule as negotiations went on week after week, trying to convince Harold's agent that the contract was a standard one that applied to all writers and always for the whole country. During this period, Harold's play *The Caretaker* opened, and the critics hailed the arrival of a new major playwright. Eventually, our contracts department convinced the agent. Finally, more than two months after it had been recorded, the episode went out on April 24, 1960. It was seen by over sixteen million viewers. It followed three plays, each one building larger audiences: Clive Exton's second play for us "Hold My Hand, Soldier," which followed Ray Rigby's second play for us "The Leather Jungle," which had followed Alun Owen's "After the Funeral."

While we all gained from this delay — Harold was now top news on the entertainment pages of the press — his agent, whom I had never met but spoke to on the phone, had left a decidedly bitter taste in my mouth.

Two years later, I was at an enormous party at the Dublin Theatre Festival, sitting quietly at a table nursing a drink. A tiny chap came along and asked if he could join me at the table. He introduced himself as Jimmy Wax. He knew who I was. He was very friendly and soon we were hitting it off, when suddenly it struck me: "Jimmy Wax? Jimmy Wax?! You're Harold Pinter's agent!"

As is my wont, I couldn't resist telling him wryly that he didn't seem the same sonofabitch who had tried to get more money out of me for "A Night Out." He laughed. "Oh, it wasn't me," he said. "It was a try-on of Harold's that I saw no harm in going along with."

We didn't find Clive Exton; he found us. He'd seen what we were doing on the air and was dissatisfied with how his previous plays had been produced by other companies. He submitted a remarkable play called "Where I Live."

On the surface, it was about the problem of what to do with old Dad who was becoming a burden living with his married daughter and her husband. The daughter feels that, unless her nouveau riche brother and his wife will take him, regretfully, Dad will have to be put into a home for the aged. A simple story about an all too common situation, but it was such a revelation in its unfolding as Exton told it.

The problem in the play has less to do with Dad, and more to do with a sibling rivalry between the brother and sister, now in their fifties, originating from their childhoods. The brother gets his comeuppance when, in the conflict between them about where the father should live, he is inadvertently revealed to their father as a hypocrite, who had always been favoured over his sister. Everybody loses. The son is unhappily shamed into taking the unwilling old man, the daughter is filled with guilt and Dad hates them both.

It sounds like a very depressing play, but it was not. The audiences were uplifted by the revelation of everyday life being so brilliantly illuminated.

I learned something pretty important from "Where I Live" — a successful play (that is, in the sense of its being popular) does not necessarily have to be a play with a conventional happy ending where everyone kisses and makes up. The truth is exhilarating when it is thought-provoking. Just give the audience a full meal of the recognizable truth of a recognizable situation that truthfully concludes a problem and above all, do it well. Ted Kotcheff did it well. We respected Exton's play, and so Ted fired up Tim O'Brien to design sets for a house so unquestionably real that you knew that the lead characters, brilliantly played by Ruth Dunning, Robert Brown and Paul Curran, truly lived, loved and raised kids in it and received the Sunday visit of relatives, Lloyd Lamble and Madge Ryan.

Around Christmas time, I had three more months to go to the end of my two-year contract. Betty and I began to think of our return to Canada, somewhat worried about pulling the kids out of school in mid-season. What worried me most was the fear that the freedoms I enjoyed at ABC had spoiled me. I would once again face knuckling down to the more narrow strictures of Canadian television, as well as miss my fine directors and my beautiful writers, the high-life, expense account — the whole shebang!

But the gods were kind. Howard Thomas asked me to stay on, and I happily agreed and signed a contract for three additional years with handsome annual increases in salary, and still, the paid-for return to Canada at the end of it.

By the end of my second season I felt pretty good. I was close to the target I had set for myself. Out of thirty-seven plays, twenty of them were original, specially commissioned by us from British writers. I had learned a helluva lot.

With a fixed time each Sunday night, I was learning something about the necessity of varying the kinds of plays we showed, to keep the loyalty of viewers. The common denominators of the plays were that they had to be fast in the telling, that they grab viewers in the first minute of the play and that they occasionally use "name" actors. Above all else, of absolute necessity to me was that the play reflect some aspect of contemporary British life — the more timely, the better.

My use of the word "reflect" does not mean to me that drama is merely an indiscriminate mirror. I use it in the meaning that Shakespeare first gave it in Hamlet's speech to his actors: ". . . to hold, as 'twere, the mirror up to nature, to show . . . the very age and body of the time his form and pressure."

In reflecting life and its pressures, the plays did so in the widest range of genre: a comedy would follow a slice-of-life play, which followed a murder-thriller, then a love story and, next, a hard-hitting social drama. Each of them involved people in different strata of society: medicine, science, the factory, the farm, department stores, ad agencies and big and small towns and cities. Ninety-five percent of them took place close to home, in the United Kingdom.

Out of bounds were plays that took seriously mysticism, astrology and extra-sensory perception. These, in my mind, cannot affect the everyday struggle for existence, and provide only a nutty means of escape.

To Peter Luke, Patrick Brawn and then Irene Shubik, whom I hired as a story editor, my aversion to plays about bullfighters made them giggle.[71] It always amazed me how this subject fascinated so many British writers. It wasn't so much the cruelty I objected to (who was I to argue about the Spanish culture?), or the impossibility of depicting in our studio the bullring's "moment of truth." My reasoning was that, since most matadors came from the working class, inevitably the Spanish hero would have to speak with some sort of working-class British accent. Now who in his sane British mind would accept the truth of a Cockney bullfighter? Not even with Michael Caine as the matador!

Also unacceptable to me were plays that referred to actual political parties (a hangover from Canada) and those with a specific political bias — the ones where the author has a hard axe to grind. I hardly ever had to lie when rejecting the latter, because they were usually bad. To make these plays work, usually the characters in them had to be distorted to suit its political message, which made them less

---

71 According to Irene Shubik in her book about producing television plays,
    Play For Today, Shubik and Luke were more amused by another aversion of
    Newman's. Shubik wrote, "I can remember Sydney Newman at a script meeting
    saying jokingly to Peter Luke, 'Don't bring me any more plays about sick old
    men,' and accusing the department of 'gerontophilia.'"

believable. I used to quote that old saying to the writer, "When you write a propaganda play, make sure the characters in it don't know it!"

The average viewer's intelligence was of no concern to me. I wasn't interested in the idea of getting down on my hands and knees to see it from his point of view. It was my assumption of the viewers' cultural awareness and education that made me get the plays to entertain them with. The very word "entertain" meant to me more than "to amuse," and I preferred its equally valid meaning of entertaining a notion, considering a concept, presenting a new and different way to look at life's possibilities.

I even took into account that the plays went out on a Sunday night. The two days of rest were coming to a close. Many had gone to church and tomorrow they would be back at work earning a living. I felt it likely that viewers would be in a somewhat contemplative mood and receptive to plays that provoked thought.

In addition to Alun Owen, Clive Exton and Harold Pinter, among the other writers who first found their dramatic voice in that second season were Angus Wilson and Peter Luke. Wilson, the distinguished British author of *Anglo-Saxon Attitudes*, was commissioned by us and wrote "After the Show," a charming social satire directed by Kotcheff with Hermione Baddeley, Ann Lynn and Jeremy Spenser playing the lead roles.

Plays that there were light and easy to take were hard to come by, and it was a problem that constantly beset us. Peter Luke thought he might try his hand at writing a drama. He had an idea about a played-out travelling salesman who falls in love with a shy widow. I became his story editor, and what a delightful play "Small Fish Are Sweet" turned out to be, as directed by Alan Cooke. That most versatile of all actors, Donald Pleasence, played the salesman who woos the beautiful Katharine Blake.

Peter, his muscles flexing after writing a few more successful plays for us, decided to take a crack at writing a full-length stage play. As his story editor, I was pretty ruthless. He managed to sell it and I went to its opening night at the Mermaid Theatre. When the curtain fell to considerable applause, Peter asked me what I thought of it. "Oh I

Peter Luke (lying centre) with Sydney, Betty, Jennifer and friends.

enjoyed it. But Peter, I think the final act is still fucked up."

The play, of course, was *Hadrian the Seventh*,[72] which played four years on London's West End, eleven months on Broadway, toured in the U.S. for two years and made Alec McCowen a star. What did I know?

The years rolled by. In the third season, of the thirty-nine plays produced, twenty-two were commissioned and an additional two were written by British writers. In March 1962, my carefully planned flow of plays became somewhat screwed up by ATV's cutting into our time slot, insisting upon doing every second play. I often wondered what kind of row Howard Thomas had with Lew Grade in trying to prevent that from happening.

Oh, they were heady times all right. It was a blur of self-discovery, meeting new people, enjoying the fruits of success with a happy family, hearing an English accent creeping into the speech of my growing

---

72 *Hadrian the Seventh* debuted in 1968. It was the beginning of Luke's career as a successful playwright.

girls. While retaining my Canadian identity, gas became petrol and elevator a lift, and Betty and I would no longer break up with laughter to my, "You're too old to become pregnant!" after she would ask me to "knock her up" in the morning.

I found myself in love with a country I felt was falling behind the times. Great Britain was an old country with hard-won traditions. When driving my car, I appreciated its roundabout mentality in contrast to my native Canada's non-stop fly-overs, forcing myself to remember that it was so tiny in area that the British Isles could not even cover Canada's Great Lakes.

CHAPTER SEVENTEEN
ABC, *THE AVENGERS* UNTIL . . . !

Several other writers come strongly to my mind. Irene Shubik found an extraordinary writer of black comedies, David Perry. His "The Trouble with Our Ivy" was a mad thing about the antagonism between two suburban London couples, which made the feuding families of Romeo and Juliet pale by comparison. To get even for an ancient hurt, one of them plants a rare South American ivy, which grows unstoppably at an alarming rate that not only envelops and crushes their neighbour's house and their own, but also clogs the main railway line to Waterloo Station. His other plays were equally mad but terribly entertaining.

One day, two young chaps came to us fresh off the boat from New York with a television musical comedy. It showed talent, but despite its charm, I thought it unsuitable for *Armchair Theatre* and so I commissioned the two of them — Steven Vinaver, the writer, and Carl Davis, the composer, to write another musical of wider contemporary appeal. "His Polyvinyl Girl" was an oddball winner — a charmingly told story with delightful music to match. It is about a man (John

Fortune) who falls in love with a department store manikin (Nyree Dawn Porter), who comes to life during the night. In high style, Philip Saville directed it.

Some journalists, especially byline article writers, have a play or more in them if encouraged by someone who wants plays of contemporary relevance. I was certainly right in commissioning Robert Muller, who was writing showbiz pieces for the *Daily Mail* when I first met him. Muller thought he would like to try his hand at a TV play about the grind of an unknown curvy actress trying to succeed in the cutthroat showbiz world of randy men. I sicced Peter Luke onto Robert and eventually we got a dandy script, which, again, Philip Saville directed most imaginatively. Janet Munro played the starlet and Ian Hendry the film director who never rises above doing TV commercials in our "Afternoon of a Nymph."

Later, Muller was to write an extraordinary play set in 1962, in which Hitler, not dead, returns to Germany with his Nordic son by Eva Braun to again attract powerful men to support him.

Whenever we produced an Alun Owen play (and we did about six of them) after "No Trams" it was an occasion, but none more so than his "The Rose Affair."

One evening, Alun and his wife Mary (a top stage designer) invited Betty and me to a bang-up dinner at their flat. Lots of drink, superb food and, in the English style, a fierce fire raging in the gas fireplace with the door to the room firmly shut against drafts. Over coffee, Alun said he had written an unusual play. He didn't think it would suit what I wanted for *Armchair Theatre*, but wondered if he might read it to me anyway. How could I refuse? And so with belly full in the stifling heat, I sat back and began listening to Alun, still the actor, reading the script aloud using all the accents he had at his command. And within five minutes I fell dead asleep.

Forty-five minutes later I awoke to hear Betty's words of praise to Alun who was staring at the fucker whom he hoped would love and produce his play but who had slept through it! Now it seems funny as hell, but thank God we were good friends and he forgave me.

The play was unusual, not just for Alun, but for any writer who doubted that television people, at that time, would ever consider producing it. Maybe the daft BBC would, seeing and doing it as a la-di-da production, if only to put a bit of cultural glitter into their annual report.

I thought, done right, it might be popular.

It was a contemporary interpretation of the old fable of Beauty and the Beast, the Beast being a guilty, eccentric capitalist. The language people spoke was in blank verse. At this time, I felt that I had sufficiently mined the areas of realism and this play, as "His Polyvinyl Girl," the Perry plays and some of Exton's represented a new stylistic approach to dramatizing the times. It was a risk and I decided to take it.

A major problem I had to face was that Kotcheff, who had directed all of Alun's plays, was away. He was on leave, somewhere in the South Pacific, directing his first feature film, *Tiara Tahiti*, with John Mills and James Mason. Alan was decidedly unhappy with his baby being given to anyone else to interpret. Eventually, I convinced him that the director I had chosen would do wonders with it. Charlie Jarrott was himself uncertain about taking it on, and I sensed he was fearful of Alun's reputation. My advice to Charles, a former actor, was to get Alun himself to read it to him, to more easily understand the nuances in the writing.

Charles did a fine and imaginative job of it. For the unique mansion in which the nearly mad capitalist lived, Voytek designed a palace that looked like Art Nouveau crossed with Gaudi. Charles's cast was spectacularly good. The lovely Natasha Parry played Beauty, the daughter of the timid manager (Naunton Wayne) in the employ of the Beast (Anthony Quayle) who had to wear a mask for most of the play to hide his tortured features. Delightful were the supporting roles, the giggle-making manservant played by Harold Lang and an equally funny Joseph O'Conor as a blarney-shooting, Irish quack doctor.

I loved that show, and so did everyone else, as proven by the readers of the *Daily Express* who voted it The Best Play of the Year. A play in blank verse! It did seem that I could do no wrong.

And then I produced one play that ran afoul of the Independent Television Authority. It was called "Three on a Gas Ring," which the public never saw. It was about three girls who live on a canal boat. The youngest (Joanna Dunham) falls in love with a laid-back, unorthodox sculptor (Alan Bates) who refuses to marry her after he makes her pregnant. The play ends on a happy high note with the three girls, led by the oldest (Sheila Allen), deciding to raise the kid when it arrives without the benefit of a father.

Sounds like pink tea today, but it caused quite a furor in the corridors of Sir Robert Fraser's shop after they had privately screened it before it was to be broadcast.[73] They were outraged. Why, they thought, it would destroy the basic institution of the family! Could they legitimize raising a fatherless child? Never!

Other than the odd niggly thing, I got along extremely well with the ITA people. Noel Stevenson, who looked after morals, violence and matters of "good taste," became a personal friend after he left to become managing director of Scottish television. The latter's major owner was Roy Thomson (the Canadian tycoon whom I first put on the air in Canada in my *Graphic* series) who suffered my disease of calling a spade a spade when he called television "a licence to print money."

I'm confident that the deputy director general, Bernard Sendall, and the director general himself, Sir Robert, both secretly liked my work even though the latter, from time to time, would josh me as to why I didn't produce more "nice plays for nice people!"

One of the biggest kicks I got out of trying to be timely in my plays was when I produced one called "The Man Out There." Being an avid reader of *New Scientist*, I was agog about what each country was doing about the international Geophysical Year. From what I read, I figured that after Sputnik, sooner or later someone was going to send a man into space. I commissioned Donald Giltinan to write the play.

The story he came up with involved a Russian doctor astronaut (Patrick McGoohan) circling the earth every ninety minutes in his space capsule giving advice each time he passed over Northern

---

73 It was screened by not only the Independent Television Authority but also the Bishop of Coventry, who was shocked by it, sounding the play's death knell. The writer David Osborn protested in the *Times*, "Many people — especially women — approved highly of this . . . defiant ending."

Canada to a mother (Katharine Blake) who is trying to save her child's life. Intercut are scenes in the Soviet space centre where experts are desperately trying, and failing, to prevent the capsule, Russia's first manned capsule, from burning up upon its re-entry into the earth's atmosphere. On the Tuesday following the play's Sunday airing, the world was stunned with the news that Gagarin had circled the world in a space capsule on the same day.[74]

I couldn't believe it. At the exact time *Armchair Theatre* audiences were watching our fictional astronaut, the world's first man in outer space was actually 19,000 miles above our heads. Never being too satisfied, I churlishly quipped, "Why couldn't I have scheduled the play on the following Sunday? By going with it first, we publicized Gagarin instead of Gagarin being advance publicity for us."

As producer of *Armchair Theatre* I also had other responsibilities as ABC's head of drama. Howard Thomas mentioned to me that it might be nice if I could come up with a children's drama serial that the commercial network could use. Being interested in outer space, I thought up a thirteen-week serial called *Pathfinders in Space*. It was about a greedy scientist, richly played by that veteran actor George Coulouris, who wants to exploit the rich minerals in a distant planet but is foiled by other scientists, one of whom was a woman (Pam Barney).

It did well and was brought back (this time called *Pathfinders to Venus*) and ran for twenty-one weeks. This serial became a testing ground for a Cambridge University group trying to determine the age of perception in children. At the group's request, after getting Thomas's approval, I had Guy Verney, the serial's producer, build into one episode twenty deliberate mistakes. One Saturday, the Cambridge people turned up with three groups of children, with ages ranging from eight to fourteen. They were then tested on the mistakes they had noticed. Because I used to teach art to children, I could have told them: kids perceive and make judgements about that which they perceive between the ages of nine and eleven. It was fun, though, being involved with a bunch of academics

---

74 Both Gagarin's flight and the broadcast of "The Man Up There" took place on April 12, 1961.

Making Pathfinders in Space, *1960.*

again as I had been before with McLuhan in Toronto. I cannot recall the public's response to the mistakes in the program.

The story of the creation of *The Avengers* is an interesting one. It started out as something almost, but not entirely, different from the Steed/Emma Peel *Avengers*.

At the beginning of my third season in 1960, I was visited by a writer I didn't know personally, but whose stuff on another commercial station I admired for its earnest feel: Julian Bond. He was with his agent, Felix de Wolfe, who, in a masterful pitch, sold me on a wonderful idea for a series by his client. It was a great idea, he said, because it "amalgamates the ideas of two of the most popular running dramas on the air: *Dixon of Dock Green* and *Emergency — Ward 10*. Cops and doctors: what could be better?"

The tricky part of the deal was that writer Julian Bond wished to be its producer. That worried me, but I took the idea to Howard Thomas, who agreed that I give it a thirteen-week run. Thus a half-hour series called *Police Surgeon* was born, about a doctor who, as part of his practice, is on first call by the police.

I made sure that Julian was given strong production support, and Dodo Watts cast Ian Hendry, a relatively unknown actor, with my approval to play Dr. Geoffrey Brent, the police surgeon. After four shows, Julian left, saying he'd rather write than produce. I needed a producer in a hurry and recalled an Englishman, Leonard White, a first-class stage director who had become a television director at the CBC in Canada. Now back in England, he had dropped into my office to say hello.

I phoned him and asked if he would like to be a producer for the final nine shows, and if so, there was a job waiting for him. "No," he said, "I want to direct. Since I'm free, and if you think I can do it, yes, I'll take on the nine shows." That appointment of mine turned out to be one of the best I ever made. A chunky-looking man with a strong-looking jawbone, suggesting a stubborn strength, Leonard turned out to be gentle, wise and open-minded while retaining his own sound opinions — the mark of a good producer.[75] As well, he knew more about theatre, acting and direction than I could learn in a thousand years.

While the series was pretty good, it somehow didn't take off. My own opinion was that it was on the air at the wrong time. But one thing was very clear: Ian Hendry was a potential star, and I was in a hurry to capitalize on his popularity. I felt that people liked his everyday good looks that radiated integrity, acute intelligence and a kind of innocence. He had another talent, too, that I accidentally discovered: he was an expert gymnast.

One day we were having a chat in my office. Ian was striding back and forth as we talked when suddenly, still talking, he leaped into the air and did two backflips in rapid succession. "Hey, Ian," I said, "that's great! Where'd you learn to do that?" He turned to me with his wry, twisted grin, "In the National Service, I was in a motorcycle team that used to do stunts. You know, handstands while beetling along at forty miles an hour or five of us on one bike, that sort of thing."

---

75 In actual fact, Newman had already been using White as producer on the series *Inside Story* and *Armchair Mystery Theatre*, the latter of which he did in tandem with *Police Surgeon*.

So, to exploit Hendry's qualities I decided to create a new, one-hour series — a fun series that would get away from the realism of *Police Surgeon*, which we had enough of in *Armchair Theatre*, and go for something melodramatic — an action adventure-thriller. I felt that I could capitalize on the current literary popularity of the John le Carré/Ian Fleming spy genre. Why not, in fact, make fun of the whole spy nonsense? I was getting somewhere.

To contrast Hendry's integrity and his physical dexterity, which I hoped to exploit, I thought of teaming him with someone — a spy, an MI-5 type, someone he wouldn't approve of so that sparks would fly between them. Perhaps someone amoral, suave and brainy who wouldn't deign to dirty himself by physically fighting, preferring a silenced gun or a sword-cane. Leonard White thought this was a good idea and agreed to remain with me as its producer. But problems remained — who would we get to play the suave spy? How could we bring the two together? What would be their common goal?

Fortunately, just arriving back in England was Patrick Macnee[76] whom I knew modestly well because he had starred in dozens of my CBC dramas. He was bang-on for the part, and happily, he was keen

---

76 The story of how Patrick Macnee came to be in *The Avengers* has been retold many times over the years, but one detail of it has never been mentioned: it might not have happened had Sydney Newman not needed some shirts from Canada. On March 3, 1960, Macnee, still living in Toronto, wrote Newman to enquire about finding an acting gig when he returned to London. "I imagine everybody in the whole world writes to you — BUT I am coming to England April 4 — after doing Arthur Hailey's 'The Queen's Peace' [on CBC] — and would very much like to work — if there is anything to keep me in mind." Macnee told Newman about his recent work in Hollywood.

Newman wrote back on March 17, "Very nice hearing from you and glad you are well. Would you perhaps do me a favour since you are coming over? I have asked a friend of mine, Ralph Ellis, to buy me a couple of shirts. If he has got them, would you perhaps bring them with you for me?" Newman added as a postscript "Mr. Leonard White is now working for me as an Associate Producer. He's great!" Macnee brought the shirts to Britain with him. Seven months later, *The Avengers* was in production, with Leonard White as its producer and Macnee as one of the leads.

*Sydney Newman (right) with Patrick Macnee (centre) and writer
John Manchip White (left) on the set of* The Avengers, *1962.*

to play it. To bring the two characters together and motivate them, I decided to take advantage of the fact that Hendry, as the police surgeon, was fond of his nurse (played by Catherine Woodville).

The script of the first show saw Hendry not as Dr. Geoffrey Brent, police surgeon, but plain old Dr. David Keel. He is engaged to his nurse who, at the end of the episode, is accidentally shot by a killer aiming at Hendry. Just when a second try is attempted, the killer is foiled by a mysterious stranger who emerges from the shadows. It is the suave, special agent John Steed who offers to assist Hendry find the killer.

I never liked the title of the series. The idea of revenge always seemed morally wrong to me, but after weeks of sweating our dozens of ideas and trying them out on anyone in sight, considering the opening story and its catchy originality, I reluctantly settled on *The Avengers*.

Howard Thomas had trouble selling it to the entire commercial network — ATV, London's station, refused to take it — but he convinced most stations to pick it up and produce it live. It miraculously went on the air five weeks after *Police Surgeon* ended. It built audiences so rapidly that ten weeks after it began, Lew Grade changed his mind, and so Londoners began to see and enjoy it as much as the rest of the UK did. Audiences didn't just watch it — they positively loved it.

The Avengers' popularity rested, I think, on more than the surface excitement of the chase, good guys and evil men, sexy women, the country in peril and Hendry's Jiu Jitsu expertise. Equally important was that most precious dramatic element — humour — which came from Hendry's near priggish suspicion of Macnee's sophistication and lack of morals as he gets sucked into one adventure after another.

The two men became national stars. The series ran for twenty-six weeks and suddenly stopped on December 30, 1961, because of a technicians' strike that hit all commercial television. As the scripts began piling up, waiting for the strike to end, the series suffered a devastating blow. Ian Hendry apologetically refused to continue because he couldn't refuse a lucrative multi-picture movie contract. That's showbiz, with a vengeance.[77]

The series format was too good to throw away, but Leonard and

---

77 The truth was, Patrick Macnee was also in jeopardy of departing. Macnee wrote Newman on December 31, 1961. "I am in the dark over a good many things," Macnee wrote. He alluded to the new season, Hendry's departure, the strike and asked if they could meet. "The irony is that you and Leonard have built up my reputation so much this year that I now find myself being offered things which I naturally am unable to accept and anyway do not want to do. Firstly, loyalty to yourselves and secondly because the new series [season] idea is excellent and I want to be associated with it." Macnee had caught wind of the plans to change the direction of *The Avengers* and approved of it. But, he added, "I do have considerable financial commitments — my children's maintenance, schooling and all the sordid alimony and what-have-you cost me £60 weekly alone." The point of Macnee's letter was that *The Avengers* being off the air with the technicians' strike meant that he needed some "reasonable financial assurance, which we can take into account when the series starts." Newman, White and Macnee were obviously able to come to terms and Macnee stayed with *The Avengers* until its end in 1969.

I could not find anyone we liked to fill Hendry's shoes. But adversity can be a spur, if exploited.

One night, watching the news on television, I saw an item that dealt with the Mau Mau[78] terrorists in Kenya. I was powerfully moved by a woman settler calmly speaking of a frightful occurrence. When she was cooking dinner, she heard screams coming from the rest of the house. As she turned to find out what it was, three terrorist Mau Mau fled past her with machetes, dripping blood as they ran out the kitchen door. She rushed into the living room to face the horrible sight of her two young sons and husband dead, the latter decapitated.

She was a woman of about forty wearing slacks and bush jacket. On her back was her baby in a papoose-like bag, but strapped around her waist was a bullet-studded belt with an enormous pistol in a holster. She and her husband had come out from England years prior to farm; she explained that the terrorist attacks were so common that all settlers' wives carried guns.

That woman was beyond my imagination. Unforgettable. And gave me the answer to the Hendry casting problem.

The next morning, I dictated a memo to Leonard saying that a woman, but with the same characteristics as Hendry, needed to be found to be Macnee's foil. I described how Steed would find her working as an anthropologist at the British Museum after her husband and children had been killed by the Mau Mau in Kenya. To protect herself there, she had become proficient at using weapons and knew Jiu Jitsu. She should be in her early thirties and be beautiful. She would be primly disapproving of Steed's amorality and Steed would always be wanting to bed her. With the exception of the sex angle, the chemistry of the two characters was to be the same as that between the old "avengers." The new sex angle would help the format.

I had an actress in mind to play the woman — Nyree Dawn Porter,[79] who had been so good as the mannequin come to life in "His Polyvinyl

---

78 The death of British Nationals during the Mau Mau uprisings in Kenya between 1952 and 1960 were in the headlines often during the late '50s and early '60s.

79 Nyree Dawn Porter had already appeared on *The Avengers* in the June 1961 episode "Death on the Slipway."

Girl." Just before I was to go off on a family holiday, Leonard White brought to me his short list of proposed actresses in order of preference. Sure enough, Nyree was on the list, but somewhere near the bottom.

Heading the list was the lovely Honor Blackman. "No! Dammit, Leonard," I cried out, "I can't stand that perpetual Rank Organization, starlet-trained, say everything with a smile kind of acting. Reverse her name with Nyree's."

When I returned from holiday, I blew up when Leonard told me that he had signed Honor to play the part of Mrs. Cathy Gale. Somewhat gracelessly I accepted his explanation that Nyree was unavailable — she was in a West End play and none of the others on the list were available. All I could do was wait for the pilot film to see how effective the chemistry was between Honor and Pat Macnee, upon which the series depended. If not good enough, I would have to dump her.

The pilot production did its job well. The chemistry was just barely visible, but it was there all right. And dammit, she did look lively, but her characterization needed fine-tuning. I said something to Leonard that, normally, would have been outrageous, but which he took with his usual forbearance: "I still can't stand that simpering Rank smile. She's not supposed to like Steed! I never want to see her smile in any episode no matter what. Never! And get rid of her cutesy bobbed hair. Get her a shoulder-length wig until her own hair grows long."

Other flaws were revealed in the pilot. Because the show was being done live and no stunt-doubles could be used, Leonard had made sure that Honor took lessons in Jiu Jitsu. She took to it like the professional she was. But in the pilot, she took a backward leap and her skirt flew up, revealing her skimpy underpants. As well, her dress tore, revealing her bra. Can't have that!

We decided that a special wardrobe needed to be designed for her to prevent showing cleavage or legs — or any body parts that might offend the sensibilities of the ITA, Mary Whitehouse not yet being in sight. Our costume lady knew that, the following autumn, leather would be the vogue attire, and so Honor was fitted out with culottes-slit pant-skirts and tight tops, all in shiny leather. Leonard and I were too innocent of the ways of the world to anticipate that we would be catering to any kinky, S&M fetishists inevitable in any audience. In no time, *The Avengers* had taken the public by storm. Honor and Patrick produced sparks — she beautiful, agile and full of integrity and Pat the lascivious dandy, whimsically the efficient killer on behalf of his country.

How Leonard, as its producer, and the actors and staff took that weekly grind evoked my fullest admiration. It was his leadership and his production team that made it work. John Bryce had the task of getting script after script filled with action and throwaway wit. Its two main directors, Peter Hammond and Don Leaver, met an impossible schedule with each of them averaging one show every two weeks with shooting that was tight and cut fast. The designers had a ball!

There were times when Pat and Honor would demand to see me so they could complain about the scripts and I would pour oil on them to keep them going. Bryce would be the first to admit that a lot of the humour was created in the rehearsal room. The fan letters sent to Pat and Honor filled mailbags week after week. These were answered mostly by Marie Donaldson's staff, because the actors couldn't handle the volume. But that wasn't the only reason.

One day, Honor came and showed me a letter, which upset her greatly. It read, "On a foggy night I love doing nothing better than undress, put on my rubber mask and go out into the foggy night, walking with the slithery rubber sliding across my bare skin as I think of you . . ." The sex of the writer was unknown because the letter was not signed. That's the showbiz you can't win.[80]

The pattern of John Steed's colleague leaving the show repeated itself, proving again the dependence of the film industry on television. After two successful seasons of fifty-two shows, Honor was snapped up by Hollywood for a multiple film contract. Her first role was Pussy Galore, in the second James Bond movie, *Goldfinger*. So *The Avengers* died for me as it did for most who worked on it.

---

80 Presumably on the grounds "if you can't beat 'em . . . ," Honor Blackman and Patrick Macnee cut a novelty single, "Kinky Boots," in 1964.

It's history, of course, that sometime later, Howard Thomas had the sense to put it on film for international distribution, with John Bryce as producer. This was great for Pat and for the new Mrs. Cathy Gale, metamorphosed by the delicious Diana Rigg into Emma Peel. Its success around the world pleased me greatly, although Thomas might have given me a credit on the air for devising it. But I had left the company by then — and that's a story that I'll recount soon.

As well as *The Avengers*, Leonard produced two other successful series we did: one summer season of *Armchair Mystery Theatre* and another one-hour series of thirteen science-fiction dramas called *Out of this World*. Irene Shubik was its successful story editor. Frankenstein's monster, Boris Karloff, topped and tailed each play.

All was well with me as head of drama at ABC. My stuff was beating the pants off every other company, including the BBC. My contentment was shattered, however, by an innocuously friendly letter that came to me in November 1961.

It was from a Mr. Kenneth Adam, director of television of the BBC.[81] He admired my work and thought it would be pleasant to meet with me for lunch. He proposed a date that my secretary might confirm with his. I thought it would be interesting to meet a senior executive of the famed broadcasting organization that had inspired the creation of my own CBC. We met at the Scandinavian Club in Kensington.

In his middle fifties, he bore no resemblance to anyone I could imagine involved with creative work. He seemed frightfully English to me and more like a lecturer of economics; he was conservatively dressed, with gold-rimmed glasses. I enjoyed the bang-up smorgasbord meal with ice-cold aquavit and lager as we got to know each other and amiably talked of the CBC, Swedish food, the state of the British theatre and Howard Thomas — a kind of pleasant, friendly, aimless chat. We parted with the hopes that we would do the same thing again.

A week later I received another letter from him. Lunch was so

---

81 "Dear Mr. Newman," wrote Kenneth Adam on November 21, 1961, "We have never met and yet I have long admired your work. It would please me very much if you could lunch with me sometime in the very near future."

pleasant; would my secretary phone his . . . ? We met, same place, same meal, same amiableness, but this time there was a little more talk about my work at ABC. I told him how happy I was working there. Then later, with feigned nonchalance, he said that he and his boss, Hugh Carleton Greene, to whom he had described our lunch, wondered if I would consider leaving ABC to join the BBC.

I was flabbergasted. I had not seen that coming. "To do what?" I asked.

"Oh," he replied, "to produce our Sunday Night dramas. You see, we admire your work and the kind of freedom we can—"

I stopped him right there, because flashing through my mind were their too often lacklustre, dated, ill-chosen, audience-alienating plays, which were no competition at all, aired at virtually the same time as *Armchair Theatre*! *If you can't beat 'em, buy 'em*, I thought, and laughed.

"No," I said. "Why should I go to the BBC to do exactly what I am now doing? As for freedom, I've got all I want. No, sir!"

He looked at me for only a split second and said, "What would make you come to us? Would you be interested in coming as our head of drama?" Clearly, he and Greene anticipated that I would turn down the producer job.

"Now you're talking," I said. "Yes, I certainly would consider that."

I thought of that nice man, Michael Barry, with his handkerchief tucked into his left sleeve. Adam read my mind and told me that Barry was leaving the corporation. "A decent, talented chap, but now D.G. wants—"

"What?" I asked, "Who's D.G.?"

He looked at me, thinking I was pulling his leg, which I wasn't. He said, "Oh, Hugh Greene. D.G.: the director general! D.G. wants somebody new. Different from what we have on the drama staff. He thinks you're the man for us."

We talked for a while about what concerned me most — the range of drama programs they were making, the scope for new ones and the kind of authority I would have over them. The answers were mouth-watering, but I needed to think. I wanted to talk to Betty.

With a promise that I would get back to him in a few days, and an agreement that the job prospect be regarded as confidential, we parted, my head awhirl with possibilities.

What was clear in talking to Betty was that I had thoroughly mined what ABC's limited two-day operation could offer. Against my present programs — *Armchair Theatre*'s one-hour contemporary plays, the occasional children's serial and *The Avengers* — were the mind-bending opportunities inherent in the BBC's seven-day output, with its promise of contemporary drama involving longer plays or serials of classical drama for both adults and children and more than one *Avengers*-type series. She and I assumed the salary would be roughly the same as at ABC. I'd be an idiot to not follow up on the offer.

On the phone, Kenneth suggested that I meet him at an obscure sherry bar on Baker Street for further discussion. When we met, he took me to a booth at the rear, cheerfully introduced me to two men, and promptly departed.

One of the men was Stuart Hood, director of television programs, who had a lean and hungry look, quickly dissipated by a slightly nervous warmth. He had a most peculiar accent, which I first took to be German but learned later was a kind of Scottish accent I had never come cross. The other man, Donald Baverstock, was considerably younger — although slight, he was built with his head hunkered down like a bull ready to charge. In recalling that meeting, I wonder if Baverstock's build determined his personality, or whether it was the other way around. Almost immediately after some pleasantries from Hood, Baverstock charged into me, questioning the values of drama as an important element in society.

A real ding-dong ensued. Thanks to Grierson, I was well armed to oppose him and, as they say, gave as good as I received. I wasn't a child of Grierson's in vain. As I learned later, the two men came out of the news/current affairs camp and, with my background, I could argue with Baverstock on his own territory; on top of that, he knew bugger all, or pretended to, about drama. They sure played the game of good cop and bad cop, Hood occasionally slowing Baverstock down.

The following evening at my home, I received a phone call from Kenneth Adam reiterating his offer and asking if I would again go to the sherry bar to meet Stuart Williams, the controller of administration, to talk contract.

Into my pocket, I slipped my ABC contract "just in case," and went to meet Williams, who turned out to be like those very nice, roly-poly, solicitorish chaps created by Dickens. We soon disposed of minor matters such as starting date and so forth, but I got the feeling that salary was going to be a bigger problem than I had anticipated. I took my ABC contract out of my pocket and asked him to read it. He demurred with an embarrassed *it's not pukka* look. But I insisted.

After he had finished reading the salient parts, he looked up at me, slightly ashen-faced. He had read that I was at present earning £7,250 a year and rising to £8,250 for my final ABC year, that I was on the top-hat tax scheme, had an interest-free mortgage on my house, a car and expenses paid for me and my family's return to Canada. Somewhat embarrassed, he said he was authorized to go only up to £6,300. We chatted, drank sherry and parted. More meetings followed, and finally I got the amount up to £7,250, the top-hat scheme, and return costs to Canada at the end of the five-year contract. No car, no interest-free mortgage.[82] But, what the hell! By now, I was hot for the job.

But I didn't have it yet. It had to be ratified by the board of governors.

Three weeks later, Kenneth phoned and asked me to come to the BBC Television Centre at 7:30 p.m., after most of the staff had left for the day. When I arrived, the commissionaires knew of my arrival and waved me into the carpark. In the vast, marbled lobby of the newly opening building, a secretary whispered a "pleased to meet you," and took me up to Kenneth's office. I was in the heart of the mother of world broadcasting — the British Broadcasting Corporation.

In the dark office lit only by a table lamp, while pouring me a

---

82 The terms of Newman's contract, which he signed on April 4, 1962, did provide him a £1,000 advance to purchase a car (for which he would have to repay the BBC over five years) and would transfer the property from Iris Productions over to them (though he would have to pay for the mortgage with interest).

drink, Kenneth said that everything had gone well with the Board of Governors and that as soon as their meeting was over, the director general himself would come and officially offer me the job.

Soon there was a rustle at the door, and Kenneth jumped to his feet. As I rose, there coming through the door and ducking his head was the tallest man I had ever seen: Hugh Carleton Greene. I had to tilt my head far back to see his round, friendly face peering down at me as he said he was glad to finally meet me. My heart went right out to him, because when he sat down opposite me, he slid his body forward, lowering his head to my level so that I would not have to look up at him. I'll never forget that. It was an augury of the kindness I would experience from him in the years ahead.

After he formally asked me to become the head of drama, and before I said I would accept, I asked whether the salary offered was the very best they could manage, and noted that I was taking a drop of between two and three thousand pounds a year and was losing both the interest-free mortgage and the car. He assured me that they had broken every rule in their salary scales to accommodate me. We shook hands. I asked, "Have you anything specific that you wish me to do?"

"Yes." He looked intently at me. "You've made *Armchair Theatre* a success by doing plays of relevance to today's audiences. You have managed to collect writers such as Pinter, Owen, Exton and Bill Naughton. They all got their start on BBC radio. I want you to get them back and find all the new voices you can so that we can reinstate the BBC's reputation as the home of the best original playwrights in the country."

After tearing home and describing in infinite detail my meeting with Greene to an eagerly listening Betty, I sat down and began drafting my letter of resignation.

Friday, the next morning, I dictated it to my unhappy secretary, Valerie. I wrote of my gratitude to Howard Thomas and praised the faith shown in me by the parent Associated British Pictures Corporation. I was leaving a happy place, not for more money — for considerably less — only because of the seven-day operation of the BBC, which offered me greater creative scope. I would always remember my happy days at ABC. And I sent my letter off to face a nerve-wracking weekend waiting for Howard's reaction on Monday.

I got it, but good! I had done something so stupid that it defies reason: I had addressed the letter to Sir Philip Warter, chairman of the board, *not* to my boss, Howard, to whom I had sent a carbon copy. Howard was right affronted, which he made clear to me on the phone. Fate had intervened, making it even worse. Sir Philip, after reading my letter early on Monday, immediately phoned Howard for his reaction. Howard didn't have any — he had not yet read his morning mail!

What a cock-up! For years I've pondered the reasons for my callous stupidity. All that makes sense to me is that, because I felt indebted to Howard, I thought he might persuade me to not leave, offer me more money, and other blandishments; I worried that I might be too weak and give in to him.

On the same phone call, Howard said that if he had his way, I would be out of the premises by noon, but he would have to wait for the executive board's approval. I tried to apologize, to explain, but he hung up on me.

The next day I received a short, curt letter from Sir Philip simply stating that the board would not agree to my leaving and that it was expected that I would fulfill the terms of my contract, which had another eighteen months to run. I was shattered and immediately sought Howard to try to convince him to end my contract.

He was calm. More in sorrow than in anger, he told me that he and C.J. Latta, the American group managing director, wanted me to go, but that the executive board refused. He agreed with my request to allow me to plead my case directly to the executive board at its next meeting.

I turned up at the parent company's headquarters in Golden Square prepared to fight for my life. Cooling my heels for a good hour before being called, I was a nervous wreck by the time I was ushered into the boardroom. As they placed me at the tail end of the polished rosewood table, I was facing not Sir Philip, who was absent, but Eric Fletcher (now Lord Fletcher), the group's deputy chairman who was heading up the meeting. Flanking him was a full turnout of the men I knew on a first-name basis, with whom I had drunk and dined, who had lavished me with praise, who controlled eleven companies, making the group one of the two largest film combines in the UK. Howard, who was not a member of the executive board but also present, looked decidedly stony-faced and refused to look at me.

Fletcher opened by stating that it wasn't in their best interests to let me go, but they thought it fair to hear me out. What did I have to say?

I rose and told them of my gratitude to the corporation, for their kindnesses to me and especially for the leadership of Howard Thomas; it was their kindness that made the creative in me flourish to the profit of ABC and the corporation. My need to leave this friendly home could not, in any fair-minded person, be regarded as disloyalty or lack of gratitude. (Howard still refused to look in my direction.) I said that Howard Thomas had no doubt reported that I would take a terrific drop in salary. Because they were in show business, they understood the creative person and therefore I hoped they would be sympathetic to my request. There was nothing to fear about the drama department I would leave behind, because it was strong with its contracted directors and writers. I ended by saying that the fair thing to do would be to let me go with goodwill. And I sat down, holding my breath.

Eric Fletcher thanked me and asked me to leave the room for a few minutes. About three minutes later, I was called back in and told that my request would not be granted.

I jumped to my feet and cried out, "You can't! It's not fair. Why? Why?!"

"Because you are under contract to us and your legal obligation to us is to fulfill it," said Eric Fletcher, the solicitor, member of the Synod of the Church of England and Labour MP.

"Contract! What's *contract* got to do with it?" I was furious. "Do you think I succeeded for you guys because of a lousy contract? You know I worked well because I liked it here and liked what I was doing."

And from my right, another solicitor, shareholder and former head of the Elstree Studios, Robert Clark, with his Scottish accent looked up at me and said, "Laddie," he said. "Hush. Ye've signed a cont-rract and that's it."

I stared at them all, feeling betrayed and totally beside myself. And then I said something so childish that I'm still ashamed of it — and I would pay for it in the months ahead: "All right! Keep me chained! But you'd better watch me closely, I tell you, because I'm going to have an actor say 'fuck' in a play!" And I turned and left the room. Traditionally, I should have slammed the door, but didn't.

No Teddington for me that day. I drove home. What a bunch of cold bastards! What a gutless, venal company. Imagine finding Audrey Hepburn, unknown, and having her under exclusive contract for seven years, never making one film with her — preferring profits earned by selling her, picture by picture, to Hollywood companies! It wouldn't be past them to have probably applied for and gotten the television franchise so that they could screw it up, just to protect their hundreds of rundown ABC cinemas. Ha! They didn't anticipate Howard's abilities to make their main profit! Christ, did I say I would have an actor say fuck on the air? I was still chewing glass when Betty greeted me.

At home, I immediately phoned Kenneth Adam and told him, "You'd better forget all about me. ABPC won't let me go."

"I see," he said. "I'm sorry. D.G. will be very disappointed. I must tell him. I'll call you back as soon as I can."

He did. "Sydney," he said, "we'll hold the job open for you." I was dumbfounded. "But Kenneth," I said, "that's for eighteen months!"

"We understand that," said Kenneth. "Hugh and I think you are worth waiting for. We'll meet in a few days when you've calmed down and we'll discuss a statement for the press."

When the story was released about my going to the BBC, a lot of ink was spilled in describing me as the prisoner of Teddington!

Normally, I roll with the punches and live fairly easily with adversity. But the frustration of waiting a year and a half for a job that came to me out of the blue, which, for two months, had so obsessed me, now found me close to a nervous breakdown. Betty spotted this and said that I must go away, leave London to try to come to peace with the inevitable.

I couldn't get Howard on the phone, but I left a message with his secretary that I was taking off for two weeks.

To spit the winter out of my system, I packed a bag of summer clothes, high-tailed it to Heathrow and took a flight to Gibraltar. There, I rented a car and drove along the coast of Spain and settled into a Spanish-type drive-in, which also had a nightclub famous for its flamenco dancers. It was Torremolinos, off-season and long before the days of the best English fish and chips in Europe and the string of skyscraper hotels.

It was too cold to swim, which I didn't like doing anyway; I read dozens of murder mysteries, dozed, slept, ate and drank well, wondered if the dancers were as hot in bed as they were on the dance floor and generally lazed around. Slowly, I began to stop licking my wounds as April Fool's Day, my forty-fourth birthday, came and went and I returned to England, knowing that any attempt to embarrass ABPC by doing something foolish on the air would only diminish me. I resolved to do even better work.

My relations with Howard were at first strained, but gradually they resumed their old cordiality — on the surface, at least. An undertone of suspicion made itself felt by the new program controller, Brian Tesler. I learned from my executive assistant, Michael Chapman, who had nosed it out that someone close to Brian was reading my *Armchair Theatre* scripts and reporting on them to him. No doubt Howard had sicced him onto this in the event that I might actually have an actor say "fuck" in a play! Silly man.

While I was sure that Howard liked me, I don't think he ever did so fully, perhaps because he felt that I worked as if I did not need him. My arm's length attitude to him put him off, I think.

In the early pre-Teddington days, when I was beginning to succeed, he asked me why it was necessary for me to always go up to our Didsbury studios when a play of mine was in production. Wouldn't it be better if I remained close to him in London, because he had "plans" for me? I explained that if I took a credit on the air, it was only right that I be there to see that things went well. And, of course, I kept right on going to Manchester, even though the weekends away from Betty and the girls were a pain in the neck. A year later, Brian, who had been our successful head of light entertainment, became ABC's controller of programs.

Brian and I, on the whole, hit it off fairly well, until the time when Clive Exton turned in two plays I had commissioned. They were both satirical, black comedies, each sending up an aspect of contemporary society. One was called "The Big Eat," which was about a plain bloke called Harold Britain, who enters a competition run by a giant food company, for which the enormous prize goes to the person who eats more food than his competitors. I decided to produce Exton's other play, "The Trial of Dr. Fancy," first.

Ted Kotcheff, just returned from his first foray into feature films (*Tiara Tahiti*), was in the middle of casting when Brian informed me that neither of Clive's plays would go out — not while he was program controller. After some discussion with him (I can't remember how heated it was), I pointed out that we were already financially committed to "Fancy." He agreed that we complete it, and later he would screen it for the ITA, and Sir Robert Fraser himself would determine whether or not it was "suitable" for mass viewing.

The entire play took place in a courtroom. Dr. Fancy, not named Fancy by Clive for nothing, is a sleek, slick surgeon being tried for the death of a patient resulting from an operation he had performed. The operation? The patient felt himself to be too tall, and Dr. Fancy obliged him, as he had efficiently obliged dozens more in his private clinic, by removing inches from the patient's legs. It also transpires that Dr. Fancy owns a share in a clothing store that caters to people who are short. Beneath the surface of the story, Exton had a ball with the whole notion of conformity — that it was bad to stand out and be noticed.

Even though it was a fine production, with Ted extracting the script's dry, devastating humour to perfection, to this day, I still cannot understand Brian's reasoning for not wanting it to be broadcast. I can only guess that it was his fear, which to me was groundless, of the medical world's reaction to the play. Whatever, it was a decision that angered me greatly. I was certain that the ITA would see no harm in it, and later heard that Sir Robert Fraser confirmed my opinion. Even so, Brian or Howard did not air it until two years after I had left the company, when it got excellent reviews with not a murmur of complaint about its satirical content.

The play's cancellation caused a minor press hoo-ha when Clive's agent, Gareth Wigan, unbeknownst to me, screened the tape of "Fancy" for some of the TV critics. Ironically, some years later, it was reported in the British press that a Swedish doctor was actually performing the same operation to make tall people shorter. Was that life copying art?

Brian stubbornly refused to allow me to produce Clive's send-up play of the consumer society, "The Big Eat." Not only did this infuriate me, but having commissioned him to write it, I felt responsible for it. On the QT, I phoned Norman Rutherford, who was acting head of drama at the BBC, holding the fort for me until I took up my job, and told him to purchase the script and have it produced, which he did.

During my agony period, waiting for the day my contract expired, work very successfully continued. *Armchair Theatre* was better and more popular than ever. The quest for new writers never let up. To give even more support to Peter Luke and Irene Shubik, I took on John Chandos. He was a former actor who usually played slimy Nazi officers, but he was also a writer, an expert on champagne and a quasi-lawyer who had a wide circle of friends.

When John told me that he might be able to get a play out of Arthur Koestler, I was overjoyed. Months passed with no concrete results. One day I was asked to see Bernard Greenhead, manager of the Teddington studios. Bernard asked me whether I examined my story editors' entertainment expense accounts before signing them. I confessed that I didn't, because I was certain that they were not inflated.

He then told me that Peter and Irene's averaged out at around £10 a week while Chandos's were way over that. He showed me some of them — Chandos was often having breakfast with Koestler, which usually included a bottle of brandy! When I berated John for this he protested vigorously, saying, "You told me to pursue him. This, I am doing. I can't help it if Arthur drinks brandy for breakfast!" Good sense made me reluctantly place an entertainment limit of £10 per week, per story editor.

Months later, at his own request, John left and at the recommendation of Howard Thomas, I replaced him with George Kerr. We never did get a play from the author of *Darkness at Noon* to help pay for the advance money and those brandy breakfasts.

Other mad events occurred during my years at ABC within my tight, wonderfully talented group of hardly more than thirty. I giggle at the recollection of the times Irene used to come into my office in tears because Peter had been rude to her; the times when the Adam's apple of my first executive assistant, Arthur Johnston, would bob up and down furiously as he tried to explain cricket to me; when Tony John, drama manager, would agree with me that the class system was bad — only because he was being polite. One incident that particularly stands out was when Michael Chapman accidentally pushed over a prop sculpture, which smashed to pieces. It was of Gitty, the girl whom the Alan Bates character in "Three on a Gas Ring" had made pregnant. I had placed it in the open space surrounded by our drama offices as an ever-present reminder of Big Brother ITA who had censored "Gas Ring."

Oh, the sweet memories. But alas, not all were sweet: there was the time a distraught Dennis Vance, five offices away from mine, stabbed the girl who had rejected him. And the time one of my directors, whose name I have not mentioned in these memories, left the company in shame because he was accused of feeling up an underage performer while auditioning her. The sad fucker tried to explain to me, "Honest, Sydney, I was only being avuncular."

Good though, was my only experience as a co-presenter of a play in the West End. Alun Owen mentioned to me that he couldn't get finance for a stage play. When I read it, I thought it good. Feeling indebted to him, I went to Howard Thomas and proposed that ABC finance its production; it would be good publicity for our company, since Owen was under exclusive contract to us.

Howard quickly agreed to put up the total amount of £8,000 to produce it. Considering today's costs, it boggles the mind, because that sum paid for everything including sets, the large-ish cast, theatre rental and publicity. Since I knew nothing about the business side of theatre, impresario Harold Fielding was selected by Howard to look after the nuts and bolts side of the venture.

The play was called *Progress to the Park*, which had a splendid cast, among whom were Billie Whitelaw, Tom Bell and Roy Kinnear. Ted Kotcheff directed it and Tim O'Brien designed the sets.

If I ever thought television was a daft, no-gamble licence to print money, the live theatre business was a licence to enter a madhouse.

Because no theatre in London was available, Fielding decided to give it a try-out production until one could be found. It opened in Blackpool, which made good sense, since the play was set in Liverpool. It was a smash hit, playing for two weeks to packed houses, nearly recouping its budget. Still waiting for a West End theatre, we moved the show to another town. And then to another, and another and another. Some of the theatres were so unsuitably large, the cast became dispirited when the house was only one-quarter full and they couldn't hear the audience breathe. Trouble, too, was the need to rejig Tim's sets — which were designed to roll on and off the stage — to accommodate each theatre's raked stages, no two of which were alike.

Eventually it got to the West End and was put into a much too large theatre, more suited to a musical comedy than Alun's intimate character play. While it got some good reviews, with its production and actors lauded, it had to close after four weeks.

Despite the live theatre's awesome roar of the crowd, I'd settle anytime for television's smell of grease paint.

A month before Christmas of 1962, Sir Philip Warter informed the staff that, because the company was in good financial shape, all employees over a named period up to December 10 would receive a bonus of two weeks' salary. Joy abounded, which I shared — but not for long. Two weeks later, four months prior to the end of my contract, I received a confidential letter advising me that my contract would be terminated on December 7. December the seventh? That was the Friday before the bonus date!

The money was not the issue! Was this a deliberate, get-even move to trick me out of the bonus, or was it a mindless bureaucracy working overtime?

Quickly, I sought out Howard Thomas, reminding him that according to our contract they were to employ me until April 1 —

and the way things were, I would hold them to the contract for the remaining months.

"But Sydney," Howard asked, "I thought you wanted to leave. What do you mean, 'the way things are'?"

I explained the matter of the dates and the bonus and said, "I will leave as offered, but only if I receive a replacement letter from Sir Philip specifying my release date as December 11, which entitles me to the bonus."

I got the letter, and the bonus, wiping out of my mind the few bad times and leaving behind the thousand good times and the staff I had carefully put together, many of whom (including the writers) had become household names and winners of awards. Ahead lay the mammoth BBC drama and script department, waiting.

CHAPTER EIGHTEEN

THAT WAS THE BBC THAT WAS

On my first day, I was met in the lobby of the BBC Television Centre on Wood Lane by Ruth Smeel, the secretary of the ex–head of drama, Michael Barry. Somewhat tentatively, she greeted me and took me to my office on the fifth floor, which, as I discovered later, housed my department of some 175 people.

I was delighted to find that my office overlooked London rather than the inside the hollow, doughnut-shaped building, which would have limited me to seeing endless offices beyond the open centre space past the giant statue of Helios balanced on its phallic post.[83] Waiting for me on the ready was a woman from administration with pencil poised and clipboard at the ready, wanting to know my

---

83 In the centre of the main block at the Television Centre was a statue designed by T.B. Huxley-Jones of Helios, the Greek god of the sun that sat at the top of a ten-foot pillar in the centre of what was supposed to be a working fountain (it was shut off because the sound echoed loudly through the atrium). The figure was to symbolize the radiation of television around the world.

Arthur Johnson and Clive Exton with Sydney in his office at the BBC.

demands for furnishing the space.

When told that I couldn't have a liquor cabinet, I mewed my disappointment. (I learned later that, years back, an overworked controller had been found so drink-sodden in his office, no employee was now allowed any drink in his office.) It was the matter of the floor covering that angered me. Apparently, at my level in the hierarchy, I was allowed a carpet of my choice, but for the same reason mine would have to stop eight inches short of the door, unlike those senior to me. What crap!

I was about to blow my stack, but Ruth endeared herself to me, as she was to do until she left to get married. Barely disguising her amusement at my attempts to buck management, she cut in to say there was a meeting I had to attend.

Was she being diplomatic, preventing me from creating a scene? Of course she was. But also, there actually was a meeting.

Ruth told me that every Wednesday morning at 10 a.m. all heads of departments, from programs through engineering to publicity, met with program controller Stuart Hood. They discussed the success or failure of the previous week's programs and noted upcoming shows that were special in some way, whether innovative or potentially contentious. Every fourth week, the meeting was extended by an hour, and Kenneth Adam, as he was to do this day, chaired a discussion on policy or, on some occasions, invited someone to give a talk.

Not knowing my way around the vast building, I was led by Ruth through the hallways and to a huge, low-ceilinged room. Entering it, I was amazed. While I knew that the BBC was big, it never occurred to me how big it really was. Seated around a huge hollow square of tables were more than fifty men and women, each in charge of staffs numbering in the hundreds!

As I looked to find a seat, Kenneth Adam spotted me and nudged Stuart Hood, who, after calling the meeting to order, welcomed me as the long-awaited new head of drama. As I found a chair I smiled foolishly at the scattered applause.

It didn't take me long to recognize that I was among the most stimulating, intellectual bunch I would ever be with. Without any visible rancour or animosity, and with commendable objectivity, programs were dissected, praised and flayed with reasons given. Department heads would explain their programs when they were criticized by the others. A complaint of an article promoting a show in the *Radio Times* was accepted by its editor, who pointed out that his staff might have received better cooperation from the show's producer. The head of enterprises (then both buying and selling programs) cried out against a program he thought most saleable abroad, but without breaks no commercial station would buy it. This led to a discussion that affirmed that the BBC audience in the UK came first and a sale abroad would have to take its chances.

Throughout the meeting, I saw the silken glove of the public's needs in the iron fist of competition. There was life in the old dog yet. Most gentlemanly, they were out to kill their competitors — the commercial ITA stations.

Kenneth Adam, the top man in the room, took a back seat and rarely spoke, but he sat next to Hood, observing his staff with benign interest. Hood kept matters on track, sometimes modifying the opinions of

Baverstock, his aggressive and vociferous BBC 1 program controller. I could easily see why many admired Baverstock. He was bright all right, although on the subject of light entertainment and drama, he was less secure — but this didn't in the least inhibit him from voicing his opinions. I would have to keep an eye on him, for sure.[84]

In those days, when a producer had concluded a long-running show, he was sometimes awarded with a three-month all-expenses paid holiday. Hugh Burnett with his *Face to Face* series (starring interviewer John Freeman), certainly deserved that, and he was to speak to the meeting about it.

He told us about the time he had spent in, of all places, Canada. To my surprise, he talked about the land of my birth as if he had been to some exotic place, like Kathmandu.

He was impressed by Canada's innovative Community Antennae System — cable TV as it was then called. Yep, the world's first TV by cable started in London, Ontario, 100 miles from where I was born.

It's tough for an Englishman to resist knocking Canada's cold winters. Burnett pitied the Canadians for not having the good sense to put bends in their streets to break the force-nine winter gales. Finished, there were questions and answers.

I thought, on my very first day, dare I get up and comment on his largely interesting talk? Well, as they say in jolly old England, in for a penny, in for a pound. I got to my feet, praised his observations and confessed that Canada was indeed bloody cold in winter and the streets were too damn straight. With deadpan, I added that it might interest those present to learn that those ruler-straight streets had been planned in the last century by British Army engineers.

Had I gone too far? No, the blessed Brits, then so full of self-confidence, could enjoy being set up. They roared with laughter at my quip. I appeared to be "a good chap" — accepted, right in the heart of the mother of world broadcasting.

---

84 Newman is being somewhat careful in his recollections. As we shall see in the accompanying essay, some of Newman's biggest fights while head of drama group were with Donald Baverstock.

That meeting made me note the dominance of the current affairs people. They were pistol hot with sharp opinions about the winds of social change and politics, these children of their acerbic boss, Grace Wyndham Goldie. She was a little old lady (at least to me, she was) who bred a bunch of tough-minded men who were to rule BBC Television for years: Baverstock, at the time controller of BBC 1; Michael Peacock, first controller of BBC 2; Huw Wheldon, famed compere and head of documentary and arts programs; Paul Fox, who later steered Yorkshire Television; and Alasdair Milne, who became director general. In the days past, Stuart Hood came from the news department and Kenneth Adam was a journalist before he joined the BBC. And so, of course, was Hugh Carleton Greene, the director general. It was clear that factual programs ruled the programming roost at the BBC.

It is good that most TV programmers in both publicly owned and commercial television see the world through literal eyes — for them actuality was the thing — live programming, whether that be a political convention, sporting event or a theatre pick-up of an opera. With my documentary background, how could I object to that? People need to know what's what in the world.

But my drama experience told me that actuality programs were not enough. They were a meal without the main course of that privately felt gut feeling, the true emotional comprehension of the day's news. An unemployment statistic rides roughshod over its human, individual impact. Current affairs and news can't ease the pain of growing up or of being out of sorts with life.

Worse, the thing that actuality programs needed was the reinforcement of laughter, tears and even anger—all of which is found in drama — to open the door of one's private imagination for a better life and the potential to live with zest.

If nothing else, I knew that my *Armchair Theatre* policy of interpreting reality was right. It would put me in good standing with my new actuality-minded bosses and, as I later learned, it was why Hugh Greene wanted me on his staff. Drama, whether a comedy, a thriller or a slice-of-life play would, I intended, do more than be escapist or blindly reflect life. I remembered Shakespeare's words in *Hamlet* again, about drama and its purpose: "to show virtue her own feature, scorn her own image, and the very age and body of the time his form and pressure."

Those words stood me well in *Armchair Theatre*, but could I succeed in doing that with children's drama, the classics and soaps, which would in some way or another sharply mirror virtue, scorn and societal pressures in contemporary Britain? If I could help it, I would get rid of the introverted, navel-gazing drama, which catered only to the literati, the author and its directors. BBC drama was going to be for the quick and not the dead. That's what Greene hired me for, and it suited me fine.

The BBC under Hugh Greene, who had become D.G. a year before I joined, was tooling up for its finest years. Huw Wheldon's *Omnibus* was already bringing culture to an audience that might think Alban Berg was an Israeli politician and Peter Pears a soap manufacturer. Wheldon's touch made creative efforts easy and attractive. Grace's *Panorama* with Richard Dimbleby was unbeatable and the eminently watchable and meaningful *That Was the Week That Was* had been a hit. Sports under Peter Dimmock was tops. Tom Sloan, head of light entertainment — that gentle and, ironically, somewhat conservative guy — was ruling the variety roost with *The Tony Hancock Show*, other innovative sitcoms, and getting ready for the outrageous and shocking *Till Death Do Us Part* and *Steptoe and Son*. And at the top of TV, Adam, Hood and the ferocious Baverstock were out to show their young, commercial competitor, the ITA network, which end was up.

But drama? Hugh Greene felt the BBC was just not with it. He thought I could make drama match the growing success of the others. Funnily enough, it never occurred to me that I would fail or succeed. I just went to work. I found I inherited a staff of about 175 people producing about 300 dramas a year, some them damn good. Rudolph Cartier never did a play that didn't get big audiences. The *Quatermass* cycle by Nigel Kneale was smashers. In fact, anything he produced and directed was an outstanding success, because he had a sharp eye for audiences. Jimmy MacTaggart, Johnny Jacobs, Alvin Rakoff and Don Taylor were doing good work along with a few others. And David Mercer, that brilliant and original writer, was loyally devoted to the Beeb.

But too damn much of it was ho-hum. While I quite liked *Maigret*, produced by Andrew Osborn, one show I was bound to kill was *Compact*,[85] a misbegotten attempt at a twice-weekly soap.

One that I would not even tamper with was David Rose's *Z Cars*, which I thought honest and tough and better than American cop shows. The only time I interfered with it was when, years later, its average weekly ratings dropped from sixteen million to eleven. I suggested to Rose that we kill the series while it was still tops, but carry its main leads, Stratford Johns and Frank Windsor, into a new police activity. David came up with *Softly, Softly* and the ratings again shot to sixteen million.

Ironically, one of the most popular dramas, Ted Willis's *Dixon of Dock Green* came not from drama but from Tom Sloan's variety department. I didn't mind the occasional crossing of departmental lines, nor did the BBC. Sloan was upset that *That Was The Week That Was* was produced by Goldie's current affairs department. He claimed it was a variety show. Grace herself was put out because my drama people had produced a play about a young homeless couple. At the weekly program review meeting, she chastised me, saying that it more properly belonged in her current affairs department. My response to her was, "Well, Grace. Why didn't you get your guys to do it?"

All in all, drama needed a good kick.

It had a fixed, aging staff, some who had actually directed cameras that couldn't move "on air" in the far-off, pre-war, "Ally Pally"[86] studios. They were more at home with the classics and writers who were already successful; they were fearful of first-time writers.

It also had a frustrated young staff that wanted a chance to flex directorial muscles.

---

85 *Compact* was a soap opera, set in the world of magazine publishing, which ran on BBC television from 1962-65.

86 "Ally Pally" was the nickname for Alexandra Palace, the site of the BBC's first television studios. The sobriquet was allegedly coined by popular actress and singer Gracie Fields.

It had a centralized script department that bought scripts (many good ones) that no director wanted. Perhaps worst of all, the prestigious single play, as a weekly series, was chosen for production without anyone seeming to know what audience it was being aimed at.

The top BBC single drama series was *The Sunday Play*. Despite the excellence of many of its productions, the department assumed its audience wanted to see, week after week, an impossible melange of cultural appeal — Shakespeare, followed by a Rattigan, followed by Ibsen, followed by David Mercer. Poor David Mercer. In terms of contemporary relevance, he could out shoot them all! Only the most ardent lovers of television drama would be loyal to that weekly fictional hash.

What bothered me even more than the aged staff, whom I couldn't get rid of even if I had wanted to, was that when I wanted a certain kind of program made, I found I didn't know who to ask in the department to make it. It seemed that I would have to deal with each director — who was his own producer — on a one-to-one basis. The vast department was organized horizontally, in which everybody was directly responsible to its head: me.

It might have been more satisfying for me personally to deal directly with the creative staff. But there being so many, it would have been utterly impossible to satisfy them individually.

I was pretty dispirited, wondering how I was to cope with the situation, until four weeks after my arrival. And then Lady Luck came to my rescue.

Kenneth Adam, director of television services, broke the startling news to me that the government had approved the creation of BBC 2, that I was to organize a whole new set of programs for it and that I would be able to increase staff by forty percent, with the same increase of above-the-line money. Michael Peacock from current affairs was to be its program controller.

To cope with all this, I had a somewhat undeveloped idea: what was required the splitting of the drama department into three to make it more manageable. With the help of Norman Rutherford, my assistant head who held the fort while I was a captive at ABC, and Elwyn Jones,

I went ahead. By April, I became head of drama group, running three more manageable departments.

Serials looked after continuing cliffhanger stories, such as the twice-weekly soaps and children's classics like Dickens. It would also later feature *Doctor Who* and, of course, *The Forsyte Saga*. Series contained those shows that were each a complete story, but which featured recurring main characters, such as *Maigret*; *Troubleshooters*; *Z Cars*; *Dr. Finlay's Casebook*; and *Softly, Softly*. Plays were each different, but catered to a specifically identified audience such as *The Wednesday Play*, *Story Parade* (dramatizations from literary sources), *Play of the Month* specials and *Thirty-Minute Theatre*. Under this was opera, which included *La Bohème*, *Billy Budd* and *Rise and Fall of the City of Mahogany*.

Each department had its own head and small admin staff with six or seven producers, each of them responsible for one run of dramas with a story editor, assigned directors and subsidiary support staff.

It was a murderous task, creating this new organization, but there was very little bloodshed in achieving it. Most, being good BBCers, accepted the reorganization like lambs.

Most controversial was the disbanding of the script department. Its staff was doled out, each editor handed over to the newly appointed producers. But what to do with the script department head, Donald Wilson, an amiable Scot who had been a successful screenwriter before being lured to the BBC by my predecessor, Michael Barry?

Thank heaven for the idea that hit me. I offered him the head of serials job, and like most writers, frustrated by the directors making a hash of their work, he grabbed at the chance of getting directly involved in controlling production. He did a terrific job, and we got along well. Later, of course, it was he who personally produced and wrote at least half of *The Forsyte Saga*.

There was no one I thought suitable to head up the plays department, so I decided to handle it myself until I could find the right person. I tried, and failed, to get Stella Richman, but she chickened out because, as she said to me, "I was frightened of that 'establishment' bureaucracy!" She went to Rediffusion and did a fine job there as head of drama. Alan Brien was flattered when I asked him, but he refused. Finally, I found Michael Bakewell, the very reputable and young assistant head of radio drama under Martin Esslin. With great regret, he left after a year, more keen to be a producer than to run a department. Finally, I succeeded in getting that excellent writer of *George and Margaret* and other successful plays, Gerald Savory, to take on the department. He worked out well except that I found him to be astonishingly "proper."

For series head, I chose Andrew Osborne, that somewhat fading, but still handsome romantic lead of feature films — not the successful producer of *Maigret*. A lovely fella and never a cross word passed between us.

The producer-director relationship was virtually unknown in the BBC and in the UK generally. In fact, directors were called producers and usually ran their own affairs. They found their own material, often bruising writers in the process.

The toughest nut to crack was perhaps appointing producers. I press-ganged some of the more mature directors to take on the producer role, tearing them away from the joys of lording it over actors. I had one helluva job in convincing them of the creative challenge of putting together a production package, from selecting a play to its promotion. I defined their jobs as mainly being the conscience of the project, and they needed to learn the hardest lesson of all: the interpretation of a dramatic work was the director's responsibility, not theirs. If a production failed it was their fault for choosing the wrong director.

The BBC brass supported all my wishes, even to the extent of making physical changes in their spanking new White City television centre.

I didn't want the producer to be in the control room while the director was at work. This was to avoid inhibiting him, and, should the need for discussion or a dispute arise between them, it would not take place in the presence of the director's assistants or technical crew. At my request, small rooms with their own video monitor, speaker and phone were built alongside each of the studio control rooms for the producers.

The arrival of BBC 2, with its demand for new programs and new talent, was a godsend. Not only was it a chance to break into new kinds of TV drama, it allowed the release of pent-up talent among young directors such as Anthony Page, Ken Loach and Waris Hussein, and the promotion of junior production assistants and floor managers. But it also opened the doors for some of the best talent at that time outside the Beeb.

Unasked by me, since I wouldn't poach from Howard Thomas at ABC-TV, and especially not from Leonard White, who took over *Armchair Theatre* after I left, many of my best people came across from ITV to join me — Philip Saville, Ted Kotcheff, Charles Jarrott, Alan Cooke, Peter Luke and Irene Shubik.

The only person I did steal was one of my ABC production assistants, Verity Lambert, and I made her producer of *Doctor Who*. But that's a success story in itself.

There were some on my staff whom I felt should leave. It was easier to pull teeth at the BBC than to achieve that. The trick I pulled was to get the powerful personnel department on my side.

In learning that the giant BBC had a department of organization, methods and grading people, who were sent into a department if senior management thought it inefficient, I decided, in effect, to use the BBC against itself. I asked, to the surprise of all, for them to investigate my own department.

They sent two chaps who virtually lived with my staff and me for two solid weeks. Very politely they pried into every aspect of our work. They were keen as mustard and excited by the task. (They told me that mail lay in my in-tray for two weeks before being answered!) One month later, I was given a full report bound in sedate gray covers loaded with tables, statistics, job descriptions and an organization chart of the devolution of authority. It was exactly what I had hoped for.

With this in my hot hands, I had no trouble with the brass and the staff changes were made like a breeze. It also helped tidy up and reorganize my shop. Another bonus was that I managed to convince John Keeble, who was the senior of the two chaps, to become my executive assistant.

My own office, I kept very sparse. I leaned very heavily on Keeble, whose organizational background combined with his non-pushy, winning personality kept me on track as he looked after the group's money, ratings, audience response and minutes of what were endless meetings. Staff problems and assignments were looked after by gentle Ayton Whitaker. My secretary, after Ruth Smeel left to marry producer Cedric Messina, was a ferociously loyal and efficient stenographer who stayed for a while before going on to bigger things.

As well as seeing departmental heads on specific problems, I'd meet with the three of them each Monday morning, all twenty-seven or so producers with their heads monthly, and as many of the entire group who could leave their work at least twice a year.

To run the vast establishment of over 400 creative drama and opera staff (about seventy-five directors and thirty story editors), I laid down two important departmental ground rules:

1) All BBC drama from comedies to melodrama, for children and adults, must, as much as possible, reflect in some way or other the world today and signal the turning points in British society, the changing relationships between parents and children, management and work force, technologist and consumer, priest and parishioner, and so on. Even classic drama was to be chosen, ideally, for its contemporary relevance.

To get this across, I pulled the corny trick of sending each producer a printed card to hang on the wall of his office. It read, "Look back not in anger, nor forward with fear, but around with awareness" (courtesy James Thurber). And I prayed that the message would sink in.

Along with the usual strictures of knowing your audience, holding to budget, I also demanded that:

2) Writers were to be paid within two weeks of the acceptance of their work. And more important, no script would be changed without the permission of the author. I held the story editor responsible for protecting the author, rather than protecting the drama department. That paid off and got us the loyalty of the best writers.

The years rolled on with many high spots to fatten my memory.

Dansk Radio came to us to jointly produce *Hamlet*, not in a studio but right in the sixteeth-century Kronborg Castle in Denmark, the

Elsinore that inspired Shakespeare. Donald Baverstock and I went to Copenhagen to negotiate the deal. Our main Danish contact, Bjørn Lense-Møller, turned out to be terrific. The Danes would provide all production facilities — two five-camera mobile units, lights and a generator, as well as the fifty or so costumed extras — and we, the interpretive elements.

I appointed Peter Luke as producer and approved Philip Saville as director, even though he had never before touched a Shakespeare play. Remembering how he had done so well with the difficult American theatrical company for *Time of Your Life*, I knew he would die rather than fail in his most chancy project. I personally laid on Christopher Plummer, a fellow Canuck, to play Hamlet.

The production problems were immense. Foolishly confident with my background in outside broadcasts, I missed out on some vital flaws in the location.[87] Half the floors in the castle were not strong enough to bear the weight of the cameras. Philip was forced to shoot around these.

Worse were the problems of sound. On one side of the castle was the ferry slip to Sweden. Every fifteen minutes intruding into a precious sound take on our sixteenth-century drama would be the alien hoot-hoot of a ferry departing or berthing — the sounds mingling with the roar of riveters coming from a shipyard on the other side of the castle. Compounding all this was fog, which lost us hours. Why? The castle was at the narrowest point of the main channel into the Baltic. Peter Luke, to this day, can still hear the blaring of foghorns of the four thousand ships that passed by each day. I wonder, if I had noticed the flaws in the recce, would I have approved the project and so missed out on the wonderful results that accrued?

Cast and crew worked eighteen hours a day, with the two technical, camera and lighting crews leap-frogging each other to save time.

In eight days, Peter and Philip, with the unflagging and patient Danish crew, got two hours and forty-eight minutes of spectacular

---

87 In additions to the problems Newman lists, the castle didn't have electricity. Huge generators would have to be sourced to power the lights.

drama in the can. Dansk Radio was terrific. They weren't able to pay the cost of half the ferry service to Sweden I'd had the nerve to request, but Lense-Møller actually got the shipyard to stop riveting for three days!

What a dream cast was put together. With Chris Plummer as Hamlet, Robert Shaw played King Claudius, Alec Clunes was Polonius and Horatio was played by Michael Caine.

Sitting in the control truck with me one day, having come from England to see how we were getting along, was Kenneth Adam. As we watched Philip on the video monitor, rehearsing with Michael Caine, who was beautifully acting his heart out, Kenneth turned, dug me in the ribs and said, "Leave it to a Canadian to cast a cockney to play an aristocrat."

"Oh really?" I replied in my best English accent.

And to play Fortinbras? Another Canuck — Donald Sutherland — in his first major appearance anywhere!

Peter Luke got a bonus out of the show (later titled *Hamlet at Elsinore*); he fell in love and married June Tobin (who played Gertrude) three weeks after the shoot. What a cast! And, what a show!

I was also in charge of opera. Imagine me in charge of a medium I had always thought good for a yawn or a laugh with its often overblown, melodramatic passions and deaths — virtually impossible to satisfy any but fanatic aficionados. I came to love it.

I was the first drama head to be given this responsibility. After about a year of Verdi, Tchaikovsky and more (we did about five major studio-originated operas a year, and a few original commissioned mini-operas), it dawned on me to ask why we weren't producing any of Britten's operas, indisputably the greatest living opera composer in the world . . . who happened to be British! I asked Cedric Messina, whom I had put in charge of opera, why the hell we had no Benjamin Britten.

I not only found out the answer to this question, but discovered the probable reason why the BBC had given opera to the drama group.

Years earlier, BBC TV had done a production of Britten's *Turn of the Screw*. The producer of it (whose name I thankfully don't

Sydney on a family holiday in Sweden, 1964.

know and don't want to know) couldn't figure out how to visualize the fifteen musical intervals, which Britten wrote to cover the scene changes in the theatre production, so the idiot cut them right out of the opera. Benjamin Britten was not amused.

BBC radio could do his stuff, but BBC television? Never again.

Fortunately, I knew Basil Coleman,[88] an English director I had helped train in television direction in Canada. He knew Britten and Pears personally, and had directed many of Britten's operas years ago, including *Gloriana* for the Queen's coronation. I phoned Basil and offered him a three-play contract if he could deliver Britten to us. Bingo! It worked, Britten was back on board and Basil directed Britten's *Billy Budd*.

It was most handsomely mounted. For the BBC's largest studio, Tony Abbott designed a ship only three feet shorter that Nelson's *Victory*, which ingeniously combined above and below deck playing areas. Its cast and chorus of eighty was star-studded, included Peter Pears as Captain Vere, Peter Glossop as Billy, Michael Langdon as Claggart and John Shirley-Quirk playing the first officer.

In the large adjacent studio, Charles Mackerras conducted the London Symphony Orchestra with Cedric Messina and I in the sound control room, keeping Britten happy. In five studio days, the opera was taped live and was unbeatable as studio opera, equal to the best stage interpretations done anywhere — verified by television and music critics.

In retrospect, I marvel at what we were encouraged to do in the BBC as it was then. To recall, that opera's budget was about £80,000 and not a complaint was ever made by my bosses when *Budd*'s minority audience numbered only 50,000 viewers. That works out to £1.60 per viewer. Who today in our market-oriented, cost-effective society would approve that production? Well today, twenty years later, with thousands of programs seen and forgotten, those who did see it still talk of the intense pleasure that production gave them.

Running the beefed-up drama operation, with its staff of over 400, left me unable to produce programs myself. Just to keep in touch, I set out to do at least one a year.

After successfully producing Hugh Leonard's *Stephen D*, directed by young Anthony Page, and Harold Pinter's *Tea Party*

---

88 Coleman would direct the last production Newman ever worked on, the 1989 adaptation of Britten's *The Little Sweep*.

directed by Charles Jarrott, I made a misstep when I produced Philip Saville's direction of the Brecht-Weill opera *Rise and Fall of the City of Mahogany*.

It was a fine and successful production all right, and even got a personal note from Hugh (now Sir Hugh) Greene saying so, but I went vastly over budget by a whopping fifty percent! I just didn't have the time to supervise it properly.

Early on in the studio, I realized that, at the rate Philip was taping, we would not be able to finish by ten o'clock, our allotted time. Even though I was one of the five most senior production executives, the bums who control the allocation of studios would not allow me a measly half-hour extension of time to finish the taping.

I knew, of course, that they were right.

I learned that one of Tom Sloan's big variety shows was due in the studio the following morning. The BBC would have to follow its usual routine of twenty-four hour studio usage, meaning that at ten o'clock, a gang of stagehands would arrive and rip the elaborate sets out of the studio as fast as they could. Then a gang of cleaners would show up, ending by washing the studio floor to rid it of the simulated painted wood, marble, rugs or whatever. When dry, scene painters would arrive around midnight and paint the floor with whatever the following days' sets required. With the paint dry around 2 a.m., the new sets would be trolleyed in and set up, touched up, furniture placed, curtains hung and sets dressed. At 7 a.m. lighting men would arrive, and at 8, the camera lenses were uncapped and cameras warmed. Sharp at 9 a.m., camera and sound crews were ready when the actors started trickling in to start rehearsals for another show.

And so, with twenty minutes of the opera still not in the can, mad as hell at myself and at Philip, I had to call a halt and release the entire London Philharmonic Orchestra, seventy performers and watch my beautiful Las Vegas sets for the opera be torn apart to clear the studio. It took me three months to get all the pieces together again to complete the opera.

After that fiasco, how could I dare whip the ass of anyone in my department who went over budget? So, with a heavy heart, I did the only sensible thing: I quit producing. It would be more than twenty years before I would produce again.

Opera was fun though, and I met the damnedest people as head of BBC TV opera because of it.

Every two years the Salzburg Festival gave a prize for the best original television opera. I went to it because we had entered. We didn't win, but while there I met Herbert von Karajan. The encounter, I'm vain enough to say, reverberated across Europe's musical world.

Herr Dr. Wilfried Scheib, director of music for Austrian State Television, asked me to join him at a cocktail party given for von Karajan, the festival director. The previous night, I had seen his powerful production of Verdi's *Macbeth* — how could I resist wanting to meet this musical giant?

Off we drove, up the winding mountain road to a vast log chalet. At the door we were greeted by a doorman dressed in an outfit looking like a flunky in the court of Louis XIV. We were then led into a vast room littered with grand pianos and harpsichords, in the centre of which were adoring worshippers encircling the great man.

"Come," said Scheib. "I'll introduce you to the Maestro." And he led me through the crowd. And as Scheib began his introductions, I was amazed to see that von Karajan was not at all like those low-angle heroic-looking shots of him on the sleeves of his LP recordings. Hell, he was even shorter than my five-foot-seven. As we shook hands, I couldn't prevent myself from blurting out, "My God, you're so small!" A gasp went up from the group, and if von K had had any Heidelberg duelling scars they would have blazed like neon tubes. A dropped pin would have been a thunderclap.

I was stunned at my gaffe, but partly recovered with a quick, hearty, ". . . to have marvellously conducted and directed that big production last night!"

Slightly mollified, he relaxed a bit, and before I knew it, we had a real ding-dong of an argument about the best way to shoot television opera. With the onlookers listening eagerly, he held to the position that the singers should mime to a playback recording of the music and singing. (I knew that he sometimes even used actors because they were better-looking to mime to the playback of the good singers' voices.) I disagreed and maintained that the most effective opera should be shot live; that singers, as well as having the right voice, must also look right for the role. It's part of the audience's expectation to see the strained lips and neck muscles of the singer.

Barely disguising his scorn, he said, "Herr Newman, you might know about pictures, but I know about sound!" and turned away.

I still think he was wrong.

One memory I will always cherish: For reasons I will never understand, the powers that be decided that I would play host to the Duke of Edinburgh, who wanted to visit Television Centre.

He turned up with a couple of equerries and Scotland Yard dicks led by BBC's deputy chairman, Hugh Greene and Kenneth Adam. I was strictly warned that I was never to take His Royal Highness out of the sight of his entourage.

After I was introduced to him, and I was leading him ahead of his minders, I asked him to call me Sydney — but for the life of me I never knew how to address him. I resisted calling him "Duke," but fell back on "Er" and the safe, "Sir."

For over three hours, I took him and his party into studios where I had a devil of a time introducing him to dozens of actors who were blanking on their names and giggling at their attempts at curtseying. In one production control room, I had to scream out to the director and technical staff to get back to work, because when we entered, to a man, they jumped to their feet even though the live drama was actually in transmission. The royal family seems to be wrapped in mystery. They look like nice people, dignified in their symbolic roles as unifiers of diverse peoples. But I've always wanted to know more, as I would guess most people do, about what they were really like, their intelligence, their sensitivity about the arts, that kind of thing.

Well, that day gave me some answers.

After leaving the studio where the Duke of Edinburgh met the cast of *Compact*, as we were striding along the corridor to the next place, we talked about the program. I was knocked out when he said to me, "*Compact*. Y'know I've often thought it more like radio, but with pictures." I couldn't have agreed with him more. And did.

To show him a control room in action meant leaving the rest of the party out in the corridor with their noses pressed against the glass window, anxiously peering in at us. Once, the Duke asked me what was beyond the far, tinted glass wall.

"The studio," I answered.

"Aren't you going to show it to me?"

What could I do? So I led him away from the sight of those in the corridor, through a soundproof door and onto the lighting gantry some thirty feet above the studio floor.

The Duke asked what the play in camera rehearsal below was about.

"Well, you see that tall chap [Nicol Williamson], he's had a homosexual relationship with the little fellow [Alfred Lynch] who is now happily married to the girl [Glenda Jackson] and the tall chap wants to continue their former relationship." I looked at the Duke and noted that on the very day of his visit we were doing the first play that overtly dealt with homosexuality.[89]

Putting me at ease, he said, "Oh, that's all right. I don't mind."

Emboldened, I then blurted out, "Oh! You should come around tomorrow when we're doing *No Exit* by Sartre. Harold Pinter's the only male in it and you can see a couple of women going at it."

He lifted his head and burst out laughing, which reverberated around the quiet studio. The actors, up to now unaware we were there, heard the laughter, looked up and saw us. Recognizing His Royal Highness, they all paused, stood straight, bowed their heads — and then went right back to rehearsing.

You just can't faze professionals, and in saying that, I am not excluding the Duke of Edinburgh.

One of my most memorable times at the BBC was when I was chosen to be one of a three-man team with David Attenborough (now Sir David), then controller of BBC 2 and Jim Redmond (now

89 The play that Newman and the Duke of Edinburgh were watching was "Horror of Darkness," a 1965 episode of *The Wednesday Play*.

Sir James), then deputy head of TV engineering. The BBC was finally getting into colour television, and our task was to find out as much about it as we could. And that, happily, meant a trip around the world!

It was a fun trip and we learned a lot. First was Canada, where colour television had just started. Then to New York and Hollywood, to see the somewhat garish, over-saturated U.S. colour system that had been in use for over five years. Then to Tokyo, where we saw the same U.S. NTSC system, but oh how different it was in the subtle hands of the Japanese.

Later, in the Japanese section of our hotel (where David insisted we stay, rather than in the Western section), the three of us soaked in a Japanese hot tub with a couple of Suntory whiskeys under our belts, chewing the fat and marvelling at the way the Japanese handled their colour by using different dichroic glass filters in the camera's beam splitter, selectively filtering colours to achieve different looks. And still not satisfied, because electronic cameras tend to intensify colour, they painted their sets not in colour, but in warm and cool shades of grey. To perk up the images with bits of pure colour, they carefully selected set dressings and people's clothes.

I couldn't have been with two nicer guys for that five-week trip. Attenborough was in a panic, because crowding his solemn concern for his BBC's program controller's duties, were his intense interests in all matters zoological, ecological and the strange ways of different cultures.

In flying from Los Angeles to Tokyo, because we had to arrive fresh, we deliberately stopped off in Honolulu to get a night's sleep.

Even though we were dead tired in the sticky heat, David insisted on going to see the U.S. Navy's famous Marine Institute, where among other things, they were training dolphins to obey commands. Although I wanted to hit the sack, Jimmy and I couldn't resist going along. We were amused by David's embarrassment when the institute's director expressed his honour at meeting the famous David Attenborough and insisted on personally showing us the place with its tanks of all sorts and sizes filled with amazing sea life.

Back in Honolulu, I couldn't forget those dolphins performing amazing feats to the underwater clicks of their trainers. Was the Navy training them for the amusement of tourists or, as I suspected, were the frisky, cheerful looking beasts being trained to self-destruct, carrying bombs to nose against enemy ships?

As we were leaving, the institute director said he would send a gift of fish to a pleased David in London. Months later, a breathless David phoned my office. Would I like to come immediately with him to Heathrow Airport? The gift of fish had arrived! It was urgent! They must be picked up and transferred to the special saltwater fish tanks David had at his house in Richmond before the oxygen ran out in the seawater-filled plastic bags containing the slowly swimming fish.

The look on David's face as he picked up the fragile bags of exotic, multi-coloured fish was worth a million bucks.

In Tokyo, after we had finished our work and were ready to fly home, David said that he was going to take part of his annual holiday by remaining in Japan for a short while and see how the locals live. Maybe, through a friend of a friend of his, Geoff Hamilton, he might be allowed to live in a Japanese religious monastery. If it could be arranged, would we like to join him?

Like a shot, Jimmy and I agreed.

Sure enough, we ended up in the Tenrikyo monastery as the guest of the Shinbashira, the Pillar of the Faith, a short, cheerful man in his sixties who looked exactly like those smiling, rotund statues of Buddha. So began five strange, incredible days for me.

We were given our own small, paper-walled-inside-a-glass-walled house within the monastery walls, and five servants to feed and look after us. During the day, we were taken to visit many of the palaces, temples, and incredible rock, moss and every other conceivable kind of garden in nearby Kyoto.

One place was certainly off to me, and I think to Jimmy. Inside were rows of bleachers on which sat some ordinary Japanese men and women, all thoughtfully gazing at a quarter of an acre of white pebbles raked in swirling patterns around five or six dark, protruding rocks. We sat and did our own gazing, Jimmy and I not having a clue as to why, but David was transfixed. We couldn't tear him away. Of course, it was part of the famous Ryoanji Temple.

Jim, with his dry Scottish humour, would occasionally tease David. As we emerged from the Temple grounds, David, at his most earnest, tried to explain that it likely represented for the Japanese a means of looking into the infinite. Jimmy, playing the role of the uncultured engineer, refused to understand and said, "Why rake it? A lawn-roller would smooth the pebbles so much more neatly."

David, exasperated by Jim's apparent obtuseness, sighed, and as he started to explain all over again, did a double take as he saw that Jimmy was sending him up. We all broke up laughing.

At the end of a day's sightseeing, on our return we'd wash ourselves and then soak in our hot tub, enjoying ourselves like slum kids at a camp. Then we'd put on a light cotton kimono followed by a thick-quilted one; we needed to keep warm because it was late in October, and the walls were thin!

We'd emerge from the bathhouse to sit on the tatami floor around a low table and be served hot saké and a mouth-watering Japanese meal. And for breakfast, out of consideration for our Western palates, they gave us bacon and eggs. We even participated in an awe-inspiring religious service.

One evening, we were invited to attend a banquet given for the Shinbashira prior to his visit to his parishioners in far-away countries. There must have been at least fifty of his friends who had come down from Tokyo, along with some ancient priests, to wish him well on his journey. We sat on the floor at low tables arranged as a large open U, with the chefs in the middle preparing and passing out the food. The gorgeous meal filled our bellies, and the drink cheerfully befuddled our minds, all fifty or so of us.

At the end of the meal, apparently it was the custom that each guest stand and entertain everybody. From the end of the U where we sat, we watched as the guest at the other end of the tables, with some difficulty (the saké!), clambered to his feet and said something, in Japanese, of course, which might have been, "A rose is a rose is a rose," and to polite applause and murmurs of *aahs*, unsteadily sat down.

As Jimmy, David and I saw each guest do his bit, we realized with horror that we would be expected to do something as well.

It wasn't until there were two men before us that we got an idea. It might have been Jim who thought of it. When we shakily got to our feet (great shtuff, saké), we put our heads together and began to sing "Old MacDonald had a farm, E-I, E-I, O." English not being understood, at first they politely stared at the mad Englishmen but we pressed on. After our "Moo Moo here," and "Quack Quack there," they got the idea of barnyard sounds and the laughter started. By the time we got to the third chorus of its "Oink Oink here," most of these middle-aged Japanese men were helplessly rolling about on the tatami mat, clutching their sides, helpless with laughter.

Back at the Beeb, work for me was all-consuming, deeply engrossing and full of challenges for anyone willing to flex his creative muscles. Very simply, I found the Beeb able to stomach failure. It was in its blood that making programs was a creative process, and therefore each program was a gamble. By careful planning, the risks were reduced to a minimum, but a gamble it was. Had the BBC thought otherwise, I wouldn't have remained. As head honcho of TV drama and opera, I ran my shop that way and somehow it worked out that I could rarely do wrong. By that, I mean I laid fewer rotten eggs than others in commercial TV who were in the same position I was.

Of course there were plenty of failures, but they were mostly decent ones, honourably inspired.

In the early days when Jimmy MacTaggart was cutting his teeth as producer of *The Wednesday Play*, he laid a most odorous egg. The intention of the play, "Fable," was to attack racial prejudice against blacks. Jimmy liked the author's intentions and the seemingly clever way of getting the story across: An imaginary UK would be peopled by black people, and an immigrant family of whites would try to settle there. When they do, they are discriminated against by the Brits. The play was well-executed, but the critics slated it. God knows what effect it had on many in the audience. *The Wednesday Play* team seemed to have produced a play contrary to its intentions: according to the bad reviews, it proved that blacks were inherently against white people!

But against the odd stinker, who can forget "Vote, Vote, Vote for Nigel Barton," "Up the Junction" and dozens more that ran week after week, freshly and lively, entertainingly making the UK real to British viewers.

To cajole a reluctant and successful director, MacTaggart, to become producer of *The Wednesday Play*, called for some mighty fine arguments on my part. He accepted only when I agreed that he could go back to directing after two years as producer.

Get a good man whom you trust to do a job, as MacTaggart was, and he can't help but gather good people around him. New writers, directors and actors by the score emerged under his direct guidance. He found Tony Garnett, then a successful actor, and made him his story editor. After a year and a half, MacTaggart begged off, and I appointed Tony to produce a number of episodes. It was he who was responsible, with Ken Loach, for what was the most memorable play of the '60s, "Cathy Come Home."

Tony in turn recommended to me that a totally unknown Kenith Trodd become his story editor. Somewhat doubtful, but trusting Tony's judgement, I agreed. Dennis Potter's *The Singing Detective* was just one of the many fine productions Trodd later produced.

Early on in joining the BBC, an opportunity presented itself for me to have some fun by creating something daffy for kids. Daffier than *The Avengers*.

My program bosses, BBC 1 Chief Donald Baverstock and Stuart Hood, his boss, were unhappy about the Saturday afternoon drop in ratings because of the traditional placement of my group's children's classic serials. They first said, rightly, that something with broader appeal was needed to follow Peter Dimmock's highly popular Saturday sports coverage and to more strongly lead into the teenage hit, *Juke Box Jury*, which followed our serial. Dramatizations of novels such as *David Copperfield* and *Nicholas Nickleby* could just as easily be moved

Sydney (right) in a meeting with Tony Garnett (centre).

to Sunday, but only if drama could devise a new, high-rating serial to bridge the two popular programs.

How could I refuse?

I asked Donald Wilson if his people could come up with something that would suit children, something with latent educational values that would be exciting enough to hold the sports loving audience and build viewers for the lovers of *Juke Box Jury*. Nothing came up that I felt confident with.

Being an old sci-fi fan, I had always been intrigued by H.G. Wells's time machine. It occurred to me that such a device might make the basis for a children's serial if it had good characters in it who were in a constant state of jeopardy.

The machine could transport characters into the past so that they would be present, say, when Caesar landed in England. What better way to make history real? Space travel being hot news in 1963, wouldn't it be exciting to also send our audience into outer space to experience what it's like to be weightless? And what was in the planets beyond ours? And in the future? Or what if our characters in the machine were on earth, but reduced to the size of ants?

Excited, I dreamed on and on, and finally got the idea down in a memorandum,[90] which I sent to Donald Wilson to consider.

In it, I described it as above, but fleshed it out with descriptions of the characters and some strictures. The time-space ship was to be a small, commonplace thing that did not look like a vehicle but was gigantic inside. It was to be operated by a refugee from outer space who had fled in terror from a dreaded enemy who had captured his home planet. He was to be 742 years old, somewhat senile but with flashes of superior intelligence. He would be crotchety and impatient (like some grandfathers), angry with himself because, while he desperately wants to go home, he can't. He just doesn't know how to run the blasted time-space ship.

Accidentally, he lands in a junkyard in London. While wandering, lost in a typical London pea-soup fog, he meets two schoolteachers shepherding home a girl student. They decide to help the lost, old duffer who cannot even remember his name. He leads them to his "ship" and invites them in. After they humour him by entering the small thing, they discover that it is vast inside. He tries to demonstrate how the ship works, presses the wrong buttons, and the time-space ship takes off to heaven only knows where, back and forward in time and space.

The memo also contained some strict injunctions. Historical journeys would have to be based on fact and outer space stories be accurate as to the most up-to-date scientific knowledge we possessed at that time. And no bug-eyed monsters! B.E.M.'s were for schlock sci-fi and not for us! As well, each serialized story was to end with the ship landing in an unknown place and be rarely longer than four episodes, each ending with a strong cliffhanger.

Donald Wilson cautiously thought the idea not bad. A lot would depend on the producer we appointed, he thought. No one

---

90 Newman's "memorandum" about *Doctor Who* is something of a mystery. Newman claimed until the end of his life that he wrote it, but if he did, it no longer exists. The earliest version of the *Doctor Who* concept is an undated draft of a format document for the series written by C.E. Webber, subsequent drafts of which were fashioned into an outline signed by Newman, Donald Wilson and C.E. Webber in April 1963. See the accompanying essay for a further discussion of this.

spectacularly right came to mind.

The fates were with me. I recalled a very bright, no-nonsense young woman who had worked as a production secretary for me at ABC. She was the kind of person who could disagree with her director (or me, for that matter) without ever being disagreeable, and would often be found to be right. And so, I gambled on a hunch. I phoned Verity Lambert[91] and asked her if she would like to become a producer. After a joyous cry of "Yes!" we met. I gave her a copy of my memo describing the serial.

"Sydney, it's good!" And then, "Yes, I think I can do it."[92]

It not being my practice to ram something down the throat of an unwilling department head, the next hurdle would be Donald Wilson accepting her. Again, with caution, he accepted her into his department.

Admin matters completed, I gave Verity a copy of the booklet describing my work at ABC with Cambridge University Group studying children's age of perception, to better understand the young. I demanded that she religiously read *The New Scientist* magazine each week for story ideas. Later, she told me that she didn't understood ninety percent of what she'd read in it. I didn't tell her that I didn't understand it either.

I also told her to use young directors, too young to be fixed in their ways. She already knew that that was why I picked her.

She took over as if she had been a producer for years, but she wasn't fully accepted by her equals for some months. I received only a whiff of the rumours. Who was she? A former, lowly personal secretary and, to boot, one from Independent Television; no doubt H.D.G. Tel's mistress, inserted into the BBC. (Every executive in the

---

91 According to Richard Marson's 2015 biography of Verity Lambert, *Drama and Delight*, Newman first tried director Don Taylor and even *Avengers* story editor Richard Bates, who turned him down. Bates claimed that he was still putting down the receiver when he heard Verity Lambert's phone ring in the next office.

92 Privately, she was less than impressed with working on a show with a juvenile audience. She told her friend Linda Agran, "I don't know any children. I don't want children. I don't fucking like children."

BBC went by initials. Mine — H.D.G. Tel — stood for head, drama group, television.) I'm not protesting too much when I say the closest Verity and I came physically was in the standard showbiz kiss kiss, hug hug accompanying a hello or congrats on a good show.

Over the months of its development I kept an eye on the series development, not, I hasten to add, as the head drama honcho, but as its deviser. Donald, as her immediate boss, gave Verity strong support, one of them by appointing Mervyn Pinfield, an electronic boffin, as her associate producer to assist in the technical wizardry the series would demand. This led her to ask for and get the series' startling opening titles created by Pinfield and Bernard Lodge and the unforgettable howling musical sounds based on Ron Grainer's music as it was arranged by Delia Derbyshire in the BBC's innovating Radiophonic Workshop.

Believe it or not, Donald and I weren't sure of the look of the title sequence but, as I had learned at ABC, what Verity wants is usually right. Donald also provided her with an experienced story editor, David Whitaker, who added a lot to Verity's own script instincts. And during the run-up period, somehow the ship became a police callbox, called the TARDIS,[93] and because the old man didn't know his own name, what better to call the series than *Doctor Who?*

What genius of hers it was to recommend to me that she cast that acidic sergeant of *The Army Game*, William Hartnell, to play the Doctor. As his foils, who were desperately wanting to get back to their Earth, Verity picked as the teachers William Russell and lovely Jacqueline Hill, both better actors than they ever had the chance to demonstrate in the series and lovely, not-so-young-as-she-looked Carole Ann Ford, who screamed like a dream.

---

93 Newman is likely speaking about the adoption of "TARDIS" as the name of the ship, which was most likely an invention of writer Anthony Coburn. In all but one of the drafts of the format documents, the time machine had always been a police box (and even the earliest draft refers to the idea of it). Newman publicly credited himself for coming up with the idea of the time machine being a police box as early as 1969, a fact independently verified by Donald Wilson's interview with writer Malcolm Hulke. See the accompanying essay for more details.

Waris Hussein, a novice director, did the first serial. The pilot production was crude as hell, and I thought Hartnell was too acidic — positively unlikeable. Minor script changes were made, and Verity made sure that Hartnell softened his crotchetiness. Hussein got four cameras for the live production. At a cost of £2,500 per episode, *Doctor Who* was launched.

The first four-episode serial got off to a reasonably good start. The characters were intriguingly interesting and the magic of the small police callbox, with its astonishing, huge interior and the trip back in time to the Neanderthal age captured everyone's imagination. From then on, I was ready to have a long-arm relationship to it — it was only one show of the dozens I was weekly responsible for. It was clear that we had a winner and I was pleased. The old dog still had it in him!

After that first serial, Betty and I and our three girls turned the TV set on the following Saturday to see what goodies Verity would bring us and millions more.

To my horror, there were the Daleks! Bloody hell! B.E.Ms!

When the episode finished, I immediately phoned Verity and expressed my displeasure.[94] I accused her of disobeying my orders: She had cheapened the series by introducing the Daleks, which were nothing but Bug-Eyed Monsters. She was to appear in my office Monday morning, and I hung up.

When she turned up, I started to rip her to pieces. Verity desperately tried to stem my anger by repeating, "They are not bug-eyed monsters. They are—" But I was unstoppable.

Finally, when I ran out of breath, Verity finished her sentence. "Sydney, they are not B.E.M.s. Inside is a human. A brain, really. They are so advanced in time that their bodies have become weakened; the casings around them are needed to replace their atrophied arms and

---

94 Newman probably didn't confront Verity Lambert about the Daleks after the broadcast of the serial now known as "The Daleks." His recounting of events in the *Daily Sketch* in May 1969 has a "timid" Lambert telling Newman about the Daleks while in his office. This was presumably while the serial was in pre-production (as Newman was away in North America while it was in production).

legs and contain their huge brains!"

Did she dream up that excuse or did she believe it? I'll never know. One thing I do know, though. It was the Daleks that made the series a whopping success.

After the first year, in examining audience figures, it was apparent that stories in the future — the sci-fi stuff — were more popular than the historical, back-in-time adventures. But Verity was as concerned as I was with the easy, educational values of the latter, and so they continued, regardless of the occasional, minor drop in ratings "hammocked" by the outer space stories.

The Doctor and his earthlings witnessed Nero fiddling while Rome burned, got involved in the French Revolution, travelled with Marco Polo and even avoided getting killed in a cowboy shootout in Tucson, all alternating with stories in the future.

Doctor Who, on at 5:15 p.m., successfully sustained the sports rating while lifting *Juke Box Jury* audience figures and the BBC captured Saturday night.

Despite its great popularity, there were complaints that some episodes frightened the heebie-jeebies out of children. At one of the Wednesday weekly program review meetings this was raised by a concerned department head, and, to my surprise, a few others agreed with her.

Thank God, Huw Wheldon was controller of programs at the time and boomed out in his best theatrical Welsh style, "Daleks frighten children? Nonsense! It's good for them, anyway. My offspring, two and four years of age, after seeing *Doctor Who*, put waste-paper baskets on their heads and rushed about shouting 'Exterminate! Exterminate!' They love it!"

No more than I would have anticipated the success of *The Avengers* could I have guessed that *Doctor Who* would become a cult program, seen in dozens of countries, with fan clubs, books and magazines dedicated to it and the sale of endless T-shirts, Dalek toys in all sizes and gee-gaws of all sorts merchandized. At the time of writing, twenty-four years later, the damn thing is still going strong.[95]

Twenty-two years later, bored with retirement, I decided that I might take a crack at becoming a producer again. It was important that I get my name before the public. Since I had never taken an on-air credit for devising *Doctor Who* (as I foolishly hadn't with *The Avengers*), I wrote to my old BBC colleague Alasdair Milne, and asked him to give me a credit on each program, as was the custom with other devisers; it would help me. He refused.[96] No doubt he was afraid that with a credit on the air I might demand royalties — a sizeable amount, considering the sales of the program over so many years.

His refusal didn't make me angry — I merely thought it mean.

Ironically, during this period, the internationally popular game Trivial Pursuit came out to screw me further. One question it asked was, "Who created *Doctor Who*?" but on the card's flip side, the answer was written as "Terry Nation." Of course, it was Terry who first wrote the Daleks and who still deserves his considerable royalties. Despite my writing Trivial Pursuit with appropriate demands, I got no more change out of them than I did from Auntie BBC.[97] C'est la vie!

Amusing to me were the howls of protest that went up when Michael Grade, upon becoming BBC's controller of TV programs,

---

95 Two years after Newman wrote this, *Doctor Who* was, in fact, cancelled by the BBC and, aside from a TV movie that aired the year before Newman died, it would remain off the air for another fifteen years before it came back in 2005 with a modern version produced by British drama writer Russell T Davies and, subsequently, Steven Moffat and Chris Chibnall. The show celebrated its 50th anniversary in 2013 and is still going strong with soon fourteen actors having played the titular Doctor thus far on screen.

96 Newman's fight for a creator credit on *Doctor Who* was slightly more involved than Newman states here. He actually fought for over two years with a number of people in the BBC hierarchy. For more detail, see the accompanying essay in this volume.

97 In fact, Newman did considerably more than just write the makers of Trival Pursuit. He sought to take legal action against the makers of the UK edition, Pallitoy. Newman's files are full of correspondence with his lawyers, though a lawsuit never proceeded from it.

announced that he was going to kill *Doctor Who*. Popular opinion forced him to rescind his order.

At the time, at a lunch, I told him he was right in disliking it; it was disgraceful. During its last seven years or so, the BBC had allowed it to degenerate into clichéd, stock, sci-fi monster fiction — escapist schlock with no redeemable social values.

Why not fix it up, I asked, by reintroducing more historical stories and a more accurate feeling for other worlds to connect it more with our world? Above all, it needed to get away from the Nietzschean, clownish-idiot image that *Doctor Who* had been developed into by misguided producers. The fun of the series always depended on the amiable conflict between the humans who wanted to come back to their home on earth and the well-meaning, though irascible, occasionally confused, old man who held them captive. Somehow, my opinions did not get through to the people who made the show. And so, after twenty-five years, it seems that *Doctor Who* finally expired.

In recounting this, I cannot help but get a crazy thought. Why not a new children's serial that will highlight the conflict between the generations? R2D2 of *Star Wars* in conflict with his parents — Mr. and Mrs. Dalek. I'm open for offers to develop it!

By the end of my second year at the BBC, Donald Wilson retired. I would miss him. He was a nice guy, and had done such a good job as my head of serials.

He came to me with an idea. Why don't we dramatize for BBC 2 in our adult classics serial *The Man of Property* by John Galsworthy, which Wilson would write and produce himself on a freelance basis in his retirement?

I refused, and obviously not because he would be the writer/producer, but because of the terms that he and I had agreed upon years ago. It not being easy to define what a classic was, we had agreed that anything esteemed today and published before 1900 was a classic; books by Zola, Dostoyevsky and the like. We also had agreed that no adaptations be longer than four, or perhaps exceptionally, six episodes.

Wilson thought that the narrative material in the book was marvellous, but I argued that under no circumstances could Galsworthy be considered a classic author. Hell, his stuff was published in the twentieth century. Maybe, I admitted, he's written one or two plays, which successfully tackled social problems, but as a novelist? He was no more than a better-than-average writer of soap novels.

Undaunted, Donald would, on spec, write an episode to prove to me how wrong I was. A month later his script of what was to be the first episode landed on my desk. Not surprisingly, it was well written, but when I saw Donald I gave him a firm *No*. I explained that it wouldn't hold an audience, that there were too many characters in it with no one for the audience to fasten on to. Besides, I reiterated, Galsworthy wasn't a classic author.

"But the narrative power, the characters!" cried Donald. "It'll hold audiences for eight episodes, easily."

"No," I replied.

"You're wrong, Sydney. I'll write another episode. You'll see." Another six weeks went by and after reading episode two I was forced to admit to Wilson that it was beginning to grab me, but I still said no.

No one ever accused me of tolerating meek mice. Wilson, somewhat red in the face, said, "Sydney, you're wrong, wrong, wrong! Those Saga books are good for at least eleven episodes, and I'm going to write two more episodes to convince you."

"Okay," I muttered. "Show me."

Another two months went by, and I liked the two scripts. I'd go with the series at ten episodes.

"Sydney, I've been studying all the books, and to do them justice, I think it must go to sixteen."

"What?!" I screamed. "Not on your Nelly will I agree!"

Boy, one sure can't keep a good man down. After much argument, I thought of a way of foiling him by making a demand he couldn't fulfill. "I'll make a deal with you, Donald: if you can come up with two good box-office names for the cast, I'll buy your sixteen episodes from those lousy books by that non-classic, hack writer. Deal?"

"Deal!" he said, and left my office.

Two days later — two days! — Donald turned up and said that Kenneth More and Susan Hampshire were delighted to play in the serial. Groaning, I said, "Okay. A deal's a deal. You're on."

But then Donald said, "It's going to have to go for twenty-six episodes. It's too good to miss."

"Wait a minute, I agreed to sixteen!" I shouted. "The deal's off!"

As usual, there was more argument. Against my better judgement, I said I would give him my decision the next day.

The only man in the BBC who was likely to turn me down was Michael Peacock, controller of BBC 2. I went to him and waited for an answer after confessing that I had just committed myself to a twenty-six-week classic serial for his channel. He frowned and asked, "What is it?"

"Galsworthy's The Forsyte Saga."

"The Forsyte Saga? Why Sydney, that's great! What a genius idea! Marvellous. Marvellous!"

I gave Donald the go-ahead.

Donald wrote most of the episodes, and over the twelve months, they were shot at the rate of one forty-five-minute episode every two weeks. I occasionally dropped into the studio and would quip to Donald, "How's your *Peyton Place* with class coming along?"

Well, the rest is history and I don't know a country that didn't buy it. On PBS in the States it would eventually spawn[98] *Masterpiece Theatre*, their still-running series of largely British, mainly BBC, dramas topped and tailed by Alistair Cooke. When Paul Fox decided to run it on BBC 1 after two runs on what was now Attenborough's BBC 2 channel, its audiences grew to an amazing 12 million each Sunday night. Some clergymen even complained that worshippers were staying home to watch it rather than attending Evensong.

Many years later, as Canadian government film commissioner, I went to the Soviet Union to learn about their amazing, 3D film system and was invited to address the exclusive Association of Film Workers, its members being mostly honoured artists of the Republic. When the

---

98 *The Forsyte Saga* first aired in the U.S. on PBS's predecessor, National Educational Television (NET) in 1969; its popularity was such that other British imports were sought, leading to the creation of *Masterpiece Theatre* in 1971.

Sydney Newman at the BBC, mid-1960s.

secretary of the club was introducing me, in Russian of course, the introduction was suddenly interrupted by tumultuous applause.

"What was just said?" I whispered to my interpreter.

"That you were responsible for *The Forsyte Saga.*"

Well, blow me down. I didn't even know it had been telecast in Russia — it turns out it was the first BBC series to be bought by that country. The next day I was given lunch by the Canadian ambassador,

Robert Ford. I told him of what had happened and asked, "Why applaud *The Forsyte Saga?*"

"Well," he replied, "there are three English authors the Russians like—"

I interrupted. "Shakespeare; Dickens, perhaps; and . . . ? Not Galsworthy, surely not Galsworthy?"

Ford nodded.

"But, in heaven's name, why Galsworthy?"

"Well, you see, the Russians study him because *The Forsyte Saga* proves the Marxian theory of the rise of the bourgeoisie, the mercantile class taking the authority of a society from the aristocracy."

Live and learn!

Oh, what heady days they were for me at the Beeb. Over the years, our dramas of all kinds won many awards for my staff who made them and the performers who were in them. It pleased me immensely when, for the first time, the BBC won the coveted and prestigious Prix Italia award for drama — for Peter Luke's production for BBC 2 of Hugh Leonard's *Silent Song*. As director, Charles Jarrott was at his most creative and inventive best.

Two years later, our production of the Tony Garnett–Kenneth Loach team of Jeremy Sanford's "Cathy Come Home" won the same award.

Nineteen sixty-seven was a banner year for us in the BAFTA award stakes when our productions seemed to win everything in sight. Best actor went to Eric Porter for his role in *The Forsyte Saga*, and the series award went to its team and producer and major writer, Donald Wilson. Judi Dench (now Lady Dench), copped the best actress award for her role in the highly unusual, four-part drama, *Talking to a Stanger* by John Hopkins, who won the best writer award. Basil Coleman won the award as director of his magnificent production of Benjamin Britten's opera, *Billy Budd*.

On that occasion, I was honoured by receiving the prestigious Desmond Davis Award for Services to Television. And earlier, the

Writers' Guild of Great Britain gave me the Zeta Award for my contribution to writers. My cup truly runneth over.

Despite all this, by the beginning of 1968, the final year of my five-year BBC contract, I began to find my job becoming too easy to do. I was an integral part of the world's finest broadcasting organization. It liked me and I liked it. The D.G., Sir Hugh Greene, let me know from time to time how pleased he was, having lured me from the fleshpots of commercial television.

One evening in Glasgow, where I had gone to see an episode of *Forsyte* being shot, I bumped into my old mentor, John Grierson, then doing his *Here and Now* program for Roy Thomson's Scottish Television. That wonderful dynamo of a man was a bit frail at the time. He still bounced, though. Apparently his lungs were as weak as wet blotting paper, and so he wasn't to drink. Seeing me, he insisted we celebrate. And so a glorious pub crawl began, he drinking Harvey's Shooting sherry and me, short malts.

At 2 a.m., we ended up at my hotel, still drinking and talking about this and that. Grierson, reasonably sober, suddenly turned to me and said, "Laddie, you've made it. You've made it good." I thanked him, mumbling something about the press being usually kind to me.

"I didn't mean that!" he said scornfully. "Anybody can get good press with good PR. You've made it because you are now a member of the British establishment: the BBC!"

I must confess that his sentiment — that great kudos went to someone who worked for the BBC — surprised me. Perhaps it was true then, but I cannot but wonder, if he were still alive now, at the time I am writing these memoirs, would he say the same about the BBC in Thatcher's UK?

And then later that evening, this man who had literally revolutionized the world with his delineation of the new uses of film for documentary, blew my mind by saying that I had discovered something he hadn't until recently. I asked him what. "The writer," he said. "I mostly thought that the director went out to shoot aided only by notes on the back of an envelope. Auteur is what they call it now. No, you discovered the writer."

*Sydney with BBC colleagues; Shaun Sutton is at the far left,
and Stuart Hood is on the right.*

Well, Grierson always made me feel like a million, even when
he bawled me out when I was a novice filmmaker. The writer bit,
however, did please me very much.

In retrospect, whether I was a member of the establishment or not, I
felt a lack of challenge. My BBC drama shop was working well. Running
the place was becoming, what? Routine. My staff, now numbering over
400 and spending over $12 million a year, was producing 370 hours of
drama, over 700 drama slots for BBC 1 and BBC 2.

The amorphous group I had cajoled into shape was so fine-tuned
that I no longer felt myself to be necessary. Keeble had my group's
money, twelve percent of television's entire budget, under full control.
When I took over in 1962, drama customarily went over budget by
ten percent a year. Now, bigger by forty percent, it was averaging an
over-budget of half of one percent — an okay overage in my mind
to annually remind my bosses that I could always use more money to
make more audience pleasers.

Andy Osborne's series department was knocking out winner after
winner over the years: *Z Cars* and its successor, *Softly, Softly*; *Dr.*

Finlay's Casebook; *The Troubleshooters*; *Adam Adamant Lives!* (another idiot's notion devised by me); *Mogul* and many more.

As a form, serials, first under Donald Wilson and then under Shaun Sutton, reached new and original heights. At one end were the Adult Classics, the best known being *The Forsyte Saga*, and the children's classics of memorable dramatizations from Charles Dickens to *Doctor Who*, *Swizzlewick* (which I loved but many critics didn't) and *The Newcomers*, to name a few.[99]

And Gerald Savory's plays department was approved by both critics and viewers. Mary Whitehouse and her miniscule Clean up Television people didn't approve, and warned against our plays of "dirt, doubt and disbelief." But they were vastly outnumbered, often by more than twelve million weekly viewers. My specifically mandated *The Wednesday Play* illuminated a changing Britain and it was heartily backed by Sir Hugh Greene and the Board of Governors.

Other single play strands, while conscious of their times, were defined by me differently. If people wanted Shakespeare, they could watch our *War of the Roses* and *Hamlet at Elsinore*. Science fiction? Irene Shubik's beautifully crafted *Out of the Unknown* brought us the Trieste Science Fiction Film Award of the Year. Dramatizations of contemporary fiction? *Story Parade* and *Thirteen Against Fate* were based on stories by Simenon. Opera-studio based productions, and not square theatre pick-ups? On average, there were about five a year, ranging from *La Bohème* to *Rise and Fall of the City of Mahogany* and some specially commissioned. Plays for first-time writers? *Thirty-Minute Theatre*. And on and on, not forgetting our entry for the EBU's largest theatre in the world, Harold Pinter's sleek and disturbing *The Tea Party*, which I commissioned and produced.

These feelings of wanting more, of further wanting to flex my creative muscles, such as they were, were vague, but present. They

---

99 At this point in his memoirs, Newman had jotted, "Note: Write story of Savory and 'I didn't know it could happen if you did it standing up!'" but further research has been unable to uncover the story Newman intended to tell here.

didn't fully come to the front of my mind until one day after my lovely secretary, Marion Franklin, told me that a Mr. Robert Clark was on the phone and wanted to talk to me.

In my days at ABC, Robert was the low man on the executive board totem pole when ABPC was in the control of Warner Bros. Pictures. With little to do, he liked to frequently come out to ABC's Teddington Studios and longingly watch me produce *Armchair Theatre*. He used to be head of their Elstree Studios, before Warner removed him from any direct connection with production. His best Elstree film was *Dambusters*. I kind of liked him.

Should I take the call? I also couldn't forget that it was he, the solicitor, at that memorable ABPC exec board meeting, who had echoed the opinion of Eric Fletcher in reminding me that I had a contract to fulfill.

I vaguely recalled hearing that, in the five years since I had last seen him, he had increased his share holdings in ABPC to the point where he had just become group-managing director.

Like him or hate him, I picked up the phone.

CHAPTER NINETEEN

IN THE SPROCKET HOLE

It wasn't Robert Clark on the phone but his secretary. She apologized that he would have talked to me himself, but he was just on a call from Hollywood. He would like to see me. A lunch, perhaps? I figured that it was likely that he'd try to send me someone for a job at the Beeb, but it might be nice to see the old guy again. Maybe I'd have enough guts to tell him what a shit he was for not releasing me from my contract.

A date was set. I was to choose a restaurant and he'd pick me up at the TV Centre.

When I came down from my office, his chauffeur was in the centre's lobby and led me to Clark, who was in his car, hunkered down as if he didn't want to be seen. The car was a Rolls Royce, an ancient one that probably was hot stuff fifteen years earlier, but was now polished down to its undercoat. When he greeted me, his usual dour, sad-dog look gave way to one of his rare, sweet smiles — something I'd seen perhaps twice before in the five years I knew him.

I took him to the somewhat faded but respectable eatery in the centre of Holland Park. While breaking bread, he sipping a wee scotch and me a double martini, we chatted about this and that, intermingled with slightly pointed questions, not about the BBC, but about *me* in the BBC.

Good Lord, I thought, he's leading up to my return to ABC. Fat chance! Not on my life. If I had itchy pants in television at the BBC, the last thing I wanted was television back at Teddington, as lovely as the place was on the banks of the Thames. These thoughts sent me back to APBC's boardroom, and so I risked telling him I remembered well his refusal to let me leave; that I was hurt, because, of all the board members, he knew me best. I added that he'd once had direct dealings with creative people, and so I had expected him to support me. Why didn't he?

"It's very simple," he said. "Why should we have given away our strongest card to our position?" He wagged a finger at me. "Someday, Newman, you'll appreciate the value of a contract." He smiled at me. "I want to talk about another contract. How long does your present one with the BBC run?"

"Why?"

"I want you to be our executive producer at Elstree." And then he went on to flatter me with what I had done in television and his expectation that I would achieve the same thing in film. He had the power now and would support me fully; British film was in a parlous state; his Elstree, with me in charge of production, would show them.

My head awhirl, we eventually parted; I promised to get back to him the following week. (And, typically, Clark didn't demur one bit, allowing me to pay for lunch. What a character!)

With plenty to think about, I left work early and drove home to tell Betty about Clark's offer. We talked for days and nights and, as usual, Betty was enthusiastic, quite accustomed to my itchy feet. She quipped, "Wherever thou goest, so goes your faithful, I."

I hired a law firm to negotiate on my behalf, and ended up with a three-year contract with annual increases of £2,500 — more money than I had ever dreamed of. I was also entitled to ten percent of the producers' net profit of any pictures I produced. I was euphoric about that until later, when I got to know more about the film business, and I discovered that the producer's *net* profit wasn't worth a pinch of 'coon shit since film distributors usually robbed talent blind. I consoled myself that since ABP were also distributors, they wouldn't do that to me.

I kept my impending departure from the BBC secret from all, with the exception of Marion, my secretary. She said if I wanted, she would be happy to leave with me. This was perfect, because she was a damn good secretary and totally loyal. In what was going to be a new and perhaps alien environment, I would need someone who was clearly on my side. We would learn the film biz together. I was able to negotiate a whopping salary for her.

Now I faced the most difficult task — how to tell my bosses and colleagues that I was leaving. I wasn't going to do the same dumb thing I did upon leaving ABC. Since my five-year contract had only three months to go, I sent a letter of regret to Kenneth Adam, director of television, that because of the challenge of film, I would not be able to accept a contract renewal were one offered me. When I personally told Huw Wheldon, controller of programs, who was now a personal friend, he raved and ranted. What a damn fool I was! The film world was full of crooks! He told me they'd eat me alive. Most, including my staff, expressed their regrets, which, in many ways, equalled my own at leaving the Beeb.

I was forty-seven and it occurred to me that I was now completing the circle. I had started in film at the NFB and after sixteen glorious years in television I was returning to it. Would I do well making feature films? While excited by the prospect, for the first time in my life, I wasn't sure. What the hell, I thought, I have nothing to lose.

I would miss the BBC much more than I missed my previous job, and not because they wouldn't let me leave when I wanted to.

At ABC, it seemed to me that, somewhat selfishly, I simply did my own thing as best I could without any particular affection or concern for the company, even though they paid me well and provided me every opportunity to excel. The only human face that meant anything to me, and for whom I still have warm feelings, was that of my boss, Howard Thomas. For the company, zilch!

At the BBC — it was in my blood. The influence of John Grierson was ever present. I cared about the place in just about the same way I cared about the National Film Board of Canada and the Canadian Broadcasting Corporation. In those organizations, the heady air of public concern for what was being created had an almost aphrodisiac effect on me. The notion of the vibes of one's work affecting audiences and enriching people's lives was, and still is, exhilarating.

And the incredibly stimulating, witty and erudite characters at the Beeb were all infused with the same sense of dedication. How they enriched me! To be in Huw Wheldon's presence was a job, whereas David Attenborough's was like being with a delightful, ever-curious child who wants to know the *why* of everything. Kenneth Adam was a sympathetic ear; Paul Fox a sturdy rock for support. Joanna Spicer was a model for Women's Lib behaviour. And in Hugh Greene's presence? I couldn't but feel humbled by his gentle humanity and the wise and wily leadership that matched his giant stature.

There are dozens more: John Keeble and so many of my glorious staff, Michael Peacock, Stuart Hood, Grace Wyndham Goldie, Tom Sloan, Dick Levin and his creative bunch, Ayton Whitaker and yes, the man I fought with but whose integrity I never underestimated: Donald Baverstock. And the many secretaries, PAs, admin types, directors and producers, the cleaning staff whom one would see leaving the television centre late at night and the mothering ladies of the hospitality suite.

So much to remember.

But I still had some time left at the Beeb.

As Britain's mandated national broadcasting voice, the BBC demanded that it have "offer of first refusal" from all the country's national theatrical organizations. It had fruitful relations with the Royal Shakespeare Company, Sadler's Wells and Covent Garden. But not the National Theatre. Word came down from Hugh Greene that this must be rectified. I, as head of drama group, should make every effort to lasso Sir Laurence Olivier and bring him into the BBC corral (my words, not Greene's).

While over the years in Britain, I had met many of the knighted performers, I had studiously avoided meeting Olivier. I thought if we did meet, he would punch me right in the nose.

When I had first come to England, I had to give many interviews. In one of them, *The Daily Mail* showbiz columnist, Robert Muller, asked me whether I intended to use any of Britain's great actors like Laurence Olivier in my *Armchair Theatre* series.

"Hell no," replied this dead-honest Canuck. "The man on the street wouldn't go and see Laurence act even if you gave him free beer and pretzels."

That sonofabitch Muller (who later wrote his first plays for me and became a friend)[100] couldn't resist quoting me exactly, and there it was, in black and white in *The Daily Mail* for all to read, including Laurence Olivier. Now, it was seven years later, and knowing how frail actors' vanities could be, I wasn't going to chance meeting him if I could avoid it. Fortunately, I knew Kenneth Tynan, who was the National's dramaturge, and we soon met.

Ken was absolutely in agreement with Hugh Greene's wishes. Both of us wanted the superb work of the National, now confined to the tiny number of Old Vic theatre seats, to be seen by the widest possible audience. We agreed to meet again after he got Olivier's agreement.

But Olivier would not give it, an unhappy Ken Tynan told me. He tried again, but Olivier was adamant. Apparently, Olivier would agree only if he received a personal fee for any production of the National we would televise.

I reported this upward through Kenneth Adam to Hugh Greene, who was so upset he phoned the National's chairman, Lord Chandos, and invited him and Ken Tynan to a dinner in the BBC's elegant hospitality suite to discuss the matter. Ken Adam and I were invited, along with one or two more from both the National and the BBC.

---

100 Nearly twenty-five years later, Muller and Newman would collaborate on a project for Channel 4 in Britain that never saw completion. See the accompanying essay in this volume for more details.

After the usual splendid meal, candles lit and all, Greene reiterated the BBC's position to Chandos over brandies and cigars.

The BBC would pay a facility fee to National for any production it televised, pay its performers and any other credited, creative people such as its designer. If Sir Laurence directed a production himself, or was a performer in one, he would receive a fee appropriate to his name. Surely though, he added, as head of the National Theatre and paid a salary out of public funds, just as the BBC staff, Sir Laurence would already be receiving a personal fee for each and every production, and to pay him an extra fee would be giving him a double salary.

Lord Chandos, not too happily, nodded his head in agreement, but he told Greene that there was nothing he could do. Hugh then asked Chandos to order Olivier to give way, but Chandos said Larry would resign. The silence was crushing. Someone then suggested that perhaps Olivier should be asked to leave the National. Chandos said he would not ask Olivier to leave.

"Why?" someone asked.

"Because," stated Lord Chandos, "Laurence Olivier *is* the National Theatre."

Except for some tense moments like those, it was a pleasant evening, but during and after my days there, the BBC never had access to a National Theatre production.

Sometime later, while at a backstage party at the Chichester Festival Theatre, I was talking to Joan Plowright — Lady Olivier. She saw her husband and suggested we go over and join him, but I begged off, still afraid Olivier might punch me in the nose.

I won't easily forget those evening dinners I was occasionally invited to. I was there to do a job. Once I was invited when the guest of honour was a senior member of Harold Wilson's cabinet, and whose wife at one time had been a rank starlet, a nice lady with whom I talked theatre while Hugh Greene, at the far end of the room, was making some kind of case to the minister.

On another occasion, Kenneth Adam invited my wife and I and two directors who knew the author to help oil the wounds of C.P. Snow, whose novels we had dramatized, and his wife, novelist Lady

Pamela Hansford Johnson. Apparently they were old friends of Kenneth Adam and his wife.

When Charles Snow was elevated to the Peerage, the newspapers had a field day knocking him when he haplessly replied to the question why he, a Labour Peer, had sent his son to Eton. He'd explained that, when his son grew up, he would be better able to get along with his equals.

The BBC's *That Was the Week That Was* could not resist that answer and did their usual — they sent him up rotten. Snow and his wife were livid with anger, and with some justification protested that Charles might be fair game as a public figure but not their young son — who now carried the brunt, being ragged daily by his fellow students at Eton. Poor Kenneth Adam. He did his best to assuage Snow's anger, but I'm not sure they left us any happier.

My last three months at the BBC seemed to go on forever, with me sneaking the odd afternoon off to drive to Elstree and meet the people there and get my office ready. There were many going-away celebrations and drinks quaffed in the BBC club by colleagues wishing me luck. Hugh Greene himself hosted a going-away dinner for me with twenty invited guests of my own choice. I felt singled out when I learned that Kenneth Adam usually hosted the parties when a senior television person left.

All I can recall of that evening, perhaps because of the wine that flowed, was that it was a happy, even riotous occasion with speeches and toasts. I flubbed my way through a speech, trying to do justice to the joys the BBC had brought me. I was given gifts, two that I cherish most. One, a framed photomontage of stills from different drama productions, and another large, framed card with the signatures of each member of my staff and those of my senior colleagues from Hugh Greene down.

Everything started well at Elstree. Jimmy Wallis, the general manager of the studios, a tiny roly-poly man with brilliant white hair and long a friend of Robert Clark's, couldn't have been kinder. Nor Andrew

Mitchel, his assistant, who later turned out to be a mine of practical knowledge, having been involved in the making of dozens of feature films, including the first ones of Sidney Furie, which starred Cliff Richard.

They quickly provided me with a most handsome set of offices. Soon Marion Franklin was hitting it off with the other secretaries and I quickly became the recipient of all the gossip in the place, which, as all bureaucrats know, is his main armour of protection.

It was an exciting place to work; that is, it was if you were gaga about film stars, to whom I was not totally immune. It wasn't hard to bump into Richard Burton coming from the MGM Borehamwood studios just up the road, to meet his wife, Elizabeth Taylor, who was being directed by Joseph Losey in our studios. Rumour had it that Mrs. Burton would not start shooting until her own private bathroom was installed, which cost the picture £10,000.

That was the moving picture business! Roger Moore was as nice a person as he looked. Then only of *The Saint* fame, he seemed to be at the studio a lot. Also on camera with us was my old *Avengers*, with Linda Thorson playing the Emma Peel part made famous by Diana Rigg. Linda, who came from my hometown, Toronto, was, I noted, even more attractive in person than she was on camera. It was great seeing my old friend Patrick Macnee again, and the original story editor of the series, John Bryce, now its producer, who parlayed my idea into a world television success. *The Avengers* came to an end while I was at Elstree. Its wrap party, to which I was invited, was a joyous bacchanalia.

With the power of electrons still in my veins, I was pleased to see that strapped to the 35mm camera shooting *The Avengers* was a tiny Vidicon TV camera. This allowed Bryce, back in a quiet office, to see and check on a monitor what his director was shooting at the same time. This was an idea that occurred to me way back in 1949 when no such tiny camera existed. I decided I would do the same when my features were shot.

For my three years at Elstree I planned very carefully, so that, by its end, I would have produced four feature films.

Year one was to be devoted to learning and preparation. Finding and commissioning scripts would be the most critical task. Year two, I would shoot only two features; year three, the last two, and then by the middle of the year hope for a renewal of contract. I'd know by then whether I could cut the mustard as a film producer — and undoubtedly, so would Clark!

He approved of the cautious and methodical way I was going about planning my work.

I had plenty to learn about making feature films. What I knew was strictly theoretical. I would have to convert what I knew about making short, documentary films with 1940s equipment and electronically shot drama of the '60s into feature films, using up-to-date technology. I was supremely confident about what I thought audiences would pay to see.

After I got into television, I had resolved to shun the movies. The tiny screen was going to be my passion and seeing movies on a giant screen might water my belief in home viewing.

Using Elstree's industry connections, I viewed a slew of features made in the previous ten years — about 200 of them. I figured that I must run like hell from the industry notion that, in film, no one ever lost his shirt by underestimating the intelligence of the public.

But the right story was what I needed. While I intended to mainly commission original scripts, it was writ that film moguls tended to finance adaptations from books. Perhaps it was because the book already had a following and was easy to read. Perhaps too, they were not able to understand a screenplay. I'm only half-joking — a script is not an easy read, nor is it always easy to visualize.

To play it safe in my first round with Clark, I bought a book that had an original and exciting idea. An action-thriller. It was about a famous mountain climber who had lost his nerve. To save the girl he loves, he must climb up the face of a skyscraper. The rights to the book were priced at £10,000 (cheap, even in those days), but I needed Robert Clark's permission to buy it. And then, of course, there was the fee for the screenwriter. Robert Clark turned out to be no easy sell. Months went by before he allowed me to go ahead.

In the files of Elstree, I found, among piles of paid-for but unused scripts, one that had a nice feel for comedy and moved fast. Its hero was an attractive, gormless, cockney member of a gang of thieves. During a robbery his mates are caught but he escapes with £120,000 in a suitcase. While fleeing, he becomes involved with two women and a young girl whom he's forced to marry, having made her pregnant. The story needed updating and the characters needed to be thickened, so I hired my old pal, Peter Luke, to rewrite the script. He needed the money and so laid aside finishing his *Hadrian the Seventh* (which later became a great success) to do this "commercial job" — something he usually scorned.

Jimmy MacTaggart had left the BBC and came to me with a good idea about a decadent, Scottish laird and his two-timing wife, which he wanted to write and direct. I said go ahead, and later he and I went up to Scotland to do a recce so I could get the genuine smell of heather in the Highlands while watching a deer hunt.

As usual with me, the daily news was a rich mine for ideas. At the time, the headline news was Dr. Christiaan Barnard performing the world's first heart transplant. Seeing him interviewed on television, one got the feeling that he acted as if he were God. What an idea! I commissioned young Hugh Whitemore, who had written some fine television plays, to take a crack at writing his first screenplay about an arrogant Harley Street surgeon who gets his comeuppance when his success goes to his head.

After nine months, I was on target. Jimmy Mac was nearly finished writing his first draft of the Scottish laird story; Whitemore was cracking away on rewrites and the mountain climber script was finished and in the stage of finding locations and budgeting.

Happily, the gormless cockney film was ready to roll, with a finalized script, locations found and a budget of a little over £700,000, which included a fee for Michael Caine to play the cockney lead. I sent it off in September to Robert Clark for approval.

By now, after trying to get to see Clark and failing many, many times, I knew he would be very slow in getting back to me. But this time, he was slower than ever. I waited and waited, becoming more and more frustrated and angry. I couldn't even get him on the phone. Little did I know what he was going through, that autumn of 1968.

While I finally got word just after Boxing Day that the project was completely approved, two weeks into 1969, I heard through the grapevine what the press later carried in full: EMI, the giant electronic and record recording company, had taken over ABPC and worst for me, my patrol, Robert Clark was out. It was tragic for him. He had waited so long to become boss of the company, starting as a poor, young lawyer coming from Glasgow in the '30s and joining Robert Maxwell's film company. Now, he had lost it just as it was in his hands. That explained why he had been so late. He was up to his ears fighting the takeover bid. I marvelled that he had found the time to approve my project.

Bernard Delfont, theatre tycoon, was the new group-managing director of the corporation with its new name, EMI. While I knew his brother Lew Grade, I had met him only casually when he presented the West End musical, *Maggie May*, when Ted Kotcheff was directing it. Perhaps his arrival would not affect me. Within two days of the takeover, Jimmy Wallis was dumped and all ABPC-originated work was frozen — including mine! When I tried to reach Delfont on the phone, his secretary said that Mr. Delfont was looking forward to meeting me and asked that I be patient and wait a week or two.

Several weeks later, all remnants of the creative staff — except me — were let go. And a month later, Delfont announced that Bryan Forbes would be the head of production at the company's Elstree Studios at a reputed salary of £30,000. Only then was I called to see him.

In a somewhat guarded but friendly way, and calling me Sydney, he said that Forbes would in future be making all recommendations to him for production of films for cinema and television. Because of my reputation, he would like me to remain as executive producer for all films made for television, but I would responsible to Forbes. Decidedly not happy with this, I accepted with as much grace as I could muster.

Well, at least I wasn't going to be tossed out. I waited for the confirming letter and press announcement of my new job.

Forbes turned up on April 1, and considering the potential

embarrassment of the situation, he was very cordial to me. He said I would have to wait awhile until he cleared with Delfont the details of the company's policy for films for television. And I waited for the press announcement.

In May, at the Cannes Film Festival, Delfont told me that my new position would be announced immediately upon our return from Cannes. One week later, Andrew Mitchel was let go. Delfont asked to see me, and he told me that with regret, they had to release me. They had decided they were not going to make any films expressly for television. Would I settle my contract with Jimmy MacDonald, the group's secretary?

On August 1, I was free as a bird, but not happy. And neither was my secretary, Marion Franklin, for whom I was able to negotiate one month of severance pay. As for me, I mentally thanked Robert Clark for his warning that, one day, I would respect the value of a contract. My contract, which still had eighteen months to run, meant that EMI owed me around £18,000, but somehow, for tax reasons, I got a cheque for £11,000; thanks to my lawyer, my nifty Jaguar was thrown in as part of the settlement.

It was around this time that David Attenborough was being promoted to become controller of programs at the BBC, because Huw Wheldon was moving up to replace Kenneth Adam, who was retiring. David phoned and asked whether he might put my name down on the shortlist as controller of BBC 2. I was touched. With much gratitude, I declined, explaining that while my future was uncertain, I felt that I had finished with television. I added that I thought the job should go to a Brit, someone who had the feel of the country by instinct and not second-hand as it was with me. I didn't tell him that the admin side of the job would have bored me to death.

Funnily, I was strangely upset when Marion got a new job within two days of our leaving Elstree, and there I was, still unemployed. In some odd way, I thought that an unkind cut, and to this day, I can't figure out my reaction to that dear person finding employment before me. A year later, she went back to the BBC as Huw Wheldon's secretary. He was a smart man.

What was I to do? I certainly wasn't short of memory, but I wanted to work. The lure of feature films was still very strong. While at Elstree, I had become friends with young James Carreras who was making the Hammer horror films. I tried to sell myself to him as a partner. In my vain fashion I thought I would give his films some "class." Jimmy, God bless him, knew the audience he was catering to and graciously refused my offer.

Over the years, thanks to my friend, literary agent Harvey Unna, and his wife, Eileen, Betty and I had become friends of the Lewensteins. Oscar was a very considerable figure in London's theatrical scene. He was a vigorous board member of the Royal Court Theatre, supporter of the theatrically courageous George Devine, and was the presenter of many outstanding plays such as *Billy Liar* in the West End. Best of all, he fostered new playwrights. Amazingly, the first film he had ever produced turned out to become a smash, worldwide success, making Albert Finney a star and winning the Academy Award. The film was the riotous, restoration comedy *Tom Jones*. After it, he had made other, but less successful films.

Oscar pleaded with me to come work with him, and said that he couldn't work with anyone else.

My choices were narrowing. But for a non-religious bloke, somehow, the Guy Up There was looking after me. In October, word that I was "between assignments" had filtered back to Canada. To my surprise and much pleasure, I received a telegram from Eugene Hallman, vice-president of the English service of the CBC. Would I come to Canada at their expense, for a job as joint head with Knowlton Nash of English television?

Well, I had had a good run in England and perhaps it was time Betty and our girls returned to Canada. It had been the best time of my life. However, a trip back to Canada was welcome. I would sound out the job. I flew back to Canada.

After the crush of people in the hurly-burly streets of London, I was struck once again by the wide spaces between people on the streets of Toronto, my hometown.

I was warmly greeted by Gene and other CBC mates. I learned

that Knowlton, who had just been brought back from Washington as the CBC's chief news correspondent, was to control all network news, current affairs and other factual programs such as sports. I would be responsible for drama, the arts, light entertainment and children's programs. There was that unloved admin thing staring me in the face again — but worse, something about the place filled me with disquiet.

Gene's ebullient enthusiasm about his reorganization didn't seem to quicken the enthusiasms of staff members who confided their doubts to me. And from outsiders, I learned that the government's revamped regulatory body, the Canadian Radio and Television Commission, was not overly enthusiastic about the CBC's present performance. I was probably wrong, but I felt that the CBC, the national centre for English language programs, was sick and didn't know it.

To check on my doubts about the CBC, I decided that since on my return to England I was going to fly via Ottawa to see my daughter Jennifer, a student at Carleton University, I should look up Pierre Juneau, whom I knew slightly. An ex–Film Boarder, he was now the head of the CRTC, and I could hear from the horse's mouth, as it were, the state of things and future fortunes of the CBC. I phoned Jenny and asked her to try to get me an appointment with Juneau on the one day I would have in Ottawa.

I left Hallman, telling him that within a week of my return to England, I would let him know whether I would accept the job.

That evening, sweet Jenny, now a handsome woman of twenty-one, met me at Ottawa's airport. I found it to be a far cry from the primitive huddle of buildings it was when I first landed there in wartime in 1940. On the way to see Betty's sister Jeanne and her husband, George Johnston, who were going to put me up for the night, Jenny excitedly told me she had spoken to Juneau himself. Saying she was my daughter got her through to him. He would be delighted to see me, but could only spare fifteen minutes if I could come to his office at 8:30 the next morning.

In the car, I couldn't help thinking of my last two visits to Ottawa. In 1966, when in Canada on the round-the-world colour trip with David Attenborough and Jimmy Redmond, I got a phone call in my hotel room before eight in the morning. The man introduced himself as Ernest Steele, undersecretary of state. His minister, Judy LaMarsh, would like to meet me. My curiosity was aroused, but I said it was impossible within our schedule; we were flying to Los Angeles the following morning.

Apparently what his minister wanted, she got. After our seeing CBC's new colour installation at Montreal's spectacular Expo, it was arranged that a car would pick me up and drive me the 125 miles to Ottawa to have dinner with LaMarsh, the secretary of state. And so it was. I sat back in a long black limo, silently speeding in the October twilight to Canada's capital.

It was dark when we arrived, and Steele, a laid-back giant of a man, met me at the designated door of the Parliament buildings and led me to the minister's suite of offices. LaMarsh, not quite as wide as she was tall and younger than me, didn't get up when I entered. Held in her plump fingers was a barrel-shaped glass, maybe an old marmalade jar.

"Hi! Glad you could get here. Have a drink. Mine's rum and Coke."

My God, I thought. *She's something!*

I nodded. "The same."

"Ernie," she rapped out, "Get him one and give me a refill at the same time."

I had heard that Judy was a real tough nut, swore like a trooper, and even though she had apparently been a first-rate minister of the important national health and welfare department, Prime Minister Pearson did not like her, the token female in the cabinet, and so he demoted her. Secretary of state was a minor department looking after the arts, protocol, the well-being of the governor general and so on.

Earlier, in the House of Commons, LaMarsh had callously described the president of the CBC, Alphonse Ouimet, as being incompetent, wasting money and unsuited to the job, implying that as an engineer by training, he did not understand programming. Of course, as a public servant, he couldn't answer back. The poor guy wanted to resign, but out of a sense of duty, didn't, until she had found a replacement the PM would approve of.

As we talked, I found that I quite liked her. I wouldn't like to be her enemy though! She said some pretty sensible things about the arts in Canada and that it was a shame that people like me who had made it good abroad — Norman Jewison, Lorne Greene, Kate Reid — didn't return to Canada.

I told her that the small population of Canada was a fact, and for that reason Canada ought not expect to do more than train good people and take pride in cheerfully giving them to the world, like Scotland does. Besides, talent needs world experience and exposure.

What about me, she asked. Would I return to Canada?

I told her that, at this time, I didn't feel inclined to.

"Even if there was a good job offered?"

"Like what?"

"Government film commissioner? Back at the Film Board where you learned your craft. As boss?"

My heart leaped, but thought no, no, no, and I answered truthfully, "I'm in the middle of my BBC contract and I like it there very much."[101]

Almost before I had finished replying, she jumped to her feet. "Ernie, get the car. Let's go eat at Madame Burger's."

When we got to the restaurant, Ernie's giant frame filled the doorway, and right behind him so did Judy's, so that I couldn't be seen. I heard the genuflections of Madame Burger as she apologized to Madame Minister that a table was not available, but the next one that became free would be hers, and that she and her party have a drink in the meanwhile.

Now, years later, sitting in the car with Jenny, she asked me why I was smiling as I remembered what then happened that night.

When the bulk of Steele and LaMarsh had passed, Madame Marie Burger, who hadn't seen me for over fourteen years, but who knew me well, since Betty and I had often eaten at her restaurant, gave a cry of delight.

"Meestaire New-man! How good to see you!" I got a warm

---

101 Newman is eliding an important point. LaMarsh asked him what job would make him break his contract. He told her becoming the president of the CBC.

embrace and kisses on both cheeks from that corseted, huge-bosomed lady, dressed, as she always was, in a shiny black dress. "Come, I have a table for you. For three? Yes?" And as we were led to the table with the other customers staring at the minister, I heard Judy mutter, not too quietly, "Jesus, here's me, a minister of the Crown, can't get a table, and this guy, from England, gets one. What's Canada coming to?"

The last time I was in Ottawa, the summer of 1967, did not leave me smiling.

One Friday morning in London, I was not in my office at the Beeb, but was at home reading some scripts when a telegram arrived signed STEELE. It read: PM WISHES MEET YOU RE CBC PRESIDENCY STOP INSTRUCTIONS AWAITING YOU AIRPORT TONIGHT REGARDS.

Now this was something I could not refuse. Betty, having earned her London teaching certificate, was away teaching primary school children at a dreadful school in the south of London. I phoned her and told her to get home fast. We had three hours to catch a plane to Canada. I reached my secretary, Marion, and begged her to do her damnedest to get me two first-class tickets to Canada.

Believe it or not, we were on a plane by 1 p.m.

In Ottawa — which was in the midst of a heat wave — there was a sealed envelope waiting for me at Uplands airport. It instructed me to take the room booked for me at the Chateau Laurier and at ten that evening to go to a certain suite and meet Jules Léger, Canadian ambassador to France.

With Jenny with us in our room and the air conditioner not working, I left after my second shower and dressed in my neatest suit, drenched in sweat, to go to meet this ambassador at one minute to ten, 2:59 a.m. by my London clock!

He was a tall, courtly and gentle French Canadian and said he was very pleased to meet me. He outlined the plans of his old friend, the prime minister, Mr. Pearson. He was to leave his post as ambassador to become chairman of the CBC, and if all went well with my meeting with Mike, as he called him, I would be the chief executive — the president. He explained that he was in Canada to host General Charles de Gaulle, who was at present in a destroyer off Quebec City, coming to celebrate Canada's centennial year.

We chatted about the problems, as he understood them, which existed in the BBC. Rather sweetly he said he would have to lean heavily on me, because I knew all about television and he didn't. Prime Minister Pearson would see me at his official Sussex Street residence on Tuesday for lunch. A car would pick me up at 12:45. He, himself, would be flying to Quebec City first thing tomorrow to be with de Gaulle who was to make a speech there — one that would later become infamous. He was sure that I wanted to get some sleep, as he did. As we said goodnight, he said he was assured that he and I could work well together as a team and he would say so to Mike.

Drenched with sweat, I returned to my room, floating on air. Both Betty and Jenny were asleep and awakened immediately as I entered the room. I told them all. Fan-tastic! I sent Jenny home in a taxi and finally fell dead asleep at 6 a.m. London time. It was certainly a day never to be forgotten. The same for the whole damn trip as it transpired.

The next morning, we were awakened by a cheerful phone call from Ernie Steele. He would look after us for the weekend. On Sunday, he took us to the ultra-exclusive fishing club in the Gatineau Hills, open mainly to deputy ministers, past and present. There I met some old friends, including Davy Dunton, the much admired past president of the CBC. From others, I got some CBC scuttlebutt.

Betty was especially glad to be in Ottawa, and spent much time with her mother and father who were living there in retirement, as well as with her sister Jeanne and of course, our daughter Jennifer.

On Monday, I visited Ernie in his office and he took me to see Judy LaMarsh. They were both on a high because of the overwhelming success of Expo and the Centennial Celebrations taking place all across Canada, for which she was responsible. Like a child, she showed me all the evidence of her work, which filled her office: dolls of all sorts made by children, including dolls that looked like Indians, RCMP coppers and Canadians in the ethnic costumes of their parents;

children's drawings; photographs of Judy with the Queen and Prince Philip and many heads of State.

She showed me a photo of herself raising the new Canadian flag on the peak of a mountain, naming it the Centennial Mountain and then tossed the very flag to me, saying, "Here, I'd like you to have it."

That afternoon, I heard from her that Mike Pearson would not allow her to have anything to do with the appointment of the new president of the CBC, even though, as secretary of state, it should have been her decision. He had rejected every person she thought suitable. And out of the blue she said, "I wouldn't recommend you!"

That knocked me for a loop. "Why?" I quietly asked, fighting hurt and anger.

"Because," she answered, "you're not tough enough!"

For some reason that made me feel better and I asked, "Who's the paragon of tough virtue you have in mind?"

"Stu Griffiths.[102] He's the man to cut out all the deadwood in the CBC."

What an extraordinary person she was. Funnily enough, I still liked her.

On Tuesday morning, as I was bracing myself to meet the prime minister, I received a phone call from his office. Regretfully the prime minister would not see me today. He'd been called away on an urgent matter of state and was meeting with his cabinet. She hoped Thursday, same time and place, was all right with me.

What had happened? Soon the press, radio and TV were full of it. Late on Monday, de Gaulle in his speech in Quebec City had proclaimed in his usual, grand rhetorical style, "Vive la Québec. Vive la Québec, Libre!" As interpreted by Pearson and the cabinet, and other Canadians, I suppose, there was a fear it would inflame Quebeckers into freeing themselves from the federal yoke.

Ernie suggested that Betty and I spend the next two days visiting

---

102 Since his time working with Newman as program director at CBLT in Toronto in the 1950s, Stuart Griffiths helped secure a license for CJOH in Ottawa, the second privately owned CTV affiliate in Canada in 1960. In spite of Judy La Marsh's intentions, Griffiths stayed at CJOH until his retirement in the 1970s.

the Expo in Montreal, which we did. There, we were treated royally and put up in a most elegant apartment that the CBC had in Moshe Safdie's architectural marvel, Habitat 67. Apparently the word had leaked out to CBCers that I was the designated president!

In Montreal on Wednesday, even though he had no doubt been made aware of the government's negative reaction to his speech, de Gaulle belted out again his Québec, Libre! cry in a speech to hundreds of dignitaries in Montreal's city hall. I wasn't surprised when I got a call on Thursday morning that lunch was off with the PM. It would have to be the following Tuesday.

On Tuesday morning, I received a call from the PM's office. This time, it was a man telling me that lunch had to be again postponed. He said his name was Marc Lalonde and perhaps he might meet me for lunch. I thought, Lalonde? Lalonde? I knew the name and asked whether he was in the Royal Commission that made recommendations about the CBC. He was, and so we were to meet at the telephones in the hotel lobby at 12:45. I kicked my heels in the sticky heat for thirty-five minutes before he arrived. With barely an apology he steered me to the pub sandwich bar next to the front desk, not one of the hotel's two elegant eateries.

Maybe it was my Londoner's sense of measuring a host's esteem for his guest by the restaurant he chose that bothered me. The place was the pits. Further, it was clear he was an important person by the toadies who waved to him and his indolent return nod. When seated, he quickly ordered a beer and a sandwich, and so I did the same.

After barely two minutes he asked how it was possible for me to run a bilingual CBC if I couldn't speak French. I said that I could — I had gone to many European Broadcast Union meetings and had no difficulties in talking to many Europeans. Besides, creative people, whether by waving hands or what, always understood one another. I added that it was my knowledge of creative programs that . . . and that's when I saw that I was talking to a stone wall. As I continued, I felt sick; the bugger had gotten me on the defensive.

I angrily shot out at him, "Surely you knew I couldn't speak French. Why the hell, then, did you bring me all the way across the Atlantic?"

The lunch was over in twenty minutes and, somewhat conciliatory, Lalonde asked me to walk back with him to his office, but first he wanted to pick up the day's newspapers in the lobby's newsstand. There, with a big, inky pile of *Le Devoir*, *Toronto Daily Star* and other papers tucked under his arm, he met someone he knew. They spoke in French for five minutes, it not even occurring to Lalonde to introduce me. I was livid and humiliated, feeling like a third wheel as I trailed them outside into the blazing sun where they paused and continued chatting. After mutual *au revoirs*, Lalonde and I more or less walked silently to the door to the East Block and said goodbye.

As fast as I could, I walked back to the Chateau, up the lift and strode into our humid room where Betty was anxiously waiting to hear how the lunch went. I yelled out, "Let's get the fuck out of here and go home!"

I phoned Ernie and gave him a pithy account of the lunch, asked him to give Judy my best wishes and thanked him for his generous hospitality. Betty and I flew out that night.

On the plane, in talking to Betty, it was clear that things were happening in Canada of which I'd been totally ignorant, being in Britain. French Canada was a fact that could not be taken for granted. If the arrogance of Lalonde was an indication of things to come, Canada was in dire trouble. England was where I had lived for over nine years and had never thought of it as home. Lalonde made me feel that Canada was no longer home, either.

Years later, I met Marc Lalonde at a party, when he was a minister in Pierre Elliot Trudeau's cabinet, and recounted that meeting to him. "Was I really like that?" he said. "You must have read me wrong." No, I did not, I thought, and changed the subject.

And years after that, at a lunch I had given for Lester Pearson after he had retired, I told him the story. Pearson, a most genial man, laughed and told me I had taken Marc too seriously. I also told Gérard Pelletier and Pierre Juneau. Each, in their own way, said that they couldn't believe it.

Now, November 1969, I was considering returning home as an executive with the CBC and ready to pick the brains of Juneau.

It was an amazing session I had with him. On seeing him, what struck me was that Pierre was now a far cry from the young NFB film distribution officer I once knew. In his still pleasant way, he radiated an air of self-confidence — a senior executive holding down a job that he knew was important.

After renewing memories of old times, discussing what he was doing and details about my life in England, about which he knew a little, I had to get down to business for the time he was giving me. I told him about the CBC job offer and asked him for his views about the future of the CBC.

It didn't take me a minute to realize that it was a dumb, futile thing to ask. It would be like asking Churchill to reveal the date of D-Day. Pierre was not so politically minded to voice an opinion. He hummed and hawed and suddenly asked, "Why don't you join me and come into the CRTC?"

I was so surprised that I didn't at first realize what he had said. Not until he was in the middle of telling me that, while he was overseeing and regulating all broadcasting in Canada, he did not have one person on his staff of about 160 people, who had ever worked in television. He wanted me to join him.

Dumbfounded, I listened to him saying that if I took charge of reporting on the program performance of the CBC and private licensed radio and television stations to his Commission, my main task would be to write the Canadian content regulations for their approval. The salary would be the best he could offer and they would pay all expenses to return me, my family and goods to Ottawa. I guess I looked doubtful, which I was, but also excited. And so he quickly added, "Only for one year?"

My fifteen-minute visit was now reaching forty-five. I said I would have a lot to think about. My wife would help me. I would let him know in about a week's time, I said, and I thanked him. I stumbled out of his office totally bewildered. And that's how I was the next morning when Betty met me at Heathrow Airport — totally bewildered.

I blurted out the news to Betty as we walked to the car and babbled on with details of the Hobson's choice facing us. In our Jag, as she

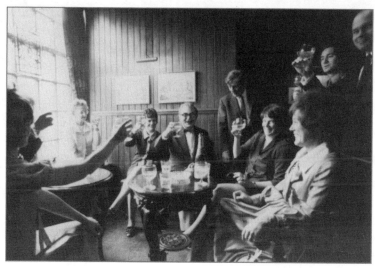

Sydney with friends, early 1970s.

expertly steered us home, I couldn't stop talking. At one point she turned to me, smiling, and said, "And Jenny? How was she?"

"Oh, lovely, terrific." And I kept on babbling about Gene, a fellow student of hers at Victoria College, my feelings about the CBC, the think job in Ottawa.

"And how are George and Jeanne? Mother and Daddy?" she asked. And so it went.

When the car came to a halt in front of our house, she turned the ignition off and turned to me. "Sydney," she said, "listening to you, it sounds as if you are homesick. You want to leave England."

"Yeah, I guess I do." I paused, and I turned to her. "Don't you?" Selfish idiot that I was, I suddenly remembered something I should not have forgotten.

In the middle of my hassle with Delfont, Betty had been suddenly stricken with a strange illness that we were told might lead to death. Polychondritis it was called. It was so rare that we learned that she was the thirtieth known victim of it in the Western world. Her London specialist was modestly succeeding in stemming its onslaught with cortisone and other drugs. To leave him might have fatal results.

That wife of mine could always read my mind long before I knew it myself. As if a burden had been lifted, she said, "Yes, I'm ready to go home. The doctors in Canada are as good as the ones here." And beaming, she added, "What'll it be, Toronto or Ottawa?"

Over the days, we weighed the odds.

In Toronto, now a Canadian-style, true cosmopolitan city warmed up by the influx of 500,000 Italians and other Europeans, we still had our nifty little house that we had never sold, and some good friends, but I'd be back to television in a senior executive job I felt dubious about.

Ottawa was a pleasant, small provincial town with its civil servants, diplomatic corps, Members of Parliament and the senate, easy access to lovely, wild countryside and a job that would be entirely new to me, which I wondered if I could handle. And not to be forgotten was that Betty, who was ill, would benefit by being close to her parents, her sister and our Jennifer.

We settled on Ottawa.

There were many parties, tearful farewells and, wonderful for me, nice press about my departure. We made a handsome profit selling our house, which would help us buy a new one in Ottawa. Farewell lovely Britain with the best television in the world. Farewell dozens of incredible, good mates. Farewell, the Isle of Skye, Cornwall, London and Alun Owen's Cardiganshire. And temporary farewell to our daughter Deirdre, an artist, who stayed behind in the UK working for Richard Williams, helping make animated films.

In Canada, the mail brought more clippings from England. It was the full column titled "Sydney of the Kitchen Sink" by Maurice Wiggin, the distinguished, and somewhat conservative, television critic for the *Sunday Times*, that pleased me most, because he rarely liked my work and ideas.

Near the end of his piece, he wrote, "I find it slightly ironical that I should be writing this valedictory interview with Sydney Newman, for I have been one of his sternest critics, though our personal relations have remained cordial."

He opened the column with:

"Sydney Newman flew back to Canada yesterday and British television will never be quite the same again. With the exception of Sir Hugh Greene, the man who liberalized the BBC, if you'll pardon the expression [Wiggin, conservative as ever, couldn't resist a bit of sarcasm], Sydney Newman probably had more influence on television in the sixties than any single individual."

And he closed with:

"He had a slogan. It was something James Thurber said. Sydney had it printed on cards and send them around to his staff. 'Let us not look back in anger, nor forward in fear, but around in awareness.' Fair enough. Good luck, Sydney."

Now vain or not, who wouldn't be pleased with that!

With our youngest daughter, Gillian, on the plane with us to Canada, and with the exception of Betty's illness, we couldn't have asked for more of Britain and certainly not more of life. It had been good. There was no reason why it wouldn't continue. Maybe, it could even be better.

CHAPTER TWENTY

HIS LIFE LAID OUT . . . WHY?

It was interesting observing this child, Sydney, or Shim as his mother called him, in his pre-perception years. One couldn't know what lay ahead of him.

Now, having read his story, it raises questions.

As best he can, he spills the beans about the major part of his life, over too many pages — that is, if there is a publisher willing to take what appears to be a rubbishly written book.

From it, though, one can only hazard a guess as to what brought about the wandering ups and downs of his life. Newman himself would claim that his reason for writing his memoirs, as he calls this mass of verbiage, was the solitary reason of finding out what made him tick. Rags to riches, newsboy to Rupert Murdoch kind of thing.

He would claim that, had he asked others, the likelihood is that he would receive evasive answers if not outright lies — flattery, suspecting that it was a case of pure vanity that motivated his question. One shouldn't discount that. But also, it might be that he had nothing else to do. What else is an old fool to do but reminisce about his past?

But his avowed reason for writing was to discover what makes him tick.

Reading his turgid prose, it is patently clear that he has done no research as any serious person would. An admirer of Anthony Burgess, Newman might claim that he, too, has total recall. Likely, he is just bone-lazy. When his memory fails him for a date or a fact (facts, he claims, are the refuge of the unimaginative), one suspects that he would phone a friend or even a former enemy on the flimsiest of excuses to weasel out the answer he needs.

One might think, reading his thousands of clichéd words, cobbled together as if a wind had blown them, that he might claim that he earned what success he had, won the wife he did, raised three fine girls — that all this came about because he was a man who knew his own mind and who figured things out right.

Nonsense! As in a Pinter play, the meaning is in the spaces between the lines. Between Newman's words the truth shines. His life was all pre-ordained.

Take his birth. Others born on April Fool's Day escaped the stigma of that day's name, but not Newman. More importantly, he didn't enter the world head-first like most other people. No, he came out ass-backwards. It cannot be anything but that which set the pattern of his life. Very simply, all the good things that ever happened to him were because he backed into them without a clue as to the consequences. Lucky stiff, I call him. No brains needed for that.

Consider his desire to be an artist. It was flattery he craved, poured on him by his sister Ruth for his crude drawings, which motivated him and quite incidentally, fed his unconscious, burgeoning sense of self.

The Art Gallery of Toronto was unknown to him until a primary school teacher entered the boy there. Okay, one cannot blame a child who does what he was told. But, at eleven years of age — the age of perception — why, one may ask, did he persist in wanting to be an artist? The answer is clear: it was pure masochism on his part. Art was his excuse for the thrilling pain he enjoyed in fighting his father's beliefs that drawing on the Sabbath was a sin and that being an artist was a romantic trip to poverty.

If he was such a promising artist, why did he stop painting? Because he had no choice. Anyone else would have taken his father's advice. It was lack of bread that forced him into filmmaking. Remember how he tried to get out of it with Arthur Lismer?

In Hollywood, he fought for and got a good job offer from Disney. Had he been able to accept it, no doubt he would have been conscripted into the U.S. Army and, like thousands of American soldiers, killed at Iwo Jima. He wanted that job desperately, but the lucky stiff backed into living many more years because the U.S. Government kept him alive — it wouldn't give the young man a work permit.

Did he become a communist in the thirties as most of his friends did? No, sheer lack of commitment — a pattern throughout his life.

To the time of this writing, the guy wouldn't commit himself to a religious belief, a school of painting, or join the Variety Club, the Kiwanis, or a London Club even if they would have him. He had no interest in belonging to anything that smacked of being one in a group,[103] even if he was paid a fortune to be there. It was only out of essential self-protection that he got around to joining the AA — not the alcoholic one but the Automobile Association. He did not know it, but he was his own man for better or for worse. Usually the former, by backing into luck.

In 1940, when he flew to Ottawa to try to get a job as a filmmaker with Grierson's National Film Board, would he have given up being a successful commercial artist and stage designer? One guesses that he applied only as an excuse to take his first flight in an airplane. One could say the plane flew him backwards into a job that changed his life.

Later, Newman correctly suspected Grierson of having hired him as a potential animator of maps because of his experience with Disney, which was in his CV. Again, luck intervened. Norman MacLaren

---

103 Newman perhaps even extended that belief to *Doctor Who* conventions, the invitations for which he turned down by the dozens in the 1980s and 1990s.

arrived, so Newman became besotted with the creative challenge inherent in filmmaking and eventually made some good films.

Trouble was, there was always a hated producer above him to tell him what to do. Newman, too smart by half, had himself promoted to get himself out from under and found that as a producer, he had to supervise others, leaving less time to make films of his own. But above him, still, was another boss — an executive producer. Fool that he was, he became one only to find that he had no time at all to direct or to be directly creative in a hands-on sense. If he was to be creative in future, he was stuck being so, but only through others.

He believed in art as self-expression, but the poor fool was seduced into Grierson's way of thinking — art for itself was small thinking; it was better to be in the service of the people.

He backed into success as a documentary film and television drama producer by his accidental acceptance of putting audiences' well-being first and his precious navel second. He left the NFB because he would not get along with his boss, Mulholland. How come this happened at precisely the time the CBC, not prompted by our hero, offered him the job as their supervising producer of television remotes? Newman avoids telling us. Isn't it clear by now that every time the guy trips, he seems to fall into a goldmine?

At the CBC, he wanted to make television documentaries, and ended up being the CBC's first sports producer. Newman was so ignorant of sports that in the dark he couldn't tell the difference between a rugby ball and a honeydew.

Did he believe in television because he thought it was a creative medium? No, he thought it was a medium for distribution. He was right, of course, as time would tell. But he cocked up his belief anyway.

After two years of sports, and the odd think program with the likes of Marshall McLuhan, he became head of television drama. The truth must out. Newman got the job because Fergus Mutrie, boss of the place, couldn't find anyone else to fill it. Newman's one-camera film mind couldn't bear to see the waste (the best art, he learned at art school, was the result of economy of means), of a studio's three cameras, each on mobile, wheeled pedestal dollies, so he made them work in a way that he thought natural, but others thought exciting and creative.

In short, there he went again. His aim wasn't to be creative but to be economical. What a character!

Did it ever occur to him that England might be a good place to live and work? Never! It took an enterprising Brit, Howard Thomas, to invite him there. When he arrived, it was lucky for him that British television drama was mired in the musty past of theatre hand-me-downs, shot by static cameras and making programs in which working-class people were comic foils. He couldn't do other than what habit and John Grierson had imprinted on his blank mind.

What his staff thought of him, one can only guess. Ted Kotcheff, whom he promoted from being a stagehand and trained, was later at ABC, and rankled at Newman's, "That's an executive order! Don't forget, chum, I brought you up from the gutter!" Newman says he doesn't remember the comment, but there is an unimpeachable witness, Verity Lambert, who heard Ted's snappy comeback: "To you is up?"

Even his best friend, Peter Luke, sent Newman up rotten and portrayed him as a vulgar, cigar-smoking, pseudo-Hollywood tycoon in his book, *Sisyphus and Reilly*. Gentle Charles Jarrott would be impelled to talk back to him. Only Philip Saville spoke kindly to him, but the truth emerged, as Newman suspected, in the newspapers, from an "unnamed" director. So often was Newman outraged by Saville's direction that at least twenty times he swore that never again would he use him. Newman backed into success, yet again, by still using Saville, because he was so good.

Was it true that Newman inspired *The Stage and Television Today* to call him the Crude Colonial, and others, King of Dustbin Drama? Yes. He was called a "purveyor of plays of dirt, doubt, and disbelief" by Mary Whitehouse, that little white-haired lady, smiling through her pearlies, who found her vision of the Almighty's morality less visible on the BBC than on commercial television.

The BBC? It never entered Newman's head the greater scope available to him there. It had to be its director general, Sir Hugh Greene, who lured him into what Grierson called The Establishment.

When his ABC bosses refused his desire to jump ship for the BBC, can one imagine any other twit threatening them with, "You'd better watch me, then. In one of my *Armchair Theatre* plays I'll have an actor say fuck on the air." That damn, foolish threat turned Brian Tesler, program controller, into a censor who later forbade the airing of two of Clive Exton's plays that Newman had commissioned, which did not contain that word.

His devising the format for *The Avengers* came about only because he wanted a change from the earnest purposes of his *Armchair Theatre*. Another worldwide success of Newman's, *Doctor Who*, came about not because he dreamt it up, but because Verity Lambert disobeyed him by introducing B.E.M.s in the form of Daleks. Even the making of *The Forsyte Saga* is positive proof that Newman's sincere convictions would have led to lost opportunity, even disaster. But no, in his case, it led to success.

The beliefs he demonstrated in his work brought him great success, even notoriety. Granted, but only as a byproduct did it give new writers, actors and directors work, and give a voice to Britain's regions and accents. The single play dramatizing the cut and thrust of a changing Britain was something he took pride in.

But, as usual with him, his sweet dreams rarely materialized. He thought that by showing life as is — its warts, scars and all — people would rid society of its ills. It didn't happen. "Cathy Come Home" might have prompted the creation of a charitable organization, Shelter, to help the homeless, but, twenty years later, there are still homeless families by the tens of thousands. There's still racial and religious persecution and more.

His plays were talked about, but only as ineffective hot air in pubs and homes all across Britain. In fact, so good were the productions, people felt that merely by seeing the problems aired, the problems had gone away — the so-called purging effect.

Perhaps he should have found a way to get the balance right. Perhaps he overestimated the power of the medium. Oh, he backed into success all right, but it was not the kind of success he wanted.

His private life is a good, final example of what did go right, despite his every effort.

He had a good wife, didn't he? It is evident that he loved her deeply. One would have thought that love might have made him overcome his aversion of commitment — marriage!

It was Betty who had to propose to him. The guy actually tried to use the war as an excuse for delaying it. One can only suppose that their love was so solid, there was no shame in her proposing rather than Newman. Too chicken to refuse Betty's proposal, he married her, and Newman was finally committed to a one-in-a-million wife.

And his kids. He didn't want any. He said they would interfere with their love for one another. But Newman caved in, and Betty got her way.

The three of them, Deirdre, Jennifer and Gillian are all reasonably normal and good-looking women, two of them mothers, two art college graduates, all three talented, able to sew and cook like a dream, and have their mother's clear mind. Newman couldn't ask for more.

One wonders if, after his scribbles, he's any wiser about what makes him tick. He needn't worry. The answer is clearly seen and proven beyond a shadow of a doubt.

One can do worse than being born ass-backwards.

FROM THE SATURDAY
SERIAL, TO THE
WEDNESDAY PLAY, TO
THE OCTOBER CRISIS,
AND BEYOND

---

by GRAEME BURK

When Sydney Newman wrote his memoir in 1987, he focused his attention on the early part of his career: his attempts to establish himself as an artist; his apprenticeship and rise through the ranks of the National Film Board of Canada; his pioneering work at the Canadian Broadcasting Corporation; his work at ABC Television in Britain producing *Armchair Theatre* and creating *The Avengers*.

While Newman does talk in his memoirs about his time as head of drama at the British Broadcasting Corporation, it was done at a quite high level. He doesn't really discuss the major achievements during his tenure (and the conflicts behind them) that impact British television even today. Indeed, Newman hardly speaks of his role in his best known creation, *Doctor Who*. Furthermore, Newman ends his memoir with his return to Canada at the end of 1969 and doesn't touch upon the remaining 30 years of his professional life.

To this end, we have offered this essay that covers much of the material Sydney Newman did not in 1987. It is done in the same spirit Newman wrote his memoir: a "warts and all" recounting of Newman's career in film and television in Canada and Britain, starting with his time at the BBC in the 1960s and moving through his time at the CRTC and the NFB, what followed in Canada in the 1970s and his return to Britain as an independent producer in the 1980s.

CHAPTER ONE
NOVEMBER 23, 1962

Saturday, November 23, 1963, is a date etched in the minds of fans of British television as the day *Doctor Who* premiered. More than five decades later, *Doctor Who* is the only program created under Sydney Newman's watch as the BBC's head of drama that continues today.

But if we were to use a time machine like the one used by *Doctor Who*'s title character and travel back a mere 365 days before *Doctor Who*'s premiere to Friday, November 23, 1962, we would find Newman sending this letter to his boss at ABC Television,[1] Howard Thomas:

---

1   ABC Television was owned by the Associated British Picture Corporation, a film studio that also owned a chain of cinemas, Associated British Cinemas (better known as ABC Cinemas). They named their independent television venture — serving the North and the Midlands regions, though mostly run from London — Associated British Corporation; it seems likely the name was devised for branding purposes so it could be known as ABC Television.

May I humbly beseech you to please let me leave the Company by January 1st.

As you know, it is now nearly eleven months since I first asked to leave. I think I have worked as hard and in the best interests of the Company during this period as I have in the past, but it has been a nightmare, really.

For the sake of the many years of our friendly and fruitful relationship, please let me go.

To understand how Newman had come to this point, we need to go back a further 365 days, to Thursday, November 23, 1961, when Newman responded to an invitation to lunch by the British Broadcasting Corporation's Head of Television, Kenneth Adam. Newman and Adam hadn't met before, though both had expressed admiration for the other. That lunch, held at the Danish Club on November 26 — Newman had developed a love for Scandinavian cuisine — led to Newman being offered the job of head of drama at the BBC. Eventually, Newman tendered his resignation to ABC around February 1962, and at first Newman seemed confident enough he would be released from his ABC contract that he began contract negotiations with the BBC, who sent him an initial contract on April 4.

But negotiations stalled when ABC's board of directors refused to release Newman from his contract and furthermore stipulated that he would have to stay at ABC for the remaining eighteen months on his contract.

Newman did not take the news well. He describes in his memoir that he threatened to embarrass his employers by having an actor swear on air. It's hard to say if he thought the threat would convince the ABC Board to terminate his contract sooner, but they didn't react to Newman's tantrum and Newman never had an actor say "fuck" on television either.

Instead, Newman got on with doing his job. He continued to produce *Armchair Theatre*, the anthology drama series he helped revivify. He had announced in the press that there would be "no more plays about 'kitchen sinks,' unless they are brilliant." Newman seemed to understand that

Honor Blackman and Patrick Macnee posing for The Avengers, *1964.* © Popperfoto/Getty Images

the popular social realism that he put into the show probably had their best days behind them, with writers like Harold Pinter moving more toward the theatre. The 1962 season of *Armchair Theatre* had episodes like "The Dumb Martian," adapted from a John Wyndham story that eventually created a science fiction anthology spin-off, *Out of This World*. He would occasionally return to social realism: Newman's discovery, Alun Owen, wrote and his old friend Ted Kotcheff directed "The Hard Knock," about an Irishman returning home after his brother was hanged. On top of this, Newman also had oversight of his friend Leonard White as he retooled the second season of *The Avengers*, which now starred Honor Blackman as John Steed's partner, Cathy Gale. For someone the press characterized as a "prisoner of Teddington," Newman was as productive as ever during 1962 — even if his relationships were strained with upper management.

But Newman's letter of November 23 had its intended effect. He was finally released from his ABC contract and, after some back-and-forth, he even received his year-end bonus. Newman finally signed his BBC contract on December 12. On Monday, January 14, 1963,[2] Sydney Newman became the British Broadcasting Corporation's head of drama.

---

2   There is some confusion regarding Sydney Newman's start date at the BBC. It was widely reported in the press that it was January 14, 1963, but there is evidence to suggest that Newman started working at the BBC immediately in December 1962, though he didn't formally begin his role until January 14.

CHAPTER TWO

AN OUTSIDER AT THE BBC

The British Broadcasting Corporation came into being by Royal Charter in 1927[3] to "inform, educate and entertain." It ruled the airwaves on radio and, in 1932, began a limited service in London, working with the new medium invented by John Logie Baird: television. It became a full-fledged service with regular television broadcasts starting in 1936. It was, at first, more of a novelty than anything. Watched by a handful of people who owned television sets, the early television service broadcast an hour of light entertainment and newsreels twice a day every day.

When the television service resumed in 1946 after being suspended during World War II, it made up for lost time, broadcasting original drama for television and original series for TV, including *The Grove Family* (one of the first British soap operas) and *Dixon of Dock Green*

---

3   It followed from the private British Broadcasting Company, which was founded in 1922.

(one of the first British police dramas). Post-war austerity kept the nation from buying televisions, but Queen Elizabeth II's coronation in 1953 provided a tipping point that led to an increase in televisions and interest in the medium. Unlike American television, whose Hollywood studios had access to resources like film, the majority of British television — children's programming, current affairs and drama — was mostly broadcast live in studio, using some material that originated on 35mm film.

By the mid-to-late 1950s, television in Britain had become more and more sophisticated. Studios, while often tiny, were more plentiful (and the BBC began building a purpose-built facility, Television Centre, in the White City area of London that would open in 1960). The technology was rapidly changing. The advent of videotape meant that live broadcast was not necessary and allowed for greater flexibility. The standard picture size was 405 lines (the high definition format of 625 coming sometime in the future) but there was more and more being broadcast. In 1955, the British government allowed for a second, independent, private broadcast network (a federation of small television companies that would be eventually collectively known as ITV), which gave the BBC competition for the first time.

Within ten years, the BBC went from an experimental service to a major broadcaster watched by 10 million viewers. It had a full schedule that started at 5 p.m. and ended at 11 p.m.[4] every day. And Sydney Newman was largely unhappy with what he saw.

"I found it to be really, absolutely asleep," Newman said in a 1984 BBC oral history project done by the BBC regarding the BBC of 1963. Newman was critical of the way they made drama from a technical perspective — he found the camera work static and stagey. He was also critical of it from a dramatic perspective — he found it elitist.

Sydney Newman was that rare breed of British television executive

---

4   The BBC television service was also on for an hour in the morning for children's programming and very occasionally showed sports during the day.

in the 1950s and 1960s: an outsider. He was a Canadian who had also worked in commercial television. He didn't tolerate people who put on airs. Former BBC executive Paul Fox said that Newman "would say 'fuck' 'round meeting tables when women were present and when nobody said 'fuck.' He had this transatlantic bravado and drive and gung-ho spirit which was needed at the BBC at this particular time."

Newman was hired because he was a showman who made ABC's anthology of plays a ratings behemoth. And, like a good showman, Newman was outspoken and willing to speak his mind in public or in private, which made him the darling of the press (who called him, with his pencil mustache and short stature, a "sawn-off Clark Gable") and the terror of any broadcaster. Newman's friend Peter Luke, who produced anthology dramas at both ABC and the BBC for him, called him "a cross between Genghis Khan and a pussycat."

But that outsider perspective was important. Irene Shubik, another friend of Newman who worked as a producer for him, noted in her book on her time in television drama, *Play for Today*, "as an outsider who had nothing to do with the evolution of the BBC drama department until that point, he could assess its position more objectively than one who had grown up in it."

The first thing Newman had to tackle upon joining the BBC was an organizational problem. Newman's new boss, Kenneth Adam, was reorganizing the BBC Television Service into a series of groups. Newman would become the head of the brand-new drama group. But Newman found the BBC's set-up for drama inefficient. There was a separate script department that provided staff writers and story editors, and also purchased scripts, which Newman felt obstructed input from directors and producers. Productions were done for series, serials, plays, even opera without any coherent structure. Complicating matters, Newman learned shortly after his arrival that a second BBC channel, which would become known as BBC 2, would start in 1964, increasing the output of the drama department by forty per cent.

Newman once said in an interview with the Canadian Broadcasting Corporation in 1966 about his work at the BBC, "The big problem in an organization this size is to eliminate the organization." Newman's solution was to decentralize and split up the different streams of drama programming into different departments: series, serials and plays. He gave each department its own head. Programs within each department would have producers assigned to them and they would have a story editor (later called a script editor) to work with writers — now freelancers, no longer staffers — that were hired directly by the program.

Newman's reputation for being bullish served him well in bringing this about — there are a number of drama department memos throughout early 1963 where Newman makes himself a nuisance with his boss, the BBC director of television, Kenneth Adam, asking when the new structure would start. Adam's memo setting out the new structure was issued March 14, an amazingly short time to change the structure of a department with several hundred jobs. Newman made himself head of drama group, an overseer of all the departments. He convinced Donald Wilson, the head of the soon-to-be-dismantled script department, to become head of serials. He hired Elwyn Jones, the writer-producer who co-created the revolutionary police drama *Z Cars*, to become head of series. Eventually, in 1964, the plays department was given to Michael Bakewell, a BBC radio producer. The changes Newman instituted became, more or less, the basis for how television was made at the BBC until the 1980s.

Even with his streamlined drama department, Newman still had a lot of work ahead in 1963. The drama department had ambitious plans, including a version of *Hamlet* recorded on location in Denmark, in Elsinore. At home there were pressing concerns; only four of the seven studios at BBC Television Centre were operational in 1963. Consequently, the logistics of filming the BBC's television schedule (much less the increased output the second channel would bring) was strained, with the BBC relying on decades-old, nearly inhospitable, former film studios at Riverside and Lime Grove for recording programs.

And, of course, there was also the problem of the Saturday serial.

CHAPTER THREE

THE SATURDAY SERIAL

It was called "the Saturday serial" for a long time in BBC internal memos, which made sense because the program was, essentially, a companion piece to the Sunday serial, a rotating set of dramas played across a number of weeks. The difference between the Sunday and Saturday serials was the audience.

By the early 1960s, Saturday schedules had settled into a familiar pattern. The BBC's popular programme of sports highlights — *Grandstand* — was broadcast all afternoon until just after 5 p.m. At 6 p.m., there was a program called *Juke Box Jury*, where a panel of musicians, actors and writers listened to songs in the pop music charts to judge whether it would be a hit. By 1963, the show was nearing the middle of a decade-long run and was popular with the teenaged demographic. From there, the programming moved on to family shows and then movies.

Bridging *Grandstand* to *Juke Box Jury* was the problem. It was felt the demographic needed to skew younger towards children given its tea-time placement. But the time slot was proving challenging. The programming boffins tried cartoons, American TV series, short-term serials (both in-house productions and overseas acquisitions) and juvenile fiction adaptations[5] . . . but none of these things caught on with the audience.

Just as Sydney Newman arrived at the BBC, the television service was planning ahead to the late summer and early autumn of 1963. Newman learned from the Controller of BBC 1, Donald Baverstock, and his second-in-command, Joanna Spicer, that they were looking for some kind of a serial to bridge the scheduling gap on Saturdays.

The first indication of what flavour the Saturday serial might have was in a memo from John Mair, the senior planning assistant at the BBC, on March 27, 1963. In this memo, full of the Orwellian *newspeak* of the BBC,[6] Mair writes "H.D.G. [Head of Drama Group — Newman] had obtained approval in principle from C.P. (BBC 1) [Controller of Programmes, BBC 1] for the Saturday serial to run 52 weeks of the year." Mair then documents that the serial would be comprised of individual serials of varying lengths but would also feature characters that would continue through the entire run.

Mair's memo also sets out the genre. "[The serial] would have a science fiction basis." Knowing the budgetary limitations this serial would have, Mair also points out, "this would be achieved by intelligent use of the Lime Grove Studios and not by extensive use of film." The budget was set at £2,000.

Thus, the Saturday serial became a science fiction show. This might

---

5   From January to August 1963 alone, the BBC showed in-house programs like *The Chem. Lab. Mystery*, made by the drama department, the U.S. drama *Zero One* and the U.S. children's series *Circus Boy*, the cartoon *Top Cat* (called *Boss Cat* in Britain), a BBC-made serial adaptation of *Just William*, a repeat showing of the BBC spy serial *Last Man Out*, a repeat run of *Harry Halliday* (a BBC children's series) and a six-part murder mystery series *Francis Durbridge Presents*.

6   Perhaps unsurprisingly, George Orwell came up with many of the ideas for *Nineteen Eighty-Four* from many of the things he encountered while working at the BBC in the 1940s.

have been, in part, because Donald Wilson remembered something he assigned to Alice Frick a year before.

In the '40s and '50s, Nora Alice Frick worked as a script editor for the Canadian Broadcasting Corporation's radio service. In 1954, she went to Britain where she joined the BBC's script department[7] and became part of its survey group. The survey group was a cluster within the BBC script department that, essentially, studied and reported on what the other side was doing in commercial television and looked into radio, film, TV and books to discern trends and to recommend writing the BBC might want to adapt or produce down the line. (The survey group, originally called the monitoring group, was an innovation of Donald Wilson back in 1960.)

In early 1962, Eric Maschwitz, the BBC head of light entertainment, asked Donald Wilson if someone in the script department could report on what could possibly be adapted from literary science fiction. Wilson referred the request to the survey group and Frick, who worked alongside one of the script department's story editors, Donald Bull.[8]

The first report by Frick and Bull, dated April 25, 1962, is somewhat cool toward the subject matter. "[Science Fiction] is overwhelmingly American in bulk," they wrote. "Inherently, SF ideas are short-winded. The interest invariably lies in the activating idea and not in character drama." Their initial conclusions were all but dismissive of literary

---

7   Before Newman disbanded it in early 1963, the BBC's script department consisted of eight story editors — each responsible for a specific area of programming — alongside ten writers (who adapted material or wrote new scripts) and a team of researchers (including the survey unit) and junior readers.

8   The use of Donald Bull in this project is not particularly unusual. In fact, *Doctor Who*'s first story editor, David Whitaker, produced a report on the success of the drama department's Sunday plays as part of his work in the script department during 1962. This would indicate that the members of the script department were treated as an in-house writing resource on top of their duties writing and editing television scripts.

science fiction as a source of adaptation (Arthur C. Clarke was said to be "a modest writer . . . able to concoct a good story and a master of the ironmongery department"; C.S. Lewis was deemed "pretentious" and "clumsy"). Worse, they felt it was a genre that didn't have much of an audience (not compared to detective and thriller fiction, they suggested). They stated it didn't have much appeal with women and was more of interest to "technically minded" younger viewers. Neither Frick nor Bull believed science fiction would be popular with a wide audience.

They concluded that "we cannot recommend any existing SF stories for TV adaptations."

Despite that less-than-ringing endorsement,[9] Donald Wilson pressed them for a list of possible works to adapt. While the second report by Frick and John Braybon, dated July 25, was a little warmer, it was still somewhat hesitant on the subject, opening with, "It is not the purpose of the comments below to suggest that a science fiction series should, or should not be undertaken." Frick and Braybon then arrived at a list of potential stories on the criteria that they avoid "Bug-Eyed Monsters," the central characters are humans and not "tin robots" and they do not "require large and elaborate science fiction type settings" and "provide an opportunity for genuine characterization in most cases." From that, they recommended five titles including Poul Anderson's time travel novel, *Guardians of Time*, Eric Frank Russell's *Three to Conquer* (about a telepath) and the short stories "Eternity Lost" by Clifford Simak, "Pictures Don't Lie" by Katherine MacLean[10] and "No Woman Born" by C. L. Moore.

---

9   Though it ends with an appended note that Frick had recently met with author Brian Aldiss and thought he could be a valuable resource. "He would be a valuable consultant — not a crank — with definite ideas of what could be achieved visually."

10 Ironically, "Pictures Don't Lie" was already in development with commercial television in Britain. On August 11, 1962, one month after Frick and Braybon sent Wilson their list of possible works for adaptation, the *Armchair Theatre* spinoff *Out of This World* broadcast an adaptation of "Pictures Don't Lie" for rival ABC. Sydney Newman was supervising producer.

The parties were thanked for their efforts and then nothing else happened.

The following March, Donald Wilson, who was now head of serials, needed a focus for his teatime serial on Saturdays. On March 26, 1963 — the day before John Mair sent his memo saying the Saturday serial would involve science fiction — Wilson convened a meeting with Alice Frick, John Braybon and a writer from the soon-to-be-dissolved script department, C.E. Webber.

Cecil Edwin Webber joined the BBC script department in 1960. From the 1940s, he had mostly worked in BBC radio as a freelancer, adapting farces and somewhat obscure stories and plays. Webber's reputation for dashing about everywhere quickly earned him the nickname "Bunny." He was brought in to flesh out the discussion into a useable idea. Since joining the script department, he had worked on a number of drama productions for the teatime slot for younger audiences — it was quite possible his work with children's serials was a reason he was asked to join the group.

The minutes for this meeting still exist, with handwritten annotations by Sydney Newman, who was on the distribution list. Frick and Braybon were quick to recommend *Guardians of Time* and *Three to Conquer*. Donald Wilson proposed a show that used a time machine, that wouldn't just travel in time but also space and "into all kinds of matter" as well. Alice Frick suggested something with a flying saucer (Newman wrote "not based in reality — or too Sunday press"). Computers were to be avoided because of the popularity of the 1961 drama *A For Andromeda*. Telepathy was mooted. There were abstract ideas tossed around: Donald Wilson wondered about doing something about creativity and genius. Bunny Webber "brought forward the idea of the continuance of thought; the idea that great scientists of the past might continue in some form of existence . . ." Newman wrote "no" beside that, presaging how out of step he and Webber would be with each other for the next few months.

Wilson established some ground rules: that it needed easily identifiable characters and perhaps two teenagers could be included. The problems were also addressed, namely how to engage a permanent cast in a widely disparate series of adventures in different settings.

In the middle of all this, John Braybon suggested "a good device would be a world body of scientific troubleshooters, established to keep scientific experiments under control for political or humanistic reasons."

Newman wrote "NO!" beside that suggestion. Which was unfortunate, as Wilson and the group assembled asked Bunny Webber to write a proposal about just that.

Webber delivered a three-page memo outlining his thoughts on a series based on Braybon's idea to Donald Wilson on March 29. (Again, the copy retained in the archival record was Newman's with his handwritten notes.)

It's clear from this, and subsequent, work that Webber had interesting ideas about television drama. The memo was full of redolent, striking phrases such as, "The essence of [science fiction] is that the wonder of the fairytale element shall be given a scientific or technical explanation. To do this there must be at least one character capable of giving the explanation. . . ." Webber has a lengthy section called "Overall Meaning of the Serial" where he posits that science fiction avoids in-depth characterizations and is "deliberately unsexual" — basically, it doesn't use women effectively. Webber also deemed that science fiction was not about moral conflicts and he insisted that "Drama is *about* moral conflicts; it is *about* social relationships. Experienced SF writers may disagree with me. Well, let them create their own live SF drama."

Webber called this putative series a "loyalty programme" (where people would come back week after week to watch) and threw in for good measure his opinion that father figures are often thrown in to these "loyalty programmes" to satisfy the needs of grown women. He also repeated Alice Frick's assertion from the previous meeting that "child characters do not command the interest of children older than themselves." Newman was unconvinced, as evidenced by his marginalia for this (he wrote "Need a kid to get into trouble [and] make mistakes") and subsequent ideas Webber discussed.

Webber continued, saying what this set-up needed was a handsome lead, a "well-dressed" thirtysomething heroine and a more mature character with some "'character' twist." These three principals would be partners in a firm of scientific consultants. They would be, to use Webber's title, "The Troubleshooters." Each character would be a specialist in a different scientific field. Webber wrote, "In fact, they have a reputation for tackling problems which no one else could handle; there is almost a feeling of Sherlock Holmes about this side of their work."

Newman was unconvinced. In his notes written in pencil in the margins, he wrote, "But no one here to require being taught." He thought even less of Webber's idea that "the Troubleshooters" could have a permanent villain, like a politician or an industrialist who was opposed to them, dismissing with the simple note: "corny."

In many ways, Webber was ahead of the curve. "The Troubleshooters" bears no small resemblance to later series such as *Doomwatch* and *Torchwood*. But Newman didn't want the type of program Webber wanted and didn't think much of his somewhat highfalutin ideas. Webber recommended eschewing easily identifiable demographic groups in the characters and Newman wanted to embrace it: Newman wanted a show with a kid that could easily get into scrapes: good-looking younger adults; and an older figure. Webber thought that the characters should be a fount of knowledge; Newman felt it was undramatic and wouldn't offer teachable moments.

At this point Newman decided to take a more direct involvement in this project. The result was *Doctor Who*.

CHAPTER FOUR

"MR. WHO?"

The first sign of what the Saturday serial was to become arrived in a rather mundane memo sent by Ayton Whitaker, an administrator who worked in the drama department, dated April 26, 1963. The memo is full of the usual alphabet soup of designations. The basic thrust of it was that the Saturday serial would be able to start recording in Lime Grove Studio D on July 5 and the first installment could be broadcast Saturday, July 27.

But the lede was buried until the last paragraph. "The serials will cost £2,300 per episode and an additional £500 will be needed to build the space/time machine[11] which will be used throughout the 52 weeks."

Sometime between March 29, 1963, when Bunny Webber sent his memo on "The Troubleshooters," and this memo of April 26, 1963, *Doctor Who* had been created.

The earliest mention of the title in BBC documentation was on May 9, when Owen Reed, the Head of Children's Programs, sent Newman a short memo recommending Leonard Chase as a director for the series, saying Chase was a bold director, with a flair for technically complex work and that he already worked with Webber. (It would seem that, as with Webber, the expectation was to use the same people who had been doing children's serials already.)[12] That said, the title cited is "Mr. Who?" which indicates either the title was in flux or, perhaps more likely, misheard.

But the more pertinent question is who: who created *Doctor Who?*

The answer is somewhat complicated and may never be completely resolved. However, until the day he died, Sydney Newman insisted that he was the sole creator of the iconic series.

Moreover, Newman insisted he wrote a memo outlining what the series was. He talked about such a memo in his memoirs and in interviews and in correspondence, including this letter to *Doctor Who* fan writer Jeremy Bentham in 1984:

> I believe I put it into a memo (I wish to hell I had a copy
> of it) addressed to Donald Wilson who I had appointed as
> my Head of Serials. I called him into my office, handed my

---

11   In the event, that spaceship set — specifically the working console — actually cost £4,378. It was an astronomical amount (caused, in part, by the inefficiencies of using the BBC's in-house design department) that nearly killed the series just as it was going into production. Assistant Controller Joanna Spicer and producer Verity Lambert worked out a deal in October 1963 that saved the series whereby a grant of £3,278 from special funds covered the majority of the cost, with Lambert kicking in £75 an episode for the first thirteen episodes and the agreement that Lambert wouldn't use the BBC to resource any further design work of a specialized nature.

12   An expectation that Newman, and later *Doctor Who*'s first producer, Verity Lambert, largely ignored, treating it as a full-on drama production.

memo to him and immodestly said, "Here's a great idea for Saturday afternoons. What do you think?"

Donald perused it, looked up at me, scratched his head, grinned and said, "Not bad! Maybe." Donald was a very cautious Scot, but his "maybe" was right. A lot of good ideas can really go to hell in production, writing, casting, direction, all being uncertain variables.

This wasn't just some anecdote Newman was presenting to the public[13]; in 1987, he contacted the BBC Archives in Caversham Park in Reading looking for it but they were unable to turn up anything. Unfortunately, the correspondence from the archive employee answering Newman indicates that his request was for a memo written in 1962, which may have affected the outcome. Also, the BBC did not have a clear records retention policy. A reasonably complete collection of files related to *Doctor Who*'s creation still exists, more through luck than anything (and largely seem to be files held by Newman or Donald Wilson). But there are still gaps. However, a 1965 memo for what became *Adam Adamant Lives!* under its original title, *Sexton Blake Lives*,[14] is retained in Newman's personal papers, so clearly Newman did write such things.

What does exist in the BBC's records are four drafts of a format document[15] for *Doctor Who*. In its final form, the format document

---

13 Others working in the BBC during that period have independently suggested Newman prepared a memo on *Doctor Who*, including director Richard Martin, who, at the time, was on attachment to the program with temporary producer Rex Tucker. Martin recalls in the 2006 DVD documentary *Doctor Who: Origins* that he met with Newman and Tucker to read over a document that Newman wrote himself.

14 Actually, it was called *S*xton Blake Lives* and Sexton Blake was called "S*xton Blake" throughout — Newman's cute way of acknowledging that the BBC didn't actually have the rights to the Sexton Blake character.

15 In early drafts it was initially called "General notes on Background and Approach" before being expanded to "General notes on background and Approach for an Exciting Adventure — Science Fiction Drama Series for Children's Saturday Viewing."

explains what the show is ("A series of stories linked to form a continuing 52 part serial; each story will run between 4 and 10 episodes"), the approach to the stories, a brief outline of the character called "Dr. Who" and the cast of characters (who became in the transmitted version Ian, Barbara and Susan but at the time were called Cliff, Miss McGovern and Sue), a brief explanation of the time-travelling spaceship and a synopsis of the first episode (which was, at the time, an adventure where the time travellers were shrunk to six inches tall).

The first draft of this document is undated and unsigned. The second draft is dated May 15, 1963. The third and fourth, final draft were dated May 16, 1963, with the note "Prepared by Donald Wilson, C.E. Webber, Sydney Newman."

So . . . who made *Who?*

Sydney Newman's version of events is quite clear. He came up with the central idea of a spaceship that was bigger on the inside and the central character being an old man who is "753 years old."[16] Probably the earliest public declaration of this was a series of behind-the-scenes articles ostensibly written by Newman that were serialized in the *Daily Sketch* on May 5, 6 and 7, 1969. These were puff-pieces designed to bolster Newman's post-BBC career as a film producer during the period when EMI was taking over the Associated British Pictures Group, and was either edited or ghost-written by writer Robert Ottaway.[17] Newman's papers still retain handwritten amendments to drafts of it. Newman says in this piece, "I toyed with the idea of space fantasy, with an improbable ship that could travel backwards and forwards in time. I thought

---

16 Curiously, in every retelling of *Doctor Who*'s origins, Newman always mentioned the Doctor's age and it usually specifically somewhere in the 700s (though never consistently applied). In the actual format document for the show, he was 650 years old.

17 It was high-powered assistance. At the time, Robert Ottaway was *Variety*'s British TV reviewer.

that the intrepid Doctor could take off in something idiotic like a Police Box."

But did Newman do this alone? Or was he helped?

The case for C.E. Webber as a creator (or co-creator) of *Doctor Who* was popularized by former *Doctor Who Magazine* editor and critic Gary Gillatt in his 1998 book *Doctor Who: From A to Z*. In many respects, Gillatt was being provocative. The case is more based on Webber's proclamations on the type of program *Doctor Who* would be, not necessarily the idea itself. Webber offers a manifesto under a section called "Quality of Story":

> . . . We are not writing Science Fiction. We shall provide scientific explanations too, sometimes, but we shall not bend over backwards to do so, if we decide to achieve credibility by other means. Neither are we writing fantasy: the events have got to be credible to the three ordinary people who are our main characters, and they are sharp-witted enough to spot a phoney. I think the writer's safeguard here will be, if he remembers that he is writing for an audience aged fourteen . . . the most difficult, critical, even sophisticated, audience there is, for TV. In brief, avoid the limitations of any label and use the best in any style or category, as it suits us, so long as it works in our medium.

The copy of this first, undated draft of the format document for *Doctor Who* that is retained in the BBC's archives was Newman's and his pencilled note on this paragraph — "not clear" — indicates he was not entirely convinced by Webber's bold assertions. And yet Gillatt, and others, point out how prescient it was: it's almost a mission statement for *Doctor Who*.

In subsequent drafts, this whole section was largely gutted except for the basics. Indeed, similar to "The Troubleshooters," what Newman disliked in this draft had more to do with Webber's exploration of what ideas the show *could* be about, rather than what the show *was* about. Webber uses the character of Dr. Who (as he was called pretty much until the show was broadcast when, on screen, the character was called only "the Doctor") to provide "continuing elements of *mystery* and *quest*." According to Webber, Dr. Who facilitated mystery and quest by having two secrets: the first "secret of Dr. Who" was that he came from a time in the far future that is a place of perfection, and that he stole his ship on a quest for an idealized past. Dr. Who is, essentially, a time-travelling anarchist, a scientist who has "opted out" according to Webber and is now trying to stop progress found in the future while searching for his idealized past. Webber felt this added a kind of cutting-edge, moral problem for the central character.

Newman, as ever, was unimpressed. "I don't like this at all," Newman wrote in the margin beside this "secret." "Dr. Who will become a kind of father figure — I don't want him to be a reactionary." But probably the most famous display of Newman's ire in *Doctor Who*'s history is reserved for Webber's "Second Secret of Dr. Who," which was that the authorities from Dr. Who's own time were more concerned that Dr. Who be stopped "monkeying with time," as his secret plan, as soon as he finds his idealized past, is to "destroy or nullify the future."

"Nuts!" wrote Newman.

Newman's note at the bottom of the draft underscores this. "I don't like this much — it all seems silly and *condescending*." Newman felt that it didn't hold to the educational principles he wanted for the series; Newman wanted a show that taught science and history "painlessly," "drama based upon . . . scientific phenomenon and actual social history," Newman also objected to Webber's philosophical bent to the character. He wanted the character to be a scientist.

Newman's marginalia on Webber's first draft indicates the frustration of someone with a clear idea of what he wants dealing with someone else who doesn't get his idea. The implication is that Newman had already communicated that idea to Webber — either verbally or, as Newman claimed for years afterward, through a memo. As with creating "The Troubleshooters" from John Braybon's idea, Webber was likely brought in to act as a dramaturge, turning another person's idea into a more fleshed-out proposal.

Nowhere is this more apparent than in Webber's discussion of Dr. Who's spacecraft. Newman's retelling of the story in 1969 indicated he dreamed up the idea of the ship looking like a police box. Webber's first draft sounds suspiciously like someone trying to talk Newman out of that idea:

> If it is a transparent plastic bubble we are with all the
> low-grade space fiction of cartoon strip and soap opera.
> If we scotch this by positing something humdrum, say,
> passing through some common object in [the] street such
> as a night-watchman's shelter to arrive inside a marvelous
> contrivance of quivering electronics, then we simply have
> a version of the dear old Magic Door.

Webber's solution was that "therefore we do not see the machine at all; or rather it is visible only as an absence of visibility. A shape of nothingness." He even suggests a technical solution to achieving it through the process of inlay[18] and suggests a rationale for it — that it's the result of light-resistant paint (Webber adds that this was an actual recognized research project!). Newman was, unsurprisingly, unconvinced. Newman scrawled above this, "Not visual. How to do? Need a tangible symbol. Don't like at all. What do we see?"

Webber's dismissal of a common object like a "night watchman's shelter" leading into a ship sounds distinctly like Webber had already been given the idea of a spaceship inside a police box by Newman and was pitching something else. The second draft of the proposal, dated May 15, features the police box.

The second and third drafts are more refinements and have edits

---

18 Inlay was kind of the green screen of its day; it involved imposing one image (usually a still photograph) onto the televised image.

by an unknown hand, presumably Donald Wilson's.[19] The fourth and final draft of the format document[20] brought back this sentiment from Webber's earliest draft: "This series is neither fantasy nor space travel nor science fiction."

It might have been Webber's only real victory with this assignment. His synopsis for the proposed first story, "The Giants," met with derision from Newman from the second paragraph, where Webber describes the time-travelling ship in a police box shrinking in front of a policeman. "NO! Impossible to do with inlay without a lot of money," replied Newman. He elaborated on this in a memo to, among others, Donald Wilson and incoming producer Verity Lambert that Webber's draft showed a complete disregard "for the fact that this was a *live* television drama serial."[21] Webber's synopsis and the two episodes he wrote were eventually written off.[22]

The question remains about Donald Wilson's contribution to *Doctor Who*. Wilson had such a storied career in film and television — particularly after his time as head of serials, when he adapted John

---

19 Several of the changes in the second draft were to situate the characters within the British class system. Sue, still just a schoolgirl and not Dr. Who's granddaughter, was "less-than-middle-class" in the new description before this was scratched out and changed to "working class." Cliff the schoolteacher had "red-brick university type" added. This certainly seems in the wheelhouse of Donald Wilson, who would go on to adapt John Galsworthy for the BBC.

20 The text from this would be reconstituted into a "series bible" later on in 1963 when they finalized the characters of Ian, Barbara and Susan. It continued to be used as late as 1966, with much the same language as when Webber, Wilson and Newman worked on it, only adding Ben and Polly as the travelling companions.

21 Newman is referring to the fact the program would be recorded "as live" with scenes unfolding in a continuous take. TV dramas had mostly moved away from live transmission by 1963.

22 Webber was paid a kill fee of fifty percent for the two episodes he wrote. That, and the BBC's calculation of how much he could receive for a script commission while working as a staff writer, meant that Webber earned £187 for his association with *Doctor Who* over and above his salary on BBC staff.

Galsworthy's *The Forsyte Saga*, which led to British television's massive success on public television in the United States — that his contributions to early *Doctor Who* were often overlooked. Wilson was never interviewed about his contribution to *Doctor Who*. The one time he was, Newman's own claim of creating *Doctor Who* was thrown into question.

In 1971, writer Malcolm Hulke, who by this time regularly contributed scripts to *Doctor Who*, was commissioned by Pan Books to work on a behind-the-scenes book about *Doctor Who*. Pan had considerable success with their books on *The Making of Star Trek* and *The Making of* 2001: *A Space Odyssey* and thought *Doctor Who* would be a logical next choice. Hulke worked on the book with *Doctor Who*'s script editor Terrance Dicks, who did it as a side project to his production work on the series.

By this time, Sydney Newman was working as the head of the National Film Board of Canada. Newman received a letter from Hulke[23] (who was called "Mac" by his friends) dated August 6, 1971. In it, Hulke stated, "I have a shrewd suspicion that *Doctor Who* was originally your idea, but that you've always been too modest to admit it. Or that at least you were in on the planning committee which gave birth to it. Anyway I wonder if you would be good enough to give me a few details of what you remember about how all it started."

Newman's reply was delayed because of a trip to Italy and wasn't sent until September 28, 1971:

> You are quite right in guessing that I had a great deal to
> do with *Doctor Who*. In fact I don't think I'm immodest in
> saying that it was entirely my concept, although inevitably
> many changes were brought about by Verity Lambert, who
> was its first producer. She would be the very best source
> of information, better than say, David Whitaker or even

---

23 Newman had worked with Hulke back during his days at ABC when Newman produced a 1960-61 science fiction series *Pathfinders* that was written by Hulke and Eric Paice. *Pathfinders* shared many elements with early *Doctor Who*, including the crotchety older scientist.

Donald Wilson, who pretty much shrugged his shoulders as head of serials and "allowed" me to deal directly with Verity, but who added things to the serial as well.

My basic concept was about three earthlings who become hopelessly involved with a senile old man, 745 years old, Doctor Who, from an unnamed planet. The latter's spaceship I conceived as being vast and remarkable in its interior but with the pedestrian exterior of a small police call box. Dr. Who, in his senility, never quite knows how to work the machine but was always trying to get back home. His earthling friends are also always trying to get back to earth.

You will recall that the original earthlings consisted of two comprehensive schoolteachers and a fourteen-year-old girl.

The main purpose of the series was to dramatize events in earth history and life on other planets. It was also part of the concept that the characters were not only able to travel backward and forward in time but equally to find themselves out of physical proportion with the environment.

One of the first group of serials was to be the return of Dr. Who and his earthling friends to the comprehensive school his earthlings had come from, but physically [were] no larger than say ¼". This concept, however, proved extremely difficult to execute in live TV terms. Interestingly enough, the stories dealing with earth history proved to be the least popular. (These short serials included the 30 Years War,[24] Nero fiddling while Rome burned etc., etc.). This was a great disappointment to me because *the*

---

24 Newman is misremembering; a 30 Years War story was possibly discussed but never made. Nero did, however, play his lyre while Rome burned in the 1965 serial "The Romans."

intention of the series was a very serious one despite its rather escapist look. I wanted to dramatize the history of mankind as well as all kinds of natural phenomena.

Anyway, despite my severe injunction to Verity and David to avoid in the characters' outer space travels the use of B.E.M. creations, ironically the Daleks were the most successful part of the series! Verity still swears the Daleks were not bug-eyed monsters!

Oh yes, one other point! The age-level appeal — or rather the intellectual appeal of the serial — was designed to bridge the BBC's Saturday afternoon sportscast with, whatever it was called, that pop-tune quiz programme that catered to the teenagers. I think we succeeded in doing this.

. . . I suppose there is one comment of mine that you want or cannot use. It relates to the young girl of the serial whom I asked before casting that she primarily have two characteristics. She should be able to scream and have big tits! (If you write this, I will kill you!)

A few days later, Mac Hulke wrote Newman again, this time on October 4. "You have posed me with a right problem!" Hulke said. Hulke had spoken to Donald Wilson as part of his research on September 8 and, according to Hulke, Wilson was claiming part credit for the basic idea of *Doctor Who*. Hulke recorded the conversation and provided a transcript of his conversation with Wilson, which he appended to his note.

Among Wilson's comments about the creation of *Doctor Who* were, "It was just Sydney and I together, chatting. At an early stage we discussed it with other people, but in fact the title, as I remember, I invented . . . This ingenious idea of the vanishing telephone box was Sydney's idea which started the whole thing off, you know."

Wilson added, "I can't really remember who thought of anything between us, but the idea of having the child with the old man . . . you know the strange child who was at a school, that's involving the two young schoolmaster and schoolmistress . . . came at an early stage and this evolved between us."

Newman was unperturbed. He responded to Hulke on October 7:

> I don't think the problem is as great as your letter would suggest. Frankly, I haven't a clue as to who thought up the title.[25] Maybe it was Donald's idea. I have no clear recollection that it was my title. I am only clear on the fact that I thought up the four-dimensional idea and that the central character be a senile old man of 70 years of age. I was also clear in my mind that the series elucidate natural phenomena, that it be very attractive on the outside and organically sincere and that it bridge the sports-loving fans of Saturday afternoon with the teenage appeal of [*Juke Box Jury*] that followed it. I am also clear that I wanted no bug-eyed monsters.
>
> Frankly Mac, it doesn't matter to me much who seems to get the credit for the program. The fact is I was Head of Drama Group at the BBC. While I feel intimately involved with *Doctor Who* (as I wasn't with *The Forsyte Saga* which was entirely Donald's idea but which I approved) it was all grist for the mill as far as I am concerned.
>
> . . . Your verbatim account of your television call with Donald doesn't seem to me to contradict much of what I have said in my last letter to you. There is no doubt in my mind that Donald had a lot to do with the serial.
>
> I am afraid, Mac, as is always the way with the writer, he is left to interpret the facts of life and of history as best he can. You have my forgiveness in advance! And you see, I can afford to be generous since there are no *royalties*

---

25 Newman does, on occasion, credit himself for coming up with the title of the show, though he just as frequently admits that he doesn't remember who came up with it. Director Richard Martin claimed that Newman came up with the title. Actor and writer Hugh David claimed in the 1980s that it came from temporary producer Rex Tucker.

From left to right, William Russell as Ian, Carole Ann Ford as Susan, Jacqueline Hill as Barbara, and William Hartnell as the Doctor gathered outside the TARDIS in the first Doctor Who *serial in 1963.* © BBC Photo Library

> whatever involved.
>   You're on your own, Mac!

Newman's argument was, essentially, that he came up with the old man and his time machine and in so doing came up with the series. It might have been in meetings with others, and Wilson may have come up with the title, but the core concept was the character we would come to know as the Doctor and the spaceship we would come to know as the TARDIS.

When *The Making of Doctor Who* was published in 1972,[26] Malcolm Hulke would give credit to both Sydney Newman and Donald Wilson

---

26 Newman was so pleased with the book when he received it, he asked Mac Hulke to drop off ten more copies at the NFB's office in London and had it shipped to Newman at the NFB's headquarters in Montreal. The receipt for shipping was kept in his papers.

as the creators of *Doctor Who*. It's interesting to note this was, in fact, the view taken by the BBC in 1963.

As *Doctor Who* ramped up toward production, the series was used as a reason to reject a children's puppet series being pitched to the children's department by an outside production company, Zenith Productions, called *The Time Travellers*. The BBC's children's department, upon learning that the drama department was doing a show that was broadly similar and featured a time machine, wrote Zenith to say that they didn't know the drama department was going to do something similar, but now that they were aware, they would have to pass on the project.

Zenith, who had already spent twelve months beating down the BBC's door on this project, was aggrieved by this, to put it mildly. In a letter to BBC Enterprises' Ronald Waldman dated July 19, 1963, Zenith producer Kenneth Cleveland wrote, "One cannot escape the inference that there has been at the very least some lack of frankness on the part of the Corporation and whether a question of plagiarism is involved depends on the contents and treatment of the idea in the BBC's version." They demanded to see a specimen script from *Doctor Who*. There was a subsequent war of words and a proliferation of internal memos that resulted in a reply from the BBC's head of copyright, R.G. Walford, on July 25, 1963. It is in this letter we see where the BBC placed creator credit on *Doctor Who*. Walford wrote, "The first important point I must make is that this *Doctor Who* series was devised jointly by Sydney Newman and Donald Wilson." Walford would go on to outline that Newman and Wilson had no knowledge of *The Time Travellers* and nor did Anthony Coburn, who by this point was writing the first ten episodes[27] of *Doctor Who*. Walford added that Coburn was commissioned to write his scripts based "on the basic format which Sydney Newman and Donald Wilson devised and which of course the BBC owns." In the end, there were more terse exchanges

---

27 At the time, Anthony Coburn was contracted to write the initial four-part serial that became known as 1963's "An Unearthly Child," followed by a six-part serial called "The Robots." In the event, "The Robots" was never made.

of words and the BBC offered Zenith Productions 100 guineas as an ex-gratia gesture of goodwill. Beyond that, it would seem, as far as the BBC in 1963 was concerned, *Doctor Who* was a co-creation of Newman and Wilson.

But Newman didn't see it that way and he never acknowledged Wilson's role in its creation beyond his presence at the birth, as it were. His view, as he stated to Mac Hulke in 1971, was that Wilson aided the process of creation along, similar to what Newman and Wilson did when Wilson developed *The Forsyte Saga*. Newman remained convinced he created *Doctor Who* until the day he died.

And yet, Newman would equally concede the point all his life that he created the *idea* of *Doctor Who*, not what *Doctor Who* actually *became*. He credited Verity Lambert for that.

Newman's ideas for *Doctor Who* were born out of his own convictions of a program rooted as much in science fact as science fiction; a program that educated kids about science and history. Much of the dramas for children that were broadcast at the CBC in the 1950s while he was supervising producer were entertaining and dramatic but also designed to "painlessly" educate children as well. We see this in Newman's bullying of Bunny Webber's proposals: anything quirky or philosophical was out. Newman wanted *Doctor Who* to teach science and history — which explains Newman's obsession with shrinking the central characters as part of the original first serial.[28]

But Newman always gave credit to Verity Lambert for the show

---

28 Having the characters shrunk down was likely a part of Newman's conception
     of the show; it was, in fact, part of the early format documents and was the basis
     for C.E. Webber's rejected script. For months, there were efforts to still include
     it as part of the show's first serial but the production team could never find a
     script that made it work. In the end, it was finally used as the debut story of
     Doctor Who's second season, "Planet of Giants" (1964). While the special effects
     were remarkable, producer Verity Lambert was unimpressed with the lack of
     dramatic incident in the final product and gave the unprecedented order to have
     it edited down from four episodes to three.

that *Doctor Who* actually became: one with adventures in space and time with monsters. In his first exchange with Mac Hulke for *The Making of Doctor Who*, Newman wrote, "Much, much credit is due to Verity as the original producer. Her casting of Bill Hartnell was sheer inspiration." In fact, in his October 7 letter responding to Hulke's questions about Donald Wilson's involvement, Newman argued, "If nothing else I demand top credit for having told Wilson to give the producership job to Verity Lambert whose capabilities I knew very well from our days together at ABC-TV." When the published book came out, Newman's one criticism was not that he was reduced to a co-creator with Donald Wilson but that Verity Lambert's role wasn't discussed. "I suppose the only criticism I can make is the somewhat sparse reference to Verity. Her wonderful enthusiasm and creative ideas did so much to whamp the series home to success." Newman publicly credited Verity Lambert for this in all his interviews.[29]

For all the sixth-form vulgarity in Newman's correspondence with Hulke about the teenaged screamer's breasts, Newman could also be astonishingly progressive for the age he lived in, recognizing the talents of women like Verity Lambert[30] and Irene Shubik, both of whom would go on to incredible careers in television, but who had their start as producers hired by Newman in the boys' club that was British television in the early 1960s.[31] And Newman had even more progressive ideas when asked to propose what to do with *Doctor Who* in 1985.

---

29 The respect was mutual. Verity Lambert praised Newman in interviews throughout her career. She even flew to Toronto to attend his funeral.

30 Even then, according to Irene Shubik in *Play for Today*, "[Newman] told me, in typical half-joking Sydney fashion, that he had [offered Lambert her job as producer] because he admired Verity's legs, her ambition and her aggressiveness."

31 While it was predominantly male, and Lambert was the BBC's first woman producer in drama, it should be noted the BBC already had trailblazing women in power including Grace Wyndham Goldie, who was in charge of current affairs at the BBC during Newman's tenure, and Joanna Spicer, the assistant controller of BBC 1, who basically ensured the survival of *Doctor Who* when her boss, Donald Baverstock, suggested euthanizing the series for cost overruns due to its spaceship set.

Producer Verity Lambert (centre) on the set of Doctor Who, *1965.* © BBC Photo Library

But more to the point, Newman credits Verity Lambert for making the series what it was by ignoring Newman's own brief for the show and bringing in the verboten "B.E.M.s" in the form of the Daleks.[32] The 1969 *Daily Sketch* article features the first published instance of Newman's much rehearsed anecdote about raining down hell on Lambert over the creation of the Daleks.

> *Doctor Who* was entrusted to a new young producer, Verity Lambert, who had worked for me as a production assistant at ABC. My only firm order to her was: "On no account will I permit any B.E.M.s — bug-eyed monsters of cheapjack fiction. They're out."
>
> Weeks later, a timid Miss Lambert came to me — and told me about the Daleks. I exploded. But she carefully

---

32 Lambert didn't just encounter resistance from Newman. Head of serials Donald Wilson also strenuously objected to Lambert proceeding with the Daleks while they were being developed.

explained they weren't *really* B.E.M.s — they were really
humans who lost their limbs, very sympathetic bits of
ironmongery. The Daleks went in — almost over my dead
body. And they became, of course, the largest single factor
in the series' popularity, with little children venting their
aggressions, screeching "Exterminate! Exterminate!" And
so much merchandising, in the form of gear and toys,[33]
that brought BBC enterprises — and Terry Nation so
much money.

Newman's greatest influence on the *Doctor Who* that was broadcast
were the notes he gave on the original pilot episode. There has been
over the years some confusion around this episode's function. On
American TV, a pilot was a program made as a one-off to attract a full-
series commission. *Doctor Who* was already a provisional commission
(though the exact number of episodes it would have would continue to
be in question for months even after it started airing). But the unseen
first episode was not, as it has been often portrayed (most recently in
the 2013 television movie *An Adventure in Space and Time*) a rejected
first episode.[34] It was, in fact called a pilot in the BBC's documentation
— a version of the first episode that would serve as proof of concept.
It might go to air if it required minimal changes (this is precisely what

---

33 *Doctor Who* historian Richard Bignell has found several memos by Newman
    where he talks about the various toys made for *Doctor Who* and the Daleks.
    (Newman joked that he "dreamt of cuckoo clocks in the form of police call
    boxes with Dr. Who popping out saying, 'Dr. Who, Who, Who,' then retreating
    hurriedly!") In fact, in a television interview he did with the CBC in 1966,
    Newman has two toy Daleks on his desk at the BBC.

34 *An Adventure in Space and Time* is heavily influenced by remarks made by
    the pilot's director, Waris Hussein, who said in interviews that he and Verity
    Lambert were expecting to get fired by Newman, with Newman (played by
    Brian Cox) saying "I should fire the pair of you" before granting them a do-over
    on the first episode. While Hussein might well have been worried about his job
    security as director, Verity Lambert didn't seem to be concerned. In fact, she had
    already instructed the scenery department to keep the sets from the pilot should
    they need them for a remount.

happened with *Fawlty Towers'* pilot, for example). But if not, the episode would serve to instruct changes for the final product and the pilot would never see the light of day. This was the case for Newman's later creation *Adam Adamant Lives!*[35] and was the case for *Doctor Who*.

When the pilot for *Doctor Who* was made on September 27, 1963, Newman had just returned from Denmark where a multinational crew was still filming *Hamlet at Elsinore*. It's not known when Newman viewed the pilot,[36] but his handwritten notes, written on the back of the last two pages of the camera script for the first episode, "An Unearthly Child," still exist in the BBC's records. They ranged from notes on the clunky direction by Waris Hussein ("What's the point of panning from back view to back view?") to the harshness of the characterization of the Doctor ("Old man not cute enough") and his granddaughter, Susan ("Can she be more cheeky? Too dour") to technical concerns ("Must be a decided change in sound and music between outside and inside"). Newman titled his notes "1st Run," which indicates that he was pretty much convinced it would have to be remade from the start.

Pretty much all of Newman's notes (and whatever instructions he gave verbally) were implemented in the final version of the first episode. The characterization of the Doctor and Susan were softened, the direction was more polished and the technical aspects, from the amount of noise of the TARDIS control room to the size of font on the credits, were dealt with overall.

Sydney Newman wasn't in Britain when the first episode aired on television in the shadow of the Kennedy assassination. One year after his note pleading to be released from his contract at ABC,

---

35 That said, parts of the pilot to *Adam Adamant Lives!* would be used in the final production.

36 In fact, one could speculate that Newman being away in Denmark might be the reason for the unusual decision to record the videotaped pilot on 16mm film — so that Newman could have a viewing copy. Whatever the reason, it resulted in one of the greatest flukes in *Doctor Who*'s history, as the film copy was retained and even managed to survive the mass junking of *Doctor Who* episodes from the 1960s.

Newman was in New York working on, among other things, attracting American interest in *Hamlet at Elsinore* with American networks and producers such as David Susskind. It was Wednesday, November 27, before Donald Wilson had the presence of mind to send Newman a telegram addressed to the Warwick Hotel, where he was staying, that read, DOCTOR WHO OFF TO A GREAT START EVERYBODY HERE DELIGHTED.

CHAPTER FIVE
POINT OF CRISIS

By Newman's estimation, when he first arrived in 1963, the BBC's drama department was producing 250 programmes a year; by the end of his tenure in 1968, that output had increased to 720 programs a year. The staff in the drama department burgeoned to 450 people.

Aside from creating *Doctor Who*, what exactly did Sydney Newman do at the BBC? He didn't produce anything himself. It was, in fact, a question posed to him in an oral history project done by the BBC in 1984. Newman answered that he assisted in programming by defining each programme's objective and its qualities, and that a lot of his work was "just generally policing it. Inspiring them. Congratulating them." On a more practical level, he supervised the BBC drama group, meeting each department head once a week and meeting with individual producers once a month.

Newman was, in the parlance of modern television, a non-showrunning executive producer. He had oversight over the people who oversaw television.

His work in developing *Doctor Who* is typical of what Newman did: he saw gaps in the BBC's output and found the means to fill them. As with *Doctor Who*, Newman approved concepts for programmes, threw in his own ideas where needed and made sure the right talent took charge of the concept from there. "[He] had a great talent for delegating to people whom he trusted," Irene Shubik wrote of Newman.

"I didn't sit on top of any programme. How could I?" Newman explained in his 1984 interview. "It would have been foolish. There were hundreds of programmes. I had to trust my people."

For example, *Hamlet at Elsinore*, which Newman more or less credits in his memoir as his crowning achievement at the BBC, was produced by Peter Luke, Newman's story editor on *Armchair Theatre* who crossed over to the BBC to follow Newman. Nonetheless, Newman was intimately involved in most details of production, including negotiating Christopher Plummer's contract, the complex negotiations with the actors' union Equity for recording abroad, the immense technical needs of the production, even attempting to sell it for broadcast in America. He was also in Denmark for several days of the recording.[37]

Every so often he would have to play "bad cop." In October 1963, in the middle of sorting out *Doctor Who*'s first episode and *Hamlet at Elsinore* and several other things, Newman sent a memo to all department heads, producers, directors and story editors titled, "Frankness in showing sexual relations." Newman began, "There is a directorial trend in our Group that's getting to be a bit of a bore." Newman was speaking of the proliferation of scenes featuring men and woman in bed together. Newman cited several incidents and asked everyone to demand people be sensible lest he be forced to give a stronger edict, adding "There are a thousand interesting ways of conveying physical attractions and relations without causing offence. A talented director will know them."

---

37 Newman even requested that bonuses be paid to several of the BBC personnel who braved the elements to record the programme in Denmark.

Mostly, Newman was hands-off in his approach — though he was always happy to venture an opinion on practically anything and everything. And he was also not one to mince words. The BBC's anthology drama *The Wednesday Play*'s 1965 production of "Alice," the story of the Oxford professor who wrote *Alice in Wonderland* under the pseudonym Lewis Carroll, is now looked upon fondly as a groundbreaking drama by Dennis Potter, already making a name for himself as a television playwright. Newman's memo shortly after the broadcast to head of plays, Michael Bakewell, and cc'd to producer James MacTaggart and story editor Tony Garnett, reveals Newman had a decidedly lower opinion of it. "What audience was in mind when 'Alice' was picked as [a season] opener? Were the boys thinking of the 8 million or so who had come to like *The Wednesday Play* or were they thinking of the critics, themselves, or what?" Newman thundered that prior discussions to get the viewer hooked in the first thirty seconds were ignored in place of what was, to Newman's mind, a dull ten-minute opening. Newman concluded with "I'm absolutely sick."

Histrionic as Newman's memo may have been, it also shows his chief concern with anything broadcast: it needed to connect to audiences. While he supported experiments in television drama — Newman was no traditionalist by any means — he despised any perceived elitism in television. He never wanted television that was beloved of the critics; he wanted viewers. Television was, for Newman, a populist medium, which was not necessarily how the in-house culture at the BBC perceived it when he arrived. Irene Shubik understood this dynamic well first-hand. "With his American and Canadian background, Sydney was perhaps more aware of the audience than those at the BBC who had enjoyed a non-commercial monopoly for so long."

"There was no real depth," Newman said in 1984 of the BBC's output in drama when he arrived. "It was all rather stagey. The material . . . didn't really cater to what I assumed to be the mass British audience." To Newman, much of the BBC's output still catered to "the highly educated, cultured class rather than the mass audience." Newman felt the dramas weren't speaking to ordinary people about common, everyday things.

Newman did have a blindspot when it came to television, and it led to some of his biggest fights at the BBC. Newman believed that the most important thing the medium could broadcast was the single play — the term used for a one-off dramatization.[38] Coming out of his background at the CBC and ABC in the 1950s, this was perhaps unsurprising. In Canada, the U.S. and Britain, the single play was the premiere form of television drama in the 1950s. Newman was a devoted disciple of this form. "There is no single activity carried out by Drama Group that is more important than the original play series," Newman declared in a memo to BBC Director of Television Kenneth Adam in June 1964.

"Throughout his plans runs the determination to represent the 'truth' about a reeling society," wrote academic Madeleine Macmurraugh-Kavanagh, "and to persevere with this strategy should this prove to be incompatible with viewer taste."

Even so, Newman was perhaps moving toward the wrong side of history. In the U.S., the anthology drama series was on the wane. *Playhouse 90*, the best known of the genre, went off the air in 1960, while others gradually faded out as the decade progressed. Series were gradually becoming the place where viewers sought entertainment that occasionally told uncomfortable truths. Newman said in repeated interviews that his model for drama was John Osborne's *Look Back in Anger*. By the mid-1960s on U.S. television, audiences were more likely looking to soapy dramas like *Peyton Place*.

It's not that Newman didn't see this tide happening in Britain. While he was working on *Armchair Theatre* for ABC, Tony Warren, a writer at Manchester's Granada Television, was creating a twice-a-week soap opera set among the working classes called *Florizel Street* — that created a sensation when it was broadcast as *Coronation Street*. A year before Newman's arrival the BBC in 1962, producer David Rose and writer Elwyn Jones brought a gritty, urban idiom to the police procedural with *Z Cars*. Newman would contribute toward retooling this series later in

---

38 This was not a play in the theatrical tradition, though it certainly did adapt theatrical plays. It was a one-off episode of television, using all the resources it had to bear.

the 1960s when it spawned a new show with its leads called *Softly, Softly*.

And Newman was happy to create escapist fare too — and not just *Doctor Who*. In 1965, Newman wrote an outline where Victorian pulp hero Sexton Blake was revived from suspended animation in the swinging sixties. When rights to Sexton Blake proved troublesome,[39] it was retooled with a differently similar hero by writer Donald Cotton and producer Verity Lambert (finally freed from *Doctor Who*) as *Adam Adamant Lives!* The show was intended as a rival to *The Avengers*, but failed to gain an audience and was cancelled after two seasons.

Newman felt that plays were the crowning jewel of the BBC and he was vocal in his disagreement with those who opposed this view. Chief among them was Donald Baverstock, who, by the time Newman had arrived at the BBC, had become the controller of what would become BBC 1.

Baverstock was a whiz kid in current affairs TV who virtually invented the format in Britain[40] before a whirlwind series of promotions elevated him to head of programming on the BBC's primary channel. His meteoric rise and lateral career moves are quite similar to Newman's, and while Baverstock was a Welshman who read history at Oxford, his mother-in-law was Enid Blyton, the popular children's author who had been the subject of a thirty-year ban by the BBC,[41] so Baverstock knew the BBC's elitist attitudes all too well. Like Newman, he was known for speaking his mind.

---

39 Newman's obsession with Sexton Blake spawned not one but two series during his tenure at the BBC; besides *Adam Adamant Lives!* there was an attempt to do a straightforward adaptation of the Sexton Blake stories — also rebuffed by the rights holders — that led to the creation of the 1964-69 anthology series *Detective*.

40 The 2011 BBC drama *The Hour*, set in the BBC of the 1950s, uses a current affairs programme in it that is essentially based on *Tonight*, the nightly current affairs show Baverstock started in 1957 with Alasdair Milne.

41 The ban was purely out of snobbery toward her work, in spite of its popularity; one memo from a radio show executive sneered that Blyton was a "second-rater."

Newman hated him. "We didn't hit it off," Newman said with some understatement in 1984. He claimed Baverstock was a blowhard and a bully who was out of his depth in areas like drama.

The conflicts between Baverstock and Newman were mostly around what Newman perceived as an attempt to do away with the single plays in 1964.[42] When Newman began at the BBC, he first attempted to duplicate the success of *Armchair Theatre* with a show called *First Night*, which was produced by John Elliot. It was shown in tandem with *Festival*, a more traditional series of highbrow adaptations of classic plays produced by Peter Luke. *First Night* went out opposite *Armchair Theatre* and Newman's later assessment was it suffered first from not understanding the competition and then by trying to copy the competition too much. "We had an endless slew of kitchen sink stuff, an endless amount of no humour, no fun and got into a lot of trouble."

However, Newman is being somewhat economical in his recollections. When *First Night* debuted in 1963 it featured a play by one of Newman's discoveries, Alun Owen (mere months before he would go on to write the Academy Award–nominated *A Hard Day's Night* for the Beatles), alongside his star director, Ted Kotcheff. This was followed up the next week with a play by Nigel Kneale. After the strong start, though, *First Night* would tail off and never succeeded in getting people to switch over from the other side.

Newman retained very little actual memoranda and correspondence from his time at the BBC. However, the documentation he did retain often featured Baverstock in some way. The first signs of trouble started

---

42 Television historians like Madeleine Macmurraugh-Kavanagh argue that the agenda of Baverstock (and indeed Head of Television Kenneth Adam) *was* in fact to eliminate single plays from the BBC's output. She writes, "All the evidence suggested that what the audience wanted in this instance were [series] in the mould of the hugely popular *Z Cars* and *Doctor Finlay's Casebook*, both of which drew a massive weekly audience outstripping any programme the rival channel could pitch against them." Baverstock and Adam, in her view, were moving to give the audience what they "wanted" (enjoyable series and serials) and not what they "needed" (single plays) — a side benefit of this would be that programming would tend to be more politically neutral and less provocative.

in a confidential letter from Newman to Kenneth Adam on January 21, 1964: "I am afraid I am beginning to find it literally impossible to work with Donald Baverstock. For months now I have been holding off coming to you with this problem in the expectation that Donald and I would achieve a more positive working relationship." The final straw, for Newman, was his discovery in a promotions meeting that Baverstock had circumvented both Newman and *First Night* producer John Elliot and demanded changes in one of the plays in the series. "I am not concerned with the merits of this decision," Newman wrote, "but I cannot help but resent his dictatorial interference in an area that involves professional judgment and not broad planning."

Things worsened by mid-1964 when *First Night* and *Festival* went into hiatus. Newman was in the middle of trying to fix the leaking boat that was the Plays department by finally securing a head of department in Michael Bakewell and then securing James MacTaggart, a director who Newman perceived had it in him to produce a hard-hitting series of plays, to succeed John Elliot as producer of *First Night*.

It was then that Newman learned from Joanna Spicer that Baverstock had decided that *First Night*, or indeed any play series, would not air until early 1965. As he recalled the incident in 1984, "Donald Baverstock was controller of BBC 1 and he immediately took the idea that single plays are out, they are no damn good and I had a tremendous row with him over it and had to fight for it."

That disagreement spilled up the chain of command to head of television, Kenneth Adam. Adam asked Newman to put his thoughts in a memo, which Newman wrote on June 26, 1964. Newman started with his characteristic dramatics: "The fact that I have been put into the position of having to define the importance to the BBC and to the country the necessity of such a [single play anthology] series makes me sick." He invoked a recent article by critic Maurice Wiggin where he complained that "the BBC has done wonders in bringing us a giant stride nearer to the American situation, where the television play is no longer an important fraction of the output."

Newman then asked Adam to recall the first time Newman met the Director General Hugh Greene for the first time, and that Greene wanted to reinstate the BBC as a home for Britain's best playwrights, getting back the discoveries from BBC radio like Harold Pinter who had been subsequently poached by Newman and others with independent television. From there, Newman then launches into a *mea culpa* that *First Night* wasn't more successful, saying he couldn't supervise single plays to the extent he felt it deserved, due to his learning curve with the organization and the challenges of increasing the drama department's output by fifty-five percent to accommodate BBC 2's arrival (along with creating new shows like *Hamlet at Elsinore* and *Doctor Who*).

And then, Newman levels his accusation on Baverstock:

> I believe I understand what motivates [Baverstock] and in a way it is flattering. He wishes and requires bigger audiences and Drama Group Serials and Series in the main provide him with these big-audience getters. Specifically, I believe the proposal to drop *First Night* is to free money and facilities for the production of a third weekly series — Kipling, Sherlock Holmes, or whatever. We want very much to do this as well as any number of other series and serials which will give the BBC bigger audiences, *but not by killing off the series which is dedicated to original writing.*

Newman asserted that under James MacTaggart as new producer, and with better publicity, *First Night* would get better ratings. He then concluded, "I did not become head of drama in order to preside over its dissolution, I hope that [Baverstock] isn't where he is for the same reason."

Baverstock took a few days before hitting back on July 1.[43] His

---

43 Neither Newman's memo to Adam nor Baverstock's were cc'd to the other — an unusual omission in the rigid formatting of BBC memoranda, which suggests that Adam might have shared Newman's memo with Baverstock privately. Both wound up in the drama department's file in the BBC archives, so perhaps they were included on the record.

response was thoughtful, considered and demonstrated a brutal sense of wit. Baverstock claimed that there were scheduling reasons and resourcing reasons for his decision, adding, "at no time have I suggested we should stop commissioning and producing a volume of new single plays every year." Baverstock slaps back at several of Newman's points with a wry sense of humour, calling Newman's bluff on his implied threats — "[Newman] can reassure himself (and the Screenwriters Guild) that of necessity I shall have to go on transmitting at least one and possibly two plays a week in future" — and bluntly disabusing Newman's notion that the appointment of MacTaggart will be the solution to all ills, pointing out MacTaggart's last anthology series wasn't a ratings smash and "did not reveal all that much showmanship or the perfect sense of his audience."

It was another two weeks before the Director of Television, Kenneth Adam, stepped in, at least in the chain of correspondence. "I am sorry that you have found it difficult to agree on this subject," Adam said, with brittle understatement. Adam pretty much sided with Baverstock and agreed with his decision to curtail single plays till 1965. Adam felt that shoring up the audience and improving ratings, particularly with a general election scheduled for October 1964, should be the priority for the corporation. But he also forced Baverstock's hand in allowing scheduling for a single play series as soon as possible in 1965, under a new title.

It was, as executive pissing matches go, fairly contained.[44] But Newman revealed in his 1984 oral history interview that it was actually more serious than what the exchange of words indicated. "I actually had to go to Kenneth Adam and say, 'Look, you either get Baverstock off my back on the question of the single play or I will

---

44 Though word of the dispute between Baverstock and Newman did get out in the press a little bit. An undated news clipping is in Newman's papers written around the time of Baverstock's resignation from the BBC in 1965 explaining what it learned "from a top TV source" the reasons why Baverstock had lost his support with the BBC, including "the big tussle with Sydney Newman, head of the drama department and cheerleader for single plays against Baverstock's preference for series."

leave. I cannot work with this man.'"

Newman certainly wasn't above such incredible demands. As 1964 progressed, Newman was even more frustrated by the low morale within the drama department. On October 27, 1964, Newman sent Kenneth Adam a strictly confidential memo where he said, point blank, "Confidence of your [head of drama group, head of plays and head of serials] in [Baverstock] is now at a point of crisis." Newman listed his complaints, which ranged from the embargo on making new plays to Baverstock's refusal to authorize production of new Sunday classic serials before angrily stating, "H.Serials, H.Plays and I must face the brutal fact that Baverstock dislikes drama, Baverstock doesn't understand drama, that Baverstock one way or another will frustrate the efforts of at least two-thirds of the people in the drama group." The missing one-third of Newman's equation was the series department, which Newman accused Baverstock of favouring to the point of vetoing any cuts to any series' budget.

Faced with a crisis in morale with his department heads and producers, Newman delivered his demand. "If the Television Service wants a first-class drama group, and that means presenting the *best* in drama as well as good drama ratings, it must do the following: 1) remove Baverstock from his post or 2) re-define his job so that whatever his influence on the areas of broadcasting he has no say in the *content* of drama." As far as Newman was concerned, the only thing the Controller of BBC 1 should offer up was an opinion on the size of the audience, the duration of the programs and the budget and resources available.

Newman summed up by saying, "Unless (1) and (2) . . . is put into action soon, we will lose all our best people, including departmental heads. For myself, I'll know that the BBC as an exciting challenge was a mistake and an illusion."

Newman effectively told his boss[45] at the BBC that the channel's

---

45 Actually, all these memos are technically to his boss' boss. They're addressed in BBC speak as "To H.Tel (as C.P. Tel)" which is to say they were written to Adam in his acting capacity as Controller of the BBC Television — a role that actually did have the authority to sack Baverstock.

controller should get out of the way and allow the drama department complete autonomy. It is an astonishing, incendiary notice that would get most people fired. But not Newman. "I've become . . . accustomed to enjoying a 'status' in this London community with its perks of privilege," Newman wrote a friend in 1969, "and, in my case, even enjoyable notoriety." The truth is Newman was the darling of the press. If Newman resigned in acrimonious circumstances it could potentially do harm to the BBC's reputation.

No one knew it at the time, but Baverstock would soon be on his way out. When Huw Wheldon became controller of the BBC's television service in 1965, one of his conditions of employment was that Baverstock move to running BBC 2, while BBC 2 controller Controller Michael Peacock would run BBC 1. (He was backed by Hugh Greene, the BBC's Director General.) Baverstock balked at this and resigned. The switch was mostly because it was felt that Michael Peacock might have been better suited to the mainstream BBC channel, but it's tempting to speculate whether what the agitating Newman was doing behind the scenes in some way contributed to this turn of events. And while it is possible Adam took Newman's concerns with Baverstock up the chain to the director general (or Newman brought it up the line himself), there is no evidence to back this up.

However, it is entirely possible that ultimatums like this and the one Newman gave in the summer of 1964 were what exacted the promise that there would be a single play anthology in the future and, perhaps, changed the face of British television in the 1960s. This war of words with Baverstock led to what was perhaps Newman's second greatest contribution to his time at the BBC after *Doctor Who*: The drama anthology series with the new title Kenneth Adam demanded — *The Wednesday Play*.

CHAPTER SIX

"AGITATIONAL CONTEMPORANEITY"

"The real breakthrough came when I had the wit to literally pressgang Jimmy MacTaggart into becoming the producer," Sydney Newman said in 1984. "I made a deal with him that he was to do it for two years and he was the one who really brought the magic."

James MacTaggart was that unusual triple threat in British television: he wrote, directed and produced. In the BBC Drama department Newman created, a person could only do one of those things at any one time, so MacTaggart mostly produced dramas and occasionally directed a single episode here and there. Alongside writers like Troy Kennedy Martin and a young director named Kenneth Loach, MacTaggart was interested in experimentation and breaking narrative conventions[46] — something that saw its climax in September 1964 with the debut of *Diary of a Young Man*, a six-part BBC serial produced by MacTaggart,

---

46 "We were going to destroy naturalism," said Troy Kennedy Martin in 1986 of himself and MacTaggart, "if possible, before Christmas."

which told the story of two working-class northern lads during their first months in London. Half the episodes were directed by Ken Loach in one of his first big breaks outside of *Z Cars*. It was edgy and used a visual grammar not seen in the usual naturalistic, performed-as-live fare on the BBC, including sequences of still images, deconstructing the order of the narrative and absurd sequences. It was hated by viewers and critics alike, but Newman loved it, telling MacTaggart in a memo he thought it was a major breakthrough. MacTaggart was just the man Sydney Newman wanted.

As with Newman's hiring of Verity Lambert for *Doctor Who*, MacTaggart was the best possible choice for the job. And, as with Lambert and *Doctor Who*, Newman largely got out of the way and let MacTaggart do his job. The memo where Newman fulminated over the choice and opening of Dennis Potter's play "Alice" also outlined Newman's goals for *The Wednesday Play*. "As I recall it, *The Wednesday Play* primarily was to do two jobs: 1) Secure the biggest audience possible. 2) Do plays that dramatize the turning points in contemporary Britain."

At a press conference in August 1966, Newman spoke "very solemnly but with enthusiasm" about the BBC's output of dramas, according to a note he sent to TV critic Philip Purser. During the conference, he spoke about the "agitational effect" some plays were having on *The Wednesday Play*. As the conversation progressed, soon the words "agitational contemporaneity" came tripping off Newman's tongue.

Newman asked the journalists present if there was such a phrase. When they replied there wasn't, Newman then said "Well, let's just say we invented it."

And "agitational contemporaneity" is just what Newman, and the British public, got.

The Wednesday Play initially started in the autumn of 1964 as a placeholder, to burn off episodes of the cancelled *Festival* that hadn't been shown yet. In January 1965, MacTaggart's version of the series began and it was already controversial within the BBC. Its third episode,

"Fable," was a play where Britain was turned into an apartheid state ruled by blacks. It was as on-the-nose as it came, and the BBC delayed broadcast by a week because of concerns that it be seen to affect the outcome of a by-election in the East London riding of Leyton that was becoming racially charged. Newman — who in his memoirs noted that he hated the episode — passed MacTaggart's complaints about this up to Kenneth Adam, who was sympathetic but unyielding.[47]

"Fable" wasn't an audience favourite[48] but it was competitive against independent television. And it marked the beginnings of 1965 as a golden year in television produced by the BBC. Dennis Potter, who would become the standard bearer of television writing with works like *Pennies from Heaven* and *The Singing Detective*, had his first works produced by *The Wednesday Play* starting in February 1965. Some of the works were satirical, like Potter's "The Confidence Course," which poked fun at Dale Carnegie-styled demagogues. Some were allegories, like "Fable," and some were character studies of a character and place, like Dennis Potter's Nigel Barton plays. Then there were character studies, like Newman's despised "Alice."

There were also moments of raw and effective social criticism. "Three Clear Sundays," which aired in April 1965, told the story of Danny, a "wide boy" — a working-class male living by his wits — who gets imprisoned for a petty crime and then embroiled in a scheme to attack a prison guard, resulting in the guard's death. The play follows Danny as he waits for his execution. It was brutal and unflinching in its exploration of capital punishment, bolstered by a script by James O'Connor and outstanding direction by Ken Loach, who became *The Wednesday Play*'s not-so-secret weapon. Loach directed ten episodes

---

47 Adam's response to Newman was that, while Apartheid was not an issue the BBC needed to remain neutral over, he did not want the play to run the risk of "being obscured by a squalid and contrived outbreak of racialism in one corner of London."

48 The Audience Appreciation Index, the BBC's internal scoring system based on a survey of audience members gave it a fifty-two, well below the average score for other plays the BBC showed up to that point of sixty-three. Newman hated it, saying in his memoirs that MacTaggart had "laid a most odourous egg."

over the next four years. For someone who eschewed naturalism in his experiments with MacTaggart in the early 1960s, Loach (and MacTaggart) now embraced it. His episodes had increased location filming and were all about situating the drama in an ordinary context. The words "documentary realism" have been bandied about ever since. Even Newman was fond of it, saying in 1969, "In the meantime, *The Wednesday Play* had begun to explore the borderline between fiction and documentary . . . extending the scope of drama by taking it out to the streets — away from the artificial studio."

Perhaps the greatest controversy of these 1965 plays was Nell Dunn's adaptation of her 1963 collection of short stories, *Up the Junction*, which aired on November 3. The play is a series of vignettes of a cross-section of youth in the Clapham Junction area of London. Loach shot it on location and, incredibly, managed to use the same *cinéma vérité* aesthetic with the studio material shot on videotape. And in an era when conventional wisdom was that you couldn't edit videotape more than twice in a half an hour, Loach and his editor, Roy Watts, blended both film and videotaped footage in a fast-paced series of montages with a pop soundtrack.[49]

It pulled no punches. One of the most striking sequences is when a salesman drives and talks conspiratorially with an unseen passenger about the tricks he uses to sell tat to the lower classes and keep them in debt. To this day, the play is best known for a sequence where a seventeen-year-old girl discovers she's pregnant and then has a backstreet abortion. The sequence employs a host of documentary techniques — the pregnancy and the decision to abort is all shown through voiceovers done like interview responses put over other footage, along with voiceover with an interview with an actual doctor[50] about the fatality

---

49 Loach did this by transferring the video footage to 16mm film and editing the film rushes, which caused arguments with the BBC's in-house engineers who said it would not be of transmittable quality. Loach won the fight in the end.

50 This was a controversial narrative technique that confounded many in the television establishment. BBC Controller of Television Huw Wheldon later told Newman he objected to this mixing of fact and fiction, particularly when it was used on "Cathy Come Home" a few years later.

statistics among back-street abortions versus hospital procedures. What little is shown of the actual abortion is *vérité* style with the camera constantly moving[51] to achieve an almost hand-held effect.

MacTaggart didn't work on the episode; famously, his story editor, Tony Garnett, developed it while MacTaggart was away on holiday.[52] For Garnett, this aspect of "Up the Junction" was personal: he had lost his mother due to a back-street abortion in the 1940s. With 10 million people watching "Up the Junction," the broadcast was claimed to have contributed to the national dialogue on abortion, which was legalized two years later, in October 1967.

"I don't support sex for titillating effect," Newman said in the *Daily Sketch* in 1969. "But when, in 'Up the Junction,' some viewers objected to the abortion scene, I think they were wrong. This wasn't put in as an irrelevance. It was completely part of the kind of life we were revealing.

"Here was a human being going through horrible pain. It was no time for smiling. And neither, very often, is life itself."

The BBC switchboard was jammed. In a report Newman wrote on *The Wednesday Play* the following June, he noted that there were 516 phone calls in total: fifty favourable and 464 complaints, mostly about the language and promiscuity. Newman himself fielded some of them. One of the letters he answered was kept in the production file for "Up the Junction":

Dear Mrs. Pratt,
 Firstly, may I say how sorry I am that you found "Up the Junction" so distasteful.

---

51 Creating this hand-held effect must have been particularly hard as this was shot in studio on a massive pedestal camera many times the size of a film camera.

52 Tony Garnett admitted in a 2006 interview with the *Independent*, "It was a case of, 'If the cat's away, the mice will play' . . . I set it in motion knowing that, if we got quite a way down the line, we would have to be allowed to make it because it would be too late to stop it and, if they did, there would be a hole in the schedule." In the event, "When MacTaggart arrived back from his holiday, he hit the roof . . . but, in the end, Jim — who was a very decent human being and a tolerant, liberal man — said that we could do it if we felt strongly about it."

As you are no doubt aware, from the comments in the Press, many people felt as you did. Again, from the Press, many, including critics, found "Up the Junction" to be entertaining, true and worthwhile.

Not only did it represent life as it is not as we would wish it to be, but many people found the play deeply moral as well. Three of our leading newspapers, *The Times, The Guardian* and *The Daily Mirror* have entirely supported this view. *The Times* described it as "a vigorous persuader to virtue"; *The Guardian* spoke of "the high moral tone of the play"; and *The Daily Mirror* said that "the abortion scene must have done its bit to keep some girl on the straight and narrow." It was in these terms that the play was conceived and produced by those who were associated with it.

Newman sent copies of his letter to Mrs. Pratt up and down the command chain with a note appended suggesting people might like to use his correspondence as a template for their own responses.

James MacTaggart left *The Wednesday Play* after a year. He was replaced by Newman's old friend, Peter Luke, who, according to Irene Shubik, "frankly avowed that he did not consider television drama a suitable platform for politics." Shubik pointed out that Luke's contributors and sources of subject matter — which included Frank O'Connor, John Betjeman and Patrick White — were "ones associated more with publishers' lists than front page stories of murder trials, abortion and massacre." But Luke retired to Spain after a year, leaving the job in the hands of Lionel Hale, who had similar tastes. Newman, however, approved the idea that Tony Garnett produce his own plays with Ken Loach within the series in order to drop occasional bombs of "ripped from the headlines" agitational contemporaneity.

Newman had to bail out *The Wednesday Play* only once. In 1967, Tony Garnett produced David Mercer's "In Two Minds," which told the story of a young woman with mental health problems who encounters everything from indifference to stigmatization from all around her — including her family, her doctors and eventually the people caring for her once she is institutionalized. Loach's direction includes lots of documentary tricks including characters talking to camera, subjective camera P.O.V. and lots of location film work, which only added to the shock value.

Newman had a basic rule with all his producers. "If you're going to get into trouble, if you think it might get the BBC into trouble . . . because you're going too far, discuss it with your head of department please, and if he in turn thinks it is worthy of my consideration, he'll bring it to me." In the case of "In Two Minds," Tony Garnett thought it was time to refer upwards. Newman himself was disturbed by the portrayal of the doctors as well-meaning but incompetent.

"I turned to the guys and I said, 'You can't do this . . . I bet in one out of every five homes in this country there's somebody who's probably mentally disturbed," Newman said in 1984. He was worried that such an incendiary portrayal would create further stigma that would prevent anyone with a mental illness from getting help. Newman himself decided to refer upwards, to the new controller of BBC 1, Michael Peacock, and the new controller of BBC television, Huw Wheldon. Newman's solution was based on what the commercial station London Weekend Television did when they showed the Canadian prison documentary *Warrendale*: have it followed by an immediate discussion of the issues. To that end, an episode of the BBC talk programme *Late Night Lineup* had an interview featuring the head of psychiatric medicine from the Middlesex hospital, Ken Loach and Ronald David (R.D.) Laing, a Scottish psychiatrist on whose writings on mental illness and schizophrenia the episode relied heavily.

Sydney Newman, for all his tendency to self-promote, was also the first to admit he was wrong when something became popular in spite of his protestations to the contrary. During Newman's tenure at the BBC in the 1960s, Newman was against the Daleks in *Doctor Who* coming into being; he was against the idea of Donald Wilson adapting John Galsworthy's *Forsyte Saga* for television; and Newman turned down what was probably the best-known television play of the 1960s in Britain, the 1966 episode of *The Wednesday Play*, "Cathy Come Home." All three were hugely popular successes.

"The greatest impact of any TV drama I've been associated with was 'Cathy Come Home,'" Newman wrote in the *Daily Sketch* in 1969. "It struck a nerve in the public conscience." Written by Jeremy Sandford[53] and directed by Ken Loach, "Cathy Come Home" was the story of a married couple who wind up indigent and homeless which ends in them squatting, living in shelters and, ultimately, having their children taken away.

Newman had been offered the script as early as 1963 by director Ted Kotcheff. "I read it in mounting gloom," Newman said, "found the story depressing and didn't feel it rose above its propaganda point, and so it was left on the shelf." Newman also felt it was too costly. The script languished. It was re-offered and passed on by Peter Luke during his apolitical year as *The Wednesday Play*'s producer before it came in front of Tony Garnett. Garnett not only saw potential in it, but he marshalled his resources to allow for even more location filming. As with the Daleks and the *Forsyte Saga*, Newman didn't block something for which a producer had a passion. "Cathy Come Home" went into production.

Ken Loach perfected the craft he would use in his later films like *Ladybird, Ladybird*, building sympathy for the very ordinary people and their tiny struggles, only to have the boom lowered on them brutally as the titular Cathy helplessly finds herself falling further and further into poverty, moving from a tidy maisonette to dingy squats to shelters to, finally, the street with two children in tow. It was filmed *vérité* style, with

---

53 Sandford was married to "Up the Junction" writer Nell Dunn. Like Dunn, Sandford was Oxbridge-educated and middle class before moving to Battersea from Chelsea. Just as Dunn wrote about the rough-and-tumble lower classes she was now living amongst in "Up the Junction," Sanford wrote "Cathy Come Home" after watching a neighbour and her children be evicted from their home and end up forcibly moved to a shelter for homeless families.

the actors overlapping and improvising dialogue, and Cathy and her husband, Reg, even though married, spoke with a frankness that seems uncomfortable for television of this era. As with "Up the Junction," Loach used interviews with social workers in voiceover throughout. The ending, where, as Cathy screams as her children are taken from her by social services at Liverpool Street Station, is a gut punch to the viewer. Loach shot it with the camera at a distance so the crowd reaction was genuine, as were the reactions of actress Carol White, playing Cathy.[54]

The response was like no other play the BBC had done before or since. It was watched by 12 million viewers and afterwards the BBC's switchboard crashed from calls by viewers wanting to know how they could help. Two weeks later, a British charity for the homeless, called Shelter, launched. Its launch was purely coincidental, but donations of millions of pounds flooded the fledgling charity as a result of "Cathy Come Home."

In 1964, Donald Baverstock scoffed at Sydney Newman's notion that bringing in James MacTaggart would make an anthology of plays a ratings' winner. And yet, within a year, that's precisely what Newman did. By the end of 1965, *The Wednesday Play* was getting 10 million viewers and figures would only go up from there.

But more than that, *The Wednesday Play* influenced television and film for decades to come. Tony Garnett, Ken Loach and Dennis Potter are among the alumni who would dominate British television and film with provocative series, serials and films during the latter half of the twentieth century. Writers like Russell T Davies have stated that *The Wednesday Play* and its successor, *Play For Today*, were influential on his work in the twenty-first century.

The single play's fortunes would wane into the 1970s.[55] But Newman not only succeeded in saving the television play in the 1960s,

---

54 Carol White's own children were playing Cathy's children, which only added to the verisimilitude in filming.

55 After Newman's departure, *The Wednesday Play*, now produced by Graeme MacDonald and Irene Shubik, would see a decline in ratings to four million viewers. The series would be reconstituted as *Play for Today*, which would stay on the air until the mid-1980s.

his decisions enabled it to thrive. "When Newman came to the BBC five years ago," a report in *The Times* stated in October 1967, "the single play was a sickly child, a pallid brother to the stage production. Today it has become, he says, 'anti-theatre' and *The Wednesday Play* has built up a regular audience of ten to twelve million."

The Wednesday Play was by far not the only show under Newman's purview; it provided thirty of the 720 or so programmes a year for which Newman's drama group produced. Newman managed to build on the success of *The Wednesday Play* and add more single-play anthologies to the mix. He also worked hard to shore up their flailing broadcasts of operas, convincing Benjamin Britten to let them adapt his opera of Melville's *Billy Budd* for television and getting Alun Owen to act as librettist for an original opera. As the 1960s progressed, Newman continued to support other plays, serials, series and their producers and their heads of departments. Often, it was nothing more than an encouraging memo.

Sometimes programmes required greater intervention. Such was the case when in 1966, the production team on *Doctor Who* decided to replace William Hartnell as his lead actor with Patrick Troughton when Hartnell had become difficult to deal with due to, as it was later revealed, a debilitating illness. The show, under its new producer, Innes Lloyd, and story editor Gerry Davis, came up with a brilliant conceit that the Doctor, due to his alien nature, could metamorphose into a different character. The question was, who would that character be like?

"I became directly involved again with the series and re-conceived Dr. Who as a kind of Charlie Chaplin, the Tramp of outer space," Newman wrote to Jeremy Bentham in April 1984. The term Newman bandied about at the time was "cosmic hobo." When others, such as Patrick Troughton, would have other ideas like playing the Doctor as a windjammer captain or even "blacked up" in swarthy makeup, Newman would go back to the "cosmic hobo." And so, Patrick Troughton played the role in a shabby version of his predecessor's costume with baggier pants, a safety-pinned bowtie and a Chaplinesque silhouette.

While Newman otherwise had little need to be involved in the day-to-day operations of his creation, often it wasn't far from his thoughts. Kept in his papers were Newman's handwritten notes from a speech he was giving in 1965 on "The Future of Television Drama." The notes start out as a straightforward speech ("The future is a long time and it's also the next second . . .") before it becomes a series of bullet points about what he would like to see happen with colour television, which was in discussion at the time. One of those bullet points was "By Autumn of '66 I want to see Dr. Who in colour sold throughout the USA." *Doctor Who* wouldn't be shown in colour until 1970 and wouldn't be sold widely throughout the U.S. until the late 1970s, but it does show Newman's confidence that the series could achieve the penetration into the U.S. market his other creation, *The Avengers*, was starting to achieve in the U.S. around the same time.

Newman didn't stay around to see it happen. By 1967, Newman received overtures from the BBC to renew his five-year contract again. Newman felt he had done all he could. "The amorphous group I had cajoled into shape was so turned [sic] that I no longer felt myself to be necessary," Newman noted in his memoirs.

When Newman left for Canada three years later, critic Maurice Wiggin said in the *Sunday Times*, "Sydney Newman flew back to Canada yesterday and British television will never be the same again." Wiggin also wrote:

> He was the impresario responsible for *Armchair Theatre* and *The Wednesday Play*. He commissioned Harold Pinter's first TV play "A Night Out." It beat *Sunday Night at the London Palladium* in the ratings. He put on "Cathy Come Home" and "Up the Junction." He raised that banner with the strange device, Agitational Contemporaneity.
>
> He caused certain conservatives with delicate stomachs to emigrate to Ireland. He brought the controversial play, deeply concerned with social issues, to millions who never

go to the theatre. Confronted with this strong meat, some threw up their hands in horror and some simply threw up.

But television drama was not wholly "kitchen sink" in the '60s. Mr. Newman was largely instrumental in creating *The Avengers* and *Doctor Who*. He was wholly responsible for creating *Adam Adamant. The Forsyte Saga*, a risk when conceived, was produced under his aegis.

Classic and contemporary, great and God-awful, fantastic and fearfully down-to-earth, British television drama in the '60s was all touched by this Canadian hand.

It was in many ways a eulogy for a way of drama, but also for the man himself. Only halfway through his career, Sydney Newman would never have this impact on the culture of a nation again.

CHAPTER SEVEN

RETURN OF THE PRODIGAL

In some ways, Sydney Newman's return to Canada happened quite suddenly. In others, it was a long time coming.

It happened suddenly in that the right job happened when Newman's job at EMI had come to an abrupt end and Newman wanted to move back home. His wife Betty had also been diagnosed with polychondritis, a severe and often painful inflammation of the cartilage, which may have informed their decision to return to familiar surroundings.

At the same time, the move to Canada also happened because Newman played a long game.

The public record shows that Newman knew the value his position as the BBC's head of drama held in Canada and he worked it to its fullest potential. His old friend and story editor from his CBC days, Nathan Cohen, was by the 1960s a theatre critic and entertainment editor of the *Toronto Star*. The two frequently corresponded. Cohen made sure that his friend received column inches while Newman lived in Britain, virtually acting as Newman's press agent. Even Newman's opinions on Toronto's newly completed City Hall — "I think it's the most beautiful City Hall in the world" — made news in 1966.

It wasn't just Cohen. Other entertainment writers on the *Star*, and to a lesser extent the *Globe and Mail*, were utterly enamoured of Newman's celebrity because it was the best kind — he was a Canadian who made good in the "mother country." A few months before Newman was publicly delighted by Toronto's new City Hall, Cohen wrote that "Everything Newman has done in England, first as head of drama for ABC and then with the BBC, are things he tried to do here, and in virtually the same language and manner. The difference is that in Canada he didn't have the producers and writers to make his ideas materialize."

Newman's well-oiled PR machine kept his name out there in Canada. And it paid off, though not quite in the way Newman wanted.

Newman wanted to return to Canada to a post like the president of the CBC. At times it seemed like he was actively campaigning for it. While Head of Drama Group at the BBC, he did an interview with reporter William Ronald for the CBC arts series *The Umbrella*, which aired on November 27, 1966. The raw footage is intriguing. Although never directly mentioning it, Ronald is clearly goading Newman to comment on the "*Seven Days* Affair," in which Patrick Watson and Laurier LaPierre's popular, maverick news program *This Hour Has Seven Days* was cancelled (Newman demurs answering). Ronald has slightly more success getting Newman to state his feelings on the lack of original dramas being produced in Canada. "I think it's tragic," he says. "Drama provides a sense of self to the audience that is easy to take and can be exciting. And for a country of Canada's size now not to have a really big and exciting drama I think is a tremendous loss to the sense of consciousness of the nation."

Newman never achieved his goal of becoming the head of the CBC, but he came infuriatingly close. During 1966 and 1967 it was an open secret that the CBC's beleaguered president Alphonse Ouimet wanted out. Newman was certainly interested. But in 1966, Secretary of State Judy LaMarsh offered Newman to be commissioner of the

National Film Board of Canada instead. Newman turned it down as he didn't, at the time, deem it a challenge worthy of breaking his BBC contract. LaMarsh asked him what role would make him break his contract and he said the CBC presidency. LaMarsh wasn't in a position to offer that, though there exists a note afterward to LaMarsh in Newman's papers, wherein he asks her if there is any interest in him in that position.

A year later, in August 1967, Newman was summoned to Ottawa to meet with Prime Minister Lester B. Pearson to discuss the CBC job. Newman flew over first class at the CBC's expense, saw Expo '67 (also at the CBC's expense), all the while fending off reporters buzzing about whether or not Newman was going to become the next CBC president.

And then it all went south. Newman's arrival in Ottawa coincided with visiting French President Charles De Gaulle creating an international incident when De Gaulle, giving a speech at Montreal City Hall, proclaimed "Vive le Québec libre! Vive, vive, vive le Canada français!" The meeting with Pearson never happened. Newman was fobbed off onto Marc Lalonde, later a cabinet minister but then an advisor in Pearson's office. Lalonde was unimpressed, snubbed Newman in a variety of ways, and Newman left insulted.[56]

In 1969, CBC Vice-President Eugene Hallman decided to split the CBC's operations into two clusters: information and entertainment. Knowlton Nash, the CBC's Washington correspondent (later the anchor of *The National*) became the director of information programs. Hallman tried to recruit Newman to head up the entertainment division. It wasn't the top job, but it would be big enough. But Newman found the rank-and-file CBC dispirited after previous regimes and he privately told Nathan Cohen that he thought Hallman was "timid" and "evasive."

---

56   In the end, the next CBC president was George Forrester Davison, a career civil servant.

But Newman got a job offer from an unexpected place while visiting his daughter who was at school in Ottawa. An old buddy from his NFB days, Pierre Juneau, was now heading up the Canadian Radio and Television Commission, a regulatory body that was just beginning to consider what requirements television and film should have in terms of Canadian content. Juneau asked Newman if he would be interested in working as a special advisor to him at the CRTC.

Newman jumped at it. In the same letter he told his pal Nathan Cohen at the *Toronto Star* that he wasn't taking the CBC job, he told him he had accepted the CRTC job. "I'm all a-twitter about it and am full of great ideas about improving Can arts used by TV," Newman wrote. "Mind you I might find it too lofty-browed after a while but the only way to find out if the water is too cold is to jump right in."

It was only a one-year contract and the pay was less than the CBC job,[57] but the CRTC would pay his moving expenses. As the job was a government position, it required permission of Treasury Board — a process where the wheels ground ever more slowly. Newman almost got cold feet. "Why the hell do I want to go home?!" he wrote a friend. But soon enough, approval was given and on December 16, 1969, Newman finally had a contract.

Sydney Newman was going home.

Just as he had done when he started at ABC and the BBC, Newman came out swinging. He gave a lively, provocative interview with the *Toronto Star* on January 9, 1970: "People are tired of being fed innocuous pap," he said. "Now is the time and Canada is the place to do something about that." Later in the same piece, Newman said, less than modestly, "I have a few ideas about broadcasting, and through the CTRC I hope to exert a little influence." Even Lee Edwards, who wrote the article, noted that was "the understatement of the year."

The CRTC had only begun its mandate two years prior, in 1968, and just before Newman's arrival they had devised what is

---

57 It was a one-year contract for $23,000 — the equivalent of $145,000 today.

now known as "Canadian content" rules, which set forth that sixty percent of television broadcast in Canada should be Canadian in origin. Newman's official title was director of broadcast programmes branch. He had a department of forty people who checked up on the activities, programming and ad content of Canadian television stations. Newman's job was to police the broadcasters. "I send letters of chastisement when the money-grubbing shits buy too many U.S. programmes or lie in commercials or distort the news," he explained in correspondence. He was now a "poacher turned gamekeeper."

The new Canadian content policy was not popular among broadcasters, who filled the airwaves with American content. In interviews, Newman was unrepentantly pugnacious. "If the broadcasters don't like the new regulations they should be blaming themselves. If they'd got up off their fannies and done the job they should have done the new regulations wouldn't be necessary."

Privately, Newman wondered if this was all it was cracked up to be. In July 1970, he wrote a long letter to his old friend Verity Lambert. "I wonder how long it's going to satisfy me personally. Frankly I can see my utter boredom with it in about six months from now. It's all so slow." Complicating matters, he found his old stomping ground, Ottawa, dull. There was a "cocktail circuit" of diplomats and arts personalities but Betty's illness had flared up badly and they stayed close to home, a newly built penthouse apartment in the Vanier district of the capital. "We would have much preferred to get a house," Newman continues in his letter to Verity Lambert, "but Betty can't count yet on expending too much energy like stairs, gardening, extensive house cleaning and so forth." Betty now required daily cortisone shots. She wasn't impressed with her specialist and they were pondering another doctor in Toronto — 450 kilometres away.

Newman was struggling with his new life. "It's all somewhat abstract and remote," he wrote Lambert, "with no tensions, no deadlines and no dealings with all those nutty, exciting guys that we all mixed it up with in the creative show-biz world."

All that would change for Newman sooner than he might have expected.

CHAPTER EIGHT

"LE BOSS UNILINGUE"

Newman's letter to Verity Lambert complaining of his restlessness and concern he wouldn't be able to stick out his job at the CRTC was dated July 8, 1970. A few days later, Newman gave six months' notice to Juneau and indicated he wouldn't work at the CRTC beyond his one-year contract.

Shortly after, Newman was away on vacation when he received a call from Gérard Pelletier, who had succeeded Judy LaMarsh as Secretary of State. Pelletier asked Newman if he wanted to become government film commissioner and head of the National Film Board of Canada.

If Newman had any concerns, he did not mention them. Newman had turned down the position once before in 1966, but at that point he was doing a job he enjoyed at the BBC. Both Pelletier and Judy LaMarsh approached Newman because he was recommended by Newman's old mentor, NFB founder John Grierson, who was now teaching at McGill University. Newman also appealed to Pelletier because the NFB was branching out to do more than documentaries and moving into dramatic shorts and feature films, and Newman's experience with producing drama in two countries would be a big advantage.

Nathan Cohen wrote in the *Toronto Star*, somewhat disingenuously given his friendship with Newman, "Certain things can be safely predicted by anyone who has followed Newman's career over a long period of time. He will certainly want to see the film board do far more feature-length productions, especially in the way of fiction."

In the time since Newman edited and later produced the *Canada Carries On* series for the National Film Board of Canada in the 1940s, the NFB had gone through massive changes and even more massive upheaval. In 1956, the NFB moved its operations away from drab Ottawa to the more cosmopolitan Montreal. By 1970, the organization employed over 1,000 people. The NFB ran its own film lab and distributed its own films. It even had offices around the globe.

Once on a visit to an NFB plant, John Grierson, horrified by what his Film Board had become, screamed down a hall "I'd fire them all!" Only Grierson couldn't do that — nor anyone else. During the 1960s, it was decided that as a government agency, salaries within the NFB were to be brought in line with government ones and the positions were also subject to the same collective bargaining process as any other within government. The result was filmmakers at the NFB had full-time permanent positions, protected by a union — a level of pay and job security most filmmakers would only find in their wildest dreams.

The difference between people at the NFB and civil service, though, was that the NFB was much more political — in every possible sense of the term.

The organization was political, first of all, in the nationalist sense. There were units for French and English filmmakers, and the Quiet Revolution[58] made its mark on the francophone filmmakers, who, as

---

58 The Quiet Revolution was a period of massive sweeping change both politically and culturally within the province of Québec that included the secularization of the former Catholic society, an emphasis on French as the majority language and the introduction of sovereigntist politics.

the 1960s progressed, became increasingly dedicated to expressing and reflecting a sense of Québécois identity in their work. With the NFB headquartered in Montreal, this reality was all-encompassing.

Secondly, it was political in an activist sense. Many of the filmmakers, both French and English, were devoted to social justice causes, which they expressed in a variety of ways ranging from left-of-centre animated cartoons to full-fledged Marxist tracts on film.[59]

Thirdly, it was political in terms of its culture. Both English and French employees belonged to the same union — Le Syndicat général des cinéastes et techniciens — and the union was vocal when it felt the rights of its employees were encroached upon.

Newman's predecessor, Hugo McPherson — who took the job instead of Newman in 1966 — had a reign that was beleaguered, to put it mildly.[60] A contemporary of Marshall McLuhan, McPherson was a professor at the University of Western Ontario who had been given a poisoned chalice almost from the start. The Liberal government of Pierre Trudeau enforced austerity measures and forced the NFB to make drastic cuts that resulted in a reduction of seventy jobs, an ugly process in which McPherson felt betrayed by Gérard Pelletier, who hadn't backed him up throughout, and was under fire from the filmmakers' union, who went behind his back and complained to Pelletier.

McPherson wasn't having an easy ride on the programming side, either. In April 1970, he made the controversial decision to not release Jacques Leduc's film *Cap d'espoir*. A documentary about Quiet Revolution–era Québec, McPherson banned it ostensibly for the swearing and vulgarity used on screen.[61]

---

59 But the nationalist politics impacted this: Academic Gary Evans points out that while English Canadians could do documentaries critical of the economic system, like the 1968 documentary *The Things I Cannot Change*, any time their French counterparts tried such a thing they were branded radicals.

60 Gérard Pelletier called McPherson "a disaster."

61 Newman kept the ban on the film when he arrived at the NFB, but the decision was his predecessor's — a distinction few of Newman's critics made, given future events.

When McPherson, bitter and burned out, finally resigned, he did so with a flair for the dramatic: he didn't show up at an event that he was officiating with Pelletier, embarrassing his minister.

This was the National Film Board that Sydney Newman was about to join.

There was one other way in which Newman was completely unprepared. In Newman's memoirs, he describes his terse meeting with Prime Minister Pearson's advisor Marc Lalonde about becoming president of the CBC. Newman says about how he felt afterward, "On the plane, in talking to Betty, it was clear that things were happening in Canada that being in Britain had made me totally ignorant of. French Canada was a fact that could not be taken for granted. If the arrogance of Lalonde was an indication of things to come, Canada was in dire trouble. England was where I had lived for over nine years and had never thought of it as home. Lalonde made me feel that Canada was no longer home, either."

Like so many English Canadians of his generation, Newman was unprepared and ill-equipped for the Quiet Revolution taking place in Québec in the late 1960s and early 1970s. The Quiet Revolution brought to light the differences between francophones and anglophones, as well as Québec and the rest of Canada. But more than that, it brought to light a conflict between a people who had grievances against the dominant powers in Canada at the time. In many ways this lack of understanding would prove to be Newman's downfall at the NFB.

Understanding that Newman might have difficulties bridging the cultural divide, Pelletier suggested that Newman take on André Lamy, who worked in the Québec film industry, as a deputy, with the understanding that Lamy could interface with the French filmmakers. Newman would grow to rely on Lamy in the coming years. But the French filmmakers were not assuaged by the presence of a Québécois in residence as second-in-command. Newman, in spite of his credentials producing television and film, was never taken seriously by the French filmmakers. Shortly after author Gary Evans finished writing his history of the National Film Board — *In the National Interest: A Chronicle of the National Film Board of Canada from* 1949 *to* 1989 — he spoke with Québécois filmmaker and author Jacques Godbout, who worked at the NFB during the 1970s. Evans told Godbout that he thought Newman wanted to steer the NFB toward more dramas.[62]

Godbout replied to Evans that Newman was regarded by the French filmmakers as "Nothing more than a bus driver."

The lack of interest became open contempt at times. Newman was called by NFB employees and outsiders "*le boss unilingue.*" It was a term he despised.[63] Newman wrote about the situation in 1976 to his old friend and colleague Peter Luke, "After all the flattery I had become accustomed to in England, can you imagine how I liked being referred to in the French press here as the . . . 'unilingue Anglophone "boss"?' Yes, the press would deliberately use 'boss' in English to nail the insult home."

Newman, writing the letter to Luke a year after he left the NFB, was surprisingly reflective and even-handed about the situation: "the trouble was that the French Canadians acted to me just as I suppose the people in Ulster act to the reps from Whitehall. Or the way Catholics used to regard (if they still don't) the head of the Ulster Constabulary! Mind you, it was not personal by intention, but being the kind of jerk I am, needing self-assurances of all kinds, I took it personally, which certainly inhibited me."

Newman explained to Gary Evans in interviews for *In the National Interest* that he tried to engage with the French filmmakers, meeting with the directors in particular once a week in his office for drinks. But,

---

62 In the event, the hope that Newman would steer the NFB to more feature film production was, in actuality, hobbled somewhat by the Canadian government's creation of the Canadian Film Development Corporation, which financed Canadian films outside the auspices of the NFB and rose to prominence during Newman's tenure.

63 In many ways, the charges of him being unilingual galvanized Newman. Newman started out at the NFB demonstrating a willingness to learn French and even took lessons. By the end of his term, he publically touted the fact he had given up trying to learn the language at all.

ultimately, Newman was disappointed in the results of these meetings. When prodded by Evans he explained why: he invited them in order to be hospitable, but they, in return, never invited him to their homes.

He was, after all, the bus driver.

In many ways, Newman was hoisted by his own petard. The self-proclaimed defender of the common man was now viewed as a conservative, upper-middle-class establishment figure. And where his outsider status enabled him to revolutionize the BBC, here, it ensured he was kept out of the revolution.

However, one of the first things Newman did upon arriving at the National Film Board of Canada was to ensure that one of the great masterpieces of Canadian film was completed.

Upon their arrival, Newman and André Lamy set up meetings to look at the films currently in production at the NFB with their directors. "Over a period of two and a half months we saw not less than 240 films — 98 hours approximately of screening time." Newman told a Parliamentary Standing Committee on Broadcasting, Films and Assistance to the Arts in April 1971. "Generally, it was impressive. Although a few of the films were somewhat incomprehensible, none were actually bad. All were competent, professionally handled as could be done in Hollywood . . . all were sincere and honest — some so that they were positively boring." (Newman was privately less censorious. He said they "stank with probity.") He said to the committee that at least fifteen to twenty per cent were "positively beautiful."

One film in particular stood out. It was a film directed by Claude Jutra that started under McPherson's reign as commissioner, when Jutra had turned down a script by screenwriter Clement Perron. Perron used the rejection as an opportunity to complain about the hard life he had, starting out in an asbestos-mining community where the mine boss would contemptuously throw out candy from his sleigh to the children on the streets at Christmas. Perron's uncle was both the town's shopkeeper and undertaker.

Jutra told Perron to write a film about that.

A co-production of the NFB and Gendron Films,[64] Jutra shot *Mon Oncle Antoine* in 1969. When Newman screened the work in progress, he had concerns about the ending of the film and offered Jutra suggestions on how to reshoot key scenes.[65] But Newman did more than make suggestions — he found the extra $40,000 so Jutra could reshoot those sequences in February 1971. When the film was released in the autumn of 1971 it proved popular with the public[66] as well as being highly acclaimed.[67] Over the succeeding decades, the film has topped multiple polls by *Sight and Sound* and the Toronto International Film Festival as the best Canadian film ever made. And yet, Newman's role in this has largely gone unheralded.[68]

Newman wanted Jutra to immediately capitalize on the success of *Mon Oncle Antoine* and make another film. Newman was following his long-honed instincts; once he saw talent, he immediately redeployed it on other projects. But where that worked on television, with playwrights like Harold Pinter and Alun Owen, the NFB was bound

---

64 With a $400,000 budget, a co-production was necessary as it was double the maximum budget for an NFB film.

65 These were primarily scenes from the climax of the film when the titular Uncle Antoine loses the coffin of a boy while transporting it at night on a sled.

66 It took until well into 1972 to get the film into a wide release. The film legendarily sat on the NFB's shelves for months after completion as Gendron Films, the co-producer who had the distribution rights, had failed to find the means to show the film in Canada initially, which meant it received acclaim long before Canadians could see it!

67 However, even here Newman and the NFB management sabotaged their relationship with the French filmmakers. According to Martin Knelman in his 1977 book on Canadian film, *This Is Where We Came In: The Career and Character of Canadian Film*, NFB restrictions around travel would permit only Jutra and Newman to attend the Canadian Film Awards ceremony, where *Mon Oncle Antoine* won. This prompted *Mon Oncle Antoine*'s screenwriter Clement Perron to send Newman a telegram, saying, "Congratulations on your success with *Mon Oncle Antoine.*"

68 Indeed, Newman's involvement in securing the extra funding for *Mon Oncle Antoine* wasn't reported on until Martin Knelman's *This Is Where We Came In*, and while it was later mentioned in Gary Evans' *In the National Interest*, it has been scarcely remarked upon since.

by its own hierarchy and systems. The French Program Committee, which determined who made what films for the Film Board, deemed that between *Mon Oncle Antoine* and *Wow* (another film Jutra made in 1970), Jutra had done enough features — it was time for other filmmakers to get a turn. The popularity of *Mon Oncle Antoine* didn't even matter.[69] Newman was helpless to change this. Jutra left the NFB shortly after to direct films on his own.

"Things sound bad in Canada from the newspapers here," Verity Lambert wrote Newman in October, 1970. "How is it affecting life there? Or do you not notice any difference. It seems unbelievable that kidnapping and political murder can happen even in Canada. Do take care!!"

In October 1970, the FLQ (Front de libération du Québec), a Québécois separatist paramilitary group that had been responsible for several acts of terrorism throughout the late '60s, kidnapped British diplomat James Cross, then kidnapped and subsequently killed a Québec politician, Pierre Laporte. For the first and only time, Prime Minister Pierre Trudeau invoked the War Measures Act during peacetime. Civil rights were suspended. It became known as the October Crisis.

Verity Lambert was right to be concerned about Newman. The NFB was headquartered in Montreal where tanks now roamed the streets and combat troops scouted the perimeter of the NFB's grounds every four hours.[70] "Then of course, Cross is kidnapped, a week later Laporte is murdered and the whole fucking Canadian army moves in," Newman said in a 1983 interview with CKVU producer Emmanuelle Gattuso. "I'm one of the most conspicuous federal presences in the province of

---

69 Or perhaps it did. The response to *Mon Oncle Antoine* was much cooler in Quebec, where its apolitical, nostalgic tone seemed out of place with the current mood.

70 "Equally absurd," Gary Evans wrote in his book *In the National Interest*, "was the sight of the [NFB's] regular security, composed of aging war-veteran commissionaires, patrolling constantly on electric golf carts."

Québec — *le commisionnaire du film* — and the Film Board is guarded. I have a black car to drive me everywhere with a little guy to look after me and my car had a siren inside with a button to press in case somebody tried to break into the car — they thought I might be kidnapped!"

Undeterred, Newman ordered the filmmakers to go outside and film everything. The French side readily agreed; the English side refused even though director Robin Spry wanted to go. Newman insisted that there be English participation and Spry was allowed. Thirty people in all filmed around Montreal, though nothing would be done with it for another three years because of the legal actions around those tried as a result.

Sydney Newman at the NFB, 1970.

Inside the NFB compound at that time, Newman and André Lamy were tending to a crisis of their own. In 1969, director Denys Arcand, now a highly regarded feature film director but then an *enfant terrible* documentary director at the NFB, shot a documentary ostensibly about the textile industry in Québec. That film came together during 1970 under the title *On est au coton*. The film was unapologetically subjective. Arcand was concerned about portraying the life of textile workers and the effect an imminent factory closure would have on those workers. After seeing a rough cut, Edward King, the head of Dominion Textiles, demanded that his interview be taken out of the film.[71] Arcand responded by reading King's request over a black screen.

It was, in many ways, the sort of political documentary American filmmakers like Michael Moore would do decades later.

But the NFB of 1970 wasn't necessarily equipped to handle that. As Gary Evans explains: "At the same time, some textile industry executives saw the film and described it as a violent class struggle . . . Some believed that it promoted class warfare and . . . abandoned any pretense of balance; others called it a Marxist propaganda tract. Most ominous of all, there was a sequence in which two members of the Front de libération du Québec were identified as they called for violence." On October 16, the day before Pierre Laporte was murdered, Newman asked NFB lawyers for an opinion. They believed sedition charges were possible.

Newman tried to broker a solution, and while Arcand complied somewhat passive aggressively (the textile executive's letter was excised but he still left the screen black), Arcand nonetheless cut the interviews with FLQ members. But even so, the Canadian Textile Institute — who cooperated with the NFB in making the film — wrote Newman in February 1971, to say that the film was, according to Gary Evans, "dishonest, disruptive and a gross representation of the Canadian textile industry." Shortly thereafter, Newman decided

---

71 Thirty years later, Arcand received permission from Edward King's son to use the interview with his late father and *On est au coton* was reinstated to its original form.

to suppress the film. "There have been criticisms about the film's objectivity[72] that have come to me from a very wide variety of sources — enough to make this action necessary."

But Newman's ban was, in many ways, meaningless. A bootleg videotape of the film made it out of the NFB and it was widely distributed and shown at "illegal" screenings at CEGEPs (community colleges) and universities in Québec. "Newman banned it and bootleg copies began to circulate," Arcand said in a *Globe and Mail* interview in December 1972. "Every junior college in Québec has a copy of it. The universities all have copies. It was even shown in Toronto by left-wing groups and the film established at one blow my reputation . . . I had no reputation before."

Newman reaped the whirlwind for his actions. His personal papers have handwritten notes for what he wrote was a "first talk to abortive meeting with FR Unit on May 3/71." The use of "abortive." indicates it did not go well. Given the incendiary language Newman uses in his notes, it's perhaps not surprising. Newman tries to defend his record thus far, but he goes after the French filmmakers for their threat to go to the press about *On est au coton*, particularly their demand that, unless a reply is given to the signatories within ten days, "the rumors of political censorship will be confirmed." Newman was apoplectic about this. "Do you that signed it and the other signatories know what the hell you are doing? That you are employing the tactics of gangsters — the blackmail of fascists?! What sort of an enemy do these think they are bravely facing? . . . I say shame on all those who signed that piece of paper — not for the search of a real problem but to the threat of blackmail."

As the film remained in limbo, its notoriety grew. In October 1971, André L'Heureux, Director of the Secretariat for Political Action for

---

72 It must be said though that Arcand never set out to make an objective film. As he quipped in a December 1972 *Globe and Mail* article, "The Film Board makes thousands of films to say that all goes well in Canada, that the western wheat fields are very beautiful and Paul Anka is an extraordinary star. So I think it is just normal that there should now and then be film which says that everything is rotten and that we live in a country that is corrupt from top to bottom."

the Confederation of National Trade Unions, wrote an open letter in *Le Devoir* that was signed by thirty-one affiliated textile workers' unions in Québec. Their letter demanded that the workers be allowed to decide for themselves if the film was inaccurate and that the NFB release the film. The letter stated that "This arbitrary and unilateral decision is unacceptable unless the NFB is actually supposed to be an instrument of propaganda for the exclusive use of the state and the employers."

Newman hit back with his own open letter in *Le Devoir*. His thesis was simple: the film was not accurate or fair. "[The film] is often moving, with moments of gritty conviction, but I am afraid does not always adhere to factual truths." Newman proceeded to correct the record on where it was claimed the film was inaccurate.[73]

But it's in an early paragraph of his open letter where Newman establishes why he feels he must suppress Arcand's film. "You ask in your letter by whose authority can a film be stopped," Newman wrote. "My answer must be by the same authority that grants permission for the film to be made in the first place — the Government Film Commissioner, who is given the responsibility by the National Film Act of the Parliament of Canada." Newman appealed to the tradition that both French and English staff make "films of significance and importance about this complicated and now troubled country of ours, sometimes with beauty but always with integrity and fairness."

Newman concludes, "I hope the workers in the thirty or so unions on whose behalf you wrote will understand that the reputation of our films and of our staff is too valuable to lose because of one film.

---

73 Among the examples Newman cites: a worker says he could make $1.25 in
the United States (according to Newman it was about the same). The old-
fashioned looms were making workers deaf (by the time the film was completed,
silent looms were apparently in operation where filming had taken place). An
employee with silicosis was not "even vaguely representative of the industry as a
whole." And Newman took particular glee in pointing out, "You are quite right
in suggesting that the textile companies have protested to me about the facts in
the film but so, Mr. L'Heureux, have trade unionists who . . . think the film does
not adequately represent an up-to-date view of the entire industry . . . it glorifies
a blood and strife view of worker-boss relations during the 1930s and '40s."

For the reasons stated above, the Film Board cannot release this film. This may be called censorship; I call it the exercise of public responsibility."

Over the years, Newman's decisions with these films have been derided as an act of political censorship. Film critic André Loiselle in the *Encyclopedia of Documentary Film* says of *On est au coton*, "The film was deemed subversive by NFB Commissioner Sydney Newman and banned." In another book on Arcand's films, Loiselle posits that Edward King "had powerful friends who put pressure on NFB Commissioner Sydney Newman to pull the plug on Arcand's already completed documentary."

However, Newman's suppression of *On est au coton* was more pragmatic than political. The same was true when, later in 1971, Newman similarly banned 24 *Heures en Plus*, a documentary by Gilbert Groulx that examined the economic system in Québec. The documentary was heavily critical of capitalist society and came to the conclusion that it was necessary to overthrow capitalism and establish a new society. Newman barred Groulx from finishing the film. "It's [the film's] content and conclusions [that] would be difficult to accept by the people who uphold our democratic society," Newman told the director of French Production at the NFB. "In the interest of all the filmmakers of the NFB and so that the NFB can continue to work throughout Canada, I can't imagine permitting the work to be finished on the film or permitting the distribution of the film." Newman then also seized the production assets and had them put into separate vaults so it wouldn't get bootlegged like *On est au coton*.

Newman was surprisingly transparent in articulating his reasons for suppressing both 24 *Heures en Plus* and *On est au coton*. By Newman's standards, these filmmakers weren't producing films independently; they were employed by a government agency and Newman was answerable for its content because the NFB was a government-funded institution. For Newman, a radical, subjective documentary could cause serious damage. "I simply have to contain the more exuberant notions about social organization. I want to rock the boat . . . but I've got to watch that we don't capsize in the process."

"One of the problems here is trying to defend the Film Board from extreme public censure which might force politicians to say, 'Well, who needs this place; sure it's a beautiful place, it makes lovely films, but if they rock the boat too bloody much, let's get rid of it.' If fifteen percent of my staff are well-politicized creative people, I have to remember the other eighty-five percent in whose work there's no overt political view. I don't want to jeopardize them."

It was a view the English-Canadian establishment could get behind. Newman's position was summarized in the *Globe and Mail* headline, "Film board head asks: Should the taxpayer subsidize a movie advocating a revolution?"

Arcand, for his part, accused Newman of being out of touch. "Sydney Newman doesn't understand what Québec is all about," Arcand told the *Globe and Mail* in 1972. "He doesn't speak to anyone who could tell him the facts."

Two months after Newman defended his decision around *On est au coton* with the open letter to the trade unions, Newman met Prime Minister Pierre Trudeau for the first time. Trudeau told him, "I admire your bravery and your answer to that scurrilous letter. I think you did the right thing."

The truth was that, ultimately, suppressing the film was the only option available to Newman. He couldn't actually fire anyone from the NFB. The iron-clad job security the Film Board offered as a unionized government agency tied Newman's hands[74] in terms of cutting out the most radical elements or, indeed, finding new blood for the organization. The only thing Newman did have power over was determining if a film would be released to the public or not.

But the struggle with these documentaries cast a pall over Newman's

---

74   And yet the benefits of a government position were also an advantage to Newman. When asked why Newman stayed for his full five-year term, NFB historian Gary Evans explained that Newman's position as government film commissioner was deemed the equivalent of a deputy minister. Having stayed his full term, Newman was eligible for a large pension.

five-year term at the National Film Board. And the heightened climate led to some precipitous — even poor — decisions on Newman's part. Newman overruled the French Programme Committee when, in 1971 they approved a feature film by Michel Brault, the cinematographer on *Mon Oncle Antoine*, about those incarcerated when *habeas corpus* was suspended during the October Crisis. Newman didn't like Brault,[75] a Québec nationalist, and Newman admitted he was "touchy" about the film's mix of fiction and documentary, which is odd, since the approach wouldn't have been out of place in a Ken Loach episode of *The Wednesday Play*. Newman's intervention made headlines in English Canada where Newman had to defend his decision. "Brault's script wasn't good enough . . . this is fraught with the most serious nationalist consequences. It is very difficult now to bring a fully rational point of view to bear on those immediate events." Brault, for his part, made the film independently and *Les Ordres* has been acclaimed as a landmark of Canadian cinema ever since its release in 1974.

As ever, Newman was gracious and admitted when he was wrong. At Cannes in 1975, Brault was celebrating following his win as best director for *Les Ordres* when a waiter brought a bottle of champagne given to him by another table. Sitting at that table, alone, was Newman. He raised his glass to Brault.

Newman did get better at handling the politics. Newman had challenges about the fairness and balance for Arcand's next film, *Québec: Duplessis et après*, but he released it anyway, even to Arcand's surprise. When Pierre Perrault made *L'Acadie, L'Acadie?!?*, a politically charged documentary about Acadian university students in Moncton and their struggle for French language rights in New

---

75 "Some of the French staff at the Film Board, a few, were being very difficult — they were kicking the shit out of me and enjoying it," Newman says in a transcript of an interview he did with CKVU's Emmanuelle Gattuso in 1983. Newman, who was editing the transcript, crossed out the lines where he says, "That's what really bothered me because . . . [Michel] Brault — well he was not . . . well, anyway they made a monkey out of me."

Brunswick, Newman told him that he liked the film so much he wanted to show it on English television on the CBC. But, as if to prove no good deed goes unpunished, the CBC asked that seventy-five minutes be cut out of the English version — and Newman was blamed for this.

For every victory Newman gained at the NFB, there would be political blowback or stony silence. One of the earliest successes Newman had was finalizing negotiations between the Film Board and the CBC that resulted in NFB films being screened during prime time. This was Newman's populist instinct at work, trying to get the NFB the largest audience possible. But the filmmakers' union, Le Syndicat, complained to Pelletier, and, furthermore, complained that Newman gave the announcement only in English and told them they could "stuff it" regarding his unilingualism. (Newman claimed he was referring to his decision about the CBC). Newman immediately called the executive of the union on the carpet, reprimanded the union and demanded — and received — a written apology. It was a move that indicated Newman would not be cowed by the union as his predecessor was.[76]

Toward the end of his first turbulent year at the NFB, Newman called his old mentor John Grierson late at night and said, "I don't know what to do. Can you help me?" Grierson came over to Newman's home and talked with him for three hours. It was the last time Newman saw him. Grierson died two months later.

In spite of his conflicts with the French filmmakers, Newman actually tried to get more work about Québec seen by English Canadians. In 1973, he helped develop a series the NFB made for television, *Adieu Alouette*, which looked at a different aspect of Québécois culture every episode. The series was acclaimed by critics. *Cinema Canada* pointed out that "one programme managed to deal with the huge question

---

76 Newman had his own methods of antagonizing Francophones. Once while an audience was listening earnestly to a speech in French, and the English members of the audience were nodding politely, Newman turned to his companion and said loudly, "Will someone please tell me what the fuck is going on!?"

of the Church in Québec in half an hour, while most controversial Québécois films are usually two, three hours long. Self-analysis is a long and painful process but even some Québécois think that those films are awfully boring." But the NFB hardly acknowledged it.

And Newman had a hand in getting one of the best documentaries about the October Crisis made and seen across Canada. By 1973, the footage the French filmmakers and Robin Spry had gathered in October and November 1970 was finally able to be used. But the French filmmakers all but abandoned it. That left Robin Spry, one of the English filmmakers, to fashion it into two films: *Reaction: A Portrait of a Society in Crisis* (about the events leading up to the October Crisis) and *Action: The October Crisis of* 1970. It was the latter film that is perhaps best known. Spry's film stitches together the events of October, 1970, and the reactions of ordinary Québecers and politicians to the unfolding events (most famously including a sequence where a shaken René Lévesque confronts reporters, moments after learning of the death of Pierre Laporte).

As he did with the French filmmakers, Newman fought Spry over the film, wanting a variety of changes. Most of them were negotiable, but the one non-negotiable change was the voiceover narration on the ending. Spry's original text was, "For Canada, the arrests, the kidnappings, the killing and the removal of civil liberties have come as a sad and costly loss of innocence. Will Québec separate?" Newman ordered the last three words cut from the film. Newman would later claim it was an artistic judgement, not a political one: he felt Spry ended on the right note with the loss of Canada's innocence. "That a province had been invaded by the Federal army was what the film was really about . . . lurid events that normally happened in foreign countries happened here. We had lost our innocence."

Newman fought hard to get *Action* shown on television. The CBC felt *Action* was precipitous and dragged their heels in showing it. Newman pressed the point during a visit to China with CBC President Laurent Picard. It was finally shown in April 1975 — over a year after it had been made.

Sydney Newman in China, September 1974.

Canadian nationalist politics weren't the only political agenda dominating the 1970s. Feminism became a dominant force, and it manifested itself in particular during Newman's final year at the NFB, when an English-Canadian filmmaker at the NFB, Kathleen Shannon, began lobbying for a separate filmmaking unit for women. At the same time, filmmaker Anne Claire Poirier was pushing for more features about women on the French side of the NFB. The filmmakers struggled to find funding. Sometimes it was just bad luck. (Their attempt to apply for a special fund for projects for the 1975 International Women's Year was foiled, as they applied a day after the deadline.) Sometimes there wasn't political will. (The Treasury Board turned down the request for a separate $1.3 million budget for women's films at the NFB.)

In spite of the lack of funds, Newman gave Shannon the go-ahead to start a women's unit,[77] with a "make-do" budget cobbled together from various sources. That led to the creation of Studio D,

---

77 Poirier's insistence that women's films have equal funding with other French productions meant that there would be no French counterpart until 1986.

a women's filmmaking unit that became a major creative force within the NFB in later decades.

And yet, providing the assist to start Studio D is not usually listed among Newman's accomplishments at the National Film Board of Canada. Nor is his work in developing dramatic feature films in English and French. Nor his critical assistance on *Mon Oncle Antoine*. History has chosen to remember that, as government film commissioner, Sydney Newman banned two films (and hobbled many others) and engaged in a series of inexorable political conflicts.

Canadian film critic Martin Knelman summed up the NFB of that era when he wrote, "The radical filmmakers would have liked Grierson's maxim, 'Public lies may not be told.' But Newman had to live by another Grierson maxim: 'The king's shilling may not be abused.'"

Newman himself felt he failed at the NFB. In 1983, Newman agreed to appear on the Vancouver TV series *Masters of Television*. For this he was "pre-interviewed" by CKVU producer Emmanuelle Gattuso, and Newman spoke with greater candour than he would on television. "I did some good things, but I didn't really in my mind turn the Film Board around — I didn't make it electric, which is what I wanted to do and thought I could do."

In this interview, conducted less than a decade after he left the NFB, Newman was blunt about what did him in. "If it wasn't for that damn kidnapping of those two guys — the coming of the War Measures Act — I might have been able to do it. But Québec, as you know, was in a state of such incredible turmoil, of ferment, and here was me trying."

Newman always loved a particular quote by James Thurber: "Let us not look back in anger nor forward in fear, but around in awareness." When Newman was at the BBC, he had this quote printed on cards and given to staff.

At the NFB, Newman wanted to do the same thing for the people who worked there. And yet, in his papers are numerous memos indicating that, despite their efforts, he and his staff struggled to find a workable French translation of the quote.

CHAPTER NINE

ONE PIECE OF ADVICE
IN TEN BEING TAKEN

It was evident to everyone that Sydney Newman would not have a second five-year term at the National Film Board of Canada. He was not bilingual and he did not have the faith of much of the organization. Even Newman himself understood this — though he was devastated and bitter. "Newman felt betrayed by the Film Board," wrote Gary Evans in his book *In the National Interest*, "and, in paraphrasing Joyce, concluded that Canada, like Ireland, was like a sow who eats her own farrow."

It was Gérard Pelletier's successor as secretary of state, Hugh Faulkner, who called it a day on Newman's time at the NFB. But Faulkner personally liked Newman and the Trudeau government possibly felt indebted Newman for weathering the storms he had for five years, so they arranged a "golden parachute" for Newman: a two-year appointment to Faulkner as special advisor to the secretary of state for film.

Newman hadn't the publicity machine he had while his friend

Nathan Cohen, who died in 1971, was still alive, but the announcement of his move was still good enough to get him on the front page of the *Toronto Star*'s entertainment section and Newman was still great for a quote. "In Canada, we lack three key elements (for filmmaking): a love of audience . . . we lack business entrepreneurs and we don't have the screenwriters." Newman's job as special advisor was to figure out ways to connect the public and private sectors and to see how the government cultural agencies could better connect with regard to film.

Privately, Newman wasn't quite so convinced about the posting. He said to Peter Luke in a 1976 letter, "I'm now handsomely paid with the rank of (in English terms) permanent undersecretary. So, for just over a year now I've been a kind of glorified bum-boy to the secretary of state, to whom film is about ninth in priority. Can you imagine *me* being an a-d-v-i-s-o-r! And living with *one* piece of advice in *ten* being taken?"

Newman talked about "flirting with offers in England" and setting up his own film company, but the job for Faulkner provided him stability, which he needed with Betty still requiring daily treatments for her illness. He proposed different things to Faulkner, like a "Cinema Canada Corporation," that might combine the National Film Board with the Canadian Film Development Corporation. This plan was reported in the press and Newman had to then deny it. Like nine out of ten of Newman's ideas as an advisor, it didn't go anywhere.

By the end of 1977, Newman had finished his term with Faulkner and was trying to figure out what to do next. He moved back to Toronto to the home he bought with Betty in the 1950s to "be quasi-retired," as he put it in a letter to his friend, writer Clive Exton. "Quasi because we just didn't have enough money."

It was the era of the tax shelter film boom in Canada and Newman worked on a film with some investors. The deal fell through, though Newman was at least paid. Around this time, Newman became convinced that having his own investment clout might help him produce films, but he could never raise the million dollars he felt necessary.

Newman was also having a crisis of confidence after his time at the NFB, and this went on for several years. "Psychologically not quite there yet," he told Irene Shubik. He also said to Peter Luke, "I've been a 'company' man, mollycoddled for so long, whose genius was to know whom to phone when I got into trouble. Who do you phone when you are on your own?"

Verity Lambert, who was now working as an executive at Thames Television, had asked if he was interested in consulting on a script Clive Exton was working on — an adaptation of Gerald Seymour's 1975 novel *Harry's Game*. Newman had hoped this could land him a bigger job, but Lambert wasn't in a position to offer anything at this juncture as it wouldn't go into production for another two years.[78] Newman finally wrote back in May 1977 and expressed his disappointment before adding, "I'm going through a most peculiar state of mind . . . of rejecting the future ... of disgust at the waste of the last ten years (or almost complete waste) . . . and what is most appalling, I'm suffering from a kind of revulsion about the group arts. To boot, my own country, or rather my reaction to it, flattens any enthusiasm I might screw myself up into having."

Verity Lambert wanted to encourage her former boss. "I feel particularly badly at not having written sooner as your letter was in some ways a 'cri-de-coeur,'" she replied in June 1977. "I've been racking my brains on ways to get you over here — there is one way that could be possible and which would take into account your expectations and earnings. If you have a good film series concept — and with ideas like *Avengers* and *Doctor Who* and *Adam Adamant* I don't think that's impossible — it would be something that you could executive produce and own a piece of it."

The problem was that even when Newman was being offered creative work, he turned it down because of what could only be described as his sense of pride. CBC head of drama, John Kennedy, offered him an executive producer job for several episodes of *For the Record*, a prestigious anthology series of docudramas made by the CBC in the 1970s. It was work in the single television play, right up

---

78   In the end, Clive Exton didn't adapt it and Thames wouldn't produce it. Yorkshire Television would eventually adapt it in 1982 working from a script by author Gerald Seymour.

his alley. The fee was good. But Newman turned them down because John Kennedy demanded script approval. He wrote to Irene Shubik, explaining the whole situation: "I told him he had the right to be fully informed on subject matter by synopsis, by word and so on . . . but why did he want to bark when he had a dog to do so, etc., etc. Within a day I turned the whole thing down."

Newman added, "Is this an example of my pure mental health or just pure vanity? It seems to me that never in my life as a departmental head or as an exec prod did I ever demand script approval." It was true — Newman did offer his employees a greater degree of trust and freedom. But the experiences in the vast empire of the BBC of the 1960s were not the same as the substantially smaller empire of the CBC of the 1970s. But Newman couldn't, or wouldn't, see the distinction.

Newman was intrigued by Verity Lambert's suggestion that he try to create a series. Eventually, in 1979, he sent her a proposal. According to his notes at the top of the document he came up with it earlier, around 1976, "one year before *Charlie's Angels* came out."

It was called *Men-Bane*.

The main theme of *Men-Bane*, according to Newman's format document, was "The battle of the sexes with women clearly victorious." Newman went on to explain, "Underlying the suspense, comedy and fast movement in a heightened, high-life, trendy world is a violent battle of the sexes in which three lusty females satirize men's attitudes to women. *Men-Bane* are stories of women hitting back at 10,000 years of male domination by using their wits, bodies and unique strengths."

The proposed series is about a secret "all-purpose crime investigation bureau that specializes in cases where women have been victimized. Bane to them are pimps, sweat-shop operators, choreographers, some evangelists and queers, television directors who take it out on their secretaries, Charlie Mansons and Jim Jones of this world — in short, all exploitive males, especially chauvinist pigs who operate with and without the law."

The organization is run by Poppy (Pops) Brite, a forty- to fifty-year-old ("built like an ox") who smokes cigars and heads up the agency. She's assisted by Liz (Lysistrata de Quincy-Jones) "about 35, a svelte, sleek, tall woman with jet black hair tightly pulled back, always immaculately dressed." An academic star and former tennis pro, she lost everything when she married a Greek shipping tycoon and then got it back while she was a croupier and then mistress of a Monaco gambling house. Finally, there's Cricket, a "diminutive dream girl with a sunny beauty" — a former crook who is naïve about men. She's forced to work for Poppy and Liz.

"The flavour of the stylistic treatment will be romantic realism with a strong send-up quality to bring out the idiocies, humour, tensions and ironies of contemporary international high-life. In short, the not-so-ordinary everyday world will be depicted in a larger-than-life fashion through Poppy (the professional), Liz (the dynamic, cynical sex tease) and the eager-for-life, innocent Cricket."

Generously, it could be said that Newman took the arch, playful style of *The Avengers* and combined it with the camp gender politics of *Charlie's Angels*. But when Newman sent the idea to Verity Lambert through a respected writers' agent, Harvey Unna, her reaction was decidedly mixed. Lambert sent word through Unna that "It really is difficult to judge this on just the breakdown. It could go many ways and although it deals with contemporary themes, it has a rather '60s feel about it. Perhaps Sydney has some ideas about script writers that might alleviate these worries." Unna added, "The lady, as you can see, needs convincing."

Discussions about *Men-Bane* continued during the summer of 1979, but in the end, the best Verity Lambert could offer was an option of "a few months" according to Harvey Unna (Newman wrote "how many?" beside that) and offered £5,000 to develop a script, of which the screenwriter would get half and the rest would be Newman's fee and travelling expenses. Lambert even offered to put up Newman at her home in London. Newman wrote "No way!" beside this, which indicates that he thought the deal was too small, or he could see that Verity was attempting to offer a "make work" project that would go nowhere.

As it was, Newman's connections in the Canadian Film Development Corporation[79] led to his next gig, first acting as a story editor before being called the CFDC's "chief creative consultant." Mostly, Newman advised on scripts sent to the CFDC for funding. "I started getting work as a consultant to the ignoramuses crawling out of the woodwork, setting themselves up as producers," he explained in a letter to writer Clive Exton. Newman offered coverage of films — the sort of work ordinarily left to younger people — for executives, and provided advice to producers about developing their scripts. He worked on other initiatives, like a program to adapt Canadian literary works for films, including Margaret Laurence's *The Diviners*, Mordecai Richler's *Joshua Then and Now* and others.

But it wasn't work Newman enjoyed. "Financially, no complaints whatsoever, but the work is really shitty. The producers (jumped-up accountants and lawyers) are, in the main, venal idiots, the Directors are ignorant and vain." And yet, "I'm the niftiest story-editor around. I am![80] By far — and that ain't hard! — considering the state of the 'art' here."

However, the job paid well,[81] allowed Newman to travel and gave him time off to engage his hobbies — he was an avid woodworker — and to take care of Betty, who, as the 1970s progressed into the 1980s, was becoming more and more frail. "She and I should be having a ball at 'our time of life,'" Newman wrote in a letter to Clive Exton in July 1981. "But Betty is not well at all. She's gone from bad to worse. No bladder, rotten lungs and a tracheotomy so that she breathes through

---

79 The CFDC was the government agency that offered funding and tax credits for films made in Canada. It is now known as Telefilm Canada.

80 Newman wasn't short-selling himself, either. In February 1982, actor, writer and director Gordon Pinsent, whom Newman worked with on developing a script by Pinsent, told André Lamy (by now the head of the Canadian Film Development Corporation) to praise Newman's work: ". . . as far as I can see, all writers should be so greatly assisted in finding their way through the long, lonely tunnel of script writing, as Sydney Newman and the CFDC have done for this writer."

81 And, for a while, CDFC, and later Telefilm Canada, paid homage by offering the Sydney Newman Prize, which went to the Genie Award winner for best adapted screenplay.

a pipe in her neck — on oxygen, 24 hours a day!" At that point, Betty had just come out of hospital after a four-month stay. Newman had set up a bedroom on the ground floor of their house and there was a regimen of nurses, therapists and housekeepers to help care for her. "Betty's strength of will and general good cheer is high — less so, I'm afraid than it was as little as six months ago but still awe-inspiring."

Newman had written Clive Exton to tell of him of his recent good fortune — he had been named an Officer of the Order of Canada. Back when Newman worked for Hugh Faulkner when he was special advisor to secretary of state, Newman sent a note in June 1977, lobbying Faulkner to get him named a Companion of the Order of Canada. "Why have an honours system if not to recognize people who have headed important national organizations?" Newman asked, adding, "I'm sure you'll forgive the chutzpah of this refugee from the creative world." In the end, Newman would have to wait four years to get the letter acknowledging he would be named — and the lower rank of Officer, rather than Companion.

Newman finally received the honour from Governor-General Edward Schreyer on April 21, 1982. But Betty would not be with him at the investiture. Newman's date book entry for December 3, 1981, has a handwritten note by Newman: "Betty's last night." Betty, who had been the one to propose to Sydney, who had stood by him in three countries,[82] who had tolerated his many tirades and who had raised their three children, died two days later on December 5, 1981.

---

82 The Canadian Press' blurb on Betty Newman's death in 1981 revealed an hitherto unknown fact: she wrote episodes of *General Motors Presents* (which was, in turn, remade as part of the *United States Steel Hour* in the U.S.) and, later, an episode of *Armchair Theatre* in the UK. She did all this under the pseudonym "Leslie Duncan." Presumably the nom-de-plume was used to get around the possible problem of having episodes written by the producer's wife. The CP blurb adds that Betty "also had plays produced in Canada and the United States."

CHAPTER TEN

YESTERDAY'S MAN

After Betty died, Newman went back to Britain in early 1982. It was a visit where he reconnected with several old friends. It began a period where he attempted to get back in the game by producing television in the country he associated with the best years of his life.

In his personal papers there are a number of letters to heads of film companies, TV channels, and drama departments in Britain that include the phrase, "is there a place for me in your organization?" For the most part, he received polite rebuffs and expressions of polite interest. But inside those organizations, Newman's requests provoked drama. Newman asked his former colleague Aubrey Singer, managing director of BBC Television, if there was a place for him in the corporation where he had made his most well-known contributions. What happened next behind closed doors was an exchange of memos in November 1982 between Singer and Graeme McDonald, who now held Newman's position as head of drama group. "Even as I read it, I know the cause is hopeless. I cannot see us re-employing him. Can you?" asked Singer.

McDonald had met with Newman on a visit earlier that year. "After the death of his wife, he is most keen to return to Britain," McDonald noted, but cautioned, "His vigour still belies his age, but I did find him, perhaps understandably, very out of touch with the way drama has gone here since he last worked in television. It's difficult, too, to see how his personality could be contained in anything but rather an important position." McDonald understood Newman all too well.

But McDonald also identified a key liability Newman had, and one that McDonald confirmed other producers had noticed and were having trouble with — that Newman was now out of touch. "It isn't really clear from his letter quite what he wants to do. The fact that he doesn't see 'gutsy dramas of contemporary England' doesn't, of course, mean we don't make them."

In the end, Singer, too, had to turn down Newman. "When you came the first time, you were the right man in the right place in the right time. Things have moved on."

Newman was finding similar barriers in Canada. When his old friend Pierre Juneau was named head of the CBC in October 1983, Newman asked if he was planning to clean the slate in drama, saying, "*You* brought me back to Canada . . . how about a crack at keeping me here?" Never one for half-measures, Newman also insisted he would not take the job "without the most solemn assurance that drama will receive top money for production, tech facilities, freedom to dump staff and a strong voice in determining the choice of air-time. England gave me these, no one got hurt and drama flourished."

It's a sign of the respect Juneau still possessed for his old friend that when he finally received Newman's letter on November 5, he immediately sent a telegram . . . that told him the drama portfolio was taken.

Newman was now sixty-six years old. It was becoming clear he would have to make his own luck.

Newman had been fascinated by the Bloomsbury Group ever since he had read about them in a play written by Peter Luke (Newman confessed to Luke he hadn't known much about them; in fact, Betty was the one who told him about Virginia Woolf's suicide). Newman's papers include several articles from British newspapers written in the early 1980s about Vita Sackville-West and John Maynard Keynes. The 1980s was the era of the television miniseries, especially on British television where Newman's friend Irene Shubik[83] had devised the successful 1984 series *The Jewel in the Crown* for Granada television that was a huge success both in Britain and the U.S. when broadcast as part of PBS' *Masterpiece Theatre*.

On his visits to Britain, Newman started pitching the idea of a miniseries about the Bloomsbury Group. One of the people he pitched to was Jeremy Isaacs, the head of Channel 4, the new private broadcaster that had begun less than two years before.

Isaacs was interested, but by this point in British television, in-house drama productions were a dying breed. Channel 4 mostly worked with outside production companies. While Newman could be the creative force behind such a series, he would need the resources of a production company and a producer to handle the money side of things. Isaacs offered Newman an "angel" for his project: Colin Callender, a former executive at Granada Television who was starting to branch out into producing television on his own. Channel 4, according to Newman, "staked him" for work in Britain through the Callender Company.

Furthermore, Jeremy Isaacs not only agreed to finance the development of *Bloomsbury*,[84] he also approached Newman and Callender about producing another series: a series of four ninety-minute films, each profiling a different person from Amnesty International's case files. The series would be eventually called *Prisoners of Conscience*.

By the end of 1984, Newman sent a resignation letter to André Lamy, now head of Telefilm Canada — the rebranded Canadian

---

83 Ironically, for a brief period during the 1980s, Shubik was Newman's flatmate. It did not go particularly well.

84 The formal title of the project was *Bloomsbury: Private Passions, Public Good.*

Film Development Corporation. "Knowing me as you do, I think you understand my joy at opportunities for me in England. At age 67 life is to start all over again!"

Newman's joy would be shortlived.

CHAPTER ELEVEN

MARKED BY LETDOWNS

Canadian film critic Martin Knelman wrote after Newman's death that "the final two decades of his life were marked by letdowns." Nowhere was this more evident than in the final years of Newman's professional career.

The frustrating thing is that Newman was often the author of his own destruction. After his disastrous time at the NFB, Newman possessed a curious sort of professional hubris — a belief that the master of the world of television in 1965 would continue that way without ever having to acknowledge things had changed.

During late 1984 and early 1985, Newman set to work on *Prisoners of Conscience* and *Bloomsbury*. The former had been conceived by Channel 4 as a prestige series that would feature top-flight writers and directors telling the stories of imprisoned activists using stories from Amnesty's files.[85] Channel 4 wanted superstar writers like David Mamet and Dennis Potter and were willing to settle for respected writers like Alan Plater and Troy Kennedy Martin. Newman attempted to enlist Arthur Miller, Harold Pinter and Gore Vidal and also tried *Rumpole of the Bailey* creator John Mortimer and Peter Luke. But everyone Newman or Colin Callender asked gave their regrets, though everyone was sympathetic to the cause.

This left Newman and Callender to reach beyond the "A" list and "B" list. They selected Robert Muller, a playwright and drama critic whose TV résumé was mostly in gothic horror and science fiction,[86] though his last TV credit was an adaptation of a Solzhenitsyn short story three years prior. Muller would adapt a story from Latin America,[87] what became known as "The Killing of Joelito."

At the same time, Newman selected Gillian Freeman, a novelist and sometime screenwriter, to write the *Bloomsbury* miniseries. Freeman had earlier written a screenplay on Virginia Woolf that Newman liked. He had asked Graeme McDonald about her while he was still the BBC's head of drama, and the assessment of the drama department was that "they feel her dramatic writing has not come anywhere near her skill as a novelist or indeed her non-fiction work. It may be that she lacks a dramatist's instinct in this area." Newman engaged her services anyway.

This proved unfortunate, as David Benedictus, Channel 4's commissioning editor for series and serials, was not particularly impressed with Freeman's work and told Colin Callender this in a letter in October 1984. "When Sydney discussed possible authors for this project with me, I said that Gillian was the least possible name of

---

85 How much this was the case in the end is somewhat debatable. There is at least one note from David Benedictus at Channel 4 complaining about the use of composite characters.

86 Muller got his break on television thanks to Newman's well-advertised search for new writers during his *Armchair Theatre* days.

87 This is perhaps a sign of how much things were in flux with this production. Previous memos indicated they had narrowed their focus to Iran, the USSR, China and South Africa.

those mentioned . . . My view is and was that this project needs a witty writer, such as John Mortimer."

Newman became defensive particularly quickly. "If my work in the past has been worthwhile, one of the main reasons was because the 'how' of the way I went about my work as a producer was never questioned." He wrote back to Benedictus. He was offended Channel 4 executives were even demanding approval of writers. Newman at least attempted to be conciliatory toward the end, and even explained his own motivation: "You must understand, David, I too have a lot at stake. I see this job of mine as a rebirth. I don't want to be crippled by having too many midwives."

"Is Channel 4 to be my co-producer?" was a phrase that appeared a lot in correspondence to both Benedictus and Channel 4's head, Jeremy Isaacs. But the fact was, by the mid-1980s, that's precisely what the TV networks were doing with outside productions. Networks gave notes. They had a say in the writers and directors hired. The *laissez-faire* management Newman practised at the BBC was long gone. Newman was perhaps willfully ignoring what decade he was living in at this point. And yet, either in deference to Newman's reputation, or just to cease the argument, Benedictus relented. Freeman would write *Bloomsbury*.

Newman would later write in his memoirs, "Basically my relations with a boss only work if he gives me a brief as to what is wanted and then leaves me alone to execute the job. I accept interference or more specific detailed instruction only if I feel he has demonstrated superior judgement, taste and experience to mine." The problem was, Newman was insisting in 1984 that his experience was superior even though he hadn't produced a television drama since 1967.

In July 1985 trouble erupted between Newman and Colin Callender. The source of contention was Robert Muller's script for *Prisoners of Conscience*, "The Killing of Joelito." Except it wasn't Muller's script anymore. Muller had written two drafts, neither of which satisfied Callender. At this point, Newman performed his own rewrite of Muller's script, physically cutting and pasting portions of it around

Newman's handwritten stage directions and dialogue.

Callender hated this draft even more and was threatening to exercise a clause in his contract that allowed him to reject the script — something that Newman saw as taking creative control on a project that was his. This also stirred up Newman's general resentments with Callender — Newman was irritated that, in spite of working through Callender's company, he had no administrative support or office space — and over July and August 1985, a general clearing of the air took place. Newman kept a diary of this experience. "It is clear that, whatever transpires between us — [Callender] is incapable of working with anyone who will not kow-tow to his judgement and opinion," Newman wrote.

At first it seemed that Callender and Newman were to come to terms. But by the end of 1985, Callender was out. The record for what transpired is scant — Newman underwent triple bypass surgery around this time — and it seems from interviews that the pair were unable to reconcile. (Callender also began working for HBO directly around this time, where he would stay for the next twenty years.) Newman was later to tell writer Stephen James Walker that when the pair split, Callender took *Prisoners of Conscience* with him. It was never made.

Newman kept *Bloomsbury*. Presumably Channel 4 found Newman a new production company to work with, and Newman joined forces with Andrew Holmes. While Newman shepherded the first draft of *Bloomsbury* through completion, he came up with the idea for another production.

Back when Newman was head of drama at the BBC, he was a champion of Benjamin Britten's operas and even convinced Britten to let the BBC adapt his *Billy Budd*. Newman loved not only that Britten wrote operas in English, but Britten's English sense of idiom and culture. He thought that Britten's 1949 opera for children, *The Little Sweep*, with its Victorian setting, had the makings of a good bit of television at Christmas.

"It seems to me that *The Little Sweep* opera will make a charming television Xmas special for Channel 4 or English equivalent," Newman said in a note in February 1986, to Andrew Holmes and his wife, Diana. "With intelligent selling, U.S. should be natural."

It was remarkably easy to pitch the idea to Channel 4. Preliminary work in securing the rights from Benjamin Britten's estate and sorting out a production was underway by the middle of 1987.

But just as *The Little Sweep* was coming together, *Bloomsbury* fell apart.

"Very mixed feelings here, I regret to say about *Bloomsbury*," Jeremy Isaacs wrote Newman on June 5, 1986. "It is ferociously difficult to bring this sort of stuff off, I know, but I still feel that wodges of it are stuffier than will ever live on the screen." Newman and Holmes begged Isaacs to reconsider, but a month later, he passed on the project.

Newman and Holmes spent the next several months re-pitching the project to various parties, including all the ITV networks and WGBH, the Boston PBS Station that produced *Masterpiece Theatre*. Newman had just had a recent tussle with the BBC brass over a creator credit on *Doctor Who* — more on this in a few moments — that had led to Newman being asked by BBC head of drama Jonathan Powell and BBC 1 Controller Michael Grade to make a proposal regarding future directions for that series. Newman tried to finesse that entrée into a pitch for *Bloomsbury*.

But everyone passed on the miniseries.[88]

Looking at the rejection letters, there are moments when David Benedictus's notes come to mind: perhaps if it had the wit of a John Mortimer, or perhaps if it had been six interconnected stories instead of a chronological retelling, it might have seem less sprawling and stuffy. Such things are perhaps easy to see in retrospect.

Newman was devastated. When he moved back to Britain, he had two drama productions to look forward to re-establish his career. Now he had the adaptation of a children's opera.

And there was also a persistent thorn in his flesh: *Doctor Who*.

---

88 Gillian Freeman would later take the scripts and adapt them into her 2006 novel, *But Nobody Lives in Bloomsbury* (the title of the TV version's first episode).

CHAPTER TWELVE

"WHO CREATED *DR. WHO*?"

When Newman's Order of Canada was announced in June 1981, he was irritated that, when the *Globe and Mail* covered it, they spoke of him as "Television and film producer Sydney Newman of Toronto, whose career in Britain included creating such series as *The Avengers* and *Doctor Who*."

"Isn't it just like the country for the [Governor-General's] office to not mention I was Government Film Commissioner?" he wrote André Lamy. "They obviously think *The Avengers* and *Dr. Who* are more important achievements!!!"

But by 1983, Newman was clearly changing his mind about the importance of *Doctor Who*. On August 24, 1983, Newman typed an astonishing letter to Alasdair Milne, who was BBC 1 Controller during the latter half of Newman's tenure as head of drama and was now director general of the BBC.

Alasdair, this will probably be the most difficult letter I

shall ever write. Perhaps after reading it you'll understand why in England I was referred to as "Newman, the Crude Colonial." You know that there are other sides to me. In this letter I'm going to be direct not crude — perhaps embarrassingly so, depending on how you read it.

I miss London, the excitement of my work there and yes, the adulation too. Somehow, for me, the memory of having made a decent contribution to the re-juvenation of the BBC in the early '60s — well, the memory, which is becoming dimmer and dimmer each day, "ain't" enough! I'm writing to ask you as D.G. to make the BBC real for me again.

I've just reached my 66th year and feel no older than when I joined the BBC — so, the hunger is still there for work and the reality of recognition. Work seems impossible with you. As you know I wrote and then phoned Aubrey [Singer]. So no dice re: work.

Well how about recognition? You know that BBC-TV is known all around the world for its drama, especial its classic series and yes, *Doctor Who*. It was I that proposed to David Attenborough that we gamble on 26 episodes of *The Forsyte Saga* — and *that* opened world markets to the BBC-TV — in fact for *all* British drama. *Doctor Who*. Did you know it was I who created the 720-year-old title character, the time-space police call [time] machine — in short, wrote the format for the show (as I did *The Avengers*)?

Jesus, I feel forgotten and that's the plain truth of it. So, dear D.G. what can the BBC do to bring me back to life, for a while anyway?

An honorary CBE? (Michael Barry[89] got it!)

Royalties for the format of *Doctor Who*? (You might think this is a lousy precedent to set, but, you know I was not on the staff of the BBC but on a five-year contract — in short, no pension and that sort of thing. So maybe it's

---

89 Michael Barry was Newman's predecessor as head of drama at the BBC.

not a precedent.) Anyway, you have no fear that I'm going to argue this in any way or fashion.

A handsome honorarium?

An October, four-week-all-expenses-paid trip to London to help celebrate *Doctor Who*'s twenty years bringing weekly delight to millions? Migod! I don't know another such long running show — the cult show of the U.S. and Canada.

Well, I couldn't be more direct, could I?

Alasdair, my twelve years in England were the best of my life. My five with you, its pinnacle.

What say?

Warmest regards to you and my mates.

Newman, the Crude Colonial.[90]

Newman added a handwritten note at the bottom, "Alasdair — after digesting the contents of this letter please, please burn it. It's for your eyes *only*. If I've embarrassed you, I apologize."

Newman's letter was a stunning bombshell of naked insecurity and sheer arrogance. It was, in a small way, the equivalent of a "drink and dial" with an ex. By the time Newman wrote this he had been turned down for practically every job he wanted in Britain, including at the BBC. He was in a low place. He wanted some kind of a blessing by his former institution, some kind of acknowledgment that he mattered.

Milne replied on September 5. It was diffident to a fault. "Many thanks for your letter which you may be reassured to know did not embarrass me in the least."

Milne reassured him that he understood that "your time with the BBC was probably the best you had." Milne also agreed that *Doctor Who* had continued to do the BBC proud and promised to think about it and see if he could "come up with something that might give you pleasure."

Milne never contacted Newman again.

---

90 Several sentences are crossed out, including a postscript, "I'm not in any financial straits whatsoever."

By 1984, Newman had found work in Britain developing *Bloomsbury* and *Prisoners of Conscience* with Colin Callender for Channel 4. But a creator credit on *Doctor Who* continued to be on his mind. This time, he asked literary agent Harvey Unna to represent him.

Unna wrote Stephen Edwards, the head of copyright at the BBC on October 26, 1984. Unna pointed out that *Doctor Who* had, by that point, earned the corporation "in excess of £500,000, either in sales via BBC Enterprises or by collecting their royalties from W.H. Allen."[91] Eventually Unna got to the crux of his argument, where he argued the point that Newman's original contract with the BBC stipulated that all his work product remained the BBC's copyright. "It will come as no surprise to you if I ask myself and your good self whether the invention or origination of television programmes is included in 'the normal duties of the post or falls within the execution of any of any other duties reasonably connected therewith or arising therefrom,'" Unna states.

Unna drew from his decades of experience with television writers and concluded that "Sydney Newman would appear to have been the only head of drama who at the same time was an inventor. Apart from *Doctor Who*, he invented, and I think you know, *The Avengers* for ABC and *Adam Adamant Lives!* for the BBC." Unna's case was essentially that Newman's creation of *Doctor Who* was outside the scope of his position as head of drama and not subject to the terms of his contract. Stephen Edwards's position, when he responded a month later on December 6, was the opposite. He believed it *was* within the scope and that the creation of any program formed part of Newman's duties as head of drama.

Edwards twisted the knife a little, though, when it came to the question of whether an ex-gratia award to Newman could be justified based on the income the programme generated for the BBC. "Our conclusion is that it could not. I should mention that one factor in our decision has been the very favourable terms afforded to Mr. Newman which are evidenced by the contract of April, 1962." And as

---

91 W.H. Allen published *Doctor Who* novels and coffee table books about the series.

if to add insult to injury, Edwards concluded with a veiled reference to Newman's letter the previous year to Milne. "I understand Mr. Newman has already raised this matter in other quarters of the BBC and I can therefore assure that it has been very fully considered."

Over the next few months, Unna pressed the matter with Edwards and even suggested arbitration, but Edwards rejected it outright. Eventually, on July 1, 1985, Unna sent Newman a note: "I have at long last and off the record discovered why the BBC does not wish to make even an ex-gratia payment: I am told that because in many departments other than drama, heads do provide and initiate programs. The Corporation is afraid of creating a precedent by giving one head preferential treatment, even though richly deserved!"

It was a view confirmed by Bill Cotton, a friend of Newman's and the BBC's managing director of television, in a note to Newman on November 15, 1985. "Much as I can understand your frustration, the Corporation cannot do anything about your association with *Doctor Who*. You, like the rest of us, had a deal that included those ideas."

For a while, this seemed to satisfy Newman. And then came Trivial Pursuit, which changed everything.

In 1985, the UK toy manufacturer Palitoy licensed Trivial Pursuit from Horn Abbot, the Canadian producers of the popular trivia game. They added trivia questions specifically for the British market, including a card with the question in the Entertainment category, "Who created *Dr. Who*?"

The answer was "Terry Nation."

Newman was livid when he found this out. He consulted his lawyers. He even wrote Daleks' creator Terry Nation, now living in California, to ask if he would assist by attesting to the fact that he didn't create *Doctor Who*.[92] Horn Abbot's lawyers responded, "One

---

92　Terry Nation's response was, "It will be my epitaph — 'He was the wrong answer in Trivial Pursuit.'" And then quipped, "Better I had been the answer to the other question on the card, 'What do you kiss to be endowed with great powers of persuasion?'"

of the UK writers relied on an erroneous source of information for the question." They promised that the question would be deleted from the game, but also commented, "Your complaint suggests that Mr. Newman's reputation and professional standing has been substantially damaged and that there has been a serious adverse effect on his earning power. It appears these allegations are pure speculation and conjecture, are not supported by any of the evidence provided and that Mr. Newman has suffered no damage whatsoever." It wasn't good enough for Newman, who kept legal proceedings — one hopes on contingency basis — going for months.[93]

In August 1986, Newman decided to make his final attempt to regain a creator credit on *Doctor Who*. The perceived slight by Trivial Pursuit certainly motivated it, but much like his first attempt at recognition for *Doctor Who* with Alasdair Milne, this time it also happened at another low point for Newman. Channel 4 had just passed on *Bloomsbury*. And with *Bloomsbury*'s demise, Newman saw his comeback in the UK slipping away.

This time Newman favoured the direct approach. On July 16, 1986, Newman wrote John Nathan-Turner, the current producer of *Doctor Who*:

> I am writing to ask that as the original deviser of *Doctor Who* you so credit me on all future episodes.
>
> I guess you know that when I dreamed up the series in 1963 I was head of drama group. I decided to not take public credit for it lest I appeared to be favouring myself over freelance writers and even members of my staff. That correct motivation has sure come back to haunt me. I guess I must live with the unhappy fact that I am denied, at a

---

93 Newman was receiving correspondence about it up until December 22, 1986, at which point the lawyer handling the case said, "If I may say so, I think we are flogging a dead horse."

time I could use some, any part of the lucrative earnings enjoyed by the BBC, others, and outside entrepreneurs over these many, many years.

Anyway, re *Doctor Who,* the final straw came a short while ago which as a creative person you will understand. Some idiot tells me that Terry Nation created *Doctor Who* and cites as evidence Trivial Pursuit. As we know, Terry created only the Daleks.

Since I am now re-establishing myself as a money-earning, active producer, executive producer or whatever, and creator of new series ideas, my names to be publically and professionally known by a new generation.

I ask that the single screen credit read:

Doctor Who Series
was devised by
SYDNEY NEWMAN

Newman cc'd his letter to BBC 1 Controller Michael Grade and the head of drama, Jonathan Powell.

Nathan-Turner wrote back on August 14 that he was referring upwards. On September 3, Ken Riddington, acting head of series / serials reiterated the party line stated to Harvey Unna (and even referring to it). "This is not in any way to gainsay that the series owes its birth to you," stated Riddington. It merely reflected the fact that any department heads who create a program for the BBC "have to be satisfied with the other rewards that flow from doing so."

Newman struck back by writing a blistering letter on September 5 to Bill Cotton, the managing director of television. "I'm feeling bitter and angry at the place I once loved and admired — the BBC, natch — that I must unload it. I've picked you not because you are the TV 'top dog' but because I feel, based on our past association, that you are the only human guy left of the old guard I know."

Newman retold Cotton his appeal to Alasdair Milne and his desire to get the credit, because Newman was re-establishing his credentials. He mentioned Trivial Pursuit and then he mentioned Ken Riddington's latest rebuff. Riddington's phrase "other rewards" particularly stung Newman.

"The reason for depriving me of my rights as the deviser of *Doctor Who* displays an ethical sickness which shames the BBC and has nothing to do whatsoever with the fact of my having been head of drama almost twenty years ago."

Bill Cotton's response, on September 29, was to be the final word on the dispute:

> I was really sad to receive your letter. Nobody knows more than I the contribution you made to the Corporation during the years you were here. You did well by the BBC, and the BBC did well by you.
>
> However, it is now over twenty years since you decided to go and you put the present administration in an impossible position asking for compensation, payment or recognition for something that should have been sorted out by you with the people running the place at the time.
>
> I know *Doctor Who* is a source of bitterness to you and I understand why.
>
> On the other hand it would set a very dangerous precedent for the Corporation if heads of output were able to claim the ideas they were responsible for and helped develop whilst they were in office or indeed when they left.
>
> I honestly cannot see how we can make any gesture to you without doing the same for others with a similar claim and who probably got even less reward when they were here.

Cotton's response was compassionate but also made the BBC's case passionately as well. But it may well be that he also found a way to offer at least something to Sydney Newman in the way of *Doctor Who*.

In 1985, *Doctor Who* had been, for a brief period, cancelled by BBC 1 Controller Michael Grade and Head of Drama Jonathan Powell. The decision prompted a deluge of negative worldwide publicity for the corporation. The series was granted a stay of execution and was given an eighteen-month hiatus instead. Newman wrote to John Nathan-Turner in the summer of 1986, as the series was about to finally come out of that hiatus, where it would face indifferent ratings and begin its death spiral. The program was not particularly loved by Grade or Powell, who felt it was tacky and past its prime.

Soon after Newman contacted John Nathan-Turner, Michael Grade reached out to Newman and asked him to lunch on September 16 at Bizanos, a restaurant near Paddington station. Newman's notes of that meeting in his diary mentioned that he was asked to "do an evaluation of *Doctor Who*. Write 500–1500 words on what it was like and what may be wrong now." Stephen Edwards, head of copyright, got in touch soon after to suggest a fee of £1,000.

The timing of all this, within mere days of Newman's latest demands for a creator credit, suggests that the higher echelons at the BBC were wanting to offer Newman something meaningful to do with *Doctor Who* — or at the very least wanted to keep him in check. It's pure speculation, but it seems possible that the thinking was, if the BBC couldn't give him an ex gratia payment, they could pay him as a consultant.

The irony was Newman wasn't enamored with the money on offer, protesting to Grade on October 2, "To offer a measly £1,000 for 'complete copyright' in my ideas and not even a hint of a percentage of the fee on signing, the rest on delivery!"

Newman continued, "I don't think I misunderstood your request. I believe you wanted me to touch on what is wrong with the series at present with *proposals for specific changes*. I *know* what the new lead character of Dr. Who himself should be and how he should behave. I *know* too the fresh and as yet untapped areas he and his earthlings would experience in their adventures to hold old audiences and find new ones. I think too I can *guarantee* more than schlock escapism. Isn't this what you want?"

There is no record as to whether or not Newman came to better terms with Grade or if Grade simply assuaged Newman's concerns.[94] But Newman delivered his "way forward" for *Doctor Who* a couple of days later on October 6, 1986. Newman first set ground rules. "In this letter I'll point the way to my concept of the direction the series ought to go to hold its present British and worldwide audiences and to increase their numbers. The copyright in any ideas expressed will be mine. Should you accept these ideas, the fee I would accept would be in the form of my being taken on and paid to be its executive producer or similar, to make sure the concept is *properly executed*. Should you not accept these ideas, an honorarium would be welcome." Newman even made an additional pitch for a creator credit.

Then Newman launched into his proposal, which was, in many ways, a return to the original proposals he worked on with Donald Wilson and C.E. Webber back in 1963. "The out-in-space, other-planet adventures are somewhat old hat," Newman complained. "Their simple good guy versus outer space monsters too rarely go beyond sheer escapism. The *best* sci-fi always has a mythic parable element that touches our own lives."

Newman proposed that "outer space stories" would take up only fifty percent of the total. The rest of it would be exploring real science and history. "Our earth, both present and past, is just as exciting as outer space, when creatively explored. The wonders of technology, science, medicine, the green earth movement and the like are hot subjects today." Newman suggested that "Dr. Who" (he never called the lead character "the Doctor") could somehow travel inside a child's body to battle cancer cells in them, or find trouble inside a NASA shuttle or be shrunken to minuscule size — the trope that drove the original first episode when the series was devised in April, 1963 — or even fight a mutiny on Christopher Columbus's

---

94 It is also possible Newman decided to accept the payment so he could establish his credentials with Grade and Powell to enlist their help on his then-ailing *Bloomsbury* project. In a letter to Jonathan Powell sent October 30, 1986, Newman says he pitched *Bloomsbury* to Michael Grade at their lunch to talk about *Doctor Who*. He sent Powell the scripts, though it was ultimately rejected by the BBC.

ship, allowing him to discover America.

"In the above," Newman explained, "the standard do-or-die, life-in-peril approach, at least our central characters will be experiencing adventures which, despite their peripheral educational values, engages the concerns, fears and curiosity of today's audiences of all ages. Don't you agree that this is considerably more worthy of a BBC than *Doctor Who*'s present, largely socially valueless escapist schlock?"

Newman's proposals for companions were straight out of his earlier proposal. "A homesick girl of twelve wearing John Lennon–type Dickensian spectacles (she's stylish)" whose defining character trait is that she plays the trumpet at various occasions ("sometimes it irritates Dr. Who when he's trying to think. 'Hush child! You're addlepating me!'") and her "Yobbo, overly self-confident brother of eighteen."

Newman's proposal for a "way forward" in *Doctor Who* is remarkably tone deaf and feels like something put together by someone who never actually watched an episode of *Doctor Who* after the pilot. It ignores the things that actually made *Doctor Who* popular in 1986: the monsters, the use of adventure, horror and comedy — the science fiction trappings. Worse, it lacked an appreciation for the demographic who watched the series in 1986 — a demographic that skewed much older than the putative audience between *Grandstand* and *Juke Box Jury*. Newman's hubris that television had not changed in the twenty years since he left Britain was once again his downfall.

But Newman also had what can be honestly termed contempt toward the modern version of *Doctor Who*. He believed that it had moved from the high-minded educational ideals he claimed he had for it. "If Verity Lambert at the start had realized my concept as the stuff [that has] appeared latterly, I would have pulled her off the show, [or] gotten someone else to produce it or torn the concept up," Newman said in a letter to *Doctor Who* fan Andrew Beech in 1993. "The fact that the series had become so incredibly popular, proves the cliché that in the production hands of some, shit is easier to sell than quality. For me, its devisor, the drama, as it became, lacked any connection with the real world of the audience. To last, it must."

While much of Newman's proposal is very old-fashioned, there was one thing that Newman put into the proposal that indicated the old populist provocateur was still there. His suggestion for the character of the Doctor was first "to see the return of Patrick Troughton — still the not-quite-there tramp from outer space." Then, "at a later stage, Dr. Who would be metamorphosed into a woman. This requires some considerable thought — mainly because I want to avoid a flashy Hollywood 'Wonder Woman' because this kind of hero[ine] has no flaws — and a character with no flaws is a bore. Given more time than I have now, I can create such a character." Newman's gambit was bold. It would take another thirty years before audiences would be comfortable with even the idea of discussing the Doctor being a woman. But Newman thought it was the logical place the character needed to go.

There is no record as to how the proposal was received or if Grade or Powell even responded.[95] What we do know is *Doctor Who* continued for another three years after 1986 and none of Newman's changes were ever implemented.

In the end, Newman's demands for a creator credit on *Doctor Who* were ignored and Newman was seemingly mollified by his participation in proposing a way forward for *Doctor Who*. What remains is the question why this was so important to Newman that he made three attempts to get a creator credit across just as many years. Newman said at various points that he did it for name recognition and because he felt he should have some participation in the profits the show was making.

But there may be another, simpler reason than that. By the mid-

---

95 Newman's proposal was sent around the time the 23rd season of *Doctor Who* completed production. Grade and Powell would soon fire the actor playing the Doctor, Colin Baker, and would offer to move producer John Nathan-Turner to another series (before rescinding that offer). The BBC executives may have been pondering clearing the decks on *Doctor Who* for Newman or, more likely, given the opinion about Newman at the BBC, someone else. In the event that never happened.

1980s, *The Wednesday Play* was long gone. *Hamlet at Elsinore* was forgotten. "Cathy Come Home" and "Up the Junction" were consigned to newspaper thinkpieces about the storied history of the BBC and nothing else.

When first Newman wrote Alasdair Milne in 1983, *Doctor Who* had reached its twentieth anniversary. Sydney Newman fought to have his name attached to the one thing he created during his time at the BBC that was still in the public eye. The Trivial Pursuit question merely underscored that even *that* achievement was anonymous.

The schedule-filling Saturday serial that Newman never quite understood after others put their imprint on it was, whether he wanted it to be or not, his legacy at the BBC.

CHAPTER THIRTEEN
UNFULFILLED

The Little Sweep was to be Sydney Newman's last television production and it spent an inordinate amount of time in development hell. By the middle of 1987, Channel 4 wanted Andrew Holmes and Newman to sort out co-production financing. Newman canvassed his contacts at the CBC to see if there was interest in it being a Canadian co-production. There was — provided there were Canadians in the cast. Newman was happy to hire Maureen Forrester, a highly regarded Canadian contralto. Even with the co-production money, Newman and Holmes needed £39,000 from Channel 4 to deficit finance the production.

At first the script was credited to Jim Goddard and Richard Hartley, the musical director, but Newman eventually took over and adapted it himself. Newman loved the idea of working with what he called the "dual reality" of the opera — where things would be shown from the point of view of Sammy, the eponymous eight-year-old sweep, in distorted, monstrous ways, as opposed to the straightforward reality of the adults surrounding him.

Newman filled the rest of his time working on his memoirs. He had also formally begun a relationship with Marion McDougall, who worked as a secretary for him at ABC in the early 1960s. Newman had attempted to strike up a romance with her at various points during the 1980s, even bringing her to Canada the summer after Betty died. By 1987, Newman moved out of London to live with her in Worthing, in suburban Sussex. Marion was devoted to Newman, and Newman, who was never domestic and faced declining health, needed looking after. Even so, Newman had profound reservations about the relationship. Being who he was, he had no problem articulating those reservations in correspondence to friends.

By the end of 1987, the financing of *The Little Sweep* was sorted out. Newman and Holmes began to work out a director, settling on Basil Coleman, who directed the BBC adaptation of Britten's *Billy Budd* under Newman two decades before. Holmes gave Newman a contract for his work on the actual production.

And then it all broke down. Again.

Newman kept in his file on *The Little Sweep* torn-out pages of his diary from 1988. On February 3: "Fight with Andrew & typical, he walked out." Andrew Holmes was having financial troubles and now claimed he had insufficient funds to work with Newman's "dual reality" approach. The row led to Holmes sending Newman and Channel 4 a letter cancelling his deal on *The Little Sweep*. Newman tried to write a conciliatory note but couldn't resist leaving a handwritten postscript that this situation could affect Newman's work permit. "It seems like blackmail but isn't. But if you want the knock-on effect of your action on your conscience, well all I can say is FUCK YOU but good."

Newman geared up for one last crisis. He approached Michael Grade, who was now CEO at Channel 4, and apprised him of the situation and asked for help. Grade agreed to continue the deficit financing offered the previous year. Newman made entreaties to other investors and managed to find interest from Ian Martin, the head of music, arts and specials at Thames Television. With Channel 4's guarantees, Martin was willing to take the fledgling production on as a Thames production.

Newman was able to save *The Little Sweep*.

The delays caused by Andrew Holmes's departure meant that *The Little Sweep* would not be ready for Christmas 1988. Production began in early 1989 and Newman was thoroughly involved in the edit. Newman was in his element, leaving director Basil Coleman notes like, "Please try and regard *Sweep* not an opera but as a musical drama . . . use the maximum amount of realistic sound effects even when selectively overriding the music and dialogue to add depth and excitement to the drama."

The Little Sweep was broadcast on Christmas Day, 1989. The *Observer* noted Newman's connection to it and called it an "entertaining adaptation."

Newman had hoped this would become a Christmas tradition, but it never aired again.

At first Newman returned to Worthing to live in retirement with Marion McDougall. But he tired of Marion's politics and was bored by life in Worthing. He moved back to Canada in 1990. Newman and Marion would break up and reunite several times during Newman's final years.

Upon his return, Newman consulted on scripts a little with the Centre for Advanced Film Studies, but mostly stayed in retirement. "You may well ask . . . why the hell I am back in Canada? It's home!" Newman wrote a friend in February 1991. "No one here in the professional film or TV world seems to give a damn about me and my background. Mind you, I haven't made any effort to sell myself and so very few people even know that I returned over a year ago."

Instead, Newman focused his energies on being retired. Now that he was back in Toronto, Newman was able to spend more time with his daughter Deirdre and his teenaged granddaughter, and he continued to remain in contact with his other daughters, Jennifer and Gillian and their respective families.

In his final years, Newman's health declined as his heart condition and then emphysema took their toll. ("I am well except for the rather nasty emphysema which inhibits any physical activity and too weak to give up smoking," Newman quipped.) Newman found happiness by going back to his first love: being an artist. "You may recall that my first hope in life was to become an artist and then I got side-tracked into the group arts," Newman wrote Frank Gillard in 1997. "Now in my decrepitude, I have gone back to my first aspirations, finding some kind of self-expression as an artist where no actor, producer and deadline can inhibit me." He continued to work with wood, he painted, and, as technology advanced, he became keen on computer design. He was an early adopter of Photoshop and enjoyed creating art using pixels. "I also work without the smell of turpentine but with the bytes of an Apple computer." He had found some measure of peace.

Sydney Newman died of a heart attack on October 30, 1997. He was eighty years old. He was remembered, and his life was celebrated, in Britain. The *Guardian*'s obituary by W. Stephen Gilbert opened with, "For ten brief but glorious years, Sydney Newman, who has died aged eighty, was the most important impresario in Britain. The period that is now conventionally referred to as the 'golden age' of television drama was presided over by this feisty Canadian who blagged his way into the industry and dared to challenge its conventions and new voices.

"His death marks not just the end of an era but the laying to rest of a whole philosophy of art."

But in Canada, his death was not nearly as recognized as it should have been. Gone were the days when even his opinions on the architecture of Toronto City Hall were published. His death was noted in the *Globe and Mail* in a one-paragraph blurb. The *Toronto Star* all but ignored him.

Eventually, the *Globe and Mail* chose to honour Newman in Canada, a month after his death, as part of their weekly "Lives Lived" column. Newman's friend, critic Martin Knelman, summed up Newman's career and particularly his final years: "The final two decades of his life were marked by letdowns . . . Sydney Newman did not endure these setbacks in silence. His grumbling had an epic quality. With justification, he felt his talent was wasted and his achievement unacknowledged. In the end, he himself had become the protagonist in a drama of the downtrodden. Paradise lost."

One obituary about the peak of his career, the other about the period after it; one written in Britain, one written in Canada. And yet, both of these eulogies on Newman's life are absolutely true. Sydney Newman encompassed the greatest successes and the greatest failures a person could have. And his contribution to television and film in two countries will only ever be partially measured.

In the end, his life could be summed up by his BBC job title: he was head of drama.

NOTES ON SOURCES

Much of this research for this was derived from primary source material from two collections: the Sydney Newman Collection, held in Library and Archives Canada (LAC) and the BBC Written Archive Centre (BBC WAC), which holds many of the BBC records including various collections, such as files for *Doctor Who*'s creation and early years (primarily the "General 1963" and "General 1964" collections), the drama department's files for 1963–64 as well as individual program and personnel files.

1. NOVEMBER 23, 1962

Newman's letter to Howard Thomas from November 21, 1963, and his correspondence with Kenneth Adam (dated November 21 and November 23, 1961) are all from LAC, as is his April 4, 1962, contract with the BBC.

Episodes of *Armchair Theatre* from 1962 can be found on its IMDB page: http://www.imdb.com/title/tt0161126/.

2. AN OUTSIDER AT THE BBC

The history of the BBC is from a variety of sources but mostly derived from an online history at the BBC, http://www.bbc.co.uk/historyofthebbc/research/general/tvstory1, with assistance provided by British TV historians Andrew Pixley and Jim Sangster.

Much of Newman's quotes for this chapter, and subsequent ones, are from an interview the BBC conducted for its BBC Oral History project, which was recorded on August 29, 1984. The transcript (with handwritten amendments made by Newman on May 2, 1997) is from the Sydney Newman collection at LAC. (Some passages of the videotaped interview appear in the 2005 documentary *Doctor Who: Origins* which appears on the *Doctor Who: The Beginning* DVD box set).

Irene Shubik's recollections of Newman come from her book about her career in television and the history of TV drama in Britain, *Play For Today: The Evolution of Television Drama* (Manchester, Manchester University Press: 2000).

Kenneth Adam's letter to Newman, January 9, 1963, and the March 14, 1963, BBC press office memo on the formation BBC Drama Group were taken from the Newman collection at LAC.

3. THE SATURDAY SERIAL

John Mair's March 27, 1963, memo is found in the BBC WAC *Doctor Who* — General 1963 collection (T5/647). Details of Nora Alice Frick's career were derived from emails with *Doctor Who* historians Richard Bignell and Stephen James Walker.

Details about *Juke Box Jury* and the other types of programming shown on Saturday afternoons in 1963 was supplied through the BBC website's "Genome" project (genome.ch.bbc.co.uk), which has taken every issue of the listings guide *Radio Times* and made it searchable. British TV historian Jim Sangster helped provide context on the nature of each production.

The details of the BBC survey group, and its function within the

BBC script department are recounted in *Doctor Who: The Handbook — The First Doctor* by David J. Howe, Stephen James Walker and Mark Stammers (Virgin Publishing, 1994). In this, Stephen James Walker worked from research he had done interviewing members of the former BBC script unit.

The sequence of events from the request by Eric Maschwicz to the Survey Group's two reports to Wilson's meeting with Alice Frick, Donald Bull and C.E. Webber has been widely subject to interpretation by *Doctor Who* fans. My reconstruction is reliant on the primary sources (as shown the memoranda retained by the BBC, particularly the General 1963 collection), as well Newman's own recollections and the sequence of events outlined in *Doctor Who: The First Doctor Handbook*. I am indebted to Andrew Pixley and Richard Bignell for providing helpful advice in piecing this together.

Alice Frick and Howard Bull, April 25, 1962, and July 25, 1962, reports on Science Fiction, minutes of Donald Wilson's meeting with Frick, John Braybon and C.E. Webber and C.E. Webber's proposal for "The Troubleshooters" are all from the BBC WAC *Doctor Who* — General 1963 collection. Many of these papers are available online at bbc.co.uk/archive/doctorwho/.

The origin of C.E. Webber's nickname were supplied by Matthew Sweet in an email to the author, while details of his payment for writing the rejected *Doctor Who* pilot comes from Webber's freelancer file at BBC WAC.

4. "MR. WHO?"
Ayton Whitaker April 26, 1963, memo, Owen Reed's May 9, 1963, memo, C.E. Webber's outline for "The Giants" with Newman's rejection of it are all found in the BBC WAC *Doctor Who* — General 1963 collection (T5/647), as are the memos from Verity Lambert and Johanna Spicer sorting out the cost of the "spaceship" set. The various drafts of *Doctor Who* format documents by Newman, Webber and Wilson (with Newman's handwritten notes) are also found here.

Newman's draft of his 1969 Daily Sketch article (which includes correspondence with writer Robert Ottaway), the letter to Newman from BBC Archives (then BBC Data), dated May 8, 1987, Newman's letter to Jeremy Bentham, dated April 12, 1984, and Newman's February 16, 1965, proposal, "S*xton Blake Lives" are all taken from the Sydney Newman collection at LAC.

Newman's correspondence with Malcolm Hulke from September–October 1971 are also in Newman's collection at LAC. The correspondence between Zenith Film Productions and the BBC, the handwritten notes on the *Doctor Who* pilot and the text of Donald Wilson's November 27 telegram to Newman are all from the BBC WAC *Doctor Who* — General 1963 collection.

5. POINT OF CRISIS

Newman's assessment of size of the BBC drama department comes from the raw footage for his 1966 interview for the CBC program *The Umbrella* and the transcript of BBC Oral History interview, which is in Newman's collection at LAC. Quotes from the Oral History interview features throughout this chapter.

Irene Shubik is quoted throughout from her book, *Play For Today*. Newman's Memo to the BBC drama group, dated October 16, 1963, on "Frankness in showing sexual relations" is from the BBC drama department, 1963 collection (T5/2239) at BBC WAC. Newman's October 14, 1965, memo to Michael Bakewell and James McTaggart, are from the BBC WAC production file for "Alice" (T5/834). Details of Newman's activities with *Hamlet at Elsinore* are in that program's production file at BBC WAC.

An examination of the roles Newman, Baverstock and Adam played in sustaining (or not sustaining) the single play can be found in Madeline McMurraugh-Kavanaugh's essay, "The BBC and the Birth of *The Wednesday Play*" in Janet Thuman (ed.), *Small Screens, Big Ideas: Television in the 1950s* (I.B. Taurus, 2002). Donald Baverstock's biography is largely derived from the obituary written by Leonard Miall in *The Independent*, March 19, 1995. Details of the BBC "Blyton ban" can be found online at bbc.co.uk/archive/blytonandthebbc/.

Newman's memoranda complaining about Baverstock and his plan to kill the single play, dated January 21, 1963, June 26, 1964, and October 27, 1964, are all from Newman's collection at LAC. Curiously, the BBC only retains the replies to this correspondence: Donald Baverstock's July 1, 1964, memo and Kenneth Adam's July 13, 1964, memo are from the BBC drama department, 1963 collection at the BBC WAC.

6. "AGITATIONAL CONTEMPORANEITY"

The transcript of Newman's Oral History interview with the BBC is from Newman's collection at LAC.

Troy Kennedy Martin is quoted from his 1986 James McTaggart lecture, "Opening up the Fourth Front: Micro Drama and the Rejection of Naturalism." Information on *Diary of a Young Man* is from the British Film Institute's webpage on that series screenonline.org.uk/tv/id/439610/. Newman's connection to James McTaggart through *Diary of a Young Man* was cited by John Hill in his essay "A 'new drama for television'?: *Diary of a Young Man*" in Laura Mulvey and Jamie Sexton (eds.), *Experimental British Television* (Manchester University Press, 2007). Biographical information on James McTaggart comes from Oliver Wake's entry for McTaggart on the British Television Drama website (britishtelevisiondrama.org.uk/?p=351).

Newman's October 14, 1965, memo about *The Wednesday Play* episode "Alice" is from the BBC WAC production file for "Alice" (T5/834). Newman's August 23, 1966, letter to Philip Purser explaining the origins of "agitational contemporaneity" and his June 15, 1966, memo about *The Wednesday Play* are from Newman's collection at the LAC. The BBC WAC production file for "Fable" (T5/1349) includes Kenneth Adam's January 28, 1965, memo to Newman and the Audience Appreciation Report.

The story of making of "Up the Junction" and "Cathy Come Home" come from an oral history, "Cathy Come Home: The True Story Behind Britain's most famous Drama" in the November 2, 2006, *Independent*. Details about Tony Garnett's mother's death come from an April 23, 2013, article in the *Guardian*.

Newman's November 9, 1965, letter to Mrs. P.E. Pratt is from the BBC WAC production file for "Up the Junction" (T16/730).

Newman's report on *The Wednesday Play*, with his statistics from the BBC switchboard for "Up the Junction," along with Newman's April 12, 1984, letter to Jeremy Bentham and his undated "Notes for Svesham" on "The Future of Television Drama" are from Newman's collection at LAC. Maurice Wiggins's column on Newman's departure from Britain was in the January 4, 1970, *Sunday Times*.

7. RETURN OF THE PRODIGAL

Newman's comments on Toronto City Hall appeared in Nathan Cohen's column in the *Toronto Star* on October 11, 1966. Cohen also wrote about Newman in his June 22, 1966, column.

The Umbrella was a Sunday afternoon program about the arts that aired on CBC in the autumn of 1966. The segment featuring Newman aired on November 27, 1966. The raw footage for this interview — which includes the entirety of Newman's interview with William Ronald, plus silent footage of Newman walking from the lobby of BBC Television Centre to his office and Newman in a television studio — can be found online at cbc.ca/archives/entry/doctor-who-creator-sydney-newman-discusses-his-career.

Newman's November 21, 1969, letter to Nathan Cohen, his December 17, 1969, letter to Pierre Juneau's secretary and his July 8, 1970, letter to Verity Lambert are from Newman's Collection at the LAC.

Articles about Newman's arrival at the CRTC includes Lee Edwards, "People tired of TV pap says Sydney Newman," *Toronto Star*, January 8, 1970, and Patrick Scott, "He'll take on all broadcast comers," *Toronto Star*, March 14, 1970.

8. "LE BOSS UNILINGUE"

Many of the details of this chapter about the National Film Board in general and Newman's tenure as its Commissioner are derived from Gary Evans's book, *In The National Interest: A Chronicle of the National Film Board of Canada from 1949 to 1989* (University of Toronto Press, 1991) and from two interviews between Gary Evans and the author on December 8, 2015, and April 14, 2016.

Throughout this chapter are quotes from a transcript of Newman interview with CKVU producer Emmanuelle Gattuso from March 1983 which are retained in Newman's collection at LAC. Details of Newman's decision to leave the CRTC and being asked to join the NFB come from that CKVU interview. Nathan Cohen's column about the Newman's appointment to the NFB is from the *Toronto Star*, August 13, 1970.

The anecdotes about John Grierson visiting the NFB's Montreal headquarters and his last conversation with Sydney Newman come from Martin Knelman's book, *This Is Where We Came In: The Career and Character of Canadian Film* (McClelland and Stewart, 1977). Newman's October 13, 1976, letter to Peter Luke is from his collection at the LAC. Newman appeared before the Standing Committee on Broadcasting, Films and Assistance to the Arts on April 22, 1971.

The story of *Mon Oncle Antoine*'s genesis has been repeated a number of places, including the 2007 episode of the documentary television series *On Screen!* which is included on the Criterion Collection DVD release of *Mon Oncle Antoine*. Verity Lambert's October 27, 1970, letter is from Newman's LAC Collection. Denys Arcand spoke about the bootlegged copies of *On est au Coton* in "Nothing's changed since Duplessis, maker of banned film says" in the *Globe and Mail*, December 27, 1973. Newman's notes "first talk to abortive meeting of FR unit" and his letter to Andre L'Heureux, Director of the Secretariat for Political Action for the Confederation of National Trade Unions, dated November 3, 1971, are both from Newman's LAC collection.

The selection of quotes from film critic André Loiselle were taken from the entry on Gilles Groulx in the *Encyclopedia of Documentary Film*, Ian Aitken (ed.) (Routledge, 2006) and Denys Arcand's *Le Déclin de L'empire Américain and Les Invasions Barbares* (University of Toronto Press, 2008).

Newman's defence of his suppression of *On est au Coton* and *Vingt-Quatre Heures on Plus* comes from "Ferment at the National Film Board," an article in the February/March 1973 issue of *Cinema Canada*. The review of *Adieu Alouette* comes from the same issue. "Film board head asks: Should the taxpayer subsidize a movie advocating revolution" was an article in the *Globe and Mail*, December 25, 1972.

Newman was quoted on decision to reject the film that became *Les Ordres* in "Sydney Newman faces NFB crisis over vetoed Quebec jail film" in the October 2, 1971, *Globe and Mail*. The incident with Michel Brault at Cannes was reported on in "Guiding light" in the August 22, 1992, *Globe and Mail*. Newman's lobbying to have *Action* shown on the CBC was reported on in "CBC indecisive on showing film on Quebec crisis" in the *Toronto Star*, February 26, 1976.

The anecdote about Newman listening to a speech in French was reported by Jay Scott in the November 15, 1977, *Globe and Mail*.

The memos about translating the Thurber quote are in Newman's collection of papers at LAC.

10. ONE PIECE OF ADVICE IN TEN BEING TAKEN

Newman was quoted in "Getting those movies moving," *Toronto Star*, December 15, 1975.

Unless otherwise noted, this chapter relies primarily on materials in the Sydney Newman collection at LAC, including his October 13, 1976, letter to Peter Luke, his May 1976 letter to Verity Lambert, January 9, 1978, letter to Irene Shubik and his June 29, 1981, letter to Clive Exton, as well as Verity Lambert's June 15, 1977, response to Newman. Also included are Newman's proposal for *Men-Bane* (from 1976) and correspondence regarding the proposal from his agent, Harvey Unna, dated April 9, 1979, and July 23, 1979.

Newman's March 5, 1976, proposal for a unified film agency in Canada includes a detailed organizational chart and even a doodle of the logo for the "Cinema Canada Corporation." This proposal was reported on in the *Toronto Star* ("Report urges consolidation of Canada's film activities," March 26, 1976.) Newman's denial to the *Toronto Star* about this proposal was featured as a letter to the editor on April 6, 1976.

Several of Newman's files on his work at the Canadian Film Development Corporation are retained in his LAC collection, which includes Gordon Pinsent's February 26, 1982, letter to André Lamy regarding Newman's work. The announcement of the CDFC's

Sydney Newman Prize was in the March 12, 1981, *Globe and Mail.*

Newman receiving the Order of Canada was first suggested in a memo from Newman to Hugh Faulkner June 3, 1977. The announcement of Newman's Order of Canada is from the June 26, 1981 *Globe and Mail.*

11. Yesterday's Man

Unless otherwise noted, this chapter relies primarily on materials in the Sydney Newman's collection at LAC, including Newman's letters from early 1982 seeking employment with various organizations and Newman's letter to Pierre Juneau from October 21, 1983, and Juneau's response by telegram from November 5, 1983.

Aubrey Singer's November 4, 1982, memo to Graeme McDonald and McDonald's memo in response from November 5, 1982, can be found in Sydney Newman's file at the BBC WAC (RAPIC: 10173510).

Newman commented on the Bloomsbury group in a letter to Peter Luke from October 13, 1976. The newspaper clippings on Vita Sackville-West and John Maynard Keynes, and several drafts of Gillian Freeman's scripts for *Bloomsbury* (and various correspondence and memoranda about it) are all retained, along with the production files, in the Newman collection at LAC.

Details of Newman's business arrangements with Colin Callender were related in an October 18, 1984, letter to David Benedictus at Channel 4. Newman's letter of resignation to André Lamy was dated December 3, 1984.

12. Marked by Letdowns

Martin Knelman was quoted from his "Lives Lived" column on Newman in the November 25, 1997, *Globe and Mail.*

Unless otherwise noted, this chapter relies primarily on materials in the Sydney Newman collection at LAC, including the production files and scripts for *Prisoners of Conscience*: "The Killing of Joelito," letters to Gore Vidal and Arthur Miller (both dated September 25, 1984), correspondence to David Bendictus (from October 12, 1984, and October 18, 1984) and Jeremy Isaacs (from October 20, 1984) and correspondence from Graeme McDonald, dated August 15, on Gillian Freeman's suitability as a writer.

Newman's LAC collection also includes Newman's hand-written journal from July and August 1985 split between Newman and Callender. Newman's explanation of the terms of the split with Callender comes from an article by Stephen James Walker, "The Forgotten Canadian" that remained unpublished until it appeared in *Talkback: The Unofficial and Unauthorised Doctor Who Interview Book Volume One: The Sixties* (Telos Publishing, 2006).

Newman outlined his ideas for *The Little Sweep* in a memo to Andrew and Diana Holmes, dated February 28, 1986. Channel 4's rejection of *Bloomsbury* was relayed in two letters from Jeremy Isaacs dated June 5, 1986, and July 21, 1986. Newman retained the rejection letters from the BBC, and Granada Television, Scottish Television, and a list of other networks that were pitched the project.

13. "Who created Dr. Who?"

Unless otherwise noted, this chapter relies primarily on materials in the Sydney Newman collection at LAC, which retains all the correspondence cited. Newman's datebook and diary for 1986 are also in this collection as well as his August 10, 1993, letter to Andrew Beech.

Newman's October 6, 1986, proposal for a "way forward" for *Doctor Who* was apparently not retained by the BBC Written Archive Centre nor is it in Newman's own papers at Library and Archives Canada. The only extant copy is a photocopy taken of it by Stephen James Walker during research for his book *Doctor Who: The Eighties* (Virgin Publishing, 1996), who kindly sent a copy to the author.

14. Unfulfilled

Unless otherwise noted, this chapter relies on materials in the Sydney Newman collection at LAC, including all the production files, correspondence and memoranda about *The Little Sweep* and the torn-out pages of his 1988 diary outlining the dissolution of his business relationship with Andrew Holmes.

Newman wrote Andrew Holmes about this situation February 2, 1988 (with a handwritten postscript), and wrote Michael Grade at Channel 4 for further financing on February 6, 1988. Newman approached Ian Martin at Thames Television as a production partner in a letter dated February 25, 1988.

Newman wrote his friend Hannah (last name unknown) about post-retirement life in Canada on October 18, 1991. He wrote to Frank Gillard, via Christine Slattery at BBC Archives, on May 4, 1997.

Newman's obituary, written by W Stephen Gilbert, appeared in the *Guardian*, November 3, 1997, while Newman was featured in the *Globe and Mail*'s "Lives Lived" column on November 25, 1997.

The author would like to acknowledge the assistance of several people in writing this essay for their assistance and willingness to not only listen to very obtuse questions but provide very cogent answers. Thanks to Andrew Pixley, Gary Evans, Richard Bignell, Steven James Walker, Toby Hadoke, Jon Arnold, Paul Cornell, Dene Kernohan, Alan Hayes and Nick Abadzis. Special thanks to Jim Sangster for his hospitality, good humour, helpful advice, vast amounts of arcane knowledge and friendship. Not necessarily in that order.

This work was supported through the Ontario Arts Council Writers' Reserve Grant.

DEIRDRE NEWMAN
AFTERWORD

My father's memoirs are of his professional life; his private life is barely mentioned. Below is my attempt at describing our family life, and to fill in his last years, from the end of his memoirs in 1987 to the end of his life in 1997. They are my memories of him, not necessarily those of my sisters.

When we moved to England in 1958, I was eleven, Jennifer, nine and Gillian, six; our parents had flown on ahead, so coincidentally, our "babysitter" on the flight was Arthur Hailey, the author of "Flight into Danger." Sydney had been but a reticent father while we were young. Therefore, my childhood memories have all to do with my mother, Betty, in a prominent role — while we, as children, were frequently in the way as he had little patience with us. He must have seen a glimmer of adulthood in us on our arrival in London, as he told us, in his usual blunt fashion, that he didn't like small children and hadn't wanted to have any. He told our mother that he was happy to finance children, but it would be up to her to do the rest! (He then joyfully adds that I was conceived under the editing room bench at the Film Board.)

So, with his work and Betty first, I barely knew him in our childhood in Canada. It wasn't until the move to England that he and I started to get to know one other, and it wasn't until after Betty's death in 1981 that I really got to know my father, as I was the one daughter living in Toronto at the time.

As a youngster, before the age of eleven, I have no memory of his playing with me, nor reading to us, except that we spent summer holidays together as a family in Georgian Bay. Ironically, the closest I remember to being close to a man was Ted Kotcheff, who picked me up in his arms — I was about eight at the time, and thought, "my father doesn't ever pick me up!"

So, until this time, it was our mother that I knew. We assumed that most fathers were as hands-off as ours, and looked with both envy and curiosity at families where the children knew their fathers. I even remember a Christmas day when he was working and not at home . . . Therefore, it is hard for me to speak about my father without my mother. She brought out all the best things in him, although also indulging him. This indulgence had both positive and negative effects; it allowed him the time to excel in his work, while at the same time gave him licence to be a distant father.

My mother was an exceptional woman; my father knew this and adored her — the expression "the little woman behind the man" was in some ways applicable. It wasn't until Betty died that, finally, our childhood fell into place, as we got to know Sydney. And to realize that we had an extraordinary father, and perhaps an even more extraordinary mother.

After a degree in philosophy at the University of Toronto, and a career at the NFB, she was a stay-at-home mother until 1965, when she took a teacher's training course and began teaching at primary school. And, though working full-time, she managed to run a house, look after three growing children and managed my father's social life beautifully.

My memory is of meeting the most interesting people through my parents — all made possible by my mother, who discovered, through our move to London, the joys of international cooking —

garlic, spices, wine — all the food that had not yet arrived in white Anglo-Saxon North America. She would cook wonderful meals for my father's guests — writers, directors, artists — and equally enjoy the evenings whether planned or impromptu. As a teenager, I was thrilled to accompany them at the table and listen and take in their conversations about television, film, theatre, art, politics; Peter Luke, Ronald Weyman and Paul Almond (when they were working in London), Robert Shaw, Michael Bentine, Leslie Hardcastle, Clive Exton, Patrick Macnee, David Attenborough, Geneviève Bujold, Tony Garnett, George Dunning and many more. We spent weekends in the country with my godmother, Marion Leigh, Alan Rawsthorne, Alan and Leslie Adamson. But none of this would have taken place without my mother.

My sister Jennifer remembers him saying "To thine own self be true" (Polonious, from *Hamlet*). If you can't be true to yourself, you can't be honest with others. And his honesty, with us, was frequently brutal. Because he hardly knew us, he would seem surprised at some accomplishment of ours, or equally, not able to understand how he had fathered a child with asthma! And in his usual blunt way, would make personal comments both cutting and complimentary! Rather like an innocent child, but in this case, a grown man who could have used some tact with growing adolescent daughters!

As we grew older, Sydney began to find us interesting. He had the capacity of complete concentration, when we would go to him with a problem — the rest of the world would disappear as he listened and delved into the issue. He was never patronizing or cynical, but wise and unassuming. He was also very supportive of our search for careers, saying that we would only succeed in a career if we were happy at it, if we were answering a need or an interest in ourselves. In all our cases, rather than following the philosophical direction of our mother, we three all took after him, two of us studying at art schools in London, the third studying art history at university in Ottawa. Again, "To thine own self be true."

He changed after our mother became ill with a rare illness called polychondritis, which the medical profession knew little about at the time, that would eventually lead to her death. Her condition became worse after their return to Canada, and it wasn't until 1973, when I moved to Toronto that I experienced, first hand, the changes in their lives. Suddenly, the hypochondria that had always been in Sydney disappeared, showing a new selflessness — clearly it came as a result of his closeness to our mother and a consciousness of her suffering and inability to carry on as before. This softness in him was new. If we were messy or left things lying about, he would remind us that Mummy could trip over them. He became a little more domesticated, but not much. Although he never learned to cook, he took a more active role in the household — puttings things away, loading the dishwasher(!) and the like. But the tension would erupt with me at times — never with Betty, or not that I knew of. When I tried to show him how to iron, he lost his temper, threw his arms up in disgust and walked away.

After the move back to Canada, he was by then at home, working freelance and was able to spend more time looking after her. However ill she was, one would never hear a squeak of complaint from her.

In fact, her entire illness was a lesson for us all; in how to suffer, and die, with dignity.

My father phoned me on a Thursday morning, saying my mother was unconscious and had been taken to hospital. As I took the bus up to their house, I was sad with a blackness I had never before experienced; I felt that my mother would die, just drift off with no conclusion to her life.

When I arrived at the house, my father told me what had happened.

After her last bout in the hospital nine months previously, she had said to him that she knew the future progress of her illness, and that she did not have much longer before she would become completely incapacitated, which would mean hospital care until she died. She did not want to be kept alive in hospital, but wanted to die at her own hand, but only if Sydney would agree. He said yes. Nothing more was said between them until now.

He described the previous day, when he had seen her writing letters, while propped up in bed. When he brought her their usual evening cocktail, she said, "Sydney, tonight I have to do it. I know I cannot last much longer before they put me in the hospital, and I do not want to be kept alive and die there." So, she took the pills she had collected and lost consciousness in my father's arms.

He said he did not sleep at all that night. The nurse for the morning shift arrived at 8 a.m., saw my mother sleeping, and went about tidying up. Eventually she wondered at my mother's not waking, realized that she was not asleep but unconscious, and had to call the doctor, the authorities and went off to the hospital with her. My mother died two days later.

The letters she had been writing were goodbye letters, to us, to Sydney and her doctors. Explaining what he knew already, but also adding — in her typical, practical way, the specific drugs she had taken, with the specific goal of saying this was a suicide and her decision, to avoid any doubt as to my father's involvement.

On hearing this, my blackness vanished abruptly and I was so happy that she hadn't just drifted into unconsciousness, that she was in control to the end — how typical of her. A good death, a positive death.

So, my father had known this was to happen for nine months, although he could not have foreseen that it would really take place.

After she died, he was never the same and we three girls could never fill the gap left in his life.

As described, he was useless domestically. I don't think I am being unkind when I say that his relationship with Marion McDougall, a former secretary in England, was purely practical.

He went back to art. He had always been practical in all the traditional men's roles — electricity, fixing things around the house — and accomplished at woodwork. In London, he had turned the dining room into a studio, and, once returned to Toronto, he built an extension on the house for a workshop, which later moved to the basement when my mother needed a ground-floor bedroom. In both places, he had fixed to the wall his favourite quotation from James Thurber, "Look not back in anger, nor forward in fear, but around with awareness."

Years previously, he had built a chest of drawers for me as a child, painting it with images of animals, the alphabet and my name; it's now being used two generations later by his great-grandchildren. After his return to Canada, he spent a lot of time making furniture and wood sculptures that he cast in bronze, kitchen utensils, and, on the lathe, he turned bowls, platters, egg cups, bread boards and knife racks that he gave as presents. He was also very proud of his collection of chisels, with which he sculpted salvaged pieces of wood. Many of these large, abstract pieces were inspired by the natural forms he found in the wood, while others were smaller and more representational.

Perhaps there was something truly innovative in his artistic curiosity. As he was fascinated by film and television in their early days, so too was he fascinated by how technology was being used in the art world; he took weekly lessons in Photoshop, Paintbrush and a variety of other software programs. In these early days of computer technology, these programs were created for commercial and graphic design purposes. And here he was, seeing the potential in computers for "fine" art. This seemed to me to be a very dignified way of retiring, and now here he was being creative in front of his beloved television "screen" — creating images both abstract and figurative. He would spend all day "drawing" on the computer, sometimes producing abstract pieces, at other times juxtaposing images with very funny results.

For someone who had started when typesetting was truly typesetting — even before Letraset, before the computer, when one traced letters from type catalogues — this use of the computer, at his age, truly impressed me. This was just a further development of the posters he designed for the films of Eisenstein in the '30s, which are some of my favourites and hang on my walls to this day.

We spent a lot of time together. I had just become a mother, so our visits included my daughter, whose passion became philosophy, which he appreciated, because she was taking after Betty. He tried working again in England, with disappointing results. He visited my godfather, his childhood friend, Jack Olsen, in Rome. They came together to visit us in Corsica, where we have a sixteenth-century stone tower. It was a difficult visit; he was unmoved by the romance of the place, ill-at-ease in a drystone tower full of stairs, crumbling plaster, vaulted ceilings, but with exquisite views over the sea and the mountains. He was uncomfortable outside his right-angled, drywalled, clean, twentieth-century existence, which was a blow to us. Why could he not see the romance as we did? Was he interested only in the here and now?

He was sad and disappointed at the end. He admitted he had made many mistakes, regretting a lot, yet at the same time was proud of his work, particularly his time spent with single plays. I saw a vulnerability then that I suspect only my mother had seen in him. What I saw in him mirrored the frailty I saw in the artists with whom I have worked in my career; high as kites one moment, very down the next. What I inherited from him has stood me well professionally; to appreciate the energy of artists, their egocentricity, their frailty, their enthusiasm, their innocence and most of all their creativity.

ACKNOWLEDGEMENTS

It has been both a poignant and fascinating time, working on my father's memoirs. Digging into the past with its many queries, I could not have succeeded without the help of the following family and friends: Jillian Marshall, Richard Stursberg, Suzanne Depoe, Catherine Gildiner, Don McBrearty, the team at ECW Press, Ted Kotcheff, Jacob Leigh, Ruth Legg Hawthorn, my two sisters Jennifer and Gillian, and for their emotional support, my partner Roy Pelletier and our daughter Jenny Pelletier, and all my cousins.

INDEX